Intellectual Property and the Law of Natio

Legal History Library

VOLUME 58

Studies in the History of International Law

VOLUME 22

The titles published in this series are listed at *brill.com/shil*

(1) (2) (3) (4) (5) (6) (7) (8) (9) (10)

The Charvet/Dufour wallpapers, *Sauvages de la mer Pacifique* ("Savages of the Pacific") displayed at the 1806 Paris Exposition and marked the introduction of water colour as an "invention" and copyright-right related activities

@WIKIMEDIA COMMONS

Intellectual Property and the Law of Nations, 1860–1920

Edited by

P. Sean Morris

BRILL
NIJHOFF

LEIDEN | BOSTON

Cover illustration: Carte de tous les Pors de Mer du Monde, Nicolas Berey, Paris circa 1650.
Credit: British Library.

The Library of Congress Cataloging-in-Publication Data is available online at https://catalog.loc.gov
LC record available at https://lccn.loc.gov/2022006621

Typeface for the Latin, Greek, and Cyrillic scripts: "Brill". See and download: brill.com/brill-typeface.

ISSN 1874-1793
ISBN 978-90-04-43981-8 (hardback)
ISBN 978-90-04-51143-9 (e-book)

This book is printed on acid-free paper and produced in a sustainable manner.

Contents

PART 2
Film and Regal Approaches to Copyright

PART 3
Trademarks, Terroir and the Colonies

Acknowledgements

The Editor would like to thank the contributors for their individual chapters and for acting as commentators to designated chapters during the "internal open peer-review" process or the very special "double-guard" process. The latter in particular selected four chapters from emerging IP scholars or papers worthy of a merit mention in order to identify scholarship. While those who served on the double-guard review team knew the identity of authors, the authors on the other hand did not know who commented on their chapter in the capacity of double-guard. It was an interesting feat of teamwork, where several stages of feedbacks by (1) designated commentators, (2) double-guard review, and (3) general open comments for all or any chapters provided further insights and challenged some assumptions and arguments. Thus, to all the contributors, your comments, critiques and insights were invaluable in guiding the chapters for a better intellectual outcome.

The double-guard review panel comprised of:

- Ainee Adam
- Johanna Gibson
- Jyh-An Lee
- Philip Johnson

In addition, special commentators for specific papers in terms of the intellectual property argument and critique were:

- Shubha Ghosh
- Zvi Rosen

We are also grateful for the comments from the external peer reviewers Brill commissioned to comment on the chapters. Their suggestions helped us to improve the chapters and make additional arguments where necessary.

The editor wishes to express his thanks to Tommi K. Kortelainen for assistance especially on the indexing.

At Brill, my sincere thanks to Wendel Scholma and the series editors for accepting my initial ideas and proposal for the project. Furthermore, Alessandra Giliberto joined the production team and all have been rather helpful in the entire publication process.

Notes on Contributors

Daniel Acquah

is a Postdoctoral researcher at the Faculty of Law, University of Turku, and a Senior Research Associate at the Institute for European Studies (IES), Vrije Universiteit Brussel (VUB). He has master's degrees in criminology and Criminal Justice (Glasgow), in law (Turku) and double doctoral degrees in law (Turku, Brussels). Acquah has spent research periods at leading intellectual property and European Union law research sites such as the Centre for International Intellectual Property Studies (CEIPI), University of Strasbourg, France, and the IES, Brussels. He is a frequent speaker at international conferences and seminars. In April 2013, he was an Erasmus visiting scholar at the University of Szeged, Hungary, where he taught a comparative law course. He has been a visiting lecturer at the University of Eastern Finland since spring 2015, and also, a guest teacher at the Hanken School of Economics since 2016. He also teaches intermittently at the IES. Acquah supervises and co-supervise masters and bachelor students working on topics linked to his research interest. He has published in reputable European and international journals relating to his area of research interest.

Ainee Binti Adam

is the Deputy Dean (Research) at the Faculty of Law, University of Malaya, a position she was appointed to in April 2019. She completed her doctoral degree in 2014 at the Faculty of Law, Monash University Australia. In 2015, she took up the position as a postdoctoral fellow at the Centre for Law and Business at the National University of Singapore. She returned in 2016 to resume her duties as Senior Lecturer. In 2019, she spent two months at Nankai University as a Confucius Institute Visiting Scholar to work on her research project. Her current research interests lie in researching the history of intellectual property rights and exploring Asian theories and philosophies to provide an alternative view/solution on contemporary intellectual property rights issues. Ainee has published several articles in journals including the *Queen Mary Journal of Intellectual Property*, *European Intellectual Property Review* and the *Hong Kong Law Journal*. Her most recent article, 'Pricing and Profiting in Copyright: An Introduction to Islamic Perspective', is published in the *Queen Mary Journal of Intellectual Property*. She is also currently the Project Leader for the team from the University of Malaya for an Erasmus Project with eight other Asian and European partners.

Louise Duncan
Barrister of Law, Melbourne, has obtained a Ph.D. in Law from Monash University (1998). She was previously a Research Fellow and Lecturer in the Law Schools of both the University of Melbourne and Monash University. She is the author of *The Role of Theoretical Debate in the Evolution of National and International Patent Protection: From the French Revolution to the Paris Convention of 1883* (Brill, 2021). Since 1998 she has been practising as a barrister in Australia, specialising in commercial litigation. Her main practice has been in the Federal Court of Australia, where she has had extensive experience in trials and appeals. The matters in which she has appeared include all aspects of patents, trade marks, designs and copyright law. She has also been briefed to appear in several disciplinary proceedings before the Professional Standards Board for Patent and Trade Mark Attorneys.

Johanna Gibson
is Herchel Smith Professor of Intellectual Property Law, Academic Director of the Intellectual Property Law LLM and the Deputy Director of the Queen Mary Intellectual Property Research Institute at the Centre for Commercial Law Studies (CCLS). She is also Editor-In-Chief of the *Queen Mary Journal of Intellectual Property* (QMJIP). She has consulted widely to industry, government, NGOs and practitioners, and has been a visiting professor to institutions around the world. Johanna's research interests are in intellectual property and the creative industries, particularly fashion and film, and animal welfare law and critical animal studies. She publishes widely, including her most recent book: *Owned, an Ethological Jurisprudence of Property: From the Cave to the Commons* (Routledge, 2020).

Phillip Johnson
is a Professor of Commercial Law at Cardiff University and a practising barrister. He has written extensively on intellectual property law and legal history and is the editor of the *Intellectual Property Quarterly* and a member of the Advisory Council on National Records and Archives. His books include Roughton, Johnson and Cook on Patents (2nd to 5th Ed), *Parliament, Inventions and Patents (2018) and Privatised Law Reform: A History of Patent Law through Private Legislation* (2017).

Jyh-An Lee
is a Professor and Executive Director of the Centre for Financial Regulation and Economic Development (CFRED) at the Chinese University of Hong Kong Faculty of Law. Professor Lee has been featured on ABC News, BBC News,

Bloomberg News, Financial Times, Fortune, South China Morning Post and Wall Street Journal as an expert on intellectual property and Internet law. His works have been cited by the U.S. Court of Appeals for the Fifth Circuit and U.K. High Court of Justice. Before starting his academic career, he was a practicing lawyer in Taiwan, specializing in technology and business transactions.

Yangzi Li
is a Ph.D. Candidate in the Faculty of Law at the Chinese University of Hong Kong. Her research interests include intellectual property law, technology law, and artificial intelligence (AI) policies. Her works have appeared in peer-review journals, such as the *European Intellectual Property Review, GRUR International* (OUP), *Journal of Intellectual Property Law & Practice* (OUP), etc.

P. Sean Morris
is a Research Scholar at the Faculty of Law University of Helsinki and an Affiliated Research Fellow at the Erik Castren Institute of International Law and Human Rights, University of Helsinki, Finland. Sean's research is in the fields of public international law and intellectual property rights. He has written extensively in both areas. Sean is the editor of two recent volumes on the Advisory Committee of Jurists (ACJ): *Transforming the Politics of International Law: The Advisory Committee of Jurists and the Formation of the World Court in the League of Nations* (Routledge, 2021); *The League of Nations and the Development of International Law: A New Intellectual History of the Advisory Committee of Jurists* (Routledge, 2021). His most recent articles on intellectual property rights are, 'Chorzow Factory: Intellectual Property and the Continuity of International Law in Investor-State Dispute Settlement' 10(2) *Queen Mary Journal of Intellectual Property* 179–199 (2020); 'The Contemporary Ideological Legitimacy of Global Intellectual Property Rights' 2020 *Intellectual Property Quarterly* 44–73 (2020).

Péter Munkácsi
is an IP expert at the senior level at the Ministry of Justice, Budapest. He obtained a Bachelor of Law from Eötvös Lóránd University, Budapest. He gained his LL.M. degree in 1993 from Ruprecht-Karls-University, Heidelberg and a second LL.M. degree was awarded by European University Institute (EUI), Florence, in 1998. From September 2021 he is a PhD researcher at Eötvös Loránd University, Budapest. He is author of more than 50 scientific publications relating copyright and IP issues in Hungarian and English, the latest is: 'Moral Rights and Cultural Aspects of Hungarian Copyright Law 1945–2000'

in: Mira T Sundara Rajan (ed.): *Cambridge Handbook of Intellectual Property In Central and Eastern Europe* (Cambridge: Cambridge University Press 2019).

Zvi S. Rosen
is an Assistant Professor at the Southern Illinois University School of Law. He holds a J.D. from the Northwestern University School of Law and a LLM in Intellectual Property Law from the George Washington University School of Law. Prior to this he was the Abraham L. Kaminstein Scholar in Residence at the United States Copyright Office, and has taught at law schools including The Maurice A. Deane School of Law at Hofstra University, the George Washington University School of Law, the University of New Hampshire School of Law, and New York Law School. He also was an Assistant Chief Counsel for Advocacy at the U.S. Small Business Administration focused on IP and trade policy for small businesses. His research focuses on the development of U.S. copyright and trademark law from its origins through today.

Devanshi Saxena
is a Ph.D. Candidate at the University of Antwerp. She works as University teaching assistant and researcher in the area of Intellectual property law. Her interests lie at the intersection of human rights law, sustainable development and intellectual property law.

Johannes Thumfart
is a Senior Researcher at the research group LSTS (Law, Science, Technology and Society) of Vrije Universiteit Brussels. He has taught or held research positions at Université Paris VIII, Berlin School of Economics and Law, Freie Universität Berlin, Universidad Iberoamericana in Mexico-City and University of Cincinnati. He is the co-editor of *Pensar Internet* (2016), one of the first Mexican anthologies about the political theory of digital technology.

Esther van Zimmeren
is Associate Professor in Intellectual Property (IP) Law and Governance at the Faculty of Law of the University of Antwerp and a member of the Research Groups Government and Law and Business and Law.

INTRODUCTION

Framing the Law of Nations in Intellectual Property in the Nineteenth Century

P. Sean Morris

The Viennese American international scholar Josef Laurenz Kunz (1890–1970) in an address to the British Branch of the Grotius Society on the 28th October 1924 pointed out, *inter alia*, that 'the history of the Law of Nations' forms part of the science of international law.[1] Kunz was not the only international legal scholar of his generation to argue on the state and jurisprudence of international law by invoking what was becoming an obsolete term or nineteenth century reference to international law in the legal scholarship. Lassa Oppenheim (1858–1919), Hersch Lauterpacht (1897–1960) and many of Kunz' contemporaries shared similar views.[2] And, as vivid Kunz observation was in 1924, so too, it is in contemporary times, to look at the 'science of international law' within the frame of 'history of the Law of the Nations.' But, more equally, it is important to examine the *subunits and systems* of the law of nations in a historical lens and how those subunits influenced the evolution of international law. One sub-unit of particular interest is that of intellectual property law and its role in shaping international law.

Yet, even framing a history of the science of international law and interjecting it in the narrative on intellectual property is a challenge. Among the

1 Kunz, Joseph L. 'On the Theoretical Basis of the Law of Nations'. *Transactions of the Grotius Society* 10 (1924) 115–143, 117. For a general reading see Vollenhoven, C. van. *The Three Stages in the Evolution of the Law of Nations* (The Hague: Martinus Nijhoff, 1919); Nussbaum, Arthur. *A Concise History of the Law of Nations* (New York: Macmillan, 1947).

2 See Nussbaum, Arthur. 'Rise and Decline of the Law of Nations Doctrine in the Conflict of Laws'. *Columbia Law Review* 42(2) (1942) 189–206. Tracing a history of international law or the law of nations as such, is not the business of this project, nor is it the purpose of this introduction, but for works that gives a "starting point" or "point zero" see e.g., Kingsbury, Benedict, and Straumann, Benjamin, eds. *The Roman Foundations of the Law of Nations: Alberico Gentili and the Justice of Empire* (Oxford: Oxford University Press, 2010); Zurbuchen, Simone, ed. *The Law of Nations and Natural Law, 1625–1800* (Leiden/Boston: Brill, 2019). I've also made a sojourn in an attempt to show how intellectual property rights is connected with the long-history of international law from a private law perspective, see Morris, P. Sean. 'The Private Foundations of International Law: Intellectual Property Rights and Pashukanis'. *Jus Gentium: Journal of International Legal History* 5(1) (2020) 37–123.

 | DOI:10.1163/9789004511439_002

challenges is the fact that two different fields of law are being discussed, or, where they intersect, and such confluence may cause sudden rapids. Another challenge is how the different tributaries of intellectual property law flow into a coherent path that show the history of the law of nations from intellectual property rivers as forming a *stream-order*. The essays in this collection are about channelling the hidden stream-orders of intellectual property law in the law of nations during the latter part of the nineteenth century (sometimes-referred to as Victorian international law) to the early part of the twentieth century (1860–1920).

For a start, the law of nations is a complex terminology that at different points in history referred to the relations between the law of nature or the inter-relations of states. As a term, the law of nations was connected with how *jus gentium* became the operative form to frame discussions on international legal relations during much of the reformation period in Europe and the latter parts of the nineteenth century. For some nineteenth-century legal scholars such as Travers Twiss (1809–1897), the law of nations proper relates to how rules govern the intercourse of natural society and political communities.[3]

There is no doubt that the law of nations is about international law, as we understood it in the modern context. Yet, writing on the evolution of various private law and norms such as those on intellectual property rights and the positive rules that governed them that emerged on the global stage in the late nineteenth century requires analogous context to the law of nations.

The narrative of intellectual property in the law of nations sets in tone the evolutionary development of specific domains in the wider realm of industrial property as part of the general maturing of the international legal system. But even then, the intellectual property narratives have a great impact on how rules and norms emerges in the same fashion one would view the evolutionary cycles of sovereignty in the law of nations. Thus, if the law of nations comprised of sovereignty or economic relations relating to property as such, then, intellectual property rights and their regulations are a subset of the grander "property"[4] relations that accompanied "sovereignty" in the formation of the

3 Twiss, Travers. *The Law of Nations considered as Independent Political Communities – On the Right and Duties of Nations in Time of Peace* (Oxford: Oxford University Press, 1861).

4 For analogies on property, sovereignty and international law see e.g., Ederington, Benjamin L. 'Property as a Natural Institution: The Separation of Property from Sovereignty in International Law'. *American University Law Review* 13(2) (1997) 263–332; Rahmatian, Andreas. 'Indirect Sovereignty Through Property Rights'. *Notre Dame Journal of International and Comparative Law* 7(2) (2017) 58–90; Garnsey, Peter. *Thinking About Property: From Antiquity to the Age of Revolution* (Cambridge: Cambridge University Press, 2007).

law of nations.[5] In other words, sovereignty and (intellectual) property relations influenced and continue to influence international legal relations. Thus, the essays in this collection aims to demonstrate some aspects of the intellectual property relations. The aim is to show the legal formation of the various intellectual property (sub)-systems of (property) that emerged alongside other forms of legal institutions in the latter nineteenth century that eventually defined how international intellectual property fully emerged within the law of nations.

The law of nations in the period under discussion in this collection was in the process of radical changes, and that process would eventually set the tone and characteristics that would come to define contemporary international law. Part of the changes the law of nations witnessed during the period was the role of 'private law' as such (including intellectual property) as having a transformative effect on international law. Recently, some works[6] (and established works)[7] have given us some insights into the operational role of private law in nineteenth century international law.[8] However, the extent which, the different *sub-systems* of intellectual property forms part of those narratives are missing. We are not pretending that we are telling the entire story of the missing sub-systems of intellectual property rights in the evolution and intersection of the law of nations in the latter part of the nineteenth century. That is not our task. Instead, we examine selective narratives in the sub-systems of intellectual property right and with diverse nations and not limited to the states in Europe, where *European international law*, as it were, often formed the entire historical discussion on international law.[9]

One of the thing that that reader must bear in mind is that the period of focus in this collection can be viewed as the era of (third) industrialization on a global scale where capitalism, innovation, trademarks and patents formed a

5 For a Vattelian discussion of sovereignty see Beaulac, Stephane 'Emer de Vattel and the Externalization of Sovereignty'. *Journal of the History of International Law* 5(3) (2003) 237–292.

6 E.g., Banu, Roxana. *Nineteenth Century Perspectives on Private International Law* (Oxford: Oxford University Press, 2018).

7 E.g., Nussbaum, 'Rise and Decline' (n. 2).

8 Banu (n. 6).

9 This observation hold true to the point that prior to the late 1990s most of the works that discussed the history of international law were rather 'euro-centric' and other civilisations were not part of the narrative, to the extent other works have been made available in English as the natural lingua of international legal literature. Naturally, the contemporary literature is abundant with various histories of international law, see e.g., van Hulle, Inge, and C.H. Lesaffer, Randall eds. *International Law in the Long Nineteenth Century (1776–1914)* (Leiden/Boston: Brill, 2019).

complex web of *industrial commodification*.[10] Intellectual property rights were therefore a necessity for industrialization to thrive and at the same time protecting the commodification of innovation and ideas in both domestic rules and at the international level. For industrialists that were looking further afield to expand their markets and production in automobiles or the protection of their innovations and inventions the rules of (international) patent law would help to create a level playing field. Conversely, *auteurs* would need to enjoy the same international level of protection for their ideas and stories in printed books and other literary mediums of public consumption.

Thus, the extent and form of how commodification occurred became a confluence of private legal rights and the obligations of states to protect such rights while honouring state-to-state legal relations as a form of civilize maturity. If international legal scholars in centuries before had paint commercial relationships among states as paramount to the law of nations[11]; then, it should be, in the same spirit, that the *industrial commodification* period as a result of the confluence of industrial property and the law of nations in the latter part of the nineteenth century must be seen. In other words, late nineteenth century industrial commodification has an analogous root in how Vattel employed the language of industrial property to promote global knowledge, industry, the arts and sciences.[12]

10 Some of the work of Tom Kemp is useful in terms of understanding the evolution of industrialization in Europe in the latter part of the nineteenth century, see e.g., Kemp, Tom. *Industrialization in Nineteenth-Century Europe, 2nd edn* (London/New York: Longmann, 1985).

11 This is perhaps one of the great takeaways from classical works such as that by Vattel, see Vattel, Emer de. *The Law of Nations, or, Principles of the law of nature, Applied to the Conduct and Affairs of Nations and Sovereigns* (London: G.G. and J. Robinson, 1797), 2.16, noting that 'Nations would communicate to each other their products and their knowledge [...] and enrich it with its invaluable fruits; industry, the sciences and the arts would be employed in promoting our happiness [...].'

12 Ibid. But see, Nakhimovsky, Isaac. 'Vattel's Theory of the International Order: Commerce and the balance of power in the Law of Nations'. *History of European Ideas* 33(2) (2007) 157–173, 167 discussing the so-called double perfection theory between states and 'the progress of the arts and sciences through commerce.' The Vattelian language on progress of the arts is reminiscent of the US Constitution and early French approaches to 'systems and privileges' as a precursor to intellectual property protection, see generally, Duncan, chapter 1 in this collection; Patterson, Ray, and Joyce, Graig. 'Copyright in 1791: An Essay Concerning the Founders' View of the Copyright Power Granted to Congress in Article I, Section 8, clause 8 of the US Constitution'. *Emory Law Journal* 52(2) (2003) 909–952; O'Connor, Sean M. 'The Overlooked French Influence on the Intellectual Property Clause'. *The University of Chicago Law Review* 82(2) (2015) 733–830. Historically, and perhaps with Vatellian language, a 1792 treatise emerged that looked at the protection of intellectual property as those of invention and innovation, see, Barnes, Joseph. *Treatise on*

It is debateable the extent how much intellectual property scholarship have remained divorce from the historical approach of scholarship on the intersection of international law. Present and past intellectual property scholarship tends to compartmentalize intellectual property scholarship by either focusing on national,[13] comparative[14] or transnational[15] (this latter reflecting late twenty-fist century methods), or international[16] legal lens. However, intellectual property scholarship does not generally show the entire confluence of intellectual property rights and the law of the nations in the late nineteenth century. The rare discussion on the subject matter is often a general reading.[17] On other occasions, the nexus between intellectual property rights, and the law of nations, in the late nineteenth century, is generally written by non-legal scholars.[18] It might be difficult to tell the various reasons for this development, but I suspect that part of the explanation may be that early (PhD) works on the matter may not have been published and are tucked away (if still available) in university libraries.[19]

---

the Justice, Policy, and Utility of Establishing an Effectual System for Promoting the Progress of Useful Arts, by Assuring Property in the Products of Genius (Philadelphia: Francis Bailey, 1792), cited in Biagioli, Mario. 'Patent Republic: Representing Inventions, Constructing Rights and Authors'. *Politics and Science: An Historical View* 73(4) 1129–1172, 1162.

13 See example, Sherman, Brad, and Bently, Lionel. *The Making of Modern Intellectual Property Law* (Cambridge: Cambridge University Press, 1999); Saiz Gonzalez, J. Patricio. 'The Spanish Patent System (1770–1907)' in Inkster, Ian, ed. *History and Technology* (London: Bloomsbury Academic, 2004) 45–80.

14 Blakeney, Michael. 'The Role of Intellectual Property in Regional Commercial Unions in Europe and Asia'. *Prometheus: Critical Studies in Innovation* 16(3) (1998) 341–350.

15 Merges, Robert, and Song, Seagull Haiyan. *Transnational Intellectual Property Law: Text and Cases* (Cheltenham: Edward Elgar, 2018).

16 Grosse Ruse-Khan, Henning. *The Protection of Intellectual Property in International Law* (Oxford: Oxford University Press, 2016).

17 E.g., May, Christopher, and Sell, Susan. *Intellectual Property Rights: A Critical History* (Lynne Rienner; Boulder, Col., 2006). I am primarily referring to how international legal scholars and intellectual property legal scholars using historical approaches would situate the origins of intellectual property rights in the law of nations, which was a more fashionably form up to the 1930s to discuss international legal developments.

18 See e.g., Grossman, Gene M., and Lai, Edwin L.C. 'International Protection of Intellectual Property'. *American Economic Review* 94(5) (2004) 1635–1653. Two other prominent US based scholars are active in this approach, especially using economic history to diagnose innovation, sample works include, Moser, Petra. 'Patents and Innovation: Evidence from Economic History'. *The Journal of Economic Perspectives* 27(3) (2013) 23–44; Khan, B. Zorina. 'Selling Ideas: An International Perspective on Patent and Markets for Technological Innovations, 1790–1930'. *Business History Review* 87(1) (2013) 39–68.

19 Early research for this collection lead me to the then unpublished PhD dissertation of Louise Duncan, which has since been published as *The Role of Theoretical Debate in the*

From an optimistic perspective though, various writers have told different narratives on the history, legal history or historical development of international cooperation to intellectual property and there is magnificent and large body of literature available.[20] Yet, broadly speaking, the events of the early 1870s leading up to two international conventions in the 1880s have secured the role of intellectual property rights as part of the broader narrative on the law of nations. The narratives in this collection captures those developments in part, but also recognises a number of other developments concerning intellectual property rights in the law of nations at the *fin-de-siciele* and leading up to the first world war and its aftermath in 1920.[21]

What unify the chapters in this collection is the object of intellectual property protection, that is, the specific legal rules pertaining to the protection of creativity and innovation; or, how states made efforts to develop rules for their protection. Against this, the story of each object of intellectual property protection is framed, implied, or explicitly discussed in different chapters and hence the notion of the *law of nations* in this collection. The law of nations in this collection is also about how the international legal protection of intellectual property rights have been transformed. Thus, while one would expect that Europe and its system of *European international law* would be the centre of attention, it is not completely the case. There are narratives on China and early colonial perspectives especially in relation to how some countries in Africa embraced (colonial) intellectual property protection through the law of nations in the latter part of the nineteenth century.

The formalization of the protection of intellectual property rights in international treaties in the latter part of the nineteenth century through to the early twentieth century have brought together nations and their interests in intellectual property conventions. Nations turned toward multilateralism and the interests of private industrialists, inventors, literary creators and states were increasingly colliding. It was the period in which industrialization leaped into a third era and states were looking toward the new twentieth century as a progressive and liberal one (for economic matters). International rules for the

---

Evolution of National and International Patent Protection: From the French Revolution to the Paris Convention of 1883 (Brill, 2021).

20 But see, May, Christopher, and Sell, Susan. *Intellectual Property Rights: A Critical History* (Lynne Rienner; Boulder, Col., 2006); Beier, Friedrich-Karl. 'On Hundred Years of International Cooperation: The Role of the Paris Convention in the Past, Present and Future'. *International Review of Industrial Property and Copyright Law* 15(1) (1984) 1–20.

21 A useful reading is also, Thomson, W.P. *Handbook of Patent Law of All Countries* (London: Stevens & Sons, 1920). This is one of the early twentieth century works that sets out the patent laws in the major countries.

protection of intellectual property were part of the arsenal to ensure that commodification of ideas and inventions take place.

The legacy of the industrial commodification brought on by intellectual property rights and the formalization of the intellectual property rules in international treaties was that a spectacular rise in multilateralism and thereby international lawmaking emerged. Intellectual property protection in other words ushered in multilateral treaty making concerning the protection of innovation and industrial property and the general relations of states in economic matters. Thus, on the one hand, the Paris Convention heralded the international system of patent protection and, on the other, intellectual property rights became an instrument of 'peace' during world conflicts. The various accounts in this collection of intellectual property in the law of nations is a starting point to remedy a deficit that exist in the literature by reflecting on certain aspects of intellectual property regulation and evolution in their international legal aspects.

It is increasingly clear that the emergence of international intellectual property law through the Paris and Berne Conventions in the latter part of the nineteenth century has been a defining moment in the modern system of international law. The Paris and Berne Conventions were two of the first multilateral treaties that shaped the positive structure of contemporary international law which, by the late nineteenth-century was shedding its natural law habits and moving from the law of nations to modern international law.

The emergence of the Paris Convention for example, began life in the early 1870s through the Vienna Patent Congress of 1873 while other significant developments in the formation of modern international law was taking place. These events include the conclusion of the Franco-Prussian War (1871) and the formation of the *Institut de Droit International* (Institute of International Law) (1873). These events have contributed to how we understand and approach modern international law.

When the industrialists and representatives of states gathered in Vienna in 1873 at a Congress to consider an international treaty for patent protection, they declared that all civilized nations required patent laws. The reference to civilized nations was on the hand echoing the tone in the invitation sent out to participants a year earlier in 1872, and, on the other, a reflection of the evolution of international law in the late nineteenth century that revolved around civilized (European) states. Moreover, it was in the same year, during the Ghent meeting that *learned* men in the science of the law of nations gathered to form the *Institut de droit International*. Thus, the 1870s was a crucial moment in the history of international law as it was a period in which the science of international law emerged. In other words, the formation of relevant societies and intellectual groups who would play a major role in the development and direction of international law as a scientific endeavour. It was also the same decade that private actors played a crucial role in the formation of international intellectual property laws through the Vienna Patent Congress of 1873. So, the idea of private-law making at the international legal sphere is not entirely new. But the question is, has intellectual property treaties served as the first area that spurned global law-making? As inviting as this question is, it is not the focus of this collection, but leaves us with room for debate about the emergence of international intellectual property law in the law of nations.

The international legal literature has blossomed in the last few years to relate to the formation and emergence of international law since the 1870s. Yet, what has been missing from the discussions was the role of international intellectual property law that emerged from the dying-clouds of the law of nations in the nineteenth-century. It is in that spirt, this collection, and some of the essays in it, approach intellectual property in the law of nations in the latter part of the nineteenth-century, and what role the international intellectual property law treaties had on the downstream formation of international legal obligations with states during the era. The essays in this collection only, in some ways, "introduce" the myriads of developments from an intellectual property perspective during the era to underpin the existence and relevance of international intellectual property law as part of the law of nations.

The treatment of the law of nations in this collection should also be seen in part, if a modern analogy is employed, with traits of "comparative international law" where contemporary scholars describe the private law forms of intellectual property rights within an international context. Hence, the law of nations, in some ways relates to comparative international law, and at the same time, it has traits similar to how some nineteenth-century writers framed it to include 'private law of nations.'[22] In this regard, one could argue that intellectual property rights as a form of private rights are not only governed by the domestic laws of nations relating to innovation but also international law. Such regulatory relationship began through the Paris and Berne Conventions in the 1880s, but have public law of nations and the private law of nations traits. As James Ram wrote in 1871: 'The law of nations in modern times has received a development unknown to the ancients, owning to the superior civilization, and constantly increasing national intercourse.'[23] This view is of course shaped in part

22 Ram, James. *The Science of Legal Judgment* (New York: Baker, Voorhis & Co., 1871) 147: 'The law of nations is usually divided by writers upon the subject into two kinds, namely, the public law of nations, and the private law of nations.'

23 Ram, ibid, 148.

by the developments from the 1870s, where an unprecedented "intercourse" among the civilized states of Europe (and to some extent, few independent peripheral states) began to take place. That relationship took into account how the positive rules of the law of nations were required for protecting international intellectual property especially those relating to "industrial property" and would culminate in the 1883 Paris Convention. These were important developments in the law of nations when one consider the fact that, the law of nations, was, among many other characteristics, derived from 'the Treaties or positive conventions of States'.[24]

By the turn of the twentieth-century, the law of nations had not yet fully gave way to the modern "international law", but it was obvious that by the time the war was over in 1918, and in its aftermath, there was much 'sophisticated skepticism' towards the law of nations.[25] Such scepticisms vary, but the tone of international legal scholars were partly to blame.[26] Furthermore, the war would fundamentally reshape global trading relations[27] and the new structure of international law, yet leaving the intellectual property system devised four decades earlier in Paris and Berne intact. If anything, the aftermath of the war reinforced the need to protect intellectual property rights. This was evident from the imposition of the Paris Convention on Germany and new areas such 'unfair competition' along with the protection of property broadly written into the Versailles Treaty.

The works in this collection shows that the evolution of intellectual property rights and the positive law approach to their regulation through treaties and domestic laws has been important for the growth of both the public and private law of nations. For contemporary purposes, both the public and private law of nations is simply international law. Thus, this collection provides the evolution and transformation of intellectual property regulation through the transformative lens of international law and also how domestic attempts arose to meet the international legal obligations. In that regard, the work is also a form of modern comparative international law, yet narrating how the private law of nations in intellectual property rights emerged.

The narratives in this collection tell the tales of intellectual property rights through different forms such as trademarks and *terroir*; copyrights in the late

24 Levi, Leone. *The Law of Nature and Nations as affected by Divine Law* (London: F.G. Cash, 1855) 59.

25 Dickinson, Edwin D. 'The New Law of Nations'. *West Virginia Law Quarterly* 32(1) (1925) 4–32.

26 Ibid, at 13.

27 On this point, see also, Calvin, Patricia, and Dungy, Madeleine. 'Trade, Law, and the Global Order of 1919'. *Diplomatic History* 44(4) (2020) 554–579.

Qing dynasty; exhibitions and diplomacy; industrial property during World War I; and the accession to the international treaties during the era. Moreover, other aspects of the narratives in this collection include countries that were not necessarily seen as part of the civilized law of nations in the late nineteenth century have since been incorporated in order to demonstrate that the positive law of nations in intellectual property rights was meant to further civilize those countries.

The narratives in this collection can help to shape how we understood what took place during the early formation of international intellectual property law and how influential the field has become over the last century. Moreover, the collection takes us right back to the beginning of law-making in international intellectual property as a joint-endeavour between states and private actors by opening up with an archival discussion on how international intellectual property law formed beginning with the Vienna Patent Congress in 1873 through the adoption of the Paris Convention in 1883. All the narratives in this collection converges around a more pluralistic understanding of the history of intellectual property rights in the law of nations.

Bibliography

Barnes, Joseph. *Treatise on the Justice, Policy, and Utility of Establishing an Effectual System for Promoting the Progress of Useful Arts, by Assuring Property in the Products of Genius*, Philadelphia: Francis Bailey, 1792.

Banu, Roxana. *Nineteenth Century Perspectives on Private International Law*, Oxford: OUP, 2018.

Beaulac, Stephane. 'Emer de Vattel and the Externalization of Sovereignty' *Journal of the History of International Law* (2003) 5: 237.

Beier, F.K. 'On Hundred Years of International Cooperation: The Role of the Paris Convention in the Past, Present and Future' *International Review of Industrial Property and Copyright Law* (1984) 15: 1.

Blakeney, Michael. 'The Role of Intellectual Property in Regional Commercial Unions in Europe and Asia' *Prometheus: Critical Studies in Innovation* (1998) 16: 341.

Calvin, Patricia, and Dungy, Madeleine. 'Trade, Law, and the Global Order of 1919' *Diplomatic History* (2020) 44: 554.

Dickinson, Edwin D. 'The New Law of Nations' *West Virginia Law Quarterly* (1925) 32: 4.

Duncan, Louise J. *The Role of Theoretical Debate in the Evolution of National and International Patent Protection: From the French Revolution to the Paris Convention of 1883* (Brill, 2021).

Ederington, Benjamin L. 'Property as a Natural Institution: The Separation of Property from Sovereignty in International Law' *American University Law Review* (1997) 13: 263.

Garnsey, Peter. *Thinking About Property: From Antiquity to the Age of Revolution*, Cambridge: CUP, 2007.

Grossman, Gene M., and Lai, Edwin L.C. 'International Protection of Intellectual Property' *American Economic Review* (2004) 94: 1635.

van Hulle, Inge and Lesaffer, Randall C.H., eds. *International Law in the Long Nineteenth Century (1776–1914)*, Brill, 2019.

Kemp, Tom. *Industrialization in Nineteenth-Century Europe, 2nd Edition*, Abingdon: Routledge, 1985.

Khan, B. Zorina. 'Selling Ideas: An International Perspective on Patent and Markets for Technological Innovations, 1790–1930' *Business History Review* (2013) 87: 39.

Kingsbury, Benedict, and Straumann, Benjamin, eds. *The Roman Foundations of the Law of Nations: Alberico Gentili and the Justice of Empire*, Oxford: OUP, 2010.

Kunz, Josef L. 'On the Theoretical Basis of the Law of Nations' *Transactions of the Grotius Society* (1924) 10: 115.

Levi, Leone. *The Law of Nature and Nations as affected by Divine Law*, London: F.G. Cash, 1855.

May, Christopher, and Sell, Susan. *Intellectual Property Rights: A Critical History*, Boulder: Lynne Rienner, 2006.

Merges, Robert, and Seagull Haiyan Song. *Transnational Intellectual Property Law: Text and Cases*, Glosuteshsire: Edward Elgar, 2018.

Morris, P. Sean. 'The Private Foundations of International Law: Intellectual Property Rights and Pashukanis' *Jus Gentium: Journal of International Legal History* (2020) 5: 37.

Moser, Petra. 'Patents and Innovation: Evidence from Economic History' *The Journal of Economic Perspectives* (2013) 27: 23.

Nakhimovsky, Isaac. 'Vattel's Theory of the International Order: Commerce and the balance of power in the Law of Nations' *History of European Ideas* (2007) 33: 157.

Nussbaum, Arthur. *A Concise History of the Law of Nations*, New York: Macmillan, 1947.

Nussbaum, Arthur. 'Rise and Decline of the Law of Nations Doctrine in the Conflict of Laws' *Columbia Law Review* (1942) 42: 189.

O'Connor, Sean M. 'The Overlooked French Influence on the Intellectual Property Clause' *The University of Chicago Law Review* (2015) 82: 733.

Patterson, Ray, and Joyce, Craig. 'Copyright in 1791: An Essay Concerning the Founders' View of the Copyright Power Granted to Congress in Article I, Section 8, clause 8 of the US Constitution' *Emory Law Journal* (2003) 52: 909.

Rahmatian, Andreas. 'Indirect Sovereignty Through Property Rights' *Notre Dame Journal of International and Comparative Law* (2017) 7: 58.

Ram, James. *The Science of Legal Judgment*, New York: Baker, Voorhis & Co., 1871.

Ruse-Khan, Henning Grosse. *The Protection of Intellectual Property in International Law*, Oxford: OUP, 2016.

Saiz Gonzalez, J. Patricio. 'The Spanish Patent System (1770–1907)' *History and Technology* (2002) 24: 45.

Sherman, Brad, and Bently, Lionel. *The Making of Modern Intellectual Property Law*, Cambridge: CUP, 1999.

Thomson, W.P. *Handbook of Patent Law of All Countries*, London: Stevens & Sons, 1920.

Twiss, Travers. *The Law of Nations considered as Independent Political Communities – on the Right and Duties of Nations in Time of Peace*, Oxford: OUP, 1861.

Vattel, Emer de. *The Law of Nations, or, Principles of the law of nature, Applied to the Conduct and Affairs of Nations and Sovereigns*, London: G.G. and J. Robinson, 1797.

Vollenhoven, C. Van. *The Three Stages in the Evolution of the Law of Nations*, The Hague: Martinus Nijhoff, 1919.

Zurbuchen, Simone, ed. *The Law of Nations and Natural Law, 1625–1800*, Brill, 2019.

PART 1

Industrial Innovation in History and Conflicts

CHAPTER 1

The Key Historical Influences Leading to the Paris Convention for the Protection of Industrial Property of 1883

Louise J. Duncan

1 The First Step towards International Patent Protection – Role of the United Kingdom

The earliest movement toward international protection of patent rights began in the United Kingdom. This point was acknowledged by the first Secretary of the International Bureau of Industrial Property, B. Frey-Godet, in a Report he made to the Second A.I.P.P.I. Congress in London in 1898.[1] He noted the work of the various U.K. Select Committees on Patents and the influence of individuals such as Henry Bessemer, Sir William Armstrong and William Siemens, who spoke of the need for an international understanding on patent law.[2]

As early as the 1850s, a small number of persons in the U.K. had turned their minds to the possibility of international patent protection. Later commentators who were involved in the 1873 Vienna Congress believed that Prince Albert, Consort of Queen Victoria, had first suggested international protection for inventions at the time of the Great Exhibition in London in 1851.[3] Modern commentators such as Plasseraud and Savignon also advanced a similar position regarding Prince Albert's key role in the initial stirrings towards international patent protection.[4] What is more likely is that Prince Albert spoke in favour of proposals to introduce temporary legal protection for inventions exhibited at the Great Exhibition in London in 1851, and this was later

1 Frey-Godet, B. "*Comparaison du texte de la Convention et de la législation britannique correspondante*" (1898) *Annuaire de l'association Internationale pour la Protection de la Propriété Industrielle* 151, pp. 151–2.

2 *Ibid.*

3 Pieper, C., and Schmid, P. *Geschichte der internationalen Union für den Schutz des gewerblichen Eigentums sammt Konvention und Staatsverträgen* (Berlin, Deutschen Vereins für den Schutz des gewerblichen Eigentums, 1894), pp. 6–7.

4 Plasseraud, Y., and Savignon, F. *Paris 1883: Genése du droit Unioniste des Brevets* (Paris, Litec, 1983), p. 121.

 DOI:10.1163/9789004511439_003

mistakenly interpreted by commentators as support for more comprehensive international patent protection.[5]

During the 1850s, however, some of the U.K. patent reform societies such as The Association of Patentees and Proprietors of Patents had a specific objective to secure international treaty arrangements for the mutual recognition of the rights of inventors.[6] However, when such societies referred to international patent protection, what they really envisaged was a series of bilateral treaties, and not a multilateral treaty such as the Paris Convention. International arrangements were also of secondary importance when compared to the compelling need for domestic patent law reform at that time.

The earliest U.K. proponent of international assimilation of patent laws was Bennet Woodcroft, Superintendent of Specifications at the U.K. Patent Office, who in 1856 was reported to have personally visited various continental states to arrange the plans for such assimilation.[7] The precise nature of Woodcroft's proposals have not been recorded in any official documents, although Thomas Webster, U.K. delegate to the 1873 Vienna Congress, noted that Woodcroft's proposals were 'the result of his own considerations and inquiries into the patent systems of other countries.'[8]

While it appears that nothing immediate came of Woodcroft's proposals, in 1858 three members of the U.K. Parliament introduced a Private Members' Bill 'To make Provisions to secure International Patent Right'.[9] The object of this Bill was to grant to foreign patentees the rights of U.K. patentees, although the duration of the U.K. patent term was linked to the duration of any prior foreign patent. The applicability of the provisions of the Bill was also limited by the fact that only nationals of States designated by Order in Council could apply for protection, which would have probably depended upon some degree

5 See further, Duncan, L. *The Role of Theoretical Debate in the Evolution of National and International Patent Protection: From the French Revolution to the Paris Convention of 1883* (Brill, 2021), pp. 206–207.

6 Davis, I.J.G. and Harrison, J. "Prelude to the United Kingdom's Accession to the Paris Convention, March 17, 1884" [1984] *Industrial Property* 395, p. 397.

7 Pieper, C. *Der Erfinderschutz und die Reform der Patentgesetze. Amtlicher Bericht über den Internationalen Patent-Congress zur Erörterung der Frage des Patentschutzes. Mit einer Einleitung von Dr. C.W. Siemens F.R.S.* (Dresden, Commission der Schulbuchhandlung, 1873), p. 260.

8 United Kingdom, Parliamentary Papers, *Vienna Universal Exhibition, 1873; Report on the International Patent Congress by Thomas Webster, M.A., F.R.S., one of Her Majesty's Counsel* (March 1874), p. 376.

9 United Kingdom, *Parliamentary Papers* (1857–58) 235, vol. II, p. 587.

of reciprocity.[10] Although the Bill was not passed, and its proposed benefits to foreign inventors were limited, nevertheless it was an early example of U.K. concern to promote international protection of inventions.

One of the earliest verified statements in favour of some form of international patent treaty (or series of treaties) was made in a submission of the Chamber of Commerce of Huddersfield to the 1862–64 U.K. Select Committee on Patents.[11] Later, in the course of the 1871 and 1872 Select Committee Inquiries, a number of witnesses spoke in favour of international assimilation of patent laws, and the 1872 Report of the Select Committee endorsed the view that the U.K. Government should promote the international assimilation of patent laws.[12] Subsequently the U.K. Government had asked its representatives in the Colonies and foreign countries to provide information as to the patent laws operating in those territories, and whether assimilation was in any way feasible.[13] It was still receiving these reports at the time when the Vienna Congress was held in August 1873.

2 The Initial Practical Experiment: Bilateral Treaties

In his work on the origins of the Berne Convention for the Protection of Literary and Artistic Works 1886, Professor Sam Ricketson argues that the development of bilateral treaties containing provisions relating to copyright was an important step which preceded the founding of the Berne Convention in 1886.[14] He states that the negotiation of bilateral treaties with precise terms under which protection was to be accorded, was considered preferable to the

10 See further, Davis, I.J.G., and Harrison, J. "Prelude to the United Kingdom's Accession to the Paris Convention, March 17, 1884" [1984] *Industrial Property* 395, pp. 396–397.

11 United Kingdom, Parliamentary Papers, *Report of the Commissioners appointed to Inquire into the Working of the Law Relating to Letters Patent for Inventions* (1864) 3419, vol. XXIX, p. 321 at 184.

12 United Kingdom, Parliamentary Papers, *Report from the Select Committee on Letters Patent; together with the Proceedings of the Committee, Minutes of Evidence, Appendix and Index* (1872) 193, vol. XI, p. 395 at v. See further Duncan, L. *The Role of Theoretical Debate in the Evolution of National and International Patent Protection: From the French Revolution to the Paris Convention of 1883* (Brill, 2021), pp. 154–158.

13 United Kingdom, Parliamentary Papers, *Reports by H.M. Secs of Embassy and Legation respecting Law and Practice in Foreign Countries with regard to Inventions* (1873) C. 741, vol. LXVI, p. 483; United Kingdom, Parliamentary Papers, *Correspondence respecting International Arrangements for Assimilation in Law and Practice in regard to Letters Patent of Inventions* (1874) C. 999, vol. LIV, p. 211.

14 Ricketson, S. *The Berne Convention for the protection of literary and artistic works: 1886–1986* (London, Centre for Commercial Law Studies, 1987), p. 25.

previous "haphazard" method of securing copyright protection on the basis of either substantive or formal reciprocity.[15] Upon the foundation of an extensive series of bilateral treaties, the Berne Convention was eventually established.

It is interesting to note that the Paris Convention of 1883 did not have the background of an extensive series of pre-existing bilateral patent treaties. As Pelletier and Vidal-Naquet state in their early, but comprehensive work on the Paris Convention,[16] before 1883, bilateral patent treaties were "*trés rares*"[17] and the only example known to the authors which specifically granted a right of "territoriality" or "national treatment" was the Austro-German treaty of 16 December 1878 (renewed in 1881 and 1891).[18] By the term "territoriality" was meant that a patent granted in one of the contracting States was only operative in that contracting State. However, the parties agreed to apply their domestic patent legislation equally to nationals and subjects of contracting States, amounting to what is now more commonly known as a right of "national treatment".[19]

It was more common for provisions relating to industrial property rights to be included in general commercial treaties, in what was known as 'dispositions accessoires'.[20] Yet only a few such treaties specifically referred to patents.[21] Moreover, any reference to patent rights in commercial treaties was usually 'bréve et précaire'[22] because '[p]ar suite de leur caractére secondaire, ces clauses son peu développées.'[23] In most cases, the patent provisions in these

15 *Ibid.*

16 Pelletier, M., and Vidal-Naquet, E. *La Convention d'Union pour la Protection de la Propriété Industrielle du 20 mars 1883 et les Conférences de Revision Postérieures* (Paris, L. Larose, 1902).

17 Translation: "very rare". *Ibid.* p. 4.

18 *Ibid.*

19 See further: *Ibid.* pp. 4–5; Milhaud, L. *Des Brevets d'invention dans les Rapports Internationaux* (Paris, Larose et Forcel, 1892), pp. 15–17.

20 Translation: "Accessory or additional provisions". Pelletier, M., and Vidal-Naquet, E., *op.cit.* p. 5.

21 Most commercial treaties which specifically included provisions relating to patents were negotiated at the instigation of the French Government. The most important were: Commercial Treaties between France and Italy of 1869 and 3 November 1881; Commercial Treaty between France, Prussia and the Zollverein of 2 August 1862; Commercial Treaty between France and Spain of 30 June 1876; Commercial Treaty between France and the U.S.A. of 10 April 1869; Commercial Treaty between France and the U.K. of 28 February 1882; Commercial Treaty between France and Austria of 7 November 1881. Source: Pelletier, M. and Vidal-Naquet, E., *op.cit.* 4–5; Plaisant, M. *Traité de Droit Conventionnel International concernant la Propriété Industrielle* (Paris, Sirey, 1949), pp. 12–13.

22 Translation: "brief and uncertain".

23 Translation: "by reason of their secondary character, these clauses were little developed". Pelletier, M., and Vidal-Naquet, E., *op.cit.* p. 5.

bilateral treaties were based on principles of reciprocity,[24] which, combined with the constant succession of amendments to these treaties, led to much variation in the treatment of foreign nationals, and consequent uncertainty for inventors.[25]

It became increasingly clear that bilateral commercial treaties were not the most appropriate way to protect any form of industrial property right. As Pelletier and Vidal-Naquet state, 'les traités de commerce sont, par leur nature, contractés pour un court laps de temps'[26] and were generally concerned to address a particular economic situation.[27] When this economic situation changed, the commercial treaty was denounced or replaced by another, which left the industrial property right holder in a difficult situation. In most cases, once the treaty had expired, the right holder was stripped of his or her rights, without access to compensation.[28]

Even in the case of trade marks and designs and models, the bilateral commercial treaty system did not offer many advantages. As with copyright, a significant number of commercial treaties included provisions relating to trade marks (and sometimes designs and models) either on the basis of 'national treatment'[29] with or without the need for reciprocity,[30] or on the basis of the treatment of the 'most favoured nation'.[31]

Bilateral commercial treaties containing provisions relating to trade marks and designs suffered the same disadvantages as those (relatively few) relating to patents, and prompted early proposals for a more unified approach. There was a growing conviction that industrial property rights were not appropriate subjects for inclusion in general commercial treaties. The Permanent Committee established by the 1878 Paris Conference[32] drafted a series of documents for submission to the French Government with the ultimate aim of establishing

24 Plaisant, M., *op.cit.* p. 13.

25 *Ibid.*

26 Translation: "commercial treaties are, by their nature, contracted for a short space of time".

27 Pelletier, M., and Vidal-Naquet, E., *op.cit.* p. 5.

28 Plaisant, M., *op.cit.* p. 13.

29 For example, the Treaty of Commerce between the U.K. and Austria-Hungary, dated 5 December 1876.

30 For example, the Treaty of Commerce between the U.K. and Belgium dated 23 July 1862.

31 For example the Declaration between the U.K. and Denmark of 28 November 1879.

32 France, Ministere de L'agriculture et du Commerce, *Comptes rendus Stenographiques publiés sous les auspices du Comité Central des Congrés et Conférences et la direction de M. CH THIRION, Secrétaire du Comité, avec le concours des Bureaux des Congrés et des auteurs de Conférences: Congrés International de la Propriété Industrielle tenu á Paris du 5 au 17 Septembre 1878* (Paris 1879), p. 719.

points of agreement to form the basis of an international treaty.[33] The second draft contained a general recommendation that '[i]l est á desirer que les stipulations de garantie réciproque de la propriété fassent l'object de conventions spéciales et indépendantes des traités de commerce.'[34] The reason for this recommendation was that there were many types of commercial treaty, their duration was subject to fluctuations in political and economic circumstances, and they were liable to cease operation without warning.[35] However, it was the Committee's view that industrial property rights should be considered more permanent, they should have 'une existence propre'[36] and should not be subject to sudden loss merely because a commercial treaty abruptly ceased, either through denunciation or expiration.[37] The only way this could be achieved was through "special conventions" dealing only with industrial property rights and providing some degree of uniformity and permanency.[38]

3 The Growth of the Spirit of Internationalism

Prior to the 1880s, there was a steady increase in what can generally be described as an awareness of potential benefits from closer international co-operation between States. Georges Maillard, a noted lawyer in Paris from 1882 and French delegate to the revision Conferences of the Paris Convention between 1911 and 1925, characterised this change in the following way:

> Dans la seconde moitié du dix-neuviéme siécle s'est manifestée entre les principaux gouvernements une tendance à substituer aux conventions particuliéres, pour le réglement des intérêts économiques dans les rapports internationaux, le systéme des conventions d'Union, c'est-à-dire des ententes liant par un même texte plusieurs nations, et pour

33 *Ibid.* p. 719. "Project d'une Union Internationale pour la Protection de la Propriété Industrielle".

34 Translation: "It is to be desired that stipulations of reciprocal guarantee of industrial property are made the object of special conventions and are independent of commercial treaties." *Ibid.* p. 723.

35 *Ibid.*

36 Translation: "an independent existence/status" *Ibid.*

37 *Ibid.* p. 145. Le comte de Maillard de Marafy, President of the Consultative Committee on Foreign Legislation of the *Union des Fabricants* in Paris, noted at the 1878 Conference that since the recent denunciation of the Commercial Treaty between France and Russia, the rights of French trade mark holders in Russia had become entirely thrown into disorder.

38 *Ibid.* See also Vidal-Naquet, E. *Des Marques de Fabrique et de Commerce et du Nom Commercial en droit International* (Paris. L. Larose, 1898) Part Three.

> le fonctionnement de ces ententes, des bureaux internationaux ... ont été créés.[39]

This desire to promote national interests through international conventions affected many areas of law, and was one of the major factors which lay behind the founding of the Paris Convention in 1883.

The spirit of internationalism which preceded the founding of the Paris Convention took two major paths. The first was the development of proposals for an international copyright treaty. The second was a more general interest in the law of nations which led to the establishment of treaties on various matters such as weights and measures and postal relations.

3.1 *Early Movements towards International Copyright Protection*

Ricketson argues that as early as 1839 support can be found for a universal law of copyright.[40] In 1858 an International Congress on Literary and Artistic Property was held in Brussels.[41] At that Congress, a number of Resolutions were passed which supported the notion of an 'international recognition of property in works of literature and art'.[42] The Congress also recommended that this principle ought to be admitted in all countries without the requirement of reciprocity,[43] and also favoured uniformity in the provisions of copyright legislation.[44]

It must be admitted, however, that support for an international copyright law did not necessarily translate into support for international treatment of any other area of intellectual property. Although in the 1850s and 1860s support for copyright was fairly universal, there were movements in some countries for

39 Translation: "In the second half of the nineteenth century there was manifested between the principal governments a tendency to replace individual treaties for the regulation of economic interests in international relations, with what is known as understandings wherein many nations comply with the same text, and in relation to the functioning of such understandings, International Bureaus ... have been created." Maillard, G. *Le Bureau International de l'Union pour la Protection de la Propriété Industrielle* (undated extract from a journal entitled *Revue Internationale du Commerce, de l'industrie et de la Banque* held at W.I.P.O. Geneva), p. 145.

40 Ricketson, S. *The Berne Convention for the protection of literary and artistic works: 1886–1986* (London, Centre for Commercial Law Studies, 1987), p. 41.

41 *Ibid.* See also Blaine, R. "On International Copyright Property in Works of Literature and the fine Arts" (1859) *Transactions of the National Association for the Promotion of Social Science* 272 (discussing the resolutions of the 1858 Brussels Conference).

42 Resolution 1 of the 1858 Brussels Congress. Blaine, R., *op.cit.* p. 272.

43 Resolution 2 of the 1858 Brussels Congress. Blaine, R., *op.cit.* p. 272.

44 Resolution 5 of the 1858 Brussels Congress. Blaine, R., *op.cit.* p. 272.

abolition of the patent system.[45] For example, in the U.K., patent abolitionists tended to support international copyright protection to allow U.K. authors access to foreign markets for their works. The patent abolitionist Robert Macfie, for example, stated in 1869 that a system of international copyright should be established to enable U.K. authors protection for their works in the U.S. market.[46] The *Athenaeum* in 1869 described the American copyright legislation as amounting to '"legalised robbery" of British copyright property in the United States'[47] and a writer in the *Law Magazine and Law Review* stated that it would be desirable to see 'one law of international copyright obtaining in all civilized countries' ... but in particular it was of primary importance to 'sham[e] the Americans into a copyright convention.'[48]

During 1873 and 1874 there were two meetings of international associations in which the question of international copyright was discussed. The first was at the meeting of the Association for the Reform and Codification of the Law of Nations in Brussels in October 1873.[49] The origins of this association lay in the United Kingdom in 1866, when at the Manchester Congress of the National Association for the Promotion of Social Science, a member, David Dudley Field, suggested the appointment of a Committee to prepare a report on the outlines of an International Code to be prepared and submitted to different governments with the 'hope of receiving their sanction'.[50] Draft Outlines were duly prepared and presented to the 1873 Norwich Social Science Congress,[51] which in turn gained international attention and were the focus of study at the Brussels meeting in October 1873.[52]

Although the major portion of the Outlines was occupied with the essential rights of nations such as their 'sovereignty, equality, perpetuity, territory, and property',[53] other provisions were inserted which impacted more clearly on the private interests of individuals. Among these, 'patents, trade marks, copyrights'

---

45 See further Duncan, L. *The Role of Theoretical Debate in the Evolution of National and International Patent Protection: From the French Revolution to the Paris Convention of 1883* (Brill, 2021). Chapters 3 and 4, pp. 105–204.

46 Macfie, R.A., ed. *Recent Discussions on the Abolition of Patents for Inventions in the United Kingdom, France, Germany, and the Netherlands: evidence, speeches and papers in its favour* (London, Longmans and Co, 1869), p. 241.

47 *Athenaeum*, 17 July 1869. Reproduced in Macfie, R.A., (ed), *op. cit.* p. 310.

48 "Anglo-American Copyright" (1868–9) 26 *The Law Magazine and Law Review* 49, p. 62.

49 Webster, T. "Reform and Codification of the Law of Nations" (1874) 3 *The Law Magazine and Law Review* (New Series) 1016, p. 1017.

50 Webster, T., *op.cit.* p. 1017.

51 Field, D., "On an International Code" (1874) 3 *The Law Magazine and Review* (New Series) 251.

52 Webster, T., *op.cit.* p. 1018.

53 Field, D., *op.cit.* p. 253–4.

were mentioned as worthy of international protection.[54] The 1873 Brussels meeting did not move beyond preliminary matters and a general espousal of the need for an International Code, but referred the question of patents, trade marks and copyright to be dealt with at the 1874 Conference.[55]

At the 1874 Conference in Geneva discussion moved to 'assimilation of Law and Procedure, and the extinction of the conflict of the Law of Nations in respect of property in intellectual labour…,' a subject described as being of world-wide interest.[56] The British delegate Thomas Webster recorded that he left the 1874 Conference confident that there would be agreement for 'a generous recognition of the claims and rights of all' in respect of copyright, and that the requirement of reciprocity would be extinguished.[57]

Even though it is clear from reports of the 1873 and 1874 Conferences that the main focus of discussion had been copyright rather than industrial property, there is no doubt that the 1873 Conference in Brussels and the 1874 Conference in Geneva did provide some initial consideration of the need for international protection of "intellectual labour" more generally.

3.2 *The Law of Nations*

It was not only the area of copyright and related industrial property issues which attracted calls for international protection during the latter part of the nineteenth century. A number of other multi-lateral treaties regulating legal relations were also established during that time. As Vidal-Naquet explained, the increasing development of communications technology, particularly by new means of transport and locomotion, permitted people separated by large distances to meet with relative ease.[58] Yet at the same time, this increasing internationalisation of business and communications resulted in greater legal difficulties, as the parties involved came into contact with the differing laws of several States. As Webster stated in 1874, '[r]ailways, steamers telegraphs, postal arrangements, and free trade, are changing the conditions and relations of intercourse and enterprise throughout the whole world. Let law and procedure be adapted to the inevitable necessity….'[59]

---

54 Field, D., *Ibid.*

55 "The Brussels Conference for the Reform and Codification of the Law of Nations" (1873) 2 *The Law Magazine and Review* (New Series) 1094, pp. 1098–1102.

56 Webster, T., *op.cit.* p. 1018.

57 Webster, T., *op.cit.* p. 1019.

58 Vidal-Naquet, E. *Des Marques de Fabrique et de Commerce et du Nom Commercial en droit International* (Paris, L. Larose, 1898), p. 196.

59 Webster, T. "Reform and Codification of the Law of Nations" (1874) 3 *The Law Magazine and Review* (New Series) 1016, p. 1019.

As early as 1865 a multilateral treaty was founded which attempted to deal with the legal problems which were consequent upon increased international communications. This was the International Telegraph Union (1865) which was followed by another multilateral treaty on communications in 1874, the Universal Postal Union. As Roubier notes, the Universal Postal Union was strongly influential in some of the early discussions over the proposals for the Paris Convention.[60] The success of negotiations over the Postal Union appeared to engender a belief that there could be international uniformity in respect of any area of law, whether this be in relation to industrial property, undersea cables, international railways, weights and measures, monetary circulation, calculation of longitude, time, or quarantine.[61]

4 International Exhibitions and the Need for Patent Protection: Vienna Congress of 1873

The first international conference devoted purely to the issue of patent protection was the Vienna Congress in 1873. The Congress was primarily a reaction to concerns about inadequate industrial property laws expressed by U.S. inventors who were unwilling to exhibit their inventions at the 1873 Vienna International Exposition. These concerns led the government of Austria-Hungary to invite delegates from various countries to meet in Vienna between 4 and 9 August 1873 to discuss this issue.[62]

Although in 1872 the Austro-Hungarian government had enacted a special law "for the provisional protection of articles introduced at the Vienna

60 Roubier, P. "Le droit unioniste de la propriété Industrielle" (1951) *Journal du Droit International* 676 (Part One); 1040 (Part two), p. 684.

61 See further: Bouvier, H. *Essais sur la Recherche de Principes Géneraux Applicables aux unions internationales pour la protection de la propriété Industrielle* (Paris, Imprimerie Moquet, 1889), pp. 8–19; Pelletier, M., and Vidal-Naquet, E., *op.cit.* 7; Field, D. "On an International Code" (1874) 3 *The Law Magazine and Review* (New Series) 251, p. 254.

62 The most complete record of the work of the Vienna Congress is contained in: Pieper, C. *Der Erfinderschutz und die Reform der Patentgesetze. Amtlicher Bericht über den Internationalen Patent-Congress zur Erörterung der Frage des Patentschutzes. Mit einer Einleitung von Dr. C.W. Siemens F.R.S.* (Dresden, Commission der Schulbuchhandlung, 1873). See also Grothe, H. *Der Internationale Patent-Congress in Wien (4–9 August 1873)* (Berlin, Julius Springer, 1873); United Kingdom, Parliamentary Papers, *Vienna Universal Exhibition, 1873; Report on the International Patent Congress by Thomas Webster, M.A., F.R.S. one of Her Majesty's Counsel* (March 1874); and for a modern commentary see Ricketson, S. *The Paris Convention for the Protection of Industrial Property* (Oxford University Press, 2015), pp. 32–37.

Exposition"[63] this law was based on earlier laws passed by the United Kingdom and France in connection with their earlier international expositions, and merely afforded temporary protection to foreign exhibitors until 31 December 1873.[64] The law did not resolve the more general problem of the harsh treatment of foreign inventors under the Austro-Hungarian patent system. As John Jay of the U.S. Legation in Vienna noted, foreign inventors who exhibited their inventions at the Vienna Exposition would be exposed to the loss of protection unless they took out patent rights in Austria within a short time after the conclusion of the exposition. It was his view that only 'mutual treaty stipulations' in respect of patent law could overcome these problems, and he considered it a 'favourable moment' for the U.S. Government to enter into discussions with the Austro-Hungarian Government on the matter.[65]

Accordingly, the Austro-Hungarian Government proposed that the issue of mutual treaty stipulations in respect of patent law should be studied at an international congress united with the Vienna Exposition.[66] The Programme of the International Congress, prepared by Archduke Régnier, President of the Organising Commission of the Vienna Exposition and Baron de Schwarz-Senborn, Chief Manager of the Vienna Exposition, was sent to a wide range of potential participants in March 1873.[67] Not only were delegates of the governments of potential exhibitors invited, but the Organising Commission encouraged the attendance of other experts, including manufacturers, scientific artisans and political economists.[68]

The Programme of the Congress referred to the desirability that a 'complete solution common to all states' should be 'accomplished by international agreement.'[69] This was the most important aspect of the Vienna Congress,

63 Appendix to letter of John Jay of the American Legation in Vienna in his Report to Washington dated 26 March 1872. United States of America, Congressional Papers, *Papers Relating to the Foreign Relations of the United States – Message and Foreign Relations 1872*, 42nd Congress, 3rd Session, H. Ex Docs VI, part 1, p. 52.

64 Programme of the International Congress for the Consideration of the Question of Patent Protection. Reproduced in United Kingdom, Parliamentary Papers, *Vienna Universal Exhibition, 1873 etc.*, p. 401.

65 United States of America, Congressional Papers, *Papers Relating to the Foreign Relations of the United States – Message and Foreign Relations 1872*, 42nd Congress, 3rd Session, H. Ex Docs VI, part 1, p. 58.

66 Programme of the International Congress for the Consideration of the Question of Patent Protection. Reproduced in United Kingdom, Parliamentary Papers, *Vienna Universal Exhibition, 1873 etc.*, p. 401.

67 *Ibid.*

68 *Ibid.* pp. 401–402.

69 *Ibid.* p. 400.

namely the search for fundamental principles for an international reform of patent legislation.

Although the Austro-Hungarian Government initially helped organise the Congress, wrote the Programme and advertised the meeting, the Congress itself had no official standing.[70] This was largely because the Austro-Hungarian Government refused to bear the expense of the Congress and its financing thus fell to private individuals, particularly those associated with the Deutsche Patentschutz-Verein.[71] Although delegates from 18 nations attended, approximately half were Germans or Austrians.[72]

In furthering the objects set down in the Programme, the Preparatory Committee set out a series of questions, having reference to:

> the international rights of inventors – the boundaries of those rights, – whether such boundaries should be international or territorial – the granting, cost, lapsing, and duration of patents – the administration of the Patent Office, and the securing of international arrangements somewhat analogous to those existing in the case of copyright.[73]

These questions were sent in advance to registered participants, and their answers assisted the Preparatory Committee in formulating a series of Resolutions and reasons in support, which were presented for discussion at the Congress.[74]

Although the original intention of the members of the Preparatory Committee was to promote international unification of patent laws, the debates that took place at the Congress made it apparent that such unification would be impossible to achieve at that time. Issues such as the compulsory licensing of patents caused considerable controversy among the delegates,[75] and the debates revealed that an international patent law would be even more

---

70 Penrose stated that the Congress was run under the "auspices" of the Austro-Hungarian Government. Penrose, E. *The Economics of the International Patent System* (Baltimore, John Hopkins Press, 1951), p. 45. Webster noted in his Report that there was some misapprehension concerning the character of the Congress, but that accredited representatives of various nations were present, although these were not official delegates. United Kingdom, Parliamentary Papers, *Vienna Universal Exhibition, 1873 etc.*, p. 340.

71 Grothe, H. *Der Internationale Patent-Congress in Wien (4–9 August 1873)* (Berlin, Julius Springer, 1873), p. 11.

72 Pieper, C. *Der Erfinderschutz und die Reform der Patentgesetze etc.*, pp. 263–267.

73 United Kingdom, Parliamentary Papers, *Vienna Universal Exhibition, 1873 etc.*, p. 342.

74 *Ibid.*

75 See further: Duncan, L. *The Role of Theoretical Debate in the Evolution of National and International Patent Protection: From the French Revolution to the Paris Convention of 1883* (Brill, 2021), pp. 233–236.

difficult to achieve than an international copyright law.[76] For this reason, the Congress decided that the more achievable plan was 'to assimilate as closely as possible the law, practice and procedure of countries by a system founded on the principles indicated in the resolutions of the Congress'.[77] As J.M. Thatcher, Assistant-Commissioner of Patents in Washington explained, it would be inadvisable and impractical to take the principles of one particular patent system, and attempt to engraft them onto the systems of other countries.[78]

The aim of the Congress then became to recommend a few principles as the proper basis for patent legislation, and then to send forth these principles 'to the world with the endorsement of [the] Congress'.[79] The Congress aimed for the harmonisation of important, general principles of patent law, but how this was actually achieved in practice 'should be left to the different countries to work out for themselves.'[80] The Congress did not envisage the introduction of any form of multilateral treaty on the subject of patent law. Yet it did establish a Permanent Executive Committee to continue its work and ensure that the Resolutions of the Congress were made known as widely as possible.[81]

Reaction to the work of the Vienna Congress varied from one country to another. In Germany, the U.K. and the U.S.A., the Congress had some influence upon domestic patent law reform, but there was certainly no evidence of harmonisation.[82] The Congress had no effect in France, largely because only three French citizens had attended the Congress and the work of the Congress remained generally unknown in that country.[83] Of more significance was the fact that in Germany and the U.K., the Congress largely put an end to the patent abolition movements.[84] In this way, it removed a major obstacle to an international patent treaty.

---

76 United Kingdom, Parliamentary Papers, *Vienna Universal Exhibition, 1873 etc.*, p. 376. See also Pieper, C., *Der Erfinderschutz und die Reform der Patentgesetze etc.*, von Baumhauer at p. 234; Werner Siemens at p. 234; Friedmann at p. 235; Pieper at pp. 237, 241; and Hartig at p. 241.

77 United Kingdom, Parliamentary Papers, *Vienna Universal Exhibition, 1873 etc.*, p. 376.

78 Pieper, C. *Der Erfinderschutz und die Reform der Patentgesetze etc.*, p. 197.

79 *Ibid.*

80 *Ibid.* (Thatcher) This statement was met with "cheers".

81 The members of the Preparatory Committee formed the Permanent Executive Committee. United Kingdom, Parliamentary Papers, *Vienna Universal Exhibition, 1873 etc.*, p. 377.

82 See further: Duncan, L. *The Role of Theoretical Debate in the Evolution of National and International Patent Protection: From the French Revolution to the Paris Convention of 1883* (Brill, 2021), pp. 238–247.

83 *Ibid.* pp. 239–240.

84 *Ibid.* pp. 242–243.

5 Growing Support for Uniform Industrial Property Legislation: The Paris Conference of 1878

Although the Paris Convention of 1883 was largely based upon a draft presented by the French Government to a diplomatic conference which took place in Paris in November 1880,[85] the unofficial 1878 Paris Conference was also important as it demonstrated growing support for comprehensive international industrial property protection, with at least a minimum of uniformity, and based upon the notion of inherent property rights in products of intellectual labour. The 1878 Paris Conference was the first truly international meeting to attempt to clarify the theoretical basis of patent protection.

5.1 *Reasons for the 1878 Paris Conference*

There were a number of factors which led to the convening of the international conference on industrial property rights in Paris between 5–17 September 1878. These included:

(a) The U.K. Government's emerging interest in international assimilation of patent laws;
(b) The work of the Association for the Reform and Codification of the Law of Nations;
(c) The work of Carl Pieper of Germany; and
(d) The Paris Universal Exposition of 1878.

Since 1872, the U.K. Government had been considering the manner in which some form of international assimilation of patent law and practice could be achieved. This interest was prompted by the recommendations of the 1872 Select Committee on Patents, and later, the work of the Vienna Congress. The 1872 Select Committee had reported that there should be an assimilation of law and practice in regard to inventions in all 'civilised countries', and recommended that the Government should undertake 'enquiries of foreign and colonial governments as to how far they would be ready to concur in such international arrangements'.[86] The U.K. Government followed up this recommendation by sending despatches to the Governors of all its colonies, asking each whether they were ready to concur in international arrangements

85 *Ibid.* Chapter 7.

86 United Kingdom, Parliamentary Papers, *Report from the Select Committee on Letters Patent; together with the Proceedings of the Committee, Minutes of Evidence, Appendix and Index* (1872) 193, vol. XI, p. 395, at v. See further details of the work of this Committee and its recommendations in Duncan, L. *The Role of Theoretical Debate in the Evolution of National and International Patent Protection: From the French Revolution to the Paris Convention of 1883* (Brill, 2021), pp. 251–252.

for assimilation of law and practice in regard to inventions.[87] Although most colonies supported assimilation of United Kingdom and colonial patent systems, the Attorney-General of New Zealand went further and reported back to London that the mode of procedure in obtaining a patent and its effect, when obtained, should be the same in all countries.[88]

The 1872 U.K. Select Committee had also affected the work of the Association for the Reform and Codification of the Law of Nations, which was established in 1873.[89] The Association's interest in industrial property and copyright law was advanced largely by the contribution of the U.K. members, many of whom had given evidence to the 1871 and 1872 U.K. Select Committees and were doubtless aware of the recommendations. However, after 1876, many non-U.K. members of the Association, particularly French nationals, promoted the cause of international patent protection.

In 1877, the Association met in Anvers, and adopted a Resolution stating that it was desirable to assimilate, as far as possible, the patent laws of the various nations.[90] It also supported in principle, the notion that the law should more readily facilitate the lodging of simultaneous applications for patents in several countries. It proposed that the filing of a patent application (and possibly also a trade mark or design application) should be effected simultaneously through deposit at foreign consulates.[91] However, as the International Bureau later noted in 1886, this solution would not have alleviated the problems of expense and inconvenience associated with making patent applications in various countries, given the difficulty of gaining access to all the required foreign consulates in one day.[92]

---

87 United Kingdom, Parliamentary Papers, *Correspondence respecting International Arrangements for Assimilation in Law and Practice in regard to Letters Patent of Inventions* (1874) C.999, vol. LIV, p. 211 at A2.

88 *Ibid.* See letter from the Attorney-General of New Zealand, James Prendergast, dated 6 February 1873.

89 Duncan, L. *The Role of Theoretical Debate in the Evolution of National and International Patent Protection: From the French Revolution to the Paris Convention of 1883* (Brill, 2021), p. 251.

90 France, Ministére de L' agriculture et du Commerce, *Comptes rendus Sténographiques publiés sous les auspices du Comité Central des Congrés et Conférences et la direction de M. CH THIRION, Secrétaire du Comité, avec le concours des Bureaux des Congrés et des auteurs de Conférences. Congrés International de la Propriété Industrielle tenu à Paris du 5 au 17 Septembre 1878* (Paris 1879) Annexe 11, pp. 498–501.

91 *Ibid.*

92 Bureau International de la Propriete Industrielle, "l'Article 4 de la Convention" (1886) 2 *La Propriété Industrielle* 17, p. 18.

References to the 1877 meeting of the Association appear frequently in the records of the 1878 Paris Conference,[93] and many of the more influential delegates to the 1877 meeting also attended as delegates to the 1878 Paris Conference.[94] One very influential figure at the 1873 Vienna Congress, the 1877 Anvers meeting and the 1878 Paris Conference was Carl Pieper, who was involved in patent law reform in Germany. He stated that he entered into communications with the French Government as early as 1876, suggesting that France should organise a general Conference on patent law at the same time as the Paris Exhibition of 1878.[95]

The French Government attributed its decision to hold the 1878 Paris Conference to its support for international social and economic development, as exemplified by the Paris Universal Exposition. The Exposition was announced by Presidential Decrees dated 4 and 13 April 1876, and was concerned not only to promote and display works of art and industry, but also to promote social progress.[96] For this reason, the Consultative Committee of the Exposition encouraged the holding of international conferences on a diverse range of subjects. There were 32 international conferences held in Paris in 1878 in conjunction with the Exposition. One of those related to legal protection for industrial property rights.[97]

93 France, Ministére de L' agriculture et du Commerce, *Comptes rendus Sténographiques etc.*, Annexes 11 and 14.

94 Duncan, L. *The Role of Theoretical Debate in the Evolution of National and International Patent Protection: From the French Revolution to the Paris Convention of 1883* (Brill, 2021), pp. 251–252.

95 Pieper, C., and Schmid, P. *Geschichte der internationalen Union für den Schutz des gewerblichen Eigentums sammt Konvention und Staatsverträgen* (Berlin, Deutschen Vereins für den Schutz des gewerblichen Eigentums, 1894), p. 7. See also Plasseraud, Y., and Savignon, F. *Paris 1883: Genése du droit Unioniste des Brevets* (Paris, Litec, 1983), p. 157.

96 United Kingdom, Parliamentary Papers, *Report of Her Majesty's Commissioners for the Paris Universal Exhibition of 1878* (1878) vol. 1, (C 2588) XXXII, p. 1 at 9.

97 The wide range of subjects covered by the Paris Conferences indicates that this was an era of internationalism. Besides industrial property, the Conferences covered the following subjects: protection of literary property, agriculture, unification and numbering of threads, Provident Institutions, demography, ethnographic sciences, geometry, statistics, improvement of the means of transportation, prevention of cruelty to animals, architecture, hygiene, mental medicine, civil engineers, monetary conferences, homeopathy, military ambulance services, legal medicine, alcoholism, anthropological sciences, commerce and industry, botany and horticulture, meteorology, geology, unification of weights, measures and coins, silk culture, relief to released prisoners, protection of artistic property, commercial geography, improvement of the conditions of the blind and deaf-mutes and Friends of Peace.

United States of America, Congressional Papers, *Paris Universal Exposition of 1878* (1878) 46th Congress, 3rd Session, H. Ex Docs vol. 20, No 42, Pt 1, p. 455 (Appendix N).

5.2 *The Work of the 1878 Paris Conference*

In his commentary upon the Paris Convention of 1883, Examiner F.A. Seeley of the U.S. Patent Office remarked that the 1878 Conference did not actually achieve anything of substance.[98] Instead, it was marked by 'an elaborate programme, largely of papers on theoretical subjects', and the plan or general idea of 'a permanent international union for the protection of industrial property' was more important to the Conference participants than the substantive points of discussion.[99] In 1886, Anthony Pollok, an official U.S. representative at the 1878 Conference, told the U.S. Senate that the Conference had been of limited value because of the large amount of time devoted to discussion of abstract subjects.[100] Like Seeley, Pollok considered that the real benefit of the 1878 Conference was that it prepared the way for later diplomatic negotiations which led to the signing of the Paris Convention in 1883.[101]

To a certain degree, the views of Seeley and Pollok were correct. The 1878 Conference spent much time discussing abstract subjects, the Programme of the Conference lacked structure, and some important matters were overlooked or dealt with in a cursory fashion. Nevertheless, two main themes ran through the work of the Conference:

(a) The recognition by delegates of natural property rights in industrial property, particularly patented inventions; and
(b) The need for uniform industrial property legislation at the international level.

5.2.1 Natural Property Rights

At a theoretical level, one of the main Resolutions of the 1878 Conference was the statement that:

> Le droit des inventeurs et des auteurs industriels sur leurs oeuvres ou des fabricants et négociants sur leurs marques est un droit de propriété. La loi civile ne le crée pas; elle ne fait que le réglementer.[102]

---

98 Seeley, F.A. *The International Union for the Protection of Industrial Property* (prepared under the direction of the Commissioner of Patents, Washington, 1 September 1887), p. 1.

99 *Ibid.*

100 Sautter, M. *La Convention Internationale pour la Protection de la Propriété Industrielle aux états-Unis: Argumentation de M.A. Pollok, de Washington, devant le Sénat Fédéral* (Paris, 1886), p. 2.

101 *Ibid.* For a modern commentary on the work of the 1878 Conference see Ricketson, S., *The Paris Convention for the Protection of Industrial Property* (Oxford University Press, 2015), pp. 37–49.

102 Translation: "the right of inventors and industrial originators in their works of manufacture and traders in their marks is a right of property. The civil law does not create it; it

In the Programme, several of the questions raised by the Preparatory Committee related to the theoretical basis of industrial property rights. Thus, comments were sought as to 'the nature of the right of the inventor', including questions of legitimacy and utility,[103] 'the nature of the right of authors in their designs and models' and the 'right of property in a trade mark'.[104] The Committee asked generally, 'Was this a right of property?', and if so, what kind of property was it?[105]

In response to the questions asked in the Programme, many individuals and organisations wrote to the Preparatory Committee with decided views that there were natural property rights in inventions, trade marks and designs.[106] The delegates sought agreement on this issue prior to any other work of the 1878 Conference.

In their discussions regarding the theoretical basis of industrial property protection, the delegates were presented with three alternatives. The original proposal was that of Pouillet[107] and Droz,[108] whose draft Resolution was the same as that eventually adopted, except that there was in addition an explicit statement that the property right was founded in natural law.[109] In contrast, a draft Resolution was proposed by an official representative of the Swiss Government, Professor Schreyer, who urged the Conference to adopt a more instrumentalist approach, accepting that it was just to accord to inventors an exclusive temporary right in their inventions for a duration sufficient to assure them remuneration for their work and expenses.[110] However, the Schreyer proposal was rejected by the majority of the delegates.[111] The Conference preferred

only regulates it." (General Section, Resolution 1). France, Ministére de L' agriculture et du Commerce, *Comptes rendus Sténographiques etc.* Resolutions, pp. 427–435.

103 "Programme due Congrés", Question 1. France, Ministére de L' agriculture et du Commerce, *Comptes rendus Sténographiques etc.*, pp. 4–10.

104 *Ibid.*

105 *Ibid.*

106 Claude Couhin, Emile Barrault, A. Poirrier, G. Leboyer, Duroy de Bruignac, the Commercial Tribunal of Saint-Etienne and the Board of Arbitration of Elbeuf. See further Duncan, L. *The Role of Theoretical Debate in the Evolution of National and International Patent Protection: From the French Revolution to the Paris Convention of 1883* (Brill, 2021), pp. 255–258; 264–265.

107 Pouillet was Parisian lawyer and the author of works on patent and trade mark law. He was one of the founders of AIPPI in 1897.

108 Droz was a Parisian lawyer.

109 France, Ministére de L' agriculture et du Commerce, *Comptes rendus Sténographiques etc.* Resolutions at p. 127.

110 *Ibid.* p. 129.

111 *Ibid.* p. 129.

the proposal of Emile Barrault,[112] that the Pouillet and Droz proposal should be adopted without specific reference to natural law.

There is no doubt that the 1878 Conference was strongly influenced by the French delegates,[113] and for that reason, it was unsurprising that the majority supported the notion of property rights in inventions. However, some delegates were cautious, and noted that the Pouillet/Droz and Barrault proposals would not readily receive support in jurisdictions outside France. Lloyd Wise, an engineer, and representative of the Society of Arts, warned that the Resolutions of the Conference would not be accepted in the United Kingdom if either of the proposals were adopted.[114] Lyon-Caen, a Professor of Law in Paris who had written extensively in the area of patent law, agreed that the Pouillet/Droz and Barrault proposals were too divisive and would never receive universal support outside the Conference.[115]

Despite the warnings of Wise, Lyon-Caen and others,[116] the Conference voted to adopt the Barrault resolution recognising industrial property rights, regulated, but not created, by civil law.[117] Acceptance of this concept in turn influenced the debates upon further resolutions of the Conference, including those concerning (a) the right of foreigners to be treated as nationals; (b) compulsory licensing; (c) forfeiture of patents for non-working; and (d) the type of inventions which should be patentable.

In regard to the notion of national treatment, the Conference adopted the simple proposition that foreigners must be treated as nationals.[118] If the inventor or industrial creator had a property right that was of an intrinsic nature, and not reliant upon domestic law for its creation, then it followed that this property right must be protected without regard to national boundaries. The main point of difference between the delegates was whether national treatment should be extended to rights other than patents.

Professor Lyon-Caen noted that it had become customary State practice for foreign inventors to be treated as nationals when applying for patents, and reciprocity was not generally required.[119] However, for trade marks and designs,

---

112 Barrault was a Parisian engineer and patent agent, active in the Association for the Reform and Codification of the Law of Nations. *Ibid.* pp. 13, 16, 127.

113 Of the 484 delegates at the Conference only 94 were not French nationals. France, Ministére de L' agriculture et du Commerce, *Comptes rendus Sténographiques etc.*, pp. 15–28.

114 *Ibid.* p. 119.

115 *Ibid.* p. 128.

116 Professor Schreyer of Switzerland, Claude Cohin of Paris and M. Demeur of Brussels. *Ibid.* pp. 119; 124–129.

117 *Ibid.* p. 130.

118 *Ibid.* p. 130.

119 *Ibid.* p. 134.

there was no such customary State practice, and for example, in France, reciprocity was still required.[120] Further, most countries considered it was in the interests of national industry to grant patents to both nationals and foreigners, in order to have timely access to new inventions. However, there was no such national imperative in relation to trade marks and designs, as the main beneficiary of such legal protection was the manufacturer, not the community.[121] Nevertheless, the Conference adopted the notion of national treatment in respect of all industrial property rights, as the majority considered that once the Conference had accepted that patents, trade marks and designs were industrial property rights, they must all be respected without regard to national boundaries or requirements of reciprocity.[122]

In regard to compulsory licensing, the Conference resolved to reject the concept, even though it had been supported at the earlier 1873 Vienna Congress. The majority supported Professor Lyon-Caen's view that compulsory licenses were inconsistent with the earlier Resolution of the Conference in support of industrial property rights.[123] If a person had a property interest, it must amount to more than merely a right to receive licence fees.[124]

The issue of forfeiture of patents for non-working surprisingly gained the support of the majority of the delegates at the Conference, despite the fact that this appeared to be inconsistent with the notion of intrinsic industrial property rights in inventions. The Conference adopted a Resolution stating that it was acceptable to allow forfeiture for non-working, provided that such forfeiture was pronounced by a competent judicial authority.[125]

It was difficult to follow the logic of the Conference, which rejected the notion of compulsory licensing (a partial restriction of property rights) but accepted forfeiture for non-working (a complete loss of property rights). However, the majority of the delegates did not recognise the contradiction. Pouillet, who proposed the forfeiture resolution, justified it on the basis that such provisions existed in many patent systems, such as those of France, Italy and Germany and were intended to protect the public interest.[126] He added that patents were granted in order to secure to the public the use of new

120 *Ibid.* p. 135.
121 *Ibid.* p. 135.
122 *Ibid.* pp. 136–137.
123 *Ibid.* pp. 248–249.
124 *Ibid.*
125 *Ibid.* p. 429 (Patents Section, Resolution 10).
126 *Ibid.* pp. 282–285.

inventions, but if the patentee did not work the invention, he did not keep his side of the bargain, and the loss of the patent was justified.[127]

Although some delegates such as Mr Selwyn,[128] M.F. von Rosas[129] and Charles Assi[130] adopted a more practical, instrumentalist approach, pointing out that complete forfeiture of a patent for non-working was worse for the inventor than compulsory licensing,[131] their views were in the minority and the Conference quickly resolved that forfeiture for non-working should be permitted.[132]

As to the types of inventions that should be patentable, there was a heated debate at the 1878 Conference as to whether chemical and pharmaceutical products should be afforded protection.[133] By an unspecified majority, the Conference finally decided that chemical products and foodstuffs were patentable, and by a majority of 46 to 38 it was decided that pharmaceuticals were also patentable.[134]

One of the reasons why some delegates resisted extending protection to chemical products was because under the prevailing French and German patent laws of the time, only chemical processes, and not products, were patentable.[135] The reason for this limitation was that it was thought right to recognise the fact that more than one inventor could discover the same chemical product, but by using different processes.[136] If a patent had been granted in relation to the product, it would prevent the exploitation of other inventions which attained the same aim, but perhaps by a more economical process.[137] The policy was that competition to discover the most economic process was advantageous to national industry.[138]

---

127 *Ibid.*

128 Mr Selwyn was a U.K. delegate and representative of the Inventors Institute. *Ibid.* p. 121.

129 M. Franz Edlen von Rosas was an influential Austrian delegate, representing many commercial associations. *Ibid.*

130 Charles Assi was a Parisian civil engineer. *Ibid.*

131 *Ibid.* pp. 282–285.

132 *Ibid.* p. 285. See further on this point: Akerman, C., *L'Obligation d'Exploiter et la Licence Obligatoire en Matiére de Brevets d'Invention* (Paris, Librairie du Recueil Sirey, 1936), pp. 58–61.

133 Note, 'Le Congrés International de La Propriété Industrielle tenu á Paris en Septembre 1878' (1878) *Journal des économistes* (4th series) 87, p. 91.

134 France, Ministére de L' agriculture et du Commerce, *Comptes rendus Sténographiques etc.*, pp. 182, 185.

135 *Ibid.* p. 174.

136 For further details see: (1885) 1 *La Propriété Industrielle* 49.

137 *Ibid.*

138 *Ibid.*

By the time of the Paris Conference in 1878, however, many had begun to question whether this policy was correct. Mr A. Poirrier, for example, a manufacturer of chemical products, pointed out that the invention of chemical products, like all inventions, required intellectual effort, work, expense, long and difficult scientific study and sometimes involved danger.[139] Similar points were made by other French delegates such as M. Limousin, M. Pouillet, and M. Meissonier,[140] and U.S. delegate A. Pollok.[141] These delegates were most concerned by the fact that excluding chemical products from patentability meant that there was nothing to prevent a person from stepping in and manufacturing the product in competition with the original inventor, thus depriving the inventor of the fruits of his labour. They also thought that there was little to encourage inventors to discover new chemical products, since they faced the constant danger of others inventing around their patent. Consequently, these views held sway and the Conference resolved that chemical products and foodstuffs were patentable.

In relation to pharmaceuticals, the opinion of the majority was reflected in the words of Professor Lyon-Caen, who stated that there was no longer any logical reason why inventors of pharmaceuticals should not benefit from the patent system.[142] He noted that in countries such as France there was a long history of excluding pharmaceuticals from patentability. The justification put forward for this exclusion was that in order to protect public health, it was thought best not to encourage charlatans selling patented medicines as the term "patented" might have implied some endorsement of quality by the State.[143] There was also a subsidiary issue that patenting pharmaceuticals might have restricted their general availability to the community.[144] Most delegates who spoke on the issue considered that inventors of pharmaceuticals should be treated the same as any other inventor, and that their property rights should be respected. Furthermore, patenting pharmaceuticals could lead to a faster pace of development in this field.[145]

139 France, Ministére de L' agriculture et du Commerce, *Comptes rendus Sténographiques etc.*, p. 174.

140 *Ibid.* pp. 180–181.

141 *Ibid.* p. 179.

142 *Ibid.* p. 178.

143 *Ibid.* pp. 175–176.

144 *Ibid.*

145 See, for example, delegates Georges Lecocq, a lawyer of Amiens and Emile Barrault, a Parisian engineer and patent agent. *Ibid.* pp. 182–184.

5.2.2 Future Uniform Industrial Property Legislation

The most enduring act of the 1878 Conference was the Resolution that:

> Un des buts de la Commission permanente créée par l'initiative privée, sera d'obtenir de l'un des Gouvernements la réunion d'une Conférence internationale officielle, á l'effet de déterminer les bases d'une législation uniform.[146]

This Resolution made clear that an important aim of the 1878 Conference was to advance the work towards an official international conference to determine the bases of uniform legislation. There was, however, a major problem with the Resolution, which was its lack of clarity as to what the Conference meant by the term 'uniform legislation'. The Conference did not make clear whether it endorsed an international treaty devoted to the regulation of industrial property law, or whether it merely wished to encourage States individually to adopt certain uniform principles in their domestic legislation, without the need for a specific international treaty. The majority of the delegates thought that the general principle of "uniformity" had merit, but did not go further in thinking about what "uniformity" really entailed. For example, Jean-François Bozérian, attorney and member of the French Senate, stated that it would be up to the Permanent Committee and the governments to advance the matters agreed at the Conference from the domain of theory to that of international practice.[147]

One reason why many delegates were satisfied to support the bare goal of uniformity, without thinking any further about its implications, was that in 1878, international uniformity in any area of law was exceptional. Before the Conference, commentators had spoken of international uniformity in industrial property legislation, but they did not specify how this should be achieved. For example, in September 1877, Charles Letort wrote in the *L'Economiste Français* that uniform patent legislation, which he termed 'an international code' was a clear goal, yet he did not address the practical issues associated with its implementation.[148] Many of those who responded to the circular of the 1878 Preparatory Committee also mentioned the need for greater international protection of industrial property rights, particularly patents, but there was no clear consensus on how this goal should be achieved.[149]

---

146 *Ibid.* p. 242.

147 *Ibid.* p. 420.

148 Letort, C. 'Une Législation Internationale sur les Brevets d'invention', *L'Economiste Français*, 29 September 1877, p. 390.

149 See for example, the submissions of Robert Macfie, Duroy de Bruignac, D.-A. Casalonga, the Consultative Chamber of Arts and Manufactures of Rethel (Ardennes), the Chamber

The 1878 Conference initially discussed the feasibility of persuading all governments to adopt a uniform industrial property code. A proposal to this effect was made by several influential French delegates, namely Albert Grodet, Count de Maillard de Marafy, Georges Lecocq, F. Tacon, C. Meissonier and L. Jaubert.[150] This proposal received the support of many delegates, who did not stop to consider how difficult it would be to achieve any degree of international uniformity in industrial property legislation.[151]

A number of delegates provided some commentary upon what they considered should be a 'minimum of uniformity' or 'minimum of understanding' in relation to industrial property legislation. De Rosas, for example, said that at a basic level, foreigners should have the ability to apply for patents in countries other than their own.[152] J. Armengaud stated that there should be uniformity in relation to such things as the duration of protection, the grant of a priority right for filing patent applications, the requirements for working of patents and the transfer of patent rights.[153] At the same session, the Conference resolved that applicants for patents, designs, models and trade marks should be able to lodge their applications at foreign consulates in their country of residence.[154] These discussions and resolutions indicated that the Conference recognised that uniformity could only initially be achieved in a very restricted sense.

However, there remained a group of delegates who considered that the adoption of a limited international treaty was the only realistic solution. Professor Lyon-Caen supported this more practical approach when he argued that it was utopian to suggest that there could be one common industrial property law operating in all countries.[155] He believed that the most the Conference could do was to determine the principal points on which there could be some later international agreement in the form of an international treaty dealing with a limited number of points on which there could be a common view. He added that it was impossible to arrive at international uniformity of industrial property laws when international relations were based on national treatment, rather than reciprocity.[156] If requirements of reciprocity had been adopted, then Lyon-Caen believed that it would have been easier to arrive at

of the Fabric Traders of Saint-Etienne, and the Chamber of First-Class Pharmacists of the Region of the Seine.

150 *Ibid.* p. 112.

151 *Ibid.* pp. 234 fwd.

152 *Ibid.* p. 239.

153 *Ibid.* pp. 241–242.

154 *Ibid.* p. 248.

155 *Ibid.* p. 139.

156 *Ibid.* p. 138.

international uniformity. Nevertheless the task would still have been extremely difficult.

A similar point was made by Edmond Imer-Schneider, a civil engineer from Berne, and one of the official Swiss delegates. He argued that any proposal for an international code was impractical, in view of the large differences in the operation of the patent systems in the various States.[157] For example, international uniformity in patent law could never be achieved so long as some countries practised substantive examination of applications, and others did not.[158] For this reason, both Lyon-Caen and Imer-Schneider referred the Conference to the recent work of the Viennese section of the Austrian Society of Engineers, which had adopted certain resolutions calling for an international treaty in the area of industrial property law.[159] The Swiss delegate, Bodenheimer, and the Austrian, Gaetner, also preferred this approach,[160] and they were supported by the U.S. delegate Pollok, the French delegates Barrault and d'Oliveira, and the Belgian delegate, Demeur.[161]

Despite the fact that at the 1878 Conference only a minority of the delegates supported an international treaty, the Permanent Committee tasked to continue the work of the Conference ultimately favoured implementation of the goals of the Conference by way of an international treaty.[162]

5.3 *The Work of the Permanent Committee*

In accordance with the resolutions of the 1878 Conference, a Permanent Committee was established 'to give effect to the propositions adopted by the Congress of Industrial Property'.[163] The proposal for a Permanent Committee had been made by one of the official Italian delegates, Romanelli, who was Director of Commerce and Industry at the Ministry of Agriculture, Industry and Commerce in Rome. The main reason for his proposal was his view that, while uniform industrial property legislation might be the ultimate goal, there were many opinions as to exactly what this entailed and how it should be achieved.[164]

---

157 *Ibid.*

158 *Ibid.*

159 *Ibid.* p. 490.

160 *Ibid.* p. 234.

161 *Ibid.*

162 Bozerian, M.J. *La Convention Internationale du 20 Mars 1883 pour la Protection de la Propriété Industrielle* (Paris, Imprimerie C. Pariset, 1885), pp. 7–8.

163 France, Ministére de L' agriculture et du Commerce, *Comptes rendus Sténographiques etc.*, p. 236.

164 *Ibid.* p. 235.

For two days after the 1878 Conference ended, on 18 and 19 September 1878, the Permanent Committee met and considered these questions. The Committee was assisted by an extremely detailed and comprehensive draft Treaty which had been prepared, largely based on the work of the Swiss member, Bodenheimer.[165] Bodenheimer's draft was, in effect the incorporation of the resolutions of the 1878 Conference into a document, and which was then renamed as an international treaty. This draft treaty was adopted by the Committee with little amendment, despite the fact that it was far too detailed for any international instrument.

When the French Section of the Permanent Committee submitted the draft treaty to the French Government, the conflict between official and private objectives became apparent. The French Government considered that the draft needed to take more account of the divergent legislation of the various States, and that the treaty should only include those articles that could be put into operation without requiring major modifications to domestic laws.[166] The French Section therefore adopted a second draft treaty, divided into parts A and B. Under part A, were provisions which the Section believed would be possible to incorporate immediately into an international treaty, and under part B were simple recommendations suggesting the direction in which national laws should in future be modified.[167]

The second draft treaty contained few substantive provisions. In particular, there was no reference to the property rights of inventors or other similar issues. The major concern of the second draft treaty was to accept the principle of national treatment in relation to patents, designs and models, trade marks and commercial names. This had been proposed by the 1878 Conference[168] and was based on the provisions of many earlier bilateral treaties, particularly those containing provisions relating to trade marks.[169] However, for the first

165 *Ibid.* p. 696.

166 France, Ministére des Affaires étrangéres, *Conférence Internationale pour la protection de la propriété Industrielle* (Paris 1880), p. 20. See also Drouets, C. "La Convention d' Union de la Propriété Industrielle: L' oeuvre de la Conférence de Revision de Londres de 1934" (1935) 134 *Bulletin de la Société d'Encouragement pour L'Industrie Nationale* 376, pp. 376–377; Pelletier, M., and Vidal-Naquet, E. *La Convention d'Union pour la Protection de la Propriété Industrielle du 20 mars 1883 et les Conférences de Revision Postérieures* (Paris, L. Larose, 1902), pp. 10–11.

167 France, Ministére de L' agriculture et du Commerce, *Comptes rendus Sténographiques etc.*, p. 721.

168 General Section, Resolution 2, 1878 Paris Conference.

169 See, for example, the Commercial Treaties between the U.K. and Austria dated 16 December 1865; the U.K. and Colombia dated 16 February 1866; the U.K. and France dated 23 January 1860; and the U.K. and the Zollverein dated 30 May 1865. These all contained

time, the second draft treaty provided for rights of priority for the filing of patents, designs and trade marks.[170] This was a departure from the earlier resolution of the 1878 Conference, which had favoured simultaneous deposit in foreign consulates.

Priority rights had been discussed at the 1878 Conference, and were supported by delegates such as Emile Barrault, Anthony Pollok, and J.-C. Colfavru. Barrault, for example, argued at the 1878 Conference that a 12 month priority period should be granted to inventors to allow them time to file their applications in foreign countries.[171] He stated that the proposal relating to simultaneous filing in foreign consulates would be useless in practice.[172] Similar points were made by Pollok and Colfavru.[173] As Barrault and Pollok were influential members of the Permanent Committee, it was to be expected that their strong views on the matter ultimately held sway.

The only other substantive provision relating to patents in the second draft treaty was the statement that subsequent patents granted in contracting States in relation to an invention should be granted for a duration of time independent of the original patent in the country of origin.[174] This provision was apparently not based on any pre-existing State practice in commercial treaties, but evolved from a resolution of the 1878 Conference that had received wide support of influential French, U.K. and U.S. delegates.[175] There were also general provisions in the second draft treaty relating to the provisional protection of inventions, designs and models, and trade marks displayed at international exhibitions, being provisions basically in accord with the resolutions of the 1878 Conference.

---

provisions according national treatment. United Kingdom, Parliamentary Papers, *Extracts from Treaties and Declarations now in force between Great Britain and Foreign Powers relating to Trade Marks, Designs, and Industrial Property, August 1888* (1888) vol. XCVIII, C. 5554, p. 745.

170 See for example, Patents Section, Article 1 of the (second) draft treaty.

171 France, Ministére de L' agriculture et du Commerce, *Comptes rendus Sténographiques etc.*, p. 245.

172 *Ibid.*

173 *Ibid.* pp. 245–247.

174 Patents Section, Article 2 of the (second) draft treaty.

175 France, Ministére de L' agriculture et du Commerce, *Comptes rendus Sténographiques etc.*, pp. 418–419. The French delegates speaking in favour of the proposal were Barrault, Pouillet, Charles Lyon-Caen, Dumoustier de Frédilly, Armengaud, Couhin, Grodet and d'Oliveira. The U.S. delegate was Pollok and the U.K. delegates were Alexander and Wise.

When the second draft treaty was submitted to the French Government, it was still considered too ambitious, and a third draft was requested.[176] It was this third draft which in August 1880 was submitted to foreign governments who had 'made known their assent to the project of meeting and have announced their intention to be represented thereat.'[177] The third draft treaty took the form of eleven Articles, divided into five sections: General Questions, Patents of Invention, Designs and Industrial Models, Trade Marks, and Commercial Names. The major points of difference between the second and third draft treaties was that the third only contained substantive provisions, and did not include any additional and non-binding Recommendations. The third draft treaty also removed any reference to the need to recognise the independence of patents, designs and models, where such rights were registered in more than one country. In the later history of the Paris Convention, when the independence of patents was debated, this proved to be a controversial topic and a corresponding article was not included in the Convention until 1900.[178]

5.4 *The 1880 Paris Conference – the First Diplomatic Meeting*

The 1880 Paris Conference was the first diplomatic conference concerned solely with the question of international legal protection of industrial property rights. At this Conference, and at the later Paris Conference of 1883, the government representatives faced the difficult task of transforming the aspirations of private individuals and groups into a diplomatic treaty.[179]

---

176 France, Ministére des Affaires étrangéres, *Conférence Internationale pour la protection de la propriété Industrielle* (Paris 1880), p. 20.

177 In August 1880, those countries which had informed the French Government of their intention to send representatives to the Conference included the U.S.A., United Kingdom, Austria-Hungary, Belgium, Italy, Russia and Switzerland. United States of America, Congressional Papers, *Report of the Commissioners appointed to Revise the Statutes relating to Patents, Trade and other Marks, and Trade and Commercial Names under Act of Congress approved June 4, 1898* (1900) 56th Congress, 2nd Session, Senate document 20, p. 233.

178 The independence of patents was raised again at the Rome Revision Conference in 1886, and was finally inserted in the Paris Convention as Article 4*bis in the Act of Brussels*, 1900. See the Debate over this matter in the records of the 1897 and 1900 Revision Conferences. Bureau International de l' union Pour la Protection de la Propriete Industrielle, *Conférence de Bruxelles: Decémbre 1897 et Décembre 1900* (Berne 1901). Even after Article 4*bis* had been inserted into the Paris Convention, there remained a significant national practice in countries such as Belgium and France which linked the duration of subsequent patents to that of the original. Note, "De l' indépendance réciproque des Brevets d'aprés l'Article 4*bis* de la Convention d' Union Revisée" (1903) 19 *La Propriété Industrielle* 97.

179 See also Ricketson, S. *The Paris Convention for the Protection of Industrial Property* (Oxford University Press, 2015), pp. 50–59.

The draft text of the 1883 Convention prepared by the 1880 diplomatic Conference contained several Articles which were in accord with the Resolutions of the private Conference of 1878. These related to the requirement of national treatment, temporary protection at international exhibitions, and the abolition of forfeiture for importation of patented goods. The 1880 Conference's acceptance of forfeiture for non-working was also generally in accordance with the Resolutions of 1878. However, there were many points where the 1880 draft text differed markedly from the 1878 Resolutions. In one respect, the 1880 draft text was an improvement upon the work of 1878. This was in its acceptance of priority rights, rather than the 1878 proposal for simultaneous lodging of applications at foreign consulates. However, the 1880 Conference failed to adequately address the meaning of the term 'industrial property', which contrasted markedly with the theoretical debates of the 1878 Conference. Further, under the 1880 draft text, non-Union nationals were denied rights, which was inconsistent with the resolutions of the 1878 Conference.

The differences between the work of the Conferences of 1878 and 1880 can be explained by the fact that the delegates to the earlier Conference were mostly experienced industrial property practitioners and rights owners, concerned to advance the concept of 'natural' industrial property rights. In contrast, the delegates to the 1880 Conference were largely career diplomats, guided by wider social, political and economic concerns. They were primarily concerned to promote the industrial developments of their own countries, and did not enter into general theoretical discussions about the basis of inventors' rights.

The 1880 Conference began with a severe limitation in the scope of its inquiry because the French Government insisted upon limiting the Programme of the Conference to the content of the third draft treaty (discussed above). However, this problem was somewhat ameliorated when the Conference voted to reject the third draft treaty, and instead adopt an alternative draft (the Jagerschmidt draft) as the basis of its discussions.

The Jagerschmidt draft had been prepared by Charles Jagerschmidt of the French Ministry of Foreign Affairs, who had no apparent experience in industrial property law, but did have experience in legislative drafting. It was his draft which, after some amendment, formed the basis of the 1883 Convention.

5.5 *Key Provisions of the 1880 Jagerschmidt Draft*

5.5.1 "Industrial Property"

The 1878 Conference had made extensive use of the term 'industrial property' to describe patents, trade marks, designs and models, and commercial names and which was reflected in General Section, Resolution 1 of the 1878 Conference. The 1880 Conference also endorsed the use of the term "industrial property" and the Jagerschmidt draft incorporated this term into the title of Convention. However, there was no real discussion of the meaning of the term 'industrial property' at the 1880 Conference.

The only limited discussion of this matter at the 1880 Conference was prompted by the statement of the Portuguese delegate, de Barros, who proposed that the Convention should have a title which summed up its aims.[180] He believed it was important that the Convention expressly recognise protection for agricultural products, particularly wines.[181] Not all delegates agreed with the proposal to include protection for agricultural products in the Convention,[182] and in an attempt to seek some compromise on the matter, the Conference agreed that only the general term 'industrial property' would be used in Article 1, but a more expansive definition would be included in the Final Protocol.[183]

5.5.2 An International "Union"

The Paris Convention was the first multilateral industrial property treaty. Yet it is strange that the crucial issue of what was meant by the terms "open" and "Union" was not discussed at the 1880 Conference except in the briefest fashion. Most of the provisions concerning the relationship between the members had been presented to the 1880 Conference in the Jagerschmidt draft, and, according to Bozérian, these aspects had been taken from earlier treaties such as the International Telegraph Union (1865) and the Universal Postal Union (1874).[184]

One of the important aims of the Convention was to include the largest possible number of States as members, and therefore, the Convention was to remain open for signature indefinitely.[185] Another feature of the "open" Union was the inclusion of specific provisions for its periodic revision. Any member

---

180 France, Ministére des Affaires étrangéres, *Conférence Internationale pour la protection de la propriété Industrielle* (Paris 1880), p. 32.

181 *Ibid.*

182 While the Russian delegate said that the words "industrial property" would include agricultural products, the Hungarian delegate said it would not. *Ibid.* p. 58.

183 *Ibid.* p. 59. Paragraph 1 of the Final Protocol, which was accepted at the 1880 Conference without further discussion stated that: "The words 'industrial property' should be understood in the broadest sense; they relate not only to the products of industry in the strict sense but also to agricultural products (wines, grain, fruit, cattle etc.), and mineral products which are put into trade (mineral waters, etc.)."

184 Bozerian, M.J. *La Convention Internationale du 20 Mars 1883 pour la Protection de la Propriété Industrielle* (Paris, Imprimerie C. Pariset, 1885), p. 27.

185 France, Ministére des Affaires étrangéres, *Conférence Internationale pour la protection de la propriété Industrielle* (Paris 1880), pp. 145–146.

States could propose amendments to the Convention which would lead to its constant improvement. As the later French commentator, Roubier, noted, these were significant features of an "open" Union, and by such mechanisms, the text of the Convention was likely to have influence on the development of laws in States not party to the Convention, and later induce them to enter into it.[186]

In the records of the 1880 Conference, there is only one reference to the delegates' views about the "Union" they were creating. This arose in the context of discussions over the tasks of the International Bureau. According to the delegates of Norway, Portugal and Uruguay, the International Bureau was the lynchpin of the Union, as it created a common bond between States.[187] The Swiss delegate, Kern, agreed, noting that the Bureau was necessary to achieve the Convention's objective of eventual unification of industrial property laws.[188] Yet, the Paris Union did not have the strong territorial connotation of the earlier postal and telegraph Conventions. In the earlier Unions, there was almost a codification of the regulations of the postal and telegraph services throughout the territory of the member States. This did not occur with the 1883 Paris Convention. Under the Paris Convention, there was only a single Union in the limited sense that national treatment had to be accorded, but this did not alter the fact that the extent of substantive legal protection for industrial property rights still varied markedly from one member State to another.

Furthermore, although the delegates considered the International Bureau as a separate organ of the Union, having an administrative office, this did not mean that the Union itself had an international legal personality independent of the separate legal existence of each contracting State.[189]

5.5.3 National Treatment

The Jagerschmidt draft, like the earlier drafts and the 1878 Conference resolutions, proposed the establishment of a right of national treatment as one of the cornerstones of the Convention. Support for the adoption of the requirement of national treatment was undoubtedly due to the fact that national treatment had figured in previous bilateral commercial treaties, and so the delegates

186 Roubier, P. "Le droit unioniste de la propriété Industrielle" [1951] *Journal du Droit International*, pp. 705 fwd.

187 France, Ministére des Affaires étrangéres, *Conférence Internationale pour la protection de la propriété Industrielle* (Paris 1880), pp. 112–115.

188 *Ibid.* p. 115.

189 See also Ricketson, S. *The Berne Convention for the protection of literary and artistic works: 1886–1986* (London, Centre for Commercial Law Studies, 1987), pp. 146–156 for a discussion of the meaning of the term "Union" under the Berne Convention of 1886.

were reasonably familiar with it.[190] Some delegates preferred the requirement of substantive reciprocity,[191] but the majority could not support it as it would have required significant amendment to national law, including, for example for countries such as Switzerland and the Netherlands which did not have patent legislation at that time. The adoption of national treatment rather than substantive reciprocity was consistent with the idea that the Convention was only the first step towards international uniformity in industrial property law. National treatment still allowed States to maintain their domestic industrial property laws without significant amendment, and Union nationals could have the benefit of these laws throughout the States of the Union.

5.5.4 Rights of Non-union Nationals

Although the 1878 Paris Conference had supported the granting of protection to all persons, without distinction of nationality,[192] this was not accepted by the 1880 Conference. As noted above, the 1878 Conference had resolved that industrial property rights were inherent in the act of creation, and thus no distinction could be made between the rights of Union nationals and foreigners: they should be treated equally. However, the 1880 Conference, attended by diplomats rather than private persons, was more concerned with practical and political issues. In particular the 1880 Conference realised that the Union would be slow to gain adherents if its benefits were extended to the nationals of countries not party the Convention.[193] However, the Conference accepted the Swedish proposal that Article 3 should be extended to foreigners established in one of the contracting States.[194] Further, as noted by Jagerschmidt, States could decide to apply the benefits of the Convention more widely if they wished, but should be under no obligation to do so.[195]

5.5.5 The Priority Period

Establishment of priority periods in which to file applications for industrial property rights was probably the most tangible benefit of the 1883 Convention.

190 See for example, the Treaty of Commerce between the United Kingdom and Austria-Hungary of 5 December 1878.

191 For example, the Portuguese delegate, de Barros: France, Ministére des Affaires étrangéres, *Conférence Internationale pour la protection de la propriété Industrielle* (Paris 1880), p. 36.

192 General Section, Resolution 2 – "Foreigners must be treated as nationals".

193 See, for example the statement by the Swiss delegate Kern: *Ibid.* p. 131.

194 *Ibid.*

195 *Ibid.* p. 130.

Jagerschmidt justified priority rights by explaining that when a person filed an application for a patent, design or trade mark in one country, there was a likelihood that the resultant publicity might allow a foreigner to improperly profit from the filing, by applying for a similar patent, design or trade mark in his own country.[196] His proposal was intended to prevent such activity by giving to the first person a right of priority of registration for a predetermined time in all the States of the Union.[197] The text of the Jagerschmidt draft relating to priority rights was debated at some length during the 1880 Conference, and amendments were made after consideration of competing drafts proposed by the Belgian and Dutch delegates.[198] The text was ultimately adopted as Article 4 of the 1883 Convention.

Although the original Jagerschmidt draft had adopted a uniform priority period for all forms of industrial property, the 1880 Conference early agreed that the priority period for patents should be of a longer duration than for other rights. Under the 1883 Convention, the priority period for patents was fixed at 6 months, with 3 months for designs, models and trade marks. However, at the 1880 Conference, several delegates supported longer priority periods, more in line with provisions in operation today.

While noting that the priority period would be a time of uncertainty when industrial competitors would be hampered by their ignorance about whether the inventor would apply for rights in a particular country, the Swiss delegate Weibel, the French delegate Bozérian and the Belgian delegate Demeur, all supported a greater than 6 month priority period for patents.[199] These delegates all supported a longer priority period for patents, for reasons such as the length of the preliminary examination in countries such as the U.S.A., and the right of opposition of 6 months that existed in the United Kingdom. Further, as pointed out by Bozérian, the normal duration before putting to work a patented invention was one year, and it was not equitable to impose on the inventor the expense of applying for a patent in a foreign land if he did not know if the invention would work or be profitable.[200]

The majority of the delegates, however, did not support a one year priority period for patents and rejected the arguments of the experienced patent practitioners Weibel, Bozérian and Demeur that a one year period was necessary

196 *Ibid.* p. 47.
197 *Ibid.*
198 *Ibid.* p. 64.
199 *Ibid.* pp. 52, 54, 55.
200 *Ibid.* p. 54.

in many countries in order for the application to pass through the many procedural stages and for the patentee to determine its value. It is unsurprising, therefore, that the Brussels revision of the Paris Convention in 1900 increased the priority period for patents to one year, with four months for designs, models and trade marks.

5.5.6 Temporary Protection at International Exhibitions

The final important general provision in the 1883 Convention was Article 11, which conferred temporary protection upon patentable inventions, industrial designs and models and trade marks in respect of goods exhibited at official or officially recognised international exhibitions. This Article was adopted from the Jagerschmidt draft with little amendment. An Italian delegate, Indelli had proposed an alternative which would have extended protection only where the inventor notified the industrial bureau of an application for a patent, design or trade mark within two months following the close of the exhibition.[201] However, this proposal was not supported by the other delegates, who preferred the more general Jagerschmidt text which left it to each State to determine the means of putting the provision into practice.[202]

5.5.7 Importation of Patented Articles and Compulsory Working

The 1880 Conference followed the 1878 Conference in adopting the general view that it was reasonable that a patent should not be forfeited merely on the grounds of importing goods from abroad. Bozérian described such forfeiture provisions as barbarous and absolutely useless,[203] (including the provisions to this effect set out in the French Law of 5 July 1844).

The records of the 1880 Conference further disclose that a majority of the delegates appeared to favour the abolition of *all* compulsory working requirements. However, this was not reflected in the final text, as the delegates of a small minority of countries such as Austria, Hungary and Switzerland still supported such provisions, and it was necessary that their views would be recognised in the Convention. Consequently, the 1880 Conference added a provision to draft Article 4 (later Article 5 of the 1883 Convention) stating that the patentee should remain under the obligation to exploit the patent in conformity with the laws of the country into which the patented articles were introduced.[204]

201 *Ibid.* p. 105.
202 *Ibid.* p. 106.
203 *Ibid.* p. 56.
204 *Ibid.* p. 69.

5.6 *The 1883 Conference – the Second Diplomatic Meeting*

Although the text of the Paris Convention of 1883 was essentially that which resulted from the work of the 1880 Conference, none of the delegates present in 1880 had their Government's authority immediately to accede to the Convention. All that was signed at the 1880 Conference was a document recording its work and stating the agreement of the delegates to submit the text of the draft Convention to their respective Governments.[205] In the period between the 1880 Conference and the subsequent meeting in March 1883, the draft text was the object of study by most of the Governments who had sent representatives to the Conference.[206]

On 6 March 1883, delegates from 20 countries met in Paris at the invitation of the French Government to consider the draft Convention and, if possible, sign their assent to the terms already established. The Convention text as signed in 1883 was little changed from that of 1880, largely because nine States sent delegates to the 1883 Conference with unrestricted authority to sign the Convention as drafted in 1880, and any changes would have had to be referred back to their Governments for consideration.[207]

By the end of the Conference, the representatives of eleven countries were able to give their signatures of assent to the terms of the Paris Convention on 20 March 1883. These countries were Belgium, Brazil, Spain, France, Guatemala, Italy, the Netherlands, Portugal, Salvador, Serbia and Switzerland.[208] On 6 June 1884, representatives of the eleven original signatories to the Convention met in Paris to deposit their Governments' instruments of ratification.[209] At that time, the instruments of ratification of the Convention were also received on behalf of the United Kingdom, Tunisia and Ecuador. These fourteen countries formed the membership of the Paris Convention which it came into force on 7 July 1884.[210]

6 The 1883 Paris Convention – a Remarkable Advance

The 1883 Paris Convention contained a number of substantive provisions which were a remarkable advance in international law at the time. Its main

205 *Ibid.* p. 147.

206 France, Ministére des Affaires étrangéres, *Conférence Internationale pour la protection de la propriété Industrielle* (Paris 1883), p. 15.

207 *Ibid.* p. 23.

208 *Ibid.* p. 51.

209 [1885] 1 *La Propriété Industrielle* 5.

210 Article 18 of the 1883 Convention stipulated that the Convention would come into effect one month after the exchange of ratifications.

achievements – the requirement of national treatment, priority rights and the concept of an 'open Union' with possibility of revision and extension of membership – were innovative features in 1883, and this Convention was to serve as a model for later international agreements in the area of industrial property law such as the Madrid Agreement Concerning the International Registration of Marks 1891, the Madrid Agreement for the Repression of False or Deceptive Indications of Source on Goods 1891, the Hague Agreement Concerning the International Deposit of Industrial Designs 1925, the International Convention for the Protection of New Varieties of Plants 1961, the Patent Cooperation Treaty 1970, the Budapest Treaty on the International Recognition of the Deposit of Microorganisms for the Purposes of Patent Procedure 1977, the Trademark Law Treaty 1994, and the Patent Law Treaty 2000.

Although many of these Agreements came into existence after failed attempts to include the relevant subjects in the text of the Paris Convention,[211] they were reliant upon the model of the Paris Convention for substantive provisions such as the requirements of national treatment, membership was often only open to Paris Union States, and the International Bureau was usually employed as the administrative organ of the Agreements.

The Paris Convention of 1883 was never intended to be the final word on international protection of industrial property rights; it was only a point of commencement. The Paris Convention was the first step in breaking down the international legal barriers which hindered the free circulation of inventions and associated manufactured goods. Before 1883 it was often difficult for inventors to secure legal protection for their inventions in foreign countries, and they also had to contend with restrictive working requirements and threats of forfeiture. The Paris Convention developed some agreed principles to ameliorate many of these problems, but there was still much work to be done. As Jean-François Bozérian told the 1880 Paris Conference, their work would be just the preface to the book that would not be completed for a long time.[212] The following chapters of this volume illustrate some of the work that has gone on since 1883 in the international legal arena to further embrace and extend these principles.

211 See for example, the difficult negotiations concerning the two Madrid Agreements of 1891. Bureau International de l 'union pour la Protection de la Propriete Industrielle, *Procés-Verbaux de la Conférence de Madrid de 1890 de l'Union pour la protection de la Propriéte Industrielle suivis des Actes signés en 1891 et ratifiés en 1892* (Berne 1892).

212 France, Ministére des Affaires étrangéres, *Conférence Internationale pour la protection de la propriété Industrielle* (Paris 1880), p. 20.

Bibliography

Commentaries and Monographs

Akerman, C. *L'Obligation d'Exploiter et la Licence Obligatoire en Matiére de Brevets d'Invention* (Paris, Librairie du Recueil Sirey, 1936).

Bozerian, M.J. *La Convention Internationale du 20 Mars 1883 pour la Protection de la Propriété Industrielle* (Paris, Imprimerie C. Pariset, 1885).

Bouvier, H. *Essais sur la Recherche de Principes Géneraux Applicables aux unions internationales pour la protection de la propriété Industrielle* (Paris, Imprimerie Moquet, 1889).

Duncan, L. *The Role of Theoretical Debate in the Evolution of National and International Patent Protection: From the French Revolution to the Paris Convention of 1883* (Brill, 2021).

Grothe, H. *Der Internationale Patent-Congress in Wien (4–9 August 1873)* (Berlin, Julius Springer, 1873).

Macfie, R.A., ed. *Recent Discussions on the Abolition of Patents for Inventions in the United Kingdom, France, Germany, and the Netherlands: evidence, speeches and papers in its favour* (London, Longmans and Co, 1869).

Milhaud, L. *Des Brevets d'invention dans les Rapports Internationaux* (Paris, Larose et Forcel, 1892).

Pelletier, M., and Vidal-Naquet, E. *La Convention d'Union pour la Protection de la Propriété Industrielle du 20 mars 1883 et les Conférences de Revision Postérieures* (Paris, L. Larose, 1902).

Penrose, E. *The Economics of the International Patent System* (Baltimore, John Hopkins Press, 1951).

Pieper, C. *Der Erfinderschutz und die Reform der Patentgesetze. Amtlicher Bericht über den Internationalen Patent-Congress zur Erörterung der Frage des Patentschutzes. Mit einer Einleitung von Dr. C.W. Siemens F.R.S.* (Dresden, Commission der Schulbuchhandlung, 1873).

Pieper, C., and Schmid, P. *Geschichte der internationalen Union für den Schutz des gewerblichen Eigentums sammt Konvention und Staatsverträgen* (Berlin, Deutschen Vereins für den Schutz des gewerblichen Eigentums, 1894).

Plaisant, M. *Traité de Droit Conventionnel International concernant la Propriété Industrielle* (Paris, Sirey, 1949).

Plasseraud, Y., and Savignon, F. *Paris 1883: Genése du droit Unioniste des Brevets* (Paris, Litec, 1983).

Ricketson, S. *The Paris Convention for the Protection of Industrial Property* (Oxford, Oxford University Press, 2015).

Ricketson, S. *The Berne Convention for the protection of literary and artistic works: 1886–1986* (London, Centre for Commercial Law Studies, 1987).

Vidal-Naquet, E. *Des Marques de Fabrique et de Commerce et du Nom Commercial en droit International* (Paris, L. Larose, 1898).

Vidal-Naquet, E. *La Convention d'Union pour la Protection de la Propriété Industrielle du 20 mars 1883 et les Conférences de Revision Postérieures* (Paris, L. Larose, 1902).

Journal Articles and Papers

"Anglo-American Copyright" (1868–9) 26 *The Law Magazine and Law Review* 49.

Davis, I.J.G., and Harrison, J. "Prelude to the United Kingdom's Accession to the Paris Convention, March 17, 1884" (1984) *Industrial Property* 395.

Drouets, C. "La Convention d'Union de la Propriété Industrielle: L'oeuvre de la Conférence de Revision de Londres de 1934" (1935) 134 *Bulletin de la Société d'Encouragement pour L'Industrie Nationale* 376.

Field, D. "On an International Code" (1874) 3 *The Law Magazine and Review* (New Series) 251.

Frey-Godet, B. "*Comparaison du texte de la Convention et de la législation britannique correspondante*" (1898) *Annuaire de l'association Internationale pour la Protection de la Propriété Industrielle* 151.

Letort, C. "Une Législation Internationale sur les Brevets d'invention" *L'économiste Français*, 29 September 1877.

Maillard, G. *Le Bureau International de l'Union pour la Protection de la Propriété Industrielle* (undated extract from a journal entitled *Revue Internationale du Commerce, de l'industrie et de la Banque* held at W.I.P.O. Geneva).

Note. 'Le Congrés International de La Propriété Industrielle tenu á Paris en Septembre 1878' (1878) *Journal des économistes* (4th series) 87.

Note. "De l' indépendance réciproque des Brevets d'aprés l'Article 4*bis* de la Convention d' Union Revisée" (1903) 19 *La Propriété Industrielle* 97.

Roubier, P. "Le droit unioniste de la propriété Industrielle" (1951) *Journal du Droit International* 676 (Part One); 1040 (Part two).

"The Brussels Conference for the Reform and Codification of the Law of Nations" (1873) 2 *The Law Magazine and Review* (New Series) 1094.

Webster, T. "Reform and Codification of the Law of Nations" (1874) 3 *The Law Magazine and Law Review* (New Series) 1016.

Official Papers and Reports

BUREAU INTERNATIONAL DE L'UNION POUR LA PROTECTION DE LA PROPRIETE INDUSTRIELLE, *Conférence de Bruxelles: Decémbre 1897 et Décembre 1900* (Berne 1901).

BUREAU INTERNATIONAL DE L'DE LA PROPRIETE INDUSTRIELLE, "l'Article 4 de la Convention" (1886) 2 *La Propriété Industrielle* 17.

BUREAU INTERNATIONAL DE L 'UNION POUR LA PROTECTION DE LA PROPRIETE INDUSTRIELLE, *Procés-Verbaux de la Conférence de Madrid de 1890 de l'Union pour la protection de la Propriéte Industrielle suivis des Actes signés en 1891 et ratifiés en 1892* (Berne 1892).

France, Ministére de L'agriculture et du Commerce, *Comptes rendus Sténographiques publiés sous les auspices du Comité Central des Congrés et Conférences et la direction de M. CH THIRION, Secrétaire du Comité, avec le concours des Bureaux des Congrés et des auteurs de Conférences: Congrés International de la Propriété Industrielle tenu á Paris du 5 au 17 Septembre 1878* (Paris 1879).

France, Ministére des Affaires étrangéres, *Conférence Internationale pour la protection de la propriété Industrielle* (Paris 1880).

France, Ministére des Affaires étrangéres, *Conférence Internationale pour la protection de la propriété Industrielle* (Paris 1883).

United Kingdom, *Parliamentary Papers* (1857–58) 235, vol. II, p. 587.

United Kingdom, Parliamentary Papers, *Report of the Commissioners appointed to Inquire into the Working of the Law Relating to Letters Patent for Inventions* (1864) 3419, vol. XXIX, p. 321.

United Kingdom, Parliamentary Papers, *Report from the Select Committee on Letters Patent; together with the Proceedings of the Committee, Minutes of Evidence, Appendix and Index* (1872) 193, vol. XI, p. 395.

United Kingdom, Parliamentary Papers, *Reports by H.M. Secs of Embassy and Legation respecting Law and Practice in Foreign Countries with regard to Inventions* (1873) C. 741, vol. LXVI, p. 483.

United Kingdom, Parliamentary Papers, *Vienna Universal Exhibition, 1873; Report on the International Patent Congress by Thomas Webster, M.A., F.R.S., one of Her Majesty's Counsel* (March 1874).

United Kingdom, Parliamentary Papers, *Correspondence respecting International Arrangements for Assimilation in Law and Practice in regard to Letters Patent of Inventions* (1874) C. 999, vol. LIV, p. 211.

United Kingdom, Parliamentary Papers, *Report of Her Majesty's Commissioners for the Paris Universal Exhibition of 1878* (1878) vol. 1, (C 2588) XXXII, p. 1.

United Kingdom, Parliamentary Papers, *Extracts from Treaties and Declarations now in force between Great Britain and Foreign Powers relating to Trade Marks, Designs, and Industrial Property, August 1888* (1888) vol. XCVIII, C. 5554, p. 745.

United States of America, Congressional Papers, *Papers Relating to the Foreign Relations of the United States – Message and Foreign Relations 1872*, 42nd Congress, 3rd Session, H. Ex Docs VI, Part 1.

United States of America, Congressional Papers, *Paris Universal Exposition of 1878* (1878) 46th Congress, 3rd Session, H. Ex Docs vol. 20, No 42, Part 1.

United States of America, Congressional Papers, *Report of the Commissioners appointed to Revise the Statutes relating to Patents, Trade and other Marks, and Trade and Commercial Names under Act of Congress approved June 4, 1898* (1900) 56th Congress, 2nd Session, Senate document 20.

Other Reports

Blaine, R. "On International Copyright Property in Works of Literature and the fine Arts" (1859) *Transactions of the National Association for the Promotion of Social Science* 272.

Sautter, M. *La Convention Internationale pour la Protection de la Propriété Industrielle aux états-Unis: Argumentation de M.A. Pollok, de Washington, devant le Sénat Fédéral* (Paris, 1886).

Seeley, F.A. *The International Union for the Protection of Industrial Property* (prepared under the direction of the Commissioner of Patents, Washington, 1 September 1887).

CHAPTER 2

Challenging the Normative Impact of Technological Innovation

From the Norm Development Process of the Paris Convention to Global Patent Justice

Johannes Thumfart

> May the invention be good or bad. The new idea that flies through the whole world with the help of the press is a flash of lightning that ignites in a hundred places. It is often worthless inventions that spread tremendous blessing and progress.
>
> WERNER SIEMENS at the Vienna Patent Congress (1873)

1 Introduction

The contemporary international framework for IP regulation, the TRIPS agreement, is to a considerable degree based on the Paris Convention of 1883. Although the first local patent regulations date back several hundred years earlier,[1] this remarkably concise document has set the international standard regarding inventors' rights. Beyond that, its concept of national treatment became one of the founding principles of the WTO.

Almost needless to say, this heritage is not uncontroversial. The Paris Convention has been drafted at the heyday of European imperialism and US expansion, when the global spread of regulatory frameworks originating from a largely unilaterally European and North American perspective[2] has not yet

1 In 1474, the Republic of Venice introduced the first patent law. The English Statute of Monopolies of 1623/24 is the oldest coherent patent law. See: Takenaka, Toshiko, and Adams, John N. eds. "History of the Patent System," in *Patent Law and Theory: A Handbook of Contemporary Research*, Research Handbooks in Intellectual Property (Cheltenham, UK; Northampton, MA: Edward Elgar, 2008), 101–31, 101f.

2 Next to classically "northern" or "western" countries, Brazil, Guatemala and El Salvador were first signatories of the Paris Convention.

 | DOI:10.1163/9789004511439_004

been understood as problematic. Accordingly, the contemporary patent system that it brought about is heavily criticized for institutionalizing global asymmetries and following a tradition of 'conquest by patent.'[3] The holders of intellectual property rights are centered in the developed world, often excluding developing nations from using patented technologies. This is particularly problematic regarding the public health situation in developing countries,[4] as recently discussed in the context of a patent waiver on COVID vaccines.

However, the current IP regime has also a negative impact on developed nations. Take the high costs of pharmaceuticals in the US due to patenting practices.[5] Also, the possibility that non-practicing entities, so-called 'patent trolls,'[6] acquire patents for the sake of patent blocking or strategic patenting contradicts the original idea that patents should provide incentives for technological innovation.[7] The complex current regime is also causing too high litigation costs.[8]

---

3 Dhavan, Rajeev; Harris, Lindsay, and Jain, Gopal. "Conquest by Patent: The Paris Convention Revisited," *Journal of the Indian Law Institute* 32, no. 2 (1990): 131–78; Galvez-Behar, Gabriel. "The 1883 Paris Convention and the Impossible Unification of Industrial Property," in Gooday, Graeme, and Wilf, Steven Robert, eds. *Patent Cultures: Diversity and Harmonization in Historical Perspective*, 1st ed., Cambridge Intellectual Property and Information Law (New York: Cambridge University Press, 2019), 38–68; Rahmatian, Andreas. "Neo-Colonial Aspects of Global Intellectual Property Protection," *The Journal of World Intellectual Property* 12, no. 1 (January 2009): 40–74, https://doi.org/10.1111/j.1747-1796.2008.00349.x.

4 Pogge, Thomas. "The Health Impact Fund: Enhancing Justice and Efficiency in Global Health," *Journal of Human Development and Capabilities* 13, no. 4 (November 2012): 537–59, https://doi.org/10.1080/19452829.2012.703172; Sunder, Madhavi. *From Goods to a Good Life: Intellectual Property and Global Justice* (New Haven [Conn.]: Yale University Press, 2012), 173f; Halliburton, Murphy. *India and the Patent Wars: Pharmaceuticals in the New Intellectual Property Regime*, The Culture and Politics of Health Care Work (Ithaca, New York: ILR Press, an imprint of Cornell University Press, 2017);

Siew-Kuan Ng, Elizabeth. "Global Health and Development: Patents and Public Interest," in Pogge, Thomas; Rimmer, Matthew, and Rubenstein, Kim, eds. *Incentives for Global Public Health*, (Cambridge: Cambridge University Press, 2010), 101–32, https://doi.org/10.1017/CBO9780511750786.007.

Ho, Cynthia M. "Current Controversies Concerning Patent Rights and Public Health in a World of International Norms," in Takenaka, Toshiko, ed. *Research Handbook on Patent Law and Theory*, Second edition, Research Handbooks in Intellectual Property (Cheltenham, UK: Edward Elgar Publishing, 2019), 419–53.

5 Richards, Kevin T. et al. "Drug Pricing and Pharmaceutical Patenting Practices" (11 February 2020) Congressional Research Service Report R46221.

6 Trerise, Jonathan. "The Influence of Patents on Science," *Politics, Philosophy & Economics* 15, no. 4 (November 2016): 424–50, https://doi.org/10.1177/1470594X16666022.

7 Lamping, Matthias et al. "Declaration on Patent Protection – Regulatory Sovereignty under TRIPS," *International Review of Intellectual Property and Competition Law* (2014) 45, 681.

8 Ibid. 680.

In addition to these concrete problems, the current patent regime initiated by the Paris Convention is epistemologically and ontologically questionable. Since it is based on the notion of individual inventorship, this framework is inadequate regarding the protection of traditional knowledge.[9] It is also doubtful whether individual inventorship is a sensible construction since multiple discoveries are rather the rule than the exception.[10] Even further-reaching ontological concerns arise out of the patenting of organisms[11] and the human genome, where the logic of patenting seems to reach an ethical threshold.[12]

This chapter approaches these contemporary problems by means of Intellectual History, Legal and Political Philosophy and the Philosophy of Technology. Before introducing the Sections of this chapter in detail, it should be briefly explained how they relate to each other and to the complex problem of the normative impact of technological innovation. Sections 1 and 2 unearth crucial components of the ideo-historical pedigree of the current patent order and identify characteristics that determine its path dependency, primarily the idea that the furthering of technological innovation constitutes a legitimate normative aim in itself. In Section 3, these insights are taken as an occasion to embark on general reflections regarding the relationship between technological innovation and legal normativity, where it is demonstrated that technological innovation cannot constitute a reasonable normative aim in itself. This leads to a final, normative Section that is dedicated to the development of a reasonable normative approach to an international patent order beyond the promotion of technological progress as a normative aim.

The Sections in detail are structured as follows: The ideo-historical discussion of the first Section focusses on the event that initiated the norm development process leading to the Paris Convention of 1883, the Vienna Patent Congress of 1873. Rather than merely shedding some light on the defining conflicts in the run-up to the Paris Convention, this serves as an exemplary case study, showing the impact of non-governmental actors and non-lawyers with transnational business ties on the development of global norms, following the

9 Karanja, Wanjiku. "The Legitimacy of Indigenous Intellectual Property Rights' claims," *Strathmore Law Review* (2016) January, 165.

10 Lemley, Mark A. "The Myth of the Sole Inventor" *Mich. L. Rev.*, (2012) 110, 5, 709.

11 Sterckx, Sigrid, and Cockbain, Julian. *Exclusions from Patentability. How Far Has the European Patent Office Eroded Boundaries?* (Cambridge, Cambridge University Press, 2012), 193–242.

12 Lever, Annabelle. "Is it Ethical to Patent Human Genes?" in Grosseries, Axel et al. ed. *Intellectual property and theories of justice*, (Palgrave Macmillan 2008), 246–64.

idea of legal history 'in the vernacular.'[13] This Section reconstructs the context of the privately funded Vienna Patent Congress and highlights the leading role of two international telegraphy entrepreneurs and inventors based in Germany and the UK, the Siemens brothers, who were, for example, the main constructors of the London-Calcutta telegraph line.

The second Section provides a detailed analysis of the concrete debate at the Vienna Patent Congress which was highly political in nature. The most important finding is that the Siemens brothers did largely ignore the opposing political views in this debate on grounds of their 'passionate tonality.'[14] Instead, they conceived of international patent regulations exclusively in terms of a solution in order to 'accelerate and secure technological progress.'[15] This decidedly apolitical and technology-centered way of arguing became characteristic of modern patent debates.

The third Section takes this exemplary case as an occasion to engage in general reflections regarding the normative impact of technological innovation on the development of legal standards. The complex relationship between technology and legal norms is discussed on the basis of the intrinsically normative nature of technology, considering the logic of the engineering process and industry standards. The exclusive focus on the normative character of technological innovation that characterizes so many debates about patent law is criticized as a "neutralization" following Carl Schmitt. Using Stiegler's philosophy of technology as a starting point, it is demonstrated that the question of regulations regarding technological innovation cannot be separated from political concerns, particularly against the backdrop of the Anthropocene and insights into the phenomenon of zootechnological coevolution.

The fourth Section proposes a remedy to the exclusive focus on technological innovation in patent debates and introduces the notion of global patent justice in critical engagement with Rawls's *The Law of Peoples* and Pogge's concept of Global Justice. It is shown that Rawls's theory allows for finding autonomous national solutions for the patent sector, for example, regarding traditional knowledge databases, the Doha Declaration or, generally, 'regulatory sovereignty,' as defined by the Max Planck Institute, which emphasizes

---

13 Cogan, Jacob Katz. "A History of International Law in the Vernacular," *Journal of the History of International Law/Revue d'histoire Du Droit International* 22, no. 2–3 (2020): 205–217, https://doi.org/10.1163/15718050-12340149.

14 Pieper, Carl, ed. *Der Erfinderschutz und die Reform der Patentgesetze. Amtlicher Bericht über den internationalen Patent-Congress* (Berlin: Commission der der Schulbuchhandlung, 1873) 46.

15 Ibid. 49.

nations' considerable degree of freedom within international regulatory frameworks.[16] However, such solutions based on nation-states are imperfect, since the patent regime is closely related to problems of global inequality and global technological entanglement. Starting from Pogge's stronger account of global justice, a global patent system based on equity is sketched. In such a system, past injustices in the context of colonialism would have to be compensated for and privileges would have to bring about advantages to the least privileged. However, such global solutions, of course, raise concerns regarding their democratic legitimacy. Around these key points, a global patent system is discussed that is, unlike TRIPS and the Paris Convention, to be negotiated as a genuinely political issue.

2 Context and Effect of the Vienna Patent Congress of 1873

The Vienna Patent Congress of 1873 that has set the agenda for the Paris Convention is closely connected to the institution of the international fair, which found its best-known early example in the British great exposition of 1851. The importance of international fairs to globalization and industrialization in the 19th century can hardly be overestimated. Considering the limited contemporary means of long-range communication in those days, the world's fairs were unrivaled "showcases for raw materials, means of production, and finished goods from all over the world" and therefore "significant vehicles of international communication among nations, manufacturers, and the millions of visitors and potential consumers."[17] Having served as places of communication, international fairs were also places of conflict and debate. In particular, around world's fairs, there were frequent discussions regarding IP law.[18]

In September 1871, shortly after the publication of the program of the international exposition to be held in Vienna in 1873,[19] the discussions about patent rights became urgent since Austria-Hungary had a particularly strong working requirement, which linked the protection of patent rights in the Habsburg Monarchy to the production of the patented product on its territory.

---

16 Lamping, "Declaration on Patent Protection – Regulatory Sovereignty under TRIPS."

17 Raizman, David, and Robey, Ethan, eds. *Expanding Nationalisms at World Fairs: Identity, Diversity, and Exchange, 1851–1915*, Routledge Research in Art History (London New York: Routledge, Taylor & Francis Group, 2018), 1.

18 Fischer, Ludwig. *Werner Siemens und der Schutz der Erfindungen* (Berlin: Springer, 1922) 49.

19 Pieper, *Der Erfinderschutz und die Reform der Patentgesetze*, p. 2.

Austria-Hungary was not unique in that. Some countries had similar working requirements, with the notable exception, however, of the US and the UK.[20]

Already on December 23, 1871, the Scientific American commented:

> It was almost equivalent to prohibition to require that the locomotive engines of Great Britain, the telegraph instruments of the United States, and the printed muslins of France shall be manufactured on Austrian soil within a year from securing the patent.

Further, the text criticized that "the value of Austrian patents issued to Americans and other foreigners can be easily escheated to the benefit of the Austrian public."[21]

In reaction to such concerns, the US government demanded patent protection from Austria-Hungary if US companies were to participate in this exhibition.[22] Consequently, the American Minister at the Austro-Hungarian Foreign office took the step to initiate a special law that protected foreign inventions from loss of rights by exhibiting at the exposition, the *Special Law for the Protection of Objects exhibited at the universal exhibition in Vienna* from 1872. This law was based on similar pieces of legislation passed in connection with international expositions by the UK and France.[23]

Additionally, it was decided to organize the International Congress of Vienna for Patent Reform, which can be considered 'the first step' leading to the Paris Convention.[24] The preceding debate on working requirements and national treatment of patents determines the outcome of the international norm development process regarding patents, which is characterized by internationalization and the concomitant easing of working requirements.

The Vienna Patent Congress had around 250 attendees, primarily governmental and private sector representatives from Germany, Austria, Britain, and the US, and a smaller number from the Netherlands, France, Belgium, Italy, Denmark, Hungary, Canada, Brazil and India.[25] Since it was not funded by the

20 Ricketson, Sam. *The Paris Convention and the Protection of Industrial Property: A Commentary* (Oxford: Oxford University Press, 2015), at 104.

21 Quoted after: Ladas, Stephen P. *The International Protection of Industrial Property* (Harvard: Harvard University Press, 1930) 73.

22 Pieper, *Der Erfinderschutz und die Reform der Patentgesetze*, p. 2f.

23 See in this volume: Duncan, Louise J. The Key Historical Influences Leading to the Paris Convention for the Protection of Industrial Property of 1883. At 23.

24 Ladas, *The International Protection of Industrial Property*, 74.

25 Ricketson, *The Paris Convention and the Protection of Industrial Property*, 125.

Austro-Hungarian Government,[26] the event depended on private individuals, particularly Prussian patent activists who later, in 1874, founded the German *Patentschutzverein* that promoted the ideas developed in Vienna.

The congress is clearly dominated by the Siemens brothers, the originally German, UK resident and inventor Charles William Siemens being its president, and his brother, Werner Siemens, being a leading German industrialist (founder of what became the Siemens AG) and patent activist in Prussia. Next to the Siemens brothers, the most influential Prussian patent activists participated in or in close collaboration with the conference's preparatory committee,[27] most notably Carl Pieper, the Secretary-General of the congress that would play a decisive role in the internationalization of patent law in the aftermath of the congress.

The Siemens brothers' engagement in regard to this issue has many layers: First of all, the Siemens brothers' multinational web of enterprises just finished the construction of the revolutionary 11.000 km telegraph line London-Calcutta in 1870. They are, therefore, on the forefront of technological and regulatory internationalization.

Second, this is crucial in regard to legal history: Britain and France were far more developed than Germany regarding patent regulations, which had no unified patent law until 1877. Consequently, this debate was much more urgent in Germany than in England and France, which also had a relatively solid philosophical tradition of legitimizing patent rights based on natural rights, which never has been comparably relevant in Germany. Germans also primarily pursued another approach than Britain and France regarding patents that has been understood as being based on a priority on the national economy and that perceived patent rights not as an absolute right, but as a means to the end of securing national welfare.

Furthermore, the issue of the internationalization of regulations was precisely urgent to German actors, because, paradoxically, internationalization constituted a 'domestic' problem between the sovereign German territories after the end of the German Empire due to the Napoleonic wars and before the founding of the Second Empire in 1871. Next to the complex system of tariffs between the different German sovereign territories, the complex system of territorial patent laws has been understood as an obstacle to industrialization. With the founding of the German tariff union in 1832, there were attempts to

26 See in this volume: Duncan, Louise J. The Key Historical Influences Leading to the Paris Convention for the Protection of Industrial Property of 1883. At 24.

27 Wilhelm André, Carl Pieper, Rudolf Klostermann and J. Rosenthal. See: Pieper, *Der Erfinderschutz und die Reform der Patentgesetze*, 4.

unify the patent system throughout the German sovereign territories, in which namely Werner Siemens had been involved.[28] However, it was the Vienna Patent Congress that ultimately led to the founding of the German *Patentschutzverein* in 1874 and, subsequently, to the establishment of its national patent law in 1877, for which the main actors of the Vienna Patent Congress, foremost Siemens and Pieper, employed the arguments developed in Vienna.[29]

Although sounding unlikely, this birth of a progressive internationalist political agenda as political compensation for a vanished feudal empire is not unusual. Take Friedrich List, who turned from advocating free trade between the German sovereign territories to a nuanced understanding of global free trade.[30] Little more than half a century later, the Austrian School Neoliberals developed their free trade agenda in order to compensate for the economic stability granted by the Habsburg Empire before its disintegration.[31] And already in the fourth century, the Greco-Syrian rhetorician Libanius formulated an extremely influential doctrine of free trade as compensation for the split of the Roman Empire between the emperors Constans and Constantius II, both sons of Constantine the Great.[32]

In its conclusion, the Vienna Patent Congress named seven reasons for the introduction of an international patent regime, including the 'sense of right among civilized nations,' the need for 'effective means of introducing new technical methods without loss of time to the general knowledge of the public,' the need to render 'the labor of the inventor remunerative,' the necessity to attract foreign capital and to prevent the emigration of inventors, and the desire to lift the veil on 'secrecy of manufacture,' characterized as 'one of the greatest enemies of industrial progress.'[33] As will be discussed in the next Section in detail, the conference proceedings show how Werner Siemens proposed five

---

28 Lührs, Philipp Moritz. *Die Entstehung des Reichspatentgesetzes von 1877 und der Versuch eines europäischen Patentrechts von 1962 im Vergleich* (PhD thesis Universität Düsseldorf 2019), 32. https://docserv.uni-duesseldorf.de/servlets/DocumentServlet?id=50527, accessed 29. December 2020.

29 Ibid. 77.

30 Daastöl, Arno Mong. "Friedrich List (1789–1846)" in Backhaus, Jürgen G., ed. *The Elgar Companion to Law and Economics*, (Cheltenham: Edward Elgar, 2005).

31 Slobodian, Quinn. *Globalists: The End of Empire and the Birth of Neoliberalism* (Cambridge: Harvard University Press, 2018).

32 Irwin, Douglas A. *Against the Tide: An Intellectual History of Free Trade*, Fifth printing, and first paperback printing, 1998 (Princeton, NJ: Princeton Univ. Press, 1998), 16.

33 Quoted after Ricketson, *The Paris Convention and the Protection of Industrial Property*, 126f.

of these seven reasons, changing the original proposal, of which the tonality was more political.[34]

The instruments for patent protection that were proposed by the Vienna Congress include primarily an abandoning of national working requirements, determined by the debate in the run-up to the congress. However, this did not yet include national treatment. The conclusion merely stated 'a patent should not be denied to a foreigner,' which, however, together with the abandoning of working requirements would produce similar results.

Before the concrete debates at the Vienna Patent Congress will be highlighted in the next Section, some words regarding its consequences: As mentioned before, regarding Germany, the Patent order for the Second German Empire can be directly traced back to the Vienna Patent Congress. And although Germany would ultimately not sign the Paris Convention until 1908,[35] the context of Prussian patent activism, namely the Siemens brothers and Carl Pieper, stayed influential in the international debate.

In the US, the congress led to the establishment of the US Patent Association (1874), which promoted the internationalization of patent regulations.[36] In 1877, the Association for the Reform and Codification of the Law of Nations, which had many British and French members, issued a list of national recommendations largely following the Vienna Patent Congress.[37] Out of the Vienna Congress came also an executive committee, which continued lobbying regarding the internationalization of patent laws.[38] The International Congress on Industrial Property on the occasion of the international exposition in Paris in 1878 underlined its continuity with the Vienna Patent Congress by appointing William Siemens honorary co-president.[39] In many of these conferences and congresses, Carl Pieper played an important role.[40]

The congress in Paris of 1878 was considerably larger, with 500 attendees and representatives from Germany, Spain, the US, Hungary, Italy, Luxembourg, Russia, Sweden, Norway and Switzerland.[41] Its central issue was the question of how an international IP regime should be achieved, whereby the discussion

34 Pieper, *Der Erfinderschutz und die Reform der Patentgesetze*, 47f.

35 Ricketson, *The Paris Convention and the Protection of Industrial Property*, 128, 153.

36 Ibid. 128.

37 Ibid. 129.

38 Pieper, *Der Erfinderschutz und die Reform der Patentgesetze*, 261.

39 Ricketson, *The Paris Convention and the Protection of Industrial Property*, 131.

40 See in this volume: Duncan, Louise J. The Key Historical Influences Leading to the Paris Convention for the Protection of Industrial Property of 1883. At 28.

41 Ladas, *The International Protection of Industrial Property*, 75.

was extended beyond patents.[42] Since, unsurprisingly, the participants could not agree on which national law to universalize, the idea of a complete international harmonization of IP law was dismissed as 'a utopia.'[43]

Nevertheless, this was a time, in which many international institutions had been set up in order to harmonize regulations regarding issues that were (or seemed to be) of less political and more technological nature. Examples are the conferences in Vienna (1868), Rome (1871) and Saint Petersburg (1875), who defined the common framework for international telegraph links,[44] the International Telegraph Union (1865), the Universal Postal Union (1874), which defined the framework for the international post system and the International Bureau for Weights and Measures (1875).[45] In this spirit, the participants also drafted the project to form a union for the protection of industrial property, which prepared the next conference on this issue.[46]

This international conference of 1880 in Paris was the first official diplomatic conference on the matter and Germany no longer participated. It widened the scope of the project by including more non-European countries, notably, former colonies that are characterized by an exclusively European understanding of nationhood: Guatemala, El Salvador, Uruguay, Brazil and Venezuela. The most important conflict of this convention originated from Switzerland and the Netherlands, which had no national legislation for the protection of inventions. And the US vehemently opposed the subordination of domestic laws to an international agreement.[47]

In the end, the conference found a compromise between national self-determination and the construction of an international legal framework by restricting itself to these points: the easing, albeit not abandoning of working requirements through national treatment and priority within the union. These aspects also concerned domestic law, but left some space for national regulatory sovereignty, for example, regarding the expropriation for public purposes.[48] The draft from 1880 became, with minor changes, the Paris Convention of 1883.

Although this was not exactly the international harmonization of the patent system that the participants of the Vienna Patent Congress had in mind,

42 Ricketson, *The Paris Convention and the Protection of Industrial Property*, 130.

43 Quoted after: Ladas, *The International Protection of Industrial Property*, 76.

44 Pascal Griset, "Innovation Diplomacy: A New Concept for Ancient Practices?," *The Hague Journal of Diplomacy* 15, no. 3 (August 19, 2020): 383–97, https://doi.org/10.1163/1871191X-BJA10036.

45 Galvez-Behar, "The 1883 Paris Convention and the Impossible Unification of Industrial Property," 38.

46 Ladas, *The International Protection of Industrial Property*, 78.

47 Ibid. 79f.

48 Ibid. 80f; Ricketson, *The Paris Convention and the Protection of Industrial Property*, 155f.

its basic idea to minimize national barriers in favor of an international patent system has been realized. This had impacts beyond formal legal obligations. For example, in the cases of Switzerland and the Netherlands, the adoption of the Paris Convention provided a nudge to develop national patent laws.[49]

The legal relationship between colonial periphery and center was more complex than a simple adaption of these rules.[50] Only with the Washington Conference of 1911, the system was formally extended to colonies and dependent territories.[51] This became, during the Stockholm Conference of 1967, subject to at least formal revisions and the reason for protests from developing and socialist countries.[52] The post-colonial critique of the international IP regime has been common, albeit not necessarily effective since then.

3 The Political Debate at the Vienna Patent Congress

Let us go back to take a closer look at the beginning of the norm development process that led to the Paris Convention. Not unusual for historical crossroads, the Vienna Patent Congress of 1873 was characterized by a plurality of viewpoints and openness of debate that has hardly ever been reached later. Corresponding to the transitional character of the 19th century, heated arguments regarding Liberalism, Feudalism, Communism and the conflicting political and legal traditions within Europe were exchanged.

In 1873, Werner Siemens commented on the resolution of the Vienna Patent Congress in the following way:

> After a number of hard fights, the international patent congress in Vienna adopted the standpoint that patent legislation should be equally reformed in all industrialized countries, in order to secure and accelerate technological progress and in order to strip patents of their functioning as monopolies inhibiting progress.[53]

---

49 Rahmatian, Andreas. "Neo-Colonial Aspects of Global Intellectual Property Protection," 40, 45.

50 Galvez-Behar "The 1883 Paris Convention and the Impossible Unification of Industrial Property," 45.

51 Ricketson, *The Paris Convention and the Protection of Industrial Property*, 423.

52 Ibid. 425.

53 "Im Wiener Internationalen Patentkongreß ist nach harten Kämpfen der Grundsatz durchgedrungen und in einer Reihe von Beschlüssen festgestellt, daß die Patentgesetzgebung in allen Industrie treibenden Ländern möglichst gleichmäßig und in dem Sinne zu reformieren sei, daß der technische Fortschritt durch sie möglichst gesichert und beschleunigt werde, und zu dem Ende den Patenten der Charakter hemmender

In his standard work, Ricketson accurately characterizes these 'hard fights' as moderately pluralist.[54] Although the majority was pro-patent, there were also other positions. Some free traders were denying the need for patents altogether. After all, the Dutch have repealed their patent law in 1869 on such grounds and the Swiss had no patent system at all in order to attract foreign industrialists.[55] Some proposed an alternative reward system.[56]

Additionally, the camp of those in favor of patent regulation was also divided: those who preferred a natural law standpoint based on absolute individual rights following British and French traditions, during the congress often dubbed as 'lawyers,' and those who preferred a utilitarian approach, often dubbed as "national economists," a position that was more important in the German discourse. This debate is clearly not technical in nature, but highly political. It is probable that its open and speculative character is owed to the fact that participants from Germany dominated this debate, which, in contrast to Britain and France, had no patent law tradition based on natural rights and, as mentioned before, at this point no national patent regulation at all.

To the most radical free traders, who opposed patents altogether, patents were 'an anachronistic relict from the age of guilds ... at odds with the freedom of business.'[57] This corresponds to the idea that before the unification of the Second German Empire, some argued for a waiver of patents, in order to facilitate technological exchange between the different sovereign German territories.[58]

Beyond that, a particularly interesting contribution from a factory owner (by no means a Socialist) criticizes the patent system for producing a new commodity for 'capitalists' to trade with, rather than providing incentives or rewards for inventors:

> Inventing requires not only the talent of the inventor but also the talent to exploit the invention. Inventors never possess this talent, or only in very rare cases. But the capitalists possess it to a very high degree, and,

---

Monopole möglichst zu nehmen sei.", Quoted after: Fischer, *Werner Siemens und der Schutz der Erfindungen*, 49.

54 Ricketson, *The Paris Convention and the Protection of Industrial Property*, 125.

55 Ibid. 95.

56 Pieper, *Der Erfinderschutz und die Reform der Patentgesetze*, 65.

57 Ibid., 45. „anachronistisches Ueberbleibsel aus der Zunftzeit", „im Widerspruch mit der Freiheit der Gewerbe."

58 Lührs *Die Entstehung des Reichspatentgesetzes von 1877 und der Versuch eines europäischen Patentrechts von 1962 im Vergleich*, 32; Ricketson, *The Paris Convention and the Protection of Industrial Property*, 96.

> gentlemen, if you look, and look honestly, you will find that in most cases of a great upswing due to new inventions, the patent buyer has had great profit, but the inventor has gone away empty-handed.[59]

From today's perspective, these arguments appear left-leaning. However, in the historical context, they probably have merely served as a justification for the agenda of a factory owner to cut costs by getting rid of patent regulations. Interestingly, during the debate, this argument was criticized for being too private-sector oriented, for being an expression of the tendency of companies to become 'states within the state' and 'completely sovereign.'[60]

On the other side of the aisle, there were few, mostly English advocates of a strong inventors' right. After all, the English were still the patent superpower at that time and setting the 'standard for (…) inventor's rights.'[61] Remarkably, they connected classical liberal natural rights theory to explicit anticommunism:

> I am among those who believe in the natural rights of invention and think it a duty of every government to protect those rights aside from any question of state interests … Those, who deny the justice of this view must – to be consistent – take refuge in communism.[62]

That position was, with slight modifications, seconded by an Austrian engineer:

> We must not deny the right of the inventor fundamentally. Especially us engineers as the commanders of the workers' corps do not want communism to take hold.[63]

---

59 Pieper, *Der Erfinderschutz und die Reform der Patentgesetze*, 65f. „Zum Erfinden gehört nicht nur das Talent des Erfinders, sondern auch das Talent, die Erfindung zu verwerthen. Dieses Talent besitzen eigentlich die Erfinder niemals oder nur in sehr seltenen Fällen. Aber in sehr hohem Grade besitzen es die Capitalisten, und, meine Herren, wenn Sie da nachsehen, und redlich nachsehen, so werden Sie finden, dass in den meisten Fällen, wo es sich um den grossen Aufschwung neuer Erfindungen handelt, der Patentkäufer wohl grossen Gewinn hatte, der Erfinder aber leer ausgegangen ist."

60 Ibid. 94, „Besonders grosse Fabrikanten sind in kleinen Ländern Staaten im Staate sie möchten vollkommen souverän sein."

61 Galvez-Behar, "The 1883 Paris Convention and the Impossible Unification of Industrial Property," 40.

62 Pieper, *Der Erfinderschutz und die Reform der Patentgesetze*, 97. English in the original.

63 Ibid. 57. „Das Erfinderrecht im Fundamente dürfen wir nicht verläugnen, und gerade wir Ingenieure als die Commandanten des Arbeitercorps und die wir nicht haben wollen, dass der Communismus Platz greife."

Against this point of view, the 'national economists' present an understanding of property rights as not being based on absolute natural law, such as the British, but as dependent on the usefulness of these rights to national welfare. This is in accordance with the split between the Anglo-Saxon Lockean, absolute understanding of property rights and the German, Kantian understanding of property rights that regards property rights as merely 'provisional' until they are ratified by a social contract.[64] In the debate, the position of the "national economists" is characterized in the following way:

> The inventor has the right to his invention only insofar as the law grants him the exclusive use of his invention. In the entire field of property law, there is no right that must exist by natural necessity. (…) The state grants rights to demands of morality only insofar as this corresponds to public benefit; therefore, the question of usefulness must be answered first and foremost.[65]

One contribution from the side of the national economists is particularly radical: a remark by a member of the congress' preparatory committee, Mathias Georg Ratkowsky, who published a monograph regarding the reform of the inventors' right in 1870.[66] There, he had proposed an entirely different patent system, which would give everyone the right to use a patent, but the user would have to buy tax stamps from a public institution for each use and the inventor would be remunerated according to the use.[67]

Although it is probably accurate that Ratkowsky's proposal is unrealistic[68] because it would have created a bureaucratic nightmare, it is interesting, since

64 See: Kant, Immanuel. *The Metaphysics of Morals, Texts in German Philosophy* (Cambridge; New York: Cambridge University Press, 1991), 257. This is precisely the ground on which Kantians such as Rawls and Pogge (Section 4) assume private property to be dependent on a mutual agreement originating from the "original position." Up to today, Kantian German law does not include absolute property rights, but limits them: "Property entails obligations. Its use shall also serve the public good." The Basic Law for the Federal Republic of Germany, Article 14.

65 Pieper, *Der Erfinderschutz und die Reform der Patentgesetze*, 75f. „Das Recht hat der Erfinder nur, soweit das Gesetz ihm die ausschliessliche Benutzung seiner Erfindung einräumt. Es giebt auf dem ganzen Gebiete des Vermögensrechtes kein Recht, welches mit Naturnothwendigkeit existiren müsste. (…) Auf Forderungen der Moral gewährt der Staat nur Rechte, sofern dies dem gemeinen Nutzen entspricht; deshalb ist vor Allem die Nützlichkeitsfrage zu beantworten."

66 Ratkowsky, Mathias Georg. *Zur Reform des Erfinderrechts* (Wien, n.n. 1870).

67 Pieper, *Der Erfinderschutz und die Reform der Patentgesetze*, 65.

68 Fischer, *Der Erfinderschutz und die Reform der Patentgesetze*, 53, footnote.

it tries to tackle the problem of remuneration and incentive-building according to public usefulness by shifting the focus from the market to public institutions. In this, Ratkowsky's historical account can be compared to Pogge's contemporary idea to organize a reward system for inventions on the basis of a global fund.[69]

The context of these opposing views not only sheds a light on the highly political nature of this debate in general but also provides a framework to understand the context of the congress's resolution. Although clearly bearing the most influence on the drafting of this resolution, the Siemens brothers did not impose their views on the other participants, but rather, they looked for a compromise.

However, this compromise is precisely defined by abandoning the contested field of political debate, which is characterized by the diverging demands of natural rights Liberalism, anti-Communism and national economy, and moving towards a merely technical understanding of international patent regulation, which includes emphasizing technological innovation as its prior normative aim.

For example, the original proposal that Werner Siemens replaced by his proposal[70] included references to 'inventions promoting the common good' and 'national welfare,' political terms that are entirely cancelled in the later proposal of the congress.[71] Siemens was aware of that move, as he argued, somewhat paradoxically, that this 'passionate tonality'[72] would not convince the fraction that tended to oppose patents exactly for the sake of national welfare.

Of course, that is primarily owed to the fact that international patent regimes cannot easily be justified along the lines of national welfare because they do not necessarily promote it. Siemens's position, in turn, is defined by his interests as an inventor and entrepreneur. However, he precisely does not justify his claims with a Lockean, absolute understanding of inventor's rights following the Anglo-Saxon tradition, which would not have been successful in this debate.

Rather, he justifies inventor's rights through a trade-off and follows the typically German and Kantian contractualist, national economist's position

---

69 Pogge, "The Health Impact Fund: Enhancing Justice and Efficiency in Global Health."

70 Pieper, *Der Erfinderschutz und die Reform der Patentgesetze*, 47f.

71 Ibid. 22. „Ein in richtiger Weise gewährter Patentschutz ist geeignet, gemeinnützige Erfindungen hervorzurufen, die Productionsmethoden zu verbessern und dadurch die Production selbst zu vermehren und zu verbilligern, die Consumtion zu vergrössern und somit die nationale Wohlfahrt zu fördern."

72 Ibid. 46.

inasmuch as he envisions the state as constituting a crucial bargaining partner in this trade. However, almost unnoticeably, Siemens switches this bargaining partner from the individual state, which has a clearly defined political interest in this bargain, to the lofty, cosmopolitan and ultimately apolitical concept of 'mankind', which clearly only serves as a rhetorical placeholder for the more likely beneficiary of this bargain, 'the whole industry'. And ultimately, since this is also just a lofty term without a concrete political referent, the mere speed of innovation becomes the real beneficiary of inventor's rights.

He lays out his basic understanding of patent rights in the following words, which clearly mark the turning point of the debate:

> The legal basis of any patent law, in my view, is this: I consider a patent just like a trade between the state as representative of the general public and the inventor. The state says: I give you protection for a certain number of years and recognize the exclusive property right of your invention under the condition that you immediately publish it faithfully. In this faithful publication now lies a tremendous impetus for the whole industry, may the invention be good or bad. The new idea that flies through the whole world with the help of the press is a flash of lightning that ignites in a hundred places. It is often worthless inventions that spread tremendous blessing and progress through rapid publication. In the granting of patents, it does not matter whether the patent is good or bad, whether it is useful or useless; the new idea contained in it should become the common property of mankind as quickly as possible. That is the root![73]

By envisioning them as two sides of a pragmatic trade ultimately entering an international level, Siemens relativizes the absolute normative roles of the inventor *and* of the individual state. Of course, he references vague normative

73 Ibid. 48. „Die rechtliche Grundlage jeden Patentgesetzes ist meiner Ansicht nach folgendes: Ich betrachte ein Patent gerade so, wie einen Handel zwischen dem Staate als Repräsentanten der Allgemeinheit und dem Erfinder. Der Staat sagt: Ich gebe dir einen Schutz auf eine bestimmte Anzahl von Jahren und erkenne das ausschliessliche Eigenthumsrecht deiner Erfindung unter der Bedingung an, dass du es sofort getreulich publicirst. – In dieser getreulichen Publication nun liegt ein ungeheuerer Antrieb für die ganze Industrie, mag die Erfindung gut oder schlecht sein. Der neue Gedanke, der mit Hülfe der Presse die ganze Welt durchfliegt, ist ein Blitz, der in hundert Gegenden zündet. Es sind oft werthlose Erfindungen, welche durch die schleunige Publication einen ungeheueren Segen und Fortschritt verbreiten. Es kommt beider Patentertheilung nicht darauf an, ob das Patent gut oder schlecht ist, ob es nützt oder unnütz ist; der neue Gedanke, der darin liegt, soll so schnell als möglich zum Gemeingut der Menschheit werden. Das ist die Wurzel!"

ideas, such as 'the state as representative of the general public.' However, these ideas are devoid of any concretely political implications, since they are immediately sublated into the higher, clearly apolitical concept of 'the common property of mankind' and, finally, 'the whole industry,' for which the publication of inventions constitutes 'a tremendous impetus.'

Clearly, although it has been developed from the conceptions of the national economists, the normative core of Siemens's proposal is the promotion of technological innovation itself, not the welfare of a particular nation. This technological progressivism is, notably, in contrast to many such claims in that epoch, not connected to a normative ideal of moral or spiritual development, since he rejects all such terms – surprisingly even the notion that 'good' ideas are worth spreading. The telegraphy entrepreneur judges an idea only by the velocity of its communication and its effects on technological innovation as such, abstracted from all human categories such as good or bad.

This mode of normative reasoning is fundamentally independent of human assessments and critical human assessment in particular since it is *a priori beyond human comprehension*. It is only in an indirect and unforeseeable way that new, good *and* bad innovations, spreading like a 'flash of lightning' provide the ground for the emergence of further innovations. In analogy to the invisible hand of the market, the technological supersystem is expected to allocate the published innovations much better than any human institution and bring them to their optimal use. By this move, Siemens replaced the moral, juridical and political arguments that have been brought forward in this debate by the mere speed of technological innovation.

Particularly during the politically heated atmosphere of the 19th century that also characterized the debates at the Vienna Patent Congress, this argumentative move must have provided relief to many participants. Obviously, at least it must have seemed so, there was an elegant exit from the deadlocks between Communism, Liberalism, Feudalism and the conflicting political and legal traditions within Europe that constituted obstacles to the internationalization of patent rights. Compatible with the authoritarian character of the time, one would simply put a higher instance in charge. One would hand all responsibility over to technological innovation itself! This, of course, deeply flawed argumentative strategy is exemplary and can serve as a starting point for general reflections on the normative impact of technology.

4 The Normative Impact of Technology

Since the very existence of the international community depends on technologies of travel, trade and communication, it is almost tautological to point out that international legal standards are strongly influenced by technological factors. In his fundamental work on the philosophy of international law, Kant argued for the necessity of global legal standards on grounds of the, at that time recent, *development* of global commerce and communication which are clearly effects of technological innovation.

> Since the narrower or wider community of the peoples of the earth has *developed* so far that a violation of rights in one place is felt throughout the world, the idea of a law of world citizenship is no high-flown or exaggerated notion.[74]

The accuracy of this conclusion can hardly be denied. Since technological innovation furthers international interdependency and exchange, technological innovation has often played a crucial role in the development of new international legal standards.

Already the theoretical formulation of modern international law at Vitoria and Grotius is owed to technologies that brought about the age of discoveries and hereby furthered international entanglement. Vitoria undertakes his research as a reflection on the legitimacy of Spanish colonialism, trade, forced labor and resource extraction in Latin America.[75] Grotius' first work on international law is commissioned by the world's first public company, the VOC, and deals with the justification of preemptive self-defense by private traders in maritime East Asia.[76] None of these reflections would have been necessary without the technologies and the related economic networks that connected Europe to the rest of the world.

The Westphalian peace, the practical source of modern international law, can likewise be understood as a product of technological innovation: The invention

---

74 Kant, Immanuel. *Toward Perpetual Peace and Other Writings on Politics, Peace, and History* (New Haven, YUP: 2006) 84.

75 Thumfart, Johannes. *Die Begründung der globalpolitischen Philosophie. Francisco de Vitorias Vorlesung über die Entdeckung Amerikas im ideengeschichtlichen Kontext* (Berlin: Kadmos, 2012).

76 Thumfart, Johannes. "On Grotius's Mare Liberum and Vitoria's De Indis, Following Agamben and Schmitt," *Grotiana* 30, no. 1 (2009): 65–87, https://doi.org/10.1163/016738309X12537002674286.

of the printing press and the spread of gunpowder[77] flooded Europe with a wave of military aggression, amplified and accompanied by religious fanaticism that has put the medieval order into question. The impact of these new technologies demanded a clearer, strictly political understanding of the limits of secular national sovereignty, which Westphalia provided. Later, the French and American revolutions and the idea of democratic self-determination and popular sovereignty that they spread slowly were significantly influenced by advances in the production of muskets.[78] In the 20th century, further international entanglement in the age of steamships brought about universal jurisdiction such as developed in the case of *S.S. Lotus, France v. Turkey* from 1927. Later, the development of air traffic required a complete reworking of the vertical extension of land ownership.[79] And, with the cultural, technological and economic globalization of the 20th and 21st centuries, legal standards became increasingly globalized.

Since technology transgresses borders, cultures and creeds, it is closely intertwined with the development of international norms. However, as these examples show, these norms are not necessarily characterized by deterritorialisation and delimitation as some believe, following Marx's famous dictum 'all that is solid melts into air.' Rather, these norms introduce new borders and limits where technology puts old ones into question.

This normative impact of technology is well understood by a particularly enlightening conclusion at the end of the Vienna Patent Congress, where an attendant argues that the universalization of this normative framework 'to secure and accelerate technological progress' becomes necessary because industrialization and inventiveness are things 'which, by their very nature, are of *cosmopolitan character*' and which 'transgress the barriers of the single nation.'[80]

77 Andrade, Tonio. *The Gunpowder Age: China, Military Innovation, and the Rise of the West in World History* (Princeton Oxford: Princeton University Press, 2016);

Tonio Andrade, *The Gunpowder Age: China, Military Innovation, and the Rise of the West in World History* (Princeton Oxford: Princeton University Press, 2016).

78 Alder, Ken. *Engineering the Revolution: Arms and Enlightenment in France, 1763–1815*, University of Chicago Press paperback ed (Chicago; London: The University of Chicago Press, 2010).

79 Lessig, Lawrence. *Free Culture: The Nature and Future of Creativity*, Reprint (New York, NY: Penguin Books, 2005), p. 21.

80 Pieper, *Der Erfinderschutz und die Reform der Patentgesetze*, 224. "Wenn er (der Übelstand unterschiedlicher Gesetze) Einrichtungen betrifft, die ihrer Natur nach einen cosmopolitischen Charakter tragen. Darüber brauchen wir aber wohl nicht zu streiten, dass in der That Industrie und Erfindungsgeist Dinge sind, die über die Schranken des einzelnen Landes sich hinwegsetzen."

Where such cosmopolitan delimitation takes place, new conflicts arise. The international patent system is a way to reintroduce immaterial borders within the increasingly borderless world of the 19th century's increasingly global technological network. These new, immaterial borders of intellectual property are not following the borders of the nation-states, but rather they transcend exactly these borders; they are also not to be understood in terms of a Luddite confrontation of technological progress, but rather, they are themselves intended to, or: at least justified as, promoting technological progress.

It would not be entirely wrong to resort to, originally Marxist, technological determinism here, which argues that the technological base determines the legal or otherwise normative superstructure. Or it would be legitimate to expand on Innis's work on how specific communication technologies bring about specific forms of imperial power, regarding reach, durability, speed and affordance[81] towards a more general understanding of the impact of technology on societal structures.

However, the relationship between technology and normativity is more complex than these approaches based on a binary understanding of the feedback between technology and society in terms of historical materialism. Rather than merely triggering normative processes by posing new problems in the material realm, technology itself has a normative character. Unlike science, technology is not descriptive, i.e. it does not describe reality, but it is prescriptive, i.e. it creates new realities. This brings it in close relation to law:

> Prescriptive knowledge not only plays a dominant role in technological practice but also is of crucial importance in many other domains of human life, such as the social domain (law) (…). Prescriptions may be effective (adequate) but not true. Within technology, these prescriptions are always hypothetical imperatives (conditioned on the desired change or state of affairs).[82]

Whilst, at least ideally, the scientist sees the world *as* it *is*, the engineer resembles the lawyer inasmuch as he sees the world as it *should be* and undertakes measures in order to close the gap between normative idea and material reality. Alder writes accordingly:

81 Innis, Harold Adams. *Empire and Communications* (London: Rowman & Littlefield, 2007).

82 Meijers, Anthonie W.M., and Kroes, Peter A. "Extending the Scope of the Theory of Knowledge," in Vries, Marc J. de; Hansson, Sven Ove, and Meijers, Anthonie W.M., eds. *Norms in Technology*, vol. 9, Philosophy of Engineering and Technology (Dordrecht: Springer Netherlands, 2013), 15–34, https://doi.org/10.1007/978-94-007-5243-6, 24.

> Where science is supposedly directed toward what is, engineering is directed toward what ought to be. (…) In principle, engineering operates on a simple, but radical assumption: that the present is nothing more than the raw material from which to construct a better future. In this process, no existing arrangement is to be considered sacrosanct.[83]

Beyond this conceptual aspect, technology has a normative dimension that is directly material. Emerging as an interdependent network, technology is, above all, built on the combinability, interchangeability and replaceability of its parts.[84] This networked nature of technology determines the nature of its components, which created the phenomenon of industrial standardization already in the 19th century.[85] Regarding the historical example, the establishment of the International Telegraph Union (1865), the Universal Postal Union (1874) and the International Bureau for Weights and Measures (1875) shows how quickly the global spread of technology led to the development of international norms. Today, similar reflections are being made regarding the impact of global digital technology on global norm development processes.[86] Even the geopolitical conflict between the US and China is increasingly understood from the perspective of a struggle for global dominance in processes of technological standard setting.[87]

Its inherent tendency toward universal norms brings technology close to law, but also law close to technology. Within modern, technology-centered debates, law becomes increasingly stripped from its legitimization in tradition and becomes itself merely a brand of social technology. Particularly patent law can be regarded as a form of technology since it can be understood as a tool providing the right framework for bringing about technological innovation.[88]

83 Alder, *Engineering the Revolution*, 12, 15.

84 Ibid. 221f.

85 Adams, C.A. "Industrial Standardization," *The Annals of the American Academy of Political and Social Science*, (1919) 8, 289.

86 C. Kettemann, Matthias. *The Normative Order of the Internet* (New York: Oxford University Press, 2020); Thumfart, Johannes. "The Norm Development of Digital Sovereignty between China, Russia, the EU and the US: From the Late 1990s to the Covid-Crisis 2020/21 as Catalytic Event," in Hallinan, Dara; Leenes, Ronald, and Hert, Paul de, eds. *Enforcing Rights in a Changing World*, Computers Privacy Data Protection (CPDP) 14 (London: Hart Publishing, 2022).

87 Seaman, John. "China and the New Geopolitics of Technical Standardization" (French Institute of International Relations, January 27, 2020), https://www.ifri.org/en/publications/notes-de-lifri/china-and-new-geopolitics-technical-standardization.

88 Biagioli, Mario, and Buning, Marius. "'Technologies of the Law/Law as a Technology,'" *History of Science* 57, no. 1 (March 2019): 3–17, https://doi.org/10.1177/0073275318816163.

That is exactly the mode how the Siemens brothers thought of legal instruments, which is exemplary for their epoch and has been a predominant point of view since then. Instead of engaging in an agonistic way with the complex political conflicts in the debate of their turbulent time, conflicts involving Communism, Liberalism and Feudalism and competing European legal and political traditions, they elevate the debate on a higher, merely technical level and elevate technological innovation to constituting the ultimate end of patent law. (See end of Section 2.) The international patent regulation that the Siemens brothers promote for meeting this end is just one more technical component of a global machine that is ideally running without human interference. The "cosmopolitan nature" of technology turns law into a cosmopolitan technology.

This way of reasoning constitutes another is-ought-fallacy, which characterizes many reflections on the relationship between law and technology up to the present day.[89] Although the motivational nature of technology is prescriptive, the statement 'technology has a cosmopolitan nature' is exactly not describing the motivational structure of technology, but is a descriptive statement, for example, regarding the factual global spread of technologies. This statement is then transformed into the normative demand that law, likewise, *ought to be* cosmopolitan.

The problem is: by their very character, descriptive statements are either true or false. They are not negotiable. This property makes them rhetorically convincing and seemingly incontestable. However, it is ultimately not possible to deduce a normative claim, which is, by definition, open to negotiation and depending on values, from a descriptive claim, which is, by definition, either true or false and not depending on values. Simply speaking: in the process of such rhetorical moves, apples (descriptive claims) are unnoticeably exchanged for oranges (normative claims). To deduce a necessary, normative character of law from a descriptive statement in this way is, therefore, clearly a fallacy.

Although such modes of arguing can be easily dismissed for these reasons, they are highly interesting from a point of view of intellectual history. The replacement of all normative claims and the abandonment of a political

89 De Hert, Paul, and Thumfart, Johannes. "The Microsoft Ireland Case and the Cyberspace Sovereignty Trilemma. Post-Territorial Technologies and Companies Question Territorial State Sovereignty and Regulatory State Monopolies," *Brussels Privacy Hub Working Papers* 4, no. 11 (July 2018), 17. https://researchportal.vub.be/files/47413975/pdh18_jt_THE_MICROSOFT_IRELAND_CASE_BPH_Working_Paper_VOL4_N11.pdf.

debate by means of technological categories is typical of what Carl Schmitt calls 'neutralization.'

Schmitt explains the logic of such neutralizations in one of the rare occasions where he develops a secular philosophy of history:

> In a theological age, everything runs smoothly if theological questions are in order (…). The same is true of other ages. In a humanitarian-moral age, it is only necessary to inculcate morals, whereby all problems become problems of education. In an economic age, one needs only to solve adequately the problem of the production and distribution of goods in order to make superfluous all moral and social questions. Mere technical thinking also solves the economic problem with new technical developments. All questions, including the economic, recede before the task of technical progress (…). The succession of stages-from the theological, over the metaphysical and the moral to the economic-simultaneously signifies a series of progressive neutralizations of domains whose centers have shifted.[90]

According to Schmitt, such 'neutralizations' are, at the same time, 'depoliticizations,' i.e. a political field of conflict is abandoned in order to find neutral common ground, the best example being the abandonment of the field of religion with the invention of secular sovereignty, its subsequent abandonment in the age of nationalism in favor of the economic, and finally, the abandonment of economic categories in favor of technology, of which the Siemens brothers can be considered a forerunner.

In this sense, history, to Schmitt, is characterized by successive neutralization, where fields of agonistic political conflict are abandoned for increasingly abstract concepts in order to find consensus and security. However, since, to Schmitt, all political reality remains, in its essence, agonistic and based on decisions, constructed values and the resulting confrontations, the remedy of neutralization is essentially illusionary and usually does not last for long. In a process of historical teleology, an increasingly higher degree of neutralization is required.

Although a critique of the authoritarian need for hierarchies would be alien to Schmitt's conservatism, it is helpful to think of this historical process of subsequent levels of neutralization in terms of an, ultimately tragic and

90 Schmitt, Carl. "The Age of Neutralizations and Depoliticizations" in *The Concept of the Political: Expanded Edition*, ed. George Schwab (Chicago, University of Chicago Press, 2007), 80–96, 86.

futile desire to transfer responsibility from individual humans to ever higher institutions. However, once the process of subsequent neutralizations has reached the level of technology for technology's sake, this logic comes to an end. Schmitt writes:

> But the neutrality of technology is something other than the neutrality of all former domains. Technology is always only an instrument and weapon; precisely because it serves all, it is not neutral ... Every type of culture, every people and religion, every war and peace can use technology as a weapon ... Consequently, no conclusions which usually can be drawn from the central domains of spiritual life can be derived from pure technology as nothing but technology.[91]

Let us interpret this again from a contemporary perspective: With the turn towards the normative predominance of technology, the, according to Freud, latently auto-aggressive human drive of the super-ego to construct hierarchical instances,[92] finds its most radical, auto-destructive expression. Technology as an instrument that becomes completely detached from the human purposes and values that might guide it is transforming into a total weapon that is directed against human life in general and *against all values* that characterized the human mode of life up to the present day.

Schmitt's reasoning, he is, after all, a legal theorist and not a philosopher of technology, stops at this tragic deadlock of humanity entering the technological age as the last plane of neutralization that leads human society to total nihilism and, possibly, auto-destruction. Since Schmitt's answers regarding this question remain vague, it is worth to further investigate why technology might have this paralyzing effect on normative reasoning.

First of all, one can detect the echo of a classical conservative argument against technology here, as also brought forward by Leo Strauss: Since technology has, like science, cosmopolitan tendencies, it

> necessarily weakens the power of the national "philosophies" and therewith the attachment of the citizens to the particular way of life, or the manners, of their community.[93]

---

91 Ibid. 91.

92 Freud, Sigmund. *Civilization and Its Discontents*, trans. James Strachey (New York: W.W. Norton, 1961), 70.

93 Strauss, Leo. *Natural Right and History* (Chicago: University of Chicago Press 1965), 257.

In other words: Although it would be an is-ought fallacy to take this as a final word, technology's intercultural character threatens traditional, culturally particular normative systems simply by showing the limits of particular traditional ways of life. Of courses, this leaves the means of rational debates to construct new modes of normativity, such as discussed in the following Section 4. However, it is true that these necessary debates are often not taking place and the normativity of technological innovation prevails. Why is that?

According to the philosopher Bernard Stiegler, human beings reach a deadlock when they reflect on technology because they wrongly assume that they reflect on something different from themselves, on technological objects to which they can relate as a subject. However, according to Stiegler, the difference between human beings and technology is not given in this drastic form, since both are essentially depending on each other. Already the process of anthropogenesis is characterized by a co-evolution of technology and humans, inasmuch as grains, firestones and human bodies form an irreducible assemblage of which the outcome would be very different if one of these elements would have different properties or be missing completely. Rather than humans creating technology, 'technical evolution results from a coupling of the human and matter, a (...) "zootechnological" determinism.'[94]

With this non-anthropocentric anthropology in mind, there is no such thing as a neutral decision on technological matters. When human beings and technology are part of the same zootechnical assemblage, every technical decision concerns the human essence. However, this technological non-human aspect of anthropology is difficult to include in traditional reasoning, because it challenges the boundaries between the biological and the technological and, therefore, transcends basic ideas of anthropocentric subjecthood:

> The problem arising here is that the evolution of this essentially technical being that the human is exceeds the biological, although this dimension is an essential part of the technical phenomenon itself, something like its enigma.[95]

Especially in regard to technological innovation, the notion of closed subjectivity and the concomitant idea of individual property seems often misleading. Already in our example of the Vienna Patent Congress, several contributors

94 Stiegler, Bernard. *Technics and Time 1: The Fault of Epimetheus* (Stanford: Stanford University Press, 1998) 46.

95 Ibid. 50.

criticize a strong notion of patent law, because multiple discoveries are rather the rule than the exception.[96]

Accordingly, Lemley writes:

> Surveys of hundreds of significant new technologies show that almost all of them are invented simultaneously or nearly simultaneously by two or more teams working independently of each other. Invention appears in significant part to be a social, not an individual, phenomenon. Inventors build on the work of those who came before, and new ideas are often either "in the air" or result from changes in market demand or the availability of new or cheaper starting materials. And in the few circumstances where that is not true – where inventions truly are "singletons" – it is often because of an accident or error in the experiment rather than a conscious effort to invent.[97]

Likewise, to Stiegler, "the logic of invention is not that of the inventor."[98] Nevertheless, inventions cannot be reduced to mere chance. Their relatively frequent simultaneity is the best argument against the idea of a contingency of inventions. According to Stiegler,

> the inventive operation cannot be said to be produced by chance, for an essential part of innovation is accomplished through transfer, whereby the functioning of a structure in a technical apparatus is analogically transposed into another domain.[99]

Following Stiegler, this logic of transposition and recombination led historically, to 'the hypothesis of a combinatory genius' inherent to technology.[100] Effectively, the Siemens brothers, too, argued in favor of the abandonment of human normative claims in favor of the blind trust in the god-like combinatory genius of technology.

Particularly regarding their normative effect, one must take the theological dimension of such ideas very seriously. Their significance becomes clear going back to Schmitt's idea of neutralization. In the context of neutralization through secular sovereignty, e.g. at Hobbes, the state became the new god. In the context of the neutralization through economy, e.g. at the Neoliberals,

96 Pieper, *Der Erfinderschutz und die Reform der Patentgesetze*, 67, 83.
97 Lemley, Mark A. "The Myth of the Sole Inventor" (2012) 110, 5 *Mich. L. Rev.* 709, 711.
98 Stiegler, Bernard. *Technics and Time 1*, 36.
99 Ibid. 34.
100 Ibid. 35.

the invisible hand of the world system acquired theological features.[101] Finally, at our age of neutralization through technology, of which the Siemens brothers are only a premature harbinger, technological progress acquired religious qualities. Today, this is, for example, expressed in the idea of the singularity,[102] in the quasi-theological beliefs of transhumanists[103] or in the idea that human activity should directly follow the normative prescriptions of technology and do 'what technology wants.'[104]

Of course, these claims are deeply unreasonable in their hidden longing for authoritarian rule and contain a sense of childlike dependency on fantasies. The individually varying,[105] yet generally human tendency towards anthropomorphic projection tends to ascribe intentionality to any kind of large, also inanimated system. Contrary to a common misconception, the nihilist technological creed is no result of too much efficiency, rationality etc.,[106] but rather, it is an example par excellence of what Kant has called the 'self-incurred immaturity' of humans, an immaturity which also Freud tried to cure. Such technology-centered ideas and ideologies should not and, ultimately, cannot provide guidance for political action and just legislation. Although this is actually a widespread, foremost unspoken belief, it is clearly foolish to blindly trust in the 'combinatory genius' of technology to cure the grave problems of the post-human Anthropocene. Stiegler's philosophy of zootechnical coevolution shows us that technology is nothing we can relate to as an external object, but that it is closely interlinked to our own intentions and, therefore, inherently depending on guidance through rational norms considering human needs and interests *above everything else*.

5 Towards Global Patent Justice

Since international treaties such as the Paris Convention and the following IP regime are ultimately human conventions, their procedural origin constitutes an adequate starting point of normative reflections. To Rawls's *The Law of*

---

101 Slobodian, *Globalists*, 87, 269.

102 Kurzweil, Ray. *The Singularity is near* (New York: Penguin, 2006).

103 Babich, Babette. "Nietzsche's Posthuman Imperative: On the Human, All too Human Dream of Transhumanism," in: Tuncel, Yunus, ed. Nietzsche and Transhumanism: Precursor or Enemy? (Cambridge: Cambridge Scholars, 2017), pp. 101–113.

104 Kelly, Kevin. *What Technology Wants* (New York: Viking, 2010).

105 Waytz, Adam; Cacioppo, John, and Epley, Nicholas. "Who Sees Human?: The Stability and Importance of Individual Differences in Anthropomorphism," *Perspectives on Psychological Science* 5, no. 3 (May 2010): 219–32, https://doi.org/10.1177/1745691610369336.

106 Gertz, Nolen. *Nihilism and Technology* (Lanham: Rowman & Littlefield International, 2018).

Peoples, which includes various ways of international cooperation, the legitimacy of such agreements as the Paris Convention is based on the assumption that representatives of peoples can represent the reasonable interests of peoples in a reasonable debate free from coercion.[107] In this procedure, domestic public reason is projected to the international level. Even if the participating peoples are neither democratic nor liberal, this kind of rational international negotiation should be based on domestic 'decent consultation hierarchy.'[108]

To Rawls's exclusively normative theory, this is only relevant as an ideal. However, one might argue that this connection between international and national public reasoning has a descriptive aspect. It describes the condition of possibility of international treaties. This means: although it might not be realized everywhere to the same degree, it would be nonsense to speak of international treaties without the assumption that representatives of peoples can somehow communicate rational choices reflecting the domestic reasoning of these peoples, which does not necessarily have to be democratic. Without this basic assumption, international treaties, which highly depend on mechanisms of representation, are merely pieces of paper.

Starting from this basic and rather uncontroversial assumption, it is evident that patent law is especially close to the interest of rational peoples and their representatives, because, as Rawls writes, 'ingenuity and invention' are examples of human rational capacities par excellence.[109] Patents, therefore, put a relatively strong limitation on individual liberties, regarding the liberty to copy and the liberty of a second, independent inventor to repeat an invention unknowingly.[110] Accordingly, other aspects of IP law have been demonstrated to be speech restrictions.[111] Furthermore, regarding nations, patents can be obstacles to improving their economic or public health situation.[112] As the historic case study in Sections 2 and 3 shows, classical liberal nations such as the Netherlands and Switzerland ranked among the last European countries to adopt patent law, because it can be understood as a considerable infringement of individual liberties. Ironically, today, Switzerland, due to its large

107 Rawls, John. *The Law of Peoples* (Cambridge: Harvard University Press, 2003) 56.

108 Ibid. 71f.

109 Rawls, John. *A Theory of Justice* (Cambridge, Harvard University Press, 1999) 374, 379.

110 Dumitru, Speranta. "Are Rawlsians Entitled to Monopoly Rights?" in Gosseries, Axel et al. eds. *Intellectual Property and Theories of Justice*, (New York: Palgrave Macmillan, 2008), 61, 69.

111 Volokh, Eugene. "Freedom of Speech and Intellectual Property: Some Thoughts after Eldred, Liquormart, and Bartnicki," *Houston Law Review*, 40:3 (2003), 698.

112 Siew-Kuan Ng, Elizabeth. "Global health and development: patents and public interest".

pharmaceutical industry, has turned into one of the prime promoters of patent law internationalization.

Additional arguments regarding the incompatibility of IP law and Rawls's philosophy have been made on grounds of a conflict between IP rights and the second principle of justice.[113] Particularly on the nation-state level, that is not very convincing, since, for example, a limited patent right might provide incentives for inventors to generate ideas that benefit the least privileged in a country and, obviously, the opportunities to develop the talent to make such an invention are equally distributed throughout a society assumed that it provides access to basic education.

However, this assessment in regard to the nation-state level is not necessarily accurate on the international level, where the least privileged developing nations most certainly do not profit from patent rights primarily held in developed nations and, due to the cumulative nature of technological progress and brain drain, also do not have equal opportunities to develop a comparable output of patents. I will come to these problems of genuinely global justice later, which are not discussed by Rawls, since, for reasons that will be explained during the next paragraphs, he does not apply the second principle of justice to the international sphere and, instead, focusses on the nation-state.

In any case, it can be summarized that, although being one of the most widely adopted international legal standards, one can by no means assume that the ratification of the Paris Convention and the following international agreements on IP law represent uncontroversial choices from the perspective of national welfare. Assumed that representatives of technologically underdeveloped peoples come to the conclusion that an international patent regime is not particularly useful below a certain threshold of technological development (such as also the history of European industrialization suggests), it would rather be reasonable for them to refrain from such a regime.

Although Rawls praises the virtues of international free trade at some occasions in his *The Law of Peoples*,[114] his liberal theory does not represent an account of economic liberalism regarding international relations. Rather, it clearly allows for national economic disentanglement. When Rawls positions himself as an opponent of the primacy of sovereignty, his rejection relates to the right to go to war and the right to treat citizens without respecting human

113 Murphy, Darryl J. "Are Intellectual Property Rights Compatible with Rawlsian Principles of Justice?," *Ethics and Information Technology* 14, no. 2 (June 2012): 109–21, https://doi.org/10.1007/s10676-012-9288-8.

114 E.g. Rawls, *The Law of Peoples*, 46.

rights.[115] Regarding economic issues, Rawls explicitly emphasizes the free choices of particular peoples.

First of all, his understanding of distributive justice relies on the nation-state and is, therefore, built on the assumption that 'a society (…) is closed: it is self-contained and has no relations to other societies.'[116] Another one of many passages where he repeats this claim: '(…) The society in question is closed, (…) taken as a self-sufficient scheme of cooperation (…).'[117]

Accordingly, when it comes to economic problems, Rawls argues that 'the crucial element in how a country fares is its political culture – its members' political and civic virtues – and not the level of its resources (…).'[118] Of course, this can be read as an evidence of Rawls's typically Kantian blindness to the realities of global economic inequality. However, he also clearly formulates a demand to find national political solutions for economic problems. Some even understand Rawls's theory therefore as encouraging economic nationalism,[119] which might be extended to the patent realm.

Furthermore, Rawls's *The Law of Peoples* explicitly *does not* conceive of an international society of peoples comparable to his domestic account, since he explicitly does not conceive of higher international sovereignty above the national level.[120] Correspondingly, he stresses an even greater need to abstain from formulating a comprehensive doctrine on the international level than on the national level, including a utilitarian doctrine, which is especially relevant to the problem of a global patent regime:

> If a reasonable pluralism of comprehensive doctrines is a basic feature of a constitutional democracy with its free institutions, we may assume that there is *an even greater diversity* in the comprehensive doctrines affirmed among the members of the Society of Peoples with its many different cultures and traditions. Hence *a classical, or average, utilitarian principle would not be accepted by peoples*, since no people organized by its government is prepared to count, as a first principle, the benefits for another

115 Ibid. 25f.

116 Rawls, John. *Political Liberalism* (Cambridge UP 1996) 67f.

117 Ibid. 301.

118 Rawls, *The Law of Peoples*, 117.

119 Schrepfer, Matthew. "A Rawlsian Case for Economic Nationalism: Globalisation and Distributional Autonomy in the Law of Peoples," *Journal of Applied Philosophy* 36, no. 1 (February 2019): 155–63, https://doi.org/10.1111/japp.12296.

120 Rawls, *The Law of Peoples*, 36; See also:
Doyle, Michael W. "One World, Many Peoples: International Justice in John Rawls's The Law of Peoples," *Perspectives on Politics* 4, no. 01 (March 2006), https://doi.org/10.1017/S1537592706060117.

> people as outweighing the hardships imposed on itself. Well-ordered peoples insist on an equality among themselves as peoples, and this insistence rules out any form of the principle of utility.[121]

One can, therefore, assume that Rawls's theory does not endorse the subordination of national welfare to the, as the previous section has shown, erratic pseudo-utilitarian ideal of promoting technological innovation. Rather, from a Rawlsian point of view, peoples could choose to abandon the patent system altogether, to nationalize it or to introduce alternate reward systems that are more suitable to promote their particular national welfare.

Whilst property rights, in general, are basic rights to Rawls, from a Kantian perspective, property rights are not absolute, but based on some form of contractualist agreement within a given nation-state (See Section 2). Although I agree that Rawls's particular conception of distributive justice does not necessarily follow from this Kantian contractualist conception of private property,[122] it is certainly the case that from a Kantian and a Rawlsian point of view alike, it would be non-sensical to assume that a nation-state would passively receive a normative framework from outside, since, as Kant wrote regarding the most drastic case of interference, 'such interference by foreign powers would infringe on the rights of an independent people struggling with its internal disease.'[123]

Regarding its refusal to formulate a global comprehensive doctrine, Rawls's account is compatible with a broader notion of what one could call *epistemic justice* regarding patent issues. The literature stresses many examples of how traditional knowledge cannot be assessed from the perspective of an incentive structure based on individual inventors competing in a market[124] which follows from the universalization of private property rights in international IP regimes.[125] With their traditional knowledge database, India, China and Peru are showing how developing nations could find unique paths to

121 Rawls, *The Law of Peoples*, 40.

122 Nance, Michael, and Platz, Jeppe von. "From Justice to Fairness: Does Kant's Doctrine of Right Imply a Theory of Distributive Justice?" in Moran, Kate A., ed. *Kant on Freedom and Spontaneity*, 1st ed. (Cambridge University Press, 2018), 250–68, https://doi.org/10.1017/9781316421888.014.

123 Kant, Immanuel. *Perpetual peace: a philosophical essay*, trans. Mary Campbell Smith (London: George Allen & Unwin, 2013), 113.

124 Karanja, Wanjiku. "The Legitimacy of Indigenous Intellectual Property Rights' claims," 165; Yu, Peter K. "Cultural Relics, Intellectual Property, and Intangible Heritage" (2008) 81:2 *Temp L Rev* 433.

125 Morris, Sean P. "The Contemporary Ideological Legitimacy of Global Intellectual Property Rights" (2019) 1 *Intellectual Property Quarterly* 44, 64.

protecting their traditional knowledge from this kind of post-colonial epistemic injustice.[126]

Likewise, the focus on national decisions regarding patent rights seems highly relevant regarding the Max Planck Institute's call for "regulatory sovereignty," which encourages nations to make use of the full scope of their liberties within the TRIPS agreement which are usually not exhaustively taken advantage of.[127] Initiatives such as the Doha Declaration have shown that developing countries can defend their interests when they are using their pooled national sovereignties.

However, one might argue that the Rawlsian focus on the capacities of individual peoples and their voluntary cooperation remains highly hypothetical since it is implicitly based on economic autarky[128] and on the assumption that states can decide free from external economic coercion. Of course, this is not necessarily the case.

Particularly the contemporary global IP regime, the TRIPS agreement, which is built on the Paris Convention, 'became a symbol of the vulnerability of developing countries to coercive pressures from the most powerful developed countries.'[129] In many cases, economic pressure, e.g. exerted by bilateral trade agreements, has been decisive for pushing developing nations towards standards that even go beyond the TRIPS agreement.[130] In light of these harsh realities, the idea that individual developing nations can decide independently may be utopian.

Another reason for abandoning the Rawlsian focus on the choices of individual peoples could be that, also besides its legal implications, of which a sovereign nation-state could theoretically opt-out, patents can have unwanted non-legal effects on other peoples. Take for example an economically significant nation allowing ethically questionable patents on biomaterial, which may affect other peoples by providing incentives to undertake possibly unethical research and spread the results from that research. For every reasonable people, it would be preferable to reach a global consensus regarding the patenting

---

126 Brahy, Nicolas. "The Contribution of Databases and Customary Law to the Protection of Traditional Knowledge," *International Social Science Journal* 58, no. 188 (June 2006): 259–82, https://doi.org/10.1111/j.1468-2451.2006.00618.x.

127 Lamping "Declaration on Patent Protection – Regulatory Sovereignty under TRIPS."

128 Rawls, *Political Liberalism*, 67f.

129 Deere, Carolyn. *The Implementation Game. The TRIPS Agreement and the Global Politics of Intellectual Property Reform in Developing Countries* (Oxford: Oxford University Press, 2009) 2, 4.

130 Ibid. 150f.

of biomaterial than to have peoples deciding autonomously on this controversial issue and possibly engaging in a race to the regulatory bottom.

Therefore, rather than leaving patent justice to individual peoples, the question of patent law internationalization must be understood in direct analogy to Rawls's considerably "thicker" domestic account of justice, which, for example, does not allow for an exit option[131] analogous to the option of turning to self-sufficient economic nationalism. Justifying an adaptation of Rawls's domestic principles to the global level, Pogge writes:

> In the modern world there are no self-contained national societies, a closed back-ground system exists only at the global level.[132]

Having fully considered Rawls's caveats regarding the applicability of his theory to the global level, one could assume a hypothetical original position under the veil of ignorance based on the globalization of these Rawlsian ideas. Considering limited essay space, I will not deeply engage with the debate of whether the parties in this global original position should be individuals, societies, peoples or nation-states, which is, from my perspective, sufficiently solved in Rawls's conception of 'peoples'. Pogge's radically cosmopolitan demand to conceive of the participants of this global original position exclusively as persons[133] makes sense from a point of view of moral philosophy. After all, nation-states, particularly unjust ones, are not necessarily object of moral duties. However, such a move (that seems to be partly corrected in Pogge's later position of 'intermediate cosmopolitanism'[134]) is unnecessary because Rawls's definition of 'peoples' already includes moral qualities beyond mere state sovereignty[135] and, in the introduction of this Section, I also stressed that the Rawlsian 'decent consultation hierarchy' is a necessary condition to speak of nations as subjects of international law and treaties at all. Furthermore, Pogge's initial move towards orthodox liberal cosmopolitanism seems to underestimate the realist and, even more importantly, ontological dimension of Kant's contractualism, which is, for example, reflected in Rawls's reference to Hegel's organic and anti-liberal conception of nationhood when

131 Rawls, *Political Liberalism*, 301: "Since I suppose the society in question is closed, we are to imagine that there is no entry or exit except by birth and death (…)."

132 Pogge, Thomas. *Realizing Rawls*, (Ithaca: Cornell University Press, 1989), p. 7.

133 Ibid. 258.

134 Pogge, Thomas. "Cosmopolitanism: A Defence," *Critical Review of International Social and Political Philosophy* 5, no. 3 (October 2002): 86–91.

135 Rawls, *The Law of Peoples*, 25f.

it comes to the respect for non-democratic peoples,[136] but also in Kant's statement (cited above) that interference with national self-determination is illegitimate because peoples should take care of their own 'internal disease' as if they formed an indivisible, organic whole. Particularly regarding the problem at hand, which concerns international contracts between participants that must be supposed to have a 'decent consultation hierarchy', going back to individuals would mean to throw the baby out with the bathwater and, in last instance, to commit a form of cosmopolitan depoliticization, which to criticize is one of the main aims of this essay.

For these reasons, I will only come back to the contentious issue of global representation in the last paragraph of this Section, where I briefly introduce the idea of the concrete, political institution of a world parliament that is in my opinion preferable to lofty cosmopolitan claims that rather counteract than strengthen grown political and societal structures.[137] For now, I assume that the participants in a global original position are representatives of peoples and that the representatives of the peoples negotiating international patent regulations would not know whether they represent a people that includes many patent holders or a people that includes no patent holders at all.

From this starting point, one would have to test the second principle of justice regarding equality of opportunity, which has been initially discussed. Is there equality of opportunity? Can every nation become a patent superpower? In principle, yes. However, it is obvious that technological progress is full of prerequisites. Developed nations have a head start regarding patents, which is, to a degree, owed to colonialist and imperialist practices in the past, of which the Paris Convention is a part. Furthermore, technological progress tends to be accumulative, so inequalities increase over time. In addition to that, the brain drain from developing to developed countries minimizes the chances of developing countries becoming innovation hubs in their own right.

In an extension of Rawls, one could argue that, in the light of such historical injustices, a neutral position would not be enough.[138] Rather, one would

136 Rawls, *The Law of Peoples*, 73, FN 13.

137 See also Section 2 and my earlier discussion of the cosmopolitical tradition in contrast to the tradition of international law: Thumfart, Johannes. "Francisco de Vitorias Philosophie: globalpolitisch, nicht kosmopolitisch," in Bunge, Kirstin; Spindler, Anselm, and Wagner, Andreas, eds. *Die Normativität des Rechts bei Francisco de Vitoria*, Politische Philosophie und Rechtstheorie des Mittelalters und der Neuzeit 2 (Stuttgart: Frommann-Holzboog, 2011), 229–54.

138 Waligore, Timothy. "Rawls, Self-Respect, and Assurance: How Past Injustice Changes What Publicly Counts as Justice," *Politics, Philosophy & Economics* 15, no. 1 (February 2016): 42–66, https://doi.org/10.1177/1470594X15599100.

have to find a position based on equity, a way to compensate peoples that can make a credible claim for having suffered from this kind of injustices, possibly by allowing selective patent waivers up to the point where these nations can, at least hypothetically, become themselves patent powers, which would be a Rawlsian 'cutoff point.'[139] For example, such patent waivers could convince companies and gifted individuals to relocate to developing countries. (The latter was the successful strategy of Swiss anti-patent politics in the 19th century,[140] as briefly discussed in Section 3.)

A similar problem would arise regarding the second principle of justice in regard to inequalities of outcome, which has been initially discussed. Does the inequality introduced by patent regimes benefit the least-advantaged members of the global society? Again, in theory, patents might produce such benefits, due to the re-investment of revenues from patents in research and development, which might produce a trickle-down effect.

However, it is one of the worst effects of the market-based incentives of the patent system that it leads to only a very small part of R&D resources being allocated to the most urgent health problems of the global poor.[141] Although working on these issues could have a great impact on global health, it is usually not very profitable. In an attempt to correct this market failure, Pogge proposed and co-founded the Health Impact Fund.[142] It disentangles incentive-building from market forces and connects it to public resources, to be allocated according to actual health gains achieved through specific pharmaceutical innovations.

A similar fund could be imagined regarding the patenting of lifeforms. Such a fund could be constructed as belonging to all individual humans. It could generate revenues for individual citizens when registered patents related to lifeforms are used by a company, with a higher share for the inventors, proportionate to the invention's merits for humanity. It is intuitively clear that planetary biodiversity should be regarded as a 'common heritage of mankind' and not within the framework of private patent rights.[143] However, without providing incentives to preserve this common wealth, the tragedy of the global

139 Rawls, *The Law of Peoples*, 119.

140 Ricketson, *The Paris Convention and the Protection of Industrial Property*, 95.

141 Pogge, Thomas et al., eds. *Incentives for Global Public Health: Patent Law and Access to Essential Medicines* (Cambridge: Cambridge University Press, 2010) 1, 4.

142 Pogge, "The Health Impact Fund: Enhancing Justice and Efficiency in Global Health."

143 International Undertaking on Plant Genetic Resources, Report of the Conference of the United Nations Food and Agriculture Organization (FAO), 22d Sess., U.N. Doc. C/83/REP (1983).

commons of biodiversity seems to be hardly stoppable.[144] A global and collective, yet property rights-based fund could constitute a middle ground between the too permissive notion of global commons and the too closed notion of an international patent system solely based on private rights.

However, regarding all such global solutions that rely on political organization beyond the nation-state, there is a serious caveat regarding their democratic legitimacy. As long as international cooperation remains almost exclusively inter-governmental, the criteria of a separation of powers on an international level and of adequate representation that initiated this Section are hardly realized to an ideal extent. When global justice goes beyond the nation-state and its legitimacy, it should be based on a world parliament along the lines of the United Nations Parliamentary Assembly.[145] Such an institution could provide democratic checks and balances to governmental actors and turn global issues into the subject of genuine political debates, challenging the normative power of technological innovation and the concomitant universalization of private rights.

6 Discussion and Outlook

This contribution traces back the Paris Convention of 1883 to an important part of its ideo-historical background, the Vienna Patent Congress of 1873, which is crucial to the path-dependency of the current global IP regime. Hereby, it becomes clear that the 19th century, a period of far-reaching social and political transformation characterized by the second industrial revolution and the beginning of globalization, is very close to our contemporary historical period that faces similarly profound transformations due to the fourth industrial revolution and accelerated globalization. Both epochs are characterized by the idea that technological innovation can constitute a normative aim in itself beyond the deadlocks of a heavily polarized political landscape.

A close reading of the debates at the Vienna Patent Congress of 1873 shows that the issue of patent law internationalization has been originally approached in a remarkably open and heated political debate. Whilst the mostly Anglo-Saxon advocates of strong inventor's rights have underlined

144 Margulies, Rebecca L. "Protecting Biodiversity: Recognizing International Intellectual Property Rights in Plant Genetic Resources Property Rights in Plant Genetic Resources" *Michigan Journal of International Law*, (1993) 14, 2, 322.

145 Bummel, Andreas, and Leinen, Jo. *A World Parliament: Governance and Democracy in the 21st Century* (Berlin: Democracy Without Borders, 2018).

their claims with anti-Communist rhetoric, others have proposed entirely different incentive structures for innovation, based on the public sector attributing rewards according to the utility of an idea. In general, the idea to subordinate patent rights to national economic interests was popular among the German-speaking participants. Some liberal free traders also have opposed patent rights altogether, because they regarded them as an antiquated obstruction of commerce by means of artificial, politically enforced monopolies which they understood as belonging to the structures of the old order of Feudalism. In short: the debate at the Vienna Patent Congress was characterized by the heated political conflicts typical of the turbulent 19th century, involving Communism, Liberalism, the critique of Feudalism and conflicting European political and legal traditions.

The Siemens brothers, being among the leading international telegraphy entrepreneurs of their time and clearly the dominating actors in this debate, intervened in this discussion and achieved consensus by elevating it to another level. This level is not political, but rather technical in nature. Their justification of patent law internationalization, which characterizes the results of the Vienna Patent Congress, is based on the idea that patent law is not a political issue, but rather should be a means to enable global technological progress. By this move from anthropocentric to technocentric modes of legitimization, they resolved the conflicted political discussion about patent law internalization, changed the outcome of the Vienna Patent Congress according to their interest and laid the groundwork for further developments that culminated in the Paris Convention of 1883. This is laid out in Sections 1 and 2.

Starting from this historical case study, Section 3 investigates the normative impact of technological innovation in general terms, discussing developments in international law inasmuch as they constitute reactions to technological developments. A special emphasis is being put on the normative impact of industry standards and the prescriptive nature of engineering. In this broad theoretical context, the Siemens brothers' arguments are interpreted as a neutralization and depoliticization in the Schmittian sense, i.e. the contested field of opposing political, anthropocentric ideas is abandoned in favor of a solution that seemingly provides a techno-centric, neutral perspective. This move is typical of debates about patents and technological innovation and still finds its echo today. According to Schmitt, however, such political neutrality is an illusion and particularly problematic regarding technology, since it leads to the dangerous, nihilist use of technology without normative ends.

Employing Bernard Stiegler's philosophy of technology, it is argued that the reason for the difficulties with having realistic debates about technological innovation in normative terms is embedded in the structure of anthropogenesis, since anthropogenesis cannot be separated from the evolution of technology. Technological innovation can therefore never be understood as a neutral process separated from human agency, but rather, it must be understood within a zoo-technical continuum. Because the fates of humans and technology are intrinsically combined, there is no such thing as a neutral technological ground independent from human concerns. Rather, this neutrality is an irrational illusion and in its religious and authoritarian connotations a perfect example of what Kant has called the "self-incurred immaturity" of humans.

As a reaction to these shortcomings of an exclusive focus on technological innovation as a normative aim, Section 4 proposes a normative discussion of the matter. In order to conceive of the outlines of normative reasoning regarding global patent justice, it uses Rawls's *The Law of Peoples*. First of all, patent law internationalization is a non-trivial problem from a, broadly speaking, Kantian point of view, since it restricts, for example, the freedom to copy or to make a discovery for the second time, which is closely related to human rational capacities and liberal freedoms. It is found that, contrary to a widespread belief, Rawls's theory encourages protectionist economic policies oriented towards national economic welfare and allows even for forms of economic nationalism. Along these lines, it is argued that peoples act reasonably to opt-out, in part or entirely, from patent regimes that do not promote their interests. Examples of the successful use of such regulatory sovereignty even within the existing TRIPS framework are the Doha Declaration and peoples' special treatment of their traditional knowledge by means of traditional knowledge databases. The latter can be regarded as an approach to establish epistemic justice beyond the paradigm of individual inventors competing in a global market, which was internationalized with the Paris Convention of 1883 and later agreements.

However, the reliance on the rational use of national sovereignty is probably not enough to guarantee global patent justice, since the problem of patenting is closely related to global economic and technological entanglement and economic coercion is not uncommon regarding trade treaties. Engaging critically with Pogge, Rawls's originally exclusively domestic theory of justice is applied to the global realm, sketching possible compensation for injustices due to colonialism and seeking for solutions to prevent the patent system from constituting an obstacle to the improvement of public health and national welfare in developing countries. Furthermore, the idea of a global fund for the patenting of lifeforms is laid out.

The ideas discussed in this chapter open up a broad horizon for future research. Regarding intellectual history, the extent to which different philosophical positions influenced the path-dependency of the development of an international patent order should be further investigated. Although it has all the qualities of an exemplary case, the Vienna Patent Congress of 1873 is just one of many events in which the course of the norm development process of the international IP regime has been set. Another specific issue to research further is the Kantian, contractualist understanding of property rights which plays a fundamental role in the debate at the Vienna Patent Congress. So far, Kant is under-discussed in regard to patent law. Regarding the normative aim of this chapter, which is equally based on Kantian ideas, the theoretical construction of global patent justice still includes the controversial issue of whether individuals, societies, nation-states or peoples should be assumed to constitute the parties in a global original position. Whilst I have made a strong case for a focus on peoples and against cosmopolitan approaches, this discussion could be extended. Also, the exact implications of global patent justice in relation to concrete cases are still to be defined. Researchers of different disciplines will have to provide detailed arguments on a case-by-case basis.

Bibliography

Adams, C.A. "Industrial Standardization," *The Annals of the American Academy of Political and Social Science*, (1919) 82:1 289–299.

Andrade, Tonio. *The Gunpowder Age: China, Military Innovation, and the Rise of the West in World History*. Princeton Oxford: Princeton University Press, 2016.

Babich, Babette. "Nietzsche's Posthuman Imperative: On the Human, All too Human Dream of Transhumanism," in: Yunus Tuncel ed., *Nietzsche and Transhumanism: Precursor or Enemy?* Cambridge: Cambridge Scholars, 2017, pp. 101–113.

Biagioli, Mario, and Buning, Marius. "'Technologies of the Law/Law as a Technology.'" *History of Science* 57, no. 1 (March 2019): 3–17. https://doi.org/10.1177/0073275318816163.

Brahy, Nicolas. "The Contribution of Databases and Customary Law to the Protection of Traditional Knowledge." *International Social Science Journal* 58, no. 188 (June 2006): 259–82. https://doi.org/10.1111/j.1468-2451.2006.00618.x.

Buchanan, Brenda J., ed. *Gunpowder, Explosives and the State: A Technological History*. Aldershot, England ; Burlington, VT: Ashgate, 2006.

Kelly, Kevin. *What Technology Wants*. London: Penguin, 2011.

Kurzweil, Ray. *The Singularity Is near: When Humans Transcend Biology*. New York: Viking, 2005.

Leinen, Jo and Bummel, Andreas. *A World Parliament: Governance and Democracy in the 21st Century*. Translated by Ray Cunningham. Berlin: Democracy Without Borders, 2018.

Cogan, Jacob Katz. "A History of International Law in the Vernacular." *Journal of the History of International Law / Revue d'histoire Du Droit International* 22, no. 2–3 (2020): 205–17. https://doi.org/10.1163/15718050-12340149.

Deere, Carolyn. *The Implementation Game: The TRIPS Agreement and the Global Politics of Intellectual Property Reform in Developing Countries*. Oxford: New York: Oxford University Press, 2009.

Dhavan, Rajeev, Harris, Lindsay and Jain, Gopal. "Conquest by Patent: The Paris Convention Revisited." *Journal of the Indian Law Institute* 32, no. 2 (1990): 131–78.

Doyle, Michael W. "One World, Many Peoples: International Justice in John Rawls's The Law of Peoples." *Perspectives on Politics* 4, no. 01 (March 2006). https://doi.org/10.1017/S1537592706060117.

Dumitru, Speranta. "Are Rawlsians Entitled to Monopoly Rights?" in *Intellectual Property and Theories of Justice*, ed. Axel Gosseries, et al. New York, Palgrave Macmillan 2008.

Fischer, Ludwig. *Werner Siemens und der Schutz der Erfindungen*. Berlin: Springer, 1922.

Freud, Sigmund. *Civilization and Its Discontents*. Translated by James Strachey. New York: W.W. Norton, 1961.

Galvez-Behar, Gabriel. "The 1883 Paris Convention and the Impossible Unification of Industrial Property." In *Patent Cultures: Diversity and Harmonization in Historical Perspective*, edited by Graeme Gooday and Steven Robert Wilf, 1st ed., 38–68. Cambridge Intellectual Property and Information Law. New York: Cambridge University Press, 2019.

Gertz, Nolen. *Nihilism and Technology*. Lanham: Rowman & Littlefield International, 2018.

Gooday, Graeme, and Wilf, Steven Robert, eds. *Patent Cultures: Diversity and Harmonization in Historical Perspective*. 1st ed. Cambridge Intellectual Property and Information Law. New York: Cambridge University Press, 2019.

Griset, Pascal. "Innovation Diplomacy: A New Concept for Ancient Practices?" *The Hague Journal of Diplomacy* 15, no. 3 (August 19, 2020): 383–97. https://doi.org/10.1163/1871191X-BJA10036.

Halliburton, Murphy. *India and the Patent Wars: Pharmaceuticals in the New Intellectual Property Regime*. The Culture and Politics of Health Care Work. Ithaca, New York: ILR Press, an imprint of Cornell University Press, 2017.

de Hert, Paul, and Thumfart, Johannes. "The Microsoft Ireland Case and the Cyberspace Sovereignty Trilemma. Post-Territorial Technologies and Companies Question Territorial State Sovereignty and Regulatory State Monopolies." *Brussels Privacy Hub*

Working Papers 4, no. 11 (July 2018), https://brusselsprivacyhub.eu/publications/BPH-Working-Paper-VOL4-N11.pdf.

Ho, Cynthia M. "Current Controversies Concerning Patent Rights and Public Health in a World of International Norms." In *Research Handbook on Patent Law and Theory*, edited by Toshiko Takenaka, Second edition, 419–53. Research Handbooks in Intellectual Property. Cheltenham, UK: Edward Elgar Publishing, 2019.

Innis, Harold Adams. *Empire and Communications*. London: Rowman & Littlefield 2007.

Irwin, Douglas A. *Against the Tide: An Intellectual History of Free Trade*. Fifth printing, and First paperback printing, 1998. Princeton, N.J.: Princeton Univ. Press, 1998.

Kant, Immanuel. *The Metaphysics of Morals, Texts in German Philosophy*. Cambridge; New York: Cambridge University Press, 1991.

Kant, Immanuel. *Perpetual peace: a philosophical essay*. Translated by Mary Smith, Campbell. London: George Allen & Unwin, 2013.

Kant, Immanuel. "Toward Perpetual Peace: A Philosophical Sketch." In *Toward Perpetual Peace and Other Writings on Politics, Peace, and History*, edited by Pauline Kleingeld, 67–109. Rethinking the Western Tradition. New Haven: Yale University Press, 2006.

Kettemann, Matthias C. *The Normative Order of the Internet*. New York: Oxford University Press, 2020.

Ladas, Stephen P. *The International Protection of Industrial Property*. Harvard: Harvard University Press, 1930.

Lamping, Matthias et al. "Declaration on Patent Protection – Regulatory Sovereignty under TRIPS." *International Review of Intellectual Property and Competition Law* (2014) 45.

Lemley, Mark A. "The Myth of the Sole Inventor" (2012) 110, 5 *Mich. L. Rev.* 709.

Lessig, Lawrence. *Free Culture: The Nature and Future of Creativity*. Reprint. New York, NY: Penguin Books, 2005.

Lührs, Philipp Moritz. *Die Entstehung des Reichspatentgesetzes von 1877 und der Versuch eines europäischen Patentrechts von 1962 im Vergleich*. PhD thesis Universität Düsseldorf 2019. https://docserv.uni-duesseldorf.de/servlets/DocumentServlet?id=50527.

Meijers, Anthonie W.M., and Kroes, Peter A. "Extending the Scope of the Theory of Knowledge." In *Norms in Technology*, edited by Marc J. de Vries, Sven Ove Hansson, and Anthonie W.M. Meijers, 9: 15–34. Philosophy of Engineering and Technology. Dordrecht: Springer Netherlands, 2013. https://doi.org/10.1007/978-94-007-5243-6.

Morris, Sean P. "The Contemporary Ideological Legitimacy of Global Intellectual Property Rights" *Intellectual Property Quarterly* (2019) 1, 44–73.

Murphy, Darryl J. "Are Intellectual Property Rights Compatible with Rawlsian Principles of Justice?" *Ethics and Information Technology* 14, no. 2 (June 2012): 109–21. https://doi.org/10.1007/s10676-012-9288-8.

Nance, Michael, and von Platz, Jeppe. *"From Justice to Fairness: Does Kant's Doctrine of Right Imply a Theory of Distributive Justice?* 1." In *Kant on Freedom and Spontaneity*, edited by Kate A. Moran, 1st ed., 250–68. Cambridge University Press, 2018. https://doi.org/10.1017/9781316421888.014.

Ng Siew-Kuan, Elizabeth. "Global Health and Development: Patents and Public Interest." In *Incentives for Global Public Health*, edited by Thomas Pogge, Matthew Rimmer, and Kim Rubenstein, 101–32. Cambridge: Cambridge University Press, 2010. https://doi.org/10.1017/CBO9780511750786.007.

Pieper, Carl, ed. *Der Erfinderschutz und die Reform der Patentgesetze. Amtlicher Bericht über den internationalen Patent-Congress*. Berlin: Commission der der Schulbuchhandlung, 1873.

Pogge, Thomas. "Cosmopolitanism: A Defence." *Critical Review of International Social and Political Philosophy* 5, no. 3 (October 2002): 86–91. https://doi.org/10.1080/13698230410001702672.

Pogge, Thomas. *Realizing Rawls*. Ithaca: Cornell University Press, 1989.

Pogge, Thomas. "The Health Impact Fund: Enhancing Justice and Efficiency in Global Health." *Journal of Human Development and Capabilities* 13, no. 4 (November 2012): 537–59. https://doi.org/10.1080/19452829.2012.703172.

Rahmatian, Andreas. "Neo-Colonial Aspects of Global Intellectual Property Protection." *The Journal of World Intellectual Property* 12, no. 1 (January 2009): 40–74. https://doi.org/10.1111/j.1747-1796.2008.00349.x.

Raizman, David, and Robey, Ethan, eds. *Expanding Nationalisms at World Fairs: Identity, Diversity, and Exchange, 1851–1915*. Routledge Research in Art History. London New York: Routledge, Taylor & Francis Group, 2018.

Ratkowsky, Mathias Georg. *Zur Reform des Erfinderrechts*. Wien, n.n. 1870.

Rawls, John. *A Theory of Justice*. Rev. ed. Cambridge, Mass: Belknap Press of Harvard University Press, 1999.

Rawls, John. *Political Liberalism*. Paperback ed. The John Dewey Essays in Philosophy 4. New York: Columbia Univ. Press, 1996.

Rawls, John. *The Law of Peoples: With, The Idea of Public Reason Revisited*. Cambridge, Mass: Harvard University Press, 1999.

Ricketson, Sam. *The Paris Convention and the Protection of Industrial Property: A Commentary* Oxford: Oxford University Press, 2015.

Schmitt, Carl. *The Concept of the Political*. Expanded ed. Chicago: University of Chicago Press, 2007.

Schrepfer, Matthew. "A Rawlsian Case for Economic Nationalism: Globalisation and Distributional Autonomy in the Law of Peoples." *Journal of Applied Philosophy* 36, no. 1 (February 2019): 155–63. https://doi.org/10.1111/japp.12296.

Seaman, John. "China and the New Geopolitics of Technical Standardization | IFRI – Institut Français Des Relations Internationales." French Institute of International

Relations, January 27, 2020. https://www.ifri.org/en/publications/notes-de-lifri/china-and-new-geopolitics-technical-standardization.

Slobodian, Quinn. *Globalists: The End of Empire and the Birth of Neoliberalism*. Cambridge, Massachusetts: Harvard University Press, 2018.

Sterckx, Sigrid, and Cockbain, Julian. *Exclusions from Patentability: How Far Has the European Patent Office Eroded Boundaries?*, 2015.

Strauss, Leo. *Natural Right and History* (Chicago: University of Chicago Press, 1965).

Sunder, Madhavi. *From Goods to a Good Life: Intellectual Property and Global Justice*. New Haven [Conn.]: Yale University Press, 2012.

Stiegler, Bernard. *Technics and Time*. Meridian. Stanford, Calif: Stanford University Press, 1998.

Takenaka, Toshiko, ed. *Patent Law and Theory: A Handbook of Contemporary Research*. Research Handbooks in Intellectual Property. Cheltenham, UK; Northampton, MA: Edward Elgar, 2008.

Takenaka, Toshiko, ed. *Research Handbook on Patent Law and Theory*. Second edition. Research Handbooks in Intellectual Property. Cheltenham, UK: Edward Elgar Publishing, 2019.

Takenaka, Toshiko, and Adams, John N., eds. "History of the Patent System." In *Patent Law and Theory: A Handbook of Contemporary Research*, 101–31. Research Handbooks in Intellectual Property. Cheltenham, UK ; Northampton, MA: Edward Elgar, 2008.

Thumfart, Johannes. *Die Begründung der globalpolitischen Philosophie. Francisco de Vitorias Vorlesung über die Entdeckung Amerikas im ideengeschichtlichen Kontext*. Berlin: Kadmos, 2012.

Thumfart, Johannes. "Francisco de Vitorias Philosophie: globalpolitisch, nicht kosmopolitisch." In *Die Normativität des Rechts bei Francisco de Vitoria*, edited by Kirstin Bunge, Anselm Spindler, and Andreas Wagner, 229–54. Politische Philosophie und Rechtstheorie des Mittelalters und der Neuzeit 2. Stuttgart: Frommann-Holzboog, 2011.

Thumfart, Johannes. "On Grotius's Mare Liberum and Vitoria's De Indis, Following Agamben and Schmitt." *Grotiana* 30, no. 1 (2009): 65–87. https://doi.org/10.1163/016738309X12537002674286.

Thumfart, Johannes. "The Norm Development of Digital Sovereignty between China, Russia, the EU and the US: From the Late 1990s to the Covid-Crisis 2020/21 as Catalytic Event." In *Enforcing Rights in a Changing World*, edited by Dara Hallinan, Ronald Leenes, and Paul de Hert. Computers Privacy Data Protection (CPDP) 14. London: Hart Publishing, 2022.

Trerise, Jonathan. "The Influence of Patents on Science." *Politics, Philosophy & Economics* 15, no. 4 (November 2016): 424–50. https://doi.org/10.1177/1470594X16666022.

Vries, Marc J. de, Hansson, Sven Ove, and Meijers, Anthonie W.M., eds. *Norms in Technology*. Vol. 9. Philosophy of Engineering and Technology. Dordrecht: Springer Netherlands, 2013. https://doi.org/10.1007/978-94-007-5243-6.

Waligore, Timothy. "Rawls, Self-Respect, and Assurance: How Past Injustice Changes What Publicly Counts as Justice." *Politics, Philosophy & Economics* 15, no. 1 (February 2016): 42–66. https://doi.org/10.1177/1470594X15599100.

Waytz, Adam, Cacioppo, John, and Epley, Nicholas. "Who Sees Human?: The Stability and Importance of Individual Differences in Anthropomorphism." *Perspectives on Psychological Science* 5, no. 3 (May 2010): 219–32. https://doi.org/10.1177/1745691610369336.

CHAPTER 3

Innovation Diplomacy

International Exhibitions and the Rise of Innovation in the Law of Nations

P. Sean Morris

> Your vigor, born of yesterday, will be so strong tomorrow that you will be able to aid the world by the benefits of commercial liberty, as you have won its admiration by the liberality of your institutions.[1]

1 Introduction

An important aspect of the evolution of international intellectual property law has been the role of exhibitions. This chapter therefore looks at the role of exhibitions during the latter part of the nineteenth century in relation to the emergence of international treaties relating to industrial innovation in particular the Paris Convention of 1883.[2] Moreover, the chapter focuses on how private merchants' lobbying, knowledge, networks and technological achievements were central to the formation of the international legal system in the 1880s on industrial innovation. Because states viewed private merchants' lobbying as a form of need to regulate the bourgeoning industrial innovation ecosystem of the nineteenth-century, the response from states was how to balance

1 French Director of Foreign Sections in his tribute to the American success of the Paris 1878 Exhibition, see Universal Exhibition of Paris, 1878: The Banquet to Richard C. McCormick, given in Paris, Nov 26, 1878 (Paris, 1878), p. 6, cited in Curti, Merle. 'America at the World Fairs, 1851–1893.' *The American Historical Review* 55(4) (1950) 833–856, 850.

2 Paris Convention for the Protection of Industrial Property (adopted 20 March 1883) 828 UNTS 305 ("Paris Convention"); see also, Duncan, chapter one, in this volume. For the purposes of clarity, this chapter deals with expositions, trade fairs, exhibitions, and other forms of public displays as the same. However, the term "exhibitions" will be the default in the discussion.

 | DOI:10.1163/9789004511439_005

the interests of the merchants and those of the states in the law of nations in the nineteenth century. This chapter refer to these developments in part as innovation diplomacy where the tact and diplomacy of private merchants intertwined with the customs and principles of nineteenth century law of nations formed a comprehensive treatification alliance.[3]

These developments in the latter part of the nineteenth century created and maintained a new era of international legal change that are present to this day as is evidenced by the two main global treaties for intellectual property rights which were adopted in the latter part of the nineteenth century: the Paris and Bern Conventions.[4] They came about in part, how interested parties such as the Vienna Congress of 1873; Victor Hugo and the then nascent Literary Association of Artists were able to lobby for their adoption. Such lobbying process is also part of the innovation diplomacy narrative that is develop in this chapter. Thus, innovation diplomacy involved, partly, lobbying and networking by non-state actors due to the rise of industrial innovation, technological advancement, the need to protect private rights in relation to industrial

3 I am primarily referring to the law of nations as international law, however, the subject matter of the law of nations is more complex in that the notion of the law of nations as such predates the latter part of the nineteenth century, where, formal links to the law of nature formed part of the how the law of nations evolved. For nineteenth century scholars, the law of nations has been seen as: 'The proper and immediate subjects of the Law of Nations being those political communities which are in a state of Independence, and the test of their Independence being their aptitude or capacity to discharge the obligations of Natural Society towards other political communities and to regulate the mode of discharging those obligations without the consent of any Political Superior, the rules which result from their mutual relations, and which govern their intercourse, resolve themselves into Natural rules and Positive rules, and the aggregate body of those rules, which admit of being enforced, constitute the Law of Nations in the most extensive sense of the term,' Twiss, Travers. *The Law of Nations considered as Independent Political Communities – on the Right and Duties of Nations in Time of Peace* (Oxford: Oxford University Press, 1861), 110. See Redlich, Marcellus von. *The Law of Nations, 2nd Edition* (Phoenix: World League for Permanent Peace, 1937), ch 1; Snow, Alpheus Henry. 'Law of Nations.' *American Journal of International Law* 6(4) (1912) 890–900; Kohler, Joseph. 'New Law of Nations.' *Michigan Law Review* 15(8) (1916) 631–638; Percy, Corbet. 'Modern Law of Nations.' *Michigan Law Review* 47(1) (1948) 67–71; Lobban, Michael. 'Custom, Common Law Reasoning and the Law of Nations in the Nineteenth Century,' in Perreau-Saussine, Amanda, and Murphy, James, eds. *The Nature of Customary Law: Legal, Historical and Philosophical Perspectives*, (Cambridge: Cambridge University Press, 2009) 256–278; Orakhelashvili, Alexander. 'The Idea of European International Law.' *European Journal of International Law* (2006) 17(2) 315–347.

4 Paris Convention for the Protection of Industrial Property (adopted 20 March 1883) 828 UNTS 305 (Paris Convention); Berne Convention for the Protection of Literary and Artistic Works, 9 September 1886, 828 UNTS 221 (Berne Convention).

innovation and copyrights which led to a change in diplomatic and legal relations among states. Moreover, the role of subjects of those states, namely private economic merchants and consumers alike, embraced regulation, innovation and the law of nations as forces of stability, especially as embodied in new commercial treaties such as the Cobden-Chevalier Treaty.[5] The Cobden-Chevalier was one of the first major commercial treaties in the late nineteenth century that would usher in a new era of commercial treaties in trade relations among the major nations of the world, and to a large degree, future multilateral trade treaties on matters of economic relations among states.[6]

Further developments such as the Franco-Prussian War (1871) would also give rise to the new science of international law, as we understood today.[7] Seemingly, it was these two major events, one on economic matters in the 1860s with the Franco-UK Trade Treaty (Cobden-Chevalier 1860) and, the other, rooted in conflict in the early 1870s that inaugurated new streams of foreign policies and free trade, and in the process gave rise to a new 'science of the legal form' as international law.[8] It was a process that takes into account treaty relations between states, power dynamics of those states and war as a 'means of negotiation'.[9] That process continued to the Hague Conventions of 1899 and 1907[10] and in

5 In part, I am referring to the beginning of a new free trade era that started with Anglo-French trade relations, Cobden-Chevalier Treaty, 23 January 1860, see also, Irwin, Douglas. 'Free Trade and Protection in Nineteenth Century Britain and France Revisited: A Comment on Nye.' *Journal of Economic History* 53(1) (1993) 146–152; Iliasu, A.A. 'The Cobden-Chevalier Commercial Treaty of 1860.' *Historical Journal* 14(1) (1971) 67–98.

6 See Gaston, Jack. 'The Free Trade Diplomacy Debate and the Victorian European Common Market Initiative.' *Canadian Journal of History* 22(1) (1987) 59–82; Fitzmaurice, Andrew. 'Liberalism and Empire in Nineteenth-Century International Law.' *American Historical Review* 117(1) (2012) 122–140.

7 International legal historians have posited that modern international law, in some ways, began in 1870, with an impulse to civilise, see Koskenniemi, Martti. *The Gentle Civilizer of Nations: The Rise and Fall of International Law 1870–1960* (Cambridge: Cambridge University Press, 2002) (tracing the development of modern international after 1870). For discussion on the Franco-Prussian War in general see Dedinger, Beatrice. 'The Franco-German Trade Puzzle: An Analysis of the Economic Consequences of the Franco-Prussian War.' *Economic History Review* 65(3) (2012) 1029–1054; Howard, Michael. *The Franco-Prussian War* (Abingdon/New York: Routledge, 2021); Wetzel, David. *A Duel of Nations: Germany, France, and the Diplomacy of the War of 1870–1871* (Madison: University of Wisconsin Press, 2012).

8 Koskenniemi, *Gentle Civilizer* (n. 7), 182.

9 Ibid.

10 See Hudson, Manley. 'Present Status of the Hague Conventions of 1899 and 1907.' *American Journal of International Law* 25(1) (1931) 114–117.

some ways culminated with the formation of the Permanent Court of International Justice (PCIJ).[11]

The events that I just described are not the entire picture as states have been interacting in different forms and markets in different epochs.[12] However, the emergence of treaties in the late nineteenth-century, such as Cobden-Chevalier or the Paris Convention and how technological advancement,[13] innovation and regulation were central to them can inform us of what was now clearly by the early twentieth century more appropriately referred to as "international law." In this new science of international law, the emergence of *sanctioned* property rights relating to creativity and inventions in the modern international legal system has been the foundational stone.

The shift in the narratives, or classification, of law of nations to international law is important; as such, a shift represents how changes were taking place in (European) societies from the late medieval period to the late nineteenth

11 Article 1 of the PCIJ Statute states in part: 'This Court shall be in addition to the Court of Arbitration organized by the Conventions of the Hague of 1899 and 1907.'. League of Nations, Statute of the Permanent Court of International Justice, 16 December 1920.

12 Commercial trading relations have been one of the core form of interactions among states, and in some ways, give rise to the legal rules that form international law, but see, Wilson, Andrew, and Bowman, Alan. *Trade, Commerce, and the State in the Roman World* (Oxford: Oxford University Press, 2017); Porras, Ileana. 'European Origins, the Doctrine of the Providential Function of Commerce, and International Law's Embrace of Economic Growth.' *Proceedings of the Annual Meeting – American Society of International Law* 107 (2013) 374–379; Gokmen, Gunes, Vermeulen, Wessel, and Vezina, Pierre-Louis. 'The Imperial Roots of Global Trade.' *Journal of Economic Growth* 25 (2020) 87–145; Morris, P. Sean. 'The Private Foundations of International Law: Intellectual Property Rights and Pashukanis.' *Jus Gentium: Journal of International Legal History* 5(1) (2020) 37–123. For discussions on other forms of interactions since the latter part of the nineteenth-century that focuses on the rise of technology and communication, see Hugill, Peter. *Global Communications Since 1844: Geopolitics and Technology* (Baltimore: John Hopkins University Press, 1999), 2: 'If information is power, whoever rules the world's telecommunications system commands the world.' See also, Landes, David. *The Unbound Prometheus: Technological Change and Industrial Development in Western Europe from 1750 to the Present* (Cambridge: Cambridge University Press, 1969).

13 The multilateral telegraph convention of 1865 help to revolutionized the spread of global communications and in that regard, the rise of technology and innovation as described in this chapter, however, the telegraphy union, although significant is not the object of this chapter, but see Codding, George. *The International Telecommunications Union: An Experiment in International Cooperation* (Leiden: Brill, 1952); Reinisch, Paul S. 'International Unions and their Administration.' *American Journal of International Law* 1(3) (1907) 579–623; Morriss, Andrew, and Nard, Craig. 'Institutional Choice & Interest Groups in the Development of American Patent Law: 1790–1865.' *Supreme Court Economic Review* 19 (2011) 143–244.

century.[14] These shifts, included, one of identity.[15] Another factor was the linguistic difference between the English common law and the continental legal system, where the latter revived the *jus gentium* tradition especially through the writings of Hugo Grotius (1535–1645),[16] Samuel Pufendorf (1632–1694)[17] and other scholastic school cohorts.[18] On the other hand, English writers such as Jeremy Bentham (1748–1832) and others framed the notion of "international law" as the common language to separate the discourse from the continental discourse and as a theoretical tool.[19] But, as Koskenniemi reminds us, it was events taking place in Europe in the 1870s, and especially around German legal thinking, that influenced the modern science of international law.[20]

American writers, in some ways initially adopted a continental approach, as was evidenced through the Alien Tort Statue (ATS)[21] and the writings of Joseph Story (1779–1845).[22] The ATS, for instance refer to the 'the law of nations'[23] and American courts have consistently remain true to that formulation.[24] From the point of view of a scholarly contribution, there is no doubt that the work of Emmerich de Vattel (1714–1767) has been instrumental in how the Americans viewed the law of nations.[25] And, Vattels' influence on the Americans, and

14 See also, Rominskyi, EV. 'Regional Traditions in Medieval International Law.' *Jus Gentium: Journal of International Legal History* 1(2) (2016) 591–604; Caenegem, RC van. 'Law in the Medieval World.' *Tijdschrift voor Rechtsgeschiedenis* 49(1) (1981) 13–46; Grewe, Wilhelm. *The Epochs of International Law* (trs Michael Byers) (Berlin/New York: Gruyter, 2000); Hall, Stephen. 'The Persistent Spectre: Natural Law, International Order and Limits of Legal Positivism.' *European Journal of International Law* 12(2) (2001) 269–307; Koskenniemi, Martti. 'The Political Theology of Trade Law: The Scholastic Contribution' in Fasenrath, Ulrich et al., eds. *From Bilateralism to Community Interest: Essays in Honour of Bruno Simma* (Oxford: Oxford University Press, 2011), 90–112.

15 Hall, ibid, 270.

16 Ibid.

17 Ibid, 273.

18 Ibid, 270–274.

19 Ibid, 279.

20 Koskenniemi, *Gentle Civilizer* (n. 391), 182; Garcia-Salmones Rovira, Monica. *The Project of Positivism in International Law* (Oxford: Oxford University Press, 2013).

21 Judiciary Act of 1789 § 9, 28 USC § 1350.

22 Story, Joseph. *Commentaries on the Conflicts of Laws, Foreign and Domestic, in Regard to Contracts, Rights, and Remedies, and Especially in Regard to Marriages, Divorces, Wills, Succession, and Judgments* (Hilliard, Gray, 1834) 19–21.

23 Judiciary Act of 1789 § 9, 28 USC § 1350.

24 E.g., The Paquette Habana, 175 U.S. 677 (1900); Kiobel v Royal Dutch Petroleum Co., 133 S. Ct. 1659 (2013).

25 Vattel, Emmerich de. *The Law of Nations*, Book 1 (London: J. Newberry, et al. 1759). Vattels' work was drawn upon by early American international jurists as the authoritative voice of international law, see Fenwick, Charles. 'The Authority of Vattel.' *American Political*

more broadly, on the intellectual nature of the law of nations, has to do with his framing of how commercial relations is relevant to the relationship states form within the context of the law of nations.[26]

Nevertheless, the law of nations has always been an idea and legal science rooted in European traditions and regulating the relationship among European states. Hence, over the centuries, or at least since the revival of Roman *jus gentium* in the eleventh and twelfth century in Europe, it took on different meanings and approaches. By the 1860s, the law of nations was transitioning to a new realm that include treaties, and in the process, diluting the traditional realm that was underpinned by a divine thought collective of natural law.[27]

In theory, the law of nations is a complex term. It is complex because, as an anglicised version of *jus gentium* – its Roman origins generally points to commercial relations between the Roman people and those from foreign lands.[28] And, on the other, the law of nations retains a normative value that gradually replaced the decline of natural law, which, by the nineteenth century, has taken currency in the legal literature.[29] In 1842 for example, scholarly legal literature painted the law of nations not only as ambiguous in terms of its science, but also, oscillates between divinity and laws of nature: '… the term "law of nations" … allows that "divine laws" are "laws or rules properly so called", now "divine laws" are synonymous and identical with the laws of

Science Review 7(3) (1913) 395–410; Mueser, Benjamin. 'The Nation and Property in Vattel's Theory of Territory.' *Global Intellectual History* 3(2) (2018) 137–155.

26 Vattel, ibid; see also, Nakhimovsky, Isaac. 'Vattel's Theory of the International Order: Commerce and the Balance of Power in the *Law of Nations*.' *History of European Ideas* 33(2) (2007) 157–173, 170 (setting out Vattel's treatment of 'commercial interests' in relation to the law of nations).

27 See Schall, James. 'Natural Law and the Law of Nations: Some Theoretical Considerations.' *Fordham International Law Journal* 15(4) (1991) 997–1030; 'Note: The Law of Nations and Treaties of the United States.' *American Law Review* 55 (1921) 877–895.

28 See generally (n. 387); Wilson (n. 396); Nussbaum, Arthur. 'The Significance of Roman Law in the History of International Law.' *University of Pennsylvania Law Review* 100(5) (1952) 678–687; Kingsbury, Benedict, and Straumann, Benjamin. 'Introduction' in Kingsbury, Benedict, and Straumann, Benjamin eds. *The Roman Foundations of the Law of Nations* (Oxford: Oxford University Press, 2011).

29 See for instance, Wheaton, *History of the Law of Nations in Europe and America: From the Earliest Times to the Treaty of Washington, 1812* (New York: Gould, Banks & Co., 1845): Hosak, John. *On the Ruse and Growth of the Law of Nations as Established by General Usage and by Treaties* (London: John Murray, 1882). It is not my intention to give a historical evolution of the term "law of nations", as that would be fruitless; I am merely pointing to its technicalities and its relevance for modern economic relationships through treaties since the latter part of the nineteenth century. But see, Verzijl, JHW. 'A Panorama of the Law of Nations.' *Nordic Journal of International Law* 21(1) (1951) 3–25.

nature, upon which the law of nations is based.'[30] The link of natural law, or its divine purpose with the law of nations, was to some extent, part of a tradition that goes back to Thomas Aquinas.[31] Nevertheless, natural law as a philosophical approach retained a prominent place in how the discourse of the law of nations evolved up to the eighteenth century and to some extent the late nineteenth century.

The rise of treaties in the relationship among states in the late nineteenth-century began to signal that states, in the same fashion people *obey* the fundamentals of domestic laws, were now bound by treaties heralding in an era of legal positivism in the law of nations. Hence, with treaties such as the Anglo-French Cobden-Chevalier representing trade and other commercial matters, the ground was set for expansion of other customs union that represented homogeneous states such as the *Zollverein* in the nineteenth century,[32] and eventually international treaties such as the Paris and Bern Conventions in the latter part of the nineteenth century. Thus, the law of nations, was now transforming into *jus gentium* like structures as originally developed in ancient Rome, as a matter of regulating commercial activities.[33]

The rise of treaties and positivism in the late nineteenth century did not separate the law of nations from its various prior incarnations since the origins of *jus gentium*. Rather, in my opinion, the turn to economic activities and the need to regulate those activities through treaties solidifies the law of nations as a global feature to better understand the state and the relationship states enjoy.[34] Furthermore, as contemporary scholars such as David Kennedy has argued, 'the nineteenth century was also the age of commerce, of liberalism,

---

30 'Definition and History of the Law of Nations.' *American Jurist and Law Magazine* 28(55) (1842) 1–34, 5 (an extract from Manning's, Commentaries on the Law of Nations). More recently, see Butler, William, and Kwon, Michael. 'Manning's Commentaries on the Law of Nations.' *Jus Gentium: Journal of International Legal History* 4(2) (2019) 621–632.

31 Schall (n. 27) 999.

32 Hancock, Kathleen. *Regional Integration: Choosing Plutocracy* (Basingstoke: Palgrave Macmillan, 2009) 61–96; Green, Abigail. 'Representing Germany? The Zollverein at the World Exhibitions, 1851–1862.' *Journal of Modern History* 75(4) (2003) 836–863; Blackbourn, David. *History of Germany 1780–1918: The Long Nineteenth Century, 2nd edition* (Malden/Oxford: Blackwell Publishing, 2003).

33 See Kingsbury and Straumann (n. 28); Mann, F.A. 'Reflections on a Commercial Law of Nations.' *British Yearbook of International Law* 33 (1957) 20–51, 34 (noting that 'the primary source of law applicable to a commercial treaty is to a large extent the treaty itself').

34 Given that the law of nations is a broad term per se, this does not mean it did not include matters relating to war or other activities, but those arguments are not the concern here, but see generally, Twiss (n. 3).

of robber barons and trusts, of revolutions in transport and technology.'[35] Therefore, to my mind, the nineteenth-century not only allowed for a revival in Roman *jus gentium* but also augmented how modern international law would be a matter of primarily economic relations. Thus, the law of nations, was also injecting into the legal relationship among states the individual economic actor[36] who sees the rule of law, as it were, the best form to engage in technological advancement and innovation. These concerns are captured in the observation made by Wilfred Jenks who argues that the law of nations represents scientific progress and technology in the world community.[37]

I now turn to how part of that scientific progress was how international exhibitions were able to showcase technological innovations in the late nineteenth century and how private merchants successfully lobbied for international rules as part of the positive law of nations for the protection of industrial property.

2 International Exhibitions and Innovation Diplomacy: Copyright Innovations

Between 1800 and 1890, several international exhibitions or trade fairs were held in various European states and other nations such as the United States.[38]

35 Kennedy, David. 'International Law and the Nineteenth Century: History of an Illusion.' *Nordic Journal of International Law* 65(3–4) (1996) 385–420, 390–1. For a general reading on the rise of technology see Kranzberg, Melvin, and Pursell, Carroll, eds. *Technology in Western Civilization, Vol. I* (Oxford: Oxford University Press, 1967).

36 I am primarily referring to other actors than states in international law, but see Jessup, Philip C. 'The Subjects of Modern Law of Nations.' *Michigan Law Review* 45(4) (1947) 383–408.

37 Jenks, C. Wilfred. 'The New Science and the Law of Nations.' *International and Comparative Law Quarterly* 17(2) (1968) 17, 327–345, 327: 'The impact of advanced science and technology is the most incisive of the decisive forces which are reshaping contemporary society on a scale and at a rate unprecedented in human experience. It has a threefold bearing on the law of nations. It has a profound, if subtle, influence on the fundamentals of legal thought; it poses a wide range of specific problems for the law; and it raises acutely the general question of the relationship of law, science and technology in the life of the world community.'

38 For preliminary readings see Auerbach, Jeffrey, and Hoffendberg, Peter, eds. *Britain, the Empire, and the World at the Great Exhibition of 1851* (Aldershot: Ashgate 2008); Geppert, Alexander. *Fleeting Cities: Imperial Expositions in Fin-de-Siecle Europe* (Basingstoke: Palgrave Macmillan, 2010); Gindriez, Charles. *International Exhibitions: Paris, Philadelphia, Vienna* (New York: Barnes & Co., 1878); Holt, Elizabeth. *The Art of All Nations, 1850–73: The Emerging Role of Exhibitions and Critics* (New Jersey: Princeton University Press, 1982); Rydell, Robert. *Wold of Fairs: The Century of Progress Expositions* (Chicago: University

These exhibitions, which included those at Paris (1806); London (1851); Paris (1867); Vienna (1873); Paris (1878); Melbourne (1880)[39]; Chicago (1893) and Brussels (1897) brought together inventors, nineteenth-century lobbyists, authors, consumers and government officials in the name of promoting the technological advancements of the century and promoting innovation.[40]

One remarkable feat about these exhibitions were the amount of inventions as such that were unveiled during the latter half of the nineteenth century. According to one recent study which looked at more than eight thousand samples of innovation at exhibitions 'between 1851 and 1915' such exhibitions were useful for how patent laws evolved since legal protection allowed for 'returns to innovation.'[41] These international exhibitions continued well into the early twentieth century. But their earlier versions, in the nineteenth century, represented a new kind of innovation diplomacy where, by the 1880s a slew of legislations were adopted at the domestic level as a result of innovation diplomacy and a response to new inventions. Thus, states such as Germany, the UK,[42] France, the US among others, significantly improved or expanded their intellectual property laws.[43]

Moreover, by the 1880s, some of those legislations were replicated at the international or were being negotiated in tandem with domestic approaches.[44]

of Chicago Press, 1993); Brown, Julie. *Health and Medicine on Display: International Expositions in the United States, 1876–1904* (The MITT Press, 2009); Ahlstrom, Goran. *Technological Development and Industrial Exhibitions, 1850–1914: Sweden in an International Perspective* (Lund University Press, 1996); Mainardi, Patricia. *Art and Politics of the Second Empire: The Universal Expositions of 1855 and 1857* (Yale University Press, 1987).

39 See Hoffenberg, Peter. 'A Science of Our Own: Nineteenth Century Exhibitions, Australians and the History of Science' in Bennett, BM, and Hodge, JM, eds. *Science and Empire: Britain and the World* (Basingstoke: Palgrave Macmillan, 2011) (discussing the Melbourne Intercolonial Exhibition of 1875); Fox, Paul. 'Exhibition City: Melbourne and the 1880 International Exhibition.' *Transition* 31 (1990) 62–71, 68.

40 It is known that a few exhibitions were held prior to 1801, such as 1756 in London; see Allen, Brian. 'The Society of Arts and the First Exhibition of Contemporary Art in 1760.' *RSA Journal* 139(5416) (1991) 265–269.

41 Moser, Petra. 'Innovation without Patents: Evidence from World's Fairs.' *Journal of Law and Economics* 55(1) (2012) 43–74, 44.

42 The Patents, Designs and Trade Marks Act 1883.

43 E.g., An Act to revise, consolidate, and amend the statutes relating to patent and copyright, H.R. 1714, 41st Cong. (1870) (U.S.).

44 This was primarily with initiatives at the Congress of Vienna in 1873 and the ensuing patent controversy including efforts by the newly established International Law Association to unify patent laws, see Field, David. *Association for the Reform and Codification of the Law of Nations: Its History and Aims* (G. Hill, 1875); ILA, *Reports of the First Conference, held at Brussels, 1873, and of the Second Conference, held at Geneva, 1874* (London: West, Newman & Co., 1903). For discussions in the field of trademarks see Duguid, Paul. 'French

Unlike a century later in the 1980s when the world was negotiating the TRIPS Agreements and states were to follow by simultaneously implementing domestic laws that were compatible with the TRIPS or were 'coerced,'[45] rather, the late nineteenth century saw the rise of innovation diplomacy that culminated in the Paris and Bern Conventions without the coercion effect.[46] Thus, in a sense of the word, the latter nineteenth century represented the first global efforts to deal with innovation and technological advancement through treaties and domestic laws that states and people obey.

Studies have shown that exhibition data based on 'innovations with and without patents' covered a range of industries.[47] Through these exhibitions, which began to gain traction at the turn of the nineteenth-century fuelled the need for private merchants to lobby and secure legal rights at the domestic and international level for industrial innovation. The first sign of what legal rights would entail centred on copyright products and the emergence of the Napoleon Civil Code in 1804. Two years later Paris held a grand exhibition where a mixture of textile and chemical sciences were on display.[48] It was

Connections: The International Progation of Trademarks in the Nineteenth Century.' *Enterprise & Society* 10(1) (2009) 3–37.

45 See Deere Birkbeck, Carolyn. *The Implementation Game: The TRIPS Agreement and the Global Politics of Intellectual Property Reform in Development Counters* (Oxford: Oxford University Press, 2008).

46 But see Wadlow, Christopher. 'The British Empire Patent 1901–1923: The Global Patent That Never Was.' *Intellectual Property Quarterly* 2006(4) 311–346.

47 Moser (n. 41), 47.

48 In fact, the first exhibition took place in 1801, followed by another exhibition in 1802 however, I am placing emphasis on the 1806 exhibition given that it emerged after the 1804 and 1804 Civil Code and Civil Procedure Codes were enacted, and the efforts to place emphasis on legal protection of inventions and innovations as an "industrial exposition". See generally, Daniels, Morna. 'Paris National and International Exhibitions from 1798 to 1900: A Finding-List of British Library Holdings.' (2013) eBLJ 2013, Article 6. For discussions on the 1806 exhibition, see Hafter, Daryl. 'The Business of Invention in the Paris Industrial Exposition of 1806.' *Business History Review* 58(3) (1984) 317–335. Daniels, ibid, for instance, citing A. Picard, Exposition Universelle Internationale de 1889 a Paris: Rapport general. Paris Imprimerie national, 1891. Illustrations. Vol. 1. Exposition de 1806 sur l'Esplande des Invalides. 7953.m.3, (Daniels p. 3) made the following observation of the 1806 Exhibition: 'In 1806 the only exhibition held under the first Empire was staged in 124 porticos built in front of the Invalides and in some rooms of the administration building of the Ponts-et-chaussees (roads and bridges) department. Many of the 1422 French exhibitors displayed textile products, including, for the first time, muslins, as well as luxury decorative items and products of the chemical and mechanical sciences. They came from 104 departements throughout the French Empire, which included at this time the left bank of the Rhine and Northern Italy. The Exhibition lasted 24 days, 25 September–19 October.' https://www.bl.uk/eblj/2013articles/pdf/ebljarticle62013.pdf.

an exhibition that signalled the rise of the new commercial age where ideas, invention would propel human kind in a new kind of excellence.

In 1806, the French also saw the need to promote their goods and inventions as the more superior compare to cheap British imports.[49] However, it was the industrial application and certification of the goods and inventions that emerged from the 1806 Paris Exhibition would trigger in part the rise of a new global movement towards legal protection. Furthermore, the revisions to the French Code Civil[50] that year to include a new Civil Procedure Code[51] sent some signals that inventions and innovations would usher in a new wave of codification that would include how states enact specific legislations (and later on treaties).[52] Thus, where the Civil Code (including the Code du commerce 1897) was a form of harmonizing instrument for French law, the 1806 Paris Exhibition in all its grandeur helped to establish a path to innovation

49 Hafter (n. 48).

50 This is due to revision of the 1804 Civil Code and 1806 Code de Procedure, see *infra* (n. 52); Ginsburg, Jane. 'A Tale of Two Copyrights: Literary Property in Revolutionary France and American.' *Tulane Law Review* 64(5) (1990) 991–1032; Schroder, Ann. 'Reversals of Power: Artistic Property, Counterfeiter, and the 1793 French Copyright Act.' *Visual Resources* 16(2) (2000) 143–154.

51 See *infra* (n. 52); Wijffels, Alain. 'Undue Delay and the French Code of Civil Procedure 1806.' Rhee, C.H. van, ed. *Within a Reasonable Time: The History of Due and Undue Delay in Civil Litigation* (Dunker & Humblot, 2010) 320–353; Crabites, Pierre. 'Napoleon and the French Code of Civil Procedure.' *Loyola Law Journal* 10(1–2) (1929) 3–12; Paris-Dobozy, Marie-Luce. 'Still Alive: Some Observations about the Two-Hundred Years of Existence of the French Civil Code of 1804.' *Irish Journal of European Law* 12(1) (2005) 72–97.

52 There are two arguments to this latter claim. The first is that the Civil Code was in fact revolutionary at the time, even though it built on the ideas of previous codes in ancient Rome. Moreover, the coverage of property in the French Code Civil it can be argued necessary included protecting individual property, such as in Article 544. The second argument however is the fact that European states were concluding treaties of various sorts and the Code Civil was a way of signalling that states can follow the example when regulating relationship with people and their commercial activities. Hence, it was not surprising that shortly after the 1806 Exhibition, the 1807 Code de Commerce emerged to complement the 1806 Code de Procedure and the original Code Civil of 1804. For discussions on the 1807 Code de Commerce see Klimaszewska, Anna. 'General Principles in the Commercial Code of France of 1807.' *Journal on European History of Law* 2(2) (2011) 91–94; Crabites, 'Napoleon and the French Code of Civil Procedure' (n. 51). For general discussion on the Code Civil see Gordley, James. 'Myths of the French Civil Code.' *American Journal of Comparative Law* 42(3) (1994) 459–506, 462 (discussing property under the Code Civil); Houin, Roger. 'Reform of the French Civil Code and the Code of Commerce.' *American Journal of Comparative Law* 4(1) (1955) 485–505; Visick, James. 'The Intellectual Influences on the *Code civil*'. *UCL Jurisprudence Review* 15 (2009) 198–221.

diplomacy.[53] Yet, by the eleventh Paris Exhibition in 1849, the French, would, by 1852, unilaterally unveiled an act for the protection of copyright.[54]

Based on the Daniels report of the 1806 Paris Exhibition[55] the most obvious inventions were those based on 'chemical and mechanical sciences.'[56] The catalogue of products (widely available in electronic format in the twentieth-century on the internet) shows that of the 124 pavilions (portico), pavilion number 124 contained an invention relating to a medical device.[57] But perhaps it was the exhibition of a certain Jean-Gabriel Charvet and his painter Joseph Dufor regarding the panoramic wallpaper drawings (and the methods of doing so) that is one of the lasting impact of the 1806 Exhibition.[58]

The Report of the 1806 Exhibition noted that a silver medal was awarded to the exhibitors of the scenic wallpapers:

---

53 It must be said that German states such as Baden around the time introduced a copyright law in 1806, that, in part, had to do with the imposition of the French Civil Code on a number of German states, see Hesse, Carla. 'The Rise of Intellectual Property, 700 B.C.–A.D. 2000.' *Daedalus* 131(2) (2002) 26–45, 39.

54 On the latter, I am primarily referring to the French International Copyright Act of 1852, offering protection to foreign works regardless of country of origin; see French Decree of 28 March 1852.

55 Daniels (n. 48).

56 Ibid.

57 See Catalogue des produits de l'industrie francaise qui sereont exposes, pendant les derniers jours de Septembre 1806, Bibliotheque national de France, (the reference to medical device is based on my non-French rough interpretation), available at https://data.bnf.fr/fr/12273521/exposition_publique_des_produits_de_l_industrie_francaise/.

58 There are conflicting reports on the origins of the wallpaper exhibitions at the 1806 Paris Exposition, however, for the purposes of consistency, I will use the Report of the Jury for citations/commentary, Rapport du Jury – Sur Les Produits – De L' Industrie Francaise, Presente, de Champagny, (Paris, 1806). See also, Costaz, Claude-Anthelme. *Notices sur les objets envoyes a l'exposition des produuits de l'industrie francaise: redigees et imprimees par ordre de S.E.M. de Champagny, minister de l'interieur an 1806* (Paris, 1806) 234 describing the "magnificent wallpapers": 'MM. Jean Zuber et compagnie, qui, ontre leur papeterie de Roppentzviller, possedent une fabrique considerable de papiers peints a Rexheim, ont compose une magnifique collection de paysages les plus interessans de la Suisse. Le coloris e nest si brilliant et tellement diversifie, qu'uun semblable travail fait au pinceuar le surpasserait difficilement. Ils se porposent d'exposer eux-membes cette collection avec d'autrers decors executes dans leurs fabriques.' But at 256, Joseph Dufour is then mentioned: 'M. Joseph Dufour, de Macon, deja connu avanta-geusement par sa fabrique de papiers peints, a expedie de nouvelles tentures, dont les sujets tires des voyages du capitane Cook, sont peut-etre ce que l'art a produit de plus curieux en ce genre; peines, soins, sacrifices pecuniares, rien n'a pu decourager M. Dufours. Des difficulties sans nombre etaient a surmonter; tout etait a creer; il est enfin arrive au but, et au point de recuillir le fruit de ses longs travaux.'

293. M. Zuber, de Rexheim, department du Haut-Rhin.

Ce fabricant fait-tres-bien les papiers peints et emploie de belles couleurs; il a fait executer des paysages qui presentent des difficultes vaincues d'une maniere utile a l'avancement de l'art.

Le jury lui decerne une medaille d'argent de 2, classe.[59]

The Charvet/Dufour wallpapers – *Sauvages de la mer Pacifique* – Savages of the Pacific – and their display at the 1806 Exhibition culminated years of design, innovation and methods for wall paper printing.[60] Thus, the early inventions and creative works that were on display at the 1806 Exhibition in France saw an increase in the need for further creative and technological revolutions that on the one hand helped to promote a consumption society but also preserve the rule of law for inventors and creators.

The relevance of the 1806 Exhibition however, in relation to the law of nations, was the presence of Belgium[61] and, to some extent, the economic effect of the Napoleonic Wars were having on trade given that a continental blockade prevented other nations from participating in the 1806 Exhibition.[62] Yet, the

59 This is my own typing and interpretation aided by machine translation. I can be wrong, so readers are asked to double check against typing and interpretation. [*My rough interpretation is as follows*: 'This manufacturer produced good wallpapers and used beautiful colours; he showed landscapes that are difficult to mount in a useful way, but nevertheless, quite a success for the advancement of art. The jury, therefore, awarded him a silver medal.'] Ive, been presented with an alternative translation by Dorothee Cambou: 'This manufacturer does wallpapers very well and uses beautiful colours. He executed (painted) landscapes which presented difficulties that he overcame in a manner that is useful to the progress of art.

The jury awarded him a silver medal of 2, clas 1.'

60 For general overview see Lythberg, Billie. 'A Pacific Macrocosm: "Les Sauvages de la mer Pacifique"' in Craciun, A., and Schaffer, S., eds. *The Material Cultures of Enlightenment Arts and Sciences* (Basingstoke: Palgrave Macmillan, 2016).

61 France in the early 1800s controlled the territory of Belgium and as such, the presence of Belgium at the 1806 exposition would further bolster the French efforts of a *grand fair* of international proportion given that France ruled Belgium between 1806–1813, but for discussions on Napoleonic Belgium see Siborne, William. *History of the War in France and Belgium in 1815* (Cambridge: Cambridge University Press, 2012). See also, Mikaberidze, Alexander. *The Napoleonic Wars: A Global History* (Oxford: Oxford University Press, 2020); Schroeder, Paul. *The Transformation of European Politics 1763–1848* (Oxford: Oxford University Press, 1994); Mokyr, Joel. *Industrialization in the Low Countries, 1795–1850* (Yale University Press, 1976).

62 See Hafter (n. 48) noting that the 1806 Exposition was in part due to the need to overcome obstacles related to conflict as much as economic. See also, Crouzet, Francois. 'Wars, Blockade, and Change in Europe, 1792–1815'. *The Journal of Economic History* 24(4) (1964)

1806 Exhibition was also part of a larger dance of the law of nations where it meant to commemorate military victories of France. However, by highlighting the presence of Belgium at the 1806 Exhibition, a further concern in relation to technological advancement during the Napoleonic Wars is whether the conflict affected economic form and the property rights associated with technology and trade in general. In other words, given the nexus between property and the rule of law as such, namely, those relating to contracts or copyrights, some form of incentives were inevitable for both countries.[63] For France and Belgium, they were able to secure temporary economic gains as a result of the conflict.[64] But the 1806 Exhibition would signal the context of future "international" exhibitions over the course of the century in different states,[65] commercial and financial legal relationships would forge even with countries at the periphery of European civilisation in the nineteenth century.[66]

Overtime as exhibitions held across the continent, London would change the dynamics with the 1851 Crystal Palace Fair as it introduced how the Western world got into the era of 'technological innovation and novelty.'[67] Officially titled, "The Great Exhibition of the Works of Industry of all Nations, 1851", the Crystal Palace Fair held on the grounds of Hyde Park London with both 'novel American ideas'[68] and 'British industrial designs'[69] which crystalized the rise of innovation and other technological advancements in the new world society

567–588, 568; Heller, Henry. *The Bourgeois Revolution in France, 1789–1815* (Bergahn Books, 2006) 136–140.

63 For analogy to contemporary debates see Barnett, Jonathan. 'Property as Process: How Innovation Markets Select Innovation Regimes'. *Yale Law Journal* 119(3) (2009) 384–457; Taalbi, Josef. 'What Drives Innovation? Evidence from Economic History'. *Research Policy* 46(8) (2017) 1437–1453; Nordhaus, William D. 'An Economic Theory of Technological Change'. *American Economic Review* 59(2) (1969) 18–28.

64 See Juhasz, Reka. 'Temporary Protection and Technology Adoption: Evidence from the Napoleonic Blockade'. *American Economic Review* 108(11) (2018) 3339–3376 (looking at mechanized technology for example in cotton farming). See also, Rosenberg, Nathan. 'Technological Change in the Machine Tool Industry, 1840–1920'. *Journal of Economic History* 23(4) (1963) 414–443.

65 See Tresch, John. *The Romantic Machine: Utopian Science and Technology After Napoleon* (University of Chicago, 1992).

66 For example, Egypt participated in the 1867 Paris Exposition and a decree authorised its representative to 'initiate laws and regulations for the internal affairs of the country', Firman (Decree) of 8 June 1867, cited in Nour, Alia. 'Egyptian-French Cultural Encounters at the Paris Exposition Universelle of 1867'. *MDCCC 1800 Luglio* (6) (2017) 35–49, note 1.

67 Ferguson, Eugene. 'Expositions of Technology, 1851–1900' in Kranzberg, Melvin and, Pursell, Carroll, eds. *Technology in Western Civilization*, Vol. 1 (Oxford: Oxford University Press, 1967) 706–726.

68 Ibid, 711.

69 Ibid, 712.

of the Victorian era. Although earlier German[70] and French exhibitions would focus on artistic and other creative forms of innovation, the French, by 1889 would wrestle the title of "great exhibition" from the British, where technological advancement was a measure of development. Hence, the 1889 *Universelle Exposition* in Paris that unveiled the Eifel Tower[71] would be a symbol of the technological progress of the nineteenth century exhibitions.

Although the focus of the 1889 Paris Exhibition was quintessentially European and American technological advancements, the presence of non-European states,[72] in particular those that were seen as having affinity to and the ability to reach European status of civilised nations, had a strong presence at the Paris Exhibition of 1889. These were primarily Latin American states which had been given pavilions of prominent exposure next to the Eifel Tower.[73] But the process of securing prestigious pavilions did not come easily, as Latin American nations had to overcome the "otherness" associated to them, when compared to Europeans.[74] Nonetheless, among the technological advancements of the Latin Americans were iron, architecture, glass, and their pavilions sought to convey 'the rationality of technology and the enhancement of decoration and artistic renditions.'[75] The presence of the Latin Americans was however also part of a broader effort in globalising the international rules for "industrial property" which had concluded a few years earlier in 1883 in Paris and the adoption by Latin American countries of a regional version of the Paris Convention, in 1889 in Montevideo (discuss further below). Arguably, the prominence of the Latin Americans at the Paris Exhibition of 1889 was part of

70 Davis, John. 'Representation, Rivalry and Transfer: The German States and 1862 Exhibition'. *Journal of the Decorative Arts Society 1850–Present* 38(2014) 162–177.

71 See Adcock, Michael. 'The 1889 Paris Exposition: Mapping the Colonial Mind'. *Context* 22(2001) 31–40, 35 questioning how, for example, 'music represented in its displays?' See also, Mainardi, Patricia. *Art and Politics of the Second Empire: The Universal Expositions of 1855 and 1867* (Yale University Press, 1987); Berthier-Foglar, Susanne. 'The 1889 World Exhibition in Paris: The French, the Age of Machines, and the Wild West'. *Nineteenth-Century Contexts* 31(2) (2009) 129–142.

72 Egypt, Japan and Latin America for example were well represented at the 1889 Paris Exhibition, see Patrick Young, 'From the Eiffel Tower to the Javanese Dancer: Envisioning Cultural Globalisation at the 1889 Paris Exhibition'. *History Teacher* 41(3) (2008) 339–362, 348 (discussing some of the colonial presence).

73 Uslenghi, Alesjandra. *Latin America at the Fin-De-Siecle Universal Exhibitions: Modern Cultures of Visuality* (Basingstoke: Palgrave, 2016), 108.

74 Ibid, 116: 'The rules of recognition within the cosmopolitan space of the exposition obliged the Latin American exhibits to engage in a complex process of negotiation that involved otherness as well as an ambivalent relation to the overwhelming criteria of universality through which national representation is always performed and materialized.'

75 Ibid, 128.

a mission to civilise through innovation diplomacy and globalizing the rules for such innovation (discuss further below). Such efforts were remarkably different from how Europeans interacted with other peripheral nation states such as those from Africa.[76]

The Paris Exhibition of 1889 was in some ways a battle between French and American technological advancements.[77] Though colonial people were present at the exhibition as exhibits themselves, in 1889, unlike previous exhibitions,[78] colonial people were no longer "exotic", rather, it was the age of inventions and technology. For the French, the unveiled Eiffel Tower would usher in 'the inventive capacities of man'[79] and honoured Thomas Edison, who had by 1889 accumulated more than three hundred patents, with his own building on the exhibition grounds.

But despite the shadow of the Eiffel Tower and the magic of Edison's light on the grounds of the 1889 Exhibition complex, the colonial exotics,[80] who were grouped into designated zones, were in some ways, representing geographical territories needed for the internationalisation of the rules that would govern the new inventions displayed at Paris in 1889. The rules for internationalisation was only taking shape in the adopted Paris Convention of 1883. But the combination of those rules and norms and practices from the previous exhibitions suggests that regulatory norms goes beyond industrial property but others for artistic and literary works given that to a great extent, France displayed in 1889 various cultural, visual arts and music items to cement its 'rapid colonial expansion during the early Third Republic.'[81] The basis for protection for those industrial innovation (and or literary and artistic works) at the international level were the two instruments that were signed by civilised states, to include,

76 This was part of a broader pattern where Europeans in the nineteenth-century would justify various actions towards non-Europeans as part of a civilisation standard, but see Linklater, Andrew. 'The Standard of Civilisations in World Politics'. *Social Character and Historical Processes* 5(2) (2016); Suzuki, S. *Civilization and Empire: China and Japan's Encounter with European International Society* (Abingdon: Routledge, 2009); Bowden, Bret. 'The Colonial Origins of International Law: European Expansion and the Classical Standard of Civilization'. *Journal of the History of International Law* 7(1) (2005) 1–24; Ledger, Sally, and McCracken, Scott. *Cultural Politics at the Fin de Siecle* (Cambridge: Cambridge University Press, 1995).

77 Berthier-Foglar, 'The 1889 World Exhibition in Paris' (n. 71).

78 Nour, Alia. 'Egyptian-French Cultural Encounters' (n. 66).

79 Berthier-Foglar (n. 71) 132.

80 For one, the colonial peoples or 'infant race' were not grouped with the 'refinements of an older civilization' where 'the white/western races occupied the buildings of the technical and artistic exhibits' and been relegated to empty spaces of 'mock foreign settings' for entertainment purposes, ibid, 137.

81 Adcock, 'The 1889 Paris Exposition' (n. 71) 40.

acceptable civilised nations, in 1883 and 1888 for international industrial property and literary and artistic works.[82]

Hence, it was easy for Europeans to accept the "otherness" of Latin America as sharing some affinity with European civilisations and could play a crucial role in globalizing the standards established in the Paris Convention in 1883. For a start, the few non-European countries that signed the Paris Convention in 1883 were to a degree, extracts of civilised nations or acceptable, from the point of view of Europeans. Those from the hinterlands, or those in Africa and parts of Asia-Pacific were not part of the society of innovative nations. Rather, they were the original source of major material necessary to drive innovation and industrialization in Europe and also to partly consume the end products.

Secondly, the *intellectual* capacities of the inhabitants in the hinterlands were also to be nurtured with other forms literary and artistic works (not the object of this discussion in this chapter).[83] But as producers, the hinterlands were also in need of technological advancement in order for Western powers to expand their production/source capacity or protect investments with military technology, and importantly, for their technological inventions to be protected within the territorial boundaries of the different colonial possessions.

By the 1880s, European civilisation had had impressive economic growth, output and industrialization, and it was time to look to new lands to both partitioned and spread the virtues of European lawmaking. While the former played out in Africa, the latter process of lawmaking or treatification was encouraged in Latin America. As international expositions held more often and in more places – so too were their relevance for how law and regulation would respond to the display of advance technologies and how the international legal implications would be addressed.

The technological changes brought by the (third) industrial revolution (circa 1870–1920)[84] and other advances in science and innovation would pose challenges to the law of nations. This was most evident by how the newly created International Law Association attempted to codify intellectual property law.[85] Another reason was the fact that technology and the associated impact on global law at the turn of the twentieth century were closely interconnected.

82 Paris and Berne Conventions.

83 But see Acquah, in this collection.

84 But see Bottomley, Sean. *The British Patent System During the Industrial Revolution 1700–1852: From Privilege to Property* (Cambridge: Cambridge University Press, 2014).

85 See Field (n. 44); Wise, Lloyd. 'Assimilation of the Laws and Practice of Various Nations in Relation to the Protection of Inventions: A paper read at the Conference of the Association for the Reform and Codification of the Law of Nations, at the Hague, September 1875'. (London: JW Last & Co., 1875).

Naturally, such relationship goes way back, however, the efforts to associate technological developments and other advances in science and innovation were only set in stone through treaties such as Paris, Berne and regional conventions such as Montevideo on "industrial property" broadly. Thus, the shift to the *treatification* of innovation as such encouraged how international law and technology evolved.[86]

The (third) industrial revolution was also pivotal for how technology evolved and the role of the individual inventor in securing legal protection and or economic benefit for their novel technological solutions. Legal protection was crucial to how inventions and other 'engineering achievements' could be patentable.[87] The move toward the *treatification* of innovations and the need for comparable domestic laws such as those on patents, copyrights and other industrial property during the late nineteenth century was because the rise of international exhibitions although with good intentions – had produce a paradox. The paradox was that "inventions" and other "innovations" that were on display at such exhibitions became "old" and inventors and other industrialists could no longer pass on their inventions as "new".[88] Thus, a growing body of private merchants and creators began to lobby for the international protection of their industrial innovations and creations.

3 International Exhibitions and Private Merchants' Quest for Protecting Literary Works

In parts of the earlier discussion it was argued how the rise of international exhibitions and their importance to trade and commercial relations with the host states and with external states was in part based on tact and lobbying. This would further increased by the time the private merchants of industrial innovation met at Vienna in 1873. Such efforts, as described in this chapter as innovation diplomacy necessary require the participation of private market

86 See Lachs, Manfred. 'Thoughts on Science, Technology and World Law'. *American Journal of International Law* 86(4) (1992) 673–699; Dellapenna, Joseph. 'Law in a Shrinking World: The Interaction of Science and Technology with International Law'. *Kentucky Law Journal* 88(4) (2000) 809–884.

87 Rae, John. 'The Invention of Invention' in Kranzberg, Melvin, and Pursell, Carroll, eds. *Technology in Western Civilization, Vol. I* (Oxford: Oxford University Press, 1967) 325, 326.

88 See similar discussions in Moser, Petra. 'How Do Patent Laws Influence Innovation? Evidence from Nineteenth Century World's Fairs'. *American Economic Review* 95(4) (2005) 1214–1236.

actors and inventors who could lobby through their networks for legal arrangements protecting inventions displayed at international exhibitions.

As international exhibitions gained popularity and became a staple of major European capitals during the late Victorian era – foreign exhibitors such as those from North America began to raise concern about the appropriation of their inventions that were on display.[89] Moreover, a number of European creators and inventors were also worried about their creative works in books and industrial inventions not being sufficiently protected in foreign lands. Two particular movements would help to transform the protection of intellectual property in the international system: the *Congress Litteraire et Artistisque Internationale*, later becoming *Association Litteraire et Artistique Internationle* (ALAI), and for broadly industrial property, the International Association for the Protection of Intellectual Property (AIPPI). These non-state actors would trigger a process in the international system that dilutes the state centric approach to lawmaking.[90]

For brevity, I will only use the ALAI for demonstrative purposes in the discussions here, before turning to patent laws as such further below. Thus, if one could argue that civilised states such as Great Britain, France, Germany, Switzerland, Belgium, and Spain along with *uncivilised* states such as Liberia, Haiti and Tunisia were responsible for the first global intellectual property treaty on artistic works in 1886, then ALAI, as a non-state actor was equally responsible. The fruit of ALAI's success was in the diplomatic conferences and congresses on copyrights and artistic works held in 1878,[91] 1883,[92] 1884,[93] 1885[94] and 1886 that eventually lead to the Berne Convention.[95]

From a legal standpoint, perhaps, it was the unwillingness of nations in the 1850s to follow the French unilateral protection of foreign works in a decree that has since relegated to the footnotes of history that in some ways gave impetus

89 Most international exhibitions would attempt or at least temporarily introduce legal protection for inventions that were on display, see (UK), Bill to Extend the Provisions of the Design Act, 1850, and to Give Protection from Piracy to Persons Exhibiting New Inventions in the Exhibition of the Works of Industry of All Nations in 1851.

90 See also, Alexander, Isabella. *Copyright Law and the Public Interest in the Nineteenth Century* (Oxford/Portland: Hart Publishing, 2010) 147 (discussing interest groups).

91 International Literary Congress, Paris 1878.

92 International Literary and Artistic Association, Berne 1883.

93 Diplomatic Conference, Berne 1884 (excluding the participation of the United States).

94 Official Conference, Berne, 1885.

95 Berne Convention for the Protection of Literary and Artistic Works, 9 September 1886, 828 UNTS 221; *see also*, Hemmungs Wirten, Eva. 'A Diplomatic Salto Mortale: Translation Trouble in Berne, 1884–1886'. *Book History* 14 (2011) 88–109.

to how private actors would lobby for global regulation in the 1870s–1880s.[96] The French issued a decree on 28 March 1852 that allowed for the protection of foreign works, albeit, without any reciprocity. A number of states avoided following in the French footsteps. The 1852 French Copyright Decree established one of the most fundamental principle in the law of nations in as much as it apply to the protection of intellectual property: national treatment. The unilateral action lead to an increase in bilateral treaties that offers reciprocity, including the Cobden-Chevalier Treaty.[97]

Bilateral treaties are strategic in that they provide for reciprocal duties and national treatment. As a progressive treaty in the 1860s, the Cobden-Chevalier Treaty was the envy of the rest of the modern nation states. France, therefore, had good reasons to extend its network of "global protection" (including for copyrights) with other European nations.[98] Thus, in France, and other nations, which France, had bilateral treaties with, authors and other creators could enjoy the same rights they had in their own countries. The law of nations, according to one nineteenth-century observer would now include patents, property and other artistic works: 'Art demands that the property in its inventions should be secured by an international law of patents. Literature, that the property in its works should be secured by international copyright' giving rise to the 'the law of nations.'[99] This observation also demonstrate the difficulties with providing protection for literary and artistic works outside of formal legal relations among nations, given that other nations laws could be applied extraterritorially. Hence, the network of bilateral treaties among the different nations, such as France, the UK, and Germany among others was one way of demonstrating how the stability of the international legal system could be secured.[100] This was to ensure that commerce flowed unhindered, and at the same time, laying the ground work for how national laws pertaining to copyright would further develop to include questions relating to literary and artistic works.

96 French Decree 1852.

97 See generally discussions in (n. 5).

98 Other European nations were also forming treaty relationships with non-European nations such as El Salvador for example, and the Spain-El Salvador Treaty of 1884 is one such. See Belido, Jose, Xalabarder, Raquel, and Casas, Ramon. Commentary on Bilateral Copyright Treaty between Spain and El Salvador (1884); Belido, Jose. 'Colonial Copyright Extensions: Spain at the Berne Conventions (1883–1889)'. *Journal of the Copyright Society of the USA* 58(2) (2011) 243–264.

99 Copinger, Walter Arthur. *The Law of Copyright in Works of Literature and Art: Including that of the Drama, Third Edition* (London: Stevens and Haynes, 1892) 565.

100 For general discussions on bilateral treaties in the late nineteenth-century see Lampe, Markus. 'Explaining Nineteenth-Century Bilateralism: Economic and Political Determinants of the Cobden-Chevalier Network'. *Economic History Review* 64(2) (2011) 644–668.

Yet, it was the efforts of some early campaigners of "human rights" including rights of authors lead by Victor Hugo (1802–1885) and other literary merchants that eventually lead to the Berne Convention. Those efforts, largely through the ALAI represented the market direction of literary work, where authors, composers and literary artists would not only benefit from international protection but also in a position to secure the economic rewards.

The ALAI from the start had been a European initiative and meetings would take place in various continental capitals. These meetings were part of an effort to contribute to the development of global rules for literary and artistic protection. Because only states were, and, still are, at the forefront of making international law, the ALAI as a non-state entity would therefore only be that of being in the driving role.[101] The ALAI's role was central as through it Victor Hugo demonstrated how influential non-state actors have been in the creation of international law by exerting and/or lobbying for the global protection of artistic and literary rights.

Another argument is that the ALAI, as led by Hugo, had other "merchant networks" among its ranks whose interests whether as literary agents, publishers or financial concerns required not only global protection but evidence of tangible economic returns. Hence, the presence of ALAI conferences and congresses in the different capitals was in part to marshal the support of the various members of ALAI and their merchant networks. In this context, one could make the further argument that the ALAI is the institutional backbone of the Berne Convention given that firstly, they achieved part of their original goal as embodied in the Berne Convention. Secondly, the Berne Convention helps to promote development in the literary and artistic innovation. Hence, while literary and artistic producers were encouraged to produce more and their works could now be freely available in other countries at an economic rate – the Berne Convention became how the merchant networks enticed other countries to benefit from the diffusion of knowledge.

Furthermore, if the knowledge networks was limited to only ALAI members, the use of exhibitions in the Victorian era that showcased innovation and other "modern marvels" of industrial advancement help to advance the language of rights protection in both the domestic and international legal system at the time. This was reflected in the multiplicity of domestic laws concerning

---

101 But see Karnell, Gunnar. 'ALAI – Initiator and Berne Copyright Convention Watch-Dog – Viewed from a Personal and Slightly Nordic Perspective' in Karnell, Gunnar et al., eds. *Liber Amicorum Jan Rosen* (Eddy.Se Ab, 2016) 414–415 noting: 'Between 1879 and 1886, the year of birth of the Berne Convention, ALAI held congress in London 1879, Lisbon 1880, Vienna 1881, Rome 1882, Conference in Berne and Congress in Amsterdam 1883, Congresses in Brussels 1884, Antwerp 1885 and Geneva 1886.'

copyrights, patents and trademarks and flourished from 1870–1911 in countries such as France, Germany, the US, UK and other jurisdictions.[102] Moreover, as earlier discussed, the Paris and Berne Conventions that emerged in the 1880s was also due to the role played by private merchants and their language of rights protection that served as a useful rhetorical device in the industrial property movement during the 1870s and 1880s which eventually produced profound changes in international intellectual property protection.

To the extent, that private merchants engaged in sustained efforts for the global protection of private rights or their industrial creativity during this era is remarkable as it speaks volume to how industrial innovation was crucial for the economic development of those countries. Yet, although most of the early exhibitions were only "international" in name, in that, few other foreign countries participated, by the late nineteenth century, when more and more foreign countries participated in larger exhibitions, a common criticism has been that inventions and other creative works were not sufficiently protected.[103] Yet, it was those criticisms that propelled the new global regulatory space for intellectual property and allow industrial innovation to strive and drive the economic development of states while promoting international trade and international law.

The lack of sufficient legal protection for intellectual property rights on a global scale (and the effects on the US in the 1880s) where the US was often seen as 'a copyright haven' for over century[104] help fuelled domestic rules on copyright. With the enactment of the Chace Act of 1891 in the US providing protection for international works, the ALAI network, which had been crusading for international legislations, could now relay to their authors how to reap the economic returns on their creative and literary works. The *Chace Act* would become critical to the rise of domestic copyright laws in many countries (the Americans would later signed up to the Berne Convention, albeit a century later in 1988) and this would add a sense of legitimacy for the protection of creative works within the major powers of the latter nineteenth century.

The global transformation of intellectual property protection was not only an incentive for inventors and creators to focus more on producing but it was also a gateway for another era in technological revolution where focus on new forms of technology and drug development would transform the economic

---

102 But see Acquah in this collection for discussions in the colonial context.

103 See earlier discussion at (n. 88).

104 Nimmer, David. 'Nation, Duration, Violation, Harmonization: An International Copyright Proposal for the United States'. *Law and Contemporary Problems* 55(2) (1992) 211–239, 212.

development of most countries.[105] Within the formal protection of industrial property was the promotion of knowledge and innovation that would developed simultaneously with professional representations in international law[106] and industrial property through patent and trademark attorneys.[107] Another observation is the fact that several other international conventions relating to industrial property would develop starting with the revisions of the Paris Convention,[108] and new conventions such as Madrid[109] and Brussels Convention to Pan American efforts on international conventions in the early twentieth century through to the 1920s.[110]

4 The Relation of Innovation to the Law of Nations

Earlier chapters in this collection (Duncan and Thumfart)[111] have set out vividly the internationalisation of patents in the early 1870s and thus, while the notion of innovation diplomacy is inextricably linked to this period, I want to frame in the next two paragraphs the internationalisation of innovation in relation to the law of nations from two defining features: national parliamentary debates and an emerging international legal order where non-state actors and individuals would become central to international law-making. I will start with the latter, that is the emerging international legal order in the 1870s and the role of non-state actors as a necessity and their participation in international law.

The Vienna Fair and subsequent Patent Congress of 1873 was largely the move toward the internationalisation of innovation. Both events were in part, a diplomatic victory for states and non-state actors. The industrialists and their supporters saw the need for internationalisation as part of an overriding objective to promote free trade and access to 1870s global markets. At the heart of that objective, the industrialists believed, should be the protection of patents under the law of nations: an international treaty. States shared that belief too

105 See Hagen, Antje. 'Patents Legislation and German FDI in the British Chemical Industry before 1914'. *The Business History Review* 71(3) (1997) 351–380; Brown, Julie. *Health and Medicine on Display: International Expositions in the United States, 1876–1904* (The MIT Press, 2009).

106 Eg, the International Law Association (n. 44).

107 Eg, formation of the German GRUR and the American INTA in the 1890s.

108 Brussels Act (1900) revising the Paris Convention.

109 Madrid Agreement for the Repression of False or Deceptive Indications of Source on Goods, 1890.

110 On the latter see Ladas, Stephen. 'Pan-American Conventions on Industrial Property'. *American Journal of International Law* 22(4) (1928) 803–821.

111 Chapters 1–2 in this collection.

and gravitated toward the need for more patent laws in the major economies of the 1870s.

The participation of the industrialists in forming and advocating a narrative for the protection of innovation at the international level would see them as emerging non-state participants in the international legal system along with the early professional international law societies. Thus, the industrialists of the 1870s found themselves between the shifting structures of the law of nations. This was in part due to the fact that after the Franco-Prussian War of 1871 a new form of international law began to emerge where the *natural law* features of the law of nations started to give way to *positive law* features.[112] Secondly, substantial efforts were being made by individuals with the formation of international societies such as the *Institut de Droit* to frame a new dimension of international law.[113] Significantly, the need for international treaties to protect the industrial property of individuals and the state-to-state protection of industrial property was critical.

The two treaties of 1883 on copyrights and the 1886 Treaty on industrial property would result in the international efforts for the general protection of innovation as such under the law of nations.[114] The 1886 Berne Convention for example, had already set out that 'exhibition' as such was subject to protection, while the Paris Convention similarly focuses on invention. International exhibitions had produce the need for not only the market for new inventions but also how protecting innovations and the associated rights would test the boundaries of domestic patent laws that were on the rebound in the 1870s in European states but also how the international legal system would respond to such protection. The use of international exhibitions to promote the need for international legal protection was by no means the only caveat toward the international protection of innovations but such exhibitions accelerated the efforts, and Vienna 1873 and Paris 1878 would bear testimony.

The Vienna exhibition and later Patent Congress of 1873[115] was key to usher in the industrialists of the 1870s as participants in the international legal

112 For arguments on the 'natural law' features of international law see Schall, 'Natural Law and the Law of Nations' (n. 27); in relation to 'natural law' and intellectual property rights, this is mostly based Lockean interpretations, but see Hughes, Justin. 'The Philosophy of Intellectual Property'. *Georgetown Law Journal* 77(2) (1988) 287–366; and for more recent discussions, see Morris, P. Sean. 'The Contemporary Ideological Legitimacy of Global Intellectual Property Rights'. *Intellectual Property Quarterly* 2006(1) 44–73.

113 Hambro, Edvard. 'The Centenary of the Institut de Droit International'. *Nordisk Tidsskrift for International Ret* 43(1–4) (1973) 9–17.

114 But see Duncan, in this collection.

115 See, Document, Universal Exhibition 1873 in Vienna, International Congress for the Consideration of Patent Protection, National Archives, Washington DC, Letters Received Concerning Patents (Box 82).

system. Yet, changes in the law of nations as such was also taking place. A radical new world image of international relations emerged after the Franco-Prussian War of 1871 and, so too, were the need for international legal rules to represent accurately the new international relations.

Industrial property owners never lost sight of the new world image and they concentrated their efforts in designing and pushing for protection of innovations and inventions both at the domestic and international level. They were equally concerned about inventions that were on display at international exhibitions and sought to ensure that such inventions would enjoy (legal) protection. Industrial property owners were traders, merchants and industrialists in the general sense of these terms and the market for their goods and inventions were beyond their domestic borders. Thus, they had to look to *foreign* lands to increase sales volumes and display their inventions. Thus, the international recognition of their industrial property rights would be paramount to the extent they can trade and display their wares in lands far afield. Bilateral treaties in areas such as trademarks[116] were already driving the consensus for the protection of inventions in other areas at the international level and was a necessity.

The industrialists that met at Vienna in 1873 were equally concerned about the similar treaties that offers protection for innovations (some industrialists with substantial inventions refused to participate in the 1873 Vienna Exhibition[117]). The fact that a number of European nations in the latter part of the nineteenth century did not have valid patent laws or suspended their patent laws would also embolden the industrialists at Vienna in 1873 to move towards facilitating the dialogues and efforts for new international rules. States such as Switzerland and the Netherlands had a rocky relationship with domestic patent laws during the era as they either suspended their domestic laws on patents or failed to enact new laws for patent protection.[118] The Vienna Exhibition and Patent Congress of 1873 was, therefore, in part, consist of efforts to ensure that patent protection both in the domestic and international

116 In the case of the UK, see eg, UK-Russia Treaty of 11 July 1871; Treaty Stipulations Between Great Britain and Foreign Powers on the Subject of Trade Marks (1872) (C. 693) 54 *Parliamentary Papers* 673.

117 The Americans also were quite hesitant in participating, see some discussions in Susan Sell, 'Intellectual Property and Public Policy in Historical Perspective: Contestation and Settlement'. *Loyola Los Angeles Law Review* 38(1) (2004) 267–322, 282. The eventual participation of the Americans in the Vienna Exhibition was successful, see Charles, Francis Adams. *Commissioner of the State of Massachusetts, Report of the Vienna Exhibition* (Boston, 1874).

118 See Doorman, Gerard. 'Patent Law in the Netherlands – Suspended in 1869 and Re-established in 1910 – Part II'. *Journal of the Patent Office and Society* 30(4) (1948) 258–271.

legal sphere would emerge. Doorman, for example, characterised the Vienna Exhibition of 1873 as follows:

> In 1873 a World Fair was to be held in Vienna. America was prepared to participate, but it was feared that by doing so a number of inventions would become known without their being protected. In order to meet this objection, the Austrian Government saw its to carry through a legal provision by which everything in the Exhibition would be afforded a temporary protection, which afterwards, on application, could be superseded by a patent with a term of 15 years. Further, the wish was expressed to table the question of international patent protection.[119]

Although the Paris Convention would eventually be drafted in 1880 and took effect in 1884, the events at Vienna in 1873 had pave the way towards international protection of innovation through the *universal act of protection* the Austro-Hungary government enacted as it covered foreign inventors as well as domestic inventions.

Another part of the narrative in relation to the changes in the law of nations in the 1870s would see how by 1878 building on the success of the 1873 Exhibition and Patent Congress, the full move toward an international treaty in explicit terms through the Paris Exhibition of 1878 and related side activities on patent reform. Building on the success of the 1873 Vienna exhibition and Patent Congress, where among other things, reforming and enacting patent laws were discussed, the state representatives and industrialists that met in Paris in 1878 for a similar exhibition and Congress produced a draft document for the international protection of patents.[120] The 1878 Paris Exhibition and Congress was more positive towards internationalisation of patent protection. From the 1878 Paris Exhibition and Congress the groundwork for negotiation an international legal instrument was set to prepare the formal meetings and drafting process for what would ultimately become the 1883 Paris Convention. Starting with a French proposal in 1878 shortly after the Paris Exhibition in 1878 through to the final version adopted in 1883.[121]

The second argument that I want to briefly point out has to do with the debates in national legislature relating to patent reform (with global implications) in the 1870s. For the purposes of the discussions here, I will rely mostly

---

119 Doorman, ibid, 259.

120 Reports of the United States Commissioners to the Paris Universal Exhibition of 1878 (Washington, 1880, 5 vols.), I.

121 But see, Duncan, in this collection.

on the debates in the British Parliament. This is primarily for practical purposes and the fact that those debates are readily available through parliamentary scripts (*Hansard*). Compare to the other developments in the 1870s, such as the 1873 Vienna Patent Congress, where industrialists as non-actors were heavily involved in the discussions, parliamentary debates are purely from states perspectives. And this allow for comparisons in some form to be made when interests collide with those of the industrialists.

Yet, perhaps, one of the significance of connecting the English parliamentary debates to innovation and the law of nations in the 1870s (late nineteenth century) has to do with the occurrence or increasingly clash of the different patent laws of different countries when the courts were called upon to adjudicate a patent infringement which had international implications. For example, the UK courts would see the patent with international implications as based on certain 'principle of interpretation'[122]; and, conversely, the US would view patent laws in England as something akin to a 'royal favour.' This was notably in *McKeever v United States* where the US Supreme Court argued that 'a patent in England was nothing more than a grant dependent in contemplation of law upon royal flavour.'[123] This observation came against the backdrop of the events of 1878 of the Paris Congress and Exhibition as starting points for an international treaty.

The industrialists of the 1870s, would of course, had more sympathy for the *McKeeerian* language of 'private property' rights as more succinct than 'royal favor' but the debates in the English parliament barely drew any distinction. For instance, during the debates on the Patents for Inventions Bill (1876), the Commons (lower house of parliament) was primarily concerned with 'fees' and 'specifications.'[124] But one of the more important moment during the UK parliamentary debates as the rise of innovation in the law of nations regarding the events of 1873 and the international exhibition in Vienna concerned the official representation of the British Government.[125] The issue of representation

---

122 E.g., Anglo-American Brush Electric Light Corporation v King, Brown & Co., UKHL 5, April 1892. For some discussion see, Stathis Arapostathis, 'Contested Inventors: British Patent Disputes and the Culture of Invention in the Late Nineteenth Century' in Araposthais, Stathis, and Dutfield, Graham, eds. *Knowledge Management and Intellectual Property: Concepts, Actors and Practices from the Past to the Present* (Cheltenham: Edward Elgar, 2013) 145–161.

123 McKeever v United States, 14 S.Ct. CL. 396, 420–21 (1878).

124 Patents for Inventions Bill (1876), Second reading.

125 Hansard, Patent Rights – International Conference, Vienna. – Question. HC Deb 31 July 1873 vol. 217 c1328, on whether a certain 'Mr. Webster, Q.C. has been authorised' to represent the British Government, and also, in another debate the issue of "Mr Webster" was raise, Hansard, Patent Rights-International Conference, Vienna. – Question, HC

was even more fascinating given that 'the Patent Laws in foreign countries' would need to be examined by the British Parliament.[126]

In terms of the Paris Exhibition of 1878, the Parliamentary debates were a mixture of procedural and the extent the UK would offer support for participants.[127] The debates reflected, few if any matters on the implications for international legal relations[128] (and, perhaps beyond belief, on the jurisdiction of cattle for slaughter) at the Paris Exhibition.[129]

By highlighting some of the debates that took place in the House of Commons on the events of 1873 and 1878, their character, from an international perspective was no doubt about how state relations on matters that were driven in part by industrialists and *artizans* became central to the internationalisation of innovation and diplomacy. Yet, these historical and practical descriptives of the parliamentary debates[130] suggests that the development of international rules and by 1883 the Paris Convention had been a clear goal for all parties: states and the industrialists of the 1870s.

It is also hugely significant to understand that the parliamentary debates clearly showed that interests of the states and those of private industrialists were one and/or the same, if one interprets the struggle over who was the official representative of the British government at the Vienna Congress in 1873. But the larger issue is that it is necessary to place the relation of innovation to the law of nations within the paradigm of the subsequent international treaty in 1883. As the efforts accelerated from 1873 to 1878, and the emergence

Deb 05 August 1873 vol. 217 c1564, and it was believed that Webster had been authorised to represent the 'Patent Law Commission at the International Patent Law Congress of Vienna.' There was also doubts as to whether the 'conference' would take place during exhibition, Hansard, Patent Laws-International Conference, Vienna. – Question, HC Deb 14 July 1873 vol. 217 cc310–1 'a conference among the Exhibition Commissioners on the subject had been mooted. It did not appear that that was to be a conference of an official or international character, and the Austro-Hungarian Government did not ask for any suggestions upon the subject,' 331. See also, Hansard, Patent Rights-International Conference. – Question, HC Deb 07 April 1878 vol. 215 c636 on earlier debates on the doubts of the conference taking place.

126 Hansard, Patent Rights – International Conference. – Question. HC Deb 07 April 1873 vol. 215 c636.

127 Hansard, The Paris Exhibition, 1878 – Assistance to English Artizans, HC Deb 16 May 1878 vol. 240 cc27–8.

128 See also, Report of the Vienna Exhibition of 1873, Vol. I–IV (23 July 1874); Report for the Paris Universal Exhibition of 1878, Vol. I–II (3rd June 1880).

129 Hansard, The Paris Exhibition – English Cattle. – Questions, HC Deb 27 June 1878 vol. 241 cc329–30.

130 For a general bibliographic metric of papers see Johnson, Philip. *Parliament, Invention and Patents: A Research Guide and Bibliography* (Abingdon: Routledge, 2018).

of a draft treaty in 1880 and subsequent adoption in 1883 those events were underpinned by both diplomacy and the clear needs of protecting innovation at the international level.

5 Patent Laws and the Mission to Civilise: Innovation in Regional Treaties

As innovative and inventive creations became popular at exhibitions and the emergence of the Paris and Berne Conventions as the capping of legalization efforts at the international level to protect inventions and creations, so too were the rise of patent laws in particular. In one sense, the popularity of exhibitions and the emergence of the international conventions in the 1880s contributed to the rise of patent laws that in some ways legalized innovation. Or to put it another way, the protection of patents under the domestic laws of states that emerged in the late Victorian era throughout Europe and some other parts of the world gave innovators the legal protection for their inventions, some of which would have first shown at exhibitions. As one observer put it:

> Americans were also concerned about the potential for intellectual piracy of their exhibits at the World's Fairs that were an important venue for commercialization of innovations. Indeed, the first international patent convention was held in the Austro-Hungarian Empire in 1873, at the suggestion of US policymakers who wanted to be certain that American technologies would be adequately protected at the International Exposition in Vienna that year.[131]

The fear of the Americans regarding the appropriation of inventions was not without merit, as the First Congress enacted The Patent Act of 1790.[132] Thus, since then Americans were well versed seeking legal remedies for possible

---

131 Khan, Zorina. 'One for All? The American Patent System and Harmonization of International Intellectual Property Laws' in Gooday, Graeme, and Wilf, Steven, eds. *Patent Cultures: Diversity and Harmonization in Historical Perspective* (Cambridge: Cambridge University Press, CUP 2020) 85, also citing, Tilton Penrose, Edith. *The Economics of the International Patent System* (John Hopkins Press, 1951). For discussions on the 1873 Vienna Congress, see Hildebrandt, A. translation of Hermann Grothe's Report, *The International Patent Congress in Vienna 1873* (London: Simpkin Marchsall & Co., 1875).

132 Patent Act of 1790, Ch. 7, 1 Stat. 109–112 (10 April 1790). See also, Walterscheid, Edward. 'The Early Evolution of the United States Patent Law: Antecedents (Part 1)'. *Journal of the Patent and Trademark Office Society* 76(9) (1994) 697–715.

appropriation of their property. But their role in the rise of patent laws is not the concern here.[133] Although, as indicated above[134] how concerned the Americans were during the exhibitions of their inventions overseas, patentization had a greater mission: *civilising*. Europeans were equally concerned about the protection of innovations and so the efforts for the Paris Convention on industrial property began in earnest. It must be said that prior to the 1880s, the rise of domestic patent laws were already taking shape in some parts of the world, or at least reforms to make patents cheap and competitive upon application.[135] So from the 1850s onwards, beginning with English patent law of 1852[136] patent reforms (or even abolition) were taking shape and culminated to changes in patent laws of different countries up to the early twentieth century.[137] But by the turn of the twentieth century, it was also a period in which international exhibitions of a grand level were waning.

The domestic laws or reforms of existing laws that the Paris Convention accelerated were in the advanced economies of Europe which had been going through the second industrial revolution.[138] The industrial revolution of the late nineteenth century was one of technological revolutions and laws as a tool of ensuring that such technological revolutions were not remove from the reward system of financial gains. Hence, the relationship between the "new" patent laws after the Paris Convention concerned how on the one hand, the state grant of "property" to private inventors that produce "public goods" would take shape, and, on the other, a modernisation of legislations that represents technological change. Thus, even countries that were at the periphery of technological change began to see improvements as a result of technological

---

133 But see, Hovenkamp, Herbert. 'The Emergence of Classical American Patent Law'. *Arizona Law Review* 58(2) (2016) 263–307.

134 Khan (n. 131).

135 This chapter is not concerned with the developments of patent laws prior to 1860. See MacLeod, Christine. 'The Paradoxes of Patenting: Invention and Its Diffusion in 18th and 19th Century Britain, France and North America'. *Technology and Cultures* 32(4) (1991) 885–910.

136 Patent Law Amendment Act of 1852 (UK). For the English, The Great Exhibition of 1851 helped spur amendments to the patent laws that ushered in the 1851 Act, later reforms in 1852 and 1855, which, by this time, 'stirred up a ferment of controversy'. See MacLeod, Christine. *Heroes of Invention: Technology, Liberalism and British Identity, 1750–1914* (Cambridge: Cambridge University Press, 2007) 3.

137 Patent Act (Sweden) (Amendment) (1914): 153–154. But see, Andersson, David, and Tell, Fredrik. 'Fighting Monopolies to Promoting Industry: Patent Laws and Innovation in Sweden 1819–1914'. *Jahrbuch fur Wirtschaftgeschichte* 60(1) (2019) 123–156.

138 See also, Burhop, Carsten, and Wolf, Nikolaus. 'The German Market for Patents During the "Second Industrialization," 1884–1913: A Gravity Approach'. *Business History Review* 87(1) (2013) 69–93.

change and the role of patent laws during the second industrial revolution.[139] At the other end, some of the more advanced countries, or at least the recently unified countries such as Germany and Italy were reaping the benefits that patents had on industrialization.[140] It was during this time that Germany became one of the most successful nation to grant patents, rivalling the US, and during the process, sow the seeds for technological roots of patent harmonization in Europe (and by extent efforts at a global level).[141]

The introduction of the German Patent Act of 1877 was one of few substantial domestic laws that emerged out of the 1880s international patent convention.[142] The German Patent Act of 1877 provided for among other things, a revocation after three years 'if the patentee fails to put his patent to use to a reasonable extent within the country.'[143] The provision also made it possible for competitive innovation and allowed for other innovators to put to use their inventions. Although there are a number of empirical evidence that points to how German firms capitalized on the Patent Act of 1877 in its early years to file for patent, studies also showed how firms were concerned 'about

139 See Andersson, David, Galaso, Pablo, and Saiz, Patricio. 'Patent Collaboration Networks in Sweden and Spain During the Second Industrial Revolution'. *Industry and Innovation* 26(9) (2019) 1075–1102. It must however be said, that other countries essential to the new global patent system that emerged out of the Paris Convention did not have patent laws at the time the Convention was sign, most notably, Switzerland, although, the situation changed in 1888 with the introduction of the Swiss Patent Law, see Dominique Ritter, 'Switzerland's Patent Law History'. *Fordham Intellectual Property, Media and Entertainment Law Journal* 14(2) (2004) 463–496, 476. And even prior to the Swiss debacle on patent laws, the Netherlands, took a radical step in 1869 to abolish patents as part of an ideological experiment to boost free trade, see further discussions in Moser (n. 88) 1229; Doorman (n. 118).

140 Empirical evidence from the economic literature suggests that Italy benefited from the rise of patenting during the second industrialization period, see Nuvolari, Alessandro and Vasta, Michelango. 'The Geography of Innovation in Italy, 1861–1913: Evidence from Patent Data'. *European Review of Economic History* 21(3) (2017) 326–356.

141 For arguments on the latter point of harmonization in Europe see e.g., Pila, Justine. 'The European Patent: An Old and Vexing Problem'. *International & Comparative Law Quarterly* 62(4) (2013) 917–940; Jorge Cruz, 'The Community Patent Convention: What Sort of Future?'. *Journal of World Intellectual Property* 1(5) (1998) 819–826.

142 Patent Act (*Patentgesetz*) of 25 May 1877. For some background on the 1877 Act *see e.g.*, Schuster, Ernest. 'The New German Patent Act'. *Law Quarterly Review* 8(1) (1892) 76–83; Donges, Alexander, and Selgert, Felix. 'Do Legal Differences Matter? A Comparison of German Patent Law Regimes Before 1877'. *Jahrbuch fur Wirtschaftsgeschichte/Economic History Yearbook* 60(1) (2019) 57–92.

143 Vonneuman, Nicholas. 'Conditionally Exclusive Patent Rights and the Patent Clause of the Constitution'. *American Journal of Comparative Law* 5(3) (1956) 391–409, 403 (providing discussions from an American point of view, but also with a reference to development in Germany).

the transfer of technology'[144] during this second industrial revolution across the continent. Thus, both for German inventors and foreign inventors, they were able to benefit from the new German Patent Act of 1877 since it provided scopes for the transfer of technology and also its common law hybridity where elements of American and British procedures and forms were also found in how some German states administered the 1877 patent law.[145]

Arguably, given that a number of foreign inventors were seeking protection in Germany, there was a legal obligation on Germany to provide such protection consistent with its international undertakings under the Paris Convention and the national treatment provision.[146] The practice of treating foreign inventors on the same grounds as local inventors under the Paris Convention not only encouraged foreigners to seek protection in other countries but also encouraged other nations to develop legislations based on the national treatment provision of the Paris Convention that would allow protection for foreign inventors on an equal and non-discriminatory basis. No more so were the efforts visible and lead to the first regional treaty than in Latin American states to develop a system similar to the Paris Convention. It was in some ways a mission to civilise.[147] This, despite the later denunciation of the Paris Convention by some Latin American countries.

With some of the larger developments taking place in Europe in the latter decades of the nineteenth-century, and with the conclusion of the Berlin Conference that partitioned Africa,[148] there was some focus towards a mission to civilise the hinterlands that had some affinity to European civilisation on the development of patent laws.[149] This effort was perhaps perpetuated

144 Burhop and Wolf (n. 138), 74.

145 For some discussions on the co-relation between Anglo-American elements in the German Patent Act of 1877 see Lehmann-Hasemeyer, Sibylee, and Streb, Jochen. 'Discrimination Against Foreigners: The Wuerttemberg Patent Law in Administrative Practice'. *The Journal of Economic History* 80(4) (2020) 1071–1100.

146 For some discussions on foreign patenting in Germany during the era see Degner, Harald, and Streb, Jochen. 'Foreign Patenting in Germany, 1877–1932' in Doze, Pierre-Yves, Nishimura, Shigehiro, eds. *Organizing Global Technology Flows: Institutions, Actors, and Processes* (Abingdon: Routledge, 2013) 17–38.

147 The Spain–El Salvador Treaty of 1884 mentioned earlier (n. 98) was a bilateral treaty and not "multilateral" in the context of the Montevideo Convention of 1889.

148 See Florestal, Marjorie. 'On the Origin of Fear in the World Trade System: Excavating the Roots of the Berlin Conference of 1884–1885'. Proceedings of the Annual Meeting: ASIL 101 (2007) 143–146; Craven, Matthew. 'Between Law and History: The Berlin Conference of 1884–1885 and the Logic of Free Trade'. *London Review of International Law* 3(1) (2015) 31–59.

149 My usage of the term "civilise" in this chapter refers to the division and rhetoric of the world in the late nineteenth century, where on the one hand European states believed

with the 1889 Paris Exhibition and the subsequent events that led to the 1911 Washington Conference on the Revision of the Paris Convention;[150] then culminated in a series of bilateral treaties on industrial property in the Americas. Such treaties were part of a mission to civilise those nations within the realm of international commercial legal relations that began in 1883 where in 1884 the only non-European signatories were states such as Tunisia, followed by the Dominican Republic in 1890. The Brazilians (white ruling class) and other Latin Americans, to a degree, share affinity with the civilised nations of Europe.

Brazil for one, was one of the few early non-European signatory to the Paris Convention. By the time the Paris Convention was being revise in 1911, Latin American treaties would now emulate the Paris Convention.[151] The Revision of the Paris Convention in 1911 also reflected this, where for example; the Bolivarinia Patents Convention also emerged.[152] However, prior to the Washington Conference in 1911 a number of significant (bilateral) Conventions relating to the protection of industrial property in the Americas, between the United States on the one hand, and on the other, Inter-Latin American initiatives on patents were signed. The most significant for the period was the Treaty on Patents of Invention 1889 (Montevideo).[153] But others include the Treaty

they were at the top of the pyramid, and as such, the standard bearer of civilisations, whilst those at the bottom of the pyramid were "savages" and/or "infant race" especially Africans and to some extent Asians, but see the classic work of Gerrit Gong, *The Standard of 'Civilization' in International Society* (Oxford: Clarendon Press, 1984).

150 Paris Convention (1883), *as revised* at Washington, 2 June 1911. One notable development in 1911 was that the Paris Convention was amended to define in Article X or state the need for all states to provide 'protection against unfair trade competition.' International Convention for the Protection of Industrial Property Signed at Washington, 2 June 1911.

151 Primarily the number of treaties on commercial law/conflicts of law signed at Montevideo in 1889 is the primary reference most of which have been translated and reproduced in Official Documents: Treaties on Private International Law (Montevideo), Supplement to the American Journal of International Law 37(3) (1943) 95–158 (hereinafter Montevideo).

152 Bolivariana Convention on Patents of Invention (Caracas, 1911).

153 Treaty on Patents of Invention (Signed at Montevideo, 16 January 1889). The signatories were Uruguay, Argentina, Bolivia, Brazil, Chile, Paraguay, and Peru. For an English language version of the text, see 'Treaty on Patents of Invention' (1943) 37 AJIL 155 (hereinafter "Montevideo Patent Convention"). Other intellectual property treaties were concluded earlier at Montevideo, but those are not the focus of the discussion in this chapter, see Treaty on Literary and Artist Property, concluded between Argentina, Brazil, Chile, Paraguay, Peru and Uruguay, signed at Montevideo, 11 January 1889; Treaty on Commercial and Industrial Trademarks, concluded between Argentina, Bolivia, Brazil, Chile, Paraguay, Peru and Uruguay, signed at Montevideo, 16 January 1889. These treaties were concluded under the auspices of the First South American Congress of Private International Law, for discussions, see Arguas, Margarita. 'The Montevideo Treaties of 1889 and 1940 and their Influence on the Unification of Private International Law in South America' in Bos,

on Patents of Invention (Mexico City)[154] or the Pan-American, to include the United States, the Buenos Aries Convention 1910.[155]

The Buenos Aires Convention for example, replicated the Paris Convention on matters relating to national treatment and priority periods. Similarly, the Montevideo Patent Convention was a *multilateral* Convention among Latin American states that allowed for patent holders reciprocal rights in another contracting state providing the patent was registered within a year.[156] One of the special features of the Buenos Aires Convention and the Montevideo Conventions was that, at the time, states that were not party to the Paris Convention could accede to the Buenos Aires or the Montevideo Conventions as they allowed for 'all' states to join. For example, Article X of the Montevideo Convention provides that 'all nations' which 'may desire to adopt' the treaty.[157]

Thus, most Latin American states that were not Party to the Paris Convention were able to enjoy international legal obligations that were similarly laid out in the Paris Convention when they signed up to the Montevideo Convention in 1899. The Montevideo Convention provides:

> Article I Any person who shall obtain a patent or privilege of invention in any of the contracting States shall enjoy in all the others the rights of inventor, if within a year at the utmost he shall cause his patent to be registered in the form prescribed by the laws of the country in which he shall ask for its recognition.
> Article II The duration of the privilege shall be that fixed by the laws of the country in which it is to take effect. This period may be limited to that prescribed by the laws of the State in which the patent was first granted, if such period be the shorter.
> Article III Questions arising as to the priority of invention shall be settled according to the date of the request for the respective patents in the country where they were granted.
> Article IV By invention or discovery shall be understood any new method, mechanical or manual apparatus, for the manufacture of industrial products; the discovery of any new industrial product, and the

Maarten, ed. *The Present State of International Law and Other Essays* (Deventer: Kluwer Press, 1973); Bewes, Wyndham. 'The Treaties of Montevideo (1889)'. *Transactions of the Grotius Society* 6 (1920) 59–79.

154 Treaty on Patents of Invention, Industrial Drawings and Models and Trademarks (Second International American Conference, Mexico City, 1902).

155 Convention for the Protection of Inventions, Patents, Designs, and Industrial Models, 20 August 1910, 155 LNTS 179 ("Buenos Aires Convention").

156 Montevideo Convention, Article 1.

157 Ibid, Article X.

application of perfected methods for obtaining results superior to any previously known.

No patents shall be granted –

(1) To inventions or discoveries already made public in any of the contracting States, or in others not bound by this treaty.

(2) To those contrary to good morals or to the laws of the country in which the patents are to be issued or recognized.

Article V The rights of the inventor shall include that of enjoying the use of his invention and of transferring it to others.

Article VI Those persons interfering in any way with the rights of the inventor shall be prosecuted and punished according to the laws of the country in which the offense may be committed.

Article VII The simultaneous ratification of all the contracting nations shall not be necessary to the effectiveness of this treaty. Those who adopt it will communicate the fact to the Governments of the Argentine Republic and the Oriental Republic of Uruguay, which will inform the other contracting nations. This formality will take the place of an exchange.

Article VIII The exchange having been made in the manner prescribed in the foregoing article, this treaty shall remain in force for an indefinite period after that act.

Article IX If any of the contracting nations should deem it advisable to be released from this treaty, or to introduce modifications in it, said nation shall so inform the rest; but it shall not be released until two years after the date of notification, during which time measures will be taken to effect a new arrangement.

Article X The provisions of Article VIII are extended to all nations which, although not represented in this Congress, may desire to adopt the present treaty.

In Witness Whereof, the plenipotentiaries of the aforesaid nations sign and seal the foregoing to the number of seven copies, in Montevideo, on the 1th day of January, 1889.[158]

The Montevideo Convention was one of the first precursor that would lead to similar conventions such as what would take place in Europe decades later with the Patent Cooperation Treaty.[159] But more importantly, the Montevideo

158 Treaty on Patents of Invention, Signed at Montevideo, 16 January 1899, as translated and reproduced in, *American Journal of International Law* 37(3), Supplement: Official Documents, (1943) 155–157.

159 Efforts largely began with the Strasbourg Convention in 1953, European Convention Relating to the Formalities Required for Patent Applications, 11 December 1953, 218 UNTS 27.

Convention had the incentive effect for patent legislations in a domestic setting for industrial property when considered against broader arguments of 'welfare effects.'[160] Thus, in some ways, although the efforts for a global system of protection of patents and inventions began in earnest at the Vienna Patent Congress 1873, and, manifested in the Paris Convention of 1883, it was the shift to the new world, to civilise their laws and cultures in the forms of visions of the old world that would launch a new phase of *treatification* in the international legal system that is to the present day revolve around industrial property rights.[161]

The Montevideo Convention represented two forms of victories: the first being, the civilising of innovation in peripheral states outside of Europe. In that sense, the broader mission of international legal relations as a civilising tool was being achieved. The second victory has to do with the extent of innovation diplomacy as developed in this chapter. In other words, the salient promoters of global innovation in the 1880s wanted to ensure that their inventions would meet the standards of legal protection as provided for in Europe and the law of nations. Moreover, the efforts by the private merchants who had the most to gain financially from international protection led the globalising efforts.

This viewpoint on the emergence of treaties relating to industrial property since 1883 including some of the modern (twenty-first century free trade agreements with substantial intellectual property provisions) should hardly be surprising given the informal role private merchants played starting with the Vienna Congress in 1873. What is however significant is that the adoption of the Paris Convention in 1883 makes the system of intellectual property in international law over the last century a more fluid and uniform progress in lawmaking by non-state actors in the international legal system.

These developments that charted the emergence of innovation in the latter part of the nineteenth and early twentieth centuries, not only demonstrate

160 Deardorff, Alan. 'Welfare Effects of Global Patent Protection'. *Economica* 59(233) (1992) 35–51; Wagner, Ulrich. 'Estimating Strategic Models of International Treaty Formation'. *The Review of Economic Studies* 83(4) (2016) 1741–1778, 1757 (arguing that countries have incentives to participate in treaties); Sokoloff, Kenneth. 'Incentive Activity in Early Industrial America: Evidence from Patent Records, 1790–1846'. *The Journal of Economic History* 48(4) (1988) 813–850; Macleod, Christine, Tann, Jennifer, Andrew, James, and Stein, Jeremy. 'Evaluating Incentive Activity: The Cost of Nineteenth-Century UK Patents and the Fallibility of Renewal Data'. *The Economic History Review* 56(3) (2003) 537–562.

161 The Paris Convention is incorporated into the TRIPS Agreement, but most bilateral and multilateral free trade agreements nowadays have substantial intellectual property rights provisions, for some contemporary discussions see Price, David. 'The U.S. Bahrain Free Trade Agreement and Intellectual Property Protection'. *Journal of World Intellectual Property* 7(6) (2004) 829–850.

how exhibitions and technical innovations were crucial to the global force of patent laws, but also allow "industrial progress" as part of how nations became civilised. The second (or third) industrial revolution and the technological flow of know-how into hinterlands also cemented how the language of "law" and/or "rules" pertaining to an "industrial society" would help mark how the science of the law of nations transform into a new language: contemporary international law based on treaties established in the late nineteenth century.

For the most part, the Paris Convention of 1833 and other intellectual property treaties from the late nineteenth century are still in operation and continues to serve as the backbone of international intellectual property protection. Moreover, the science of international law is still dependent on how one can *refer* to and/or *situate* those multilateral treaties in the economic relations of states.[162] Hence, the attraction of protecting "industrial property" in the international legal system is a form of commercial necessity that the forces of nature or war will not diminish, but rather, drive the wheel of 'human activities stretching from the accumulation of knowledge about the myriad relationships of the physical universe and the world of man.'[163] In that regard, whatever the inventions of man, whether during war or peace, such inventions will need regulation, and such regulations are often driven by the initial inventors through how they lobby for rules in their domestic legal system and then into the international legal sphere where legal regulation can enjoy 'a decisive influence on the further development of international law in world-wide dimension.'[164] This is an important insight by Lachs when applied to the evolution of the protection of intellectual property rights or those relating to industrial innovation as developed in this chapter. In a number of ways contemporary intellectual property rights has shown decisive influence as

162 Oppenheim, Lassa. 'The Science of International Law: Its Task and Method'. *American Journal of International Law* 2(2) (1908) 313–356, 320 (discussing lawmaking treaties).

163 Malina, Frank. 'Some Reflections on the Difference Between Science and Art', in Hill, Anthony, ed. *Data: Directions in Art, Theory and Aesthetics* (New York: Graphic, 1968) 134.

164 Lachs, 'Thoughts on Science' (n. 86), 676. See further at 679 noting that since the nineteenth century: '[T]echnology became the mediator that methodologically translated theory into deeds and began to feed practice, which was transformed from the helpmate of the artisan into the ever-ready "toolmaker" of scientific invention. Together, science and technology, working in harness, opened up new economic prospects.' The extent to which technological innovation has served to increase the economic expansion of countries and/or international trade is well covered in the literature, but for preliminary reading see Murmann, Johann. *Knowledge and Comparative Advantage: The Coevolution of Firms, Technology, and National Institutions* (Cambridge: Cambridge University Press, 2003); Khan, Zorina. 'Selling Ideas: An International Perspective on Patenting and Markets for Technological Innovations, 1790–1930'. *The Business History Review* 87(1) (2013) 39–68.

developed in international law over the last century: the actual *behaviour* of intellectual property rules is something that transcends the nation state. Yet, by the turn of the twentieth century, the role of intellectual property would affect peace treaties.

The ensuing developments after the World War did not change the trajectory and development of international intellectual property rules as conflicts merely put those rules on a "pause", as suggested by Johnson in this volume.[165] As the world was engulf in an armed conflict for much of the time between 1914–1918, a series of treaties brokered at Versailles included an economic clause that among other things required Germany 'to adopt all the necessary legislative and administrative measures to protect goods the produce or manufacture.... from all forms of unfair competition in commercial transactions'[166] was part of the decisive influence of intellectual property. However, it is Article 286 of the Versailles Treaty that is even more salient. Article 286 provides for the application of the Paris and Berne Conventions on German Territory 'in so far as they are not affected or modified'.[167] When the provisions of Articles 274 and 286 of the Versailles Treaty are taken into account, from an intellectual property rights perspective, then, war merely facilitated the continuity of intellectual property rules. The imposition of the concept of unfair competition and obligations for Germany to adhere to the Paris and Berne Conventions sealed the fate of private property rights such as those on industrial property as part of the fabric of contemporary international law regardless of war or peace.

6 Conclusion

This history of innovation and the international efforts to provide legal protection under patent laws has been one of the major developments in the latter part of the nineteenth century where an explosion of patent laws contributed to the globalisation of intellectual property rights. By turning to the nineteenth

165 See also Johnson, in this collection; but see, Zhang, Yue. 'Customary International Law and the Rule Against Taking Cultural Property as Spoils of War'. *Chinese Journal of International Law* 17(4) (2018) 943–990.

166 Peace Treaty of Versailles, Article 274. See also Banerjee, Arpan, and Beldiman, Dana. 'International Trade Mark Enforcement under the Versailles Treaty: A Case Study of Sanatogen' in Ghosh, Shubha, ed. *Forgotten Intellectual Property Lore: Creativity, Entrepreneurship and Intellectual Property* (Cheltenham: Edward Elgar, 2020).

167 Versailles Treaty, Article 286. See also, Article 297-Annex (paragraph 5 on the effects of trademarks).

century to excavate some of the historical records to highlight the various efforts by private actors, the participation of states and how innovation and those displayed at exhibitions contributed to industrialization and economic growth it was shown that the incentive effect relates to a broader mission to civilise cultures on protecting innovation. Thus, the chapter examined how international exhibitions in the latter part of the nineteenth century contributed to the globalisation of innovation and patent laws. By combing through some of the available historical records, especially the reports of the some of the major exhibitions, the efforts for a global treaty for protecting industrial property, and the widespread adoption of patent laws to protect innovation the chapter demonstrated that most states were faced with an incentive effect to adopt global patent standards and protection in the late nineteenth century. One of the major contribution of this chapter is the civilising mission argument that the 1883 Paris Convention had on non-European states. In other words, states such as those in Latin America were eager to adopt global standards for patent protection based on international standards that were set out in the Paris Convention and the chapter outlined how the Montevideo Convention of 1889 was one of the first multilateral convention to embrace the trajectory set by the Paris Convention.

Acknowledgements

I am grateful for the comments received from two anonymous reviewers and the contributors in this collection. All other errors remain yours truly.

Bibliography

Cases, Legislations and other Primary Sources

Universal Exhibition of Paris, 1878: The Banquet to Richard C. McCormick, given in Paris, Nov, 26, 1878 (Paris, 1878).

Paris Convention for the Protection of Industrial Property (adopted 20 March 1883) 828 UNTS 305.

Berne Convention for the Protection of Literary and Artistic Works, 9 September 1886, 828 UNTS 221 (Berne Convention).

League of Nations, Statute of the Permanent Court of International Justice, 16 December 1920.

Judiciary Act of 1789 § 9, 28 USC § 1350.

The Paquette Habana, 175 U.S. 677 (1900).

Kiobel v Royal Dutch Petroleum Co., 133 S. Ct. 1659 (2013).

The Patents, Designs and Trade Marks Act 1883 (UK).

An Act to revise, consolidate, and amend the statutes relating to patent and copyright, H.R. 1714, 41st Cong. (1870) (U.S.).

ILA, Reports of the First Conference, held at Brussels, 1873, and of the Second Conference, held at Geneva, 1874 (London: West, Newman & Co., 1903).

Firman (Decree) of 8 June 1867 (France).

International Copyright Act of 1852 (France).

Decree of 28 March 1852 (France).

Catalogue des produits de l'industrie francaise qui sereont exposes, pendant les derniers jours de Septembre 1806, Bibliotheque national de France.

Rapport du Jury – Sur Les Produits – De L' Industrie Francaise, Presente, de Champagny, (Paris, 1806).

Claude-Anthelme Costaz, Notices sur les objets envoyes a l'exposition des produuits de l'industrie francaise: redigees et imprimees par ordre de S.E.M. de Champagny, minister de l'interieur an 1806 (Paris, 1806).

Picard, A. Exposition Universelle Internationale de 1889 a Paris: Rapport general. Paris Imprimerie national, 1891. Illustrations. Vol. I. Exposition de 1806 sur l'Esplande des Invalides. 7953.m.3.

Bill to Extend the Provisions of the Design Act, 1850, and to Give Protection from Piracy to Persons Exhibiting New Inventions in the Exhibition of the Works of Industry of All Nations in 1851 (UK).

Brussels Act (1900) revising the Paris Convention.

Madrid Agreement for the Repression of False or Deceptive Indications of Source on Goods, 1890.

Document, Universal Exhibition 1873 in Vienna, International Congress for the Consideration of Patent Protection (National Archives, Washington DC, Letters Received Concerning Patents (Box 82).

UK-Russia Treaty of 11 July 1871.

Treaty Stipulations Between Great Britain and Foreign Powers on the Subject of Trade Marks (1872) (C. 693) 54 Parliamentary Papers 673.

Reports of the United States Commissioners to the Paris Universal Exhibition of 1878 (Washington, 1880, 5 vols.), I.

Anglo-American Brush Electric Light Corporation v King, Brown & Co., UKHL 5, April 1892.

McKeever v United States, 14 S.Ct. CL. 396, 420–21 (1878).

Patents for Inventions Bill (1876), Second reading.

Hansard, Patent Rights – International Conference, Vienna. – Question. HC Deb 31 July 1873 vol. 217 c1328.

Hansard, Patent Rights-International Conference, Vienna. – Question, HC Deb 05 August 1873 vol. 217 c1564.

Hansard, Patent Laws-International Conference, Vienna. – Question, HC Deb 14 July 1873 vol. 217 cc310-1.

Hansard, Patent Rights-International Conference. – Question, HC Deb 07 April 1878 vol. 215 c636.

Hansard, Patent Rights – International Conference. – Question. HC Deb 07 April 1873 vol. 215 c636.

Hansard, The Paris Exhibition, 1878 – Assistance to English Artizans, HC Deb 16 May 1878 vol. 240 cc27-8.

Hansard, The Paris Exhibition – English Cattle. – Questions, HC Deb 27 June 1878 vol. 241 cc329-30.

Report of the Vienna Exhibition of 1873, Vol. I–IV (23 July 1874).

Report for the Paris Universal Exhibition of 1878, Vol. I–II (3rd June 1880).

Patent Act of 1790, Ch. 7, 1 Stat. 109–112 (10 April 1790) (US).

Patent Law Amendment Act of 1852 (UK).

Patent Act (Sweden) (Amendment) (1914).

Patent Act (Patentgesetz) of 25 May 1877 (Germany).

Spain-El Salvador Treaty of 1884.

Paris Convention (1883), as revised at Washington, 2 June 1911.

International Convention for the Protection of Industrial Property Signed at Washington, 2 June 1911.

Bolivariana Convention on Patents of Invention (Caracas, 1911).

Treaty on Patents of Invention (Signed at Montevideo, 16 January 1889).

Treaty on Literary and Artist Property, concluded between Argentina, Brazil, Chile, Paraguay, Peru and Uruguay, signed at Montevideo, 11 January 1889.

Treaty on Commercial and Industrial Trademarks, concluded between Argentina, Bolivia, Brazil, Chile, Paraguay, Peru and Uruguay, signed at Montevideo, 16 January 1889.

Treaty on Patents of Invention, Industrial Drawings and Models and Trademarks (Second International American Conference, Mexico City, 1902).

Convention for the Protection of Inventions, Patents, Designs, and Industrial Models, 20 August 1910, 155 LNTS 179 ("Buenos Aires Convention").

European Convention Relating to the Formalities Required for Patent Applications, 11 December 1953, 218 UNTS 27.

Peace Treaty of Versailles, Article 274.

Literature

Adcock, Michael. 'The 1889 Paris Exposition: Mapping the Colonial Mind'. *Context* 22(2001) 31–40.

Ahlstrom, Goran. *Technological Development and Industrial Exhibitions, 1850–1914: Sweden in an International Perspective* (Lund University Press, 1996).

Alexander, Isabella. *Copyright Law and the Public Interest in the Nineteenth Century* (Oxford/Portland: Hart Publishing, 2010).

Allen, Brian. 'The Society of Arts and the First Exhibition of Contemporary Art in 1760.' *RSA Journal* 139(5416) (1991) 265–269.

Andersson, David, and Tell, Fredrik. 'Fighting Monopolies to Promoting Industry: Patent Laws and Innovation in Sweden 1819–1914'. *Jahrbuch fur Wirtschaftgeschichte* 60(1) (2019) 123–156.

Andersson, David, Galaso, Pablo, and Saiz, Patricio. 'Patent Collaboration Networks in Sweden and Spain During the Second Industrial Revolution'. *Industry and Innovation* 26(9) (2019) 1075–1102.

Arapostathis, Stathis. 'Contested Inventors: British Patent Disputes and the Culture of Invention in the Late Nineteenth Century' in Araposthais, Stathis, and Dutfield, Graham, eds. *Knowledge Management and Intellectual Property: Concepts, Actors and Practices from the Past to the Present* (Cheltenham: Edward Elgar, 2013).

Arguas, Margarita. 'The Montevideo Treaties of 1889 and 1940 and their Influence on the Unification of Private International Law in South America' in Maarten Bos (ed.), *The Present State of International Law and Other Essays* (Deventer: Kluwer Press, 1973).

Auerbach, Jeffrey, and Hoffendberg, Peter, eds. *Britain, the Empire, and the World at the Great Exhibition of 1851* (Aldershot: Ashgate 2008).

Barnett, Jonathan. 'Property as Process: How Innovation Markets Select Innovation Regimes'. *Yale Law Journal* 119(3) (2009) 384–457.

Banerjee, Arpan, and Beldiman, Dana. 'International Trade Mark Enforcement under the Versailles Treaty: A Case Study of Sanatogen' in Shubha Ghosh (ed.), *Forgotten Intellectual Property Lore: Creativity, Entrepreneurship and Intellectual Property* (Cheltenham: Edward Elgar, 2020).

Belido, Jose, Xalabarder, Raquel, and Casas, Ramon. Commentary on Bilateral Copyright Treaty between Spain and El Salvador (1884).

Belido, Jose. 'Colonial Copyright Extensions: Spain at the Berne Conventions (1883–1889'. *Journal of the Copyright Society of the USA* 58(2) (2011) 243–264.

Berthier-Foglar, Susanne. 'The 1889 World Exhibition in Paris: The French, the Age of Machines, and the Wild West'. *Nineteenth-Century Contexts* 31(2) (2009) 129–142.

Bewes, Wyndham. 'The Treaties of Montevideo (1889)'. *Transactions of the Grotius Society* 6 (1920) 59–79.

Birkbeck, Carolyn Deere. *The Implementation Game: The TRIPS Agreement and the Global Politics of Intellectual Property Reform in Development Counters* (Oxford: Oxford University Press, 2008).

Blackburn, David. *History of Germany 1780–1918: The Long Nineteenth Century, 2nd edition* (Wiley-Blackwell, 2002).

Bowden, Brett. 'The Colonial Origins of International Law: European Expansion and the Classical Standard of Civilization'. *Journal of the History of International Law* 7(1) (2005) 1–24.

Bottomley, Sean. *The British Patent System During the Industrial Revolution 1700–1852: From Privilege to Property* (Cambridge: Cambridge University Press, 2014).

Brown, Julie. *Health and Medicine on Display: International Expositions in the United States, 1876–1904* (The MITT Press, 2009).

Burhop, Carsten, and Wolf, Nikolaus. 'The German Market for Patents During the "Second Industrialization," 1884–1913: A Gravity Approach'. *Business History Review* 87(1) (2013) 69–93.

Butler, William, and Kwon, Michael. 'Manning's Commentaries on the Law of Nations.' *Jus Gentium: Journal of International Legal History* 4(2) (2019) 621–632.

Caenegem, R.C. van. 'Law in the Medieval World.' *Tijdschrift voor Rechtsgeschiedenis* 49(1) (1981) 13–46.

Charles, Francis Adams. *Commissioner of the State of Massachusetts, Report of the Vienna Exhibition* (Boston, 1874).

Codding, George. *The International Telecommunications Union: An Experiment in International Cooperation* (Leiden: Brill, 1952).

Copinger, Walter Arthur. *The Law of Copyright in Works of Literature and Art: Including that of the Drama, 3rd edition* (London: Stevens and Haynes, 1892) 565.

Crabites, Pierre. 'Napoleon and the French Code of Civil Procedure.' *Loyola Law Journal* 10(1–2) (1929) 3–12.

Craven, Matthew. 'Between Law and History: The Berlin Conference of 1884–1885 and the Logic of Free Trade'. *London Review of International Law* 3(1) (2015) 31–59.

Crouzet, Francois. 'Wars, Blockade, and Change in Europe, 1792–1815'. *The Journal of Economic History* 24(4) (1964) 567–588.

Cruz, Jorge. 'The Community Patent Convention: What Sort of Future? *Journal of World Intellectual Property* 1(5) (1998) 819–826.

Curti, Merle. 'America at the World Fairs, 1851–1893.' *The American Historical Review* 55(4) (1950) 833–856.

Daniels, Morna. 'Paris National and International Exhibitions from 1798 to 1900: A Finding-List of British Library Holdings.' (2013) eBLJ 2013, Article 6.

Davis, John. 'Representation, Rivalry and Transfer: The German States and 1862 Exhibition'. *Journal of the Decorative Arts Society 1850 – Present* 38(2014) 162–177.

Deardorff, Alan. 'Welfare Effects of Global Patent Protection'. *Economica* 59(233) (1992) 35–51; Ulrich Wagner, 'Estimating Strategic Models of International Treaty Formation'. *The Review of Economic Studies* 83(4) (2016) 1741–1778.

Dedinger, Beatrice. 'The Franco-German Trade Puzzle: An Analysis of the Economic Consequences of the Franco-Prussian War.' *Economic History Review* 65(3) (2012) 1029–1054.

Dellapenna, Joseph. 'Law in a Shrinking World: The Interaction of Science and Technology with International Law'. *Kentucky Law Journal* 88(4) (2000) 809–884.

Degner, Harald, and Streb, Jochen. 'Foreign Patenting in Germany, 1877–1932' in Pierre-Yves Doze and Shigehiro Nishimura (eds.), *Organizing Global Technology Flows: Institutions, Actors, and Processes* (Abingdon: Routledge, 2013) 17–38.

Donges, Alexander, and Selgert, Felix. 'Do Legal Differences Matter? A Comparison of German Patent Law Regimes Before 1877'. *Jahrbuch fur Wirtschaftsgeschichte/ Economic History Yearbook* 60(1) (2019) 57–92.

Doorman, Gerard. 'Patent Law in the Netherlands – Suspended in 1869 and Re-established in 1910 – Part II'. *Journal of the Patent Office and Society* 30(4) (1948) 258–271.

Duguid, Paul. 'French Connections: The International Progation of Trademarks in the Nineteenth Century.' *Enterprise & Society* 10(1) (2009) 3–37.

Fenwick, Charles. 'The Authority of Vattel.' *American Political Science Review* 7(3) (1913) 395–410.

Ferguson, Eugene. 'Expositions of Technology, 1851–1900' in Melvin Kranzberg and Carroll Pursell (eds.), *Technology in Western Civilization*, Vol. I (Oxford: Oxford University Press, 1967) 706–726.

Field, David. *Association for the Reform and Codification of the Law of Nations: Its History and Aims* (G. Hill, 1875).

Fitzmaurice, Andrew. 'Liberalism and Empire in Nineteenth-Century International Law.' *American Historical Review* 117(1) (2012) 122–140.

Florestal, Marjorie. 'On the Origin of Fear in the World Trade System: Excavating the Roots of the Berlin Conference of 1884–1885'. Proceedings of the Annual Meeting: ASIL 101 (2007) 143–146.

Fox, Paul. 'Exhibition City: Melbourne and the 1880 International Exhibition.' *Transition* 31 (1990) 31, 68.

Gaston, Jack. 'The Free Trade Diplomacy Debate and the Victorian European Common Market Initiative.' *Canadian Journal of History* 22(1) (1987) 59–82.

Geppert, Alexander. *Fleeting Cities: Imperial Expositions in Fin-de-Siecle Europe* (Basingstoke: Palgrave Macmillan, 2010).

Ginsburg, Jane. 'A Tale of Two Copyrights: Literary Property in Revolutionary France and American.' *Tulane Law Review* 64(5) (1990) 991–1032.

Gindriez, Charles. *International Exhibitions: Paris, Philadelphia, Vienna* (New York: Barnes & Co., 1878).

Gokmen, Gunes, Vermeulen, Wessel, and Vezina, Pierre-Louis. 'The Imperial Roots of Global Trade.' *Journal of Economic Growth* 25 (2020) 87–145.

Gong, Gerrit. *The Standard of 'Civilization' in International Society* (Oxford: Clarendon Press, 1984).

Gordley, James. 'Myths of the French Civil Code.' *American Journal of Comparative Law* 42(3) (1994) 459–506.

Green, Abigail. 'Representing Germany? The Zollverein at the World Exhibitions, 1851–1862.' *Journal of Modern History* 75(4) (2003) 836–863.

Grewe, Wilhelm. *The Epochs of International Law* (trs Michael Byers) (Berlin/New York: Gruyter, 2000).

Hagen, Antje. 'Patents Legislation and German FDI in the British Chemical Industry before 1914'. *The Business History Review* 71(3) (1997) 351–380.

Hafter, Daryl. 'The Business of Invention in the Paris Industrial Exposition of 1806.' *Business History Review* 58(3) (1984) 317–335.

Hall, Stephen. 'The Persistent Spectre: Natural Law, International Order and Limits of Legal Positivism.' *European Journal of International Law* 12(2) (2001) 269–307.

Hancock, Kathleen. *Regional Integration: Choosing Plutocracy* (Basingstoke: Palgrave Macmillan, 2009).

Heller, Henry. *The Bourgeois Revolution in France, 1789–1815* (Bergahn Books, 2006).

Hemmungs Wirten, Eva. 'A Diplomatic Salto Mortale: Translation Trouble in Berne, 1884–1886'. *Book History* 14 (2011) 88–109.

Hesse, Carla. 'The Rise of Intellectual Property, 700 B.C.–A.D. 2000.' *Daedalus* 131(2) (2002) 26–45.

Hildebrandt, A. translation of Hermann Grothe's Report, *The International Patent Congress in Vienna 1873* (London: Simpkin Marchsall & Co., 1875).

Hoffenberg, Peter. 'A Science of Our Own: Nineteenth Century Exhibitions, Australians and the History of Science' in B.M. Bennett and J.M. Hodge (eds.), *Science and Empire: Britain and the World* (Basingstoke: Palgrave Macmillan, 2011).

Holt, Elizabeth. *The Art of All Nations, 1850–73: The Emerging Role of Exhibitions and Critics* (New Jersey: Princeton University Press, 1982).

Hosak, John. *On the Ruse and Growth of the Law of Nations as Established by General Usage and by Treaties* (London: John Murray, 1882).

Houin, Roger. 'Reform of the French Civil Code and the Code of Commerce.' *American Journal of Comparative Law* 4(1) (1955) 485–505.

Hovenkamp, Herbert. 'The Emergence of Classical American Patent Law'. *Arizona Law Review* 58(2) (2016) 263–307.

Howard, Michael. *The Franco-Prussian War* (Abingdon/New York: Routledge, 2021).

Hudson, Manley. 'Present Status of the Hague Conventions of 1899 and 1907.' *American Journal of International Law* 25(1) (1931) 114–117.

Hugill, Peter. *Global Communications Since 1844: Geopolitics and Technology* (Baltimore: John Hopkins University Press, 1999).

Hughes, Justin. 'The Philosophy of Intellectual Property'. *Georgetown Law Journal* 77(2) (1988) 287–366.

Irwin, Douglas. 'Free Trade and Protection in Nineteenth Century Britain and France Revisited – A Comment on Nye.' *Journal of Economic History* 53(1) (1993) 146–152.

Iliasu, A.A. 'The Cobden-Chevalier Commercial Treaty of 1860.' *Historical Journal* 14(1) (1971) 67–98.

Jenks, C. Wilfred. 'The New Science and the Law of Nations.' *International and Comparative Law Quarterly* 17(2) (1968) 17, 327–345.

Jessup, Philip C. 'The Subjects of Modern Law of Nations.' *Michigan Law Review* 45(4) (1947) 383–408.

Johnson, Philip. *Parliament, Invention and Patents: A Research Guide and Bibliography* (Abingdon: Routledge, 2018).

Juhasz, Reka. 'Temporary Protection and Technology Adoption: Evidence from the Napoleonic Blockade'. *American Economic Review* 108(11) (2018) 3339–3376.

Karnell, Gunnar. 'ALAI – Initiator and Berne Copyright Convention Watch-Dog – Viewed from a Personal and Slightly Nordic Perspective' in Karnell, Gunnar et al., eds. *Liber Amicorum Jan Rosen* (Eddy.Se Ab, 2016) 414–415.

Kennedy, David. 'International Law and the Nineteenth Century: History of an Illusion.' *Nordic Journal of International Law* 65(3–4) (1996) 385–420.

Khan, Zorina. 'Selling Ideas: An International Perspective on Patenting and Markets for Technological Innovations, 1790–1930'. *The Business History Review* 87(1) (2013) 39–68.

Khan, Zorina. 'One for All? The American Patent System and Harmonization of International Intellectual Property Laws' in Gooday, Graeme, and Wilf, Steven, eds. *Patent Cultures: Diversity and Harmonization in Historical Perspective* (Cambridge: Cambridge University Press, CUP 2020) 85.

Kingsbury, Benedict, and Straumann, Benjamin. 'Introduction' in Kingsbury, Benedict, and Straumann, Benjamin, eds. *The Roman Foundations of the Law of Nations* (Oxford: Oxford University Press, 2011).

Kohler, Joseph. 'New Law of Nations.' *Michigan Law Review* 15(8) (1916) 631–638.

Koskenniemi, Martti. *The Gentle Civilizer of Nations: The Rise and Fall of International Law 1870–1960* (Cambridge: Cambridge University Press, 2002).

Koskenniemi, Martti. 'The Political Theology of Trade Law: The Scholastic Contribution' in Fasenrath, Ulrich et al., eds. *From Bilateralism to Community Interest: Essays in Honour of Bruno Simma* (Oxford: Oxford University Press, 2011), 90–112.

Kranzberg, Melvin, and Pursell, Carroll, eds. *Technology in Western Civilization, Vol. I* (Oxford: Oxford University Press, 1967).

Klimaszewska, Anna. 'General Principles in the Commercial Code of France of 1807.' *Journal on European History of Law* 2(2) (2011) 91–94.

Lachs, Manfred. 'Thoughts on Science, Technology and World Law'. *American Journal of International Law* 86(4) (1992) 673–699.

Ladas, Stephen. 'Pan-American Conventions on Industrial Property'. *American Journal of International Law* 22(4) (1928) 803–821.

Landes, David. *The Unbound Prometheus: Technological Change and Industrial Development in Western Europe from 1750 to the Present* (Cambridge: Cambridge University Press, 1969).

Lampe, Markus. 'Explaining Nineteenth-Century Bilateralism: Economic and Political Determinants of the Cobden-Chevalier Network'. *Economic History Review* 64(2) (2011) 644–668.

Ledger, Sally and McCracken, Scott. *Cultural Politics at the Fin de Siecle* (Cambridge: Cambridge University Press, 1995).

Lehmann-Hasemeyer, Sibylee and Streb, Jochen. 'Discrimination Against Foreigners: The Wuerttemberg Patent Law in Administrative Practice'. *The Journal of Economic History* 80(4) (2020) 1071–1100.

Linklater, Andrew. 'The Standard of Civilisations in World Politics'. *Social Character and Historical Processes* 5(2) (2016).

Lobban, Michael. 'Custom, Common Law Reasoning and the Law of Nations in the Nineteenth Century,' in Perreau-Saussine, Amanda, and Murphy, James, eds. *The Nature of Customary Law: Legal, Historical and Philosophical Perspectives*, (Cambridge: Cambridge University Press, 2009) 256–278.

Lythberg, Billie. 'A Pacific Macrocosm: 'Les Sauvages de la mer Pacifique" in Craciun, A., and Schaffer, S., eds. *The Material Cultures of Enlightenment Arts and Sciences* (Basingstoke: Palgrave Macmillan 2016).

MacLeod, Christine. 'The Paradoxes of Patenting: Invention and Its Diffusion in 18th and 19th Century Britain, France and North America'. *Technology and Cultures* 32(4) (1991) 885–910.

MacLeod, Christine. *Heroes of Invention: Technology, Liberalism and British Identity, 1750–1914* (Cambridge: Cambridge University Press, 2007).

Macleod, Christine. Tann, Jennifer, Andrew, James, and Stein, Jeremy. 'Evaluating Incentive Activity: The Cost of Nineteenth-Century UK Patents and the Fallibility of Renewal Data'. *The Economic History Review* 56(3) (2003) 537–562.

Mainardi, Patricia. *Art and Politics of the Second Empire: The Universal Expositions of 1855 and 1857* (Yale University Press, 1987).

Malina, Frank. 'Some Reflections on the Difference Between Science and Art', in Hill, Anthony, ed. *Data: Directions in Art, Theory and Aesthetics* (New York: Graphic, 1968).

Mann, F.A. 'Reflections on a Commercial Law of Nations.' *British Yearbook of International Law* 33 (1957) 20–51.

Mikaberidze, Alexander. *The Napoleonic Wars: A Global History* (Oxford: Oxford University Press, 2020); Schroeder, Paul. *The Transformation of European Politics 1763–1848* (Oxford: Oxford University Press, 1994).

Mokyr, Joel. *Industrialization in the Low Countries, 1795–1850* (Yale University Press, 1976).

Morris, P. Sean. 'The Contemporary Ideological Legitimacy of Global Intellectual Property Rights'. *Intellectual Property Quarterly* 2006(1) 44–73.

Morris, P. Sean. 'The Private Foundations of International Law: Intellectual Property Rights and Pashukanis.' *Jus Gentium: Journal of International Legal History* 5(1) (2020) 37–121.

Morriss, Andrew, and Nard, Craig. 'Institutional Choice & Interest Groups in the Development of American Patent Law: 1790–1865.' *Supreme Court Economic Review* 19 (2011) 143–244.

Moser, Petra. 'Innovation without Patents: Evidence from World's Fairs.' *Journal of Law and Economics* 55(1) (2012) 43–74.

Moser, Petra. 'How Do Patent Laws Influence Innovation? Evidence from Nineteenth Century World's Fairs'. *American Economic Review* 95(4) (2005) 1214–1236.

Mueser, Benjamin. 'The Nation and Property in Vattel's Theory of Territory.' *Global Intellectual History* 3(2) (2018) 137–155.

Murmann, Johann. *Knowledge and Comparative Advantage: The Coevolution of Firms, Technology, and National Institutions* (Cambridge: Cambridge University Press, 2003).

Nakhimovsky, Isaac. 'Vattel's Theory of the International Order: Commerce and the Balance of Power in the *Law of Nations*.' *History of European Ideas* 33(2) (2007) 157–173.

Nimmer, David. 'Nation, Duration, Violation, Harmonization: An International Copyright Proposal for the United States'. *Law and Contemporary Problems* 55(2) (1992) 211–239.

Nordhaus, William D. 'An Economic Theory of Technological Change'. *American Economic Review* 59(2) (1969) 18–28.

Nour, Alia. 'Egyptian-French Cultural Encounters at the Paris Exposition Universelle of 1867'. *MDCCC 1800 Luglio* (6) (2017) 35–49.

Nussbaum, Arthur, 'The Significance of Roman Law in the History of International Law.' *University of Pennsylvania Law Review* 100(5) (1952) 678–687.

Nuvolari, Alessandro, and Vasta, Michelango. 'The Geography of Innovation in Italy, 1861–1913: Evidence from Patent Data'. *European Review of Economic History* 21(3) (2017) 326–356.

Oppenheim, Lassa. 'The Science of International Law: Its Task and Method'. *American Journal of International Law* 2(2) (1908) 313–356.

Orakhelashvili, Alexander. 'The Idea of European International Law.' *European Journal of International Law* (2006) 17(2) 315–347.
Paris-Dobozy, Marie-Luce. 'Still Alive: Some Observations about the Two-Hundred Years of Existence of the French Civil Code of 1804.' *Irish Journal of European Law* 12(1) (2005) 72–97.
Penrose, Edith Tilton. *The Economics of the International Patent System* (John Hopkins Press, 1951).
Percy, Corbet. 'Modern Law of Nations.' *Michigan Law Review* 47(1) (1948) 67–71.
Pila, Justine. 'The European Patent: An Old and Vexing Problem'. *International & Comparative Law Quarterly* 62(4) (2013) 917–940.
Porras, Ileana. 'European Origins, the Doctrine of the Providential Function of Commerce, and International Law's Embrace of Economic Growth.' *Proceedings of the Annual Meeting – American Society of International Law* 107 (2013) 374–379.
Price, David. 'The U.S. Bahrain Free Trade Agreement and Intellectual Property Protection'. *Journal of World Intellectual Property* 7(6) (2004) 829–850.
Rae, John. 'The Invention of Invention' in Melvin Kranzberg and Carroll Pursell (eds.), *Technology in Western Civilization, Vol. I* (Oxford: Oxford University Press, 1967).
Redlich, Marcellus von. *The Law of Nations, 2nd Edition* (Phoenix: World League for Permanent Peace, 1937).
Reinisch, Paul S. 'International Unions and their Administration.' *American Journal of International Law* 1(3) (1907) 579–623.
Ritter, Dominique. 'Switzerland's Patent Law History'. *Fordham Intellectual Property, Media and Entertainment Law Journal* 14(2) (2004) 463–496.
Rominskyi, E.V. 'Regional Traditions in Medieval International Law.' *Jus Gentium: Journal of International Legal History* 1(2) (2016) 591–604.
Rosenberg, Nathan. 'Technological Change in the Machine Tool Industry, 1840–1920'. *Journal of Economic History* 23(4) (1963) 414–443.
Rovira, Monica Garcia-Salmones. *The Project of Positivism in International Law* (Oxford: Oxford University Press, 2013).
Rydell, Robert. *World of Fairs: The Century of Progress Expositions* (Chicago: University of Chicago Press, 1993).
Sell, Susan. 'Intellectual Property and Public Policy in Historical Perspective: Contestation and Settlement'. Loyola Los Angeles Law Review 38(1) (2004) 267–322.
Schall, James. 'Natural Law and the Law of Nations: Some Theoretical Considerations.' *Fordham International Law Journal* 15(4) (1991) 997–1030.
Schuster, Ernest. 'The New German Patent Act'. *Law Quarterly Review* 8(1) (1892) 76–83.
Schroeder, Paul. *The Transformation of European Politics 1763–1848* (Oxford: Oxford University Press, 1994).
Schroder, Ann. 'Reversals of Power: Artistic Property, Counterfeiter, and the 1793 French Copyright Act.' *Visual Resources* 16(2) (2000) 143–154.

Siborne, William. *History of the War in France and Belgium in 1815* (Cambridge: Cambridge University Press, 2012).

Snow, Alpheus Henry. 'Law of Nations.' *American Journal of International Law* 6(4) (1912) 890–900.

Sokoloff, Kenneth. 'Incentive Activity in Early Industrial America: Evidence from Patent Records, 1790–1846'. *The Journal of Economic History* 48(4) (1988) 813–850.

Story, Joseph. *Commentaries on the Conflicts of Laws, Foreign and Domestic, in Regard to Contracts, Rights, and Remedies, and Especially in Regard to Marriages, Divorces, Wills, Succession, and Judgments* (Hilliard, Gray, 1834).

Suzuki, S. *Civilization and Empire: China and Japan's Encounter with European International Society* (Abingdon: Routledge, 2009).

Taalbi, Josef. 'What Drives Innovation? Evidence from Economic History'. *Research Policy* 46(8) (2017) 1437–1453.

Tresch, John. *The Romantic Machine: Utopian Science and Technology After Napoleon* (University of Chicago, 1992).

Twiss, Travers. *The Law of Nations considered as Independent Political Communities – on the Right and Duties of Nations in Time of Peace* (Oxford: Oxford University Press, 1861).

Young, Patrick. 'From the Eiffel Tower to the Javanese Dancer: Envisioning Cultural Globalisation at the 1889 Paris Exhibition'. *History Teacher* 41(3) (2008) 339–362.

Uslenghi, Alesjandra. *Latin America at the Fin-De-Siecle Universal Exhibitions: Modern Cultures of Visuality* (Basingstoke: Palgrave, 2016).

Vattel, Emmerich de. *The Law of Nations*, Book 1 (London: J. Newberry, et al., 1759).

Verzijl, J.H.W. 'A Panorama of the Law of Nations.' *Nordic Journal of International Law* 21(1) (1951) 3–25.

Vonneuman, Nicholas. 'Conditionally Exclusive Patent Rights and the Patent Clause of the Constitution'. *American Journal of Comparative Law* 5(3) (1956) 391–409.

Wadlow, Christopher. 'The British Empire Patent 1901–1923: The Global Patent That Never Was.' *Intellectual Property Quarterly* 2006(4) 311–346.

Wagner, Ulrich. 'Estimating Strategic Models of International Treaty Formation'. *The Review of Economic Studies* 83(4) (2016) 1741–1778.

Walterscheid, Edward. 'The Early Evolution of the United States Patent Law: Antecedents (Part 1)'. *Journal of the Patent and Trademark Office Society* 76(9) (1994) 697–715.

Wetzel, David. *A Duel of Nations: Germany, France, and the Diplomacy of the War of 1870–1871* (Madison: University of Wisconsin Press, 2012).

Wheaton. *History of the Law of Nations in Europe and America: From the Earliest Times to the Treaty of Washington, 1812* (New York: Gould, Banks & Co., 1845).

Wijffels, Alain. 'Undue Delay and the French Code of Civil Procedure 1806.' Rhee, C.H. van, ed. *Within a Reasonable Time: The History of Due and Undue Delay in Civil Litigation* (Dunker & Humblot, 2010) 320–353.

Wilson, Andrew, and Bowman, Alan. *Trade, Commerce, and the State in the Roman World* (Oxford: Oxford University Press, 2017).

Wise, Lloyd. 'Assimilation of the Laws and Practice of Various Nations in Relation to the Protection of Inventions: A paper read at the Conference of the Association for the Reform and Codification of the Law of Nations, at the Hague, September 1875'. (London: JW Last & Co., 1875).

Zhang, Yue. 'Customary International Law and the Rule Against Taking Cultural Property as Spoils of War'. *Chinese Journal of International Law* 17(4) (2018) 943–990.

CHAPTER 4

Mr Patent Goes to War!

Industrial Property and the Breakdown of the International Order during World War I

Phillip Johnson

1 Introduction

The First World War, the Great War as it was once know, was a total war[1]; militarily, but more importantly economically. It is usually said that the British had begun the war hoping that overall it would remain "business as usual"[2] with a contemporary writer in 1914 suggesting:

> it is important to keep in mind two principles ... first that war should not interrupt business relations further than is necessary to prevent assistance being given to the enemy; and secondly, that war and its effects should be confined as far as possible to the armed forces of the belligerents.[3]

The German war plan had been to achieve victory within six weeks,[4] and despite popular belief few in Britain really thought it would be 'over by Christmas'.[5] These contrasting views of the war – the Central Powers seeing

1 Saint-Amour, Paul. "On the Partiality of Total War" *Critical Inquiry* (2014) 40:420.

2 This was partly based on the government thinking that it could avoid any significant involvement with a land war and keep the conflict at sea: French, David. 'The Rise and Fall of Business as Usual' in Burk, Kathleen, ed. *War and the State: The Transformation of British Government, 1914–1918*, (George Allen & Unwin, 1982), Ch 1; also see Broadberry, Stephen and Howlett, Peter. 'The United Kingdom during World War I: Business as Usual?' in Broadberry, Stephen, and Harrison, Mark, eds. *The Economics of World War I*, (Cambridge University Press, 2005), Ch 7; McDermott, John. "'A Needless Sacrifice' British Businessmen and Business As Usual in the First World War" *Albion* (1989) 21: 263.

3 Anon, "Alien Enemies as Plaintiffs" *Solicitors Journal* (1914) 59:83 at 84.

4 For a copy the plan and a critique see Ritter, Gerald. *The Schlieffen Plan: Critique of a Myth* (Oswald Wolff 1958); however, it may have been accepted by the military that a longer war (of at least six months) was inevitable: Herwig, Holger. "Germany and the 'Short-War' Illusion: Toward a New Interpretation?" *Journal of Military History* (2002) 66:681.

5 Hallifax, Stuart. "'Over by Christmas': British popular opinion and the short war in 1914" *First World War Studies* (2010) 1:103.

 DOI:10.1163/9789004511439_006

it as a rapid conflict with the Allies viewing it as a longer drawn out war – can also be seen in the approach each took to industrial property. This chapter[6] explores how two of the Allies (the United Kingdom and France[7]) and two Central Powers (Austria[8] and Germany) adopted economic strategies, which included restricting and modifying industrial property[9] owned by enemies, thereby bringing them into direct conflict with obligations under international treaties and norms. While the number of countries in the war was much greater – thirty in all – some came to the conflict much later,[10] others were not members[11] of the Paris Convention for the Protection of Industrial Property[12] and some had a industrial property system little used by foreigners.[13] The war was a battle of economic as well as military might and the Allies started with an economic advantage which only became greater as the belligerents changed.[14] This was not the case, however, in relation to patents where German companies were much more active at filing patents overseas than any of the other belligerents in the pre-war years as the following table demonstrates:

6 There has been a recent discussion of what occurred in Australia: Bond, Catherine and Lai, Jessica. "'A Process of Experimentation': Intellectual Property, War and Defence in Australia" in Ghosh, Shubha, ed. *Forgotten Intellectual Property Lore*, (Edward Elgar 2020), p. 376; Bond, Catherine. "'This is not a Bill to legalize looting': Wartime Regulation of Enemy-Owned Intellectual Property in Australia" *Intellectual Property Quarterly* (2015) 79.

7 While the approach the United States took to restricting industrial property was as drastic, if not more so, than that of France and the United Kingdom, as it entered the war so late the battle lines over industrial property had long been set.

8 The other half of the Dual Monarchy (Hungary) will not be substantively considered in this discussion. It had a separate Patent Office from Austria, but the filing activity of France and the United Kingdom was lower there than even for Austria (in the two years leading up to the war there was an average of 106 and 77 patent applications each year: *La Propriété Industrielle* 1916, p. 134). Nevertheless, where Hungary took a significantly different path to Austria this will be noted. For a discussion of the Dual Monarchy see Chapter 5.

9 There were also special war rules relating to copyright, but by the First World War in all four countries this was an unregistered right and so presented quite different issues which will not be considered here.

10 Eg the USA declared war on Germany on 6 April 1917 (and Austria-Hungary on 7 December 1917).

11 Russia was not a member.

12 The Paris Convention was established in 1883.

13 Serbia was a member of the Paris Union from its beginning, but it only had a trade mark law before 1920: for a contemporary short history see Jan Vojáček "Jugoslavia: A New Patent Territory" *Patent and Trademark Review* (1922) 20:259.

14 Broadberry, Stephen, and Harrison, Mark, eds. *The Economics of World War I* (Cambridge 2005), p. 5; highlighting the need for Germany to win quickly (p 9).

TABLE 4.1 The average number of patents filed in the Austrian, French, German and British Patent Office 1909–1914 by nationality[a]

Patent Office \ Applicant	Austria	France	Germany	United Kingdom
Austria	1,592	224	2,091	288
France	307	7,050	2,835	1,153
Germany	435	613	8,606	593
United Kingdom	331	1,049	3,014	19,963

a All data taken from Bureaux Internationaux Réunis pour la Protection de la Propriété Intellectuelle (BIRPI, now WIPO), *La Propriété Industrielle*: 1911, p. 42; 1912, p. 104, 118 and 180; 1913, 15; 1914, p. 63 and 80; 1915, 11 and 94; 1916, p. 15 and 100; 1917, p. 67. There are no figures for French filings in 1912 and the French figures include France and its colonies, and the UK figures cover the British Isles only.

Thus, at the beginning of the war, the German authorities had the greatest desire to leave the industrial property system out of the conflict. Conversely, the British and French could hit harder with restrictions on German rights holders[15]; Austria, on the other hand, was not country which attracted significant foreign filings or filed much overseas yet throughout the war it tended to follow its ally. It was therefore a war of attack by the Allied Powers with counter-attacks by the Central Powers[16] even though the retaliation was for political reasons, rather than for any particular useful effect.[17] Yet all were part of a broader international picture.

2 The International Picture

The Paris Convention for the protection of industrial property, which remains to this day central to the industrial property system globally, was approved on 20 March 1883.[18] By 1914, the Convention had already been repeatedly

15 There was a broad (although not total) consensus in Germany not to attack patents in the early days of the war: Mächtel, Florian. *Das Patentrecht im Krieg* (Mohr Siebech 2009), p. 244.

16 Mächtel, *Das Patentrecht im Krieg*, p. 237.

17 Mächtel, *Das Patentrecht im Krieg*, p. 249.

18 There were two other significant treaties relating to industrial property, but both had only a limited membership so will not be considered here. The system of international

revised[19] and had attracted twenty-two parties.[20] When the world turned upside down in early August 1914 as the major powers in Europe declared war on each other all four countries had become parties to the Convention.[21] Indeed, another recent instrument, the Hague Convention (IV) respecting the Laws and Customs of War on Land,[22] provided that a state party may not "declare abolished, suspended, or inadmissible in a court of law the rights and actions of the nationals of the hostile party"[23] so it might have been expected that any industrial property rights owned by enemies would continue as before.

But the obligations the Paris Convention imposed were challenged, and even disregarded, during the First World War. Yet it was not that simple, for as Florian Mächtel puts it, the belligerents enacted "laws [which] violated – seemingly paradoxically – the Paris Convention and at the same time respected it."[24] Some international obligations presented more difficulties than others. For instance, the requirement of national treatment (or non-discrimination),[25] that is treating nationals of other contracting parties no worse than you treat your own, clearly creates tension when those same nationals are targets on the battlefield; likewise, the rules of priority whereby a date of filing for a patent, design or trade mark can be taken from the first filing in a foreign (possibly enemy) country[26]; and the requirement to accept marks registered in other countries for registration in your own[27] ensuring enemy brands to be

---

trade mark registration under the Madrid Agreement Concerning the International Registration of Marks (1891) had only been ratified by France (1892) and Austria (1908), but not Germany or the United Kingdom; and the Madrid Agreement for the Repression of False or Deceptive Indications of Source on Goods (1891) had been ratified by France and the UK (1892), but not Germany or Austria.

19 Conferences of revision were held in Rome 1886; Madrid in 1890 and 1891; Brussels in 1897 and 1900; and Washington 1911; the text was only revised in Brussels in 1900 and Washington in 1911. For a history, see Ricketson, Sam. *The Paris Convention for the Protection of Industrial Property: A Commentary* (Oxford 2015), Ch 3 and 4.

20 At the time, this would have included a significant part of the world as France and the United Kingdom's ratification included the whole of the French and British Empires.

21 Ratifications: Britain and France (1884); Germany (1903) and Austro-Hungry (1909).

22 Established 1907; ratifications: Austria, Germany and United Kingdom (1909); France (1910).

23 Article 23 of the IV Hague Convention, 1907; there was a view that because of the varying ratifications of this Convention it did not apply to anyone: see Pillet, Antoine. "La Guerre Actuelle et le Driot des Gens" *Revenue Générale de Droit International Public* (1916) 23:5 at 21.

24 Mächtel, *Das Patentrecht im Krieg*, p. 204 ("Diese Gesetze verletzten – scheinbar paradoxerweise – die PVÜ und respektierten sie gleichzeitig").

25 Paris Convention (Washington 1911), art 2.

26 Paris Convention (Washington 1911), art 4.

27 Paris Convention (Washington 1911), art 6.

protected – difficult things to accept in a time of total war. All the belligerents eventually adopted a strategy which respected and protected property, but not the proprietor[28]; ensuring the rights could continue after the war, but that the right holder got no benefit from them in the meantime. However, as we will see, it was the British who were the first to separate the holder from the right, and other countries followed somewhat reluctantly. The extensive breakdown in these international obligations was almost inevitable as was the great complexity when peace eventually came.

3 The Peace Treaties

The Peace Treaties between the Allied Powers and Germany (the Treaty of Versailles) and between the Allies and Austria (the Treaty of Saint Germain) made provision to put the countries' industrial property regimes back together after the war.[29] The remainder of this chapter will explore why those provisions became necessary,[30] and what it was that belligerent States had done to their industrial property laws which needed remedying. So while the story will be told as the laws developed (the tit-for-tat retaliation) it will be told through the lens of what was needed afterwards to put everything back together again. This is a story which can be broadly divided into seven sections.

First, there was a question of whether the Paris Convention continued in effect throughout the war or needed to be brought back into effect when peace came.[31] Secondly, there was provision to restore ownership to pre-war proprietors and to deal with the unpicking the numerous state sanctioned appropriations and licences as well as the anti-evasion measures that had been taken.[32] Thirdly, there was a general right for right holders to extend time limits where the application or right existed before the war thereby reviving many long

28 For a contemporary discussion of policy development see the discussion of the Memorandum to the German Patent Office President: see Mächtel, *Das Patentrecht im Krieg*, p. 252.

29 Treaty of Versailles (German and Allies), arts 286, 306–311; Treaty of Saint Germain (Austria and Allies), art 237, 258 to 262; also see Treaty of Trianon (Hungary and Allies), art 220 and 241–245.

30 Initially, there had been consideration of a separate treaty to put the industrial property laws back together under the umbrella of BIRPI: see BIPRI, *La Protection Internationale de La Propriété Intellectuelle et la Guerre Mondiale* (1919), p. 74. As will be seen this was overtaken by events.

31 Treaty of Versailles, art 306(1); Treaty of Saint Germain, art 258(1).

32 Treaty of Versailles, art 309 and 310; Treaty of Saint Germain, art 261 and 262.

dead rights.[33] Fourthly, the period of priority was extended between belligerent powers.[34] Fifthly, the requirement to work an invention or use a mark were turned off for the war.[35] Sixthly, the Allied Powers (although not the Germans or Austrians) were indemnified for any government use of any industrial property right.[36] Finally, while not dealt with in the Peace treaties, the war also had a long term effect the on patents relating to national security ("secret patents"). We begin[37] by considering the continuing effect (or otherwise) of the industrial property conventions.

3.1 *Conventions*

There were members of the Paris Union who remained neutral during the war, and there were countries who only declared war on some, but not all, of the opposing belligerents.[38] This presented a question as to the continuing application of any international obligations under the Paris Convention during wartime. The opinion of jurists on whether the obligations subsisted diverged,[39] but the view of the Bureaux Internationaux Réunis pour la Protection de la Propriété Intellectuelle (BIRPI)[40] was that the Convention should be respected

33 Treaty of Versailles, art 307; Treaty of Saint Germain, art 259.

34 Treaty of Versailles, art 308; Treaty of Saint Germain, art 260.

35 Treaty of Versailles, art 307; Treaty of Saint Germain, art 259.

36 Treaty of Versailles, art 306(3); Treaty of Saint Germain, art 258(3); the laws depriving enemies of rights also remained in force: art 306(2) and art 258(2).

37 Many of these laws were made under war time enabling powers.

38 For full details see: BIPRI, *La Protection Internationale de la Propriété Intellectuelle et la Guerre Mondiale* (1919), p. 8–9.

39 See generally, Ladas, Stephen. *Patents, Trademarks, and Related Rights: National and International Protection* (Harvard 1975), Vol. 3, [966]; as to the different perspectives: Pillet, Antoine. "La Guerre Actuelle et le Driot des Gens" *Revenue Générale de Droit International Public* (1916) 23:5 (Part 1) and 203 (Part 2) at 225 (the Conventions cease to have effect between all parties whether at war or not); Renault, Louis. "Les Unions Internationales" *Revue Générale de Droit International Public* (1896) 3:14 at 21 ("It is quite obvious that the Treaty of Union [a different Union] would continue to operate, during the war, between the neutrals and each of the belligerents"; "Il est bien évident que le traité d'Union continuerait à fonctionner, pen dant la guerre, entre les neutres el chacun des belligérants"); Westlake, John. *International Law: Part II War* (2nd Ed, Cambridge 1913), p. 34 (treaties involving third parties, such as Unions, cannot be abrogated by war); Poltitis, Nikolaos. "Effets de la Guerre sur les Obligations Internationales" *Annuaire de l'Institut de Droit International* (1911) 24:200 at 214 (Conventions remain in force, but their execution may be effected).

40 Bureaux Internationaux Réunis pour la Protection de la Propriété Intellectuelle, which was the forerunner of the World Intellectual Property Organisation (WIPO) and administered the Paris Convention.

and continued to be applied as far as possible.[41] Indeed, the view that the Convention continued in effect was supported by Austria and Germany[42] and their courts[43] both holding that the private rights of enemy nationals under the Convention continue under municipal law (even if not international law) as war is waged against the State and not the citizens of that state, who in turn continued to enjoy full civil rights.

However, as we shall see, even the governments in these states took steps to change the domestic law and to remove the rights of foreign enemies whilst preserving the industrial property rights themselves. When peace came it does not appear that the belligerents were entirely sure whether the Paris Convention had continued in effect. Even BIRPI seemed to have become uncertain of it status proposing a draft text which stated the Convention should continue to have effect in the form it had before the war.[44] The Peace Treaties themselves refer to the Convention "coming again into effect"[45] suggesting it ceased to have effect at some point.[46] While its application or otherwise might reflect an interesting question on the law of treaties, it is clear that in certain key respects the Convention was not effective in practice and we will begin with the redistribution of ownership.

3.2 *Restoring Ownership*

The Peace Treaties restored the rights of the person who owned the individual industrial property right at the outbreak of war as well as returning ownership of pending applications.[47] The belligerent countries had spent the war appropriating the industrial property rights of each other's nationals and restricting the transfer and grant of rights. Not only ignoring the non-discrimination rule in the Paris Convention, but also the rules on civil rights in the Hague

41 BIRPI, *La Propriété Industrielle* (1914), p. 131.

42 BIRPI, *La Propriété Industrielle* (1915), p. 5 and 45.

43 Reichsgericht, 26 October 1914 (1914) 85 RGZ 374; it appears that this decision was not followed by all German courts and some took the contrary view for a time: Mächtel, *Das Patentrecht im Krieg*, pp. 190–194; it was followed in Austria however: Oberster Gerichtshof, 4 December 1916 (1917) *La Propriété Industrielle* 65.

44 BIPRI, *La Protection Internationale de la Propriété Intellectuelle et la Guerre Mondiale* (1919), p. 75 'Traité de Paix', art 1 and 2. It also sent out a circular asking whether countries treated the Convention as continuing Circular 148, 14 September 1914 but it never got any answers: ibid, p. 72.

45 Treaty of Versailles, art 286; Treaty of Saint Germain, art 237.

46 Ladas, Stephen. *Patents, Trademarks, and Related Rights: National and International Protection* (Harvard 1975), [974].

47 Treaty of Versailles, art 306(1); Treaty of Saint Germain, art 258(1) (all actions done during the war under the special measures stayed in effect however).

Convention. Each of the four belligerents had started the discrimination against enemies early on and all progressed to no longer granting enemies industrial property rights at all.[48] The British, with their view it would be a long war, began by allowing the prosecution of enemy[49] applications, but refusing to grant any patent or register any trade mark or design.[50] Initially, applications were suspended before publication, but in 1916 this is was changed to suspending it afterwards to enable the technology to be made available to the public.[51] This might seem like an aggressive stance but it probably made little practical difference as, even if granted, an enemy alien could not sue[52] for infringement in Britain as they had no standing before the court.[53] Therefore, an enemy patent or other right was essentially unenforceable[54] during the conflict[55]; this was, in itself, contrary to the non-discrimination rule of the Paris Convention. Critically, however, the strategy protected the property – insulating it as it were – as once the suspension was lifted the application could proceed to grant. This would both facilitate reconstruction after the conflict and allow some technological information to transfer to Britain in the meantime.[56]

---

48 A book was produced for the peace negotiations which provided in English most, although not all, of the laws (in translation) passed by the belligerents during the war: Langner, Lawrence, and White, William. *Basic Patent and Trade-Mark Laws of the Principal Belligerent Powers together with War Legislation* (Washington 1919) ("Langner and White"); a less comprehensive collection (but which includes some different material) was Armstrong, J.W. Scobell. *War and Treaty Legislation* (Hutchinson 1921)("Armstrong").

49 The rules changed to extend the meaning of enemy patents and trade marks to rights which were beneficially owned by an enemy: Patents, Designs and Trade Marks (Temporary) (Amendment) Rules 1915 (SI 1915/591); following the Act: Patents, Designs, and Trade Marks Temporary Rules (Amendment) Act 1914 (4 & 5 Geo 5. c. 73).

50 Patents, Designs and Trade Marks (Temporary) Rules 1914 (SI 1914/1255), r 2; Trade Marks (Temporary) Rules 1914 (SI 1914/1256); and Designs (Temporary) Rules 1914 (SI 1914/1327); the "Procedure to be Followed" was set out in the *Illustrated Official Journal* (*Patents*), 26 August 1914, No 1336, p. 1197 (and the necessity of filing evidence emphasised soon afterwards: *Illustrated Official Journal* (*Patents*), 9 September 1914, No 1338, p. 1255); a revised practice was adopted on 1 June 1915: *Illustrated Official Journal* (*Patents*), 2 June 1915, No 1376, p. 600.

51 *Thirty-Third Report of the Comptroller* 1916 (1916 HC Papers 58), Vol. 14, p. 463, p. 3.

52 But an enemy could be sued (if present in the jurisdiction to be served the writ necessary to start the legal process): *Porter v. Freudenberg* [1915] 1 KB 857, 863; and Anon "Status of Enemy Aliens in Courts of Justice" (1918) 31 *Harvard LR* 470, 473.

53 For a contemporary summary see, Picciotto, Cyril. "Alien Enemy Persons, Firms and Corporations in English Law" (1917) 27 *Yale LJ* 167.

54 Accordingly, it would also be impossible to licence.

55 The suspension of trade marks was more restricted, and did not cover figurative (pictorial) marks: *Illustrated Official Journal* (*Patents*), 11 November 1914, No 1347, p. 1492.

56 See Cave, Sir George. 108 Parl. Deb, H.C. (5th ser.) (11 Jul 1918), cols 534–535.

In contrast, in Austria and Germany[57] the basic position was that an enemy retained a right to sue (and be sued) during wartime; albeit enforcement was restricted.[58] Initially, therefore, the Austrian decision to allow patents from friends or enemies to proceed to grant was significant, particularly as it was also possible for an *applicant* to request that the grant be suspended for a year.[59] A measure which would benefit its own nationals as well as enemy subjects (to the extent the latter was practically able to apply); thus Austria began the war by protecting both property and proprietor. However, a little under a year[60] later both the Austrians[61] and Germans followed the British lead and left only the property protected by allowing prosecution of enemy patent applications (and in Germany, trade marks and utility models applications) up to, but excluding, grant[62]; in Austria, where there was registered design

57 Albeit this might have been subject to reciprocity see Anon "Status of Enemy Aliens in Courts of Justice" *Harvard Law* Review (1918) 31:470, 472.

58 No. 4487 Bundesratsverordnung betreffend die Überwachung ausländischer Unternehmungen [Ordinance on the Supervision of Foreign Enterprises], 4 September 1914 (Reichsgesetzblatt, p. 397). [The title of all non-English language legislative material is given with a summary title in English.]

59 No 232 Verordnung womit für die Zeit der kriegerischen Verwicklungen Ausnahmsbestimmungen auf dem Gebiete des Patentwessens getroffen warden [Ordinance Making Exceptional Patent Law Provision in Wartime], 2 September 1914 (Reichsgesetzblatt, p. 981; Langner and White, p. 83), art 7 it was possible to suspend it for up to 6 months under the normal law: Patentgesetz [Patent Law] (No 30 of 11 January 1897)(Reichsgesetzblatt, p. 35; Langner and White, p. 36, art 57).

60 It appears that Germany had suspended the grant of enemy patents much earlier (by 29 September 1914) albeit this was probably just administrative: Mächtel, *Das Patentrecht im Krieg*, p. 245.

61 The Hungarians only allowed the prosecution of existing applications and not new ones: see No 297 A m. kir. minisztérium 1916. évi 2.706. M. E. számú rendelete, egyes ellenséges államok részéről ipari tulajdonjogi téren tett korlátozó intézkedések megtorlásáról [Decree on Retaliation in the Field of Industrial Property], 15 August 1916 (Magyarországi Rendeletek Tára, p. 1063; Langner and White, p. 332).

62 "Berichte und Mitteilungen" [Reports and Communications], *Österreichisches Patent Blatt*, 1 May 1915, p. 120 (Langner and White, p. 91); the legal basis of the approach adopted in this Notice is unclear. It was confirmed by a Regulation a little under year later: Regulation No 82 Verordnung über die Unterbrechung des Verfahrens bei der Erteilung von Patenten [Ordinance on the Interruption of Patent Procedure], 24 March 1916 (Reichsgesetzblatt, p. 180; Langner and White, p. 98); later by No. 258 Verordnung über Vergeltungsmaßregeln auf dem Gebiete des gewerblichen Rechtschlußes [Ordinance on Retaliation in Commercial Matters], 16 August 1916, art 6 (Reichsgesetzblatt, p. 613; Langner and White, p. 101); Germany: Ordinance No. 4790 Bundesratsverordnung über gewerblich Schutzrechte feindlicher Staatsangehöriger [Ordinance on Enemy Propety], 1 July 1915 (Reichsgesetzblatt, p. 414; Langner and White, p. 202), art 2 (arts 5 and 7 defines enemies, and a different approach was adopted for Russian enemies).

protection, the term was simply suspended and would restart after the war.[63] Around the same time, the French took a similar step. So while it is unclear whether an enemy could sue in a French court,[64] it did not matter as by the autumn of 1915 all Austrian and German enemies had their industrial property rights suspended[65] or abandoned.[66] So, by a more explicit method, the French stopped enemies having rights in the industrial property but kept the property itself in stasis.

Subsequently, the British took matters further in January 1916 by allowing enemy patents to be granted to the public custodian[67] and permitting the seizure of enemy property, including industrial property.[68] Both of these measures enabled enemy industrial property to be appropriated and thereby entirely sidestepping future proprietorship issues. It appears the mechanism was infrequently used and so some nexus between the owner and the property was maintained for most of the war[69]; but on the eve of peace this changed when all patents and applications held by enemies finally vested in the Public Custodian.[70] This was clearly a way of controlling and simplifying the peace

---

63 No 152 Verordnung womit anläßlich des Kriegszustandes Ausnahmsbestimmungen auf dem Gebiete des Musterschutzwesens getroffen warden [Ordinance Making Exceptional Design Law Provision in Wartime], 2 June 1915 (Reichsgesetzblatt, p. 261; Langner and White, p. 94), art 1 (it applied retrospectively, but granted third party rights if the design had already lapsed, art 3; it was also possible to extend the term of a design if it was within 2 years of expiring, art 5); Germany protected designs under an unregistered system at the time and so is outside the scope of this discussion.

64 Garner, James. "Treatment of Enemy Aliens" *American Journal of International Law* (1919) 13:22, 47–56.

65 Loi établissant des règles temporaires en matière de propriété industrielle, notamment ence qui concerne les brevets d'invention appurtenant aux ressortissants des empires d'Allemagne et d'Autriche-Hongrie [Law Establishing Temporary Rules for Patents for German and Austro-Hungarians], 27 May 1915 (*Journal Officiel*, p. 3414; Langner and White, p. 162), art 1.

66 See p. 163 below.

67 Trading with the Enemy Amendment Act 1916 (5 & 6 Geo 5. c. 105), s. 6.

68 Trading with the Enemy Amendment Act 1916, s. 4.

69 By 24 July 1916, three had been granted to the public custodian: 84 Parl. Deb. H.C. (24 July 1916), col 1298; as it was the practice to vest those applications or patents only where it was necessary because they were going to be dealt with (assigned or licensed) imminently: Armstrong, p. 116. However, it may be that the number went up quickly as there were over 2,000 by July 1918: see *Comptroller's Thirty-Fifth Report* 1917 (1918 HC Papers 87), Vol. 12, p. 537, p. 2.

70 Order of the Board of Trade in the matter of the trading with the Enemy Amendment Acts, 1916 and 1918, 30 October 1918 (Armstrong, p. 391); see: "Patent and Patent Applications Vested in Public Trustee" Notice (1918) 101 *Board of Trade Journal*, p. 575 and "Enemy Interests in United Kingdom Patents", *Illustrated Official Journal (Patents)*, 13 November 1918,

negotiations (after all, they were all returned in the Peace Treaties[71]). It can be seen that the fundamental rule of the Paris Convention had been not only broken but some of the belligerents pulled in entirely the opposite direction by wrenching proprietorship from enemy nationals. On the other hand the approach in relation to licences was more consistent between the belligerents.

3.2.1 Licences

With the peace came an amnesty for all infringements which had occurred during the war[72] along with a cancellation of all licences between residents of the states which had been at war[73] (eg between a British and German company) and a mechanism whereby a licence could be reclaimed within six months of the relevant Treaty taking effect.[74] This mechanism helped to regularise the myriad war time procedures the belligerent states had instigated to cancel existing licences and to allow the compulsory licensing of enemy industrial property.

Licensing was, and is, one of the central ways the holder of an industrial property right makes money. So removing the ability to exploit a right from an enemy by ending existing licences – or going further and granting compulsory licences to nationals – once more represents separating property from proprietor. Critically, however, revoking a right barely ever happened[75]; a more robust strategy to terminate patents, for instance, would have enabled anyone to work the invention. But as before the strategy was to protect the property at the expense of its pre-war owner, rather than making the invention, design or mark, freely available to be worked. This was clearly less drastic than revoking the right and also more straight forward to remedy when peace returned. It was done in various ways. First, as a licence, or assignment, usually[76] involves a contract, the validity of pre-war contracts was critical to establishing any war

No 1556, p. 996 (the fact this notice was published after the Armistice shows how close to the end of the war it was issued).

71 Cf Mächtel, *Das Patentrecht im Krieg*, p. 229.

72 Treaty of Versailles, art 297; Treaty of Saint Germain, art 249 as to the problems applying this to third nations see Ladas, Stephen. *Patents, Trademarks, and Related Rights: National and International Protection* (Harvard 1975), Vol. 3, [983]; in the UK, pending cases involving enemies might have been stayed: *Actiengesellschaft Für Anilin Fabrikation in Berlin v. Levinstein Ld* (1921) 38 R.P.C. 277 at 281.

73 Treaty of Versailles, art 310; Treaty of Saint Germain, art 262; as to contracts behind licences see Treaty of Versailles, art 299; Treaty of Saint Germain, art 251.

74 Treaty of Versailles, art 310; Treaty of Saint Germain, art 262.

75 The British revoked (avoided) only two patents: see fn 86 below.

76 But a contract is not essential for an industrial property licence as it is merely permission to do what would otherwise infringe.

time right. However, the basic position in contract law varied with British[77] and French law[78] nullifying any contract with an enemy; whereas this was not the case in Austria[79] or Germany.[80] In addition, the Austrians, British and Germans allowed for licences to be suspended in the public interest on petition[81] (by contrast, the French ultimately allowed some enemies to grant industrial property licences).[82] This restriction on the right to exploit was often accompanied by the government being able to appropriate the right to licence from enemy proprietors (the exclusive rights as it were) thereby ignoring the requirement for national treatment.

Once more, it was the British who moved first and they did so within a few days of the war beginning. The comptroller was empowered to grant a licence to a third person to work a patent or use a trade mark owned by an enemy alien[83] to ensure the inventions could still be worked and that products essential to the war effort or civilian life would be available.[84] It was not possible for licence fees to be paid to companies incorporated in enemy countries as this would be trading with the enemy: any royalties were therefore paid to the public custodian.[85] At this point, it was only the British who took these steps with other countries taking longer to negative the proprietary rights.[86] The French

77 Baty, Thomas, and Morgan, John. *War: Its Conduct and Legal Results* (Dutton & Co 1915), Part IV, Ch II (explaining it to be the common law position).

78 Décret relatif à l'interdiction des relations commerciales avec l'Allemange et l'Autriche-Hongrie [Decree Prohibiting Trade with Germany and Austia-Hungary], 27 September 1914 (*Journal Officiel*, p. 8069; Langner and White, p. 160), art 2.

79 Curti, Arthur. *Handelsverbot und Vermögen in Feindesland. Gesetzgebung und Praxis von England, Frankreich, Deutschland, Italien, Österreich und Rußland während des Krieges 1914/15* (Heymann, 1916), p. 108.

80 See n. 595 and Mächtel, *Das Patentrecht im Krieg*, p. 238.

81 Verordnung No 258 of 16 August 1916, art 1 and 4; Bundesratsverordnung No. 4790 of 1 July 2015, art 1; also see Ordinance No 5619 Bundesratsverordnung betreffend Verträge feindlicher Staatsangehöriger [Ordinance on Contracts with Enemies], 16 December 1916 (Reichsgesetzblatt, p. 1396; Armstrong, p. 27), Trading with the Enemy Act 1916 (5 & 6 Geo 5, c 105), s 2.

82 Loi 27 May 1915, art 2.

83 It was expanded to cover beneficial interests later: see fn 49.

84 *Illustrated Official Journal (Patents)*, 11 November 1914, No 1347, p. 1492.

85 Created under Trading with the Enemy Amendment Act 1914 (5 Geo 5, c 12), s 1.

86 There were only 14 patents suspended and 2 avoided during the whole war (and 787 licences granted): see Comptroller's Reports: *Thirty-Second Report 1914* (1914–16 HC Papers 160), Vol. 32, p. 1; *Thirty-Third Report 1915* (1916 HC Papers 58), Vol. 14, p. 463; *Thirty-Fourth Report 1916* (1917–18 HC Papers 79), Vol. 17, p. 823; *Thirty-Fifth Report 1917* (1918 HC Papers 87), Vol. 12, p. 537; *Thirty-Sixth Report 1918* (1919 HC Papers 172), Vol. 27, p. 31; also see Mächtel, *Das Patentrecht im Krieg*, p. 223; it was suggested in Germany that the licence fees charged were below the economic value of the licence: ibid, p. 222.

followed its ally's lead in 1915 by allowing the government to licence enemy patents.[87] Soon after, the Germans launched what might now be seen as a long delayed counter-attack[88] albeit by this point, after some initial hysteria, it was accepted the effect of the British measures on German industrial property had not been as "frightening" as feared.[89] Like the British and French, the Germans provided that the Chancellor could grant licences to third parties[90] and a year later still, in 1916, the Austrian's joined the assault and allowed the licensing of enemy industrial property rights in the public interest.[91] Once more the pattern emerging was the Allies taking any right to exploit an industrial property right away from enemy nationals, but retaining the property itself. The Central Powers, on the other hand, tried to maintain the distinction between private citizen and state but ultimately like the Allies they decided to protect the property but took away the rights of the proprietor.

3.2.2 Assignments

Once restrictions on enemies holding or suing for infringement of industrial property rights took effect, it was inevitable that those affected would try to pass their rights to companies in neutral or friendly countries to enable exploitation to continue. But governments took steps to prevent such evasion. So, for example, the British provided that any assignment of industrial property to, or for, an enemy whether directly or through a neutral[92] was void unless the Board of Trade had consented.[93] Later, there were concerns within the British government over patent rights being used to restrict the production of war materials. Accordingly, in 1916 a restriction was imposed to prohibit any dealing in any patent, design or process relating to war materials without the permission of the authorities.[94] Likewise, Austria and Germany[95] required

87 Loi 27 May 1915, art 3.

88 Bundesratsverordnung No. 4790 of 1 July 1915.

89 Ferchland, Paul. *Der internationale gewerbliche Rechtsschutz im Kriege* (Berlin 1915), p. 8 ("nicht gerade als erschreckend bezeichnet warden").

90 Bundesratsverordnung No. 4790 of 1 July 1915, art 1 and 2; very few appear to have been granted: five decisions are set out in "Entscheidungen des Reichskommissars für gewerbliche Schutzrechte" (1916) GRUR 249–251.

91 Verordnung No 258 of 16 August 1916, art 1 and 4.

92 See *Weld v Früling* (1916) 32 T.L.R. 469; *Moss v Donahue* (1916) 32 T.L.R. 343.

93 Trading with the Enemy Amendment Act 1914, s 6.

94 Defence of the Realms Regulation, reg 30A; inserted by Order in Council, 24 September 1915: *London Gazette*, 24 September 1915, Iss 29307 p. 9426.

95 There were also anti-avoidance provisions whereby some assignments by enemies were ignored: Bundesratsverordnung No. 4790 of 1 July 1915, art 3.

government consent to assign any enemy property,[96] the French, on the other hand adopted a different approach, whereby enemy property was treated as abandoned and so could on application be sequestered by the courts (until such time, it was suspended).[97] Thus, once more, the measures taken restricted the rights of the owner but did not undermine the property itself.

3.3 *Extension of Time Limits*

It is often the mundane that needs the most attention in war time and so it was with industrial property. Any industrial property system based on examination, rather than deposit, involves applicants being required to meet deadlines; and both type of system require (renewal) fees to be paid at the right time to maintain the right. The moment war was declared it became more difficult for deadlines to be met as communications between enemy states were purposely broken down and so fees and other requirements went unmet.[98] Eventually, under the Treaties of Peace, applications and industrial property rights which existed when the war began,[99] but which had lapsed due to time limits expiring, fees not being paid or other formal requirement not being met because of the war, were revived.[100] This simple rule provided the utmost possible protection to industrial property, but in doing so merely followed a four-year trend of doing the same thing, which began within days of war being declared.

96 No 439 Verordnung über die Anmeldung und Sperre des in Österreich befindlichen Vermögens feindlicher Staatsangehöriger und die Anmeldung des im feindlichen Auslande befindlichen Vermögens österreichischer Staatsangehöriger [Ordinance on Registration and Control of Enemy Property in Austria], 31 October 1917 (Reichsgesetzblatt, p. 1211; Armstrong, p. 91), art 13 and 14; No 4905 Bundesratsverordnung über die Anmeldung das im Inland befindlichen Vermögens von Angehörigen feindlicher Staaten [Ordinance on Registration of Enemy Property in Germany], 7 October 1915 (Reichsgesetzblatt, p. 633; Armstrong, p. 47), art 7 and 8.

97 Garner, James. "Treatment of Enemy Aliens" *American Journal of International Law* (1918) 12: 744 at 747–9.

98 See comment in *Thirty-Third Report of the Comptroller 1916* (1916 HC Papers 58), Vol. 14, p. 463, p. 3.

99 The English courts rejected the argument this applied to applications being treated as filed where it would have been made but for the war: *In The Matter of Ucar's Patent* (1922) 39 R.P.C. 269.

100 Treaty of Versailles, art 307; Treaty of Saint Germain, art 259 (there was a one-year period after the Treaties came into effect to remedy this). As third parties might have been using the inventions, designs or marks for many years by this time there was also protection provided for third party who had used the invention or mark in the interim. In the UK, unusually in a dualist nation requiring treaties to have implementing legislation, the right more or less had direct effect: see *Cooksley v. Crowthorn Engineering Company Ltd* (1921) 38 R.P.C. 294.

On 4 August 1914, the German Patent Office extended all time limits for patent and trade mark matters for three months[101] – it was the day after Britain had declared war and within days of the declaration by France; this clearly fits with the official German position that the conflict would be resolved within three months. It also fits with the trend of protecting industrial property; additionally, as with the Central Powers generally, it was an attempt to preserve the distinction between enemy state and enemy national.

The French, acted in the following week, simply suspending a few specified time limits, rather than a more general extension[102]; although, as the French system was a deposit based there were only a handful of time limits which could be missed. The British approach, which arrived a few days later still, had a clear long-term "war footing".[103] Instead of a blanket extension,[104] a power was given to the comptroller (the head of the British Patent Office) to extend any time limit in two circumstances.[105] The first, where it a person was prevented from doing an act by reason of active service or enforced absence from the country and this justified an extension, and the second where by reason of the war doing the act would be prejudicial to any applicant, patentee or proprietor.[106] All "enemies" had enforced absence from the country (as they no longer had a right of entry into the country) and it appears the intention was to allow them to apply for extensions. Indeed, as explained already, "enemy" applications could be prosecuted up until grant.[107] This preserved the industrial property,

101 Bemerken No 162 Maßnahmen zur Berhütung von härten gegenüber Anmeldern und Inhabern gewerblicher Schuzrechte während der Dauer des Kriegszustandes [Measures to Prevent Hardship to Applicants and Holders of Industrial Property], 26 August 1914 (1914) 20 *Blatt für Muster und Zeichenwesen*, p. 251 (Langner and White, p. 193).

102 Décret suspendant les délais en matiére de brevets d'invention et de dessins et modèles [Decree Suspending Patent and Design Time Limits], 14 August 1914 (*Journal Officiel*, p. 7453; Langer, p. 159–160), art 3 (time limits relating to international exhibitions and filing for drawing or designs whether publicly and secretly).

103 There was also a general delegation of the Board of Trade's powers: Patents, Designs and Trade Marks (Temporary) Rules 1914, r 5; Trade Marks (Temporary) Rules 1914, r 3; Designs (Temporary) Rules 1914, r 3.

104 See Response of United Kingdom to Circular 158/1351 of the International Bureau (1915) 211 *Official Gazette of United States Patent Office* 288 (Langner and White, p. 284).

105 Also see "Procedure to be Followed under Rules 2 and 3 of the [Patents, Designs and Trade Marks (Temporary) Rules 1914]" *Illustrated Official Journal* (*Patents*), 26 August 1914, No 1336, p. 1197, [3 and 4] (Langner and White, p. 277). This broad power meant there was a notice on (almost) every Patents Journal during the war giving a warning that patents and applications which appear to have lapsed might not have done so (the first warning appeared in the *Illustrated Official Journal* (*Patents*), 9 September 1914, No 1338, p. 1253).

106 Patents, Designs and Trade Marks (Temporary) Rules 1914, r 3.

107 Suspended under the Patents, Designs and Trade Marks (Temporary) Rules 1914, r 2 just before grant; "Procedure to be Followed under Rules 2 and 3", [2].

but left its owner in a place of uncertainty. These measures were followed at the end of the month by a BIRPI circular asking all contracting states to show "tolerance" to applicants caused problems by the war[108]; something three of the four states had already done weeks earlier.

The fourth state, Austria, first moved in September 1914[109] and did so to address renewals only[110] and the Central Power's general "civility" continued with the Germans also extending the renewal fee deadline in the same month,[111] but also allowing for the reinstatement of applications which have been terminated[112] due to the war.[113] Six months later, the Germans continued by allowing applicants to delay the grant of their patents for a year[114] (and later allowing for further extension).[115] Eventually, the British allowed a time extension where the doing of an act as part of the prosecution of an industrial property right would, by reason of the war, be prejudicial to the public interest.[116] Thus, all sides were happy to provide mechanisms to keep rights alive: protecting the property as it were. A greater challenge came from the requirement to pay fees directly to enemy institutions, that is "enemy" Patent Offices.

108 Circular No. 144, 24 August 1914: see BIPRI, *La Protection Internationale de la Propriété Intellectuelle et la Guerre Mondiale* (1919), p. 71.

109 This is somewhat surprising as about a month earlier the Hungarian government included patent renewal in its general moratorium: No 160 A m. kir. minisztérium 1914. évi 6.045. M. E. számú rendelete, magánjogi kötelezettségek teljesítésére halasztás (moratórium) engedéséről [Decree Granting Moratorium on Fulfilling Private Law Obligations], 12 August 1914 (Magyarországi Rendeletek Tára, p. 1467; Langner and White, p. 324). It continued the effect of this moratorium through an assortment of laws until after the end of the war.

110 See below, p. 168.

111 See below pp. 168–9.

112 No 4491 of 10 September 1914 Bundesratsverordnung betreffend vorübergehende Erleichterungen auf dem Gebiete des Patent Gebrauchsmuster und Warenzeichenrechts [Ordinance on Temporary Relief in Relation to Patents, Utility Models and Trade Marks], art 1; (Reichsgestzblatt, p. 403; Langner and White, p. 193–4), art 2; there is also reference to the right to reinstatement in the Bürgerliches Gesetzbuch, BGB (the Civil Code), art 233.

113 See below pp. 139–40.

114 Bundesratsverordnung No 4704 of 31 March 1915, art 4 (the period under (No 1947) *Patentgesetz* [Patent Law], 7 April 1891 (Reichsgestzblatt, p. 79) art 23(4)); Later still, a general extension of varying lengths was given to everybody: No 95 Bekanntmachung, 7 May 1915 (1915) 21 *Blatt für Muster- und Zeichenwesen*, p. 142 (Langner and White, p. 201).

115 No 5147 Bundesratsverordnung über Erleichterungen im Patent, Gebrauchsmuster und Warenzeichenrechts [Ordinance on Facilitation of Patent, Utility Models and Trade Mark Law], 13 April 1916 (Reichsgestzblatt, p. 278; Langner and White, p. 205).

116 Patents, Designs, and Trade Marks (Temporary) (Second Set) Rules 1915 (SI 1915/1011).

3.3.1 Fees: Trading with the Enemy

The conduct of patent proceedings, and the payment of fees could involve trading with the enemy. A simple example would be a British Patent Agent taking a fee from an Austrian client for filing a form during the prosecution of a patent before the British Patent Office. In Britain the common law rule was that any existing contract with an enemy alien was dissolved once war was declared[117] and thereafter a licence was required before any commercial intercourse with an enemy alien was permitted.[118] This common law rule was buttressed by Royal Proclamations prohibiting anyone who is in British Territory trading with the enemy.[119] The complexities of when something was trading with the enemy are well beyond the scope of this discussion[120] but it is clear that a German company, *absent a licence*, could no longer take steps to instruct a British Patent Agent.[121] A general licence was forthcoming, however, being granted in September 1914,[122] and from April 1915 it was permissible for any person to take money from royalties on enemy industrial property rights for

117 *Janson v Driefontein Consolidated Mines* [1902] 1 *Appeal Cases* 484 (relating to the South African Boar War); this presented a tension with the Hague Convention on the Legal Rights of Belligerents, art 23(h); see William Trotter, *The Law of Contract During and After the War* (3rd Ed Hodge 1919), p. 25–26.

118 See *"The Mashona"* [1900] 17 Buchanan 135.

119 The Original Proclamation was issued on 5 August 1914 (A Proclamation Relating to Trading with the Enemy, *London Gazette*, Second Supplement to 4 August 1914, p. 6166), but it was superseded by one on 9 September 1914 (A Proclamation Relating to Trading with the Enemy, *London Gazette*, Second Supplement to 9 September, p. 7177). These were extended as more countries declared war.

120 See generally, Roxburgh, Ronald. "The Alien Enemy in English Law" *Journal of Comparative Legislation and International Law* (1920) 2:269; Clive Parry "The Trading with the Enemy Act and the Definition of an Enemy" *Modern Law Review* (1941) 4:161.

121 The payment had to come from the company and not an agent: see Board of Trade Announcement to Patent Agents, *Illustrated Official Journal* (*Patents*), 24 November 1915, No 1401, p. 1303.

122 Trading with the Enemy: Payment of Patents, Designs, and Trade Marks Fees, 23 September 1914 (*Illustrated Official Journal* (*Patents*), 30 September 1914, No 1341, p. 1328; Armstrong, p. 211); following the Royal Proclamation of 8 October 1914 a further licence was issued on 4 November 1914 (*Illustrated Official Journal* (*Patents*), 11 November 1914, No 1347, p. 1492; Armstrong, p. 212); it was replaced by a new licence on 7 December 1915 (*Illustrated Official Journal* (*Patents*), 22 December 1915, No 1405, p. 1402; Armstrong, p. 213), which was amended on 5 September 1917 (*Illustrated Official Journal* (*Patents*), 12 September 1917, No 1495, p. 758; Armstrong, p. 216). Permission was also made to receive payments from those on the prohibited list (from whom payment could not usually be taken): "Interests of British and Enemy Subjects in Patents, Trade Marks, and Designs" *Illustrated Official Journal* (*Patents*), 25 April 1917, No 1475, p. 328.

the prosecution of applications and paying renewal fees.[123] But in the closing phase of the war there was an about-face as payments to enemy Patent Offices and from enemies were finally forbidden[124] and any further proceedings relating to enemy patents were suspended.[125]

The common law rule by its nature existed before the outbreak of war, but it was matched in other countries with a statutory ban in September 1914 on trading with the enemy by France[126] and soon after payments to enemy countries from Germany[127] and from Austria were banned.[128] But as in Britain, the payment of industrial property fees were eventually excluded from prohibitions on trading with the enemy in France[129] and Germany,[130] but unusually it appears not in Austria. While fees were due at numerous stages in the application process for patents, trade marks and designs, it was maintenance (or renewal) fees for granted rights where the pressure was most extreme. The collection of fees from overseas enemies could bring in much needed money to the government; more so for the allies as there were so many more German industrial property rights registered in France and Britain than there were the other way around. But beyond these financial gains, the approach once more

123 "Alien Enemies, Patents, Designs, and Trade Marks (Temporary Rules) Act 1914", *Illustrated Official Journal (Patents)*, 28 April 1915, No 1371, p. 456 (this notice was included in most editions of the journal thereafter until it was modified just before the end of the war when payment regarding enemy patents was generally forbidden: see *Illustrated Official Journal (Patents)*, 23 October 1918, No 1553, p. 924).

124 "Patents, Designs and Trade Marks" (1918) 101 Board of Trade Journal p. 78; "Trading with the Enemy", Notice 15 July 1918, (*Official Journal (Patents)*, 24 July 1918, No 1541, p. 653; Armstrong, p. 217). Any fees already remitted to agents had to be paid to the public custodian: "Remittances by Enemies for Payment of Patent, &c. Fees", *Illustrated Official Journal (Patents)*, 11 September 1918, No 1547, p. 797.

125 Notice, *Illustrated Official Journal (Patents)*, 31 July 1918, No 1540, p. 672.

126 Décret of 27 September 1914.

127 No 4504 Bekanntmachung, betreffend Zahlungsverbot gegen England [Notice of Payment Ban Against England], 30 September 1914 (Reichsgetzblatt, p. 421); extended to France: Ordinance No 4515 Bekanntmachung, betreffend Zahlungsverbot gegen Frankreich, 20 October 1914 (Reichsgetzblatt, p. 443).

128 No 291 Verordnung über die Erlassung eines Zahlungsverbotes gegen Großbritannien und Frankreich [Ordinance Imposing Ban on Payments to Great Britain and France], 22 October 1914 (Reichsgetzblatt, p. 1148); it had previously only banned it on a reciprocal basis: Martin Schennach "The Effects of World War I on Austrian Private Law" *Comparative Legal History* (2014) 2:215 at 238.

129 "France: Payement de taxes relatives à la propriété industrielle" (30 November 1914) *La Propriété Industrielle*, p. 152 (Langner and White, p. 162).

130 Bekanntmachung No 4 of 28 December 2016 (2017) 23 *Blatt für Muster- und Zeichenwesen* p. 2.

was an attempt to preserve the property in enemy countries, even though the rights of the proprietor could not be exercised.

3.3.2 Fees: Suspension and Exemption

In addition to allowing payment of renewal fees to enemy Patent Offices another step was taken to preserve property otherwise at risk. Time limits for paying renewal fees were extended. In Britain this was dealt with by the general power, but elsewhere provision was made separately. For instance, soon after war was declared, the French suspended the deadline for the payment of renewal fees until the end of the war[131]; although this was later restricted to where there was a reciprocal extension.[132] The Austrians provided an open ended extension for patent renewal fees, and to allow a lapsed patent or trade mark to be restored by those involved in military service[133] or where the difficulty with payment was caused by wartime interruptions in communications reaching the Patent Office.[134] For trade marks, at least initially, a registration was continued to the end of the war without a requirement to do anything[135]; once more on the basis of reciprocity.[136] This might have been part of a broader expectation that the war would be over quickly, or more likely a holding position to protect the property. After the initial extension,[137] the Germans allowed a further long extension (of up to nine months from the outbreak of war, which

131 Décret of 14 August, art 1.

132 Loi 27 May 1915, art 5.

133 Verordnung No 232 of 2 September 1914, art 5.

134 Verordnung No 232 of 2 September 1914, art 3 and 4; Regulation No 257 Verorduung womit aus Aulaß der friegeritchen Berwictlungen Ausuahmsbestimmuungen auf dem Gebiete des Markenschußwesens getroffen warden [Ordinance on the regulation of foreign undertakings relating to trade marks], 24 September 1914 (Reichsgetzblatt, p. 1021; Langner and White, p. 87), art 5.

135 Verordnung No 257 of 24 September 1914 (1 February 1915), but extended to 1 August 1915 by Verordnung No 355 betreffend eine Ergänzung der Verordnung, womit aus Anlaß der kriegerischen Verwicklungen Ausnahmebestimmungen auf dem Gebiete des Markenschutzwesens getroffen werden [Decree Establishing Exceptional Arrangements for Trade Marks During Wartime], 24 December 1914 (Reichsgetzblatt, p. 1351; Langner and White, p. 91) and to a date to be fixed by Regulation No 177 Verordnung betreffend eine Ergänzung der Verordnung vom 24. September 1914, womit aus Anlaß der kriegerischen Verwicklungen Ausnahmebestimmungen auf dem Gebiete des Markenschutzwesens getroffen warden [Ordinance Supplementing that of 24 September 1914], 24 June 1915 (Reichsgetzblatt, p. 312; Langner and White, p. 95).

136 Verordnung No 257 of 24 September 1914, art 6.

137 See p. 164.

was later extended further[138]) where a person could not pay renewal fees,[139] but this was also contingent on reciprocal protection.[140] This even led to some moves to try and persuade the British to give similar protection.[141] These steps acknowledge once more that the desire of all the belligerents was to preserve the existence of foreign industrial property even though in most cases the rights were not being exercised by friend or foe. The blanket approach was also demonstrated in the related post-war issue of term extension.

3.3.3 Patent Term Extension

The war meant that many inventions could not be worked, because it was difficult accessing raw materials, and there was a diminished market for goods. But patents lasted for a comparatively short time, 14 or 15 years,[142] and this meant with a war lasting over four years much of that monopoly was lost. In the closing months of the war, this loss of exclusivity was being questioned, particularly in Britain,[143] and while patent term was not part of any peace negotiations all

138 No 4704 Bundesratsverordnung betreffend weitere Erleichterungen auf dem Gebiete des Patent und Gebrauchsmusters [Ordinance Simplifying Patent and Utility Model Law], 31 March 1915 (Reichsgestzblatt, p. 212; Langner and White, p. 199), art 2 (the right to extend also applied to another deadline relating to utility models: art 1).

139 Bundesratsverordnung No 4491 of 10 September 1914, art 1; see No 282 Auslegung der Verordnung des Bundesrats vom 10 September, betreffend vorübergehende Erleichterungen auf dem Gebiete des Patent-, Gebrauchsmuster-, und Warenzeichenrechts, in der Praxis des Steuerlichen Patentamts [Interpretation of Law of 10 September 1914] (1914) 20 *Blatt für Patent-, Munster- und Zeichenwesen*, p. 383 (Langer, pp. 197–8), paragraph 1 (it needed to be supported by facts, not mere assertion: Notice, paragraph 3). The German Office also made it clear that those who got the right enjoyed national treatment and not the rights from the country of origin: Bekanntmachung No 71, betreffend Erleichterungen auf dem Gebiete des Patent-, Gebrauchmuster- und Warenzeichenrechts [Notice Concerning Relief in Patent, Utility Models and Trade Mark Law], 31 March 1915, (1915) 21 *Blatt für Muster- und Zeichenwesen*, p. 118 (Langner and White, p. 200).

140 Bundesratsverordnung No 4491 of 10 September 1914, art 3; a notice was published setting out who was entitled: Bekanntmachung No 28, betreffend Erleichterungen auf dem Gebiete des Patent-, Gebrauchmuster- und Warenzeichenrechts in ausländischen Staaten [Notice Regarding Relief in Patent, Utility Model and Trade Mark Law], 20 February 1915 (1915) 21 *Blatt für Muster- und Zeichenwesen*, p. 24 (Langner and White, p. 198).

141 Letter of Dr Hamburger, 15 October 1914, *Patent and Trade Mark Review* (1914) 13:38.

142 Patentgesetz 1891, Art 7 (15 years); Patentgesetz 1897, art 14 (15 years) and Loi 5 July 1844, art 4 and 8 (15 years) and the Patents and Designs Act 1907, s 13 and 17 (14 years).

143 Various questions were asked in the House of Commons: 109 Parl. Deb, H.C (5th ser.) (5 Aug 1918), col 941W; 110 Parl. Deb, H.C (5th ser.) (24 Oct 1918), col 958W, 115 Parl. Deb, H.C (5th ser.) (14 May 1919), col 1579 and (15 May 1919), cols 1811–1812W.

four countries extended term one way or another.[144] Highlighting again how each belligerent wanted to maintain the value of the patent whether owned by allies or enemies. A similar desire is evident from the steps taken in relation to the preservation of priority.

3.4 *Priority*

The system of priority under the Paris Convention had become well developed by 1914. Essentially, the Convention provided that a person could file an application in one convention country and then use that first filing (priority date) in another country for the purposes of assessing registrabilty. The periods varied for designs, trade marks and patents (inventions) ranged from 4 to 12 months.[145] The effect of priority can be profound. For example, a patent application which was first filed in Germany on 6 July 1913 could be subsequently filed in Britain on 12 May 1914 and the novelty of that application would be judged from 6 July 1913. A competitor could not invalidate the patent, therefore, if it transpired that an identical product had first been sold in England in January 1914. The outbreak of war presented two challenges to this system. The first was whether the obligation to recognise priority from a filing in an enemy country should be honoured (as has already been discussed there was a somewhat mixed view as to the continuing effect of the Paris Convention). The second was more practical: could a filing physically be made (eg could it be posted or otherwise delivered between enemy countries) and was it possible to establish priority (for instance, filing a certified copy of the earlier application[146]).

While the four countries had made some provision to address the difficulties with priority during the war, the Peace Treaties went much further extending the periods of priority to six months after the Treaties came into

144 Patents and Designs Act 1919 (9 & 10 Geo 5. c. 80), s 7; Germany: No 771 Gesetz, betreffend eine verlängerte Schutzdauer bei Patenten und Gebrauchsmustern sowie die Wiedereinsetzung in den vorigen Stand im Verfahren vor dem Reichspatentamt [Law Extending Patent and Utility Model Term and Reinstating Status for Proceedings], 27 April 1920, (Reichsgetzblatt, p. 675); France: Décret modifiant les délais précis par le décret du 27 janvier 1920 conformément à l'arrangement international du 30 juice 1920 pour la conservation of le rétablissement des droit de propriété industrielle [Decree for Conservation and Restoration of Industrial Property], 11 January 1921 (Journal Officiel, p. 778); Austria, Regulation No. 267 Bundesgesetz über eine Verlängerung der Höchstdauer von Patenten [Law Extending Maximum Duration of Patents], 26 April 1921 (Reichsgetzblatt, p. 829).

145 Patents, 12 months; designs and trade marks, 4 months: Paris Convention (Washington 1911), art 4(c).

146 E.g. Patents Rule 1908 (SI 1907/949), r 16.

effect.[147] Thereby granting a massive opening up to overseas filings. This generosity reflected a benevolent mood during the war to assist with priority claims, something BIRPI had push for throughout the conflict[148]; demonstrating once more the general willingness to try and save industrial property where possible (at worst based on reciprocity). In the early days of the war neither France nor Germany made any special provision for priority, but in Britain it was covered by the general power to extend time limits.[149] The Austrians adopted a special rule extending time early on, in September 1914,[150] and later relaxed the requirements to file documents establishing entitlement to priority,[151] before providing general extensions of the priority period for certain countries.[152] Originally, the Austrian law applied to any person entitled to claim priority under the Paris Convention, whether or not an enemy.[153] In 1915 and 1916, Austria,[154] Germany[155] and France[156] took steps similar to those eventually adopted in the Peace Treaties and suspended the period of priority until the

147 Treaty of Versailles, art 308(1); Treaty of Saint Germain, art 260(1).

148 See BIPRI, *La Protection Internationale de la Propriété Intellectuelle et la Guerre Mondiale* (1919), p. 75.

149 Patents, Designs, and Trade Marks (Temporary) Rules 1914, r 3.

150 No. 233 Verordnung betreffend die Verlängeruug der Frist zur Beibringung der sum Nachweise des Brioritätsrechtes bei Patent, Muster und Merkenanmeeldunten erforseelixhen Belge [Ordinance Extending Priority Deadlines] (Reichsgesetzblatt, p. 983; Langner and White, p. 82).

151 No 353 Verordnung betreffend die Verlängerung der Frist zur Beibringung der zum Nachweise des Prioritätsrechtes bei Patent-, Muster- und Markenanmeldungen erforderlichen Belege [Ordinance Further Extending Priority Deadlines], 1 December 1915 (Reichsgesetzblatt, p. 881; Langner and White, p. 88); the decision was delayed until grant: "Berichte und Mitteilungen", *Österreichisches Patent Blatt*, 1 May 1915, p. 120 (Langner and White, p. 91).

152 Kundmachung über Ausnahmsbestimmungen für die im Pariser Unionsvertrag zum Schutze des gewerblichen Eigentums festgestzten Prioritätsfristen zu Gunsten der Angehörigen ausländischer Staaten [Notice on Exceptional Priority Period], *Österreichisches Patent Blatt*, 15 December 1915, p. 276 (Langner and White, p. 96).

153 No. 349 Verordnung über Ausnahmsbestimmungen für die im Pariser Unionsvertrag zum Schutze des gewerblichen Eigentums festgesetzten Prioritätsfristen anläßlich des Kriegszustandes [Ordinance on Exceptional Provisions Concerning Priority Periods], 1 December 1915, (Reichsgesetzblatt, p. 879; Langner and White, p. 89), art 1(2) made it retrospectively on 1 December 1915.

154 Verordnung No. 349, 1 December 1915 (it was retrospective, art 3).

155 No 4728 Bekanntmachung, betreffend die Verlängerung der im Artikel 4 der revidierten Pariser Übereinkunft zum Schutze des gewerblichen Eigentums vom 2. Juni 1911 vorgesehenen Prioritätsfristen [Notice Extending Priority Periods], 7 May 1915 (Reichsgesetzblatt, p. 272; Langner and White, p. 200).

156 Loi 27 May 1915, art 7.

end of hostilities[157] but only for nationals of countries who were doing the same (a reciprocal basis); Britain continued to rely on individual applications being made to extend the priority period. While relying on reciprocity, the war time approach once more involved countries taking all possible steps to retain the validity (that is the novelty) of industrial property rights irrespective of whether owned by an enemy or ally: protecting the property over almost everything else. This mindset is further demonstrated by the suspension of the requirement to work a patent.

3.5 *Requirement to Work*

The law of France had long required that a patentee work the invention or risk it being revoked,[158] and a similar rule was (very controversially) introduced in Britain.[159] The Central Powers, Austria[160] and Germany,[161] had a more moderate approach whereby non-working could lead to a compulsory licence. Clearly when war broke out foreign companies, whether enemy, allied or neutral, might struggle to work the invention.[162] Indeed, in France it became *unlawful* for an enemy subject to work a patented invention or use a trade mark[163] and in Austria it was provided that a person could petition in the public interest to suppress enemy a company's rights to use an invention[164] and similar provision was made in Germany.[165] It was agreed in the Peace Treaties that the requirement to work the invention should be treated as having been suspended during the war.[166] This largely reflects the position that had been adopted by the Allies during the conflict (the Central Powers had no need to do anything). The French had suspended the period for non-working almost immediately

157 Germany initially extended it to 30 June 1916, but this was extended it to the end of the war: No 5138 Bekanntmachung, betreffend die verlängerten Prioritätsfristen [Notice Regarding Extending Priority Periods], 8 April 1916 (Reichsgesetzblatt, p. 259; Langner and White, p. 205).

158 Loi 5 July 1844 sur les brevets d'invention [French Patent Law 1844] (Recueil Duvergier, p. 553), art 32(2) (non-use a ground of revocation).

159 Patents and Designs Act 1907, s 27. It was one of the most debated provision when the Bill was before Parliament: see 172 Parl. Deb. (4th ser.) (17 Apr 1907), cols 1016–1017, 1027, 1031–1032, 1036, 1037, 1041, 1044–1045, 1053–1054 (Cl 10); 180 Parl. Deb. (4th ser.) (9 Aug 1907), cols 663–668; 181 Parl. Deb. (4th ser.) (20 Aug 1907), cols 421–422; (23 Aug 1907), cols 1356–1357.

160 Patentgesetz 1897, art 27 (three years non-use).

161 Patentgesetz 1891, art 21.

162 See question of Sir Frederick Crawley, 65 Parl. Deb. H.C. (5th ser.) (10 Aug 1914), col 2249.

163 Loi 27 May 1915, art 1.

164 Verordnung No 258 of 16 August 1916, art 4.

165 Bundesratsverordnung No. 4790 of 1 July 1915, art 1.

166 Treaty of Versailles, art 307; Treaty of Saint Germain, art 259.

after hostilities broke out[167] a measure which could be seen as maintaining the status quo and protecting the patent for future exploitation, and likewise the British suspended the working requirements in November 1915[168] to protect the post war value of the patent. In both countries, the working requirement applied to both friendly and enemy patents. On the one hand, this shows adherence to the Convention rules on non-discrimination, but it is better viewed as fitting the clear pattern of preserving the property right against any possible challenge arising from the war.

3.6 *Government Use*

The Peace Treaties indemnified the Allied Powers for government use of any industrial property rights owned by nationals of the Central Powers.[169] This played into long standing government rights of use. The British had allowed for the government use of patents upon payment of compensation (Crown use)[170] which could be invoked in peace time as well as during the war.[171] Thus, there was little need to expand on this power during the war although an obligation to provide the government with information about inventions (whether patented or not) was introduced in 1916.[172] On the other hand, the French government had no right to use a patent until 1916; when the Ministers of War and the Navy were permitted to grant compulsory licences in respect inventions in the interest of national defence.[173] The royalty paid was by agreement or settled by arbitration.[174] This approach largely follows that of its British ally. The use of enemy owned patents by Allied Powers were exonerated when peace came. Having spent the entire war preserving enemy patents it would have been entirely unacceptable to a war weary country to then have to pay former

167 Décret of 14 August 1914, art 2; it was continued on a restricted reciprocity basis under Loi 27 May 1915, art 5.

168 Patents and Designs (Partial Suspension) Act 1915 (5 & 6 Geo b5. c. 85), s 1.

169 Treaty of Versailles, art 306(3); Treaty of Saint Germain, art 258(3); the laws depriving enemies of rights in the Allied Powers also remained in force: art 306(2) and art 258(2).

170 Patents and Designs Act 1907, s 29; it was extended to designs during the war however: Defence of the Realm Regulations, r 8C: inserted by Order in Council 28 July 1915, *London Gazette*, 30 July 1915, Iss 29247, p. 7463.

171 In practice, most payments were deferred and paid after the war following a claim being made to the Royal Commission on Awards to Inventors (whose work only finished in 1937); a list of the Commission reports can be found in Johnson, Phillip. *Parliament, Inventions and Patents: A Research Guide and Bibliography* (Routledge 2018), p. 614.

172 Defence of the Realm Regulations, r 8CC; inserted by Order in Council, 7 September 1916: *London Gazette*, 12 September 1916, Iss 29745, p. 8973.

173 Loi 12 April 1916, art 1.

174 Loi 12 April 1916, art 1.

enemies for infringing industrial property rights which were necessary to win the war.

There were similar provisions allowing government use under German law[175] and that of Austria.[176] However, it appears that before and during the war[177] the German provision was hardly ever used and there is some evidence that patents were simply ignored by the military.[178] So as it could not be proved which patent were used by the Central Powers, the absence of an indemnity would probably have made little difference. The Treaties already had a requirement to pay reparations and these were (theoretically) set to what the German and Austrian governments could afford to pay.[179] These was, therefore, no more money left in the pot. This futility provides a contrast to the other government activity that of keeping some patents secret.

3.7 *Secret Patents*

The disclosure of an invention,[180] by the outbreak of World War I, was seen as a central paradigm of patent law. After all, patents were usually published[181] and it would not be too difficult for the enemy to get a copy of the specification whether through espionage or a neutral power. So it is hardly surprising that in the early years of the First World War many high ranking Germans expressed serious concern about "patent espionage".[182] This was despite the fact the German law already allowed for patents to be excluded from publication where they were owned by the state.[183] This system had problems, however, as certain information was still published, such as the fact the patent had been granted,[184] making it quite clear which inventions the government wanted kept secret.[185] Further, private applications could not be kept secret leaving a significant loophole. This was addressed in a 1915 Notice where it was said that

175 Patentgesetz 1891, art 5(2).
176 Patentgesetz 1897, art 15.
177 It had been used three times: Mächtel, *Das Patentrecht im Krieg*, p. 161.
178 Mächtel, *Das Patentrecht im Krieg*, p. 149–50 (although Mächtel doubts it was widespread).
179 See further, Marks, Sally. "The Myths of Reparations" *Central European History* (1978) 11:231.
180 Johnson, Phillip. *Privatised Law Reform: A History of Patent Law through Private Legislation, 1620–1907* (Routledge 2017), Ch 7.
181 Loi 5 July 1844, art 24; Patentgesetz 1897, art 64; Patentgesetz 1891, art 23 and 27; Patents and Designs Act 1907, s 6 (public inspection).
182 Mächtel, *Das Patentrecht im Krieg*, pp. 46–49.
183 Patentgesetz 1891, art 19 and 23.
184 Patentgesetz 1891, art 26.
185 Mächtel, Florian. *Das Patentrecht im Krieg* (Mohr Siebeck 2009), p. 25.

disclosing such patent applications would be treated as treason.[186] In 1917, the Germans eventually set out a mechanism for restricting publication of patent applications which needed to remain secret in the national interest.[187] The Austrian law likewise provided for government patents to be excluded from publication when war broke out,[188] and it followed some of the steps taken by its ally to reiterate that disclosing certain patents would be treason.[189] The Allied Powers took a someone different approach.

In Britain it had been acknowledged for over fifty years that some inventions needed to be kept secret, but the law has a similar pitfall to Germany in that it applied only where the invention was assigned to the government.[190] Accordingly, this rule was expanded in 1915 to restrict publication of *any* patent or design where its publication would be detrimental to the defence of the realm or public safety.[191] In France, by contrast, there were no secret patents at the outbreak of war but it was possible to delay publication for one year[192] upon request (a time period which was suspended on the outbreak of war).[193] After two years of warfare, it too introduced provisions to keep patents secret.[194]

---

186 No 209 Bekanntmachung, Bert. Wahrung der Landesverteidigungsinteressen bei der Rachjuchung von Patenten im Kriege [Notice on Patent Retaliation], 10 October 1915 (1915) 21 *Blatt für Patent, Munster, und Zeichewesen* p. 242; Langner and White, p. 204; reference is made to (No 651) Reichsstrafgesetzbuch, 15 May 1871 [Criminal Code], art 89 (assisting an enemy); for a discussion of the notice's gestation see Mächtel, *Das Patentrecht im Krieg*, pp. 49–52.

187 No 22. Bekanntmachung über den Auschluß der Öffentlichkeit für Patente und Gebranchsmuster [Notice Restricting Patent Inspection], 8 February 1917 (1917) 23 *Blatt für Patent, Munster, und Zeichewesen*, p. 13 (Langer and White, p. 207).

188 Patentgesetz 1897, art 65; the protection of secret designs was only instituted in Verordnung No 152, 2 June 1915, art 2.

189 For a discussion of the Austrian approach see Mark Cornwall "Traitors and the Meaning of Treason in Austria-Hungary's Great War" *Transactions of the Royal Historical Society* (2015) 25:113.

190 Patents and Designs Act 1907, s 30; Patents Rules 1908, rr 97–100; Patents for Inventions Act 1859 (22 Vict. c. 13); see more generally, O'Dell, Thomas. *Inventions and Secrecy: A History of Secret Patents in the United Kingdom* (Clarendon 1994).

191 Defence of the Realm Regulations, reg 18B(1); inserted by Order in Council, 14 October 1915, *London Gazette*, 15 October 1915, Iss 29328, p. 10133. When this Order was revoked it meant that applications could be accepted back to this date: see *Official Journal (Patents)*, 18 December 1918, No 1561, p. 1112.

192 Loi 5 July 1844, art 11 (as amended by Loi modifiant divers articles de la Loi du 5 juillet 1844 sur les brevets d'invention [Law Modifying the Patent Law 1844], 7 April 1902 (*Journal Officiel*, p. 2607; Langner and White, p. 139).

193 Décret of 14 August 1914, art 3(2).

194 Loi relative aux inventions intéressant la défense nationals 12 April 1916 [Law of National Defence], art 2: (Journal Officiel, p. 3140; Langner and White, p. 165).

In parallel with rules prohibiting publication, Britain and France adopted restrictions on filing patent applications abroad.[195] To achieve the same ends, German and Austria relied on their treason law and in the case of the latter it was expressly stated[196] that where filing a patent overseas might assist the enemy it would constitute the military offence of "crimes against the war power of the state"[197] carrying a potential death penalty.[198] The restrictions on filing overseas and secret patents while known before the war were made more robust as the conflict progressed. In contrast to almost every other type of war time measure, there was no attempt to require disclosure of secret patents when peace came, the Peace Treaties specifically permitted restrictions on industrial property rights for the purposes of national defence or the public interest to continue.[199] It was one of the few cases where the desire was not to protect the property but to protect the state; indeed, by setting the bar so high it can be seen as a way of normalising and protecting as much of the industrial property as possible.

4 Conclusion

The role of industrial property in the economic war might have taken many turns. The belligerents could have revoked enemy industrial property rights

195 Defence of the Realms Regulation, reg 18B(2); inserted by Order in Council, 14 October 1915: *London Gazette*, 15 October 1915, Iss 29328, p. 10133 (but as there was a special rule where Patents were excluded from the restrictions on sending printed material overseas: Defence of the Realms Regulation, reg 24B(1); inserted by Order in Council, 19 July 1917: *London Gazette*, 20 July 1917, Iss 30192, p. 7338) provided there were permission from the Board of Trade; previously special permission had been given to file in South Africa: "Applications for Patents in Union of South Africa", (*Illustrated Official Journal* (*Patents*), 14 February 1917, No 1465, p. 115); France: Loi 27 May 1915, art 6 (restricted filing abroad to where reciprocal prohibition in place); Loi relative aux inventions intéressant la défense nationale [Law on Inventions Relating to National Defence], 12 April 1916 (*Journal Officiel*, p. 3140; Langer and White, p. 165), art 3 (banning filing overseas where relates to national security). It was punished as a breach of the law of espionage: Loi tendant à établir des pénalitès contre l'espionnage [Espionage Law], 18 April 1886 (*Journal Officiel*, p. 1821), art 5 (5 years imprisonments and fine).

196 Mitteilung des k. k. Ministeriums für Landesverteidigung vom 1. Mai 1916 über die Anmeldung und due Verwertung von Patenten in feindlichen und in neutralen Staaten [Notice on Registration and Use of Patents in Enemy and Neutral States], *Österreichisches Patent Blatt*, 15 May 1916, p. 88 (Langer and White, p. 98).

197 "Verbrechen wider die Kriegsmacht des Staates".

198 Militärstrafgesetz über Verbrechen und Vergehen [Military Criminal Code], 15 January 1855, §§327–329.

199 Treaty of Versailles, art 306(5); Treaty of Saint Germain, art 258(5).

and so made them free to use for all. The intangible nature of the rights gave governments great freedom. Inventions could have been no longer protected by patents, designs not registrable and trade marks pushed out the market. When there was wartime economic hardship, removing enemy patent and design protection from enemies might have opened up opportunities for domestic and friendly companies. Yet none of the four belligerents took this path of increasing access, rather each ensured that industrial property survived the war and ultimately it was returned to its pre-war owner.

Each time the belligerents protected the property at all costs by giving procedural flexibility to applicants and proprietors ensuring that the patents, trade marks and designs survived. Even when attacks were made it was against the proprietor and not the property. Peace saved the industrial property rights still in existence, but the Treaties went further reviving many more. The disproportionate number of German patents filed in the Patent Offices of the Allied Powers meant it was one of the few areas where Germany gained more from the peace than its erstwhile enemy. It would have been expected that when industrial property rights went to war the causality would be the right itself but it turned out enemy patents, designs and trade marks were seen as too important and were protected even if the proprietor was not.

Acknowledgements

I would like to thank Péter Munkácsi for his comments on an earlier draft of this chapter.

Bibliography

Anon. "Status of Enemy Aliens in Courts of Justice" *Harvard Law Review* (1918) 31: 470.

Anon. "Alien Enemies as Plaintiffs", *Solicitors Journal* (1914) 59:83.

Baty, Thomas, and Morgan, John. *War: Its Conduct and Legal Results*, New York, Dutton & Co, 1915.

Bond, Catherine. "'This is not a Bill to legalize looting': Wartime Regulation of Enemy-Owned Intellectual Property in Australia" *Intellectual Property Quarterly* (2015) 79.

Bond, Catherine, and Lai, Jessica. "'A Process of Experimentation': Intellectual Property, War and Defence in Australia" in *Forgotten Intellectual Property Lore*, edited by Shubha Ghosh, Cheltenham: Edward Elgar 2020, 376–406.

Broadberry, Stephen, and Harrison, Mark, (eds.). *The Economics of World War I*, Cambridge: Cambridge University Press 2005.

Broadberry, Stephen and Howlett, Peter. 'The United Kingdom during World War I: Business as Usual?' in *The Economics of World War I*, edited by Stephen Broadberry and Mark Harrison, Cambridge: Cambridge University Press, 2005.

Bureaux Internationaux Réunis pour la Protection de la Propriété Intellectuelle, *La Protection Internationale de La Propriété Intellectuelle et la Guerre Mondiale* (1919).

Cornwall, Mark. "Traitors and the Meaning of Treason in Austria-Hungary's Great War" *Transactions of the Royal Historical Society* (2015) 25: 113.

Curti, Arthur. *Handelsverbot und Vermögen in Feindesland. Gesetzgebung und Praxis von England, Frankreich, Deutschland, Italien, Österreich und Rußland während des Krieges 1914/15*, Heymann, 1916.

Ferchland, Paul. *Der internationale gewerbliche Rechtsschutz im Kriege*, Berlin, 1915.

French, David. 'The Rise and Fall of Business as Usual' in *War and the State: The Transformation of British Government, 1914–1918*, edited by Kathleen Burk, Ch 1, George Allen & Unwin, 1982.

Garner, James. "Treatment of Enemy Aliens" *American Journal of International Law* (1919) 13: 22.

Garner, James. "Treatment of Enemy Aliens" *American Journal of International Law* (1918) 12: 744.

Hallifax. Stuart. "'Over by Christmas': British popular opinion and the short war in 1914" *First World War Studies* (2010) 1: 103.

Herwig. Holger. "Germany and the "Short-War" Illusion: Toward a New Interpretation?" *Journal of Military History* (2002) 66: 681.

Johnson, Phillip. *Parliament, Inventions and Patents: A Research Guide and Bibliography*, Abingdon: Routledge, 2018.

Johnson, Phillip. *Privatised Law Reform: A History of Patent Law through Private Legislation, 1620–1907*, Abingdon: Routledge, 2017.

Ladas, Stephen. *Patents, Trademarks, and Related Rights: National and International Protection*, Cambridge: Harvard University Press, 1975.

Langner, Lawrence, and White, William. *Basic Patent and Trade-Mark Laws of the Principal Belligerent Powers together with War Legislation*, Washington, 1919.

Mächtel, Florian. *Das Patentrecht im Krieg*, Tübingen, Mohr Siebech 2009.

Marks, Sally. "The Myths of Reparations" *Central European History* (1978) 11: 231.

McDermott, John. "'A Needless Sacrifice' British Businessmen and Business As Usual in the First World War" *Albion* (1989) 21: 263.

O'Dell, Thomas. *Inventions and Secrecy: A History of Secret Patents in the United Kingdom*, Oxford: Clarendon 1994.

Parry, Clive. "The Trading with the Enemy Act and the Definition of an Enemy" *Modern Law Review* (1914) 4: 161.

Picciotto, Cyril. "Alien Enemy Persons, Firms and Corporations in English Law" *Yale Law Journal* (1917) 27: 167.

Pillet, Antoine. "La Guerre Actuelle et le Driot des Gens" *Revenue Générale de Droit International Public* (1916) 23: 5 and 203.

Poltitis, Nikolaos. "Effets de la Guerre sur les Obligations Internationales" *Annuaire de l'Institut de Droit International* (1911) 24: 200.

Renault. Louis. "Les Unions Internationales" *Revue Générale de Droit International Public* (1896) 3: 14.

Ricketson, Sam. *The Paris Convention for the Protection of Industrial Property: A Commentary*, Oxford: Oxford University Press, 2015.

Ritter, Gerald. *The Schlieffen Plan: Critique of a Myth*, London: Oswald Wolff, 1958.

Roxburgh, Ronald. "The Alien Enemy in English Law" *Journal of Comparative Legislation and International Law* (1920) 2: 269.

Saint-Amour, Paul. "On the Partiality of Total War", *Critical Inquiry* (2014) 40: 420.

Schennach, Martin. "The Effects of World War I on Austrian Private Law" *Comparative Legal History* (2014) 2: 215.

Scobell Armstrong, John Warneford. *War and Treaty Legislation*, London: Hutchinson, 1921.

Trotter, William. *The Law of Contract During and After the War*, 3rd Edition, Hodge, 1919.

Vojáček, Jan. "Jugoslavia: A New Patent Territory", *Patent and Trademark Review* (1922) 20: 259.

Westlake, John. *International Law: Part II War*, 2nd Edition, Cambridge: Cambridge University Press, 1913.

PART 2

Film and Regal Approaches to Copyright

CHAPTER 5

Stuck in a Waltz

The Austro-Hungarian Monarchy and Its Imperial Approach to the Berne Convention

Péter Munkácsi

1 Introduction

> Through whirling clouds, waltzing couples may be faintly distinguished. The clouds gradually scatter: one sees an immense hall peopled with a whirling crowd. The scene is gradually illuminated. The light of the chandeliers bursts forth at the fortissimo. Set in an imperial court, about 1855.

The French composer, Maurice Ravel laid out the scenario for *La valse, poème chorégraphique pour orchestre* (a choreographic poem for orchestra) in the score published in 1920, but all was not quite as delightful as it seemed. In the Vienna of 1855, the Habsburg court maintained a show of glittering *joie de vivre* and the city swayed to the waltzes of the Strauss family. Yet, despite of a culturally brilliant and economically prosperous period for the Austrian Empire, for London and Paris issues related to Vienna were not of primary concern. As the Hungarian historian István Diószegi aptly observed, in world politics, Europe has long been synonymous with England and France. In fact, in this period, the continent's international role was pretty much reduced to nothing more than English and French activity, since this covered the whole globe.[1]

A series of defeats, including the Italian wars of 1859 and 1866 and, particularly, the Prussian war of 1866, clearly demonstrated that Austria was no longer the major military power that it had once been. Prussia exploited the historical moment and independently asserted its influence over other German states within the 1815 German Confederation (*Deutscher Bund*). The international status of the Austrian Empire was increasingly dependent upon its unavoidable internal, structural reorganization, which reflect the conflicting social agendas

1 Diószegi, István. *Nemzetközi kapcsolatok története 1919–1939*. Kézirat [History of International Relations 1919–1939. Manuscript] (Tankönyvkiadó 1979).

 | DOI:10.1163/9789004511439_007

of this vast East-Central European realm.[2] The 1867 agreement of constitutional law known as the Austro-Hungarian *Ausgleich* or "Compromise" transformed the Austrian monarchy into the dual monarchy of Austria-Hungary. Tibor Frank rightly observed that the Austro-Hungarian Compromise was the last, and perhaps the most fundamental, reorganization of the Habsburg Empire.[3]

As a consequence of the Compromise, the bargaining between the Hungarian political elite and the dynasty (backed, by the Austrian political-economic elite) restored the supremacy of the Hungarian nation over the ethnic groups who lived in Hungary. It gave the Hungarian ruling class powers to administer the country's affairs that it had not had for more than 300 years, along with influence to shape the monarchy's external relations, which had previously been inaccessible. From 1875, the respective governments in Hungary followed the policy of linguistic assimilation and "Hungarianization", which played a significant role in an antidemocratic and retrograde distortion of public life.[4]

The rise and fall of the Austro-Hungarian monarchy coincided with a global expansion in the mass production and international trade of books, sheet music and works of art. Modern reproduction techniques resulted in an increased dissemination, reception and, inevitably, exploitation of literary works, raising the question of their use abroad.[5] With the blossoming of literature under the

---

2 Frank, Tibor. 'The Austro-Hungarian Compromise of 1867 and its Contemporary Critics'. *Hungarian Studies* 193, 14/2 (2000) <http://www.epa.hu/01400/01462/00024/pdf/193-200.pdf> last accessed on 15 August 2021.

3 Ibid 193.

4 Herczegh, Géza. *Európa közepén és Európa peremén. Magyarország nemzetközi kapcsolatainak története 896–1945.* [In the middle of Europe and on the edge of Europe. History of Hungary's international relations 896–1945] (Hága: Mikes International 2003) 148 <http://mek.oszk.hu/01000/01099/01099.pdf> last accessed on 15 August 2021.

5 Wiesner, J(akob). *The History of the Hungarian Book-Trade* (Organizing Committee of the Eight Session of the International Publisher's Congress, 1913) 9. Wiesner explained that there was a gratifying revival of industry, trade, art, and literature. The Hungarian book trade also began to revive. This was the starting point of the second period of the history of the Hungarian book-trade. A quieter and more peaceful epoch follows the period of the pioneers, the time of development, which lasted until the 1890s. Every bookseller was at the same time a publisher. Bookselling firms arose one after the other, and moreover, kept abreast of the latest literary innovation. The time was come for the bookseller to lend wings to literary activities. From this moment the real life of the book-trade may be said to have started. And although several booksellers' businesses were already established in the earlier decades, such as Charles Geibel's (AKA Geibel Károly Frigyes) in 1841, Maurice Ráth's (AKA Ráth Mór) and Charles Osterlamm's (AKA Osterlamm Károly) in 1857, nevertheless the intensive growth of the Hungarian book-trade only dates from the year 1867.

monarchy, the publication of original works became the focus of the publishing houses and had a decisive influence on its development.

The modern sense of the term 'author' is the product of the rise in the 18th century of a new group of individuals: writers who sought to earn their livelihood from the sale of their works to a rapidly expanding reading public. The industrialisation of the eighteenth century had led to an increased commodification of culture, including textual culture.[6] One century later writers and artists gave rise to voices for the general legal regulation of the property question. There was a time which produced a series of laws for the new, rising bourgeoisie could be realized. In the field of copyright, the second half of the 19th century was particularly decisive.[7] The questions raised were answered multilaterally with the establishment of the Berne Convention for the Protection of Literary and Artistic Works in 1886 (1886 Berne Convention).

In the beginning of the period of bilateral convention-making, before the birth of the 1886 Berne Convention, the Austro-Hungarian monarchy took a less active part in these activities. According to Sam Ricketson and Jane C. Ginsburg, the reason seems to have been more to do with the chaotic arrangement of the internal laws of its component parts and the difficulty of entering international agreements, which would require changes them.[8]

This chapter provides a comprehensive picture of the missed opportunity of the Austro-Hungarian monarchy to join the first and the most important multilateral treaty in the field of copyright, the 1886 Berne Convention. The issues of the international legal personality and foreign relations of the monarchy are reviewed and particular attention is paid to the failed accessions of Austria and Hungary, which were finally achieved by the Paris Peace Treaties in 1919–1920.

6 Rhodes, Jacqueline. 'Copyright, Authorship, and the Professional Writer: The Case of William Wordsworth', *Cardiff Corvey: Reading the Romantic Text 8* (*June 2002*) 3. <https://sites.cardiff.ac.uk/romtextv2/files/2013/02/cc08_n01.pdf> last accessed on 15 August 2021.

7 Gerhartl, Sybille. *"Vogelfrei" – Die österreichische Lösung der Urheberrechtsfrage in der 2. Hälfte des 19. Jahrhunderts oder warum es Österreich unterließ, seine Autoren zu schützen.* [, *"Vogelfrei"* – The Austrian solution to the copyright question in the second half of the 19th century or why Austria failed to protect its authors] (Diplomarbeit Wien 1995) 11. <https://www.wienbibliothek.at/sites/default/files/files/buchforschung/gerhartl-sybille-urheberrecht.pdf> last accessed on 15 August 2021.

8 Ricketson, Sam and Ginsburg, Jane C. *International Copyright and Neighbouring Rights: The Berne Convention and Beyond* vol. 1 (2nd edn, OUP 2006) 1. 31.

2 The Legal Context of the Austro-Hungarian Monarchy in Relation to the International Negotiations – the Monarchy's International Legal Personality

The Austro-Hungarian Compromise provided an organizational and political structure for the monarchy's domestic politics. But the arrangement inherently reflected the problems of nationality, which also made things more complicated for domestic rule and foreign policy. Both unifying and divisive, the Compromise created overlapping political authorities. After 1867, Austria-Hungary consisted of two separate nations, each with its own parliament and prime minister and connected in a real union by a single monarch, who was both Emperor of Austria and King of Hungary. A common army and navy, foreign policy and a customs unit (with their bureaucracies) held the two halves together.[9]

The Compromise was regulated differently by the Austrian and Hungarian laws. Pursuant to Hungarian law,[10] the part of foreign affairs is common to 'which together belong to the countries under His Majesty's reign'. However, Austrian law made the whole foreign policy a common cause as it laid down:

> Foreign affairs, including diplomatic and commercial representation abroad, as well as any decisions that may be necessary in relation to international treaties.[11]

---

9 Williamson, Samuel R. *Austria-Hungary and the Origins of the First World War* (MacMillan International Higher Education 1990) 13.

10 Article 8 of Act XII of 1867 (1867. évi XII. törvénycikk a magyar korona országai és az Ő Felsége uralkodása alatt álló többi országok között fenforgó közös érdekü viszonyokról, s ezek elintézésének módjáról. 8. §: „A pragmatica sanctióból folyó közös és együttes védelemnek egyik eszköze a külügyek czélszerü vezetése. E czélszerü vezetés közösséget igényel azon külügyekre nézve, melyek az Ő Felsége uralkodása alatt álló összes országokat együtt illetik. Ennélfogva a birodalom diplomaticai és kereskedelmi képviseltetése a külföld irányában és a nemzetközi szerződések tekintetében fölmerülhető intézkedések, mindkét fél ministeriumával egyetértésben és azok beleegyezése mellett, a közös külügyminister teendői közé tartoznak. A nemzetközi szerződéseket mindenik ministerium saját törvényhozásával közli. Ezen külügyeket tehát Magyarország is közöseknek tekinti, s kész azoknak közösen meghatározandó költségeihez azon arány szerint járulni, mely az alábbi 18., 19., 20., 21. és 22. pontokban körülirt módon fog megállapittatni.)".

11 Article 1 of Law of 22 December 1867 (Das Gesetz vom 22. Dezember 1867, RGBl. 146, betreffend die allen Ländern der österreichischen Monarchie gemeinsamen Angelegenheiten und die Art ihrer Behandlung. „§ 1. Nachfolgende Angelegenheiten werden als den im Reichsrathe vertretenen Königreichen und Ländern und den Ländern der ungarischen Krone gemeinsam erklärt:

Thus, Hungarian law recognised the community of foreign affairs only to the extent necessary for common defence. However, the content of common foreign affairs had not been established, but instead the tasks of the Joint Foreign Minister included that 'the diplomatic and commercial representation of the empire towards the rest of the world and measures arising from international agreements'.[12] In other words, what the Austrian Act referred to as a common cause in foreign affairs was defined by the Hungarian law as the joint foreign minister. Austrian law did not allow the Austrian Government any influence or interference in foreign affairs, but Article 8 of the Hungarian Act ensured the influence of the Hungarian and Austrian Governments in the management of common foreign affairs. It required a common foreign minister to pursue common foreign policy in agreement and with the agreement of the governments of the two parties.[13] Since Act XII 1867[14] made common only the foreign policy necessary for common and joint protection deduced from *Pragmatica Sanctio*.[15] Hungary was fully independent in foreign affairs not covered by the common foreign affairs.[16] It did not affect the fact that in such cases also the common foreign minister[17] represented Hungary in international relations.[18]

The Austro-Hungarian monarchy itself was not a state. It had no sovereignty and no authority to exercise supreme power, because it had no organs that could take binding decisions on the bodies of the two parties, Austria and Hungary, without their consent. The Austro-Hungarian monarchy was made up of two sovereign states, whose citizens were mutually foreign nationals in

a) Die auswärtigen Angelegenheiten mit Einschluß der diplomatischen und commerziellen Vertretung dem Auslande gegenüber, sowie die in Betreff der internationalen Verträge etwa nothwendigen Verfügungen, wobei jedoch die Genehmigung der internationalen Verträge, in soweit eine solche verfassungsmäßig nothwendig ist, den Vertretungskörpern der beiden Reichshälften (dem Reichsrathe und dem ungarischen Reichstage) vorbehalten bleibt; […])".

12 Article 8 of Act XII of 1867 (n. 11).

13 Ibid.

14 Ibid.

15 *Pragmatica Sanctio* was an edict issued by Emperor Charles VI. in 1713 in order to ensure that the Austrian throne and Habsburg lands would be inherited by Emperor Charles VI.'s daughter, Maria Theresa.

16 The full independence in foreign affairs is more of a theoretical finding because, unlike the wording of the laws, in practice it was almost entirely under the direct control of the Vienna court.

17 During the existence of the Austro-Hungarian monarchy, 6 Austrian and 5 Hungarian origin held the office of the common foreign ministers.

18 Szabó, Szilárd. 'Magyarország nemzetközi jogalanyiságának kérdése az 1907. évi gazdasági kiegyezés kapcsán' [The issue of Hungary's international legal personality in connection with the 1907 economic compromise]. *Jogtörténeti Szemle* 1 (2012), 57.

each other's territories. Therefore, the Austro-Hungarian monarchy had international legal personality not as a state, but as an international treaty alliance, a confederation with international legal entities established by an international treaty. In order to achieve the objectives set out by sovereign states, it took part in international relations as a federation. The limited legal personality of the monarchy for common purposes and, in parallel, the independent international legal personality of the two states increased. This is illustrated by the fact that the Austrian Empire was a signatory in 1865 for both states to the 1865 International Telegraph Convention, but Austria and Hungary were individual contractual parties to the first International Radiotelegraph Convention in 1906.[19] In matters not jointly affecting the two states, Hungary could independently conclude (and, in fact, concluded) international agreements with third states.[20]

3 Particularities of Austro-Hungarian Developments in the Field of Copyright

In the absence of any Austro-Hungarian common copyright law, this section reviews the development of the legislative tendencies of each nation in relation to the Berne Convention. Nevertheless, as will later be discussed, it cannot be unequivocally stated that imperial law-making was missing. After the suppression of the Hungarian Revolution and War of Independence (1848–1849) and the Compromise (1867), laws that were essentially Austrian were applied to Hungary.

3.1 *Hungarian Copyright Developments*

As a result of the Revolution, the first attempt at Austrian copyright legislation, the 1846 legal patent for authors[21] (Austrian Copyright Act of 1846) did not come into force in Hungary. Nevertheless, Article VII of the Emperor's Decree[22]

19 Weller, Mónika. 'Az Osztrák- Magyar Monarchia kialakulásával és fennállásával kapcsolatos egyes nemzetközi kérdésekről' [On certain international issues related to the formation and existence of the Austro-Hungarian Monarchy]. *Állam- és Jogtudomány* 1, XXXVIII/1–2 (1996–1997), 97–99.

20 Copyright Convention Between the United States of America and the Kingdom of Hungary. Signed at Budapest, January 30, 1912; ratifications exchanged September 16, 1912. U.S. Treaty Series, No. 571.

21 Das Kaiserliche Patent vom 19. Oktober 1846 Nr. 992 J G S.

22 Decree of November 29 1852: RGBl. 246/1852.

ordering application in Hungary of the Austrian Civil Code (*Allgemeines bürgerliches Gesetzbuch* – ABGB) also brought the Austrian copyright law into force in Hungary (as of May 1 1853).[23] As far as the copyright protection of foreign citizens was concerned, the principle of reciprocity was enshrined in the Decree. It was also prescribed that the bilateral treaties concluded by Austria, in particular the bilateral treaty between Austria and Sardinia in 1840, were also applicable to Hungary.

The history of Hungarian copyright law is characterised by attempts at codification, although aborted bills failed due to changes in historical circumstances rather than the standard of proposals. Following the age of imperial patents and decrees, after the Compromise (1867), the Society of Hungarian Writers and Artists put forth an unsuccessful motion for regulation. However, the Commercial Code Act XXXVII of 1875 devoted a separate chapter to the regulation of publishing activities. The first (independent) Hungarian copyright law, Act XVI of 1884, was made following László Arany's[24] initiative, István Apáthy's[25] motion.[26]

The Act based on the 1870 German Copyright Act,[27] incorporating the concept of autonomous copyright. The scope of the protection, extending the one determined by László Arany, included all literary and artistic forms known at the time.[28] In his assessment of the Act, István Apáthy emphasized the necessity of creating a copyright law which was justified, among other things, by

23 Mezei, Péter. 'The Development of Hungarian Copyright Law until the Creation of the First Copyright Act (1793–1884)', in Rajan, M. Sundara, ed. *Cambridge Handbook of Intellectual Property in Central and Eastern Europe*, (CUP 2019), 37–50.

24 László Arany was a Hungarian poet and folktale collector, the son of the poet and famous Hungarian Shakespeare translator, János Arany. A literary society in Pest (The Kisfaludy Society) mandated László Arany in 1876 with preparing the Copyright Bill and he published it in the same year.

25 István Apáthy was a Hungarian legal expert, academic professor, member of the Hungarian Academy of Sciences, Member of Parliament. When the Copyright Bill was submitted to the Lower House of the Parliament Apáthy was appointed as rapporteur.

26 Nótári, Tamás. 'Remarks on Early Hungarian Copyright Regulation', in *Geistiges Eigentum und Urheberrecht aus der historischen Perspektive* [Intellectual property and copyright from a historical perspective], ed. Éva Jakab (Pólay Elemér Alapítvány Lectiones Iuridicae; 10. 2014) <http://www.juris.u-szeged.hu/download.php?docID=30110> last accessed on 15 August 2021.

27 Gesetz, betreffend das Urheberrecht an Schriftwerken, Abbildungen, musikalischen Kompositionen und dramatischen Werken. Vom 11. Juni 1870. [Statute concerning author's rights to works of literature, illustrations, musical compositions and dramatic works. Of 11 June 1870].

28 Mezei, The Development of Hungarian Copyright Law 2019 (n. 23) 49.

fulfilling its legislative obligations based on the previous legislation, honouring multiple, long lasting legislative attempts before the adoption of the Act and, *inter alia*, matching the ambition of adherence to future international treaties.[29]

In addition to its significance, it should be mentioned the provisions of the 1884 Copyright Act concerning the right of translation. According to the law (§ 7), the right of translation belongs to the author. A translation of a work without the consent of the author considered as a copyright infringement. The then Hungarian law established strict formalities and conditions regarding the exclusive right of translation. First of all, the author had to reserve the right of translation on the title page or at the beginning of the original work. The law allowed the author a short time to exercise this right, as it made it a condition that the publication of the translation begin within one year of the publication of the original work and be completed within three years. In case of dramatic works the condition was even stricter: the translation had to be completed within six months of the original work being published. The beginning and the completion of the translation had to be presented for registration to the competent authority at the time (in case of the bilateral copyright agreement with France[30] the competent authority was the common Ministry of Foreign Affairs), within the deadline set by law.

3.2 *Austrian Copyright Developments*

The bilateral treaty between Austria and Sardinia in 1840 was described as the first international copyright treaty intended to resolve reprinting conflicts between 'Sardinian' publishers from Turin and 'Austrian' publishers from Milan and Venice; it also banned the import of unlicensed reprints into Lombardy. Elements of modern copyright theory, such as a general, abstract concept of the protected 'work' and a *post mortem auctoris*, can trace their history to 1840.[31] The treaty went on to form a major part of the Austrian Copyright Act

29 Apáthy, István. *A szerzői jogról szóló törvény (1884. XVI.t.cz.) méltatása jogi és gazdasági szempontból. (székfoglaló értekezés)* [Appreciation of the Copyright Act (1884. XVI.t.cz.) from a legal and economic point of view (inaugural)]. (Magyar Tudományos Akadémia 1885), 13–14.

30 Act III of 1879 on extending the Shipping Convention, the Consular Convention, the Convention on the Regulation of Heritage and the Convention on the Ownership of Intellectual and Artistic Works, concluded with France on 11 December 1866.

31 Kawohl, Friedmann. 'Commentary on the Bilateral Treaty between Austria and Sardinia (1840)', in Bently, Lionel and Kretschmer, Martin, eds. *Primary Sources on Copyright (1450–1900)*, (2008) <http://www.copyrighthistory.org/cam/tools/request/showRecord?id=commentary_d_1840> last accessed on 15 August 2021.

of 1846 and was incorporated into the domestic legislation of the Kingdom of Sardinia and soon acceded to by the other five Italian states (Lucca, Modena, Parma, Rome and Tuscany) and Hungary.[32]

While the impact of the agreement with Sardinia on the development of international copyright was decisive,[33] the same cannot be said for the development of domestic law. The Austrian Copyright Act of 1846 remained in force and unchanged for nearly half a century. Efforts in the first half of the 19th century were recurrently undermined and delayed, especially for the Austrians. After decades of an undisguised reprinting policy in Austria, in the early 1860s they were finally ready to give in and wanted to take the leadership without significant Prussian influence.[34]

Nevertheless, it appeared that the problems in the area of authorship for the Austrian government moved to the background, copyright issues were of less relevance. In 1886, due to the urgency of the matter, the Association of the Austro-Hungarian book, art and music traders took matters into their own hands. Many of the reform ideas of the forthcoming years remained unrealized while in 1891 the Ministry of Justice drafted a concept and on July 12, 1892, the government introduced the corresponding bill to the upper house, the House of Lords (*Hohen Herrenhaus*). After a slow negotiation process, the proposal finally reached the Imperial Council (*Reichsrat*) in 1895. Critical voices saw the emerging law primarily as a deviation from the European path concerning the legislative trends in the field. Therefore, changes were needed, which were ultimately only minimal; the House of Lords also approved the improved proposal of the House of Deputies (*Abgeordnetenhaus*) on December 20, 1895, so nothing stood in the way of the imperial sanction of the law from December 26, 1895 and Austria's copyright law came into force on 31 December 1895.[35]

---

32 The Convention of 13 May 1846 between Prussia and Great Britain regarding international copyright (involving a state from the German Confederation) was also of great importance for the multinational legal development.

33 Ricketson and Ginsburg *International Copyright* 2006 (n. 8) 1. 29. Ricketson stressed the decisive factor of the treaty from the point of the development of the international copyright. Article 27 of the treaty provided that both governments were free to invite the other governments of Italy (of which there were number at this time) as well as the Swiss canton of Ticino to accede to the treaty.

34 Gerhartl, *Vogelfrei* 1995 (n. 7) 19.

35 Gerhartl, *Vogelfrei* 1995 (n. 7) 28.

4 Institutionalisation of Culture in the 19th Century

The revolutions and wars of the middle of the 19th century were followed by a general stabilization of the international situation. This is especially important given that the unification of the Italian Peninsula and the end of the Franco-Prussian war marked the emergence of a unified Germany. Small states disappeared from Europe, the territory of which was basically occupied by great powers: Germany, Russia, Great Britain, France and the Austro-Hungarian Empire. Additional mention should be made of Italy, which aspired to superpower status and threatened the Turkish Empire. The simplification of the political map of Europe helped to maintain peace formally recognized by the 1814/1815 Congress of Vienna. It was not as if there were no profound contradictions between the great powers, but the balance of power that had arisen meant they all needed to be careful. The possibility of expansion in Europe had disappeared and any military action would have clashed directly with another great power. Continental conquests were replaced by colonization which captured the attention and energy of the great powers.

Decades of stabilization resulted in fundamental changes in social and cultural life, such as metropolisation, the separation of elite and mass culture and the concomitant unauthorized reproduction and use of foreign works.[36] Following the 1793 French Decree of the National Convention, from the middle of the 19th to early 20th century almost all of the great powers provided regulations at the national level to protect the copyright of literary and artistic works.[37]

4.1 *Birth of the Berne Convention and the Austro-Hungarian Monarchy*

The *Association littéraire internationale*, a non-governmental organization, founded in 1878 in Paris, was the original proponent of what then was called *une convention universelle* for the protection of literary and artistic property and the foundation of a *Union de propriété littéraire*. In its Congress, held in Rome in 1882, the Association decided to meet in Berne in 1883. The Swiss Government hosted the 1883 Congress of the Association and delegated to it one of its ministers, Numa Droz. The Congress, presided over by Droz, took place in Berne in September 1883. It lasted four days (September 10 to 13) and

36 These traditional issues of popular culture fall into the field of popular culture studies.

37 Munkácsi, Péter-Kiss, Zoltán. 'Magyarország 1922-es csatlakozása a Berni Egyezményhez' [Hungary's Accession in 1922 to the Berne Convention], in Pogácsás, Anett, ed. *Quaerendo et creando, Ünnepi kötet Tattay Levente 70. születésnapja alkalmából* [In Honour of Levente Tattay in the Occasion of his 70th Birthday], (Szent István Társulat 2014) 285–308.

concluded with the adoption of the draft of a multilateral treaty with the title *Convention pour constituer une Union générale pour la protection des droits des auteurs sur leurs œuvres littéraires et artistiques* (Convention Establishing a General Union for the Protection of the Rights of Authors in their Literary and Artistic Works). It consisted of ten articles.[38]

The Federal Council of the Swiss Confederation sent the draft, on December 3 1883, to the governments of "all civilized nations" and informed them of the plans of a diplomatic conference in 1884 to adopt a treaty. The treaty should, according to the circular sent to these countries, result in 'on the one hand, to the universal recognition of the rights of authors without regard to their nationality and, on the other hand, to the desirable uniformity of the principles governing such protection'.[39]

But the number of favourable replies was sufficient for the Swiss Government to decide the convocation of the first diplomatic conference. Its dates were fixed from September 8–19, 1884, and the venue fixed was the room of the *Conseil des Etats*, the upper house of the Swiss Parliament, in Berne. The Conference took place as planned. The countries represented were Austria-Hungary, Belgium, Costa Rica, France, Germany, Great Britain, Haiti, Italy, the Netherlands, Paraguay, El Salvador, Sweden-Norway and Switzerland.

Dr. Emil Steinbach[40] and Jules Zador[41] represented Austria-Hungary with separate votes[42] and Steinbach appointed also for a member of the Drafting Committee.[43] Austria and Hungary mainly participated in the discussion of the question of translation rights. The proposal in the draft convention concerning these in Article 6 was considerably more cautious than the preparatory proposals. The committee considered the text proposed by the German and Swedish delegations. This provided for a limited period of protection, on condition that the translation was done within certain period following the publication of the original work.[44] In the debate, Austria-Hungary took the position that they would vote against the article, whereas it was contrary to then adopted Hungarian copyright law, Act XVI of 1884.[45] During the vote on the whole of

38 Bogsch, Arpad. 'The First Hundred Years of the Berne Convention for the Protection of Literary and Artistic Works' in *The Berne Convention for the Protection of Literary and Artistic Works from 1886 to 1986* (WIPO Publication No.877 1986) 11–81.

39 Ibid.

40 Dr. Emil Steinbach was a Ministerial Counsellor at the Ministry of Justice of Austria.

41 Jules Zador (AKA Zádor Gyula) was a Counsellor at the Ministry of Justice of Hungary.

42 Bogsch, The First Hundred Years 1986 (n. 38) 88.

43 Bogsch, The First Hundred Years 1986 (n. 38) 90.

44 Ricketson and Ginsburg, *International Copyright* 2006 (n. 8) 2. 29.

45 Bogsch, The First Hundred Years 1986 (n. 38) 97. Dr. Steinbach said the following in his own name and on behalf of Counsellor Zádor, his counterpart from Hungary: 'We have to

Article 6 the provision was adopted[46] as proposed by the Committee by six countries (Germany, Costa Rica, France, Sweden, Norway and Switzerland) to three (Austria, Hungary and Haiti).[47] The Conference agreed on a new draft which the delegates took home as a basis for preparing themselves for the second diplomatic conference.

The attitude of Austria-Hungary to the diplomatic conference of 1884 was ambivalent from the start. A distinction must be made from the outset between the Ministry of Foreign Affairs and the two ministries of Justice in Austria and Hungary. After Hungary had already indicated that it would hardly participate in such an agreement, Austria joined this scepticism.[48]

The report on the diplomatic conference by Steinbach, illustrates the situation well:

---

vote against Article 6 of the Convention, because new Hungarian legislation on authors' rights is in contradiction with that Article regarding the formalities to be complied with for the acquisition of the exclusive right of translation and as to the duration of that right.' On the same grounds the delegation of Austria-Hungary voted against the second paragraph of Article 11. According to the provision the authors of dramatic or dramatico-musical works shall, throughout the duration of their exclusive right of translation, be mutually protected against unauthorized public performance of translations of their works. Nevertheless, the article was adopted according to the proposals of the Drafting Committee.

46 Article 6 as adopted: Authors who are nationals of one of the countries of the Union shall enjoy, in all the other countries of the Union, the exclusive right of translation in relation to their works for ten years after the publication, in one of the countries of the Union, of the translation of their work authorized by them.

In order to enjoy the benefits of the above provision, the complete authorized translation must appear within three years following the publication of the original work.

For works published in instalments, the period of three years specified in the foregoing paragraph shall be calculated only as from the publication of the last instalment of the original work.

Where the translation of a work appears in instalments, the ten-year term provided for in the first paragraph shall also be counted only as from the appearance of the last such instalment.

In the case of works composed of several volumes published at intervals, and also for bulletins or collections published by literary or scientific societies, or by private persons, each volume, bulletin or collection shall, with regard to the periods of ten and three years, be considered a separate work.

It is understood that the exclusive right of translation shall not extend beyond the language or languages in which an authorized translation has appeared.

47 Bogsch, The First Hundred Years 1986 (n. 38) 97.

48 Dillenz, Walter. 'Warum Österreich-Ungarn nie Berner Übereinkunft beitrat' [Why Austria-Hungary never acceded to the Berne Convention], in Wadle, Elmar, ed. *Historische Studien zum Urheberrecht in Europa* [Historical Studies on Copyright in Europe], (Berlin: Duncker & Humblot 1993), 167–191.

> But now the Hungarian government has come to the realization, due to its completely new legislation, that the cultural conditions of the country do not allow the works of foreigners in general and in particular against translations more extensive protection, which the Hungarian law granted to the works of the nationals and then rejected to attend the conference. This attitude makes our approach very easy. We can only join Hungary's position, whereby we can privately admit that for the non-German internationalities of Austria in particular, the extension of the foreigners' authorship rights is only a tribute to the higher culture.[49]

The second diplomatic conference took place a year later in the absence of Austria-Hungary, again in Berne, from September 7 to 18, 1885 and Droz continued as president. The draft texts agreed upon were now three in number: the Convention, an "Additional Article" and a "Final Protocol." But they were still only drafts and served as a basis for the third diplomatic conference. The third and final diplomatic conference in Berne took place from September 6 to 9, 1886.[50] In his opening address Numa Droz also mentioned specifically those states that did not participate in the conference:

> We also regret not seeing the representatives of two countries that took part in the previous Conferences, namely Austria-Hungary and the Netherlands; however, the state of their legislation does not allow them to accede at the present time. They will no doubt lose no time in joining us.[51]

With some amendments, it adopted these texts and they were signed by: Belgium, France, Germany, Great Britain, Haiti, Italy, Liberia, Spain, Switzerland and Tunisia.

Following the conference, on October 12, 1886, the Swiss government sent a letter to the common ministry of foreign affairs of the monarchy informing it of the adoption of the convention, with a strong reference to Article 18 thereof. According to the provision the countries that are not party to this Convention, and provide in their domestic law for legal protection against the violation of the rights that are the subject of this Convention, shall be allowed to accede to it at their request. Austria-Hungary did not respond to the information received.[52]

---

49 Ibid 173.
50 Bogsch, The First Hundred Years 1986 (n. 38) 19.
51 Bogsch, The First Hundred Years 1986 (n. 38) 131.
52 Dillenz, Warum Österreich-Ungarn 1993 (n. 48) 177.

5 "Beings That Cannot Adapt Will Scrape By or Waste Away" – Accession Efforts to the Berne Convention at the Dawn of the 20th Century

5.1 *1900/1901 – Possible Years of Accession?*

In 1901, a short study was published in Hungary by Viktor Ranschburg, Secretary General of the Association of Hungarian Book Dealers.[53] It was based both on the agenda item of the Austro-Hungarian monarchy and the Berne Convention from the 4th International Publisher's Congress held that year in Leipzig and a the book published by Carl Junker a year earlier.[54] At the congress a decision was made regarding Austria-Hungary: Fourth International Publishing Congress, to entrust the permanent office with the task of taking the appropriate steps at the Imperial Royal Austrian and Royal Hungarian Governments to encourage the monarchy to begin joining the Berne Union as soon as possible.[55] It should be also noted that following the earlier debate in the Austrian House of Representatives from March 1901 and the recommendation of the rapporteur (Dr Arthur Skedl[56]), the government of the Monarchy did not lose sight of the question of the accession of Austria-Hungary to the Convention of International Union.[57]

Ranschburg quoted Junker's statement that Hungary's accession "is undoubtedly based on both our literary interests and our national character".[58] The Secretary General's intention, however, in discussing and shedding light on the issue, does not intend to be guided by the impact of this polite statement, but as he wrote, "only our own domestic relations, our own cultural interests, the vocation and future of our domestic literature keep in mind".[59]

The Ranschburg study continues with a description of the history of the Convention, followed by Chapter III, which partially analyses the domestic situation, presenting the contradictions between the Convention and the current copyright regulations regarding the right to translation. In addition to

53 Ranschburg, Viktor. *A szerzői jog nemzetközi védelmére alkotott berni egyezmény vonatkozással Magyarországra* [Berne Convention for the International Protection of Copyright with respect to Hungary] (Eggenberger-féle könyvkereskedés 1901) 91.

54 Junker, Carl. *Die Berner Convention zum Schutze der Werke der Litteratur und Kunst und Österreich-Ungarn* [The Berne Convention for the Protection of the Works of Literature and Art and Austro-Hungary] (Alfred Hölder 1900) 108.

55 *Le Droit d'Auteur* Quatorzième année – No. 7 15 Juillet 1901, 81.

56 Arthur Skedl (Dr.) was an Austrian lawyer, professor and politician.

57 *Le Droit d'Auteur* Quatorzième année – No. 5 15 Mai 1901, 49–51.

58 Ranschburg, *A szerzői jog* 1901 (n. 53) 12.

59 Ibid.

joining the Berne Convention, the author's argument was considered valid years later,[60] just as his calculations for accession in terms of surplus cost (25,000 crowns) was still cited a decade later.

5.2 *The Debate of Hungarian Lawyers' Society (Magyar Jogászegylet) in 1906*

From the point of view of legal history, it is inevitable that the debate of the Hungarian Lawyers' Society (*Magyar Jogászegylet*) held in 1906, on the fundamentals of the regulation of then copyright law, must be considered. During the debate three participants, renowned experts, lawyers of the era such as Géza Kenedi,[61] Emil Szalai[62] and Sándor Marton also addressed the issue of Hungary's accession to the Berne Convention.

According to Géza Kenedi, at the time of the Hungarian copyright act, at the end of the 1800s, the foundations of the Berne Convention had already been laid; nevertheless, a law was enacted in Hungary that was not in line with the convention. By 1906, most of the European states had ratified the convention, except for Austria-Hungary. The core of the Berne Convention is that it provides the author's right of translation in his own state; abroad, it allowed ten years for starting translation. If a translation has been started, it provided the same rights as were enjoyed at home. Ultimately this means much greater security for literary works. By this regulatory method valuable Hungarian literary works could obtain foreign markets, so it would be important to integrate the rules of the Convention in the reform, a view shared by traders and publishers. At the relevant time, while it was in the interest of Hungary to ratify the international agreement, it was aborted by the Czechs and the Poles to hinder the breakthrough of German culture in Austria.[63] At the end of his speech Géza Kenedi notes that it is very difficult for our law making machinery to adopt the act, although it would be of utmost importance to adapt to the needs

---

60 Ibid 35–39.

61 Géza Kenedi was a Doctor of Laws and Political Science, lawyer and editor of Newspaper *Pesti Hírlap*. He was the vice-president of the Budapest Association of Journalists, the vice-president of the national literary expert committee, and a regular member of the Dugonics Society in Szeged.

62 Emil Szalai worked in Budapest as a copyright lawyer. In the 1920s and 1930s, he managed the affairs of the Hungarian Stage Authors 'Association, the Budapest Actors' Association and the Philharmonic Society. From 1923 to 1938, he was the editor of the journal *Jogállam* [Rule of Law]. He was taken to Auschwitz in 1944, where he also died.

63 Dillenz, Warum Österreich-Ungarn 1993 (n. 48) 182 on the background of the opposition by the Czechs and the Poles.

of the nation: "Beings that cannot adapt will scrape by or waste away: this is a law of nature".[64]

Emil Szalai referred to the chain of thoughts in Géza Kenedi's speech that Hungarian literature is not significant in exports, its imports are all the more significant. He thinks it should be considered whether it is the domestic interests and values or the works of otherwise well-paid authors that should have priority. It is pointless to make efforts as soon as possible to pay increasingly high customs duties to countries that import books duty free, in the form of author's royalty through regulation of translation rights and international agreements. This was a stumbling block to Hungary joining the Berne Convention – therefore, Szalai did not support accession to the Berne Convention either.

He was also of the opinion that in the reform special emphasis should be placed on the need to revise the copyright act so that Hungary could obtain financial benefit from imported works, instead of the regulation at the time, under which foreign authors' works flow into the country without payment of any customs duty; this shift would give a chance to publishers, translators to have foreign literature flowing in huge volumes marketed in Hungarian and, thereby, it was hoped, generate profit.

The positions of Sándor Marton and Géza Kenedi regarding treaties were completely identical: the issue of treaties is an economic one. The first treaty that Hungary concluded with France in 1866 on the subject of copyright is considered a false move because the term of protection for translation of French works was unlimited, whereas Hungarian works did not receive any protection. In the absence of statistical data, he refers to his knowledge and claims that about five hundred literary works in foreign languages and about forty plays are translated for the stage in Hungary every year. These lawyers were opposed to the fact that Hungary had to pay a large sum of money abroad to acquire translation rights, but only a fraction came back to the country. They were of the view that it would be worthwhile to follow the German legislative practice and restrict the rights of authors "from an industrial policy point of view".[65]

5.3 *1913 – Another Possible Year in View of the Hungarian Accession?*

Despite the feverish debates of previous years, it seemed for a long time that there had been no substantive reflection from the government on accession to

64 Nótári, Tamás. 'Debates and proposals of Hungarian jurisprudence on copyright in the first decades of the 20th century'. *Publicationes Universitatis Miskolcinensis Sectio Juridica et Politica* Tomus XXX/1 93 (2012), 102.

65 Ibid 103 and 107.

the Berne Convention. Therefore, it was a significant turning point that Jenő Balogh, the Minister of Justice of the Lukács Government, made a firm statement on the issue of accession to the Convention in January 1913. After a personal meeting with the Minister, the Association of Hungarian Book Dealers and the Association of Hungarian Stage Authors received a positive promise about the intention to join and the drafting stage of the Accession Bill, which had become particularly interesting in light of the forthcoming International Publishers Congress.[66]

5.3.1 Discussion on Accession at the Hungarian Academy of Sciences from 1913

At a plenary meeting of the Hungarian Academy of Sciences (*Magyar Tudományos Akadémia* – MTA) held on May 26, 1913, the description made by the Hungarian Royal Minister of Commerce to the MTA was discussed regarding accession to the Berne Convention.[67] The Minister's submission stated that the Hungarian entry into the Berne Convention should be subject to a reservation on the right of translation. The rules of the Convention would not apply during the transitional period not just works that became public domain in the country of origin at the time of our entry due to the expiry of the term of protection, but also for works that became public domain for other reasons e.g. as a result of non-compliance with the prescribed formalities or conditions.

In its comments on the submission, the Board of the Hungarian Academy of Sciences stated that Hungarian intellectual life had grown used to the framework of the then valid copyright law, which did not protect the interests of "intellectual production workers"[68] effectively enough, given the difficulties in the path of comprehensive reform, the Hungarian Academy of Sciences had succeeded in the narrower reform of copyright, insofar as it serves the fuller protection of authors.[69] The report included Hungary's accession to the Berne Union, especially considering that, in contrast to thirty years ago (at the time of the preparation of the 1884 Hungarian copyright act), the works of Hungarian authors were in high demand abroad, which justified the protection of the financial interests of Hungarian writers abroad. Because the Berne Convention provided the authors of the contracting states much greater protection than in the Act XVI 1884, according to the report, it was not fair that "Hungarian

66 Munkácsi-Kiss, Magyarország 1922-es csatlakozása 2014 (n. 37) 300.

67 Corvina (1913) 35, 116.

68 The term is synonymous in Hungarian with "creator" from the 19th century.

69 Munkácsi-Kiss, Magyarország 1922-es csatlakozása 2014 (n. 37) 301.

authors receive greater, more effective protection in trading abroad than in Hungary."[70]

5.3.2 8th International Publisher's Congress, June 1913 Budapest

In a crisis-ridden[71] domestic political, environment preparations for the International Publisher's Congress began in early 1913. Nevertheless, the Congress was held with the participation of about 300 mostly foreign publishers and chaired by Viktor Ranschburg, then director of the Athenaeum Publishing.[72] At the congress, the Minister of Justice was represented by Gusztáv Tőry, the Under-secretary. In his welcome speech, he stated that the bill on Hungary's accession to the Berne Convention was fully completed, as was the proposal to revise the parts of Hungarian copyright related to the Berne Convention. At the congress, the legal protection of photographs; the regulation of the legal relationship between the publisher and phonograph; the plan for an international publishing museum; the establishment of national libraries and houses of culture; price reductions for retailers, and the issue of the discount of publications were discussed.[73]

During the congress, under the government of László Lukács, the mood in the Parliament was pugilistic and the Prime Minister resigned on June 10, 1913.[74] The issue of accession was again postponed indefinitely and the situation would change due to World War I and the subsequent peace treaties.

---

70 Ibid.

71 The post-effects of the constitutional and government crisis between 1904–1906, on further elements of the crisis 'text to n 74'.

72 Athenaeum Publishing was one of the largest book publishers in Hungary. From its founding in 1841 until 1948, the publisher published works by the most significant writers and poets of the age and thus played a decisive role in Hungarian literature.

73 Munkácsi-Kiss, Magyarország 1922-es csatlakozása 2014 (n. 37) 300.

74 Although the incapacity of the contemporary opposition proved, they obstructed draft laws passed by the ruling party, such as the vote on a new defence forces law to increase the number of recruits and increase military spending, which was justified by arms race and instability in the Balkans. Due to the impracticability of the obstruction, the governments followed each other frequently at that time, and in 1912 László Lukács, former Minister of Finance, became Prime Minister. The culmination of the parliamentary struggle was the forced adoption of the new Defence Forces Act (in Hungarian: *Véderőtörvény*) on 4 June as well as 7 June. An opposition MP attempted to assassinate István Tisza, Speaker of Parliament, in the Chamber. It should be noted that behind the Lukács-cabinet were the political ideas of István Tisza, with preparations for war, a moderate, conservative reform of the suffrage and popular representation. In the end, the opposition defeated Lukács not in politics and in the Chamber, but in the press: back in 1912, an opposition MP called the Prime Minister "Europe's greatest panamist" who sued him for defamation. However, the court dismissed the representative, so László Lukács resigned on June 10, 1913.

6 The Developments Leading Up and Participating in the Events after World War I

The Berne-based the United International Bureaux for the Protection of Intellectual Property (*Bureaux internationaux réunis pour la protection de la propriété intellectuelle*),[75] with the acronym BIRPI derived from the French title, understood the contradiction between the union of international publishers during and after World War I and as a player in international cultural and intellectual property policy, which has become part of the reorganization of Europe through the peace treaties.[76]

The early 20th century and, in particular, World War I caused a major reordering of the European state system. A number of new states emerged from the disintegration of the Austro-Hungarian monarchy (and other empires) and moved to engage in the international order. The majority of them joined to the Berne Convention.

6.1 *Austria – Peace Treaty of Saint Germain-en-Laye in 1919*[77]

This peace treaty was signed in the Parisian suburb of St Germain-en-Laye between the Allied powers and Austria under the framework of the Paris Peace Conferences. Although the negative attitude within the Austrian government had been overcome before the start of the war and the new Compromise (*Ausgleich*) laws in 1908 were now more dependent on Hungary's approval, the competent authorities still relegated on a previous amendment to the national copyright law. A corresponding draft was to have been completed in the spring of 1918, but due to the turmoil of war it was no longer subject to parliamentary treatment.[78] Section 239 of the Treaty of Saint Germain "ordained" Austria's accession to the Berne Convention.[79]

---

75 More details about BIRPI in recent literature Davies, Gillian and Ricketson, Sam. 'The foundation of the World Intellectual Property Organization: what came before', in *Research Handbook on the World Intellectual Property Organization. The First 50 Years and Beyond*, ed. Sam Ricketson (Edward Elgar 2020) 496.

76 Munkácsi-Kiss, Magyarország 1922-es csatlakozása 2014 (n. 37) 288.

77 Treaty of Peace between the Principal Allied and Associated Powers and Austria, signed at Saint Germain-en-Laye, September 10, 1919 coding by Staatsvertrag von Saint-Germain-en-Laye vom 10. September 1919. StGBl 303/1920.

78 Gerhartl, *Vogelfrei* 1995 (n. 7) 77.

79 Article 239: Austria undertakes, within twelve months of the coming into force of the present Treaty, to adhere in the prescribed form to the International Convention of Berne of September 9, 1886, for the protection of literary and artistic works, revised at Berlin on November 13, 1908, and completed by the additional Protocol signed at Berne on March 20, 1914, relating to the protection of literary and artistic works.

After a corresponding amendment of the domestic legal norms in 1920, which was an improvement for the foreign author compared to the domestic author in each case, The Republic of Austria acceded to the Bern Convention on 1 October 1920.

The existing obligation under international law to join the Berne Convention generated divided reactions from the lawyers. On the one hand, the accession had already wanted to take place voluntarily, but now it was forced. On the other hand, the obligation was perceived as preaching to the choir and there was no need for compulsion.[80]

6.2 *Hungary – Peace Treaty of Trianon 1920*[81]

The Peace Treaty of Trianon, as with the other peace treaties of World War I, separated the questions of multilateral and bilateral treaties. Articles 217–221, or Sections 217–221 of the Peace Treaty of Trianon, provided a long list of all those multilateral agreements, which were revived by the peace treaty and would be applicable again.[82]

Hungary was obliged by Section 222 to accede to the Berne Convention within twelve months, which had been *de facto* in progress since 1913.[83] The relevant bill had been drawn up, but the outbreak of World War I prevented

---

Until her adherence, Austria undertakes to recognise and protect by effective measures and in accordance with the principles of the said Convention the literary and artistic works of nationals of the Allied and Associated Powers.

In addition, and irrespective of the above-mentioned adherence, Austria undertakes to continue to assure such recognition and such protection to all literary and artistic works of the nationals of each of the Allied and Associated Powers to an extent at least as great as upon July 28, 1914, and upon the same conditions.

80 Dillenz, Warum Österreich-Ungarn 1993 (n. 48) 185.

81 Treaty of Peace between the Allied and Associated Powers and Hungary, signed at Trianon, June 4, 1920, coding by the Act XXXIII of 1921.

82 Szalai, Anikó. 'Effects of the World Wars on International Treaties of Hungary'. *Miskolc Journal of International Law* 5 No. 2 (2008), 99.

83 Article 222: Hungary undertakes, within twelve months of the coming into force of the present Treaty, to adhere in the prescribed form to the International Convention of Berne of September 9, 1886, for the protection of literary and artistic works, revised at Berlin on November 13, 1908, and completed by the Additional Protocol signed at Berne on March 20, 1914, relating to the protection of literary and artistic works.

Until her adherence, Hungary undertakes to recognise and protect by effective measures and in accordance with the principles of the said Convention the literary and artistic works of nationals of the Allied and Associated Powers.

In addition, and irrespective of the above-mentioned adherence, Hungary undertakes to continue to assure such recognition and such protection to all literary and artistic works of the nationals of each of the Allied and Associated Powers to an extent at least as great as upon July 28, 1914, and upon the same conditions.

the law from being enacted. Moreover, the chaotic domestic and international conditions after the war made it impossible to submit the bill to the legislature. The bill was finally submitted in 1921, and was approved by the National Assembly on 23 December 1921; it was promulgated on 25 February 1922 (after Hungary acceded to the Union). Hungary announced its accession to the government of the Swiss Confederation on 14 February 1922. In Hungary, the law providing for the above was published in the 4 February 1922 issue of the National Statute Book, under the title Act XIII 1922 "on Accession of Hungary to the International Berne Union Founded for Protection of Literary and Artistic Works."[84]

7 Conclusion

There are many lessons learnt from the bumpy road of Austria and Hungary's accession to the Berne Convention. As a consequence of the 1867 Austro-Hungarian Compromise the Hungarian ruling class received more power in the administration of the country's affairs and influence on the shaping of the monarchy's external relations.

In the economic field, Hungary's development accelerated after the Compromise compared to "Cisleithania", the unofficial name of the Viennese side of the monarchy named after the River Leitha as a natural border-line. There was also no problem with economic development, which was favourable compared to other European countries, but rather with the development of the political situation. The dualism defended tooth and nail by Hungarian politicians made it impossible for any rational policy concerning nationalities to be made.

Leaving aside this important historical moment, the Hungarian foreign policy during the period of the birth of the Berne Convention can be characterized by the following elements: anti-Germanism; fear of pan-Slavism; rejection of federalism; a conflict between national and imperial consciousness; a lack of an international horizon, and an uncertain search for a place on a world stage dominated by Western European powers.

Foreign policy issues were completely undermined by public law debates. The Hungarian public did not recognize the changing international power relations. Hungary was always a subordinate of a major power, and perhaps for this reason it was unable to appreciate the benefits resulted from its situation.

84 Nótári, Remarks on Early Hungarian Copyright Regulation 2014 (n. 26) 96; Munkácsi-Kiss, Magyarország 1922-es csatlakozása 2014 (n. 37) 308–309.

The lack of autonomy in international relations made the foreign policy orientation more difficult.

On the Hungarian side these petty politics and, on the Austrian side, excessive bureaucracy did not allow for the emerging global expansion in the mass production and cross-border trade of books. Austria and Hungary represented itself at a first diplomatic conference in Berne, 1884, and no one from the country took part in the diplomatic conference establishing the convention two years later. Participation in revision conferences of the international instrument did not come to the fore in the following decades either. Thus the protection of intellectual property and copyright at the international level was not engaged with and, ultimately, the value of accession to the Berne Convention was underestimated by the monarchy. On the other hand the little matter of joining an international copyright agreement illustrates the fundamental problem of the dual monarchy.

Different economic level differences, but similar socio-political tensions, internal and external contradictions led to World War I. Despite decades of efforts, only the mandatory provisions of the Peace Treaties sealed the fate of Austria and Hungary that the two countries joined the convention of modern international copyright law, the weight and significance of which were difficult to recognize after the war, disintegration and trauma.

To return to Ravel: the premiere of *La valse* took place on 12th December 1920 in Paris with great success. This is a piece with one central idea, according to the English composer of classical music and conductor, George Benjamin, whether or not it was intended as a metaphor for the predicament of European civilisation in the aftermath of the Great War, its one-movement design plots the birth, decay and destruction of a musical genre: the waltz.[85] Just as Ravel's waltz disappears before our eyes, the three-beat pulse is itself destroyed in the last two measures, the difficulty of acceding to the Berne Convention shows the monarchical bureaucracy collapsing under its own increasingly ponderous weight.

Acknowledgements

I would like to express my gratitude to Laura R. Ford, Phillip Johnson, Péter Mezei, Anikó Szalai for their comments, remarks on earlier version of this chapter.

85 Benjamin, George. 'Last Dance. George Benjamin Revisits La valse, and Argues the Case for Ravel's Orchestral Masterpiece'. *The Musical Times*, 135, No. 1817 (1994), 432–435.

Bibliography

Apáthy, István. *A szerzői jogról szóló törvény (1884. XVI.t.cz.) méltatása jogi és gazdasági szempontból. (székfoglaló értekezés)*. (Budapest: Magyar Tudományos Akadémia 1885).

Benjamin, George. 'Last Dance. George Benjamin Revisits La valse, and Argues the Case for Ravel's Orchestral Masterpiece'. *The Musical Times*, 135, No.1817 (1994), 432–435.

Bogsch, Arpad. 'The First Hundred Years of the Berne Convention for the Protection of Literary and Artistic Works', in *The Berne Convention for the Protection of Literary and Artistic Works from 1886 to 1986* (Geneva: WIPO Publication No.877 1986), 11–81.

Dillenz, Walter. 'Warum Österreich-Ungarn nie Berner Übereinkunft beitrat', in Wadle, Elmar, ed. *Historische Studien zum Urheberrecht in Europa* [Historical Studies on Copyright in Europe], (Berlin: Duncker & Humblot 1993), 167–191.

Diószegi, István. *Nemzetközi kapcsolatok története 1919–1939*. Kézirat (Budapest: Tankönyvkiadó 1979).

Frank, Tibor. 'The Austro-Hungarian Compromise of 1867 and its Contemporary Critics'. *Hungarian Studies* 193,14/2 (2000), available at: http://www.epa.hu/01400/01462/00024/pdf/193-200.pdf (last accessed on 15 August 2021).

Gerhartl, Sybille. *"Vogelfrei"- Die österreichische Lösung der Urheberrechtsfrage in der 2. Hälfte des 19. Jahrhunderts oder warum es Österreich unterließ, seine Autoren zu schützen.* (Diplomarbeit Wien 1995), available at: https://www.wienbibliothek.at/sites/default/files/files/buchforschung/gerhartl-sybille-urheberrecht.pdf (last accessed on 15 August 2021).

Herczegh, Géza. *Európa közepén és Európa peremén. Magyarország nemzetközi kapcsolatainak története 896–1945*. (Hága: Mikes International 2003), available at: http://mek.oszk.hu/01000/01099/01099.pdf (last accessed on 15 August 2021).

Junker, Carl. *Die Berner Convention zum Schutze der Werke der Litteratur und Kunst und Österreich-Ungarn* (Wien: Alfred Hölder 1900).

Kawohl, Friedmann. 'Commentary on the Bilateral Treaty between Austria and Sardinia (1840)', in Bently, Lionel and Kretschmer, Martin, eds. *Primary Sources on Copyright (1450–1900)*, (2008), available at: http://www.copyrighthistory.org/cam/tools/request/showRecord?id=commentary_d_1840 (last accessed on 15 August 2021).

Mezei, Péter. 'The Development of Hungarian Copyright Law until the Creation of the First Copyright Act (1793–1884)', in Rajan, M. Sundara, ed. *Cambridge Handbook of Intellectual Property in Central and Eastern Europe*, (Cambridge: CUP 2019), 37–50.

Munkácsi, Péter-Kiss, Zoltán. 'Magyarország 1922-es csatlakozása a Berni Egyezményhez' [Hungary's Accession in 1922 to the Berne Convention], in Pogácsás, Anett, ed. *Quaerendo et creando, Ünnepi kötet Tattay Levente 70. születésnapja alkalmából* [In Honour of Levente Tattay in the Occasion of his 70th Birthday], (Szent István Társulat, 2014) 285–308.

Nótári, Tamás. 'Debates and proposals of Hungarian jurisprudence on copyright in the first decades of the 20th century'. *Publicationes Universitatis Miskolcinensis Sectio Juridica et Politica* Tomus XXX/1 93 (2012).

Nótári, Tamás. 'Remarks on Early Hungarian Copyright Regulation', in *Geistiges Eigentum und Urheberrecht aus der historischen Perspektive*, ed. Éva Jakab (Pólay Elemér Alapítvány Lectiones Iuridicae; 10. 2014), 91–108, available at: http://www.juris.u-szeged.hu/download.php?docID=30110 (last accessed on 15 August 2021).

Ranschburg, Viktor. *A szerzői jog nemzetközi védelmére alkotott berni egyezmény vonatkozással Magyarországra* (Budapest: Eggenberger-féle könyvkereskedés 1901).

Rhodes, Jacqueline. 'Copyright, Authorship, and the Professional Writer: The Case of William Wordsworth'. *Cardiff Corvey: Reading the Romantic Text 8 (June 2002)*, available at: https://sites.cardiff.ac.uk/romtextv2/files/2013/02/cc08_n01.pdf (last accessed on 15 August 2021).

Ricketson, Sam, and. Ginsburg, Jane C. *International Copyright and Neighbouring Rights: The Berne Convention and Beyond* vol. 1(Oxford: 2nd edn, OUP 2006).

Szabó, Szilárd. 'Magyarország nemzetközi jogalanyiságának kérdése az 1907. évi gazdasági kiegyezés kapcsán'. *Jogtörténeti Szemle* 1 (2012), 57–61.

Szalai, Anikó. 'Effects of the World Wars on International Treaties of Hungary'. *Miskolc Journal of International Law* 5 No. 2 (2008), 98–108.

Weller, Mónika. 'Az Osztrák- Magyar Monarchia kialakulásával és fennállásával kapcsolatos egyes nemzetközi kérdésekről'. *Állam- és Jogtudomány* XXXVIII/1–2 (1996–1997), 97–99.

Wiesner, J(akob). *The History of the Hungarian Book-Trade* (Organizing Committee of the Eight Session of the International Publisher's Congress, 1913).

Williamson, Samuel R. *Austria-Hungary and the Origins of the First World War* (London: MacMillan International Higher Education 1990).

CHAPTER 6

The Man behind the Curtain

Developing Film's Double Exposure of Intellectual Property

Johanna Gibson

> Pay no attention to that man behind the curtain[1]

1 Introduction

> To talk about film was like making them. What I'm saying is not nostalgic, it's historical.[2]

The early days of film and its subsequent accommodation within copyright show a particular constellation of forces in the history of copyright as well as in the interaction with patents and intellectual property more widely. First, film is exemplary in the articulation of the relationship between industrialisation, new technologies, and the impact on both creative industries and their consumers. Secondly, film's initial incorporation into international copyright law was a response not to its product but to its technology; that is, film as a means of reproduction of a wholly other copyright, as it were, in theatrical productions. Finally, film put both the product, and the protection of that product, on the move. Arguably, the protection of film is the first challenge to the discrete boundaries of copyright, its objects, and place. A highly collaborative cultural form, the multiplicity of film is at the same time somewhat obscured both by film traditions (and the auteur) and by the law. Who makes a film? Or perhaps more tellingly, what makes an auteur?

The time and movement of film is arguably the first real disruption to copyright's creative landscape as well as providing much needed insight into the

1 The Wizard of Oz, in *The Wizard of Oz* (1939), Victor Fleming (dir).

2 Jean-Luc Godard in interview in Godard, J.-L. (2003) *The Future(s) of Film: Three Interviews 2000/01*, Gachnang & Springer, Zurich, p. 14.

 | DOI:10.1163/9789004511439_008

mythology underpinning the colonialist narrative of invention during the industrial revolution.[3] The development of film and modern cinema provides a fascinating perspective in that the invention and dissemination of the first film technologies coincide with the development of copyright as an international relationship through the Berne Convention. The birth of cinema may be 1895 (with disclaimers to follow), but 1908 is one of the most important years for the law of film.[4]

And as much as the history of film speaks to copyright, similarly it has much to say about the way in which narratives of invention are reconstructed both socially and within the intellectual property framework itself. The story of the invention of cinema itself comprises an obfuscation of the innovation narrative, presenting a coherent linearity where there is nothing but reels and reels of innovation mysteries and shadows. In reality, from the Lumières to Edison's Motion Picture Patents Company, the story of cinema and the law is one of broken tracks and way objects.

The conventional history of the invention of film technology streamlines the distributed and cacophonous inventive landscape into a linear progress of innovation mythology and cultural modernity.[5] Indeed, it is perhaps no accident that the originary and exemplary figure of film's origins is the arrival of a train, 'a motif which, more than almost any other, allows us to engage with the modern experience of visuality,'[6] an exemplary trope of industrialisation, modernity and invention. Marian Aguiar writes, 'As a technological object, the train acted as metonym for modernity – its very existence testified to the presence and legitimacy of the modern; modernity was rendered imaginatively through the materials of technology. The railway became modernity's most prominent emblem … As we view the mobilization of modernity's rhetoric in

3 To an extent, the current debates over vaccine nationalism, in the wake of Covid, reflect similar tensions and at the same time invoke intellectual property (patents) before they have even begun to characterise the landscape.

4 Several critical events of 1908 precipitated a new status for film as both art and property: the founding of le Film d'art (January); the Berlin Conference of the Berne Convention for the Protection of Literary and Artistic Copyright (October–November); the establishment of the Motion Picture Patents Company (December); and the commencement of the so-called *Ben Hur* litigation (November), *Kalem Co v Harper Brothers*, 222 US 55 (1911).

5 Viva Paci states, "The emergence of cinema was part of the euphoria of modernity": Paci, V. (2006) The Attraction of the Intelligent Eye: Obsessions with the Vision Machine in Early Film Theories, in Strauven, W. (ed.) (2006) *The Cinema of Attractions Reloaded*, Amsterdam University Press, Amsterdam, pp. 121–138: p. 125.

6 Blümlinger, C. (2006) Lumière, the Train and the Avant-Garde, in Strauven, W., ed. (2006) *The Cinema of Attractions Reloaded*, Amsterdam University Press, Amsterdam, pp. 245–264: p. 245.

postcolonial national building, we can trace it through the representation of technology.'[7]

The late nineteenth-century emphasis on visual technologies runs through the relationship between industrialisation and film, consumer culture and cinema. Viva Paci links cinema's modernity to other iconic visual technologies, such as the microscope, including the train and flight as part of this visual revolution in that they provide new perspectives upon the landscape.[8] And Tom Gunning has identified links between cinema and the entertainment carnival, describing the way early cinema even absorbed the train into its physical exhibition apparatus: 'Perhaps most extreme is the Hale's Tours, the largest chain of theatres exclusively showing films before 1906. Not only did the films consist of non-narrative sequences taken from moving vehicles (usually trains), but the theatre itself was arranged as a train car with a conductor who took tickets, and sound effects simulating the click-clack of wheels and hiss of air brakes.'[9]

This chapter looks at the relationship between two great phenomena of industrialisation – railroads and films. Both the railroad (the tracks and the train) and cinema (the technology and the film) demonstrate the bifurcation in the industrial narrative of the *fin de siècle*, one that would be imported into intellectual property law itself. At the same time, both are also interpreted through and as phenomena of colonialism, with long-reaching consequences for contemporary intellectual property critique.

Film characterises the curious, almost Cartesian divided logic of intellectual property. There is the creative identity of the film product itself, and at the same time the industry of its reproduction and projection. There is the technology of the inventions of projection and the industry built upon the relationships between protection, rather than between instruments and apparatus. And strikingly, the early days of cinema were not merely the patent wars of Edison's company, or the copyright wars of cinematography and theatre. They played

7 Aguiar, M. (2008) Making Modernity: Inside the Technological Space of the Railway, *Cultural Critique*, 68, 66–85: p. 71. See further the discussion of the train as a symbol of modernity (as well as mobility and technological advancement) in Indian cinema, in Gopal, S. (2015) Some Brief Reflections on Technology, Cinema, and the Postcolonial Uncanny, *Pacific Coast Philology*, 50(2), 198–208. See further the train as symbol of modernity and mobility in Argentine cinema and the representation of rural space and society in Losada, M. (2011) Argentine Cinema and Rural Space, *Chasqui*, 40(2), 18–32.

8 Paci, V. (2006) The Attraction of the Intelligent Eye: Obsessions with the Vision Machine in Early Film Theories, in Strauven, W. (ed.) (2006) *The Cinema of Attractions Reloaded*, Amsterdam University Press, Amsterdam, pp. 121–138: p. 125.

9 Gunning, T. (2006) The Cinema of Attraction(s): Early Film, Its Spectator and the Avant-Garde, in Strauven, W. (ed.) (2006) *The Cinema of Attractions Reloaded*, Amsterdam University Press, Amsterdam, pp. 381–388: p. 383.

out as geopolitical wars between patents and copyright themselves – a division in emphasis that arguably continues to characterise national film industries to this day. It is the contention of this chapter that, for the makings of intellectual property, film provides the first glimpse of the man behind the curtain.

2 Making the First Move

> When I speak of the invention of gunpowder, of the telegraph, of railroads, etc., I mean, of course, the group of accumulated and yet distinguishable and numerable inventions which have been necessary for the production of gunpowder, or telegraphy, or railroads.[10]

Like other innovations of the industrial era, the invention of film was a highly distributed affair and at the same time a wholly intimate labour of contact. Film was both borne out of shared innovation and provided (and continues to provide) much of the impetus to other consumer innovation through the very circumstances of its communication; that is, the contact that is necessary for further innovation. Gabriel Tarde, writing in the same period, emphasises contact and imitation as instrumental not only to innovation but also to its diffusion: 'Lack of communication in social physics plays the same role as lack of elasticity in physics. The one hinders imitation as much as the other, vibration. But the imitative spread of certain well-known inventions (railroads, telegraphs, etc.), tends to diminish, to the benefit of every other invention, this insufficiency of mental contact.'[11] Film is thus part of the important machinery for innovation and the diffusion of invention, as well as the advertising of industrialisation's consumer culture and the spread of desire. Tarde writes, 'To develop mines, railroads, and cotton mills is to give new hands to the industries that are born of modern inventions.'[12] And from fashion to domestic appliances, film gave 'new hands,' new contact, to new industries of modernity and has continued to touch new inventions and products. And what better contact than through the society, the gatherings of cinema? Arguably, film and its audiences provide an exemplary history and sociology of the proliferation of "producers"

10 Tarde, G. (1890/[1903]) *The Laws of Imitation*, E.C. Parsons (trans), Henry Holt & Co, New York, p. 11.

11 Tarde, G. (1890/[1903]) *The Laws of Imitation*, E.C. Parsons (trans), Henry Holt & Co, New York, p. 115.

12 Tarde, G. (1890/[1903]) *The Laws of Imitation*, E.C. Parsons (trans), Henry Holt & Co, New York, p. 122.

in any one product, the society of a product, a film's many directors.[13] When it comes to understanding the contact achieved by the spread of these two key inventions, film and the railroad, the technologies of film and of the railroad have curiously intertwined but almost inevitably familiar histories.

In the story of film's invention, there is no clear consensus on the first film. And there is no clear inventor of a discrete technology, or an irrefutable start date. Film's premiere, as it were, was actually quite incremental. Nevertheless, many if not most commentaries on film cite 28 December 1895 as 'the birth of cinema'; that is, the experience of film and the cinematic apparatus.[14] This is in acknowledgement of Auguste and Louis Lumière's short programme of documentary films (or actualities) that was exhibited on this day to a paying audience in Paris. The programme reportedly included the single shot film, *L'Arrivée d'un train en gare de la Ciotat*, which has gone on to become the exemplary product of the invention of film.[15] But in fact, there is no record of the film being included in the printed matter to accompany that particular screening. The first public screening was actually recorded a month later in Lyon, 25 January 1896.[16] Already there is some uncertainty in the "creation story" of film. But the charisma of cinema's first train appears to have overwhelmed any concerns about this; indeed, in part this may even have been the motivation for this consolidated history of cinema's first moment. But more on this – in another moment.

In the story of film's invention there is also no clear consensus on the "invention." The Lumière brothers' apparatus was not completely revolutionary; rather, it was profoundly indebted to earlier as well as other contemporary

13 Bruno Latour, responding to Tarde, advocates critique that undertakes "a multifarious inquiry launched with the tools of anthropology, philosophy, metaphysics, history, sociology to detect *how many participants* are gathered in a *thig* to make it exist and to maintain its existence." See Latour, B. (2004) Why Has Critique Run out of Steam? From Matters of Fact to Matters of Concern, *Critical Inquiry*, 30(2), 225–248: p. 246.

14 Cousins, M. (2020/[2004]) *The Story of Film*, updated edition, Pavilion Books, London, p. 25.

15 Cousins, M. (2020/[2004]) *The Story of Film*, updated edition, Pavilion Books, London, p. 25. See further Loiperdinger, M. (2004) Lumière's "Arrival of the Train": Cinema's Founding Myth, *The Moving Image: The Journal of the Association of Moving Image Archivists*, 4(1), 89–118.

16 Vue No 653, *L'Arrivée d'un train en gare de la Ciotat* https://catalogue-lumiere.com/arrivee-train-a-la-ciotat/. See further the IMDB record at https://www.imdb.com/title/tt0000012/. A record of the original program is available from L'Institut Lumière which shows the absence of *L'Arrivée d'un train en gare de la Ciotat* – http://www.institut-lumiere.org/musee/les-freres-lumiere-et-leurs-inventions/premiere-seance.html.

techniques, including: Georges Demenÿ's bioscope (1894)[17]; Léon Bouly's 'cinématographe' (1893)[18]; Louis Aimé Augustin Le Prince's photo-camera and stereopticon (1888)[19]; Émile Reynaud's use of perforated bands (1888)[20]; and Edison's slightly later use of perforations in 35mm strips (1889).[21] Le Prince's contribution is actually one of the great mysteries in the story of film and once again a train is central to one of film history's enigmatic episodes. Le Prince disappeared in 1890, after boarding a train to Paris just before he was due to premiere his invention in New York.[22] Le Prince's body and luggage were never found, leading to a flurry of theories, even including one explanation of his disappearance as an outcome of a patent war with Edison.[23]

The uncertainty over the exact date of "the birth" is not in itself the interesting or even frustrating element of this history. Rather, the intrigue and insight are to be found in the circumstances of that uncertainty – the constructed nature of the story of film's invention, the phenomenon of myth making around the history of film, and the uncertainty (or even multiplicity) surrounding the provenance of the invention of film and film projection. Cinema,

---

17 Mannoni, L., Campagnoni, D.P., and Robinson, D. (1995) *Light and Movement: Incunabula of the Motion Picture 1420–1896*, Le Giornate del Cinema Muto, Pordenone Italy, pp. 397–398.

18 Mannoni, L., Campagnoni, D.P., and Robinson, D. (1995) *Light and Movement: Incunabula of the Motion Picture 1420–1896*, Le Giornate del Cinema Muto, Pordenone Italy, p. 351.

19 USPTO No 367,247, 10 January 1888. See further the documentation for Le Prince's US Patent for improvements to his method, reproduced in Mannoni, L., Campagnoni, D.P., and Robinson, D. (1995) *Light and Movement: Incunabula of the Motion Picture 1420–1896*, Le Giornate del Cinema Muto, Pordenone Italy, pp. 369–377.

20 Mannoni, L., Campagnoni, D.P., and Robinson, D. (1995) *Light and Movement: Incunabula of the Motion Picture 1420–1896*, Le Giornate del Cinema Muto, Pordenone Italy, p. 251.

21 Mannoni, L., Campagnoni, D.P., and Robinson, D. (1995) *Light and Movement: Incunabula of the Motion Picture 1420–1896*, Le Giornate del Cinema Muto, Pordenone Italy, pp. 325, 399. The authors argue that Demenÿ's contribution was especially instrumental. Between 1893 and 1895, Louis Lumière corresponded with Demenÿ and "Demenÿ proposed to Lumière a mechanism capable of resolving the difficult problem of the projection of chronophotographic films," which he presented to Lumière in original drawings: "These sketches suggest that the development of the Lumière cinématographe, between December 1894 and February 1895, might have been due not only to the Edison kinetoscope but also thanks to the suggestions of Georges Demenÿ" (pp. 387–388).

22 Rawlence, C. (1990) *The Missing Reel: The Untold Story of the Lost Inventor of Moving Pictures*, Atheneum, New York, pp. 50–56. See also *The First Film* (2015) David Wilkinson (dir). For a commentary on the film see Hannaford, A. (2015) The mystery of Leeds's long-lost movie pioneer, *The Telegraph*, 24 June.

23 Rawlence, C. (1990) *The Missing Reel: The Untold Story of the Lost Inventor of Moving Pictures*, Atheneum, New York, p. 11. Edison's role in the growth of the US film industry, particularly in the establishment of the Motion Picture Patents Company in 1908, is discussed in more detail later in this chapter.

as the public exhibition of film, charts an almost feverish period in the emergence of the modern entertainment consumer and the rise of consumer culture across a range of cultural forms, all in the context of an emphasis on the visual.[24] During this period of rapid proliferation of forms of consumption and entertainment, cinema was all but inevitable in securing the effort involved in establishing modern consumer culture. And film technology is itself a crystallisation of diverse contributions and the acceleration of a shared effort with a "pre-history" far more extensive and complex than is perhaps ordinarily acknowledged.[25]

While it may well be that 28 December 1895 was a significant demonstration in what was to become the preferred technology of early cinema, it certainly was not the first public exhibition, or even the first exhibition of film to ticketed consumers. More than a year earlier, in February 1894, Jean Aimé Leroy reportedly staged the first public exhibition of films, outside the Riley Brothers optical shop in New York.[26] But although details on Leroy are scant,[27] there are still several other examples of public exhibitions before the legendary date of 28 December 1895. In August the same year, Birt Acres held public exhibitions in Barnet, London[28]; in September 1895, Thomas Armat and Charles Francis Jenkins demonstrated to the public their phantoscope at the Cotton

24 Kristin Thompson and David Bordwell note that "The nineteenth century saw a vast proliferation of visual forms of popular culture," largely supported by the mass production of images made possible by the industrial era. See Thompson, K. & Bordwell, D. (2010) *Film History*, 3rd ed, Mc-Graw Hill, New York, p. 3.

25 See for example the extensive and comprehensive pre-history in Mannoni, L., Campagnoni, D.P., and Robinson, D. (1995) *Light and Movement: Incunabula of the Motion Picture 1420–1896*, Le Giornate del Cinema Muto, Pordenone Italy.

26 Sauvage, L. (1985) *L'Affaire Lumière: du mythe a l'histoire, enquête sur les origines du cinéma*, Lherminier, Paris, pp. 142–144.

27 Indeed, Leroy has been all but erased from cinematic history, with very few if any histories mentioning his contribution or this reported event. Compare the recovery of Leroy in cinematic history in Sauvage, L. (1985) *L'Affaire Lumière: du mythe a l'histoire, enquête sur les origines du cinéma*, Lherminier, Paris.

28 Birt Acres produced one of the world's first news films, filming the Oxford-Cambridge Boat Race and the Derby horse race, and exhibited these through the summer at the Empire of India Exhibition, Earl's Court. Notably, the public exhibition used kinetoscopes and so did not approach the communal audience achieved by the Lumières. See further Mannoni, L., Campagnoni, D.P., and Robinson, D. (1995) *Light and Movement: Incunabula of the Motion Picture 1420–1896*, Le Giornate del Cinema Muto, Pordenone Italy, pp. 416–417. Thompson and Bordwell note that although Acres gave other demonstrations, "he did not systematically exploit his projector and films." See Thompson, K. & Bordwell, D. (2010) *Film History*, 3rd ed, Mc-Graw Hill, New York, p. 9.

States Exposition in Atlanta[29]; and on 1 November 1895, Max Skladanowsky produced the first public show with his Bioskope at the Wintergarten Berlin,[30] the same day as filing a patent for the device.[31] But amidst the frenetic activity of the period, the Lumière brothers were conscientious not only in presenting their innovations in Paris, but also in publicising their technology: 'The Lumière brothers dispatched films and projectionists to every continent with such speed that within one to two years audiences in most countries had seen the famous train arriving in La Ciotat.'[32]

Thus, notwithstanding the cultural and historical impact of the Lumière brothers' exhibition, the "invention" of cinema, that is, the apparatus of this public exhibition, was less a spectacular premiere than it was the marvellous finale of centuries of innovation in moving images, 'a limp anti-climax, in contradiction of the mythology which seeks to make it the climax of the dangerous adventure of invention.'[33] Jacques Aumont maintains, 'Lumière did not invent anything except a radical conceptual shift, which he was unaware of himself, and a perfect adaptation of the machine to its exploitation, whose

29 Mannoni, L., Campagnoni, D.P., and Robinson, D. (1995) *Light and Movement: Incunabula of the Motion Picture 1420–1896*, Le Giornate del Cinema Muto, Pordenone Italy, p. 379.

30 Mannoni, L., Campagnoni, D.P., and Robinson, D. (1995) *Light and Movement: Incunabula of the Motion Picture 1420–1896*, Le Giornate del Cinema Muto, Pordenone Italy, p. 408. Ultimately, the superiority of the Lumière cinématographe eclipsed the Skladanowsky Bioskope and the various other demonstrations that preceded the Lumière event. Although the Skladanowsky brothers also toured Europe until 31 March 1897, their technology was overtaken by the Lumières: Mannoni, L., Campagnoni, D.P., and Robinson, D. (1995) *Light and Movement: Incunabula of the Motion Picture 1420–1896*, Le Giornate del Cinema Muto, Pordenone Italy, p. 409. David Parkinson notes that "it is this date [28 December 1895] that historians hold sacred," arguing that "The Lumières merit elevation above their peers." See Parkinson, D. (2012) *History of Film*, 2nd ed, Thames & Hudson, New York, pp. 16–17.

31 The patent was ultimately granted, 21 October 1896, No 88599. See further Mannoni, L., Campagnoni, D.P., and Robinson, D. (1995) *Light and Movement: Incunabula of the Motion Picture 1420–1896*, Le Giornate del Cinema Muto, Pordenone Italy, pp. 408, 410.

32 Cousins, M. (2020/[2004]) *The Story of Film*, updated edition, Pavilion Books, London, p. 25. Cousins notes: "By 1900 the Lumière films had reached audiences in Senegal (Dakar) and Iran, including the Shah in his mirrored Qajar Palace" (26). According to Cousins, in 1896 alone the film had been exhibited in cities in Italy, Russia, Hungary, Romania, Serbia, Denmark, Canada, India, Czechoslovakia, Uruguay, Argentina, Mexico, Chile, Guatemala, Cuba, Japan, Bulgaria, Thailand and the Philippines (pp. 25–26). It is recorded that in about eighteen months, the film had reached every continent except Antarctica: Rosen, M. (1987) "Lumière," in Wakeman, J., ed. (1987) *World Film Directors: Volume I, 1890–1945*, The HW Wilson Company, New York, pp. 700–709: p. 705.

33 Païni, D. (1995) Foreword: The Spiral of Inventions, in Mannoni, L., Campagnoni, D.P., and Robinson, D. (1995) *Light and Movement: Incunabula of the Motion Picture 1420–1896*, Le Giornate del Cinema Muto, Pordenone Italy, pp. 13–18: p. 15.

ultimate consequences he was also unaware. Is this to have invented cinema? We hardly care any more.'[34]

Indeed, we hardly do care, as this minor incursion upon the history is somewhat obscured by the mythology of cinema and the consolidation of its relationship to modernity. What is notable about the emphasis on this particular date is that it anchors the common representation of cinema as a phenomenon of the industrial revolution, with frequent reference to a culmination of innovative effort identifying the late nineteenth century as the historical and momentous birth of motion pictures: 'The 1890s were, it was generally agreed, the period that gave birth to moving images.'[35] The received history of cinema is thus conventionally accepted as a phenomenon of the industrial revolution. Cinema is said to have '*appeared* in the wake of the industrial revolution.' And, as a "new" technology of the industrial era, film 'became the basis of a large industry.'[36] The origin story of 1895 is thus fraught with plot holes. But if this perceived coincidence between film and the 1890s is such an inaccurate account, why has it endured with such constancy and authority? Answering this question is arguably the undercurrent of this chapter.

However, perhaps even more striking than the technical development, is that the Lumières' device was to be forever firmly associated with the charisma and spectacle of their film, not its operation as such: 'Lumière's most noteworthy contribution was not in the technological domain, still less in the scientific. What he saw, no doubt unconsciously, was that priority should be given not to the travel mechanism over the film, but to the film over the mechanism. It was the film, its perfect regularity of movement, its stability, that counted – and it was to ensure these that he made his only innovation.'[37] In other words, the "origin myth" was to be forever characterised not by the technology but by the film and the event of communality in audience.[38] The "invention" was the

34 Aumont, J. (1996) Lumière revisited, B. Brewster (trans), *Film History*, 8(4), 416–430: p. 417. On this unawareness of both the technology and the commercial growth of cinema, Lumière is said to have stated, rather contemptuously it would seem (and not inconsistently with his appeal to exclusivity), "Had I been able to foresee what the cinema would become ... I would never have invented it." Quoted in Puttnam, D. & Watson, N. (1997/[1999]) *Movies and Money*, Random House/Vintage, New York, p. 18. See further Sauvage, L. (1985) *L'Affaire Lumière: du mythe a l'histoire, enquête sur les origines du cinéma*, Lherminier, Paris, p. 169.

35 Huhtamo, E. (2011) Natural magic: a short cultural history of moving images, in Guynn, W. (ed.) (2011) *The Routledge Companion to Film History*, Routledge, Abingdon, pp. 3–15: p. 3.

36 Thompson, K. & Bordwell, D. (2010) *Film History*, 3rd ed, Mc-Graw Hill, New York, p. 3.

37 Aumont, J. (1996) Lumière revisited, B. Brewster (trans), *Film History*, 8(4), 416–430: p. 417.

38 Puttnam and Watson credit Louis Lumière's device with the introduction of communal viewing: "instead of being limited to a single viewer, allowed large groups of people to

cinematic apparatus, as it were.[39] And in taking their train around the world, they branded cinema forever with the Lumière name, and the Lumières with cinematography.

Even the provenance of the terminology itself, cinematography, the term that would go on to signify the whole industry, is a tale of frustrated patent maintenance and personal rebranding. Léon Bouly coined the term, cinematographe, as applied to his French patent granted 1894.[40] However, when Bouly was unable to afford the fees to maintain the patent, he sold the rights to the invention and the name to the Lumières.[41] The term cinematography was subsequently adopted as a terminological standard, including in the

---

watch the images it project. Thus was born the idea of communal viewing, which would remain at the heart of the cinemagoing experience." See Puttnam, D. & Watson, N. (1997/[1999]) *Movies and Money*, Random House/Vintage, New York, p. 15. Although an instrument designed for single viewing, it was possible to adapt the kinetoscope for an audience but to do so was impractical (see Musser, C. (1991) *Before the Nickelodeon: Edwin S Porter and the Edison Manufacturing Company*, University of California Press, Berkeley, pp. 36–37). The seamlessness of the Lumières' device was considered superior. Putting this communality at the heart of the cinematic experience is nevertheless tested by contemporary streaming and communality in the "aftermath," as it were, of social media discussion (particularly in the current circumstances of a pandemic, during which this chapter is being written). Nevertheless, it is arguable that approaching this communality remains a priority of contemporary forms of exhibition and distribution, deriving novel community through other means.

39 That is, in introducing the conventional architecture of the cinematic projection and positioning of the viewing subject, we both film's community in audience, and at the same time the ideology of representation that made film such a critical tool of colonialism, empire, and indeed imperious viewpoints today. See further the discussion of the cinematic apparatus in one of the founding works in this area, Baudry, J.-L. (1970/[1974–1975]) Ideological Effects of the Basic Cinematographic Apparatus, A. Williams (trans), *Film Quarterly*, 28(2), 39–47 (Translated from the 1970 article originally published in *Cinéthique*, No 7/8, 1–8). It is worth noting Baudry's observation that the cinematic image is premised upon the same assumptions of presentation as traditional western painting: "The dimensions of the image itself, the ratio between height and width, seem clearly taken from an average drawn from Western easel painting" (p. 41). This resonates with the discussion later in this chapter of cinema's reliance upon an affinity with the high arts in order to establish its credibility as a mass-produced art.

40 The text of the patent, deposited 27 December 1893 and ultimately granted 16 March 1894, is reproduced in Mannoni, L., Campagnoni, D.P., and Robinson, D. (1995) *Light and Movement: Incunabula of the Motion Picture 1420–1896*, Le Giornate del Cinema Muto, Pordenone Italy, pp. 352–354 with further commentary available p. 351.

41 Auer, M. & Ory, M. (1979) *Histoire de la caméra ciné amateur*, Éditions Big; Geneva, pp. 44, 46–47. Compare the interpretation of events provided in Puttnam, D. & Watson, N. (1997/[1999]) *Movies and Money*, Random House/Vintage, New York, where the authors claim that Antoine Lumière favoured the term, "Domitor," but that the brothers insisted on "Cinématographe" (p. 15).

introduction of film to international copyright in the 1908 revision of the Berne Convention.[42] Thus, the "authorship" of the industry is readily consolidated to the romantic notion of the inventive genius, thus establishing the origin myth of the Lumières. The origin story of film in lights, the Lumières, and the iconic image of the train.[43] The birth of cinema was thus an event – the arrival of the train as both the end, and the beginning, of film.

3 An Invention with No Future

> The cinema is an invention without a future.[44]
> So Art is limited to the infinite, and beginning there cannot progress.[45]

The opening scene of Jean-Luc Godard's 1963 film, *Le mépris*,[46] recollects the Lumières' *L'Arrivée d'un train en gare de la Ciotat*. A woman is approaching the screen accompanied by director with camera and crew. The camera travels along on a dolly in pace with the woman towards the audience, the perspective

---

42 Discussed in more detail later in this chapter.

43 Jacques Aumont, noting the train's referencing and legacy in cinema history states, "With these filmmakers, Lumière has found his true posterity: not that of the 'Lumière line' to which he has been confined, but that, quite simply, of cinema pictures." See Aumont, J. (1996) Lumière revisited, B. Brewster (trans), *Film History*, 8(4), 416–430: p. 429. Jacques Aumont notes Jean-Luc Godard's referencing of *L'Arrivée d'un train en gare de la Ciotat* in two films – *Les Carabiniers* (1963) and *Hélos pour moi* (1993) (see p. 429). He then adds *Pierrot le fou* (1965) in a footnote (see *fn* 28). But I would also add *Le mépris* (1963), not only for its quotation of Louis Lumière's legendary phrase, but also, and perhaps even more importantly, for its opening scene, as discussed in the next part of this chapter.

44 This phrase was most widely accepted as uttered by Louis Lumière and this belief is found throughout the literature and in film itself, as in Godard's *Le mépris*. See further Puttnam, D. & Watson, N. (1997/[1999]) *Movies and Money*, Random House/Vintage, New York, p. 9. But the phrase has also been attributed to Louis's father, Antoine, or even simply to "the Lumières" (Parkinson, D. (2012) *History of Film*, 2nd ed, Thames & Hudson, New York, p. 289). And a similar sentiment has also been attributed variously to Louis's brother, Auguste, and also to his father, Antoine, both of whom have been reported to have said that the invention "has no commercial value whatsoever" (for example, the phrase is attributed to Antoine Lumière in Myrent, G. (1985) When Movies Began and No One Came, *The New York Times*, 29 December). Despite uncertainty over whether it was said and by whom, it has become an apocryphal statement of film history, forever linked to the Lumières.

45 Jean-Luc Godard in interview in Godard, J.-L. (2003) *The Future(s) of Film: Three Interviews 2000/01*, Gachnang & Springer, Zurich, p. 114.

46 *Le mépris/Contempt* (1963), Jean-Luc Godard (dir), Alberto Moravia (novel), Jean-Luc Godard (screenplay, uncredited).

mapping clearly onto the Lumières' train. The woman then moves out of shot, and the camera turns and lowers to face the audience. Godard has long been preoccupied with the making of film itself, with what goes on behind the curtain, and has been critical of the contrived separation of film's industrial and aesthetic dimensions: 'If we studied the way a film is made, those 30 people who come together, then part, the financial, social, sexual ties, you would see quite a lot.'[47] And *Le mépris* is compelling in its study of cinema and its critique of the story and history of cinema that is told.

It is not insignificant that *Le mépris* is a film within a film, and an adaptation within an adaptation. The film dramatises the making of a film, the cinematic adaptation of the novel, *Il dispresso*[48]; which is itself a novel about the writing of a script; which is itself an adaptation of the story of Homer's *Odyssey* for a cinematic production. In that delicious intimacy of proliferative imitations and reiterations is the story of cinema. As well as the multiciplicity of inventions that constitute the "invention" of cinema, and the communal creativity that constitutes the "auteur," *Le mépris* sets out the self-seeking of early cinema in establishing itself as a discrete art, rather than a mere technology of reproduction.[49] At the centre of this is Homer's *Odyssey*, a classic of the western canon, and its adaptation a manifest declaration of cinema as art. Indeed, as discussed later in this chapter, for the early days of cinema this very practice of adapting classical works of theatre and literature was part of an express attempt to establish cinema's validity as a cultural form and set the groundwork for the development of the authorial and auteurial social and legal rendering of film. Film's own odyssey, as it were.

In the screening room scene, the director of the film within the film, Fritz Lang, is joined by the producer, Jeremy Prokosch (Jack Palance), to view the progress of the film. The shots are all of statues of gods, reproducing "scenes," as it were, of a classical work. Prokosch becomes frustrated at the film and leaps up in rage, standing in front of the screen to address Fritz. On the masking beneath the screen behind Prokosch is the following text, 'Il cinema è un

47 Jean-Luc Godard in interview in Godard, J.-L. (2003) *The Future(s) of Film: Three Interviews 2000/01*, Gachnang & Springer, Zurich, p. 29. This almost adversarial approach to organising knowledge runs through the history and philosophy of science (as seen in C.P. Snow's canonical work, *The Two Cultures* – Snow, C.P. (1969) *The Two Cultures*, Cambridge University Press, Cambridge) and indeed in contemporary approaches to interdisciplinarity in the academy and the presumed (and spurious) theory/practice divide in pedagogy.

48 Alberto Moravia, 1954. Moravia is also credited as the writer for *Le mépris*.

49 A preoccupation which is revisited later in this chapter around the momentous developments of 1908, and how they influenced not only the productions, but also the protection emerging in this period of early cinema's complex of inferiority.

invenzione senza avvenire,' with an attribution to Louis Lumière included below the text. This is the famous phrase, 'Cinema is an invention without a future.' This is also the moment in *Le mépris* where the authorship or auteurship is at once confounded in that it is a combat between director, producer, screenwriter, and, to some extent, the public. The scene appeals to a shared history and taste through the expectations attached to the high art presented by Homer's *Odyssey*, a kind of exclusivity, yet one that is at once everywhere. The very dilemma of film as an emerging art of mass-production and mass spectatorship.

The surrounding legend of Louis Lumière's famous utterance is instructive in interpreting this presentation of film's history. Amidst an uncertain commercial environment, the Lumières were known for guarding their technology and refusing to sell to any potential competitors: 'A daily flood of inquiries from inventors poured into the Monplaisir factory. All were anxious to acquire one of the new machines, but Louis and Auguste, wary of piracy, refused to contemplate selling to anybody.'[50] Even the Edison Manufacturing Company made a request to purchase in January 1896, to which they received no response.[51] Antoine Lumière is reported as having said, 'It's a big secret, this device, and I don't want to sell it. I want to develop it myself, exclusively.'[52] It would seem that the famous phrase, cinema is an invention without a future, might have been uttered as a refrain of secrecy with which to refuse the many potential buyers.[53]

As well as simply refusing to sell the technology, Louis Lumière excelled at promoting the brand and the mythology of the inventive genius: 'Lumière always cultivated his image as an inventor, by hook or by crook ... he never tired of the tale of the "stroke of genius" in his invention (the sewing machine

50 Puttnam, D. & Watson, N. (1997/[1999]) *Movies and Money*, Random House/Vintage, New York, p. 15. The authors report that following the famous exhibition of 28 December 1895, "the director of the Folies-Bergère, one of the most powerful figures in the French entertainment world, offered Lumière 50,000 francs for a single machine. Antoine, fearing piracy, was adamant, insisting that no amount of money would induce him to sell" (p. 17).

51 Rittaud-Hutinet, J. & Dentzer, Y. (eds.) (1994/[1995]) *Auguste and Louis Lumière Letters: Inventing the Cinema*, P. Hodgson (trans), Faber and Faber, London, p. 96.

52 Quoted in Rosen, M. (1987) "Louis Lumière," in Wakeman, J., ed. (1987) *World Film Directors: Volume I, 1890–1945*, The HW Wilson Company, New York, pp. 700–709: p. 705.

53 Notably, the efforts at exclusivity somewhat compromised the Lumières' prominence when cinema began to develop rapidly. See further Mannoni, L., Campagnoni, D.P., and Robinson, D. (1995) *Light and Movement: Incunabula of the Motion Picture 1420–1896*, Le Giornate del Cinema Muto, Pordenone Italy, pp. 399–400.

that came to his mind on a sleepless night, as a sudden illumination).'[54] As his brother Auguste described it, 'In one night, my brother had just invented the Cinématographe.'[55]

The mythology surrounding Louis Lumière's flash of genius is characteristic of *fin-de-siècle* thinking and the rupture with the past through the modernity of cinema, at once revolutionary and untranslatable. Cinema is an invention without a future. It is both the beginning and end of history. If it is true that Lumière once said that his intention was to 'reproduce life,'[56] it is a curious result that life is deferred by the image. What is modernity if not a future that is always yet to arrive? But the historical discontinuity of both film's development and its records is disguised by the apparatus itself: 'The original Lumière films, after all, document not only the 1890s but the origins of movies; the simple shot of the Lyon train pulling into the station … has been since the 1920s a film about the genesis and evolution of film. The Lumière films had a distinctive look, too – all flicker and deep shadows and nitrate nimbi – that, it turns out, is not simply a matter of age; the new films all glow with the same delicate texture, a grain and contrast and metastable movement we've long taken to be exclusively *fin-de-siècle*.'[57] Indeed, had Louis Lumière known what was to come, he would never have invented it.[58]

At the end of his life, Louis Lumière reportedly acknowledged the contributions of others, the distributed, collaborative, and incremental story of cinema's invention: 'What have I done? It was in the air.'[59] But the myth was nevertheless recuperated: 'All the ideas that led to the Cinématographe of

54 Aumont, J. (1996) Lumière revisited, B. Brewster (trans), *Film History*, 8(4), 416–430: p. 419. See further Parkinson, D. (2012) *History of Film*, 2nd ed, Thames & Hudson, New York, p. 17; Puttnam, D. & Watson, N. (1997/[1999]) *Movies and Money*, Random House/Vintage, New York, p. 15. Compare the more iterative development suggested through exchanges with Georges Demenÿ: Mannoni, L., Campagnoni, D.P., and Robinson, D. (1995) *Light and Movement: Incunabula of the Motion Picture 1420–1896*, Le Giornate del Cinema Muto, Pordenone Italy, pp. 387–388.

55 Quoted in Rosen, M. (1987) "Louis Lumière," in Wakeman, J., ed. (1987) *World Film Directors: Volume I, 1890–1945*, The HW Wilson Company, New York, pp. 700–709: p. 701.

56 As said to Georges Sadoul and quoted in Rosen, M. (1987) "Louis Lumière," in Wakeman, J., ed. (1987) *World Film Directors: Volume I, 1890–1945*, The HW Wilson Company, New York, pp. 700–709: p. 702.

57 Atkinson, M. (1997) Lumière & Company: The Future of the Invention, *Film Comment*, 33(3), 72–73, 75: p. 73.

58 Louis Lumière is reputed to have said: "*Le cinema? Je n'y vais plus. Si j'avais pu prévoir qu'on en viendrait là, je ne l'aurais pas inventé!*" Quoted in Sauvage, L. (1985) *L'Affaire Lumière: du mythe a l'histoire, enquête sur les origines du cinéma*, Lherminier, Paris, p. 169.

59 Quoted in Rosen, M. (1987) "Louis Lumière," in Wakeman, J., ed. (1987) *World Film Directors: Volume I, 1890–1945*, The HW Wilson Company, New York, pp. 700–709: p. 709.

Louis Lumière were in the air for fifty years, but it was he who made it all seem clear, who developed the invention decisively and with absolute perfection.'[60] That such clarity on the cinema (and indeed on the paradox of progressive innovation itself) emerged from 'The kingdom of shadows'[61] is an almost perfect moment of the *fin-de-siècle*.

4 Reels and Railroads

While it can be seen that the conventional story of the invention(s) of the technologies of film and film-making is attributed somewhat artificially and narrowly to the 1890s, this is not by reason of the Lumières' charisma alone. Even where there is some attempt to acknowledge the inventive provenance of film, it is done so in the context of a 'pre-history' to a momentous invention, 'the impression of a sudden technological and cultural rupture,'[62] rather than recognised as part of the fundamental history of cinema and indeed a larger history of moving image.[63] The link between film and modernity is thus cemented in this resilient narrative of 'a sharp break between the Victorian and the modern society.'[64] This self-conscious insistence on historical rupture is also seen in the early twentieth-century films themselves, including Cinema

60 Maurice Bessy and Jean-Louis Chardans quoted in Rosen, M. (1987) "Louis Lumière," in Wakeman, J., ed. (1987) *World Film Directors: Volume I, 1890–1945*, The HW Wilson Company, New York, pp. 700–709: p. 709.

61 The reported response of the writer, Maxim Gorky, to the screening of *L'Arrivée d'un train en gare de la Ciotat* in Moscow in 1896. Quoted in Parkinson, D. (2012) *History of Film*, 2nd ed, Thames & Hudson, New York, p. 27.

62 Huhtamo, E. (2011) Natural magic: a short cultural history of moving images, in Guynn, W., ed. (2011) *The Routledge Companion to Film History*, Routledge, Abingdon, pp. 3–15: p. 57.

63 Indeed, Erkki Huhtamo argues that cinema is perhaps just one moment in a larger and ongoing history of media, with precursors in the very earliest innovations in moving images: "Labeling all the developments that took place before the emergence of cinema as pre-cinema has begun to feel unjustified, not the least because early forms considered so far as 'primitives' of the cinema are now seen to have contained seeds of very different media forms than the ones generally projected via cinema. If the dominance of the cinema was really just a stage in a much longer and broader trend, it is time to rethink the history of moving images." See Huhtamo, E. (2011) Natural magic: a short cultural history of moving images, in Guynn, W., ed. (2011) *The Routledge Companion to Film History*, Routledge, Abingdon, pp. 3–15: p. 4.

64 Huhtamo argues that this "sharp break" is "extolled in its most extreme form by the manifestoes of the Italian Futurists calling for the destruction of past culture and the erection of a new one amidst its smoldering ruins." See Huhtamo, E. (2011) Natural magic: a short cultural history of moving images, in Guynn, W., ed. (2011) *The Routledge Companion to Film History*, Routledge, Abingdon, pp. 3–15: p. 7.

Futurista (Italy) and French and German expressionism, arguably answering in the films the predominant contemporary social movements of *fin-de-siècle* thinking.

Film's history is thus, in part, a history of modernity. And as such, it becomes bound also to colonial imperatives in entertainment, communication and copyright; modernity is itself 'an instrument of empire' and 'has been inculcated with a colonial past and the promise of a national future.'[65] In that flash of Lumière, as it were, the technology of film is given a linear and rational narrative of modernity. This story-making of technologies and their revolution characterises contemporary developments as well. Indeed, a similar rationalism of authorship is identifiable in contemporary representations of the development and innovation landscape of artificial intelligence as an uncomplicated progress narrative of secular modernity.

Arguably, the link between cinema and industrialisation is also propagated by a kind of filmic colonialism, as it were, that continues to endure to this day. Indeed, the emphasis on the Lumière brothers' train in this history and the surrounding mythology of that first exhibition of *L'Arrivée d'un train en gare de la Ciotat* is similarly framed by *fin de siècle* thinking and the lens of colonialism. Even the subject matter itself, the arrival of a train, was and continues to be recognisable as a colonialist and industrialist trope.[66] But it is the way in which this experience of the Lumière exhibition is reported and misreported, and the legend of the audience's reaction, that arguably leaves as unambiguous the assumption of the imperiousness of film and the purported naivety and passivity of film audiences.

As legend has it, the first screening of *L'Arrivée d'un train en gare de la Ciotat* caused audiences to flee in terror from the image of the oncoming train: 'Today, we cannot comprehend the terror that gripped the 1895 audience facing the Lumière brothers' arriving train – this first film with which they gave birth to documentary film.'[67] Despite the acceptance that these reports

65 Aguiar, M. (2008) Making Modernity: Inside the Technological Space of the Railway, *Cultural Critique*, 68, 66–85: p. 66.

66 For example, see the discussion in Aguiar, M. (2008) Making Modernity: Inside the Technological Space of the Railway, *Cultural Critique*, 69, 66–85. Importantly, Aguiar notes the train as both an instrument of colonialism and at the same time a technological imaginary of fluid modernity: "Although colonial rhetoric of the railway equated technology with the progress of a secular nation, the train's symbolic form allowed it more changeability in practice" (p. 71).

67 Exhibition brochure for *100 Jahre Kinobiscum*, 1995–1996, quoted in Loiperdinger, M. (2004) Lumière's "Arrival of the Train": Cinema's Founding Myth, *The Moving Image: The Journal of the Association of Moving Image Archivists*, 4(1), 89–118: p. 89.

were exaggerated or that it did not even happen at all, the 'apocryphal myth' persists.[68] The folkloric status of this story not only reaffirms the notion of film's momentous ushering in of modernity, but also seemingly restores over and over the dominant perception of the passivity and irresponsibility, as it were, of the audience. This resonates with the discourses of innovation and colonialism of the late nineteenth and early twentieth centuries, whereby the audience is portrayed as being reduced 'to a state usually attributed to savages in their primal encounter with the advanced technology of Western colonialists, howling and fleeing in impotent terror before the power of the machine.'[69] And in what is possibly the first example of a film within a film, *The Countryman and the Cinematograph* (1901)[70] brings together the iconic image (the train) and the iconic word (cinematograph) in a depiction of the legendary audience hysteria as a kind of distinction of both education and class. In the surviving fragment of this British silent short, there is a man in country attire watching *L'Arrivée d'un train en gare de la Ciotat* who becomes so panicked by the oncoming train that he runs out of the frame. While no doubt a satirical take on the Lumière event, nevertheless the uneducated, rural population is represented according to stereotype as incapable of interpreting the new technology, reaffirming the place of both the cinematograph and the Lumières' train in the discourse of modernity and progress.

Film and a presupposed colonising perspective in order to educate the masses in the advancement and progress of modernity are thus seemingly forever bound together in the mythology of cinema's first train, which 'still stalks

68 Brown, W. (2012) Has film ever been Western? Continuity and the question of building a "common" cinema, in Bâ, S.M. & Higbee, W., eds. (2012) *De-Westernizing Film Studies*, Routledge, London, pp. 166–177: p. 167. Tom Gunning notes that there are no accounts of any such panic: "As with most myths of origin, the source for these accounts remains elusive. It does not figure in any report of the first screening at the Salon Indien of the Grand Café that I have located." See Gunning, T. (1989/[2016]) An Aesthetic of Astonishment: Early Film and the (In)Credulous Spectator, in Braudy, L. & Cohen, M., eds. (2016) *Film Theory and Criticism*, 8th ed., Oxford University Press, Oxford, pp. 645–659: p. 645; reprint of Gunning, T. (1989) An Aesthetic of Astonishment: Early Film and the (In)Credulous Spectator, *Art and Text*, 34, 31–45. However, that may have much to do with the "myth of origin" of the very screening itself of *L'Arrivée d'un train en gare de la Ciotat* itself, which was not a part of the programme. See further Grundhauser, E. (2016) Did a Silent Film About a Train Really Cause Audiences to Stampede? *Atlas Obscura*, 3 November.

69 Gunning, T. (1989/[2016]) An Aesthetic of Astonishment: Early Film and the (In)Credulous Spectator, in Braudy, L. & Cohen, M., eds. (2016) *Film Theory and Criticism*, 8th ed, Oxford University Press, Oxford, pp. 645–659: p. 645; reprint of Gunning, T. (1989) An Aesthetic of Astonishment: Early Film and the (In)Credulous Spectator, *Art and Text*, 34, 31–45.

70 *The Countryman and the Cinematograph* (1901), Robert W. Paul (dir), Paul's Animatograph Works.

the imagination of film theorists who envision audiences submitting passively to an all-dominating apparatus, hypnotised and transfixed by its illusionist power.'[71] And at the same time, the historical reconstruction of film firmly situates this imperious perspective in the "progressive" and "modern" west. At the same time, the cinema is thus emphasised as a high (albeit technical) art, while audiences are naïve or even primitive, positioning the creator (the author, the director) in a kind of paternal role over the infantilised consumer.[72]

This relationship between colonialism and modernity that insists in the early days of film and the railroad has been imported into the narratives of innovation and of intellectual property and copyright that continue to characterise contemporary debate. Indeed, it is the same mythology that arguably is a frequent resort in attempts to derail reform in user "rights" and relationships in digital environments.[73] In other words, the producer/consumer dynamic is similarly recast as a paternal relation, within which the hapless consumer is not only indolent but also presented with a kind of childlike dependence upon the producer. In many respects, the story of film goes to the heart of copyright's prejudice, as it were, its own certain tendency.[74]

5 Film's Work of Art

For internationalism, film, and intellectual property, 1908 was a momentous year. If 1895 was the birth of cinema, rightly or wrongly, then 1908 was the birth of the cinematic industry's international intellectual properties.[75] 1908 precipitated a series of important events in relation to film and intellectual property,

71 Gunning, T. (1989/[2016]) An Aesthetic of Astonishment: Early Film and the (In)Credulous Spectator, in Braudy, L. & Cohen, M., eds. (2016) *Film Theory and Criticism*, 8th ed, Oxford University Press, Oxford, pp. 645–659, reprint of Gunning, T. (1989) An Aesthetic of Astonishment: Early Film and the (In)Credulous Spectator, *Art and Text*, 34, 31–45.

72 In *Le mèpris* (1963), the privileged perspective of the creator is played out in dialogue from Prokosch, the producer. When the scene of a naked woman swimming is explained to him as a representation of a mermaid, a visibly titillated Prokosch says to the director, Fritz Lang, "Fritz, that's wonderful for you and me, but do you think the public is going to understand that?"

73 Indeed, an examination through film of the relationship between film, copyright, and the nationalistic tensions that continue to inhere in that relationship, provides particular insight into contemporary discourse on the decolonisation of copyright.

74 To borrow from Truffaut's famous title – Truffaut, F. (1954) Une certaine tendance du cinéma français, *Cahiers du Cinema*, 31 (January).

75 These developments arguably were in response to the production of longer films and the introduction of specific retail outlets for film, rather than housing them within theatres and fairs as a peripheral novelty. See further the discussion in Bakker, G. (2003)

largely in response to the separation anxiety, so to speak, between the popular and mass-produced lowliness of cinema, and the lofty ideals of the high arts of theatre and literature. The crisis was one of both author and audience; that is, of producer and consumer.[76] On the one hand, there was a tension between the authors of traditional, classical cultural forms (such as theatre and paintings) and the potential reproduction in film. And, on the other hand, there was the perceived need to educate a new audience for cinema through stronger connections with the prestige of the high arts. This became a preoccupation of France and the United States in particular, the two dominant industries.[77]

The first notable development in connection with this was in January with the establishment of the production company, le Film d'art in France,[78] which

---

The Emergence of the International Film Industry, 1890–1940, *Enterprise & Society*, 4(4), 579–585.

76 David Andrews describes the "socioeconomic pressure" at this time and "many film producers and distributors were anxious to protect the cinema by elevating its status through specialized forms": Andrews, D. (2013) *Theorizing Art Cinemas: Foreign, Cult, Avant-Garde, and Beyond*, University of Texas Press, Austin, p. 5. See also, in a note on its collection, the Eye Filmmuseum, The Netherlands, describes a "crisis in international film production" in 1907 that could be attributed to loss of cinema audiences once the novelty of the first films had subsided: "Cinema attendance stagnated. Higher-educated viewers lost interest in the simple slapstick and comical one-act films that dominated the theatres at that time". The Art Film, Eye Filmmuseum, Netherlands, https://www.eyefilm.nl/en/collection/film-history/article/the-art-film. These factors were to be significant in the introduction of longer films and the birth of the "feature."

77 But while film sought out the arts, the arts were not necessarily as receptive, and the association with film was frequently reported as a kind of downgrading of the arts. One interesting example of the early cynicism in response to such "co-branding" (a business model which nevertheless continues today) is found in a reader's letter of 1916, in the United States. The letter comments on an art competition in which students drew nudes of a movie star, to be displayed in the lobby where her film was to be exhibited, and the entries were to be judged by a jury of prominent American painters: "It is indeed surprising that painters ... should lend their aid and names to such a cheap advertising scheme." See Letter (1916) Artists Lower Their Art, *American Art News*, 15(12), p. 4.

78 Established 18 January 1908. Similarly, conscientious moves towards an association with the high arts can be recognised in other countries, including the United States. In 1909, the Vitagraph Company of America (a member of Edison's Motion Picture Patents Company) produced an adaptation of Victor Hugo's *Les Misérables*, the first feature film produced in the United States: *Les Misérables* (1909), J. Stuart Blackton (dir), the Vitagraph Company of America. Japanese film also grew out of a close relationship to and representation of traditional theatre. However, the short but considerable impact of le Film d'art is of particular note, especially due to the historical prominence of the French film industry and the considerable influence of the French theatre industry on legal developments, as will be seen in the next section on the 1908 Revision to the Berne Convention. See further the influence of le Film d'art on United States production in Puttnam, D. & Watson, N. (1997/[1999]) *Movies and Money*, Random House/Vintage, New York, pp. 55–56.

generated a wider genre of films also known as films d'art. Le Film d'art was founded not by filmmakers but by an entrepreneur, Paul Lafitte,[79] at the behest of la Comédie Française. The primary objective of le Film d'art was to broaden the audience horizons for cinema and to achieve for cinema the status of a legitimate art form.[80] In an effort to promote film as an art form with cultural value in its own right, le Film d'art 'identified itself with elite tastes,'[81] and sought to produce adaptations of canonical works of dramatic art and literature. Thus, films became necessarily longer and more substantial in pursuit of a new market: 'it was partially in order to be recognized as an art form that the cinema began to develop its faculties for narration.'[82]

Although the movement was ultimately a financial failure, and le Film d'art was sold off in 1911,[83] nevertheless 'the film d'art movement created a precedent for looking at cinema as an aspirational form that could potentially enjoy the same high-art culture status enjoyed at the start of the century by elite forms of theater.'[84] However, this alignment with theatre was both strategic and self-defeating, and has been criticised 'for having failed to innovate in a cinematic (as opposed to a theatrical) vein.'[85] A rather damning indictment from Berys Gaut illustrates this point quite clearly: 'These films consist of recordings in long shot of great actors of the day, such as Sarah Bernhardt, emoting (silently) in a conventional theatre-like setting, while the camera sits stationary, like a spellbound spectator agog at the thespian brilliance enacted before him … these films had the ambition of showing that film could be an art because of the artistry of what is shown. But, of course, these films show no such thing:

---

79 Paul Lafitte (1864–1949) was an American-born French financier and entrepreneur.

80 Aumont, J. et al. (1983/[1992]) *Aesthetics of Film*, R. Neupert (trans), University of Texas Press, Austin, p. 70. The authors note a similar self-consciousness in the contemporary film industry, in the use of terms such as "independent," which "also expresses this privileging of the artistic element" (p. 73). See further the discussion in Andrews, D. (2013) *Theorizing Art Cinemas: Foreign, Cult, Avant-Garde, and Beyond*, University of Texas Press, Austin, pp. 5–6.

81 Thompson, K. & Bordwell, D. (2010) *Film History*, 3rd ed, Mc-Graw Hill, New York, p. 23.

82 Aumont, J. et al. (1983/[1992]) *Aesthetics of Film*, R. Neupert (trans), University of Texas Press, Austin, p. 70.

83 Thompson, K. & Bordwell, D. (2010) *Film History*, 3rd ed, Mc-Graw Hill, New York, p. 24.

84 Andrews, D. (2013) *Theorizing Art Cinemas: Foreign, Cult, Avant-Garde, and Beyond*, University of Texas Press, Austin, p. 6.

85 Andrews, D. (2013) *Theorizing Art Cinemas: Foreign, Cult, Avant-Garde, and Beyond*, University of Texas Press, Austin, p. 6. A similar interaction between theatre and film was also in evidence in Germany, and resulted in considerable conflict between the theatre and film industries in somewhat of a war over the consumer and market share: Hansen, M. (1983) Early Silent Cinema: Whose Public Sphere? *New German Critique*, 29, 147–184: pp. 164–165.

they are only *recordings* of an art, not art themselves.'[86] The screening room scene in *Le mépris* appears to reference and stage this tension of cinema's early artistic ambitions, through the filming of statues of gods from classical mythology. During the scene, the director, Fritz Lang, explains to the producer that, 'It's a fight against the gods ... the gods have not created man, man has created gods.'[87] But who has created cinema?

The perceived lack of cinematic innovation at this time was significant not only artistically and theoretically, but also legally. For both theoretical and legal approaches to film, the cinematic is 'that which is capable of appearing *only* in films.'[88] In other words, for copyright to subsist in film as a work in and of itself, the film cannot simply be a recording of a dramatic work. Rather, through editing, filmic time and space, it becomes a representation of something that is possible only inside the film. The deference to the classics of theatre and literature led to problems for film both as art and legally.[89] Film's aspirations to be recognised for its own aesthetic and cultural value saw the territories marked out on an international scale, when film made its premiere at the 1908 Conference of the Berne Convention for the Protection of Literary and Artistic Works.[90]

6 Berne's Trolley Problem

In 1908, France made a proposal at the Berlin Conference of the Berne Convention for the Protection of Literary and Artistic Works, to include

86 Gaut, B. (2010) *A Philosophy of Cinematic Art*, Cambridge University Press, Cambridge, p. 304.

87 Fritz Lang in *Le mépris* (1963), Jean-Luc Godard (dir).

88 Aumont, J. et al. (1983/[1992]) *Aesthetics of Film*, R. Neupert (trans), University of Texas Press, Austin, p. 73.

89 Richard Abel explains that it "created an aesthetic problem for writers in clearly distinguishing the cinema from the theatre. Whereas the legal differences between the two seem to have been resolved rather quickly, the aesthetic differences took a good deal of time to work out." See Abel, R. (1988) *French Film Theory and Criticism: Volume I, 1907–1939*, Princeton University Press, Princeton NJ, p. 19.

90 The Berne Convention for the Protection of Literary and Artistic Works was first adopted in 1886 and was the first multilateral copyright agreement towards a "universal law of copyright." See Ricketson, S. & Ginsburg, J.C. (2005) *International Copyright and Neighbouring Rights: The Berne Convention and Beyond, Vol I*, 2nd ed, Oxford University Press, Oxford, p. 42. The Convention has since gone through seven further stages, including the revision of the Berlin Conference of 1908. See further Ricketson, S. & Ginsburg, J.C. (2005), Chapter 3.

cinematographic works.[91] Interestingly, the motivation came less from the desire to protect film and more from the reaction to film as a new technology of "reproduction." That is, the proposal was not driven by cinematographers but largely by dramatists who complained against the use of their work through cinematography.

In the Report of the Committee Chairman and Rapporteur, Louis Renault,[92] it was noted that while it was no doubt unnecessary to mark cinematography out separately with new rules, the French authorities had requested specific provisions.[93] This was in response to the perception of the cinematograph as both a technology of reproduction, as well as a work in and of itself, thus introducing at the very beginning the curious commingling of technology and art in film's character, at the same time endorsing what has become the persistent division between industry and aesthetic. Much of the pressure for this came from the dramatists and the specific concern for protection *against* cinematographs, rather than lobbying from within the film industry for protection *for* the cinematograph: 'A literary work can be appropriated by means of the cinematograph; this is the case when the cinematograph produces scenically an idea taken from a novel or a dramatic work ... By means of the cinematograph, there may well be an indirect appropriation which is only the reproduction of a literary work in the same form or in another form without essential additions or alterations.'[94] To emphasise the point even further, the Report includes extracts from five French judgments,[95] including explicit reference to piracy

91 The 1908 membership of Berne included Belgium, France, Germany, Italy, Spain, Switzerland, Tunisia, United Kingdom, Luxembourg, Monaco, Norway Japan, Denmark, and Sweden. The United States was not a member and did not become a member until 1989, relying instead upon the Universal Copyright Convention and before that a network of bilateral agreements (International Copyright Act of 1891, 26 Stat. 1106).

92 Louis Renault (1843–1918) was a professor of public international law and co-winner of the 1907 Nobel Peace Prize for his work on international law in the service of the promotion of peace. See further his participation in the 1908 Conference of Berne in the World Intellectual Property Organization (WIPO) Publication celebrating the Centenary of Berne, *The Berne Convention for the Protection of Literary and Artistic Works, 1886–1986.*

93 The Berne Convention, Records of the Conference, Convened in Berlin October 14 to November 14, 1908. Reproduced in Ricketson, S. & Ginsburg, J.C. (2005) *International Copyright and Neighbouring Rights: The Berne Convention and Beyond, Vol I*, 2nd ed, Oxford University Press, Oxford, Appendix 26, pp. 178–223: p. 211.

94 The Berne Convention, Records of the Conference, Convened in Berlin October 14 to November 14, 1908. Reproduced in Ricketson, S. & Ginsburg, J.C. (2005) *International Copyright and Neighbouring Rights: The Berne Convention and Beyond, Vol I*, 2nd ed, Oxford University Press, Oxford, Appendix 26, pp. 178–223: p. 212.

95 Judgments of 7 July 1908 of the Civil Court of the Seine (First Chamber). The proceedings emanated from the theatre industry, "instituted by various authors who complained

through cinematographic projections and to the reproduction of scenes. The latter is interesting in that it anticipates the perceived critical division between directors as scenarists (mere technicians of recording) and auteurs (as artists).

In so doing, the Report sets out the potential ethical dilemmas of Berne's trolley problem[96] with film (or, given that it is film arriving at the station, Berne's dolly problem). In this way, the copyright narrative and the very first insistence upon film, imposes a consequentialist approach to the interaction between cultural forms and to innovation itself. Berne thus shifted the tracks and the Report delivers the conclusion that 'it was considered preferable to make an Article concerning cinematographs which would be complete in itself. It will be more convenient for the parties concerned who have not necessarily penetrated the depths of our subject.'[97] Thus, the awkward peripherality and dissociative character of cinema was set:

> We have just seen the cinematograph being used for purposes of reproduction or adaptation. It can also serve to give form to a creation. The person who takes the cinematographic shots and develops the negatives will also be the person who has imagined the subject, arranged the scenes and directed the moves of the actors ... [W]e have here a dramatic work

that their works had been reproduced without their authorization by means of cinematographic adaptation." The Berne Convention, Records of the Conference, Convened in Berlin October 14 to November 14, 1908. Reproduced in Ricketson, S. & Ginsburg, J.C. (2005) *International Copyright and Neighbouring Rights: The Berne Convention and Beyond, Vol I*, 2nd ed, Oxford University Press, Oxford, Appendix 26, pp. 178–223: p. 212.

96 The Trolley Problem is a thought experiment whereby a subject responds to a series of ethical dilemmas generally requiring a sacrifice in one place to protect something in another place. Judith Jarvis Thomson, who is credited with coining the term, explains the namesake dilemma as follows: "Suppose you are the driver of a trolley. The trolley rounds a bend, and there come into view ahead five track workmen, who have been repairing the track. The track goes through a bit of a valley at that point, and the sides are steep, so you must stop the trolley if you are to avoid running the five men down. You step on the brakes, but alas they don't work. Now you suddenly see a spur of track leading off to the right. You can turn the trolley onto it, and thus save the five men on the straight track ahead. Unfortunately, Mrs. Foot has arranged that there is one track workman on that spur of track. He can no more get off the track in time than the five can, so you will kill him if you turn the trolley onto him. Is it morally permissible for you to turn the trolley?" See Thomson, J.J. (1985) The Trolley Problem, *The Yale law Journal*, 94(6), 1395–1415: p. 1395. See further, Thomson, J.J. (1976) Killing, Letting Die, and the Trolley Problem, *The Monist*, 59(2), 204–217.

97 The Berne Convention, Records of the Conference, Convened in Berlin October 14 to November 14, 1908. Reproduced in Ricketson, S. & Ginsburg, J.C. (2005) *International Copyright and Neighbouring Rights: The Berne Convention and Beyond, Vol I*, 2nd ed, Oxford University Press, Oxford, Appendix 26, pp. 178–223: p. 213.

> of a particular genre which it must not be possible to appropriate with impunity. It is not the question of monopolizing an idea or a subject but of protecting the form given the idea or the development of the subject.[98]

In other words, the new "work" of film was itself also a new technology of reproduction.[99] To frame it in the context of the later concept of the auteur, it was both the technology of the scenarists, and the imagination and direction, as it were, of an auteur. Protection of rights in one sector can thus be interpreted as promotion of rights and protection in another; the creation of intellectual property rights to protect one sector can also be engaged in the development of another industry altogether. In other words, value generated in one place may be deferred and displaced to recuperation in another. In the case of film's acknowledged entry into copyright, the objective of protecting theatre and literary copyright also facilitated the creation of value in the "reproduction" of those cultural industries.

That the first film copyright proceeded from the perspective of the technology of distribution was portentous. The effect of copyright in this respect is to establish rights in other contexts, in other artefacts. Indeed, the operation of the public domain mirrors the kind of dual protection anticipated in film. The entry of a work into the public domain, regardless of jurisdiction, does not necessarily facilitate access. It simply opens the market to the creation of new editions and so on; that is, new "recordings," new artefacts in which new copyright will subsist. This dual nature of copyright is to be found not just in neighbouring rights in film and sound recordings; it can be understood throughout copyright, and arguably this divided thinking became part of copyright's logic through its early interaction with film. Copyright insists upon a binary logic that is in service of the technologies of distribution, separating out the industrial and the aesthetic, at the same time facilitating substitution. Arguably, this accounting in film is a perspective that continues to overwhelm attempts to

---

98 The Berne Convention, Records of the Conference, Convened in Berlin October 14 to November 14, 1908. Reproduced in Ricketson, S. & Ginsburg, J.C. (2005) *International Copyright and Neighbouring Rights: The Berne Convention and Beyond, Vol I*, 2nd ed, Oxford University Press, Oxford, Appendix 26, pp. 178–223: p. 213.

99 This is interesting in the contemporary copyright environment as well, where we see new technologies of reproduction actually leading to new products, new uses and new user experiences (most recently, perhaps, has been the very similar debate that developed over the emergence of 3D printing, and the same kind of self-conscious division when it came to its reckoning with copyright). Thus, the history of film and its relationship to intellectual property provides important insight that can be applied in other areas of intellectual property and the creative industries, and indeed in new technologies of reproduction and perceived challenges to intellectual property protection.

deal with new technologies of reproduction, and to address protection in a digital context, as the discourse remains almost entirely preoccupied with distribution. And perhaps nowhere is this more clear than in the consumption of visual images through film and photography: 'We were producing in order to distribute.'[100] The problem with copyright is the trolley.

7 The Great Train Robbery

At the same time that members of the Berne Convention were addressing the industry of film through copyright, the United States was attempting to secure its control over foreign competition through patents. Where Berne sought to facilitate the industry through a kind of universalism in copyright, Thomas Edison engineered the new and enduring dominance of the United States film industry in a form of geopolitics of protectionism through an emphasis on patents. And the pivotal event in this process was the establishment of the Motion Picture Patents Company in 1908.[101]

One of the first films to be made by Thomas Edison's studios was *The Great Train Robbery*,[102] a silent western that was produced and distributed by the Edison Manufacturing Company in 1903. While considerable debate surrounds its claimed priority as a western, or its significance to cinema, it is perhaps most notable for its iconic image of the actor, Justus D Barnes, firing his pistol directly at the camera. In this final shot of the film, Barnes stares straight at the camera and fires repeatedly, surrounded by smoke as his pistol discharges. The image is curiously resonant with both the imagery and the mythology surrounding the Lumières' arriving train and its aura of smoke. And it is seemingly acknowledged also in Godard's turning and pointing of the camera at the audience in *Le mépris*. From the very beginning, cinema appealed to the audience for its impact and its legacy.

The Great Train Robbery was a product of the strategy and policy in the film industry of early twentieth-century United States, and the geopolitical war for territory in the international film industry that endures. The reported competition between inventors is largely documented as a nationalistic battle between France and the United States. And this battle is personalised in the figures of

100 Jean-Luc Godard in interview in Godard, J.-L. (2003) *The Future(s) of Film: Three Interviews 2000/01*, Gachnang & Springer, Zurich, p. 22.

101 Musser, C. (1991) *Before the Nickelodeon: Edwin S Porter and the Edison Manufacturing Company*, University of California Press, Berkeley, p. 13.

102 *The Great Train Robbery* (1903), Edwin S Porter (dir), Edison Manufacturing Company.

Edison and the Lumières, the star protagonists, at least according to legend.[103] Antoine Lumière has been described as a 'fervent French nationalist,' who 'had already developed a fierce antipathy toward the Americans.'[104] And intellectual property was deployed as the armoury of choice in this contest for cinema: for France, considerable importance was attached to copyright and revising Berne; for Edison, the preferred cannonry was patents,[105] and this had a significant impact on the burgeoning film industry in the United States.

In the context of this purported rivalry, Edison established the Edison Manufacturing Company in 1889 under his sole ownership and transferred all manufacture and sale of the kinetoscope to the Company in 1894.[106] Edison became notorious for his indefatigable litigation of his patent portfolio,[107] including against the American Mutoscope Company, popularly known as the Biograph Company after the name of its projector.[108] Biograph was established in 1895 by Edison's former assistant and inventor, William Kennedy Dickson, becoming the major competitor for the Edison Manufacturing Company.[109] But the two companies faced a major potential rival in Lumière, and there are various reports of some extraordinary measures taken to oust the French competition before it could become established in the United States. There are even suggestions that 'Lumière's head of operations in America had been forced to flee the country, secretly paddling by canoe to board a French liner waiting in the Hudson.'[110] The history of film would make a good movie.

At the same time, an emphasis on protectionism for the domestic industry curtailed the early success of foreign film companies in the United States. In 1890, the McKinley Tariff Act was passed, increasing protective tariffs to 49.5%

---

103 Puttnam, D. & Watson, N. (1997/[1999]) *Movies and Money*, Random House/Vintage, New York, pp. 14–24.

104 Puttnam, D. & Watson, N. (1997/[1999]) *Movies and Money*, Random House/Vintage, New York, p. 14.

105 Although patent litigation was Edison's primary commercial strategy, he did also sue for copyright infringement: *Edison v Lubin*, 122 Fed. 240 (1903); and *American Mutoscope Co v Edison*, 137 Fed. 262 (1905).

106 Musser, C. (1991) *Before the Nickelodeon: Edwin S Porter and the Edison Manufacturing Company*, University of California Press, Berkeley, p. 44.

107 Musser, C. (1991) *Before the Nickelodeon: Edwin S Porter and the Edison Manufacturing Company*, University of California Press, Berkeley, pp. 114–116. See further Puttnam, D. & Watson, N. (1997/[1999]) *Movies and Money*, Random House/Vintage, New York, p. 21.

108 Musser, C. (1991) *Before the Nickelodeon: Edwin S Porter and the Edison Manufacturing Company*, University of California Press, Berkeley, p. 91.

109 Puttnam, D. & Watson, N. (1997/[1999]) *Movies and Money*, Random House/Vintage, New York, p. 20.

110 Puttnam, D. & Watson, N. (1997/[1999]) *Movies and Money*, Random House/Vintage, New York, p. 20.

to protect local industry from foreign competition.[111] The Biograph Company reportedly had 'close ties to some of the more fervent protectionists who dominated McKinley's administration' and ultimately the company even adopted the Republican Party slogan – "America for Americans" – as its own.[112] This programme of protectionism, together with Edison's patent litigation, had two likely unintended consequences. First, this environment resulted in the reduction of the United States industry to just two major production companies – the Edison Manufacturing Company and the Biograph Company. At the same time, however, this actually led to having greater foreign product on the market rather than less, as other companies started to import more French and British films instead of producing American product: 'Since Edison's patent litigation threatened American producers more than their foreign competitors, it greatly facilitated foreign domination of the American screen.'[113] Edison's business model unduly emphasised the technologies of production and to a large extent, although not completely, did not anticipate the importance of the product itself. As one newspaper report commented in August 1908: 'In the long run the best output of subjects will prove the most profitable – that is, providing patent litigation does not wipe out one side or the other.'[114]

Edison's aggressive patent strategy eventually led to the establishment of the Motion Picture Patents Company (MPPC) in 1908, both to dominate the market and to pool patents.[115] The Company was incorporated in September and Edison replaced his vice-president and general manager with Frank Dyer, his chief patent lawyer, arguably making clear the strategic direction of his business model when just three months later he was made President of

111 An Act to reduce the revenue and equalize duties on imports, and for other purposes, 1890, Ch 1244 (McKinley Tariff Act). See further the discussion in relation to the film industry in Puttnam, D. & Watson, N. (1997/[1999]) *Movies and Money*, Random House/Vintage, New York, p. 14. According to Puttnam and Watson, Antoine Lumière reported on the 1893 World's Columbian Exhibition, "It is not an entrance duty which hits our products ... it is a form of prohibition, while we have left our own door almost completely open" (Quoted p. 14).

112 Myrent, G. (1985) When Movies Began and No One Came, *The New York Times*, 29 December.

113 Musser, C. (1991) *Before the Nickelodeon: Edwin S Porter and the Edison Manufacturing Company*, University of California Press, Berkeley, p. 335.

114 *New York Dramatic Mirror*, 1 August 1908, cited in Musser, C. (1991) *Before the Nickelodeon: Edwin S Porter and the Edison Manufacturing Company*, University of California Press, Berkeley, p. 381.

115 Puttnam and Watson note that the constant litigation was in danger of bankrupting the Edison and Biograph companies and that this was a significant factor in the creation of the MPCC, together with Edison's "downright predatory aims." Puttnam, D. & Watson, N. (1997/[1999]) *Movies and Money*, Random House/Vintage, New York, p. 40.

the MPPC. Indeed, Dyer is said to have 'reorganized the Kinetograph department and the entire film industry' in the process.[116] The MPPC concluded agreements with nine producers (both United States and local operations of foreign companies) including Biograph and Edison.[117] The foreign members included, perhaps most importantly, Pathé, which later went on to undermine a similar European objective at the Paris Film Congress of 1909.[118] The members assigned their patents to the MPPC,[119] thereby creating a patent pool as a barrier to external competition and new entrants on the market. And the consequent monopoly created by the MPCC restored local productions to dominance in the United States market.[120]

However, once again, Edison's aggressive strategy had unintended consequences: first, the mobilisation of independents to cooperate to improve production and distribution[121]; and secondly, the industry shift in emphasis from the East Coast to the nascent industry on the West Coast. It may well be that, in

116 Musser, C. (1991) *Before the Nickelodeon: Edwin S Porter and the Edison Manufacturing Company*, University of California Press, Berkeley, p. 13.

117 Musser, C. (1991) *Before the Nickelodeon: Edwin S Porter and the Edison Manufacturing Company*, University of California Press, Berkeley, pp. 437–439. The foreign members included, perhaps most importantly, Pathé. The French film production and distribution company, Pathé, was growing rapidly in dominance prior to the establishment of the MPCC. See further Puttnam, D. & Watson, N. (1997/[1999]) *Movies and Money*, Random House/Vintage, New York, pp. 34–44. When, in response to the development of the MPCC, European film producers and distributors considered a plan similar at the Paris Film Congress of 1909, Pathé (a member of the MPCC) was somewhat obstructive and resolutions to establish a similar trade body were ultimately not adopted, and that this ultimately assisted the dominance of the United States in the British film industry: Burrows, J. (2006) When Britain Tried to Join Europe: The Significance of the 1909 Paris Congress for the British Film Industry, *Early Popular Visual Culture*, 4(1), 1–19. See further the discussion of the British pre-emptive formative of the Cinematograph Trade Protection Society (CTPS) in March 1909 in Shail, A. (2008) The Motion Picture Story Magazine and the Origins of Popular British Film Culture, *Film History*, 20(2), 181–197.

118 The French film production and distribution company, Pathé, was growing rapidly in dominance prior to the establishment of the MPCC. See further Puttnam, D. & Watson, N. (1997/[1999]) *Movies and Money*, Random House/Vintage, New York, pp. 34–44.

119 Musser, C. (1991) *Before the Nickelodeon: Edwin S Porter and the Edison Manufacturing Company*, University of California Press, Berkeley, p. 438.

120 Puttnam and Watson note that by 1912, 80% of all new releases in the United States were American productions: Puttnam, D. & Watson, N. (1997/[1999]) *Movies and Money*, Random House/Vintage, New York, p. 63.

121 Alvarez, M. (2007) The Motion Picture Distributing and Sales Company, *Film History*, 19(3), 247–270. This was also assisted in 1911 when Kodak began making Eastman stock available to producers outside the MPPC monopoly (p. 262).

attempting to control the industry through patents, the monopoly of the MPCC was instead instrumental to the sudden growth of Hollywood.

8 "Jerusalem Rebels at Roman Mis-Rule"[122]

In November 1908, a critical copyright case commenced in the United States.[123] *Ben Hur* (1907),[124] a fifteen-minute, unauthorised film adaptation of Lee Wallace's 1880 book, *Ben Hur: A Tale of Christ*, was to become perhaps the most important catalyst in the introduction of copyright protection of cinematographic works in the United States. The unauthorised adaptation is an example of the fashion of the day for adapting classical works of literature and theatre. And just as the theatre industry pursued film at the Berlin Revision Conference of Berne, part of the background to this litigation was an authorised stage adaptation of *Ben Hur*, for which the film might have posed some competition.[125] It is in this tale of copyright, that the European traditions in some way arrive in the United States in *Kalem v Harper Brothers* (1911).[126]

In 1908, the United States did not recognise copyright in film other than as a photograph. The consequence of this was that protection was available only to the entire film taken to be one photograph.[127] The position of film was still not resolved in the landmark Copyright Act of 1909, where film remained omitted. Meanwhile, the producers of *Ben Hur* (1907) were sued for copyright infringement of *Ben Hur*, the 1880 novel, by Harper and Brothers (Wallace's publisher), Klaw & Erlanger (the theatrical production), and Henry Wallace (the author's son) in *Kalem Co v Harper Brothers*.[128] The 1911 judgment found that a film was capable of copying a book; however, much more significantly,

122 The opening frame from *Ben Hur* (1907), Frank Oakes Rose & Sidney Olcott (dirs), Kalem Company.

123 *Harper & Bros v Kalem Co.*, No. 2-160 (SDNY Nov 2 1908), reprinted in Transcript of Record, *Kalem v Harper Brothers*, 222 US 55 (1911).

124 *Ben Hur* (1907), Frank Oakes Rose & Sidney Olcott (dirs), Kalem Company.

125 *Harper & Bros. et al v Kalem Co. et al*, 169 Fed. 61 (1909): at 63.

126 *Kalem Co v Harper Brothers*, 222 US 55 (1911).

127 *Edison v Lubin*, 122 Fed. 240, (1903): "What was thus copyrighted was a single celluloid sheet, on which a number of objects had been photographically printed or reproduced" (at 242); *American Mutoscope Co. v Edison*, 137 Fed. 262.

128 *Kalem Co v Harper Brothers*, 222 US 55 (1911); *Harper & Bros et al v Kalem Co et al*, 169 Fed. 61 (1909).

the litigation led to the specific inclusion of film for the first time[129] in the Townsend Amendment to copyright law in 1912.[130]

By 1911, the MPCC's "mis-rule" was waning and in 1912 the Department of Justice would commence the antitrust prosecution of the members of the MPCC, ultimately leading to its closure in 1917.[131] But the inattention of film was to come to an end in the wake of the *Kalem* litigation. In arguments before the Committee of the House of Representatives, the decision in *Kalem* was debated at length,[132] and the challenge from film as a technology of reproduction ultimately led to the clarification of film as a work of copyright and its inclusion in the 1912 amendment.[133]

The circumstances are remarkable for returning this tale to the beginning. The fifteen-minute adaptation is a striking example of the stationary camera, the theatrical staging, and the adaptation of a literary work – all the characteristics of le Film d'art. And just like le Film d'art and others, this production ultimately provided the same provocation for reform to film protection that motivated the 1908 revision of Berne. Film was finally protected in order to clarify infringement; that is, to protect a different industry. Film became art, for art's sake.

9 The Auteur, Copyright's Certain Tendency

> Prokosch (the Producer): "Oh gods. I like gods. I like them very much. I know exactly how they feel. Exactly."[134]
>
> "People like to say, 'What do you mean exactly?' I would answer, 'I mean, but not exactly.'"[135]

129 Peter Decherney writes, "When Congress failed to address film in the 1909 revision of the Copyright Act, the Supreme Court intervened and took on the *Ben-Hur* case. Film had grown into a major industry, and someone needed to negotiate between the publishers, the Broadway producers, and the film companies. Finding a solution required a sophisticated understanding of the art of film and the state of American popular culture in addition to legal doctrine." See Decherney, P. (2012) *Hollywood's Copyright Wars: From Edison to the Internet*, Columbia University Press, New York, p. 47.

130 37 Stat. 488.

131 In 1912, the Department of Justice would commence an antitrust prosecution of the members of the MPCC: *United States v Motion Pictures Patents Co et al*, 225 Fed. 800 (E.D. Pa. 1915). This would be later appealed but the appeal was not pursued: 247 U.S. 524.

132 Townsend Copyright Amendment: Complete File of Arguments on HR 15263 and HR 20596 Before the H Comm on Patents Commencing Jan 24 1912, 62d Cong. (1912).

133 37 Stat. 488.

134 *Le mépris* (1963), Jean-Luc Godard (dir).

135 Jean-Luc Godard in interview with Gavin Smith (1996) Interview: Jean-Luc Godard, *Film Comment*, March–April.

This remarkable story of film's development and the historic appeal to taste through the presentation of "high art" plays out in *Le mépris* in the film-within-a-film's adaptation of *The Odyssey*. The representations of the gods, together with Prokosch's proclamation, "I know exactly how they feel," assert the link between the discourse of high art, the figure of the auteur, and copyright's ultimate trolley problem – the audience. Just as film history is often popularly consolidated into the marvellous event of the Lumières' train, the concept of the auteur summarises or even obscures the different contributions to film. The figure of the auteur becomes a kind of personality of copyright's story of film.[136]

The tension between the United States industry and the French industry shadows and foreshadows the rise of the auteur. Explicitly distinguishing themselves from the perceived scenarists of the American industry, French auteurists strove to reestablish production at the heart of what had become an enterprise of distribution. While the United States industry emphasised patents and control over the distribution of technology, the French industry continued to champion authors' rights and the development of the product. In the contemporary context, this dissociative identity of film persists. The separation of industrial (and an emphasis on economic rights in the United States) and aesthetic (and an emphasis on authors' rights in France and other civil law jurisdictions) continues to characterise national identities (and intellectual properties) in the international film industry: 'It's very striking that nowadays you can't talk about a film without saying. "It did well," "It didn't do well," "It did such and such at the box office." When Rohmer was shooting <Bérénice> in 16 mm black-and-white, he had twelve viewers. He wasn't thinking in terms of success or failure.'[137] Indeed, *who makes a film*?

What is also striking is that neither perspective addresses the audience. Indeed, auteurism is as validly criticised for the deferral and even erasure

136 As Charles Musser remarks, "We often forget that Sergei Eisenstein had a co-director, Grigori Alexandrov, on *October* and *Old and New* … *Un chien andalou* by Luis Buñuel *and* Salvador Dali, *Entr'acte* by René Clair *and* Francis Picabia" (Musser, C. (1991) *Before the Nickelodeon: Edwin S Porter and the Edison Manufacturing Company*, University of California Press, Berkeley, p. 476). And to this one might add *Tout va bien*, directed by Jean-Luc Godard *and* Jean-Pierre Gorin.

137 Jean-Luc Godard in interview in Godard, J.-L. (2003) *The Future(s) of Film: Three Interviews 2000/01*, Gachnang & Springer, Zurich, pp. 13–14. Godard explores the relationship between the commercial environment (including intellectual property) for film and the film-making in many of his films, including in particular the co-directed *Tout va bien* (1972) (Jean-Luc Godard & Jean-Pierre Gorin (dirs.)) where the overlaying of meaning through the construction of property in film is set out explicitly and implicitly throughout, while at the same time deploying the theatrical staging of Brechtian theatre.

of the audience, as much as economic approaches that promote the will of investment. Beware. One train may hide another.

10 Making the Next Move

> In a poem, one line may hide another line,
> As at a crossing one train may hide another train.
> That is, if you are waiting to cross
> The tracks, wait to do it for one moment at
> Least after the first train is gone. And so when you read
> Wait until you have read the next line –
> Then it is safe to go on reading.[138]

The early days of film and its various intellectual properties are compelling in the retelling, as it were, of future questions. The protection of film, and the consternation of copyright in particular, rethinks technology as an imaginary, from reproduction to creativity. The arrival of the train is just the beginning. Film, like the railroads, has made everything possible.

> You think, Now it is safe to cross and you are hit by the next one. It can be Important
> To have waited at least a moment to see what was already there.[139]

Bibliography

Abel, R. (1988) *French Film Theory and Criticism: Volume I, 1907–1939*, Princeton University Press, Princeton NJ.

Aguiar, M. (2008) Making Modernity: Inside the Technological Space of the Railway, *Cultural Critique*, 68, 66–85.

Alvarez, M. (2007) The Motion Picture Distributing and Sales Company, *Film History*, 19(3), 247–270.

Andrews, D. (2013) *Theorizing Art Cinemas: Foreign, Cult, Avant-Garde, and Beyond*, University of Texas Press, Austin.

138 Koch, K. (1994) One Train May Hide Another, in Koch, K. (1994) *One Train: Poems*, Alfred A Knopf, New York, 3–4: p. 3.

139 Koch, K. (1994) One Train May Hide Another, in Koch, K. (1994) *One Train: Poems*, Alfred A Knopf, New York, 3–4: p. 4.

Atkinson, M. (1997) Lumière & Company: The Future of the Invention, *Film Comment*, 33(3), 72–73, 75.

Auer, M., & Ory, M. (1979) *Histoire de la caméra ciné amateur*, Éditions Big; Geneva.

Aumont, J. (1996) Lumière revisited, B Brewster (trans), *Film History*, 8(4), 416–430.

Aumont, J. et al. (1983/[1992]) *Aesthetics of Film*, R. Neupert (trans.), University of Texas Press, Austin.

Bakker, G. (2003) The Emergence of the International Film Industry, 1890–1940, *Enterprise & Society*, 4(4), 579–585.

Bâ, S.M., & Higbee, W., eds. (2012) *De-Westernizing Film Studies*, Routledge, London.

Baudry, J.-L. (1970/[1974–1975]) Ideological Effects of the Basic Cinematographic Apparatus, A. Williams (trans.), *Film Quarterly*, 28(2), 39–47 (Translated from the 1970 article originally published in *Cinéthique*, No 7/8, 1–8).

Braudy, L., & Cohen, M., eds. (2016) *Film Theory and Criticism*, 8th ed, Oxford University Press, Oxford.

Blümlinger, C. (2006) Lumière, the Train and the Avant-Garde, in Strauven, W. (ed.) (2006) *The Cinema of Attractions Reloaded*, Amsterdam University Press, Amsterdam, pp. 245–264.

Brown, W. (2012) Has film ever been Western? Continuity and the question of building a "common" cinema, in Bâ, S.M. & Higbee, W. (eds.) (2012) *De-Westernizing Film Studies*, Routledge, London, pp. 166–177.

Burrows, J. (2006) When Britain Tried to Join Europe: The Significance of the 1909 Paris Congress for the British Film Industry, *Early Popular Visual Culture*, 4(1), 1–19.

Cousins, M. (2020/[2004]) *The Story of Film*, updated edition, Pavilion Books, London.

Decherney, P. (2012) *Hollywood's Copyright Wars: From Edison to the Internet*, Columbia University Press, New York.

Gaut, B. (2010) *A Philosophy of Cinematic Art*, Cambridge University Press, Cambridge.

Godard, J.-L. (2003) *The Future(s) of Film: Three Interviews 2000/01*, Gachnang & Springer, Zurich.

Gopal, S. (2015) Some Brief Reflections on Technology, Cinema, and the Postcolonial Uncanny, *Pacific Coast Philology*, 50(2), 198–208.

Grundhauser, E. (2016) Did a Silent Film About a Train Really Cause Audiences to Stampede? *Atlas Obscura*, 3 November.

Gunning, T. (1989/[2016]) An Aesthetic of Astonishment: Early Film and the (In) Credulous Spectator, in Braudy, L. & Cohen, M., eds. (2016) *Film Theory and Criticism*, 8th ed, Oxford University Press, Oxford, pp. 645–659: p. 645; reprint of Gunning, T. (1989) An Aesthetic of Astonishment: Early Film and the (In)Credulous Spectator, *Art and Text*, 34, 31–45.

Gunning, T. (2006) The Cinema of Attraction(s): Early Film, Its Spectator and the Avant-Garde, in Strauven, W., ed. (2006) *The Cinema of Attractions Reloaded*, Amsterdam University Press, Amsterdam, pp. 381–388.

Guynn, W. (ed.) (2011) *The Routledge Companion to Film History*, Routledge, Abingdon.
Hannaford, A. (2015) The mystery of Leeds's long-lost movie pioneer, *The Telegraph*, 24 June.
Hansen, M. (1983) Early Silent Cinema: Whose Public Sphere? *New German Critique*, 29, 147–184.
Huhtamo, E. (2011) Natural magic: a short cultural history of moving images, in Guynn, W., ed. (2011) *The Routledge Companion to Film History*, Routledge, Abingdon, pp. 3–15.
Koch, K. (1994) One Train May Hide Another, in Koch, K. (1994) *One Train: Poems*, Alfred A. Knopf, New York, 3–4.
Latour, B. (2004) Why Has Critique Run out of Steam? From Matters of Fact to Matters of Concern, *Critical Inquiry*, 30(2), 225–248.
Loiperdinger, M. (2004) Lumière's "Arrival of the Train": Cinema's Founding Myth, *The Moving Image: The Journal of the Association of Moving Image Archivists*, 4(1), 89–118.
Losada, M. (2011) Argentine Cinema and Rural Space, *Chasqui*, 40(2), 18–32.
Mannoni, L., Campagnoni, D.P., and Robinson, D. (1995) *Light and Movement: Incunabula of the Motion Picture 1420–1896*, Le Giornate del Cinema Muto, Pordenone Italy.
Musser, C. (1991) *Before the Nickelodeon: Edwin S Porter and the Edison Manufacturing Company*, University of California Press, Berkeley.
Myrent, G. (1985) When Movies Began and No One Came, *New York Times*, 29 December.
Myrent, G. (1985) When Movies Began and No One Came, *The New York Times*, 29 December.
Paci, V. (2006) The Attraction of the Intelligent Eye: Obsessions with the Vision Machine in Early Film Theories, in Strauven, W. (ed.) (2006) *The Cinema of Attractions Reloaded*, Amsterdam University Press, Amsterdam, pp. 121–138.
Païni, D. (1995) Foreword: The Spiral of Inventions, in Mannoni L, Campagnoni DP, and Robinson D (1995) *Light and Movement: Incunabula of the Motion Picture 1420–1896*, Le Giornate del Cinema Muto, Pordenone Italy, pp. 13–18.
Parkinson, D. (2012) *History of Film*, 2nd ed, Thames & Hudson, New York.
Puttnam, D., & Watson, N. (1997/[1999]) *Movies and Money*, Random House/Vintage, New York.
Rawlence, C. (1990) *The Missing Reel: The Untold Story of the Lost Inventor of Moving Pictures*, Atheneum, New York.
Ricketson, S., & Ginsburg, J.C. (2005) *International Copyright and Neighbouring Rights: The Berne Convention and Beyond, Vol I*, 2nd ed, Oxford University Press, Oxford.
Rittaud-Hutinet, J., & Dentzer, Y., eds. (1994/[1995]) *Auguste and Louis Lumière Letters: Inventing the Cinema*, P. Hodgson (trans.), Faber and Faber, London.
Rosen, M. (1987) "Louis Lumière," in Wakeman, J., ed. (1987) *World Film Directors: Volume I, 1890–1945*, The HW Wilson Company, New York, pp. 700–709.

Sauvage, L. (1985) *L'Affaire Lumière: du mythe a l'histoire, enquête sur les origines du cinéma*, Lherminier, Paris.

Shail, A. (2008) The Motion Picture Story Magazine and the Origins of Popular British Film Culture, *Film History*, 20(2), 181–197.

Smith, G. (1996) Interview: Jean-Luc Godard, *Film Comment*, March–April.

Snow, C.P. (1969) *The Two Cultures*, Cambridge University Press, Cambridge.

Strauven, W., ed. (2006) *The Cinema of Attractions Reloaded*, Amsterdam University Press, Amsterdam.

Tarde, G. (1890/[1903]) *The Laws of Imitation*, E.C. Parsons (trans.), Henry Holt & Co, New York.

Thompson, K., & Bordwell, D. (2010) *Film History*, 3rd ed, Mc-Graw Hill, New York.

Thomson, J.J. (1976) Killing, Letting Die, and the Trolley Problem, *The Monist*, 59(2), 204–217.

Thomson, J.J. (1985) The Trolley Problem, *The Yale law Journal*, 94(6), 1395–1415: p. 1395.

Wakeman, J., ed. (1987) *World Film Directors: Volume I, 1890–1945*, The HW Wilson Company, New York.

CHAPTER 7

The Untold Story of the First Copyright Statute of China

Exploring the 1910 Copyright Code of the Great Qing Dynasty

Jyh-An Lee and Yangzi Li

1 Introduction

Determining when China first adopted a copyright regime is controversial. Many believe that copyright protection in China can be traced back to the Song Dynasty (960–1279) when publishers claim that book copying was not allowed[1] and that those who copied a book without publisher permission were subject to fines and corporal punishment.[2] However, the 1910 Copyright Code of the Great Qing Dynasty ("Qing Copyright Code") was indubitably the first comprehensive copyright statute in China.[3] Although the Qing Copyright Code was short-lived because the Qing Dynasty was overthrown in the 1911 Revolution led by Dr Sun Yat-sen,[4] it influenced later Chinese copyright legislation in terms of basic principles and statute language.[5] In 1912, the government of the new Republic of China announced an extension of the term of

1 Lam, Philip H. 'Copyright Protection of Foreign Computer Software in the People's Republic of China: Significant Progress in Two Years'. *Loyola of Los Angeles International and Comparative Law Journal* 17(4) (1995), 865; Yang, Yiping. 'The 1990 Copyright Law of the People's Republic of China'. *UCLA Pacific Basin Law Journal* 11(2) (1993), 262.

2 Lazar, June Cohan. 'Note, Protecting Ideas and Ideals: Copyright Law in the People's Republic of China'. *Law and Policy in International Business* 27(4) (1996), 1186.
Yang, 'The 1990 Copyright Law' (n. 1), 262; Wu, Shulin. 'The Conditions of the Judicial and Administrative Protection of Copyright in China'. *Duke Journal of Comparative & International Law* 9(1) (1998), 241.

3 Declet, Jr., Rafael A. 'Protecting American Intellectual Property in China: The Persistent Problem of Software Piracy'. *New York International Law Review* 10(2) (1997), 61; Lam, 'Copyright Protection' (n. 1), 865; McIntyre, Stephen. 'The Yang Obeys, But the Yin Ignores: Copyright Law and Speech Suppressions in the People's Republic of China'. *UCLA Pacific Basin Law Journal* 29(1) (2011), 87.

4 McIntyre, 'The Yang Obeys' (n. 3), 87.

5 Lazar, 'Protecting Ideas and Ideals' (n. 2), 1186; Lam, 'Copyright Protection' (n. 1), 865; Lula, Katie. 'Neither Here Nor There But Fair: Finding An International Copyright Legal System Between East and West, Past and Present'. *Asian-Pacific Law & Policy Journal* 8(1) (2006), 120; Yang (n. 1), 263.

 | DOI:10.1163/9789004511439_009

the Qing Copyright Code to 1915.[6] The Northern Warlord then holistically imitated the Qing Copyright Code and enacted the *Copyright Law of the Northern Government* on 7 November 1915.[7] Later, the Kuomintang government followed the basic framework of the 1915 Copyright Law, the same as that of the Qing Copyright Code, and promulgated the *Law on Authors' Rights* in 1928,[8] which later became the Copyright Act of Taiwan.

Part 2 introduces the background and contributing factors of copyright legislation in the late Qing Dynasty. Because copyright was a foreign concept to China in the late nineteenth century, various international factors contributed to the legislation, including foreign pressure for more legal protection and the diffusion of Western copyright concepts in the country. In the meantime, Chinese policymakers, authors and publishers also started to become aware of the value that a copyright regime could bring the Chinese society. The international and domestic setting provided a friendly atmosphere for copyright legislation. Part 3 analyses the structure and key provisions of the Qing Copyright Code. The definitions of copyright and copyright work reflect the cultural and technological development at that time. The law required registration as a precondition for copyright protection and introduced modern copyright concepts of joint-authorship, terms and limitations, and exceptions to China. Part 4 discusses whether foreign works were protected under the Qing Copyright Code. Although requests for and debates over protected foreign works were important driving forces of copyright legislation in the late Qing Dynasty, hindsight suggests that foreign works were not effectively protected under the Qing Copyright Code. Part 5 concludes this chapter.

2 Political Economy of the Legislation

The path to the Qing Copyright Code was meandering. The Ministry of Commerce (商部) started to prepare for the legislation by translating foreign copyright statutes, such as the Japan Copyright Act, German Copyright Law, U.S. Copyright Act and Copyright Statute of the Great Britain,[9] in January

6 Zhou, Lin and Li, Mingshan. *Research Documents on The History of Copyright in China* (中国版权史研究文献) (Beijing: China Fangzheng Press, 1999), 133.

7 Li, Yufeng. *Law at Gunpoint: A Study on History of Copyright in China* (枪口下的法律: 中国版权史研究) (1st edn, Beijing: Intellectual Property Publishing House, 2006), 123.

8 Ibid., 130.

9 Han, Dong. 'Can I Own My Writings and Sell Them Too? A Brief History of Copyright in China from The Late Qing Era to Mao's China'. *Chinese Journal of Communication* 3(3) (2010), 335; Feng, Qiuji. 'Western Theories and the Legislation of Copyright Law in Late Qing Dynasty' (西人论说与晚清版权立法). *Jiangxi Social Sciences* 8 (2005), 210.

1904.[10] The Ministry of Commerce completed the first draft of the copyright law in 1905, which was later submitted to the Ministry of Education (學部) for further review and public discussion.[11] However, the Ministry of Education concluded that the draft was far from satisfactory and thus required a thorough revision.[12] The draft was then shelved by the Qing government, which prioritised regulations on the publishing industry and news censorship.[13] This deference of copyright legislation signals the Qing government's priority of controlling the publication industry than protect copyright. Therefore, some scholars believe that the Qing Copyright Code was later enacted to supplement the regulations of the publication industry.[14]

The legislation process of copyright law resumed in 1907 and was led by the Ministry of Civil Affairs (民政部), which was established in 1906 and became the highest administrative authority in charge of civil affairs in the country.[15] In the meantime, legal scholars, such as Tao Baolin, also actively urged the government to study foreign copyright principles and enact the copyright law as soon as possible.[16] In 1910, the Ministry of Civil Affairs published a document explaining the necessity of copyright legislation and important principles that should be included in the copyright code, such as the definition, scope and duration of copyright.[17] The document also referred to foreign copyright laws, such as the German Copyright Act.[18] In the same year, the Ministry of Civil Affairs completed a draft of the Qing Copyright Code, which was later reviewed by the Constitutional Compilation Bureau (憲政編查局) and the

10 Zhang, Xiaoli. 'The Copyright Code of The Great Qing Dynasty' (《大清著作权律》述论). *Academic Research* 9 (2005), 108.

11 Yang, Ming. 'Legal System vs. Documents: The Historical Examination on Copyright Law of Qing Dynasty' (制度与文本:《大清著作权律》的历史审视). *Journal of Huazhong University of Science and Technology (Social Science Edition)* 27(5) (2013), 62.

12 Zhang (n. 10), 108; see also 'Ministry of Education Deliberates Copyright' (學部慎重版權) *Ta Kung Pao* (6 April 1906).

13 Cong, Shijian. 'Difficulties and Progress: Modernization of the Copyright Law in Late Qing Dynasty' (曲折与进步：清末著作权法的近代化). *Journal of Chongqing Normal University Edition of Social Sciences* 6 (2014), 15–18.

14 McIntyre, 'The Yang Obeys' (n. 3), 87.

15 Cong, 'Difficulties and Progress' (n. 13), 15–18.

16 Tao, Baolin. 'The Necessity to Enact Copyright Law and Publishing Law' (論著作權法出版法急宜編訂頒行) in Zhou and Li, *Research Documents* 1999 (n. 6), 82–86.

17 'Ministry of Civil Affairs' Letter to Central Advisory Council on The Reason For Drafting Copyright Code' (民政部為擬具著作權律草案理由事致資政院稿) (1910) in Zhou and Li, *Research Documents* 1999 (n. 6), 86.

18 Ibid.

Advisory Council (資政院).[19] Finally, the Qing Copyright Code was officially enacted on 17 November 1910.[20]

Scholars have different accounts of the driving forces behind the first copyright statute in China. Some believe that it was a result of the Qing government's strong intention to control the publication industry and speech[21]; others contend that the law was enacted in response to foreign pressures.[22] However, we argue that this legislation is influenced by both the external and internal political economy faced by the Qing government.

2.1 *External Factors*

2.1.1 Treaty Protections of Foreign Works

Western powers had sought various protections of legal rights and prerogatives in China since the country's devastating defeat by Britain in the First Opium War (1840–1842).[23] Indeed, the protection of copyright had become an international trend in the latter half of the nineteenth century,[24] so it is unsurprising that among other legal rights, foreign countries paid increasing attention to copyright issues during their interaction with China because of the enactment of the *Berne Convention for the Protection of Literary and Artistic Works* (Berne Convention) in 1886 and the rising number of copyright works translated and distributed in China.[25] These foreign countries therefore requested the Qing government to include copyright clauses in treaties. For example, Article 5 of

19 'Ministry of Civil Affairs Letter on Discussion on The Drafting of The Copyright Code of The Great Qing Dynasty' (民政部為擬定著作權律清單請旨交議事奏摺) (1910) in Zhou and Li, *Research Documents* 1999 (n. 6), 88.

20 Ibid., see also 'Ministry of Education's Letter to Ministry of Civil Affairs on The Copyright Code Drawing Attention from Foreign Press' (學部為著作權律已引起外國出版界重視致民政部呈文) (1911) in Zhou and Li, *Research Documents* 1999 (n. 6), 97.

21 *See, e.g.*, McIntyre, 'The Yang Obeys' (n. 3), 87.

22 Liang, Zhiwen. 'Between Freedom of Commerce and Protection of Moral Rights: The Chinese Experience and a Comparative Analysis'. *Journal of the Copyright Society of the U.S.A.* 57 (1–2) (2010), 114.

23 Li, Yufeng. 'Copyright Reform in China'. *Intellectual Property Journal* 22(2) (2010), 203–4; Wang, Wei. 'Historical Evolution of National Treatment in China'. *International Lawyer* 39 (2005), 760.

24 Burger, Peter. 'The Berne Convention: Its History and Its Key Role in the Future'. *Journal of Law and Technology* 3 (1988), 69.

25 For example, during 1902 to 1904, there were 533 foreign books, including 89 in English, 24 in German, 17 in French, and 321 in Japanese, were translated and distributed in China. See Feng, Qiuji. 'Reason and Situation: The Dilemma of Copyright Protection Policy in The Late Qing Dynasty' (理与势：晚清版权保护政策的两难选择). *Henan Social Sciences* 17(5) (2009), 166.

the 1903 Supplementary Treaty of Commerce and Navigation between China and Japan (中日續議通商行船條約) stipulated that

> The Chinese government likewise agrees to make such regulations as are necessary for affording protection to registered copyrights held by Japanese subjects in the books, pamphlets, maps, and charts written in the Chinese language and specially prepared for the use of Chinese people.[26]

Article 11 of the 1903 Treaty Respecting Commercial Relations between China and the United States (中美續議通商行船條約) similarly stipulated that

> Whereas the Government of the United States undertakes to give the benefits of its Copyright Laws to the citizens of any foreign State which gives to the citizens of the United States the benefits of copyright on an equal basis with its own citizens –
>
> Therefore the Government of China, in order to secure such benefits in the United States for its subjects, now agrees to give full protection, in the same way and manner and subject to the same conditions upon which it agrees to protect trade-marks, to all citizens of the United States who are authors, designers, or proprietors of any book, map, print, or engraving especially prepared for the use and education of the Chinese people, or translation into Chinese of any book, in the exclusive right to print and sell such book, map, print, engraving, or translation in the Empire of China during ten years from the date of registration. With the exception of the books, maps, specified above, which may not be reprinted in the same form, no work shall be entitled to copyright privileges under this Article. It is understood that Chinese subjects shall be at liberty to make, print, and sell original translations into Chinese of any works written or of maps compiled by a citizen of the United States. This Article shall not be held to protect against due process of law any citizen of the United States or Chinese subject who may be author, proprietor, or seller of any publication calculated to injure the well-being of China.[27]

---

26 Supplementary Treaty Commerce and Navigation Between Japan and China [8 October 1903] in *Hertslet's China Treaties: Treaties, etc., Between Great Britain and China in Force on the 1st January, 1908*, ed. Godfrey E.P. Hertslet (vol. 1, Cambridge: Cambridge University Press, 2012), 385.

27 Treaty Between China and The United States Respecting Commercial Relations [8 October 1903] in Hertslet, *Hertslet's* 2012 (n. 26), 573–574.

Certain implications are observable from the copyright provisions in these two treaties. First, both provided reciprocal copyright protection; that is, citizens of foreign countries could enjoy copyright protection in China as much as Chinese citizens could enjoy that same protection in their countries. Second, because China lacked a copyright law at that time, Chinese citizens' works were not protected like foreigners' were, so the reciprocal copyright protection in these treaties actually created super-national treatment for foreign authors.[28] In other words, under these treaties, only foreigners could enjoy copyright protection whereas Chinese authors' works were not subject to copyright protection in the absence of domestic copyright law. The asymmetric treatment for domestic and foreign authors may have amplified the motive for the Qing government to enact a national copyright law to protect Chinese authors. Third, the treaty above between China and the United States did not completely favour American copyright owners because it specifically stipulated that Chinese citizens could legally translate copyright work owned by American citizens. Last but not least, since Britain and other Western powers had obtained 'most favoured nation' treatment from China in previous treaties, the copyright protection for Japanese and American authors mentioned below had been automatically applied to those other Western powers.[29]

2.1.2 Legal Reform to Relinquish Extraterritoriality

In the face of Qing weakness and eventual collapse, foreign powers increasingly gained extraterritoriality through their treaties with China[30] because they regarded Chinese law as 'barbaric'.[31] With these extraterritoriality provisions in

---

28 Super-national treatment means the treatment is more favorable to a foreigner than a similarly-situated national. *See, e.g.*, Beauvais, Joel C. 'Regulatory Expropriations under NAFTA: Emerging Principles & Lingering Doubts'. *New York University Environmental Law Journal* 10(2) (2002), 265; Feng, Xiaoqing and Huang, Frank Xianfeng. 'International Standards and Local Elements: New Developments of Copyright Law in China'. *Journal of the Copyright Society of the U.S.A.* 49(4) (2002), 919; Graham, Edward M. 'Regulatory Takings, Supernational Treatment, and the Multilateral Agreement on Investment: Issues Raised by Nongovernmental Organizations'. *Cornell International Law Journal* 31(3) (1998), 603.

29 Li, Yufeng and Ng, Catherine W. 'Understanding the Great Qing Copyright Law of 1910'. *Journal of the Copyright Society of the U.S.A.* 56(4) (2009), 770; Chen, Kai. 'The Legislation of Copyright in the Late Qing Dynasty: The Game Between Right Protection and Instrumentalism' (晚清著作权立法：权利保护与工具主义的博弈). *Intellectual Property* 5 (2014), 45.

30 Evans, Justin W. 'Explaining China's Legal Flexibility: History and the Institutional Imperative'. *Pace International Law Review* 31(1) (2018), 212; Szto, Mary. 'Gender and the Chinese Legal Profession in Historical Perspective: From Heaven and Earth to Rule of Woman?'. *Texas Journal of Women and the Law* 18(2) (2009), 228.

31 Evans, 'Explaining China's Legal Flexibility' (n. 30), 215.

treaties, foreigners in China were subject only to their nation's laws enforced by relevant consular officials.[32] An important drive for the Qing to advance law reform in the late nineteen contrary was that foreign powers promised to relinquish extraterritoriality if China revamped its legal system to comply with Western standards.[33] Britain explicitly expressed such an expectation in its 1902 Mackay Treaty with China:

> China having expressed a strong desire to reform her judicial system and to bring it into accord with that of Western nations, Great Britain agrees to give every assistance to such reform, and she will also be prepared to relinquish her extra-territorial rights when she is satisfied that the state of the Chinese laws, the arrangement for their administration, and other considerations warrant her in so doing.[34]

The legislation of the Qing Copyright Code was set against this backdrop. While the Qing Copyright Code was not the only law enacted as a result of this legal reform aiming to abolish foreign extraterritoriality, the Qing government's desire to regain sovereignty and international dignity certainly played a deciding role in the copyright legislation.

2.1.3 Copyright Awareness Promoted by Foreigners

Modern copyright law was not endogenous to China under Qing governance. Therefore, it is quite important to understand how the Chinese society was able to accept and incorporate the Western concept of copyright. Notably, foreign missionaries, whose footprints had spread across China, played an important role in disseminating Western values and ideas in the late Qing Dynasty.[35] Among those missionaries, Young John Allen, an American Methodist

32 Eyster, James Parry. 'Antigone in China: Teaching American Law and Lawyering in Shenzhen'. *Asian-Pacific Law & Policy Journal* 12(1) (2010), 51.

33 Hsieh, Pasha L. 'The Discipline of International Law in Republican China and Contemporary Taiwan'. *Washington University Global Studies Law Review* 14(1) (2015), 106; Wang, Tay-sheng. 'Translation, Codification, and Transplantation of Foreign Laws in Taiwan'. *Washington International Law Journal* 25(2) (2016), 317.

34 Treaty Between Great Britain and China Respecting Commercial Relations (Mackay Treaty) [5 September 1902] in Hertslet, *Hertslet's* 2012 (n. 26), 82.

35 Cohen, Paul A. *China and Christianity: The Missionary Movement and the Growth of Chinese Antiforeignism, 1860–1870* (Cambridge: Harvard University Press, 1963), 63–76; Lackner, Amelung, Kurtz, Lackner, Michael, Amelung, Iwo, and Kurtz, Joachim, *New Terms for New Ideas: Western Knowledge and Lexical Change in Late Imperial China* (Leiden: Brill, 2001), 57, 80,153, 304.

missionary with the Chinese name Lin Lezhi (林樂之), was an active advocate for establishing a copyright regime in China.[36]

In 1868, Allen founded the *Church News* (教會新報), later renamed the *Global Magazine* and *Review of the Times* (萬國公報),[37] which was a religious journal with broad readership.[38] This journal actively disseminated Western knowledge concerning geography, history, civilisation and many other fields,[39] and Allen used it as a vehicle to publish his proposal of a copyright regime in China.[40] Allen persuaded local Qing government officials in 1896 through American counsel to release a public notice prohibiting the reprinting of works by missionaries.[41] He later reproduced this notice in the *Review of the Times* to indicate that the local government supported his copyright claim.[42]

In 1903, Allen and his friend Fan Yi published the essay 'General Rules of Copyright' (版權通例) in the *Global Magazine*, examining the definition, functions and durations of copyright in Western countries.[43] They argued that copyright was an instrument to reward authors' hard work and that any unauthorised excerpt and reprint of copyright works should be prohibited and penalised by law.[44] They also believed that all copyright works should be free of use if their terms expire.[45] They argued in another article, 'The Relation of Copyright' (版權之關係), that copyright should be conferred to authors as a private right and that the government should take the lead in copyright protection.[46] They contended that copyright should be designed to reward authors' efforts and to induce their further creation.[47] They also suggested that the adoption of Western copyright protection rules was an inevitable trend that

36 Han, 'Can I Own My Writings And Sell Them Too?' (n. 9), 331; Li and Ng, 'Understanding the Great Qing Copyright Law of 1910' (n. 29), 776.

37 *See* China National Newspaper Index (全国报刊索引) – The Church News (中国教会新报), available at: https://www.cnbksy.com/home (last accessed on 12 January 2021).

38 Li and Ng, 'Understanding the Great Qing Copyright Law of 1910' (n. 29), 776.

39 Bennett, Adrian A. *Missionary Journalist in China: Young J. Allen and His Magazines, 1860–1883* (Athens: University of Georgia Press, 1983), 96–225.

40 Li and Ng, 'Understanding the Great Qing Copyright Law of 1910' (n. 29), 776.

41 Ibid., 777; Han, 'Can I Own My Writings and Sell Them Too?' (n. 9), 331.

42 Li and Ng, 'Understanding the Great Qing Copyright Law of 1910' (n. 29), 777.

43 Young John Allen, 'The Review of the Times No. 177' (1903) (Restated by Yi Fan) in Zhou and Li, *Research Documents* 1999 (n. 6), 77.

44 Ibid.

45 Ibid.

46 Young John Allen, 'The Review of the Times No. 183' (1903) (Restated by Yi Fan) in Zhou and Li, *Research Documents* 1999 (n. 6), 82.

47 Ibid.

could rejuvenate the nation.[48] While Allen was not entirely against other newspapers reproducing his editorials, he demanded that they should acknowledge their source.[49] Therefore, Allen unsurprisingly wished that Chinese copyright could protect the right of attribution.[50]

While Allen's endeavours to advance copyright knowledge in China originated in his own interest as an author,[51] he had successfully facilitated social awareness of the copyright system and its benefit to society.

2.2 *Internal Factors*

2.2.1 Public Sector

Because most high-level government officials and politicians were intellectuals or scholars in the Qing Dynasty, they were usually authors as well, so most did not object to establishing a copyright regime that protected authors. Unlike other reforms concerning the abolition of slavery and fornication, building a copyright system was much less controversial among Qing government officials.[52] Influential politicians, such as Ministers Sheng Xuanhuai and Lu Haihuan, urged that China should establish a copyright regime which explicitly defined the scope of protection and penalties for infringement.[53]

While government officials and politicians did not significantly disagree with the protection of domestic authors, they had different views on whether and to what extent that copyright should protect foreign authors.[54] While a group of politicians led by Zhang Zhidong and Liu Kunyi supported a copyright regime providing limited protection for foreign works,[55] other politicians led by Minister Zhang Baixi insisted that China should not protect foreign authors' copyright.[56] As the Minister of Education, Zhang Baixi was opposed to protecting foreign works in China's treaties with other countries because

48 Ibid.

49 Li and Ng, 'Understanding the Great Qing Copyright Law of 1910' (n. 29), 776.

50 Ibid., 777.

51 Ibid., 776.

52 Wang, Yangchuan and Nie, Shihai. 'Turning over The Dusty History – Stories of The Copyright Code of the Great Qing Dynasty' (翻开尘封的历史 – 《大清著作权律》的那些故事). *Fortune Today-China Intellectual Property* 11 (2010), 35–36.

53 Cong, 'Difficulties and Progress' (n. 13), 15–18; 'Lu Haihuan's Memorial on Copyright Issues' (吕海寰為版權事奏稿) in *China Modern History Series – Memorials of Lu Haihuan* (中國近代史料叢刊·呂海寰奏稿), ed. Yunlong Shen (Taiwan: Taiwan Wenhai Press, 1990).

54 Han, 'Can I Own My Writings and Sell Them Too?' (n. 9), 330.

55 Cong, 'Difficulties and Progress' (n. 13), 15–18; 'Viceroy Kunyi Liu's Reply to Baixi Zhang's Telegram' (前江督劉坤一複電) in *Research Documents* 1999 (n. 6), 42–43.

56 Cong, 'Difficulties and Progress' (n. 13), 15–18.

he believed such clauses would hinder access to foreign knowledge and thus thwart modern education in China.[57]

2.2.2 Private Sector

2.2.2.1 *Publishers*

2.2.2.1.1 Lian Quan and the Wenming Press

The case of the Wenming Press (文明書局) illuminates the difficulty faced by private publishers in the late Qing Dynasty. The Shanghai-based Wenming Press was once the largest private publisher of textbooks in Qing Dynasty,[58] but it suffered significant losses due to unauthorised reproduction, not only by private parties but also, more importantly, by government agencies. Most notably, the Beiyang Official Newspaper Bureau (北洋官報局), a governmental publisher, was the one that extensively copied and sold Wenming Press's publications for profit.[59] Consequently, a founder of the Wenming Press, Lian Quan, filed a petition in 1902 to the Viceroy of Zhili (直隸總督) and the Minister of Beiyang (北洋大臣) Yuan Shikai to seek copyright protection.[60] Yuan then released an official document in 1903 confirming that the government would protect the copyright of publishers.[61] Nevertheless, Yuan's declaration did not stop the Beiyang Official Newspaper Bureau from copying Wenming Press's publication at all. Even worse, Zhang Xiaoqian, the Director of the Beiyang Official Newspaper Bureau, justified the bureau's reproduction by claiming that no law in China prohibited unauthorised copying and that its copying was in the public interest.[62] Zhang also asked Yuan to revoke the protection of Wenming's publications because the content therein was incorrect, ill-mannered and illegal.[63] Yuan then turned a blind eye to the Beiyang Official Newspaper Bureau's unauthorised copying activities.[64]

---

57 Li and Ng, 'Understanding the Great Qing Copyright Law of 1910' (n. 29), 782–783.

58 Li and Ng, 'Understanding the Great Qing Copyright Law of 1910' (n. 29), 776; Liu, Guifang and Hong, Gang. 'Copyright Legislation of Textbook during Late Qing Dynasty and the Republic of China' (晚清及民国时期教科书版权立法述论). *Library and Information Service* 23 (2009), 137–140.

59 Li, Mingshan. 'Pirate Printing in Beiyang Official Newspaper Bureau and the Formulation of Late-Qing Copyright Law' (北洋官报局盗版与晚清版权律的制定). *Journal of Nantong Teachers College (Social Science Edition)* 3 (2001), 147, 147–152.

60 Ibid., 149.

61 Li, 'Pirate Printing' 2001 (n. 59), 149; 'The Advices from Minister of Beiyang Government Yuan Shikai to The Governors of Wenming Press' (北洋大臣袁宫保為文明書局諮各督撫文), *Ta Kung Pao* (19 January 1903).

62 Li, 'Pirate Printing' 2001 (n. 59), 149; 'Investigation on The Wenming Press' (查辦書局咨文) *Ta Kung Pao* (3 March 1903).

63 Li, 'Pirate Printing' 2001 (n. 59), 149.

64 Ibid.; 'Petition on Revocation of Fallacy on Copyright' (論直督請撤銷版權之謬), *Ta Kung Pao* (8 March 1904).

Lian Quan filed a similar petition to Zhang Baixi, then the Minister of Education, in May 1903, to seek government protection of private publications.[65] Minster Zhang responded to Lian Quan's petition by stating the importance of curbing piracy and promising to grant copyright to the press if its printed works were registered at the Ministry of Education.[66] Unfortunately, Zhang's response did not effectively deter unauthorised reproduction.[67]

Eventually, Lian Quan filed a complaint with the Ministry of Commerce in April 1904 reclaiming the Beiyang Official Newspaper Bureau's misbehaviour of reproduction and rebutting the accusation by Zhang Xiaoqian.[68] Lian Quan argued that government agencies, such as the Beiyang Official Newspaper Bureau, should not compete with private publishers for profit and that the misappropriation of Wenming Press's published content was certainly not non-profit charity for education.[69] More importantly, Lian Quan urged the government to enact copyright law in the interest of the whole society.[70] The story of the Wenming Press and Lian Quan well illustrates the demand for copyright legislation in the private sector under the Qing Dynasty.

2.2.2.1.2 Zhang Yuanji and the Commercial Press

Zhang Yuanji was another remarkable reformer in the publishing industry in pre-modern China. He actively promoted the Western concept of copyright and implemented copyright practice in his publishing business. In January 1902, Zhang launched the newspaper *Diplomacy* (外交報) in Shanghai, which later became an important platform advocating copyright protection in the country.[71] From 1902 to 1909, *Diplomacy* published a series of reports introducing the 1886 Berne Convention and its subsequent amendments in Chinese.[72]

Zhang later became the chairperson and a primary investor in the Commercial Press (商務印書館), the largest modern publishing house at that time. Zhang initiated the publication of China's first monograph on copyright law,

65 Lian, Quan. 'Lian's Petition to The Chief of Education Department on Copyright' (廉部郎上管學大臣論版權事) in Zhou and Li, *Research Documents* 1999 (n. 6), 45–46.

66 Zhang, Baixi. 'Reply to Lian's Petition on Copyright' (管學大臣批答廉惠卿部郎呈請明定版權由) in Zhou and Li, *Research Documents* 1999 (n. 6), 46.

67 Li, 'Pirate Printing' 2001 (n. 59), 148–149.

68 Lian, 'Lian's Petition' (n. 65), 45–46; Li, 'Pirate Printing' 2001 (n. 59), 149.

69 Li, 'Pirate Printing' 2001 (n. 59), 150.

70 Ibid.

71 Lei, Yanlin. 'Zhang Yuanji and Copyright Protection in Pre-modern China' (张元济与中国近现代的著作权保护). *China Edit* 4 (2011), 92–94.

72 *See e.g.* Diplomacy Newspaper (外交報) no. 3 (1902), 8–12; no. 4 (1902), 8–13; no. 5 (1902), 6–12; 'Discussion on Berne Convention' (論萬國會議保護著作權), *Diplomacy Newspaper* (no. 252, 1909), 13–25.

FIGURE 7.1
Copyright stamp of the commercial press

Copyright Overview (版權考), by the Commercial Press in 1903.[73] The book, which covered the origins and development of copyright laws in the Western world,[74] successfully helped the Chinese society understand the copyright regime from an international perspective.

In addition to promoting the value of copyright law via publication, Zhang also incorporated copyright practice in his publication business in the absence of the law. The Commercial Press included a copyright notice of 'All Rights Reserved' (翻印必究) in its published books as early as 1904, when Yan Fu's translation of *English Grammar Annotated* (英文漢詁) was published.[75] Apart from the notice of 'printed and published by the Commercial Press Shanghai' (上海商務印書館印行), the copyright notice specified that 'the underlying copyright is owned by Yan' (侯官嚴氏版權所有).[76] This historical fact suggests that Zhang and the Commercial Press valued copyright protection not only from the perspective of a publisher but also from that of an author.

In 1905, Zhang published an editorial suggesting that an ideal copyright law code would provide limited protection to foreign works.[77] Moreover, he

73 Zhou and Li, *Research Documents* 1999 (n. 6), 50–77.

74 Ibid.

75 Ibid.

76 Wang, Qing. 'The Commercial Press and Copyright Protection in Pre-modern China (Part 2)' (商务印书馆与中国近代版权保护（下）). *Publishing Research* 1 (1993), 55; Li, Bo. 'Translation and Copyright Legislation in Late Qing China (1900–1910)'. *Translation Quarterly* 65 (2012), 96.

77 Lei, 'Zhang Yuanji' (n. 71), 93; Wang, Qing. 'A Preliminary Study of Yan Fu and Zhang Yuanji's Copyright Thoughts' (严复、张元济版权思想初探). *Law Science Magazine* 4 (1992), 39–40.

opined that textbooks should be protected by copyright law after registration with government authorities.[78] Obviously, he shared the same view on this as Lian Quan at the Wenming Press.

2.2.2.2 *Authors*

In addition to foreign authors in China, such as Young John Allen, Chinese authors were also keen for more copyright protection for their works. Yan Fu was one of the most active supporters of copyright protection in the country. A prominent scholar, writer and translator, Yan introduced many fields of Western knowledge, from political science[79] to economics,[80] law[81] and science.[82] As a prolific author and translator, Yan believed that he suffered enormous financial loss in the absence of copyright protection.[83] Yan particularly cared about the relations between authors and publishers. At that time, once an author provided his work to a publisher for a price, he assigned the ownership of the work to the publisher and therefore no longer owned it.[84] Yan did not entirely agree with such a copyright practice and believed that authors should be entitled to part of the profits generated from the publication.[85]

Yan therefore actively negotiated royalty arrangements in his publication agreements with publishers. In his correspondence with Zhang Yuanji, who was then the Dean of the College of Translation at the Nan Yang Public School, Yan expressed his wish to obtain 20% of the total profits generated from the publication of his translation of *The Wealth of Nations* for 20 years.[86] Yan explained that the royalties could incentivise more scholars to produce new works.[87] Yan's translation of *The Wealth of Nations* was eventually published by

78 Ibid.

79 Yan, Fu. *Shehui tongquan* (社會通詮) (1903), translated from A History of Politics by Edward Jenks.

80 Yan, Fu., *Yuan fu* (原富) (1901), translated from The Wealth of Nations by Adam Smith.

81 Yan, Fu. *Fayi* (法意) (1904–1909), translated from The Spirit of the Laws by Montesquieu.

82 Yan, Fu. *Tianyan lun* (天演論) (1896–1898), translated from Evolution and Ethics by Thomas Henry Huxley.

83 Yan, Fu. 'Petition to Minster of The Ministry of Education on Copyright' (與管學大臣論版權書) in Zhou and Li, *Research Documents* 1999 (n. 6), 46–48.

84 Yan, Fu. 'Letters to Yuanji Zhang No.8' (与张元济书（八）) in *Yan Fu Collection*, ed. Shi Wang, vol. 3 (Shanghai: Chung Hwa Book Company, 1986), 538.

85 Ibid., see also Han, 'Can I Own My Writings and Sell Them Too?' (n. 9), 336; Zhang, Jinqiu and Jin, Mei. 'The History of Chinese Copyright Legislation' (中国著作权立法史述论). *Legal Review* 2 (1994), 79–83.

86 Yan, 'Letters to Yuanji Zhang No.8' (n. 84), 544; Zhou and Li, *Research Documents* 1999 (n. 6), 20–21.

87 Yan, 'Letters to Yuanji Zhang No.8' (n. 84), 544.

the Nan Yang Public School Press in 1900, and Yan obtained 20% of the profit as a royalty on top of the initial remuneration of 2,000 silver dollars.[88]

Two years later, Yan authorised the Wenming Press to publish his translation of Herbert Spencer's book *The Study of Sociology*. According to Lian Quan's letter to Yan, Yan and the Wenming Press co-owned the copyright of the translation.[89] Yan would obtain 75 cents per piece published as royalty.[90] Moreover, the publisher had to return the copyright to Yan if the former sold out the stipulated volume of 6,000 copies or failed to pay the latter royalties.[91] Should the publisher have failed to include the copyright notice provided by Yan, the omission would be viewed as an infringement incurring a harsh penalty of 2,000 taels of silver on the publisher.[92]

Yan signed the first written publication agreement in China with the Commercial Press in 1903 when he authorised it to publish his translation of Edward Jenks's book *A History of Politics*.[93] This agreement stipulated that Yan and the Commercial Press co-owned the copyright of the translation, that Yan was entitled to 40% of the total profits from the publication[94] and that each copy would include a copyright notice as illustrated in Figure 7.1[95]; otherwise the publisher would be subject to a penalty of 2,500 silver dollars.[96]

Aside from striving for copyright from publishers as an author, Yan also actively persuaded Qing policymakers, such as Minister Zhang Baixi, to build a modern copyright regime in China.[97] Yan forcibly argued that disrespect of copyright would discourage the translation of foreign works and therefore

88 Han, 'Can I Own My Writings and Sell Them Too?' (n. 9), 333–334; Wang (n. 77) 39–40.

89 Yan, Fu. 'Letter from Quan Lian' (廉泉《与严复书》) in *Supplement of Yan Fu Collection* (严复集补编), eds. Yingxiang Sun and Houfeng Pi (Fuzhou: Fujian Renmin Press, 2004), 373–379.

90 Ibid.

91 Ibid.

92 Ibid.

93 Han, 'Can I Own My Writings and Sell Them Too?' (n. 9), 333.

94 'Yan Fu and The Copyright of Chinese Books' (严复与中国书籍版权), *Renmin Zhengxie Bao* (人民政协报) (7 July 2008), available at: https://www.rmzxb.com.cn (last accessed on 8 January 2021).

95 Ni, Siting. 'The Earliest Royalty Contract in China' (我国最早的“版税合同). *E-Zhicai* (4 September 1994), available at: http://www.ezhicai.com/news/38980.htm (last accessed on 12 January 2021).

96 Ibid.

97 Yan, Fu. 'Discussion on Copyright with Baixi Zhang' (與管學大臣論版權書) in Zhou and Li, *Research Documents* 1999 (n. 6), 46–48.

undermine China's access to Western knowledge.[98] Yan believed that a robust copyright regime would enhance China's national competitiveness.[99]

2.3 *Summary*

External and domestic factors mutually contributed to the legislation of the Qing Copyright Code in 1910. While foreign powers fought for their own copyright interests in China, Chinese publishers and authors also actively promoted the idea of creating a copyright regime in the country. The legislation did not happen overnight; instead, Western copyright values were promoted by both foreign and Chinese authors for several decades, and copyright was gradually protected in the publication agreements between publishers and authors before the legislation was enacted. The political economy of this legislation reflects the challenges faced by the late Qing government and the aspirations of Chinese intellectuals for a new legal order for the country in a fast-changing world.

3 Structure and Key Provisions of the Qing Copyright Code

As mentioned above, the Qing government extensively referred to foreign copyright laws to prepare the draft of the code, a common legislative approach in the late period of the Qing Dynasty after Western powers forced China to open its gates.[100] At that time, China finalised law reforms primarily based on existing foreign laws,[101] and the legislation of the Qing Copyright Code was no exception. German and Japanese copyright laws were particularly important sources for the legislation of the Qing Copyright Code.[102] One comparative study even found that 91% of the Qing Copyright Code was transplanted from Japanese copyright law.[103]

The Qing Copyright Code of the Great Qing Dynasty had five chapters and fifty-five articles. It generally defined the concept, scope, duration, formality and limitations of copyright and penalties for copyright infringement.

98 Ibid.

99 Ibid.

100 Ma, Herbert H.P. 'The Chinese Concept of the Individual and The Reception of Foreign Law'. *Journal of Chinese Law* 9(2) (1995), 214.

101 Ibid.

102 Qin, Ruijie. 'The Interpretation on The Copyright of The Great Qing Dynasty' (著作權律釋義) in Zhou and Li, *Research Documents* 1999 (n. 6), 104.

103 Han, 'Can I Own My Writings and Sell Them Too?' (n. 9), 335; Wang, Lanping. *The Growth of Copyright Law in Modern China: 1913–1910* (Beijing: Peking University Press, 2006), 99–132.

Chapter 1 provided a general definition of copyright and stipulated copyright registration. 'Copyright' referred to an exclusive reproduction right over works, and copyright works encompass literature, paintings, pamphlets, calligraphy, photographs, sculptures and models.[104] A copyright had to be registered at the Department of Civil Affairs.[105] The application for copyright registration had to include two copies of the work submitted directly to the Department of Civil Affairs or via local governments (衙門).[106] Registration was a prerequisite for copyright protection.[107]

Chapter 2 defined copyright duration in different scenarios. While authors enjoyed lifetime copyright protection, their successors owned the inherited copyright for another thirty years.[108] The successors of joint-authored work could also own the inherited copyright for thirty years starting from the death of their heirs,[109] which would start when the successor reported the death of the last surviving author.[110] The thirty-year duration was applied to three other scenarios as well: (1) a successor owning the copyright of a posthumous work if he published it[111]; (2) works published under the name of an entity, such as government agency, company, school, etc.[112]; and (3) anonymous work.[113] Copyrights of photographs were protected for ten years,[114] which was shorter than normal terms. Scholars have claimed that this provision was codified based on the Japanese copyright law on account of the creation photographs taking less labour and time than other types of copyright work.[115]

Chapter 3 specified the reporting obligations of authors and their successors to the designated departments or bureaus.[116] Chapter 4 had three sections. The first was on copyright ownership, which included the ownership of joint work,[117] compilations,[118] commissioned work,[119] speech[120] and derivative

104 Qing Copyright Code, art. 1.
105 Ibid., art. 2.
106 Ibid., art. 3.
107 Ibid., art. 4.
108 Ibid., art. 5.
109 Ibid., art. 6.
110 Ibid., art. 15.
111 Ibid., art. 7.
112 Ibid., art. 8.
113 Ibid., art. 9.
114 Ibid., art. 10.
115 Zhou and Li, *Research Documents* 1999 (n. 6), 106.
116 Qing Copyright Code, arts. 16–13.
117 Ibid., art. 24.
118 Ibid., art. 25.
119 Ibid., art. 26.
120 Ibid., art. 27.

work.[121] The law particularly granted copyright to translators who translated foreign works into Chinese.[122] Furthermore, the law listed four types of uncopyrightable subject matter: (1) laws, regulations and governmental documents; (2) exhortations for confraternity preaching; (3) newspapers reporting political and current affairs; and (4) speech at public associations.[123] Another four types of work were viewed as 'public interest', which could be understood as in the public domain under the law: (1) works whose copyright terms had expired; (2) works whose authors had passed away without any successors; (3) works circulated for a long period; and (4) works whose authors agreed on unconditional reproduction.[124] These works were free from copyright protection.

The second section of Chapter 4 elucidated the copyright infringement and misappropriation prohibited by the law. The reproduction of a registered copyright work was a major infringement.[125] The law protected authors' rights of integrity, rights of attribution,[126] and rights against false attribution.[127] This legislation reflected a strong moral-right tradition implemented in the civil law systems, and it conferred exclusive rights to textbook authors to publish answers to the questions in the book.[128] Additionally, the law prohibited creditors from taking debtors' unpublished works to offset their debt without their permission.[129] Nonetheless, the following uses of copyright works were exempted from infringement liability if they were accompanied by acknowledgement: (1) excerpting and compiling the works of numerous authors for to prepare a textbook; (2) quoting others' works for research and citation; and (3) producing a sculpture based on another's painting and vice versa.[130] The last section of Chapter 4 provided penalties for copyright infringement and misappropriation.[131]

Chapter 5 contained supplementary provisions about retroactive applications and various registration fees.[132] The liability imposed on infringers in

121 Ibid., art. 29.
122 Ibid., art. 28.
123 Ibid., art. 31.
124 Ibid., art. 32.
125 Ibid., art. 33.
126 Ibid., art. 34.
127 Ibid., art. 36.
128 Ibid., art. 37.
129 Ibid., art. 38.
130 Ibid., art. 39.
131 Ibid., art. 40–50.
132 Ibid., art. 51–55.

the Qing Copyright Code was only fines.[133] In other words, infringers were not obliged to compensate the author's loss, nor was there any confiscation of infringing materials.

4 The Protection of Foreign Works

As mentioned in Part 2 of this chapter, one external factor contributing to the legislation of the Qing Copyright Code was foreign pressure on the Qing government to protect foreign works. While Qing officials had different views on whether foreign works should be protected by copyright law, the Qing Copyright Code was silent on this issue, with no specific provision governing the protection of foreign works.

In *Ginn & Co. v. Commercial Press*, the plaintiff claimed infringement of copyright over its book *General History for Colleges and High Schools* against the defendant.[134] The Mixed Court of the International Settlement in Shanghai ("Mixed Court") ruled that since the book was a foreign work, it was not protected by the Qing Copyright Code.[135] The court further explained that because China did not sign the Berne convention, it did not have an obligation to protect foreign works.[136] Instead, the issue should be governed by Article 11 of the 1903 Treaty Respecting Commercial Relations between China and the United States, which provided that the Chinese government should give copyright protection 'to all citizens of the United States who are authors, designers, or proprietors of any book, map, print, or engraving especially prepared for the use and education of the Chinese people, or translation into Chinese of any book'.[137] The court eventually held in 1911 that the book was not prepared especially for the use and education of the Chinese people, so the defendant's unauthorised copying of the book did not constitute copyright infringement in China.[138] Although foreign authors and publishers continued to seek copyright protection for their works in China after the Qing Dynasty was overthrown, they

133 Ibid., art. 40–43.

134 Zhou and Li, *Research Documents* 1999 (n. 6), 146; Li, *Law at Gunpoint* 2006 (n. 7), 121.

135 Li, *Law at Gunpoint* 2006 (n. 7), 121; Wang, 'The Commercial Press' (n. 76), 57; see also Zhou and Li, *Research Documents* 1999 (n. 6), 146–151.

136 Zhou and Li, *Research Documents* 1999 (n. 6), 147–8.

137 Treaty Between China and the United States respecting Commercial Relations [8 October 1903] in Hertslet, *Hertslet's* 2012 (n. 26), 573–574.

138 Li, *Law at Gunpoint* 2006 (n. 7), 121; Wang, 'The Commercial Press' (n. 76), 57; see also Zhou and Li, *Research Documents* 1999 (n. 6), 146–51.

did not succeed because of the limitation 'especially prepared for the use and education of the Chinese people' in the 1903 Treaty Respecting Commercial Relations between China and the United States.[139] Therefore, although foreign powers substantially influenced the legislation of the Qing Copyright Code, hindsight reveals that the law did not provide sufficient protection for foreign works in China. Chinese copyright law did not provide explicit protection for foreign works until the enactment of *Law on Authors' Rights* in 1928.[140]

It should be noted that the Mixed Court was established in 1864 with the purpose of protecting 'foreign interest … concerned in cases either civil or criminal, ….'[141] As Thomas P. Stephens noted, the Mixed Court was 'a branch office of the Qing government's Shanghai magistracy, located within the settlement limits, for the more expeditious disposal of police charges arising locally against Chinese nationals residing in the settlement.'[142] It became a typical instrument for the enforcement of extraterritoriality given by a series of Sino-foreign treaties signed in late 19th century.[143] In addition, the Mixed Court also provided an important platform for Chinese authorities and citizens to learn western legal concepts and judicial practices.[144] The jurisdiction of the Mixed Court covered all kinds of commercial, civil, and criminal matters.[145] In light of intellectual property cases, an empirical study revealed that from 1909 to 1913, the Mixed Court accepted and heard nine cases on trademark and one case on copyright, which were filed by U.S. consulate in Shanghai.[146]

---

139 Wang, 'The Commercial Press' (n. 76), 57; see also Zhou and Li, *Research Documents* 1999 (n. 6), 146–51.

140 Detailed Implementing Rules of the 1928 Copyright Law of the Republic of China, art.14.1 ("[f]oreign works exclusively prepared for the use of Chinese nationals can be registered for copyright protection under the law").

141 Barton, Sydney. 'The Shanghai Mixed Court'. *Chinese Social and Political Science Review* 4(1) (1919), 33.

142 Stephens, Thomas P. *Order and Discipline in China: The Shanghai Mixed Court 1911–27* (Seattle: University of Washington Press, 1992), 44.

143 Meighen, John FD. 'International Mixed Court of Shanghai'. *Commercial Law League Journal* 31(11) (1926), 530.

144 Yu, Huachuan. 'Clashes and Reconciliation of Chinese and Western Legal Systems and Thinking – View from the Perspective of The Mixed Court of the International Settlement at Shanghai' (从上海公共租界会审公廨看中西法律制度和思想的冲突与融合) (DPhil thesis, East China Normal University, 2005), 122.

145 Kroll, Stefan. 'Zooming in on Norm Research: Towards a Suitable Scale for the Shanghai Mixed Court'. *Global Constitutionalism* 5(3) (2016), 391.

146 Cai, Xiaorong 'Mixed Claims and Negotiation between Chinese and American Merchants in the Shanghai Mixed Court in the Late Qing Dynasty and Early Republic of China' (清末民初上海会审公廨中美商民的混合诉讼及交涉). *Historical Research* 1 (2019), 89.

5 Conclusion

The Qing Copyright Code was the first modern copyright legislation in China. Although its life was rather short because of the collapse of the Qing Dynasty, it offers insight into the complicated political and economic challenges faced by the country in the late nineteenth century. Unsurprisingly, a rising number of foreigners sought legal privileges and protection in China after the country was forced to open its doors to the world. Foreigners' push for better copyright protection in China was also influenced by the adoption of the Berne Convention in Europe in 1886. In the meantime, China started to learn the value of Western knowledge and legal institutions, and copyright law was indubitably an important idea that China slowly absorbed for decades. Chinese intellectuals also realised that the goal of building a robust copyright system was not to protect foreigners but to foster more knowledge dissemination, improve education and eventually enhance China's competitiveness.

Bibliography

Barton, Sydney. 'The Shanghai Mixed Court'. *Chinese Social and Political Science Review* 4(1) (1919), 31–41.

Beauvais, Joel C. 'Regulatory Expropriations under NAFTA: Emerging Principles & Lingering Doubts'. *New York University Environmental Law Journal* 10(2) (2002), 245–296.

Bennett, Adrian A. *Missionary Journalist in China: Young J. Allen and His Magazines, 1860–1883* (Athens: University of Georgia Press, 1983).

Burger, Peter. 'The Berne Convention: Its History and Its Key Role in the Future'. *Journal of Law and Technology* 3 (1988), 1–70.

Cai, Xiaorong. 'Mixed Claims and Negotiation between Chinese and American Merchants in the Shanghai Mixed Court in the Late Qing Dynasty and Early Republic of China' (清末民初上海会审公廨中美商民的混合诉讼及交涉). *Historical Research* 1 (2019), 86–104.

Cohen, Paul A. *China and Christianity: The Missionary Movement and the Growth of Chinese Antiforeignism, 1860–1870* (Cambridge: Harvard University Press, 1963).

Cong, Shijian. 'Difficulties and Progress: Modernization of the Copyright Law in Late Qing Dynasty' (曲折与进步:清末著作权法的近代化). *Journal of Chongqing Normal University Edition of Social Sciences* 6 (2014), 15–18.

Chen, Kai. 'The Legislation of Copyright in the Late Qing Dynasty: The Game Between Right Protection and Instrumentalism' (晚清著作权立法:权利保护与工具主义的博弈). *Intellectual Property* 5 (2014), 43–49.

Declet, Jr., Rafael A. 'Protecting American Intellectual Property in China: The Persistent Problem of Software Piracy'. *New York International Law Review* 10(2) (1997), 57–76.

Evans, Justin W. 'Explaining China's Legal Flexibility: History and the Institutional Imperative'. *Pace International Law Review* 31(1) (2018), 173–262.

Eyster, James Parry. 'Antigone in China: Teaching American Law and Lawyering in Shenzhen'. *Asian-Pacific Law & Policy Journal* 12(1) (2010), 43–92.

Feng, Qiuji. 'Reason and Situation: The Dilemma of Copyright Protection Policy in The Late Qing Dynasty' (理与势：晚清版权保护政策的两难选择). *Henan Social Sciences* 17(5) (2009), 165–167.

Feng, Qiuji. 'Western Theories and the Legislation of Copyright Law in Late Qing Dynasty' (西人论说与晚清版权立法). *Jiangxi Social Sciences* 8 (2005), 205–210.

Feng, Xiaoqing, and Huang, Frank Xianfeng. 'International Standards and Local Elements: New Developments of Copyright Law in China'. *Journal of the Copyright Society of the U.S.A* 49(4) (2002), 917–948.

Graham, Edward M. 'Regulatory Takings, Supernational Treatment, and the Multilateral Agreement on Investment: Issues Raised by Nongovernmental Organizations'. *Cornell International Law Journal* 31(3) (1998), 599–614.

Han, Dong. 'Can I Own My Writings and Sell Them Too? A Brief History of Copyright in China from The Late Qing Era to Mao's China'. *Chinese Journal of Communication* 3(3) (2010), 329–346.

Hertslet, Godfrey E.P. (ed.) *Hertslet's China Treaties: Treaties, etc., Between Great Britain and China in Force on the 1st January, 1908* (vol.1, Cambridge: Cambridge University Press, 2012).

Hsieh, Pasha L. 'The Discipline of International Law in Republican China and Contemporary Taiwan'. *Washington University Global Studies Law Review* 14(1) (2015), 87–130.

'Investigation on The Wenming Press' (查辦書局咨文). *Ta Kung Pao* (3 March 1903).

Kroll, Stefan. 'Zooming in on Norm Research: Towards a Suitable Scale for the Shanghai Mixed Court'. *Global Constitutionalism* 5(3) (2016), 383–404.

Lam, Philip H. 'Copyright Protection of Foreign Computer Software in the People's Republic of China: Significant Progress in Two Years'. *Loyola of Los Angeles International and Comparative Law Journal* 17(4) (1995), 861–890.

Lazar, June Cohan. 'Note, Protecting Ideas and Ideals: Copyright Law in the People's Republic of China'. *Law and Policy in International Business* 27(4) (1996), 1185–1212.

Lackner, Amelung, Kurtz, Lackner, Michael, Amelung, Iwo, and Kurtz, Joachim, *New Terms for New Ideas: Western Knowledge and Lexical Change in Late Imperial China* (Leiden: Brill, 2001).

Lei, Yanlin. 'Zhang Yuanji and Copyright Protection in Pre-modern China' (张元济与中国近现代的著作权保护). *China Edit* 4 (2011), 92–94.

Li, Bo. 'Translation and Copyright Legislation in Late Qing China (1900–1910)'. *Translation Quarterly* 65 (2012), 85–103.

Li, Mingshan. 'Pirate Printing in Beiyang Official Newspaper Bureau and the Formulation of Late-Qing Copyright Law' (北洋官报局盗版与晚清版权律的制定). *Journal of Nantong Teachers College (Social Science Edition)* 3 (2001), 147–152.

Li, Yufeng. 'Copyright Reform in China'. *Intellectual Property Journal* 22(2) (2010), 203–221.

Li, Yufeng, and Ng, Catherine W. 'Understanding the Great Qing Copyright Law of 1910'. *Journal of the Copyright Society of the U.S.A.* 56(4) (2009), 767–788.

Li, Yufeng. *Law at Gunpoint: A Study on History of Copyright in China* (枪口下的法律: 中国版权史研究) (1st edn, Beijing: Intellectual Property Publishing House, 2006).

Lian, Quan. 'Lian's Petition to The Chief of Education Department on Copyright' (廉部郎上管學大臣論版權事) in Zhou and Li, *Research Documents* 1999, 45–46.

Liang, Zhiwen. 'Between Freedom of Commerce and Protection of Moral Rights: The Chinese Experience and a Comparative Analysis'. *Journal of the Copyright Society of the U.S.A.* 57 (1–2) (2010), 107–[ii].

Liu, Guifang, and Hong, Gang. 'Copyright Legislation of Textbook during Late Qing Dynasty and the Republic of China' (晚清及民国时期教科书版权立法述论). *Library and Information Service* 23 (2009), 137–140.

Lula, Katie. 'Neither Here Nor There But Fair: Finding An International Copyright Legal System Between East and West, Past and Present'. *Asian-Pacific Law & Policy Journal* 8(1) (2006), 96–137.

'Lu Haihuan's Memorial on Copyright Issues' (呂海寰為版權事奏稿) in *China Modern History Series – Memorials of Lu Haihuan* (中國近代史料叢刊·呂海寰奏稿), ed. Yunlong Shen (Taiwan: Taiwan Wenhai Press, 1990).

Ma, Herbert H.P. 'The Chinese Concept of the Individual and The Reception of Foreign Law'. *Journal of Chinese Law* 9(2) (1995), 207–218.

McIntyre, Stephen. 'The Yang Obeys, But the Yin Ignores: Copyright Law and Speech Suppressions in the People's Republic of China'. *UCLA Pacific Basin Law Journal* 29(1) (2011), 75–134.

Meighen, John F.D. 'International Mixed Court of Shanghai'. *Commercial Law League Journal* 31(11) (1926), 529–531.

'Ministry of Civil Affairs' Letter to Central Advisory Council on The Reason For Drafting Copyright Code' (民政部為擬具著作權律草案理由事致資政院稿) (1910) in Zhou, Lin and Li, Mingshan. *Research Documents on The History of Copyright in China* (中国版权史研究文献) (Beijing: China Fangzheng Press, 1999), 86.

'Ministry of Education Deliberates Copyright' (學部慎重版權). *Ta Kung Pao* (6 April 1906).

'Ministry of Education's Letter to Ministry of Civil Affairs on The Copyright Code Drawing Attention from Foreign Press' (學部為著作權律已引起外國出版界重視

致民政部呈文) (1911) in Zhou, Lin and Li, Mingshan. *Research Documents on The History of Copyright in China* (中国版权史研究文献) (Beijing: China Fangzheng Press, 1999), 97.

Ni, Siting. 'The Earliest Royalty Contract in China' (我国最早的"版税合同"). *E-Zhicai* (4 September 1994), available at: http://www.ezhicai.com/news/38980.htm (last accessed on 12 January 2021).

'Petition on Revocation of Fallacy on Copyright' (論直督請撤銷版權之謬), *Ta Kung Pao* (8 March 1904).

Qin, Ruijie. 'The Interpretation on The Copyright of The Great Qing Dynasty' (著作權律釋義) in Zhou and Li, *Research Documents* 1999, 104.

Stephens, Thomas P. *Order and Discipline in China: The Shanghai Mixed Court 1911–27* (Seattle: University of Washington Press, 1992).

Supplementary Treaty Commerce and Navigation Between Japan and China [8 October 1903] in *Hertslet's China Treaties: Treaties, etc., Between Great Britain and China in Force on the 1st January, 1908*, ed. Godfrey E.P. Hertslet (vol. 1, Cambridge: Cambridge University Press, 2012), 383–391.

Szto, Mary. 'Gender and the Chinese Legal Profession in Historical Perspective: From Heaven and Earth to Rule of Woman?'. *Texas Journal of Women and the Law* 18(2) (2009), 195–262.

Tao, Baolin. 'The Necessity to Enact Copyright Law and Publishing Law'(論著作權法出版法急宜編訂頒行). in Zhou, Lin and Li, Mingshan. *Research Documents on The History of Copyright in China* (中国版权史研究文献) (Beijing: China Fangzheng Press, 1999), 82–86.

'The Advices from Minister of Beiyang Government Yuan Shikai to The Governors of Wenming Press' (北洋大臣袁宫保為文明書局諮各督撫文), *Ta Kung Pao* (19 January 1903).

Treaty Between China and The United States Respecting Commercial Relations [8 October 1903] in *Hertslet's China Treaties: Treaties, etc., Between Great Britain and China in Force on the 1st January, 1908*, ed. Godfrey E.P. Hertslet (vol. 1, Cambridge: Cambridge University Press, 2012), 566–578.

'Viceroy Kunyi Liu's Reply to Baixi Zhang's Telegram' (前江督劉坤一複電) in Zhou, Lin and Li, Mingshan. *Research Documents on The History of Copyright in China* (中国版权史研究文献) (Beijing: China Fangzheng Press, 1999), 42–43.

Wang, Lanping. *The Growth of Copyright Law in Modern China: 1913–1910* (Beijing: Peking University Press, 2006).

Wang, Qing. 'The Commercial Press and Copyright Protection in Pre-modern China (Part 2)' (商务印书馆与中国近代版权保护(下)). *Publishing Research* 1 (1993), 55–58.

Wang, Qing. 'A Preliminary Study of Yan Fu and Zhang Yuanji's Copyright Thoughts' (严复、张元济版权思想初探). *Law Science Magazine* 4 (1992), 39–40.

Wang, Tay-sheng. 'Translation, Codification, and Transplantation of Foreign Laws in Taiwan'. *Washington International Law Journal* 25(2) (2016), 307–330.

Wang, Wei. 'Historical Evolution of National Treatment in China'. *International Lawyer* 39 (2005), 759–780.

Wang, Yangchuan, and Nie, Shihai. 'Turning over The Dusty History – Stories of The Copyright Code of the Great Qing Dynasty' (翻开尘封的历史 –《大清著作权律》的那些故事). *Fortune Today-China Intellectual Property* 11 (2010), 34–36.

Wu, Shulin. 'The Conditions of the Judicial and Administrative Protection of Copyright in China'. *Duke Journal of Comparative & International Law* 9(1) (1998), 241–248.

Yan, Fu. 'Petition to Minster of The Ministry of Education on Copyright' (與管學大臣論版權書) in Zhou, Lin and Li, Mingshan. *Research Documents on The History of Copyright in China* (中国版权史研究文献) (Beijing: China Fangzheng Press, 1999), 46–48.

Yan, Fu. 'Discussion on Copyright with Baixi Zhang' (與管學大臣論版權書) in Zhou and Li, Zhou, Lin and Li, Mingshan. *Research Documents on The History of Copyright in China* (中国版权史研究文献) (Beijing: China Fangzheng Press, 1999), 46–48.

Yan, Fu. 'Letters to Yuanji Zhang No.8' (与张元济书（八）) in *Yan Fu Collection*, ed. Shi Wang, vol. 3 (Shanghai:Chung Hwa Book Company, 1986), 538.

Yan, Fu. 'Letter from Quan Lian' (廉泉《与严复书》) in *Supplement of Yan Fu Collection* (严复集补编), eds. Yingxiang Sun and Houfeng Pi (Fuzhou: Fujian Renmin Press, 2004), 373–379.

Yang, Ming. 'Legal System vs. Documents: The Historical Examination on Copyright Law of Qing Dynasty' (制度与文本:《大清著作权律》的历史审视). *Journal of Huazhong University of Science and Technology (Social Science Edition)* 27(5) (2013), 58–66.

Yang, Yiping. 'The 1990 Copyright Law of the People's Republic of China'. *UCLA Pacific Basin Law Journal* 11(2) (1993), 260–284.

Yu, Huachuan. 'Clashes and Reconciliation of Chinese and Western Legal Systems and Thinking – View from the Perspective of The Mixed Court of the International Settlement at Shanghai' (从上海公共租界会审公廨看中西法律制度和思想的冲突与融合) (DPhil thesis, East China Normal University, 2005).

Zhang, Baixi. 'Reply to Lian's Petition on Copyright' (管學大臣批答廉惠卿部郎呈請明定版權由) in Zhou, Lin and Li, Mingshan. *Research Documents on The History of Copyright in China* (中国版权史研究文献) (Beijing: China Fangzheng Press, 1999), 46.

Zhang, Jinqiu, and Jin, Mei. 'The History of Chinese Copyright Legislation' (中国著作权立法史述论). *Legal Review* 2 (1994), 79–83.

Zhang, Xiaoli. 'The Copyright Code of The Great Qing Dynasty' (《大清著作权律》述论). *Academic Research* 9 (2005), 106–111.

Zhou, Lin, and Li, Mingshan. *Research Documents on The History of Copyright in China* (中国版权史研究文献) (Beijing: China Fangzheng Press, 1999).

PART 3

Trademarks, Terroir and the Colonies

CHAPTER 8

The Crystallization of International Norms

A Case Study on Diffusion of Trademark Norms in Early-20th Century China

Ainee Adam

1 Introduction

Trademark protection is inherently territorial in nature. The first wave of globalization in the 19th century, however, saw a marked increase in the trade of merchandises between nations. This inevitably raised concerns regarding trademark, its infringement as well as remedies for such infringements in foreign lands.

The growing importance of trademark protection subsequently persuaded governments to include reciprocal trademark protection clauses in bilateral commercial treaties. This meant that Nation A would provide protection to trademarks from Nation B as per Nation B's law and Nation B would extend similar protection to trademarks from Nation A. While reciprocal protection may, at times, result in better protection for foreign trademarks, it may also result in lesser protection as compared to those given to the local trademarks. This is highly dependent on the level of protection provided by the laws of both Nations A and B.

This method of ensuring international protection of trademarks, however, created convoluted domestic systems of trademark protection as multiple foreign trademark laws operate within one single territory. Therefore, it became necessary to establish an 'international' practice/standard of protecting foreign trademarks without relying on reciprocal clauses in bilateral treaties. This would provide the necessary assurance that foreign trademarks are protected regardless of the territory in which they operate and subsequently further promote international trade. To this end, delegates from various nations participated in discussions for an international treaty and this eventually culminated in the Paris Convention for the Protection of Industrial Property of March 20, 1883 ('Paris Convention').[1]

1 Paris Convention for the Protection of Industrial Property (adopted 20 March 1883) 828 UNTS 305.

 | DOI:10.1163/9789004511439_010

Adopted and signed in 1883 by 11 nations, the Convention ensured that foreign trademarks receive protection similar to those made available to national trademarks in the territory of any of the nations who are party to the Convention. This is achieved via Article 2 of the Convention which provides as follows:

> The subjects or citizens of each of the contracting States shall, as regards patents, industrial designs, trademarks, and trade names, enjoy the advantages that their respective laws now grant, or may hereafter grant, to nationals. Consequently, they shall have the same protection as the latter and the same legal remedy against any infringement of their rights, provided they observe the formalities and conditions imposed upon nationals by the domestic legislation of each State.

Despite the national treatment clause in the Convention, it is acknowledged that foreign trademark owners may still be at a disadvantage due to the first-to-file system used in some nations. With registration being given to those who first filed their application, trademark owners experiencing delays in registering trademarks in foreign countries (due to factors such as time taken to translate the documents to be filed) could potentially lose out in the event an application for the registration of similar mark was filed before the former could do so.

Consequently, the Paris Convention incorporates an additional measure to assist merchants in protecting their trademarks internationally in the form of Article 4. The clause essentially provides trademark owners, who had filed their application for registration in one nation and are applying to file their application in another, with the right to be treated as though they had filed their later application on the same day as the first application was filed. This right, however, is only available for a period of four months from the date of filing of the first application.

These two Articles, therefore, can be seen as the first step towards establishing an international norm for the protection of foreign trademarks. Nevertheless, the norm is only accepted and applied by parties to the Convention. By the turn of the 20th century, only 19 nations have signed the Convention.[2] The

2 The nations consist of Belgium, Brazil, Italy, France, Netherlands, Portugal, Spain, Switzerland, Tunisia, the United Kingdom, Norway, Sweden, the United States, Dominican Republic, Japan, Denmark. Note that Ecuador, Salvador and Guatemala signed the Convention in 1884 but denounced shortly thereafter. See World Intellectual Property Organization, *The Paris Convention for the Protection of Industrial Property from 1883 to 1983* (Geneva: International Bureau of Intellectual Property, 1983) 123.

limited number of nations adhering to the rules or norm in Articles 2 and 4 meant that there was a need for the norm to be accepted by more nations. It is only at that point that the norm would be crystalised as an international norm.

The question that arises, then, is how does one ensure that a norm is accepted by others? One method would be by encouraging more nations to accede to the Paris Convention. The other method would be by way of diffusing the norm to non-signatory nations. The chapter focuses on the latter method as it examines the ways in which the norm is diffused to other nations.

Twining observed that scholarship on diffusion of law, more often than not, are confined to studies involving the transfer of laws at a national level from a developed nation to a less developed nation, be it due to colonialism or otherwise.[3] These studies have created expectations and assumptions such as law is diffused in a structured manner, materializing in the enactment of statutes.

He, however, cautioned against presuming that all diffusion take place within these parameters. According to him, while the above studies represent an ideal model of diffusion of law, it is nonetheless a simplistic (and sometimes, misleading) model. This is because several possible variants may feature in any study of diffusion of law. These include situations where (1) legal concepts or norms (as opposed to statutory law) are diffused and are, therefore, less structured; (2) the diffusion occur in an informal manner; and (3) the recipient nation received the subject matter of diffusion from multiple sources or nations. Therefore, a comprehensive study of the diffusion of law should consider and include these variants, where relevant.[4]

Bearing in mind Twining's observations, this chapter looks at early-20th century China as a case study. China presents an interesting case study. Driven to introduce trademark law by its complex relationship with various foreign powers, China's experience with trademark protection is fraught with conflicts and disagreements.

3 Note that scholars have used terms such as 'legal transplant' and 'legal reception' as well as 'diffusion of law' in studying the movement of law from one place to another. See for example Nelken, David. "The Meaning of Success in Transnational Legal Transfers" *Windsor Yearbook of Access to Justice* 19 (2001): 349; Orucu, Esin. "Law as Transposition," *International & Comparative Law Quarterly* 51, no. 2 (2002): 205; Graziadei, Michele. "Legal Transplants and the Frontiers of Legal Knowledge," *Theoretical Inquiries in Law* 10 (2009): 723. Twining used the term 'diffusion' to cover all terms used by other scholars to 'underline its potential connection with the study of diffusion in other social sciences.' See Twining, William. "Diffusion of Law: A Global Perspective," *Journal of Legal Pluralism and Unofficial Law* 49 (2004): 1, 5.

4 Twining, "Diffusion of Law: A Global Perspective" 17–34.

There are also potentially various means in which the general concept of trademark protection (including the protection of foreign trademarks) may have been diffused into China. Aside from the formal legal transplant which subsequently resulted in the enactment of the first Chinese trademark law, it is also possible that diffusion could have taken place informally due to interactions between: (1) the foreign consuls and their officers involved in negotiating and drafting the provisions of the first Chinese trademark law and their Chinese counterpart; and (2) foreign missionaries and merchants to the locals.

While these pose interesting possibilities to the study of diffusion of trademark protection concept in China, it is, regrettably, not possible to examine the role of each and every variant in this chapter. Nevertheless, as will be seen later, although the chapter primarily focuses on the diffusion via the first Chinese trademark law and the events surrounding the introduction of this law, the chapter will highlight instances and opportunities for informal diffusion where possible.

Furthermore, while the special focus of this chapter is on the diffusion of the norm of protection of foreign trademarks via the national treatment principle and the right of priority, it is only natural that the general concept of trademarks protection is simultaneously diffused with the norm. Therefore, parts of the chapter discuss the diffusion of the general concept of trademark protection when relevant.

It bears noting that this chapter uses the terms 'diffusion' and 'legal transplant' in its study of the movement of the norm of protection of foreign trademarks into China. These terms are not used interchangeably. The term 'diffusion' is used to broadly cover both the formal and informal spread of the norm into China whereas the term 'transplant' is used to refer specifically to the formal transfer of the norm into China through the enactment of statutory provisions.

Confining its examination to the period between 1902–1905, the chapter is divided into 5 parts. Part 1 consists of the introduction. Part 2 of the chapter first outlines China's relationship with foreign powers between mid-19th century to early-20th century to provide an insight into the reason why China agreed to protect foreign trademarks. Part 3 subsequently analyses the means in which the norm is diffused in China by examining the Experimental Regulations for Trademark Registration 1904 in general and provisions related to protection of foreign trademarks specifically. Part 4 looks at the events that transpired shortly after the introduction of the Regulations. Part 5 concludes the chapter.

It should be noted that due to the existing in-depth historical studies tracing the introduction of trademark law into China during the turn of the

20th century,[5] the chapter will not re-trace this history. It will, instead, rely on these historical accounts in its analyses of the diffusion of the norm of protection of foreign trademarks in early-20th century China.

2 The Qing Government and Its Treaties with Foreign Powers

Ruling China from 1644 to 1912, the Qing Dynasty has generally been opposed to opening China up to foreign trade. Employing the Canton system, the Qing government restricted foreign trade solely to the port in Canton and such trade was permitted only with a group of Chinese merchants licensed by the imperial court.[6]

This, however, changed when foreign merchants began selling opium to the Chinese. Recognizing the destructive effects of opium to China, its economy and its people, the Qing government took measures to stop the sale of opium in China. This later brought about the first Opium War (1839–1842) between China and Britain.[7]

Greatly outmatched by the British military forces, the Qing government was defeated and was subsequently compelled to sign the Treaty of Nanking 1842 ('1842 Treaty') with Britain to end the war.[8] The Treaty, among other things, saw the Qing government granting the right to British merchants to engage in trade freely in Canton, Amoy, Ning-po, Foochow-fu and Shanghai, heralding China's first official trade relationship with foreign powers.

In order to govern the execution of the 1842 Treaty, the Qing government further signed the Supplementary Treaty of the Bogue 1843 ('Supplementary Treaty 1843') which effectively saw it granting British subjects with extraterritorial rights. These rights essentially grant: (1) British subjects residing and

5 See for example Heuser, Robert. "The Chinese Trademark Law of 1904: A Preliminary Study in Extraterritoriality, Competition, and Late Ch'ing Law Reform," *Oriens Extremus* 22, no. 2 (1975): 183; Alford, William P. *To Steal a Book is an Elegant Offence: Intellectual Property Law in Chinese Civilization* (Stanford: Stanford University Press, 1995); Motono, Eiichi. "Anglo-Japanese Trademark Conflict in China and the Birth of Chinese Trademark Law (1923) 1906–1926," *East Asian History* 37 (2011): 9.

6 See Carroll, John M. "The Canton System: Conflict and Accommodation in the Contact Zone," *Journal of the Royal Asiatic Society Hong Kong Branch* 50 (2010): 51 for more on the Canton system.

7 See Cassan, Benjamin. "William Jardine: Architect of the First Opium War," *Historia* 14 (2005): 106 for more on the first Opium War.

8 See for example Nield, Robert. "Treaty Ports and Other Foreign Stations in China," *Journal of Royal Asiatic Society Hong Kong Branch* 50 (2010): 123 for more on the Treaty of Nanking 1842.

trading in China immunity from local criminal laws; and (2) the British consul with the right to enforce English criminal laws on them. The Supplementary Treaty further granted Britain with most favoured nation treatment which eventually saw the Qing government expanding the scope of the immunity to cover civil laws.[9]

These two treaties marked the beginning of a series of what is later known as 'unequal treaties' as the Qing government then entered into multiple bilateral commercial treaties with various foreign powers. Many, if not all, of the subsequent treaties included clauses granting either extraterritorial rights and/or most favoured nation treatment to that foreign power.[10]

The special status granted to these foreign residents, deemed to be an affront to the Qing government and its sovereignty, could be said to have been the precursor to the introduction of trademark law in China. This, however, is a matter to be discussed shortly in the chapter. At this point in time, it is useful to briefly turn our attention to the concept of trademark in China.

Historians have found evidence that trademarks were used in China even as early as the Warring States period (403–221 BC) while there were recorded accounts of judgments on trademark infringement from the 16th century.[11] Nevertheless, trademarks and their protection was a highly localized matter, governed primarily by the industry itself and commercial guilds. This system was understandably adequate in an era where local merchandises were the primary subject matter of trade.

Historical accounts of mid-19th century China, however, tell of growing Chinese interests in foreign goods, be it imported or produced locally in foreign-owned factories.[12] This, among other things, led to unauthorised uses

---

9 Read together Article VIII of the Supplementary Treaty of the Bogue 1843 with Article XXV of the Treaty of Wangxia (1844) signed between the Qing Government and the United States which granted, among other things, the latter with jurisdiction to try both civil and criminal cases involving American subjects residing and trading in China.

10 See for example the Treaty of Whampoa 1844 between the Qing Government and France and the Sino-Portuguese Treaty of Peking 1877 between the Qing Government and Portugal.

11 Shao, Ke. "Look at My Sign! – Trademarks in China from Antiquity to the Early Modern Times," *Journal of the Patent and Trademark Office Society* 87, no. 9 (2005): 683. Scholars, however, have more popularly regarded the 'white rabbit' logo used during the Northern Song Dynasty (960–1127) to be the first trademark in China. See for example Ran Ruixue, "Well-known Trademark Protection in China: Before and After the TRIPS Amendments to China's Trademark Laws," *Pacific Basin Law Journal* 19, no. 2 (2002): 231, 232; Eckhardt, Giana M., and Bengtsson, Anders. "A Brief History of Branding in China," *Journal of Macromarketing* 30, no. 3 (2010): 210, 215; Peng Yang 彭洋, "Zhongguo jindai shangbiao lifa yanjiu 中国近代商标立法研究_彭洋 [Study on the Legislation of Trademark in Modern China]" (Master Thesis, Zhengzhou University 2013) 5.

12 Alford, *To Steal a Book is an Elegant Offence*, 34.

of foreign trademarks, frustrating foreign trademark owners. Although foreign merchants turned to their Consulates for protection, it soon became clear that the Consulates were not able to protect their nationals' trademark effectively without cooperation from the local enforcement authorities.

The British government then took the step to negotiate with the Qing government for a commercial treaty which included a provision on trademark protection. This culminated in the signing of the Treaty between Great Britain and China Respecting Commercial Relations, etc in 1902 ('1902 Britain–China Treaty'). Article VII of the Treaty provides as follows:

> Inasmuch as the British Government afford protection to Chinese trademarks against infringement, imitation, or colorable imitation by British subjects, the Chinese Government undertake to afford protection to British trade-marks against infringement, imitation, or colorable imitation by Chinese subjects.
>
> …

As can be seen, the clause compelled the Qing government to ensure that protection is provided to British trademarks against infringement, imitation and colorable imitation by Chinese subjects. In return, the British Government would provide reciprocal protection to Chinese trademarks.

Considering that China had some form of localized trademark protection and somewhat benefitted from counterfeit goods, it may appear strange for the Qing government to agree to protect foreign trademarks to its detriment. This is even more so when the protection of Chinese trademarks in foreign land was probably not a matter of great concern to the Qing government at that time.[13]

Article XII of the 1902 Britain–China Treaty, however, sheds more light onto the Qing government's decision to sign the treaty:

> China having expressed a strong desire to reform her judicial system, and to bring it into accord with that of Western nations, Great Britain agrees to give every assistance to such reform, and she will also be prepared to relinquish her extraterritorial rights when she is satisfied that the state of the Chinese laws, the arrangement for their administration, and other conditions warrant her in so doing.

13 At that time, China was grappling with issues such as the influx of foreign treaties and the various terms of the treaties affecting China and its sovereignty. Furthermore, relatively few Chinese immigrants were in foreign land with most of them being labourers and not traders. It is, therefore, unlikely that trademark protection in foreign land was a matter of any urgency to the Chinese and their Government. See also ibid fn 54, 144.

As discussed earlier, extraterritorial rights provided immunity to foreign residents living and trading in China from the operation of Chinese laws. The rights also resulted in, in some instances, the establishment of Consulate courts hearing cases and enforcing laws other than laws of the territory. At times, even Chinese subjects were subjected to foreign laws where disputes involved both Chinese subjects and foreign residents.[14] Therefore, the offer to relinquish its extraterritorial rights was understandably attractive to the Qing government.

Nevertheless, it bears noting that the British government's offer came at a cost. By signing the treaty, the Qing government agreed to introduce trademark law capable of protecting foreign trademarks. Furthermore, and perhaps more importantly, the law and its implementation should first receive approval from the British government before the extraterritorial rights were relinquished. This effectively bound China to some indirect form of colonialism.

In the following year, China entered into bilateral treaties with Japan and the United States ('US'). Similar to the 1902 Britain–China Treaty, the Japanese and the US governments offered to relinquish their extraterritorial rights as a quid pro quo for the introduction of trademark law and protection of foreign trademarks.[15]

These treaties thus marked the Qing government's first formal and international obligations to introduce modern trademark law into its legal system. The following part focuses on the diffusion of the norm of protecting foreign trademarks into Chinese territory through the first Chinese trademark law.

3 Experimental Regulations for Trademark Registration 1904 (China)

Shortly after the Qing government signed the treaties with Britain, Japan and the US, the Chinese Ministry of Commerce delegated the task of drafting a set of trademarks regulations to the Chinese Maritime Customs Office ('Customs Office'). It is worth noting that the Customs Office, at that time, was not only largely under the control of the foreigners but it was also headed by a British.[16]

---

14 See Quigley, Harold Scott. "Extraterritoriality in China," *The American Journal of International Law* 20, no. 1 (1926): 46, 57–59; Alford, *To Steal a Book is an Elegant Offence*, 32–33.

15 See Articles v and xi of the Sino-Japan Treaty for the Extension of Commercial Relations, 1903, Articles ix and xv of the Treaty between the United States and China for the Extension of Commercial Relations between Them, 1903.

16 Qiang, Hou 侯强. "Jindai Zhongguo Shangbiao Lifa de Tezheng Ji Qi Shehui Xiaoying 近代中国商标立法的特征及其社会效应_侯强 [Characteristics of Modern China's Trademark Legislation and its Social Effects]" *Zhongguo Kuangye Daxue Xuebao* (*Shehui*

It is, therefore, not surprising that the draft submitted by the Customs Office (specifically, Sir Robert Hart, the Inspector-General of the Customs Office) primarily protected British interests. Neither Chinese nor other foreign powers' interests were adequately addressed in the draft. The draft was naturally rejected by the Ministry of Commerce as well as other foreign powers. The chapter will occasionally refer to this first draft ('Hart's Recommendations') when relevant.[17]

The Ministry of Commerce then, with the aid of two Japanese advisors, drafted and introduced its own set of trademarks regulations: Experimental Regulations for Trademark Registration 1904 ('1904 Regulations'). While it was designed to regulate the registration of trademarks as well as their protection thereof, the 1904 Regulations was provisional in nature, meant to serve only as trial regulations. This is probably due to the clause in the 1902 Britain–China Treaty (and its counterparts in the treaties with Japan and the US in 1903) which required the law introduced to first meet their approval prior to relinquishment of extraterritoriality rights.

With a total of 28 Articles and 23 other supplementary rules, the 1904 Regulations is relatively intricate. Nevertheless, for the purposes of the current discussions, the chapter focuses only on selected provisions which are directly related to the norm of protection of foreign trademarks.

3.1 *National Treatment Principle*

Beginning with Article 1 of the 1904 Regulations, the provision defined trademark as those possessing particularly distinctive graphics, words and/or marks. It also made it mandatory for all merchants (Chinese and foreigners) to register their marks with the trademark registration bureau. The right to exclusive use of the trademarks is granted upon such registration.

An important point is established by this provision, that is, the 1904 Regulations do not discriminate between foreign and local trademarks. In other words, it essentially incorporates the principle of national treatment as per the 'international' norm at that time.

The approach taken by the 1904 Regulations marked a significant departure from that which is observed to have been adopted in Hart's

---

Kexue Ban) 1 (2009): 114, 115; Zuo, Xu Chu 左旭初. "Woguo Di Yi Bu Shangbiao Fagui Dansheng Shimo 我国第一部商标法规诞生始末_左旭初 [The Beginning and the End of my Country's First Trademark Legislation]" *Zhonghua shangbiao* 4 (2014): 61, 62.

17 The author was not able to obtain a copy of the full text of Hart's Recommendations despite all efforts to do so. All references to Hart's Recommendations in this article are, therefore, based on available literature referring to the same, for example, Heuser, "The Chinese Trademark Law of 1904" 183.

Recommendations. Heuser, in his study of the 1904 Regulations, observed that Hart's Recommendations was drafted to protect the various marks used in China including those which fall outside the definition of trademark in the UK.[18] While Chinese trademarks were included in the Recommendations, the inclusion was noted to have been merely perfunctory and that most of the protection measures were directed at foreign trademarks.[19] It is, therefore, evident that Hart's Recommendations was primarily aimed at protecting British interests and not to establish a set of trademark regulations which is consistent with the trademark norms at that time.

Based on this, it can be said that the principle of national treatment in Article 1 of the 1904 Regulations could not be attributed to Hart's Recommendations. The question that arises, then, is, how was the norm diffused to China or phrased differently, to whom can we attribute this diffusion? Scholars have noted that the Ministry of Commerce was reportedly dissatisfied with the categories of marks recognized in Hart's Recommendations due to the apparent biasness towards British marks.[20] The dissatisfaction thus prompted the Ministry to remove the categories and accorded every mark with fair treatment in the 1904 Regulations.

Therefore, it is possible that Article 1 was drafted without any specific reference to the Paris Convention or any other foreign trademark laws. Yet, it is also possible that the Ministry of Commerce had adopted the approach in Article 1 from other foreign trademark laws as it had referred to several other foreign trademark laws in drafting the 1904 Regulations.[21] The source of Article 1 or the

18 Heuser, "The Chinese Trademark Law of 1904" 193.

19 Ibid; Alford, *To Steal a Book is an Elegant Offence*, 38; WenTing, Cheng. 'China: Rule-taker or Rule-maker in the International Intellectual Property System?' (PhD Thesis, Australian National University 2018) 42.

20 See part 3(b) for more on the types of marks in Hart's Recommendations. See also Hai, Cui Zhi 崔志海. "Zhongguo Jindai Di Yi Bu Shangbiao Fa De Banbu Ji Qi Yaozhe 中国近代第一部商标法的颁布及其夭折 [The Promulgation of Modern China's First Trademark Law and its Termination]" *Lishi Dang An* 3 (1991): 105, 107; Hai, Qu Chun 屈春海. "Qingmo Zhongwai Guanyu Shangbiao Zhuce Shiban Zhangcheng Jiaoshe Shishi Kaoping 清末中外关于_商标注册试办章程_交涉史实考评_屈春海 [Evaluation of the History of Negotiations Regarding 'Experimental Regulations for Trademark Registration 1904 (China)' between China and Foreign Countries in the late Qing Dynasty]" *Lishi Dang An* 4 (2012): 87, 89.

21 Rong, Cai Xiao, and Ping, Wang Guo 蔡晓荣. "Wanqing Shiqi de Shewai Shangbiao Qinquan Jiufen 晚清时期的涉外商标侵权纠纷_蔡晓荣 [Foreign Trademark Infringement Disputes in the late Qing Dynasty]" *Xueshu Yanjiu* 9 (2005): 101, 104; Lan, Yao Xiu 姚秀兰 and Lin, Zhang Hong 张洪林. "Jindai Zhongguo Shangbiao Lifa Lun 近代中国商标立法论_姚秀兰 [A Study on Modern Chinese Trademark Legislation]" *Fazhi Lun Cong* 21 no. 2, (2006): 85; Peng, "Zhongguo jindai shangbiao lifa yanjiu" 3, 6.

national treatment principle in the first Chinese trademark law is, therefore, currently indeterminate.

3.2 *First-to-File System and the Right of Priority*

Article 6 of the 1904 Regulations provides that in the event that there are two or more applications for registration of the same mark for the same or similar product, the first application filed will be registered.

It is clear from this provision that the 1904 Regulations expressly adopts the first-to-file system. Again, this is unlike the approach incorporated into Hart's Recommendations. While the Recommendations allow for registration of trademarks, it also provides trademark protection to unregistered trademarks through the first-to-use system.[22] This is evident in Article 8 of the Recommendations which extended protection to: (1) foreign trademarks registered in foreign countries and used in China; as well as (2) foreign trademarks used in China but unregistered in foreign countries. Therefore, the first-to-file system could not have originated from the Recommendations.

Motono, in his study of Japan's role in the drafting of the 1904 Regulations, highlighted that the Qing government's decision to introduce the first-to-file system may be attributed to the Japanese advisors who assisted the Chinese Ministry of Commerce in preparing the 1904 Regulations and subsequently, the Trademark Law of Japan 1899 ('1899 Japanese law').[23] According to him, the advisors were instructed by the Japanese government to transplant this system (which is also used in the 1899 Japanese law) into China's trademark law to protect Japan's interests. He explained that Japanese merchants, at that time, were counterfeiting Western merchandises while the Chinese merchants, on the other hand, were producing counterfeits of Japanese merchandises.

Therefore, the use of the first-to-file system in the 1904 Regulations arguably facilitates Japanese merchants in protecting their trademarks provided they registered the trademarks (albeit forged or counterfeit) first. This would protect their merchandises from being counterfeited and yet enable them to continue producing counterfeits of Western merchandises.[24] Unsurprisingly,

---

22 Qu, "Qingmo Zhongwai Guanyu Shangbiao Zhuce Shiban Zhangcheng Jiaoshe Shishi Kaoping" 89.

23 See Article 8 of the Trademark Law of Japan 1899 which similarly provides for the first-to-file system.

24 Motono, "Anglo-Japanese Trademark Conflict in China and the Birth of Chinese Trademark Law" 11. See also Heuser, "The Chinese Trademark Law of 1904" 209; Peng, Zhang 张鹏. "Guizhi Shangbiao Eyi Qiangzhu Guifan de Tixihua Jiedu 规制商标恶意抢注规范的体系化解读 [Systematic Interpretation of the Regulations that Regulate the Standard of Malicious Registration of Trademarks]" *Zhishi Chanquan* 7 (2018): 17, 18. It should

the Western powers were unhappy about this and objected to the implementation of 1904 Regulations. This, however, will be discussed later in the chapter.

Prior to proceeding further in examining the 1904 Regulations, it must be pointed out here that Motono's account sheds some light on to the trademark situation in the East Asian region in the early 20th century. While historical accounts commonly relate locals' understanding and appreciation for local trademarked goods, it is apparent that local merchants were aware of the value of foreign trademarked goods and the opportunities to be had seeing that foreign trademarked goods were relatively 'unprotected'. The absence of laws protecting foreign trademarks, coupled with demand from locals and in some circumstances, government support, created a chain of chain of counterfeiters in the region. It is, therefore, unsurprising that foreign merchants and their governments viewed trademark protection to be a matter of particular urgency.

Although the 1904 Regulations embodied the first-to-file system, there are several exceptions to it. Article 8(c), for example, bars the registration of trademark if the mark has been publicly used by another in China for a period of more than two years prior to the present application. Based on this, it can be seen that notwithstanding the first-to-file system, the 1904 Regulations provides some measure of protection to trademarks which were unregistered but in use.

Nevertheless, this protection is somewhat limited as Article 8(c) further provides that if such mark has been registered for a period of three years without any objection, then the registration of that trademark will not be annulled. This means that if the mark has been registered by an infringer and the owner failed to object to such registration within a period of three years from the date of the registration, the owner is deemed to have lost his right to that trademark.

Another exception, and the focus of this chapter, is Article 7 which provides as follows:

> For a trademark that has already been registered in a foreign country, within four months from the date of its registration, the applicant who petitions the trademark for registration may recognize the date of its original registration in the foreign country.

At first glance, the provision may seem unremarkable. It essentially incorporates the right of priority and allows applicants a grace period of four months to file its application to register their trademarks and yet be given priority over

be noted that majority of the literature on the drafting history of the 1904 Regulations do not mention Japan's role in the drafting.

other applications. However, a closer look at the provision from the historical and comparative aspects would show that Article 7 is fascinating.

Firstly, as discussed earlier, the first-to-file system in the 1904 Regulations seemed to have been transplanted from the 1899 Japanese law. It would, therefore, be reasonable to assume that Article 7 could similarly be attributed to the 1899 Japanese law.

At this juncture, we should turn our attention briefly to Japan. Historical accounts of intellectual property law in Japan relate that, similar to China, the Japanese government entered into several bilateral (unequal) treaties with foreign powers in the late-19th century. The treaties essentially required the Japanese government to either permit the registration of foreign patents or accede to the Paris Convention as well as the Berne Convention for the Protection of Literary and Artistic Works. Deeming that accession to the Conventions would be a better option for Japan, the Japanese government became party to the Conventions in 1899.[25]

This promptly led to the amendment of the Japanese trademark law. A clause on the right of priority, consistent with the requirements in Article 4 of the Paris Convention, was thus incorporated into the domestic trademark system in the form of Article 9 of the 1899 Japanese Law.

Based on this, a rough trail of the diffusion of the concept of right of priority can be mapped. Starting as a concept embodied in an international convention, the right of priority was first diffused to Japan due to the treaties signed between the Japanese government and foreign powers and its subsequent accession to the Paris Convention. Upon adoption in the 1899 Japanese Law, the concept, then, arguably, found its way to China via the Japanese advisors to the drafting team at the Chinese Ministry of Commerce.

Secondly, a careful comparison between Article 7 of the 1904 Regulations with its counterparts in the Paris Convention, the Patents, Designs and Trademarks Act 1883 (UK) ('1883 UK Act') as well as the 1899 Japanese Law would show that the Chinese provision is surprisingly revolutionary.

Article 4 of the Paris Convention provides as follows:

> [1] A person who has duly filed an application for … the registration of a trade mark, in one of the Contracting States, shall enjoy, for the purpose of filing in the other States, and subject to the rights of third parties, a right of priority during the periods hereinafter stated.
>
> [2] …

25 Ganea, Peter, and Nagaoka, Sadao. "Japan," in Goldstein, Paul, and Straus, Joseph. *Intellectual Property in Asia: Law, Economics, History and Politics*, (Heidelberg: Springer, 2009) 130, 134.

> [3] The above-mentioned periods of priority shall be … three months … for trade marks. They shall be increased by one month for overseas countries.

Section 103 of the 1883 UK Act, on the other hand, provides as follows:

> If Her Majesty is pleased to make any arrangement with the government or governments of any foreign state or states for mutual protection of … trade marks, or any of them, then any person who has applied for protection for any … trade mark in any such state, shall be entitled … to registration of his … trade mark … under this Act, in priority to other applicants; and such … registration shall have the same date as the date of protection obtained in such foreign state.
>
> Provided that his application is made, … in the case of trade mark within four months, from his applying for protection in the foreign state with which the arrangement is in force.

Finally, Article 9 of the 1899 Japanese Law provides as follows:

> Any person filing an application for registration of a trademark in a country of the Paris Convention for the Protection of Industrial Property Rights shall file an application for registration of the same trademark within four months, provided that such application shall have the same effect as if it had been filed on the date of the initial application.

As can be seen, there are obvious similarities between Article 7 of the 1904 Regulations and Article 4 of the Paris Convention, Section 103 of the 1883 UK Act and Article 9 of the 1899 Japanese Law. There is, however, a slight but significant variant in these provisions.

Referring first to Article 4 of the Paris Convention and Article 9 of the 1899 Japanese Law, it is clear that the respective provisions are available only to trademark owners whose nations are party to the Convention. Section 103 of the 1883 UK Act, on the other hand, expressly provides that the right is available only to applicants whose governments had agreement with the British Government for mutual protection of trademarks. Therefore, similar to the Paris Convention and the Japanese Law 1899, the right of priority granted by the 1883 UK Act is limited to applicants from certain nations.

Turning back to Article 7 of the 1904 Regulations, it is interesting that there is no such limitation and a further examination of the 1904 Regulations as a whole yields the same result. This is significant when considering that the existing norm was to grant right of priority only to trademark owners from selected nations. This is despite the Paris Convention's general objective for establishing the norm, that is, to provide international protection to trademarks.

From one perspective, it may be argued that Article 7 of the 1904 Regulations appeared to be more advanced than its counterparts. It could even be said that the provision realized the Paris Convention's objective, even more so than the Article 4 of the Convention itself.

However, a look at the history of China provides a more sobering speculation. As discussed in part 2, foreign trade was permitted in some ports in China as a result of the Qing government's defeat in the first Opium War and the subsequent signing of treaties. Furthermore, the 1904 Regulations was introduced due to pressure from the foreign powers via the treaties and not due to an internal need for such law. It is, therefore, unlikely that the 1904 Regulations could incorporate measures superior to the Paris Convention and embodying the very objective of the Paris Convention. It is more likely that the Chinese drafters of the 1904 Regulations were unfamiliar with, among other things, the legal terminology used and were, consequently, unaware of the significance of the clause. It may also be possible that the drafters were ill-advised by their foreign advisors who stand to benefit from the broadly drafted clause.

In the absence of evidence or documents shedding light onto the matter, however, the possible rationale(s) underpinning the drafting of Article 7 is likely to remain as mere speculation. Nevertheless, Article 7 is most likely sourced from the 1899 Japanese Law, which in turn, came from the Paris Convention.

4 Events Transpiring after the 1904 Regulations

Notwithstanding the intentional or unintentional advancement made by the 1904 Regulations to the trademark system, the Regulations was met with resistance from both the Chinese and Western powers. Again, all parties were dissatisfied with the set of regulations introduced.

The Chinese viewed the 1904 Regulations to be too foreign-centric.[26] For example, on the face of it, the 1904 Regulations does not discriminate between Chinese and foreign trademarks, thereby protecting both Chinese and foreign interests. However, bearing in mind that the Chinese merchants were most

26 Peng, "Zhongguo jindai shangbiao lifa yanjiu" 3, 6; Zuo, "Woguo Di Yi Bu Shangbiao Fagui Dansheng Shimo" 61.

probably unfamiliar with the Western concept of trademark registration,[27] the 1904 Regulations, arguably, placed them at a disadvantage. This is further accentuated by Article 19 which provides for the payment of compensation in the event of trademark infringement.

The Western powers, on the other hand, were against provisions such as the mandatory registration requirement. One of the reasons for this is that registration fee of all existing trademarks would potentially cost the owners between 10,000 to 20,000 taels, an amount considered to be prohibitive by many. This is even more so when the Western merchants were not willing to incur any costs to avail themselves to trademark protection in China.[28]

Furthermore, the Western powers were quick to realize that the registration system would greatly benefit the Japanese merchants who were forging their trademarks and producing counterfeits. This ran counter to their initial objective for requiring the Qing Government to introduce trademark law.

The objections from various parties resulted in the postponement of the implementation of the 1904 Regulations. Therefore, on this front and at this point in time, the Regulations' role in introducing trademark law into Chinese domestic legal system came to a premature end.

Although the 1904 Regulations never came into effect, the issue of trademark regulation continued to be a point of conflict between the Qing government and other foreign powers. A consortium of five nations, consisting of Britain, Italy, Germany, Austrio-Hungary and France was formed. The consortium amended the 1904 Regulations which effectively provided foreign trademarks with protection more than those provided in Hart's Recommendations and submitted the amendment to the Ministry of Commerce in 1905 ('1905 Draft').[29]

27 Note that although the 1904 Regulations never came into effect, the registration offices in Tianjin and Shanghai remained open and continued to receive applications for registration of trademarks. It was noted that in the span of 20 years after the 1904 Act was first introduced, majority of the trademarks registered in China were foreign trademarks. See Hong, Zhao Yong 赵永红. "Zhishi Chanquan Fanzui Yanjiu 知识产权犯罪研究 [Intellectual Property Crime Research]," (China Legal Publishing House, 2004) 210.

28 Heuser, "The Chinese Trademark Law of 1904" 201–202. Heuser also noted that the Japanese merchants have applied for the registrations of trademarks even before the Regulations' projected date of coming into force.

29 Alford, *To Steal a Book is an Elegant Offence*, 40; Sheng, Li Yong 李永胜. "Qingmo Zhongwai Shangbiao Baohu Jiaoshe Shulun 清末中外商标保护交涉述论_李永胜 [A Study on the Negotiation of Trademark Protection between China and Foreign Countries in the late Qing Dynasty]" *Anhui shixue* 6 (2012): 29, 34; Qu, "Qingmo Zhongwai Guanyu ShangbiaoZhuce Shiban Zhangcheng Jiaoshe Shishi Kaoping" 93.

For example, the 1905 Draft was noted to have included, among other things, the recognition (and exemption thereof from registration), of marks used in China prior to 1903.[30] In effect, the 1905 Draft could be said to have incorporated both the first-to-use system – for trademarks used pre-1903 as well as the first-to-file system – for trademarks used post-1903. This is comparable to Article 8(c) of the 1904 Regulations which limits the application of the first-to-use system as discussed earlier in Part 3(b) of this chapter.

In some ways, the recognition of marks used in China pre-1903, or in other words, the first-to-use system, understandably could be seen as a response to the first-to-file system embodied in the 1904 Regulations and to safeguard existing trademarks from the possibility of losing their trademarks due registration by infringers. Yet, it could also be seen as an attempt to diffuse the first-to-use system commonly used in some European nations into China.[31]

The Ministry of Commerce, however, considered the draft to be foreign-centric and rejected it. It sought to negotiate for a more balanced set of trademark regulations, by stating that 'all points affecting the commercial interests of the various nations, as well as those affecting the sovereign rights of China, should be taken into consideration equally and regarded equally.'[32]

As the foreign powers as well as the Qing government failed to come to a compromise,[33] it was only in 1923 that the Chinese trademark law finally came into operation. It should, however, be noted that although the norm of protection of foreign trademarks failed to materialize in the form of national law in the early-20th century, this does not necessarily mean that foreign trademarks remained unprotected in China. This is because the foreign powers had continued to rely on reciprocal trademark protection via bilateral treaties.

The US, for example, in its correspondence with France in October 1905, offered to protect registered French trademarks against infringement by Americans in China provided the French Government reciprocates this protection to registered American trademarks. The protection offered was in the nature of civil proceedings for damages against American infringers at the American Consular Courts. The French Government agreed to this offer and committed to protecting registered American trademarks, with the French

30 Alford, *To Steal a Book is an Elegant Offence*, 40.

31 Ibid.

32 Heuser, "The Chinese Trademark Law of 1904" 203.

33 Li, "Qingmo Zhongwai Shangbiao Baohu Jiaoshe Shulun" 36; Cui, "Zhongguo Jindai Di Yi Bu Shangbiao Fa De Banbu Ji Qi Yaozhe" 104.

Consular Courts being made open for complaints in the event of infringement of registered American trademarks by French citizens.[34]

It is evident from this correspondence that the US and France were committed to protecting trademarks belonging to the other nation even without any involvement from the Qing government. Instances of infringements would be managed by the relevant Consulate.

Nevertheless, considering that the infringements as well as the actions taken to remedy such infringements would take place in China, it would seem reasonable to speculate that these events would be reported or at least made known to those in the trade. Therefore, there is some measure of likelihood that, informally, the diffusion of the concept of trademark (local and foreign) protection would have taken place in some way or another in China by virtue of these private agreements between the foreign powers.

5 Conclusion

The chapter essentially tracks the progression of a set of rules which is originally binding on a limited number of nations (by virtue of the Paris Convention) to being crystallized as an international norm through bilateral treaties and informal means. Focusing on early-20th century China as case study, the chapter examined the circumstances bringing about the introduction of the first Chinese trademark law, the 1904 Regulations and the events transpiring soon thereafter.

The examination has revealed four interesting points. Firstly, while Britain (through the Hart's Recommendations) as well as Japan (through the Japanese advisors to the Ministry of Commerce) tried to transplant their trademark law, these attempts proved to be unsuccessful as neither the Hart's Recommendations nor the 1904 Regulations came into force.

Secondly, as Twining noted, legal norms and concepts could be diffused, instead of statutory law. The diffusion could further take place informally, and not formally. Therefore, although the legal transplant of trademark law was unsuccessful due to the rejection of the Hart's Recommendations, the 1904 Regulations as well as the 1905 Draft, it is arguable that the failure does not necessarily mean that the diffusion of the norm is unsuccessful.

Based on the examination in parts 3 and 4 of the chapter, it is arguable that the entire process of negotiating and drafting the trademark provisions in

34 See Exchange of Notes in regard to the Reciprocal Protection of Trade-Marks in China, October 3, 1905 between France and the United States.

China would have likely provided Qing government officials and Chinese merchants privy to the process, with some exposure and a measure of familiarity with the concept of trademark protection. This, in itself, could amount to an informal form of diffusion of norm.

Thirdly, Twining has observed that multiple sources or nations could be the diffusion agents of a single norm. This is clearly demonstrated in this chapter from the examination of the general perspective of the situation in China as well as the specific provisions in the 1904 Regulations.

From a general standpoint, it can be said that diffusion of the general concept of trademark (local and foreign) protection may be attributed to both the British (through the Hart's Recommendations) as well as the drafting team (including the Japanese advisors) from the Ministry of Commerce. Although the team from the Ministry of Commerce promoted the use of the first-to-file system whereas the British advocated the first-to-use system, it bears noting that the different systems promoted the same objective and diffuses the same norm.

Furthermore, as discussed in part 4, while the drafting of the 1904 Regulations seemed limited to the British and Japanese involvement, other foreign powers such as Italy and France were actively involved in the drafting of the 1905 Draft. The robust discussions between the foreign powers and the Qing government concerning the measures for protecting (foreign) trademarks denotes that French and Italian officials could have potentially contributed to the informal diffusion of the norm. This similarly applies to the private agreements between the foreign powers for reciprocal protection of trademarks.

The detailed examination of the 1904 Regulations in part 3, however, demonstrates that there are two possible sources for the diffusion of the national treatment principle in the 1904 Regulations: the Japanese advisors or the Ministry of Commerce itself. The diffusion of the concept of the right of priority, on the other hand, could potentially be attributed to the Japanese advisors and the 1899 Japanese Law.

Finally, and most importantly, as highlighted in part 3, Articles 1 and 7 of the 1904 Regulations appeared to have embodied the very essence and objective of the Paris Convention. Although it is of no consequence now whether this was done intentionally or otherwise, the matter remains that (1) the Qing government officials were relatively unfamiliar with Western-styled trademark laws; (2) the 1904 Regulations was drafted to satisfy the Qing government's international obligation; (3) the foreign powers exerted relentless pressure on the Qing government for expeditious drafting and introduction of a set of trademark regulations; and (4) the foreign powers were primarily concerned about maximizing their interests. Considering these factors and the Qing government officials' endeavours to protect Chinese interests the best they could, Articles 1 and 7 of the Regulations are remarkable.

In summary, the chapter has outlined the possible paths where formal and informal diffusion of the norm of protection of foreign trademarks could have taken place in early-20th century China by focusing on the first Chinese trademark law and the events surrounding it. At the same time, the chapter marks the crystallizing process of a norm into an international norm.

Acknowledgements

The author is grateful to Professor Luo ChuanYu and Wendy P'ng Yuen Li for their invaluable assistance in accessing and translating Chinese literature. Any mistakes in the chapter are the author's.

Bibliography

Alford, William P. *To Steal a Book is an Elegant Offence: Intellectual Property Law in Chinese Civilization*. Stanford: Stanford University Press, 1995.

Cai, Xiao Rong, and Wang, Guo Ping 蔡晓荣, 王国平. "Wanqing Shiqi de Shewai Shangbiao Qinquan Jiufen 晚清时期的涉外商标侵权纠纷_蔡晓荣 [Foreign Trademark Infringement Disputes in the late Qing Dynasty]" 9 *Xueshu Yanjiu* (2005): 101–5.

Carroll, John M. "The Canton System: Conflict and Accommodation in the Contact Zone." *Journal of the Royal Asiatic Society Hong Kong Branch* 50 (2010): 51–66.

Cassan, Benjamin. "William Jardine: Architect of the First Opium War." *Historia* 14 (2005): 106–17.

Cheng, WenTing. "China: Rule-taker or Rule-maker in the International Intellectual Property System?" PhD Thesis, Australian National University, 2018.

Cui, Zhi Hai 崔志海. "Zhongguo Jindai Di Yi Bu Shangbiao Fa De Banbu Ji Qi Yaozhe 中国近代第一部商标法的颁布及其夭折 [The Promulgation of Modern China's First Trademark Law and Its Termination]."*Lishi Dang An* 3 (1991) 105–9.

Eckhardt, Giana M., and Bengtsson, Anders. "A Brief History of Branding in China." *Journal of Macromarketing* 30, no. 3 (2010): 210–21.

Experimental Regulations for Trademark Registration 1904 (Qing).

Ganea, Peter, and Nagaoka, Sadao. "Japan." In *Intellectual Property in Asia: Law, Economics, History and Politics*, edited by Paul Goldstein and Joseph Straus, 129–54. Heidelberg: Springer, 2009.

Graziadei, Michele. "Legal Transplants and the Frontiers of Legal Knowledge." *Theoretical Inquiries in Law* 10 (2009): 723–43.

Heuser, Robert. "The Chinese Trademark Law of 1904: A Preliminary Study in Extraterritoriality, Competition, and Late Ch'ing Law Reform." *Oriens Extremus* 22, No. 2 (1975): 183–210.

Hou, Qiang 侯强. "Jindai Zhongguo Shangbiao Lifa de Tezheng Ji Qi Shehui Xiaoying 近代中国商标立法的特征及其社会效应_ 侯强 [Characteristics of Modern China's Trademark Legislation and its Social Effects]." *Zhongguo Kuangye Daxue Xuebao (Shehui Kexue Ban)* 1 (2009): 114–8.

Ke, Shao. "Look at My Sign! – Trademarks in China from Antiquity to the Early Modern Times." *Journal of the Patent and Trademark Office Society* 87, No. 9 (2005): 654–82.

Li, Yong Sheng 李永胜. "Qingmo Zhongwai Shangbiao Baohu Jiaoshe Shulun 清末中外商标保护交涉述论_李永胜 [A Study on the Negotiation of Trademark Protection between China and Foreign Countries in the late Qing Dynasty]." *Anhui Shixue* 6 (2012): 29–36.

Motono, Eiichi. "Anglo-Japanese Trademark Conflict in China and the Birth of Chinese Trademark Law (1923) 1906–1926." *East Asian History* 37 (2011): 9–26.

Nelken, David. "The Meaning of Success in Transnational Legal Transfers." *Windsor Yearbook of Access to Justice* 19 (2001): 349–66.

Nield, Robert. "Treaty Ports and Other Foreign Stations in China." *Journal of Royal Asiatic Society Hong Kong Branch* 50 (2010): 123–139.

Orucu, Esin. "Law as Transposition." *International & Comparative Law Quarterly* 51, no. 2 (2002): 205–223.

Paris Convention for the Protection of Industrial Property, as last revised at the Stockholm Revision Conference, Mar. 20, 1883, 828 U.N.T.S. 305.

Patents, Designs and Trademarks Act 1883 (UK).

Peng, Yang 彭洋. "Zhongguo jindai shangbiao lifa yanjiu 中国近代商标立法研究_彭洋 [Study on the Legislation of Trademark in Modern China]"(Master Thesis, Zhengzhou University 2013).

Qu, Chun Hai 屈春海. Qingmo Zhongwai Guanyu Shangbiao Zhuce Shiban Zhangcheng Jiaoshe Shishi Kaoping 清末中外关于_商标注册试办章程_交涉史实考评_屈春海 [Evaluation of the History of Negotiations Regarding "Experimental Regulations for Trademark Registration 1904 (China)" between China and Foreign Countries in the late Qing Dynasty]" *Lishi Dang An* 4 (2012): 87–95.

Ran, Ruixue. "Well-known Trademark Protection in China: Before and After the TRIPS Amendments to China's Trademark Laws." *Pacific Basin Law Journal* 19, no. 2 (2002): 231–62.

Supplementary Treaty of the Bogue, Britain-China, October 8, 1843.

Trademark Law of Japan 1899 (Japan).

Treaty between Great Britain and China Respecting Commercial Relations, etc., Britain-China, September 5, 1902.

Treaty of Nanking, Britain-China, August 29, 1842.

Twining, William. "Diffusion of Law: A Global Perspective" *Journal of Legal Pluralism and Unofficial Law* 49 (2004): 1–45.

World Intellectual Property Organization. *The Paris Convention for the Protection of Industrial Property from 1883 to 1983*. Geneva: International Bureau of Intellectual Property, 1983.

Yao, Xiu Lan, and Zhang, Hong Lin 姚秀兰，张洪林. "Jindai Zhongguo Shangbiao Lifa Lun 近代中国商标立法论_姚秀兰 [A Study on Modern Chinese Trademark Legislation]" *Fazhi Lun Cong* 21 no. 2 (2006): 85–9.

Zhang, Peng 张鹏. "Guizhi Shangbiao Eyi Qiangzhu Guifan de Tixihua Jiedu 规制商标恶意抢注规范的体系化解读 [Systematic Interpretation of the Regulations that Regulate the Standard of Malicious Registration of Trademarks]" *Zhishi Chanquan* 7 (2018): 17–32.

Zhao, Yong Hong 赵永红. "Zhishi Chanquan Fanzui Yanjiu 知识产权犯罪研究 [Intellectual Property Crime Research]." China Legal Publishing House, 2004.

Zuo, Xu Chu 左旭初. "Woguo Di Yi Bu Shangbiao Fagui Dansheng Shimo 我国第一部商标法规诞生始末_左旭初 [The Beginning and the End of my Country's First Trademark Legislation]" *Zhonghua shangbiao* 4 (2014): 61–3.

CHAPTER 9

The Unusual Extension of Imperial Intellectual Property Laws to Colonies in Africa

Daniel Opoku Acquah

1 Introduction

Despite a growing body of scholarship on the history of intellectual property law in Great Britain, little has been said about the history of intellectual property law in the British colonies. Scholarship that explores the issue has focused on the "white settler" colonies like Australia and New Zealand, those American colonies who attained independence in the eighteenth and early nineteenth centuries, or the Caribbean and Asia[1] (unless otherwise studied from a global perspective).[2] The picture is rather grim when one turns attention to Africa. Compared to other British colonies, the history of intellectual property in Africa is the least explored. The few scholarships that focus on the subject either approach the issue at a more general level (that is, from the perspective of European imperialism), a survey of regional intellectual property organizations and economic communities, or by way of specific treatment of individual countries or topics.[3]

1 *See for instance* Bently, Lionel. "The 'Extraordinary Multiplicity' of Intellectual Property Laws in the British Colonies in the Nineteenth Century," *Theoretical Inquiries in Law* 12, no. 1 (January 2011); Bently, Lionel. "Copyright, Translations, and Relations Between Britain and India in the Nineteenth and Early Twentieth Centuries," *Chicago-Kent Law Review* 82, no. 3 (June 2007): 1181; Suthersanen, Uma, and Gendreau, Ysolde, eds. *A Shifting Empire: 100 Years of the Copyright Act 1911* (Cheltenham: Edward Elgar, 2013); Gervais, Daniel. "The Emergence and Development of Intellectual Property Law in Canada," in Dreyfuss, Rochelle, and Pila, Justine, eds. *The Oxford Handbook of Intellectual Property Law*, (Oxford: Oxford Daniel Acquah, University Press, 2018); Moyse, Pierre-Emanuel. "Canadian Colonial Copyright: The Colony Strikes Back," in ed. Ysolde Gendreau. *An Emerging Intellectual Property Paradigm: Perspectives from Canada*, Gendreau, Ysolde, ed. (Cheltenham: Edward Elgar, 2008); Bond, Catherine. "'Cabined, Cribbed, Confined, Bound in': Copyright in the Australian Colonies," in Alexander, Isabella, and Gómez-Arostegui, H. Tomás, eds. *Research Handbook on the History of Copyright Law*, (Cheltenham: Edward Elgar, 2016).

2 Deere Birkbeck, Carolyn. *The Implementation Game: The TRIPS Agreement and the Global Politics of Intellectual Property Reform in Developing Countries* (Oxford: Oxford University Press, 2008).

3 Yankey, George Sipa-Adjah. *International Patents and Technology Transfer to Less Developed Countries: The Case of Ghana and Nigeria* (Aldershot: Avebury, 1987); Acquah, Daniel.

 | DOI:10.1163/9789004511439_011

This chapter contributes to the literature by examining the extension of Imperial intellectual property laws in the field of technology and culture – namely patents and copyrights – to British colonies in Sub-Saharan Africa[4] from the late nineteenth century to the early twentieth century, critically appraising how British dominion shaped domestic intellectual property laws and culture, and its impact on the social and economic development of Sub-Saharan African nations. It argues that contrary to the narrative that there was no apparent imperial strategy as to the development of colonial intellectual property laws, there seems to have been a certain arrangement regarding Africa, which cannot be merely coincidental. Intellectual property laws were imposed on Sub-Saharan Africa, not borrowed,[5] and there must have been a reason for this. Yet unlike other Crown colonies,[6] the Imperial government did not build local capacity nor institutions for intellectual property in Africa.

"Intellectual Property, Developing Countries and the Law and Policy of the European Union: Towards Postcolonial Control of Development" (PhD diss., IPR University Center, 2017); Okediji, Ruth L. "The International Relations of Intellectual Property: Narratives of Developing Country Participation in the Global Intellectual Property System," *Singapore Journal of International & Comparative Law* 7 (2003); Kongolo, Tsimanga. "Historical evolution of copyright legislation in Africa," *WIPO Journal* 5, no. 2 (2014); Kongolo, Tsimanga. "Historical developments of industrial property laws in Africa", *WIPO Journal* 5, no. 1 (2013); Sikoyo, George M., Nyukuri, Elvin, and Wakhungu, Judi W. *Intellectual Property Protection in Africa: Status of Laws, Research and Policy Analysis in Ghana, Kenya, Nigeria, South Africa and Uganda* (Nairobi: Acts Press, 2006); Ncube, Caroline B. "Three Centuries and Counting: The Emergence and Development of Intellectual Property Law in Africa," in Dreyfuss, Rochelle, and Pila, Justine, eds. *The Oxford Handbook of Intellectual Property Law*, (Oxford: Oxford University Press, 2018).

4 While the specific scope for this article is Sub-Saharan Africa, for the sake of convenience, I use Sub-Saharan Africa interchangeably with Africa.

5 An exception to this was the South African colonies, which became a dominion in 1910. Known as the Union of South Africa, some of the states had their local copyright laws by 1880. According to the Encyclopaedia Britannica, dominion was the status, prior to 1939, of each of the British Commonwealth countries of Canada, Australia, New Zealand, the Union of South Africa, Eire, and Newfoundland. Although there was no formal definition of dominion status, a pronouncement by the Imperial Conference of 1926 described Great Britain and the dominions as 'autonomous communities within the British Empire, equal in status, in no way subordinate one to another in any aspect of their domestic or external affairs, though united by a common allegiance to the Crown and freely associated as members of the British Commonwealth of Nations.' https://www.britannica.com/topic/dominion-British-Commonwealth.

6 According to an internet source, a Crown Colony was a British overseas territory under the direct authority of the British Crown. As such, a Crown Colony did not possess its own representative government and was not represented in the British Parliament. The colony was administered by a governor appointed by the Crown and responsible to the colonial office (or its forerunners) and, from 1966 onward to the Foreign and Commonwealth Office in London. https://www.encyclopedia.com/history/encyclopedias-almanacs-transcripts-and-maps/crown-colony.

This led to displaced local knowledge governance and innovation systems, and countries ill-equipped to handle the pressures of the twenty-first-century intellectual property system – contributing to adherence and compliance overdrive in the post-TRIPS era.

To address these points, the chapter draws attention to four developments during this period. Since imperialism and imposition of law underlies aspects of the argument in this chapter, the second Section explores briefly a theory of imperialism and imposition of law. The third Section then examines Africa's pre-colonial contact with European countries, the systems of innovation and knowledge governance in place and how this system stood in contrast to the Western conception of intellectual property. Section four addresses the question of the devolution of Imperial intellectual property laws in the dominions (and special Crown colonies) during the nineteenth century, pointing to the degree of autonomy that these "special" colonies enjoyed from Britain. This permits us to compare the variations in how Imperial intellectual property laws were extended to the African colonies during the latter part of the nineteenth century and early twentieth century. Section five thus focuses on the unusual[7] extension of Imperial intellectual laws to the British colonies in Africa. Section six reflects on the implication of the imposition of colonial intellectual property laws on Africa, and in the final section, I conclude.

2 A Theory of Imperialism and the Imposition of Law

European imperialism reached its height during the nineteenth century,[8] the period that many agree international law became a global legal order.[9] For the peoples and scholars of the colonized world, international law expanded when international legal rules, doctrines or ideas were imposed outside Europe to

7 By "unusual", I mean to uncover the level of deviation of Britain when it comes to the extension or application of its intellectual property laws to the African colonies during the period under investigation – compared to, for instance, how it was done in the dominions.

8 Anghie, Antony. "Imperialism and International Legal Theory," in Orford, Anne, and Hoffmann, Florian, eds. *The Oxford Handbook of the Theory of International Law*, (Oxford: Oxford University Press, 2016), 158.

9 Becker Lorca, Arnulf. "Universal International Law: Nineteenth-Century Histories of Imposition and Appropriation," *Harvard International Law Journal* 51, no. 2 (Summer 2010); Anghie, Antony. "Finding the Peripheries: Sovereignty and Colonialism in Nineteenth Century International Law," *Harvard International Law Journal* 40, no. 1 (Winter 1999). For a general discussion, *see also* Anghie, Antony. *Imperialism, Sovereignty, and the Making of International Law* (Cambridge: Cambridge University Press).

enable and justify formal or informal colonialism.[10] For them, imperialism was a central feature of international law that was continuously deployed against them by European states to further their interest.[11] Yet, for international lawyers mostly from Europe, international law expanded when non-European nations were added as new members of the international community.[12] Eager to make their contribution to the management of colonial relations, these scholars who are understood to constitute the canon of the discipline,[13] had to grapple with questions about the personality of non-European entities, the relationship between law and "civilization" and the universality of norms they associated with international law.[14] In this regard, Antony Anghie argues that colonial questions or problems were seen as largely incidental, practical or administrative.[15] Yet, Anghie also contends that "some of the most central concerns of international legal theorizing cannot be properly explored without taking imperialism into account."[16] Thus, in recent times, there has been a call for the recognition of the expansion of international law to be seen both as an expansion through admission and imposition, that is, acknowledging the coexistence of the regimes of equality and inequality.[17]

Indeed, during the period when the non-European world was colonized or subjected to informal imperialism, international law recognized the sovereignty of Western states while denying legal personality to non-Western societies, legalizing the acquisition of overseas territories, based on discovery and occupation, or through treaties in which the societies ceded sovereignty or jurisdiction to Western powers.[18] For example, international law redefined overseas territories as *terra nullius* – that is, territories that are not subjected to the authority of any sovereign and thus can be acquired through occupation.

---

10 Anghie, "Finding the Peripheries," (see n. 9). *See also* Anghie, *Imperialism, Sovereignty* (see n. 9).

11 Anghie, "Imperialism and International Legal Theory," 159 (see n. 8).

12 Lorca, "Universal International Law," 476 (see, n. 9).

13 Anghie, "Imperialism and International Legal Theory," 156 (see, n. 8). (Mentioning eminent scholars such as Francisco de Vitoria, Hugo Grotius, Emer de Vattel and other greats such as John Westlake, James Lorimer, Johann Kaspar Bluntschli).

14 Anghie, 158. (Emphasis added).

15 Anghie, 159.

16 Anghie, 157.

17 Lorca, "Universal International Law," 476 (see, n. 9); Anghie, "Imperialism and International Legal Theory," (see, n. 8).

18 Lorca, "Universal International Law," 477 (see, n. 9). In fact, Lorca argues that Western international lawyers and diplomats, representing their merchants' interests or their states' expansionist policies, deployed the idea of an exclusively European international law to justify the exclusion of non-European entities from the privileges of an international legal order based on sovereign equality.

Once an overseas territory was occupied either through conquest or a treaty, the colonizer could then impose its laws from the metropole on the colonized. Each major colonial power developed a legal rationalization for the imposition of laws – in one form or another of a doctrine of the colonizers' superiority and the alleged inferiority of the colonized.[19] As Schmidhauser asserts, "fundamentally, it was the convergence of modes of conquest and subsequent policies of the imposition of the colonizer's legal culture and institutions which established the enduring influence of the imposed legal system."[20]

Writing in the context of international law and poverty creation, Jason Beckett fervently argues that "international law was forged in the heat of the colonial encounter with others, in the need to justify the exploitation of those others and the expropriation of their natural resources and wealth."[21] Schmidhauser affirms that legal imperialism universally imposed law where economic penetration – whether land tenure or modern trade and commercial development – was at issue.[22] In the field of intellectual property, the Paris and the Berne Conventions could be said to have further facilitated this process regarding Africa.[23] The award of patents in, for instance, the Gold Coast[24]

---

19 Schmidhauser, John R. "Legal Imperialism: Its Enduring Impact on Colonial and Post-colonial Judicial Systems," *International Political Review* 13, no. 3 (July 1992): 331. *See also* Section 5.

20 Schmidhauser, 331.

21 Beckett, Jason. "Creating Poverty," in Orford, Anne, and Hoffmann, Florian, eds. *The Oxford Handbook of the Theory of International Law*, (Oxford: Oxford University Press, 2016), 989.

22 Schmidhauser, "Legal Imperialism," 328 (see, n. 19).

23 The two principal international treaties for intellectual property protection were concluded in 1880s respectively: the first was the Paris Convention for the Protection of Industrial Property, Mar. 20, 1883, 13 U.S.T. 2, 828 U.N.T.S. 107, as last revised at the Stockholm Revision Conference, July 14, 1967, 21 U.S.T. 1538, 828 U.N.T.S. 303 [hereafter Paris Convention]. The Paris Convention governed 'patents, utility models, industrial designs, trademarks, service marks, trade names, indications of source or appellations of origin, and repression of unfair competition.' The second was the Berne Convention for the Protection of Literary and Artistic Works, Sept. 9, 1886, as last revised July 24, 1971, 25 U.S.T. 1341, 828 U.N.T.S. 221. [hereafter Berne Convention], which governed copyright and related rights. For a detailed discussion of the Paris and the Berne Conventions, *see* Section 5.2.

24 In 1821, the United Kingdom Parliament, acting under pressure from anti-slavery interests, dissolved the Company of Merchants and assumed direct control of the Gold Coast forts. On October 17, 1821, Letters Patent were issued giving effect to 1 & 2 Geo IV c.28 and creating a colony called the West African Settlements consisting of the Gold Coast settlements, Sierra Leone and the Gambia with its seat at Freetown. *See* Goldman, Neal M. "Fallible Justice: The Dilemma of the British in the Gold Coast, 1874–1944" (PhD diss., Graduate Center, City University of New York, 2016). For convenience, I use Gold Coast and Ghana interchangeably.

(now Ghana) and Nigeria at a time when there were no local inventions or industrial activities that would meet the requirements for the grant of patents are a telling example.[25] Patenting, which was concentrated in wealthy plantation or gold mining colonies that sought greater productivity, was, therefore, a key part of the economic development of the British Empire.[26] Critics of the intellectual property system, therefore, lament that while the system generates revenue for developed countries, it represents a cost for developing countries that have to pay to access technologies developed by the former.[27]

During the nineteenth century, international law was explicitly allied with power and this power relied on the law to legitimize itself in justifying conquest and dispossession.[28] In the area of intellectual property, this did not end with the decolonization process in Africa during the 1950s and 1960s. Instead, institutional mechanisms put in place by former colonial nations and allied international organizations (such as the World Intellectual Property Organization and the World Trade Organization) ensured neo-colonial penetration.[29] For instance, Schmidhauser, in testing the persistence of legal imperialism and economic penetration post-World War II, found that of the 142 existing countries, 74 (52 per cent) provided legal training similar to that of the former colonial nation; 11 (8 per cent) had their legal professionals trained in the former colonial nation, and 106 (74.6 per cent) had adopted a legal system similar to that of their former colonial nation.[30]

Regarding Great Britain, however, it may be fair to note that its colonial policy was pragmatic in terms of the adaptation of British law. Bryce, has, for instance, observed that British law was imposed in those sectors of each colony where stability, tax revenue, and the flow of inter-colonial and transitional commerce were needed.[31] In Africa, in particular, the British could not also

25 Yankey, *International Patents* (see, n. 3). For a detailed discussion on the subject, *see* Section 5.

26 Graham, Aaron. "Patents and Invention in Jamaica and the British Atlantic Before 1857," *The Economic History Review* 73, no. 4 (July 2020): 940–963. (Emphasis added); Yankey, *International Patents*, 104 (see, n. 3).

27 Melo Araujo, Billy A. *The EU Deep Trade Agenda: Law and Policy* (Oxford: Oxford University Press, 2016), 139; Acquah, "Intellectual Property," (see, n. 3).

28 Anghie, "Imperialism and International Legal Theory," 159 (see, n. 8).

29 Acquah, Daniel. "Technical Assistance as a Hedge to IP Exclusivity," in Griffins, Jonathan, and Mylly, Tuomas, eds. *Global Intellectual Property Protection and New Constitutionalism: Hedging Exclusive Rights*, (Oxford: Oxford University Press, 2021). Available on SSRN at https://papers.ssrn.com/sol3/papers.cfm?abstract_id=3682646.

30 Schmidhauser, "Legal Imperialism," 331 (see, n. 19).

31 Bryce, James. *Studies in History and Jurisprudence* (New York: Oxford University Press, 1901).

eliminate indigenous legal systems. Instead, they generally imposed major elements of their legal system upon the indigenous systems reducing the latter to a secondary status, and further leading to a dual legal system in many areas of law.[32] Even so, when one considers the enduring impact of the imposition of laws, it seems legitimate to ask whether there was any plausible basis for the extension of Imperial intellectual property laws to Africa. Imperialism, when viewed from the perspective of those who have been its subjects, "generates a new epistemology and a new set of questions."[33]

3 Africa's Contact with Europe, Innovation and Knowledge Governance Systems in the Pre-colonial Era

In 1553 the first British ship reached the shores of the Benin River, following the Portuguese who had been trading with the Binis since 1485.[34] The primary reason for the European presence in West Africa was trade, from the time of the Portuguese arrival in the late fifteenth century until the end of the nineteenth century.[35] An ancillary objective was to spread Christianity as part of the European civilizing mission.[36] Thus much of what is known about the innovation and knowledge governance systems of ancient African states and kingdoms come from the works of African historians who rely on the records of the European traders and missionaries,[37] archaeologists, anthropologists, and

32 For a detailed discussion on the duality of colonial legal regime in Africa, *see* Merry, Sally Engle. "Law and Colonialism," *Law & Society Review* 24, no. 4 (1991).

33 Anghie, "Imperialism and International Legal Theory," 159 (see, n. 8).

34 Ryder, Alan Frederick Charles. *Benin and the Europeans 1485–1897* (New York: Humanities Press, 1969); Elias, Taslim Olawale. *Africa and the Development of International Law*, ed. rev. Richard Akinjide (Dordrecht: Nijhoff Publishers, 1988), 12.

35 Feinberg, H.M. "Benin and the Europeans 1485–1897 by A.F.C. Ryder," review of *Benin and the Europeans 1485–1897*, by Alan Frederick Charles Ryder, *African Studies* 4, no. 2 (1971).

36 The doctrine of the 'standard of civilization' has a particular genealogy. As the law of peoples, it emerged in the fifteenth century under a natural law conception and shifted progressively to become a formalized legal order underpinned by positivist legal thought. Western legal scholars developed the doctrine of the standard of civilization to delimit international law's scope and validity. The nineteenth-century positivist international law of civilized nations did not include any formal procedure to determine the 'civilized' status, leaving the admission of new members to the determination of international legal scholars. Positivism and the distinction between civilized and uncivilized peoples served the interest of Western imperialism and colonialism. *See* Lorca, "Universal International Law," 495–6 (see, n. 9).

37 Lorca, 495–6.

development economists.[38] Ryder, for instance, shares an interesting detail about the city of Benin from the account of a missionary who sent a letter through Lourenco Pinto, the captain of a Portuguese ship that carried missionaries, to the Sacra Congregazione at the instance of one Father Montelcone:

> Great Benin, where the king resides, is larger than Lisbon; all the streets run straight and as far as the eye can see. The houses are large, especially that of the king which is richly decorated and has fine columns. The city is wealthy and industrious. It is so well governed that theft is unknown and the people live in such security that they have no doors to their houses. The artisans have their places carefully allocated in the squares which are divided up in such a manner that in one square he counted all together one hundred and twenty goldsmith's workshops, all working continuously.[39]

Taking the period into consideration, the above description reflects an innovative community. Indeed, as noted by Austen and Headrick, the introduction of agriculture and metallurgy to Africa is prehistoric, autonomous and revolutionary process. Ironmaking developed alongside agriculture in West Africa, Ethiopia and the Great Lakes area, and the craft rapidly reached a level of sophistication that rivalled contemporary European and Middle Eastern metallurgy in at least its smelting processes.[40] Forbes account supports the above claim: "outstanding among the negroid African's industries is his work in smelting iron and in manufacturing from the crude metal the tools and weapons upon which depend his agriculture, the fabrication of his wooden utensils, and his supply of weapons for fishing, hunting, and warfare."[41]

On the water, we hear of the dugout canoe, some of which measured up to 80 feet in length and was capable of carrying 100 men or more.[42] There were other types of craft with limited diffusions such as reed boats on Lake Chad, plank boats on the Niger River and dhows on the East African coast.[43] Some of these crafts were said to have reached the size of Viking long-boats or Greek galleys although not as seaworthy as their European counterparts.[44] A structure

38 Austen, Ralph A., and Headrick, Daniel. "The Role of Technology in the African Past," *African Studies Review* 26, no. 3–4 (December 1983): 165.

39 Ryder, *Benin and the Europeans*, 113 (see, n. 34).

40 Austen and Headrick, "The Role of Technology," 165 (see, n. 38).

41 Forbes, Robert J. "The Black Man's Industries," *Geographical Review* 23, no. 2 (April 1933).

42 Forbes.

43 Forbes.

44 Austen and Headrick, "The Role of Technology," 167 (see, n. 38).

in Namoratunga, a megalithic site in northwestern Kenya, constructed around 300 BC suggested that a prehistoric calendar based on detailed astronomical knowledge was in use in eastern Africa.[45] Similarly, Africans possessed wide-ranging knowledge about the therapeutic or medicinal value of plant and biological materials, which is known today as traditional medicinal knowledge, rich cultural life in the art, music, dance, and artefacts, commonly referred to as traditional cultural expressions or folklore.[46]

Arguably, while the mode and systems of technological innovation in medieval Africa was analogous to contemporaneous development in other regions of the world, the communal way of life and systems of social organization as governed by indigenous law – what would later become known as "customary law" in colonial times[47] – would lead to the outcome that while advances were being made in, for instance, technological innovations in Europe, the opposite was happening in Africa.[48] For example, as early as the 15th century, patents were being awarded to inventors in the Republic of Venice.[49] Pamela Long even assert that there is evidence of a few patents in the 13th century.[50] Yet in Africa,

---

45 Lynch, B.M., and Robbins, L.H. "Namoratunga: The First Archeoastronomical Evidence in Sub-Saharan Africa," *Science* 200, no. 4343 (May 1978).

46 Ncube, "Three Centuries and Counting," 411 (see, n. 3).

47 Merry, "Law and Colonialism," 897–98 (see, n. 32). Merry argues that the law of colonized peoples recognized by colonial governments was generally labelled "customary law" and was considered to be indigenous law. Hence, far from being rules handed down from the precolonial period, customary law was a historical product created by the colonial institutions – the outcome of complex intersections of pre-colonial African polities, British law as understood by early administrators, and the creative efforts of emerging African elites who shaped the law to meet needs under changing political and economic conditions.

48 Austen and Headrick, "The Role of Technology," 165 (see, n. 38). Austen and Hedrick asked the difficult question that has also preoccupied historians of ancient Greek and Roman technology, why Africans failed to adopt various "free-floating" technologies that were available to them in pre-colonial and colonial times. To answer this, they identify three stages in the development of African technology to shed light on why things are the way they are: first, the fairly rapid and autonomous emergence and spread of what may be called classical African agricultural and metal-using technologies. Second, a long period of contact with the outside world in which various elements of European and Asian proto-industrial technology (most notably the wheel and the plough) were not adopted, and finally, the last century of colonial and post-colonial regimes, when imported advanced industrial technology entered Africa without being effectively integrated into locally-based system.

49 Long, Pamela O. "Invention, Authorship, 'Intellectual Property,' and the Origin of Patents: Notes Toward a Conceptual History," *Technology and Culture* 32, no. 4 (October 1991): 875–880.

50 Long, 875–880.

pre-colonial commercial legal arrangements with European nations marked its first encounter with Western practices related to intellectual property.[51] Thus, intellectual property rights as conceived in the modern sense did not exist in pre-colonial Africa[52] – although pre-colonial Africans innovated, just as their modern constellations.

Customary law provided and, to an extent, continues to provide knowledge governance systems.[53] Customary law is an established system of immemorial rules which has evolved from the way of life and natural wants of the people.[54] It is said to be living in the sense that communities adapt the rules to their changing circumstances and needs.[55] A distinction can be made between this pre-colonial, organic customary law and the one historically constructed in the colonial era – fixed, formal and written rules enforced by native courts.[56]

While there are many commonalities in the customary laws of indigenous communities, they are all unique. Among these are usually special rules about knowledge governance, the bulk of which is not reduced to writing or even disclosed orally beyond that community,[57] and dating back to the pre-colonial times. An example is the kente cloth of Ghana whose manufacture is the preserve of the Ashanti and Ewe tribes of Ghana. There are rules about when to wear and how to wear Kente cloth for both male and female adults. Similarly, the special *Kete* and *Adowa* dance of Ghana and the *Nwumkoro* music ensemble has been designated as the preserve of Akan tribes. In East Africa, specific composers are regarded to be the custodians of their musical compositions, and some types of artwork and designs are owned by specific community members.[58] Such examples (and countless others which cannot

51 Okediji, "The International Relations," 323 (see, n. 3).

52 See Okediji; Kongolo, "Historical developments of industrial property laws," (see, n. 3); Kongolo, "Historical evolution of copyright," (see, n. 3); Ncube, "Three Centuries and Counting." (see, n. 3).

53 Ncube, "Three Centuries and Counting," 412 (see, n. 3).

54 Ncube, 412 (see, n. 3), citing J.C. Bekker, ed., *Seymour's Customary Law in Southern Africa*, 5th ed. (Cape Town: Juta, 1989).

55 Merry, "Law and Colonialism," 897 (see, n. 32); Himonga, Chuma and Nhlapho, Thandabantu, eds. *African Customary Law in South Africa: Post-Apartheid and Living Law Perspectives* (Cape Town: Oxford University Press Southern Africa, 2014), 27.

56 Merry, "Law and Colonialism," 897–98 (see, n. 32).

57 Ncube, "Three Centuries and Counting," 412 (see, n. 3).

58 Ouma, Marisella. "The Policy Context for a Commons-Based Approach to Traditional Knowledge in Kenya," in Beer, Jeremy de, Armstrong, Chris, Oguamanam, Chidi, and Schonwetter, Tobias, eds. *Innovation and Intellectual Property Collaborative Dynamics in Africa*, (Claremont: University of Cape Town Press, 2014), 132.

be enumerated here due to their oral nature) are what has led some scholars to advocate that customary law continue to have a key role in the regulation of traditional knowledge. In particular, in the design of the appropriate regimes for traditional knowledge, especially, sui generis systems, regardless of the community's location.[59]

According to Oguamanam, traditional knowledge is affirmed in the customary laws and norms of indigenous peoples and categories of local communities as an aspect of their sovereignty and self-determination.[60] Thus, in many indigenous worldviews, the conceit of humankind as an unbridled determiner of the fate of all biotic and abiotic resources is renounced.[61] This may explain why the appropriation logic does not have an exact parallel in indigenous worldviews.[62] In these communities, knowledge is produced and largely held in a context akin to a trust, with balance and sensitivity to virtually all recognized interests in the prevailing socio-cultural and socio-legal order.[63] Also, intangible assets like know-how (for example, knowledge of medicinal products or active ingredients from aerial or underground parts of plants or other plant material or the combination of them, whether in the crude state or as plant preparation or containing natural organic or inorganic active ingredients which are not of plant origin) are often kept as trade secrets or confidential information traditionally.[64]

59 Ncube, "Three Centuries and Counting," 412 (see, n. 3); Kuruk, Paul. "The Role of Customary Law under Sui Generis Frameworks of Intellectual Property Rights in Traditional and Indigenous Knowledge," *Indiana International & Comparative Law Review* 17, no. 1 (2007): 81–83; Dutfield, Graham. "Traditional Knowledge, Intellectual Property and Pharmaceutical Innovation: What's Left to Discuss?" in David, Matthew, and Halbert, Debora. *The Sage Handbook on Intellectual Property*, (Los Angeles: Sage Publications, 2014), Sage.

60 Oguamanam, Chidi. "Wandering Footloose: Traditional knowledge and the 'Public Domain' revisited," *The Journal of World Intellectual Property* 21, no. 3 (March 2018): 2.

61 Oguamanam, 6.

62 Oguamanam, 6.

63 Oguamanam, 6; Okediji, Ruth L. "Negotiating the Public Domain in an International Framework for Genetic Resources, Traditional Knowledge and Traditional Cultural Expressions," in Robinson, Daniel F., Abdel-Latif, Ahmed, and Roffe, Pedro, eds. *Protecting traditional knowledge: The WIPO Intergovernmental Committee on Intellectual Property and Genetic Resources, Traditional Knowledge and Folklore*, (London: Routledge, 2017).

64 Houghton, Peter J., and Mensah, Abraham Y. "Herbal Practitioners and Pharmacists in Ghana," *The Pharmaceutical Journal* 271, no. 7258 (2003): 93–94. *Also see* Manteaw, Samuel O. "Patents and Development in Ghana: Proposals for Change," *University of Ghana Law Journal* 24 (2008–2010): 13–14.

4 Variations in Imperial Devolution of Intellectual Property Laws in the Nineteenth Century – Focus on the Dominions and Other Special Colonies

The extension and application of Imperial intellectual property laws to the colonies varied according to region. A review of some of the literature on the role of law in the colonial process reveals that the British treated their colonies differently in place, time and situation.[65] This is particularly apparent when one looks at the history of intellectual property law in some of the British dominions and colonies. Lionel Bently, however, argues that colonies under British tutelage in the nineteenth century experienced a period in the development of intellectual property law that was uncoordinated and unplanned.[66] Accordingly, there was no imperial law of patents, designs or trademarks.[67] However, upon payment of a small additional fee, letters patent could be extended to include "all His [after 1837 'Her'] Majesty's Colonies and Plantations abroad,"[68] reflecting a desire that the grant has imperial application.[69] The only exception, however, was copyright in books although not without considerable controversy.[70] The above claim gives reason for a closer look at how Britain related to its colonies in intellectual property law-making and the variations thereof. To be able to strike the appropriate comparison, the remainder of this section will focus on the development of patent and copyright laws of the dominions and other colonies apart from the African colonies.

4.1 *Patents*

In the early to the mid-nineteenth century, there emerged serious discussion about the value and effectiveness of extending a patent granted in England to

65 Merry, "Law and Colonialism," 891 (see, n. 32).

66 Bently, "The 'Extraordinary Multiplicity'," 162 (see, n. 1). This Section relies to a large extent on Bentley's contribution to the topic and also Gervais, "The Emergence and Development," (see, n. 1). It is therefore not entirely original.

67 Bently, "Copyright, Translations, and Relations," 163 (see, n. 1).

68 Barrigar, Robert H., and Robinson, Christopher. "Some Notes on the Historical Development of Patent law in Colonial Canada and Other British Colonies," *Intellectual Property Journal* 5 (1990): 392; Bently, "Copyright, Translations, and Relations," 163 (see, n. 1), citing Macleod, Christine. *Inventing The Industrial Revolution: The English Patent System, 1660–1800* (Cambridge: Cambridge University Press, 1988); Select Committee on the Law Relative to Letters Patent for Inventions, 1829, H.C. 332, at 173–75 (examples), 213–16 (forms).

69 Bently, "The 'Extraordinary Multiplicity'," 163 (see, n. 1).

70 Bently, 163.

the colonies.[71] One camp advocated for the need for the colonies to choose for themselves whether to grant patent rights and, if so, their scope.[72] The other camp argued for patents to be applied in the colonies – justifying that the colonies would benefit from such a regime while its absence could undercut businesses in Britain.[73] In the aftermath of the 1852 Patent Law Amendment Act, which streamlined the grant of a single British patent, the question arose within the Patent Office whether these unitary patents should be extended to the colonies. It was decided that British grants should not, in general, be extended and none were.[74]

Despite the decision not to extend British patents, there was certain indirect coordination of legislation with the colonies. Even if "unintended", a consequence of the latter was the formulation of local laws. Bently has noted, for example, how a circular issued by the Colonial Office could "inform a colony of a particular change in British law, inspiring perhaps a local legislative response, or request information on the protection available to a British citizen, thus suggesting, perhaps, that such protection was necessary or desirable."[75] In the early 1850s, for example, the Lord Chancellor, Lord St. Leonards, sent a circular to the colonies asking for information concerning local laws. Many of the colonies responded by formulating patent laws modelled after the English Act of 1852. The effectiveness of this policy could be seen in the fact that by

71 Bently, 163. Noting that in evidence to the Select Committee on Patents of 1829, the patent agent John Farey suggested that such rights were of limited value and, in many cases, had no legal effect.

72 *See* the Select Committee of the House of Lords Appointed to Consider of the Bill, Intituled, "An Act Further to Amend the Law Touching Letters Patent For Inventions"; And also of the Bill, Intituled, "An Act For The Further Amendment of the Law Touching Letters Patent For Inventions"; And to Report Thereon to the House, Report and Minutes of Evidence, 1851, H.C. 486, at 305–06 (Lieut-Col Reid, QQ. 2268–69). The different colonies had different populations (in terms of size, wealth, racial makeup, and literacy), different cultures, languages, economies, industries, legal traditions and neighbors. Action might be needed in Britain, but have wholly different effects in a colony. Protection of patents in a colony might, equally, increase the prices of commodities, placing the colony at a disadvantage vis-a-vis a foreign neighbour (to which the patent would not apply). Moreover, levels of mechanical knowledge varied from place to place, so that it was not possible to assume that an invention that lacked novelty in Britain would also lack novelty in a colony, or vice versa.

73 *See* the Select Committee of the House on the Bill, at 151 (Robert Macfie, Qq. 980, 997).

74 Bently, "The 'Extraordinary Multiplicity'," 163 (see, n. 1), citing the Royal Commission, Report of the Commissioners Appointed to Inquire into the Working of the Law Relating to Letters Patent for Inventions, 1864, C. (1st series) 3419, at 30 (Lewis Edmunds).

75 Bently, "The 'Extraordinary Multiplicity'," 186 (see, n. 1).

1864, seventeen British colonies had patent laws,[76] ahead of many European countries.

How was this achieved? Partly, the colonial governments assumed that what was appropriate in Britain was also appropriate in the colony. This was particularly the case in the non-white colonies since, in many cases, their colonial legislatures or Councils were dominated by British appointees.[77] For example, the first Indian patents Act VI of 1856, which had the objective of encouraging inventions of new and useful manufactures, was subsequently repealed by Act IX of 1857 since it had been enacted without the approval of the British Crown.[78] On the other hand, India was also a colony that enjoyed some goodwill and autonomy from Great Britain. Often considered an empire in its own right, by 1918, it was already clear that India, alongside Australia, New Zealand, South Africa and Canada would establish their government scientific departments, scientific societies, and universities.[79] In this regard, India's patent Act of 1859 established an independent grant system such that it required an invention to be new in the sense that it had not been used in Britain nor India.[80] It also excluded the possibility of the invention by "importation" (unless the importer was the inventor).[81]

Correspondingly, some colonies specifically passed local laws as alternatives to any British grant that had explicitly been made applicable to the colony.[82] Others also gave no effect to British grants made after the introduction of the colonial law unless they complied with conditions under the colonial law.[83] Canada was an example of legislative autonomy. It showed early on that it

76 Bently, 186, citing the 1864 Royal Commission On Patents, n 50, at 30 (Lewis Edmunds). For instance, Patent Acts and Ordinances adopted in New South Wales and Barbados in 1852, Victoria in 1854, India in 1856, Jamaica in 1852 and 1857, Tasmania in 1858, Ceylon and South Australia in 1859, New Zealand and the Cape of Good Hope in 1860, British Guinea in 1861, and British Honduras in 1862, among others.

77 Bently, "The 'Extraordinary Multiplicity'," 184 (see, n. 1). (Emphasis added).

78 "History of Indian Patent System," Office of the Controller General of Patents, Designs and Trademarks, Department for Promotion of Industry and Internal Trade, Ministry of Commerce and Industry, Government of India, page last updated December 20, 2019, http://www.ipindia.nic.in/history-of-indian-patent-system.htm.

79 Michael Worboys, "British Colonial Science Policy 1918–1939," in *Les Sciences Coloniales: Figures and Institutions*, ed., Patrick Petitjean (ORSTOM: 1996), 99–112.

80 Act No. 15 of 1859, § 19 (India).

81 Act No. 15 of 1859, § 19 (India).

82 Ordinance to Regulate the Granting of Patents in This Colony, No. 13 of 1861, § 19 (British Guiana).

83 Patent Law Amendment Act, 1862, 26 Vict., c. 2, § 44 (British Honduras); Act to Provide for the Granting, in this Colony, of Patents for Inventions, No. 17 of 1860, §§ 14, 35 (Cape of Good Hope) (section 35 was entitled "English patents subject to this Act").

wanted to forge its policies irrespective of how far the laws deviated from Britain.[84] In 1824, Lower Canada adopted the first general legislation for the grant of local patents.[85] It was followed by similar legislation adopted in Upper Canada,[86] Nova Scotia,[87] New Brunswick,[88] and Prince Edward Island.[89] All of these statutes provided that patents could only be granted to residents of the colony (province) concerned.[90] The problematic nature of such a provision led to the 1850 case of *Adams v Peel*, where it was held that a British patent had no force in Canada after the passing of the provincial Patent Act of 1824.[91] Consequently, "Her Majesty's subjects in England or other Colonies could not obtain patents in the Colonies unless they proceeded by private bill."[92]

In 1929, the Lower Canada Act was amended to allow residents to obtain a patent on an invention imported from abroad but not invented by the applicant.[93] Even so, the colonial legislatures could and did make special exceptions to the residency requirement.[94] In 1869 when Canada adopted its first federal patent statute,[95] it was unique among British colonies in adopting the first-to-invent standard.[96] The Act also required applicants to have been residents of Canada for at least one year before the date of application.[97]

---

84 Gervais, "The Emergence and Development" (see, n. 1); Bently, "The 'Extraordinary Multiplicity'," 186 (see, n. 1).

85 Gervais, 285 (see n. 1), citing SLC 1824 c 25.

86 SUC 1826 c 5.

87 SNS 1833 c 45.

88 SNB 1834 c 27.

89 SPEI 1837 c 21.

90 Barrigar and Robinson, "Some Notes," 393 (see, n. 68).

91 Gervais, "The Emergence and Development," 285 (see, n. 1), citing 1850, 1 LCR 130. This seems to have been confirmed by the English Act of 1852. *See* Lund, Henry. *A Treatise on the Substantive Law Relating to Letters Patent for Inventions* (Pennsylvania: T. & J.W. Johnson, 1851).

92 Gordon Asher, *The Development of the Patent System in Canada Since 1767* (Agincourt: Canada Law Book Company, 1965). Photocopied from *the Canadian Patent Reporter* 43 (1965): 56–75. (reviewing the exchanges of the letters between various officials and the inventors desiring to obtain the colonial patents in the 1850s).

93 9 Geo IV c 47. *See also* Asher, "The Development," 61 (see, n. 92); Barrigar and Robinson, "Some Notes," 396 (see, n. 68). A survey of the first 62 patents granted in Lower Canada showed that 20 of those patents were for imported, not locally invented technology.

94 Gervais, "The Emergence and Development," 286 (see, n. 1). See also Barrigar and Robinson, "Some Notes," 395 (see, n. 68); Asher, "The Development," 64 (see, n. 92).

95 SC 1869 c 11.

96 Gervais, "The Emergence and Development," 286 (see, n. 1).

97 Gervais, 286.

4.2 *Copyright*

At the outset, British dominions and colonies were not subject to British copyright. The statute of Anne 1710, which introduced a statutory right to control the reprinting of books *only applied throughout Britain.*[98] Following the Union of the two kingdoms of Great Britain and Ireland, the Statute of Anne was extended by the copyright Act of 1801 so that it applied throughout the United Kingdom and "any part of the British dominions from Europe."[99] This changed in 1814 when the passage of the Literary Copyright Act[100] finally extended copyright in books to British dominions and colonies. This Act provided that where a book was first published in Britain, the owner of copyright was able to bring an action against "any bookseller or printer, or other person whatsoever, in any part of the United Kingdom of Great Britain and Ireland, in the Isles of Man, Jersey or Guernsey, or in any other part of the British Dominions, [who] shall ... print, reprint, or import ... any such book or books...."[101] From then on, the copyright for works published in Britain was capable of being infringed anywhere in the British Empire,[102] thus securing protection within the imperial market. The imperial scope of copyright was reaffirmed in the Literary Copyright Act of 1842,[103] which extended coverage to even future colonies. In short, the Act extended copyright protection to books first published in the United Kingdom throughout the colonies but did not protect colonial works in Britain or other colonies.[104]

Despite it being uniquely imperial in its application, Bently argues that there was considerable room for the exercise of colonial variation in copyright – citing three reasons. Firstly, the 1842 Copyright Act was significantly modified through the Foreign Reprints Act of 1847 – based on protest from the Canadian colonies. Secondly, the 1842 Act only applied to books first published in the United Kingdom, and colonies were free to formulate laws for books first published in their jurisdictions. Thirdly, the Act only applied to books and music,

98 Act for the Encouragement of Learning, 1710, 8 Ann., c. 19.

99 Copyright Act, 1801, 41 Geo. 3, c. 107, § 1. For a detailed discussion, *see* Bently, "Copyright, Translations, and Relations," (see, n. 1).

100 Act to Amend Several Acts for the Encouragement of Learning, 54 Geo. 3, c. 156, § 4.

101 Act to Amend Several Acts for the Encouragement of Learning, 54 Geo. 3, c. 156, § 4.

102 Bently, "The 'Extraordinary Multiplicity'," 172 (see, n. 1).

103 Literary Copyright Act, 1842, 5 & 6 Vict., c. 45 (Imperial). Under this Act, if a book was first published in the United Kingdom by an author who was a resident in one of the British possessions, the book would benefit from copyright throughout the British dominions, defined as "all parts of the United Kingdom of Great Britain and Ireland, the islands of Jersey and Guernsey, all part of the East and West Indies, and all the colonies, settlements and possessions of the Crown which are now or hereafter may be acquired."

104 Gervais, "The Emergence and Development," 270 (see, n. 1).

allowing colonies the room to develop their regimes for the protection of artistic works, dramatic works and related rights.[105] On the contrary, in 1847, when India considered adopting a local copyright law, having regarded the Imperial Copyright Act of 1842 as being insufficient, the chief minister involved recommended that the local legislation mirror the imperial, explaining that it would be "improper in a subordinate legislature" to deviate from the imperial regime.[106] Similarly, when in 1872, a Bill was tabled in the Canadian Parliament to allow reprints of British books to be subject to a flat duty of 12.5 per cent[107] – something we might today call a compulsory license – it received significant opposition in Britain on the basis that it conflicted with Imperial copyright. The Bill was disallowed.[108]

Two possible scenarios can be deduced from the development of colonial copyright regarding the dominions or special colonies: either the local government in the colonies enacted copyright laws in protest to imperial copyright or as a supplement to it. For example, Canada remonstrated the effects of the 1842 Imperial Copyright Act,[109] which led the United Kingdom to pass the Foreign Reprints Act of 1847.[110] Canada, however, again protested the Foreign Reprints Act by adopting a Copyright Act in 1847, signalling that it wanted to bring copyright (and book importation) policy back to Canada.[111] The Canadian Act protected British authors, but only if they printed and published their works in Canada. This text could not legally supersede the existing Imperial Act adopted by Westminster and thus had little practical legal effect.[112]

105 Bently, "The 'Extraordinary multiplicity'," 174 (see, n. 1).

106 Bently, 174, citing the Minute of Charles Hay Cameron, Legal Member of the Council (1843–48), and President of the Council of Education (July 5, 1847) (IOL F4/2256 Board's Collections (1847–48), vol. 2256 113858–114023, at No. 113864).

107 Seville, Catherine. *The Internationalisation of Copyright Law: Books, Buccaneers and the Black Flag in the Nineteenth Century* (Cambridge: Cambridge University Press, 2006), 103.

108 Gervais, "The Emergence and Development," 271 (see, n. 1), citing McKeown, John. *Fox on Canadian Law of Copyright and Industrial Designs*, 4th ed. (Toronto: Carswell, 2003), 30.

109 Seville, *The Internationalisation of Copyright Law*, 79–86 (see, n. 107). Purportedly, the 1842 Act had been accompanied by a Customs Act (Customs Act 1842, 5 & 6 Vict., c. 24 (Imperial)) that required customs authorities to enforce imperial copyright law by preventing the importation of books that had been printed without the authorization of the copyright holder.

110 Act to Amend the Law Relating to the Protection in the Colonies of Works Entitled to Copyright in the UK, 1847, 10 & 11 Vict., c. 95 (Imperial).

111 Gervais, "The Emergence and Development," 270 (see, n. 1).

112 Gervais, 270.

New Zealand was another example of a colony that adopted a local copyright law for books in 1842.[113] This law was modelled after the British Act of 1814 and, and unlike the Lower Canada law of 1832[114] (or the Province of Canada law of 1841),[115] which only conferred copyright where the author was a person "resident in the province",[116] the New Zealand law contained no explicit restriction on residence.[117] The above examples show the degree of autonomy or room for manoeuvre granted to some of the colonies on intellectual property policy and legislation. It also shows the level of resistance to imperial laws in the colonies. Arguably, to be able to require or exhibit this level of autonomy or resistance entails some level of human, social and economic development as well as institutional capacity, the very constituents lacking when one looks at the African colonies in terms of the development of intellectual property laws.

5 The Unusual Extension of Imperial Intellectual Property Laws to Africa

Law has been described as the cutting edge of colonialism[118] as it was central to the "civilizing mission" of imperialism, particularly British imperialism of the nineteenth and early twentieth centuries.[119] For the British colonies in Africa and India, British law represented to the colonizers a substantial advance over the "savage" customs of the colonized.[120] Law was thus conceptualized as "the gift we gave them."[121] This gift inherently challenged and transformed traditional conceptions of property, time, space, marriage, work and the state.[122]

113 Ordinance to Secure the Copyright of Books to Their Authors, No. 18 of 1842 (N.Z.), reprinted in Copies of the Law and Ordinances Passed by the Governor General of New Zealand, 1841–42, 1844, H.C. 61, at 51.

114 Act for the Protection of Copy Rights, 1832, 2 Will. 4, c. 53 (Lower Can.).

115 An Act for the protection of Copy Rights in this Province 1841 (4–5 Vict c 61).

116 Bently, "The 'Extraordinary Multiplicity'," 176 (see, n. 1); Gervais, "The Emergence and Development," 269–270 (see, n. 1).

117 Gervais, 178.

118 Merry, "Law and Colonialism," 890 (see, n. 32). Citing Chanock, Martin. *Law, Custom, and Social Order: The Colonial Experience in Malawi and Zambia* (Cambridge: Cambridge University Press, 1985).

119 Darby, Philip. *The Three Faces of Imperialism* (New Haven: Yale University Press), 1987.

120 Merry, "Law and Colonialism," 890 (see, n. 32); Bently, "The 'Extraordinary Multiplicity'," (see, n. 1).

121 Fitzpatrick, Peter. "Custom as Imperialism," in Abun-Nasr, Jamil M., Spellenberg, Ulrich, and Wanitzek, Ulrike, eds. *Law, Society and National Identity in Africa*, (Hamburg: Helmut Buske Verlag, 1990).

122 Merry, "Law and Colonialism," 891 (see, n. 32).

Intellectual property law was part of this colonial legal apparatus. As Ruth Okediji notes, "intellectual property law was not merely an incidental part of the colonial legal apparatus, but a central technique in the commercial superiority sought by European powers in their interactions with each other in regions beyond Europe."[123]

There are three related reasons why I consider the extension of Imperial intellectual property laws to Africa as unusual.[124] First, as discussed above, the United Kingdom to a large extent devolved intellectual property law-making to its colonies. However, with regards to its African colonies, there was no devolution of intellectual property law-making and administration (except South Africa, which became a self-governing dominion in 1910).[125] Second, the latter part of the nineteenth century saw the conclusion of two international agreements in the field of intellectual property. International harmonization of intellectual property law came with consequences for the African colonies and protectorates. Third, there emerged efforts at uniform imperial intellectual property laws after the international harmonization of intellectual property became a reality in the nineteenth century. Whiles uniformity in law further led to increased autonomy in legislation for the British dominions (and special colonies), it further perpetuated the imposition of imperial laws on Africa. These are elaborated in turn.

5.1 *No Devolution of Intellectual Property Law-Making and Administration in Africa*

As noted earlier, during the nineteenth century, many of the particularly white settler colonies had gained increasing amounts of autonomy and practical independence from Westminster,[126] perhaps, due to deep concerns about Britain's imperial mandate, and the reaction of some of the colonies to the revision of laws, especially, copyright law.[127] One would think that this devolution would naturally transfer to the African colonies. Except for a slight

123 Okediji, "The International Relations," 324 (see, n. 3).

124 From 1871–1900, Britain gained control over or occupied what is now known as Egypt, Sudan, Kenya, Uganda, South Africa, Gambia, Sierra Leone, northwestern Somalia, Zimbabwe, Zambia, Botswana, Nigeria, Ghana, and Malawi. Great Britain also got southern and northeastern Africa from the Berlin conference 1844–1845.

125 In what is today the Republic of South Africa, the provinces of Cape Colony, Natal, Orange Free State, and the Transvaal were united to form the Union of South Africa, which was granted autonomy and thus began to be self-governed in 1910.

126 Bently, "The 'Extraordinary Multiplicity'," 191 (see, n. 1).

127 Suthersanen, Uma. "The First Global Copyright Act." Queen Mary School of Law Legal Studies Research Paper No. 106/2012. 2012. Available on SSRN, https://ssrn.com/abstract=2022878.

deviation in the case of the Gold Coast, this was not the case.[128] Contrary, it was a situation of Great Britain looking for new territories to expand its power and claim sovereignty, impose its laws and further its economic interest.

The development of patent law in the Gold Coast makes an interesting case study. Until 1899, the Gold Coast had no patent law. In January 1898, the British Secretary of State for the Colonies sent a dispatch to the then Acting Governor of the Gold Coast enquiring about the procedure for obtaining patent protection in the Gold Coast colony.[129] Since there was no patent legislation in the colony, the Secretary of State for the Colonies asked the Board of Trade for advice on the need for a patent law for the Gold Coast.[130] In the following year, the British Parliament passed the Gold Coast Patent Ordinance in 1899[131] – modelled on the British Patents, Designs and Trade Marks Act 1883.[132] Exceptionally, this Ordinance operated as an independent patent registration system with a Patent Office under the control of a registrar.[133] It had provisions for patent applications and procedures for obtaining patents in the Gold Coast without recourse to the United Kingdom Patent Office.[134]

However, after more than two decades in operation, the 1899 Ordinance was repealed in 1925 and replaced by the Patents Registration Ordinance (Cap. 179).[135] This Ordinance restructured the patent system of the Gold Coast by effectively terminating the autonomous system of the 1899 Ordinance, and merely extended the validity of all patents registered in the United Kingdom to the Gold Coast colony.[136] In so doing, it incorporated the Gold Coast's patent

128 Again, an exception to this was some of the self-governing South African colonies. Most of them already had local patent and copyright laws by 1860–1880. *See for example* Law to Provide for the Granting in this Colony of Patents for Inventions, No. 4 of 1870, (Natal); Act to Provide for the Granting, in this Colony, of Patents for Inventions, No. 17 of 1860, (Cape of Good Hope); Act to Protect and Regulate the Rights of Authors in Respect of their Works, No. 2 of 1873 (Cape of Good Hope).

129 Yankey, *International Patents*, 98 (see, n. 3), citing Dispatch No.52 of January 28, 1898 in C.O. 96 Gold Coast 1898 Vol. XXVII, 336, and noting that the dispatch so transmitted was a copy of a letter inquiry from patent agents Messrs. H. & W. Pataky.

130 Manteaw, "Patents and Development in Ghana," 4 (see, n. 64).

131 *See* Gold Coast Patent Ordinance 1899, No. 1 of 1899.

132 Yankey, *International Patents*, 100 (see, n. 3), citing the Board of Trade's letter dated 16 May 1898 in C.O. 96 Gold Coast 1898, Vol. XX, 329.

133 Manteaw, "Patents and Development in Ghana," (see, n. 64).

134 Yankey, *International Patents*, 114 (see, n. 3); Manteaw, "Patents and Development in Ghana," (see, n. 64).

135 Patents Registration Ordinance, 1925 (Cap. 179).

136 Yawson, Robert M. "Technology commercialisation and intellectual property rights in Ghana," (paper presented at the International Conference on TRIPS – Next Agenda for Developing Countries), 7, https://mpra.ub.uni-muenchen.de/id/eprint/33185.

system into that of the United Kingdom and rendered the existing local patent office a mere registration centre for the United Kingdom patents.[137] Section 4 of Cap 179 provided that:

> Any person being the grantee of a patent in the United Kingdom, or any person deriving his right from such grantee by assignment, transmission or other operation of law, may apply within three years from the date of issue of the patent, to have such patent registered in the Gold Coast.

What this meant was that the grant of a patent in Ghana was only to United Kingdom patent holders and that to have patent protection for an invention made in Ghana, one needed to apply for the grant first in the United Kingdom before having it re-registered in Ghana. The application for registration of such a grant in Ghana had to be made within three years from the date of issue of the United Kingdom patent. This procedure applied to Ghanaians and non-Ghanaians, that is, other Africans desiring patent protection in Ghana. The privileges and rights of such a patent grant in Ghana dated from the date of the patent in the United Kingdom, "and shall continue in force only so long as the patent remains in force in the United Kingdom…."[138] Thus, any extension or annulment of the United Kingdom grant automatically applied to the Ghana registration.[139]

Reflecting on the rationale for the enactment of patent legislation for the Gold Coast, a significant factor was the protection of the imperialist interest in the mining industry, especially, gold mining.[140] Communication between the Colonial Office and the Board of Trade points to this. In a letter dated April 30 1898, the Colonial Office noted that:

> There is at present no patent legislation in force in the colony (Gold Coast), but in view of the development of the gold mining district of Tarkwa, and the consequent introduction of machinery etc. Mr Chamberlain (Colonial Secretary) thinks it would be well to take steps to afford protection to invention.[141]

137 Manteaw, "Patents and Development in Ghana," (see, n. 64).

138 Section §7(2) of the Patents Registration Ordinance, 1925 (Cap. 179).

139 Manteaw, "Patents and Development in Ghana," 5 (see, n. 64).

140 Yankey, *International Patents*, 104 (see, n. 3); Manteaw, "Patents and Development in Ghana," 6 (see, n. 64).

141 Yankey, 105 (see, n. 3), quoting Colonial Office's letter of April 30, 1898 to the Board of Trade in C.O. 96 Gold Coast 1898, Vol. IV, March 9–31, 313.

A second letter to the Acting Governor of the Gold Coast colony from the Secretary of State for the Colonies was even more precise and conclusive: "I have under consideration, the advisability of enacting patent legislation for the Gold Coast in view of the introduction of patented machinery and processes which will probably follow on the development of the mining industry."[142] Thus, "patent protection was provided for the machinery necessary for the exploitation of gold and other mineral resources."[143] All the patents registered during this period belonged to foreign individuals or firms.[144] For 70 years and almost 36 years after Ghana's independence,[145] the country maintained the colonial law on patents and continued the tedious process of prosecuting patents through the United Kingdom and merely registering the United Kingdom-granted patent in Ghana until 1993 when the Patent Law, 1992 (P.N.D.C.L. 305A) was adopted. This law has been replaced by the Patents Act, 2003 (Act 657).

The 1899 Patent Ordinance of the Gold Coast was replicated in other British West African colonies. Its replication in other colonies and protectorates, however, raised questions about its benefits since the legislation was not meant to spur local innovation, research and development, or transfer of technology, which would have enhanced, for example, access to medicines and other technologies.[146] For example, the above ordinance became the foundation of patent law in Nigeria. The colonial office sent copies of the legislation to the colony of Lagos, the Southern and Northern protectorate Nigeria (now constituting present-day Nigeria)[147] with the specific instruction to pass a similar ordinance.[148] It is on record that the Governor of the Lagos Colony stated that the Patent Ordinance of Lagos Colony was "based on the imperial statute and Gold Coast Ordinance dealing with the matter."[149] Until this development,

142 Yankey, *International Patents*, 105, quoting Colonies' Sec. of State letter, 25 May 1898, C.O. 98 G.C. 1898, Vol. XX, 329.

143 Timothy Umahi, Okechukwu. "Access to Medicines: the Colonial Impacts on Patent law of Nigeria," 22 December 2011, SSRN, 7, http://papers.ssrn.com/sol3/papers.cfm?abstract_id=1975928.

144 Yawson, "Technology commercialisation," (see, n. 136).

145 Ghana gained her independence from Great Britain on 6 March 1957.

146 Umahi, "Access to Medicines," 7–8 (see, n. 143). (Emphasis added).

147 Umahi, 7–8. This extension resulted in the enactment of the Patents Ordinance No. 17 of 1900 for the Lagos Colony; the Patents Proclamation Ordinance No. 27 of 1900 for Southern protectorate Nigeria, amended by the Patents Amendment Ordinance No. 19 of 1901; and the Patents Proclamation Ordinance No. 12 of 1902 for Northern Protectorate Nigeria.

148 Yankey, *International Patents*, 104 (see, n. 3), citing C.O. 96 Gold Coast 1899.

149 Yankey, 107, citing C.O. 147 Lagos 1900, Vol. 14 151 Despatches Nos. 235–332, 21 Sept–31 Dec.

however, patents registered in the United Kingdom in the late nineteenth to early twentieth centuries were by Order in Council made applicable in Nigeria.[150]

In 1914, the Southern and Northern Nigeria colonies and protectorates were merged to form the Colony and Protectorate of Nigeria. This amalgamation resulted in the repeal of the Patents Ordinance for Lagos and the Patents Proclamation Ordinances for Northern and Southern Nigeria, ushering in the Patents Ordinance No. 30 of 1916, which was amended in 1925 to become the Registration of United Kingdom Patents Ordinance No. 6 of 1925. The Ordinance of 1925 provides for the registration in Nigeria of patents granted in the United Kingdom provided the application for registration was made within three years from the date of the issue of the patent. The rights conferred in Nigeria dated from the date of the grant of the patent in the United Kingdom and remained in force so long as the patent was in force in the United Kingdom. This remained the status quo even long after Nigeria became independent in 1960.[151]

In Kenya, until 1989 when the first national Industrial Property Act was passed,[152] the Patents Registration Act Cap. 508 established a registration procedure similar to Ghana.[153] A certificate of registration conferred on the applicant privileges and rights as though the patent had been granted in the United Kingdom with an extension to Kenya.[154] An application had to be made within three years from the date of the United Kingdom grant and the patent would remain in force as long as the patent remained in force in the United Kingdom.[155] Concerning copyright, the 1897 East Africa Order in Council extended the application of the 1842 English Copyright Act, the International Copyright Act of 1844, the Fine Arts Copyright Act of 1862 and the Copyright (Musical Compositions) Act of 1888 to Kenya.[156] As Sikoyo et al. put it, these laws were essentially designed and extended to protect the monopoly rights of British publishers in Kenya, restrict the growth of the publishing industry in the country, provide censorship for publications that colonialists termed

150 Sikoyo et al., *Intellectual Property*, 19 (see, n. 3). (Emphasis added).

151 Even though Nigeria gained its political independence from Great Britain on 1 October 1960, it only introduced national intellectual property laws from 1965, starting with the Trademarks Act of 1965, the Patents and Design Act of 1970 and the Copyright Act of 1970.

152 The Industrial Property Act Cap 509 (Kenya). Repealed by Industrial Property Act, No 3 of 2001.

153 Patents Registration Act, Cap 508, § 4 (Kenya).

154 Patents Registration Act, Cap 508, § 4 (Kenya), § 7.

155 Patents Registration Act, Cap 508, § 4 (Kenya), § 8.

156 Chege, John Waruingi. *Copyright Law and Publishing in Kenya* (Nairobi: Kenya Literature Bureau, 1978).

seditious, blasphemous, immoral or contrary to government policy and propagate the ideology of colonial superiority among the natives.[157] Kenya adopted its first national copyright law in 1966[158] after the country had gained independence.[159] This Act has been amended severally to meet the needs and demands of the local market and the country's international obligations under international treaties.[160]

5.2 *International Harmonization of Intellectual Property*

5.2.1 Late Nineteenth-Century to Early Twentieth Century

In the late nineteenth century, a distinct legal development on intellectual property happened at the international level that would impact African countries as well. Countries that were net exporters of knowledge and information goods began to seek international agreements for the protection of intellectual property, as it had become obvious that transnational commercial activities required more than mere national intellectual property protection. Initial agreements included mainly European countries, most of whom were then major colonial powers (United Kingdom, France, Germany, Spain, Italy and Belgium). The first agreement was the Paris Convention and the second was the Berne Convention.[161] The Paris and the Berne Conventions further consolidated the participation of developing countries and Africa, for that matter, in the international intellectual property system through the agency of colonial rule. Simultaneously, the continent was annexed through the Berlin West Africa Conference of 1884–1885. Chief among the goals for the Berlin Conference was the control of African markets.[162] Intellectual property was used to control creative and industrial markets in the interest of European rights holders.[163]

In the absence of their African colonies (except Tunisia and Liberia[164] in Berne) and without their consent, the contracting European countries to the

157 Sikoyo et al., *Intellectual Property*, 17 (see, n. 3). (Emphasis added).

158 The Copyright Act, Chapter 130, 1966 (Kenya).

159 Kenya gained her independence from Great Britain on 1 June 1963.

160 See Act No. 5 of 1975; Act No. 5 of 1982; Act No. 14 of 1989; and Copyright Act Chapter 130 of the Laws of Kenya (CAP 130).

161 See, n. 23.

162 General Act of the Berlin Conference, 26 February 1885, C 4361 1885 (Preamble).

163 Peukert, Alexander. "The Colonial Legacy of the International Copyright System," in Röchenthaler, Ute, and Diawara, Mamadou, eds. *Copyright Africa: How Intellectual Property, Media and Markets Transform Immaterial Goods*, (Canon Pyon: Sean Kingston Publishing, 2016).

164 Liberia was officially colonized by the United States from 1820 to 1847 – the date of its independence. In 1886, Liberia as an independent country signed the Berne Convention

Paris and Berne Conventions decided to incorporate their colonial territories into the new intellectual property Unions as 'Countries of the Union' without being regarded members thereof.[165] In the case of Tunisia, it is asserted that a French law professor represented the country in Berne, while French diplomats represented Tunisia in Madrid and The Hague.[166]

The precise method of utilizing this procedure comprised two steps. The first entailed the submission, by the colonizing state, of a declaration of the application of the applicable international agreement to the colonized state. Declarations of the application of the Berne Convention were made following Article 19 of the original text of the convention.[167] Declarations of the applicability of the Paris Convention were made in terms of Article 16 *bis* (1)–(2) of the London Act of 1934 and the Lisbon Act of 1958 of the convention.[168] Today, this provision can be found in Article 24 of the 1979 Act of the convention – albeit in a refined language. This procedure was further adopted in Article XIII of the 1952 Universal Copyright Convention (UCC)[169] and Article 27 of the 1961 International Convention for the Protection of Performers, Producers of Phonograms and Broadcasting Organizations.[170] It is noteworthy, however, that Great Britain sought the consent of Canada and the other dominions as well as India before acceding to the Berne Convention on their behalf.[171]

---

and ratified it in October 1908. Liberia had its first copyright law in 1911 (Libéria, Loi concernant le droit d'auteur du 22 décembre 1911, Droit d'auteur, August 1912, p. 106).

165 Peukert, "The Colonial Legacy," (see, n. 163). *See also* Kongolo, "Historical developments of industrial property laws," 105 (see, n. 3). It should be noted that this procedure was mostly utilized in the Berne Convention, for that matter, copyright. However, as noted, it applied in the case of patents as well.

166 Beer, Jeremy de, Baarbé, Jeremiah, and Ncube, Caroline B. "The Intellectual Property Treaty Landscape in Africa, 1885 to 2015," Open AIR Working Paper 4, 2017, 16.

167 Kongolo, "Historical evolution of copyright," 165 ff. (see, n. 3). Article 19 carried that "the countries acceding to this Convention also have the right to accede at any time for their colonies or foreign possessions."

168 Kongolo, "Historical developments of industrial property laws," 115 (see, n. 3).

169 Universal Copyright Convention, signed at Geneva on 6 September 1952, http://www.wipo.int/wipolex/en/other_treaties/text.jsp?file_id=172836, adopted in Geneva in 1952, is one of the principal copyright conventions. It was developed by the United Nations Educational, Scientific and Cultural Organization (UNESCO) as an alternative to the Berne Convention for those countries that disagreed with aspects of the Berne Convention, but still wished to participate in some form of multilateral copyright protection. The UCC was responsive to the specific needs of developing countries but also stressed the fundamental principle of exclusive copyrights.

170 International Convention for the Protection of Performers, Producers of Phonograms and Broadcasting Organisations, done at Rome on October 26, 1961, http://www.wipo.int/wipolex/en/treaties/text.jsp?file_id=289795.

171 Bently, "Copyright, Translations, and Relations," 1217 (see, n. 1).

Secondly, the declaration of applicability of the international conventions was then followed by the extension of the colonizing states copyright or patent legislation to the colony, or the enactment of legislation applicable only to the colonized territory.[172] The Berne Convention was extended to the colonies in Africa through declarations made by Great Britain, France, and Spain at the time of signing or ratification.[173] Consequently, as Kongolo asserts, "the British Copyright Laws of 1911 and 1956, the French Copyright Laws of 1791, 1793 and 1957, the Spanish Copyright Law of 1847 and the Belgian Copyright Law of 1886 were deemed to be mutatis mutandis the copyright laws of their colonies unless otherwise provided."[174] This act of incorporating the colonies made it possible for right holders from the Member Countries to enjoy protection not only within Member Countries of the Unions but in all overseas territories. Such actions would lay the foundation for an enduring influence on legal and economic development in African countries and on how law and development are perceived and understood.

5.2.2 After Mid-Twentieth Century When Colonies Became Independent[175]

The decolonization process in the 1950s and 1960s subjected the fate of the numerous contracts between post-colonial states and private investors from European countries to the mercy of transnational law.[176] As newly independent states moved to promulgate national intellectual property laws, one question that arose was whether the new states had to formally accede to the intellectual property Unions or whether they were already members of the club. The former colonial powers took action to ensure stability and continuity of their colonial agenda. Various legal and political efforts were undertaken to stabilize the foundations of the colonial intellectual property regime during the decolonization period. Fearing that the international intellectual property system might break down, the United International Bureaux for the Protection of Intellectual Property (BIRPI), in charge of administering the Berne and Paris Unions, moved swiftly to facilitate a system whereby newly independent states

172 Kongolo, "Historical developments of industrial property laws," 106–107 (see, n. 3).

173 Kongolo, "Historical evolution of copyright," 163 (see, n. 3).

174 Kongolo, 163.

175 While the period under discussion goes beyond the early twentieth century, it nonetheless cover issues that relates to development in the late nineteenth century and early twentieth century. It thus sets the context for understanding the implication of some of these early development and the issues being discussed in this chapter.

176 Singh, Prabhaka, and Mayer, Benoît. *Critical International Law: Postrealism, Postcolonialism, and Transnationalism* (Delhi: Oxford University Press, 2014), 12.

in Africa and Asia that were no longer bound by Berne's colonial clause could issue "declarations of continued adherence."[177] Many developing countries declared their adherence to or acceded to the Berne Convention.[178]

In the area of patent law, BIRPI did not assume that newly independent states were still bound by colonial obligations.[179] Instead, it came out with a Model Law for Developing Countries on Inventions in 1964, whose emphasis was on inventions for developing countries.[180] This model law had been drawn in response to pressure from industrialized nations for developing countries to join the "community of nations" in the Union. This Model Law was forwarded to 69 developing countries[181] and many of them modelled their patent and design laws on BIRPI's Model Law, Nigeria being an example.[182] Umahi suggests that Nigeria, just like many other developing countries, adopted the Model Law because they believed that it was an opportunity for them to gain access to patented foreign technology, increase competitiveness in trade and foreign direct investment.[183] However, achieving the essence of the policy behind the patent system proved elusive for many African countries.

In Africa, regional arrangements in the aftermath of independence facilitated the enduring influence of former colonial powers and WIPO on intellectual property laws. Today the only continent to have two regional intellectual property organizations is Africa. In 1976, WIPO and the United Nations Economic Commission for Africa (UNECA) facilitated the creation of the African Regional Intellectual Property Organization (ARIPO) for Anglophone countries and served jointly as the Secretariat of ARIPO until 1981 when the

177 Ricketson, Sam. *The Berne Convention for the Protection of Literary and Artistic Works: 1886–1986* (London: Centre for Commercial Law Studies, Queen Mary College, 1987), 799–806.

178 Peukert, "The Colonial Legacy," (see, n. 163); Deere Birkbeck, *The Implementation Game* (see, n. 2); and Kongolo, "Historical evolution of copyright," (see, n. 3); Ncube, Caroline B. *Intellectual Property Policy, Law and Administration in Africa: Exploring Continental and Sub-regional Co-operation* (Oxon: Routledge, 2016).

179 Bodenhausen, Georg H.C. *Guide to the Application of the Paris Convention for the Protection of Industrial Property* (Geneva: BIRPI, 1968), 19.

180 United International Bureaux for the Protection of Intellectual Property (BIRPI), *Model Law for Developing Countries on Inventions*, BIRPI Pub. no. 801(E) (1965); Greenberg, Suzanne F. "The WIPO Model Laws for the Protection of Unpatented Know-How: A Comparative Analysis," *International Tax & Business Lawyer* 3, no. 52 (1985), 54.

181 Harbers, Michael J. "International Patent Cooperation," *Stanford Law Review* 20, no. 5 (May 1968): 1013; Penrose, Edith. T. "International Patenting and the Less-developed Countries," *The Economic Journal* 83, no. 331 (September 1973): 779–83.

182 Umahi, "Access to Medicines," 5 (see, n. 143); Dinwoodie, Graeme B. et al. *International Intellectual Property Law and Policy* (San Francisco: Matthew Bender & Company, 2001), 412.

183 Umahi, "Access to Medicines," 5 (see, n. 143). (Emphasis added).

organization established an independent Secretariat.[184] Similarly, the French National Patent Rights Institute and WIPO assisted former French colonies to create the Organization Africaine de la Propriété Intellectuelle (OAPI), establishing a unified intellectual property system with a central patent office for Francophone countries. The OAPI system serves as the equivalent of regional intellectual property law for most aspects of intellectual property and derives primarily from French intellectual property laws. The ARIPO system co-exists with the national intellectual property laws in its member states and draws primarily from British intellectual property law.[185] Besides, since their inception to date, WIPO has offered technical assistance to the two organizations. WIPO's assistance has been criticized as a basis for the adherence and compliance overdrive being witnessed in the majority of African countries regarding intellectual property law in recent times.[186]

5.3 *The Move towards Uniformity in Empire Intellectual Property Laws*

The latter part of the nineteenth century and the early part of the twentieth century saw a shift in favour of uniformity concerning just about all fields of intellectual property within the Empire.[187] One explanation for this development was the advent of international intellectual property relations – the Paris and the Berne Conventions. By signing on to these treaties (and especially, concerning subsequent revisions), the United Kingdom was required to make some adjustments to its laws and in particular, its relations to its colonies. The idea of uniformity shifted the interest away from imperial devolution of laws to a more unified system, especially, at a time when the self-governing dominions enjoyed increasing autonomy.[188] Contrastingly, in Africa, this served as a catalyst for the further imposition and to an extent, harmonization of intellectual property laws.

From 1887 to about 1922, a series of colonial conferences were held to fashion out a possibility for uniform patent law. While the idea of imperial patent law came close to being realized,[189] it never materialized. However, uniformity in the area of copyright law did materialize.[190] Canada is credited to have

184 Acquah, "Technical Assistance," (see, n. 29).

185 Deere-Birkbeck, *The Implementation Game*, 38–39 (see, n. 2).

186 Acquah, "Technical Assistance," (see, n. 29).

187 Bently, "The 'Extraordinary Multiplicity'," 188 (see, n. 1).

188 Bently, 188.

189 Wadlow, Christopher. "The British Empire Patent 1901–1923: The 'global' patent that never was," *Intellectual Property Quarterly*, no. 4 (2006). (Noting that an interim scheme came within one vote of being adopted at the 1923 international conference).

190 Bently, "The 'Extraordinary Multiplicity'," 188–198 (see, n. 1).

been the cause of the failure of creating a unified patent system for the British Empire at the London Imperial Economic Conference in 1923.[191] As Wadlow notes, that all of the Dominions "instinctively took a negative and defensive attitude to patents, reflected in the fact that the main preoccupation of their legislation was less to reward or encourage innovation, than to avoid having their economy dominated by foreigners."[192] Copyright came up in colonial conferences at the beginning of the twentieth century, gathering momentum especially after the struggles of the United Kingdom during the Berlin revision of Berne.[193] The Berlin revision of the Berne Convention provided a reason and an opportunity to fix the United Kingdom's domestic copyright law and to attempt to address questions of British copyright relations with its colonies.[194] A committee set up to consider whether British copyright law should be reformed to enable the Government to give effect to the Berlin revision, the Gorell Committee, recommended that Britain should adhere to the Berlin revision and that there needed to be uniform copyright law throughout the empire.[195]

This led to a conference in 1910. Only the self-governing colonies were invited to the colonial conferences.[196] Thus, the African colonies were not invited or represented – except for South Africa. India, although not a self-governing dominion, was invited at the last minute to join the conference. It did so by assigning Sir Thomas Raleigh, former legal member of the government of India's Legislative Council[197] to attend on its behalf.[198] Agreements and commitments made at the conference led to Bills being introduced in the House of

191 Gervais, "The Emergence and Development," 288 (see, n. 1).

192 Wadlow, "The British Empire Patent," 335. (see, n. 189).

193 Wadlow, 269, 272.

194 Bently, "Copyright, Translations, and Relations," 1220 (see, n. 1).

195 Bently, "The 'Extraordinary Multiplicity'," 190 (see, n. 1), citing Report of the Committee on the Law of Copyright, 1910, Cd. 4976, p. 29.

196 Bently, "Copyright, Translations, and Relations," 1221 (see, n. 1).

197 Bently, 1221. Noting that Raleigh (1850–1920) had been in India between 1899 and 1904, where he had spearheaded Lord Curzon's reforms of the university system (much to the dislike of the educated Indian constituency). He joined the Council of India in 1909. Prior to his appointment to the Viceroy's Council, Raleigh had been a Fellow of All Souls College, Oxford, and Reader in English Law.

198 Bently, 1221, citing Letter from Herbert Hope Risley, India Office, to Gov't of India (Apr. 22, 1910) (India Office Library, located in the British Library, St. Pancras, London, L/PJ/6/993, file 898 with file 4609/11).

Commons in 1910 and 1911.[199] Thereafter, the 1911 Copyright Act was adopted[200] to replace a tapestry of existing statutes on 4th June 1912.[201] This Act came with variations in the treatment of colonies. For instance, while the self-governing dominions had complete freedom as to whether to accept or reject the whole or part of it, all colonies were bound by the terms of the Act.[202]

Section 27 of the Copyright Act, however, provided British possessions with a little leeway to vary the operation of that Act in its application to the colony in question. As Bently notes, "this flexibility was primarily intended to allow for adaptations necessary in the light of differences in matters relating to legal procedure and remedies.[203] Insofar as a colony wished to tamper with the substance, Section 27 of the Copyright Act limited such variations to "works the authors whereof were, at the time of the making of the work, resident in the possession, and to works first published in the possession." India took advantage of this provision in 1914.[204] However, it is to be noted that India was an exception in that among other colonies, she received preferential treatment from Great Britain.[205]

Except for South Africa, the extension of the 1911 Copyright Act was a one-way street for the colonies in Africa. (The instance of Kenya described earlier is a good example). In Ghana, the Copyright Ordinance of 1911 made the United Kingdom Copyright Act applicable to the Gold Coast colony. A post-independence copyright Act of 1961 brought an end to the application of the Imperial Copyright Act.[206] However, this Act was essentially a mere

199 *See* Bill to Amend and Consolidate the Law Relating to Copyright, 1910, Bill [282] (Imperial). This was only introduced with a view to consideration. For 1911, *see* Bill to Amend and Consolidate the Law Relating to Copyright, 1911, Bill [149] (Imperial). After Amendments by Select Committee, Bill to Amend and Consolidate the Law Relating to Copyright, 1911, Bill [296] (Imperial). After House of Lords Amendments, Bill to Amend and Consolidate the Law Relating to Copyright, 1911, H.L. Bill [384] (Imperial).

200 Copyright Act 1911, 1 & 2 Geo. 5., c. 46.

201 Gervais, "The Emergence and Development," 269 (see, n. 1).

202 Copyright Act 1911, 1 & 2 Geo. 5., c. 46. § 25(1). This Act ... shall extend throughout His Majesty's dominions.

203 Bently, "Copyright, Translations, and Relations," 1225 (see, n. 1).

204 Proclamation, Oct. 31, 1912 (India); Copyright Act, 1914 (India).

205 Even though India was not a self-governing dominion, it was consulted and its consent was sought by the United Kingdom for the International Copyright Act of 1886, the Act giving effect to the Berne Convention in the United Kingdom. It was also invited to the series of colonial conferences on uniform copyright law – paving the way for the 1911 Copyright Act. India's consent was also sought for the ratification of the Berlin Act of the Berne Convention, and colonial administrators did take measures to foster the development of a cadre of local intellectual property experts. For details about this and others, see Bently, "Copyright, Translations, and Relations," 1217 ff. (see, n. 1).

206 The Copyright Act, 1961 (Act 85). Section 17 provided that 'the Copyright Act, 1911 of the United Kingdom shall cease to have enact in Ghana and the Copyright Ordinance (Cap. 126) is accordingly hereby repealed.'

re-enactment of the existing law in the United Kingdom[207] – providing somewhat limited protection for authors in their works. The 1961 Act was repealed and replaced by the Copyright Law 1985, PNDC Law 110 (Law 110). Section four of the latter law expanded the scope of copyright to include "expressions of folklore," defining the folklore very broadly to include not only oral culture but also elements of material culture like adinkra and kente cloth designs.[208] This was the first time Ghana weaned itself of colonial copyright. The 1985 law has been replaced with the Copyright Act, 2005 (Act 690).[209]

In Nigeria, the situation was not very different. By an Order in Council No. 912 of 29th June 1912, the English Copyright Act of 1911 was extended and became applicable in the Southern Protectorate of Nigeria.[210] According to Ola, it is without contention that the extension of the English Copyright Act formally introduced a copyright framework into Nigeria's legal system.[211] While providing the first legislative framework for Nigeria's administration of copyright, it also served as a basis for further development of Copyright law in Nigeria. This Act remained in force through independence until 1970 when the first indigenous Copyright Act was promulgated. The Copyright Act 1970 being the first indigenous act was expected to protect the Nigerian interest and be reflective of the peculiarities of her people as well as their culture and traditions. However, concerning the administration of copyright, there was no effective structure under the 1970 Act until a new Copyright Act was adopted in 1988, which is embodied in the laws of the Federation 2004.[212]

6 The Implication of the Imposition of Imperial Intellectual Property Laws on Africa

The imposition of British institutions, norms, and systems – including patent and copyright – on the cultural, economic, and legal landscape of its African colonies was an expansion of the colonial enterprise and had nothing to do

207 Sikoyo et al., *Intellectual Property*, 16 (see, n. 3).

208 Boatema Boateng, "The Hand of the Ancestors: Time, Cultural Production, and Intellectual Property Law," *Law & Society Review* 47, no. 4 (December 2013): 943.

209 The purpose of the new Copyright Act was to bring Ghanaian copyright law into conformity with the Ghanaian Constitution, to help strengthen protection of copyrights and related rights in Ghana and to bring Ghana into compliance with its international obligations.

210 Ola, Kunle. "Evolution and Future Trends of Copyright in Nigeria," *Journal of Open Access to Law* 2, no. 1 (2014): 7.

211 Ola, 8. (Emphasis added).

212 First Schedule, Copyright Act Cap C28 Laws of the Federation 2004.

with stimulating indigenous creativity and innovation.[213] If anything, Imperial intellectual property laws dissipated local innovation and knowledge governance systems in Africa since they did not fit the Western concept of privately held rights over intellectual property. Colonial administrators held customary laws of their colonies in low regard, particularly because they did not serve the commercial interests of colonizers determined to extract as much wealth from the colonies as they could.[214] Thus, local laws were enacted specifically not to protect (or promote) the cultural knowledge, creations and innovations of the citizens of the colonies. Rather, they were promulgated to benefit British inventors, creators and writers.

For example, it is obvious from the discussion above that the 1899 Gold Coast Patent Ordinance, which was adopted in its entirety in other former British West African colonies, was never meant to encourage either indigenous inventive activity, local research and innovation or to accomplish an effective technology transfer. Rather, it was geared towards the protection of property rights in machine technology relevant to the exploitation of the gold and other mineral resources of the Colony.[215] In this regard, it sanctioned a policy of protecting the transfer of technology to the colony in pursuit of an extractive scoop and ship investment policy.[216] Samuel Manteaw has, for instance, argued that the nature of the patent legislation might have contributed to Africa's asymmetrical vulnerability dependence on raw materials and natural resources.[217]

The above development affected indigenous participation in the patent and copyright system. It also affected local and indigenous creativity and innovation, especially those embedded in traditional knowledge and biodiversity, as they were not regarded as worthy of protection and hence were not encouraged. However, Africa is most likely to receive substantial benefits from the protection of traditional knowledge, traditional cultural expressions and genetic resources. Since the 1960s, there has been agitation for and a growing sense in

213 Ezejiofor, G., "Sources of Nigerian Law," in *Introduction to Nigerian Law*, ed. Cyprian Okechukwu Okonkwo (London: Sweet & Maxwell, 1980). (Emphasis added).

214 Carolyn Deere-Birkbeck, "Developing Country Perspectives on Intellectual Property in the WTO: Setting the Pre-TRIPS Context," in *Research Handbook on Intellectual Property Law and the WTO*, ed. Carlos Correa (Oxford: Edward Elgar, 2009), 2. Available at SSRN: https://ssrn.com/abstract=1405430.

215 Yankey, *International Patents*, 106 (see, n. 3).

216 Manteaw, "Patents and Development," 7 (see, n. 64).

217 Manteaw, "Patents and Development," 7 (see, n. 64). For a general discussion, *see* Kojo Yelpaala, "In Search of a Model Investment Law for Africa," *African Development Bank Law for Development Review*, Forthcoming, Available at SSRN: https://ssrn.com/abstract=1011166.

developing countries that folklore embodied creativity was part of the cultural identity of indigenous and local communities.[218] It was therefore seen as worthy of intellectual property protection, especially since new technologies were making folklore increasingly vulnerable to exploitation and misuse.[219] Yet, for more than twenty years, Africa and other developing countries have engaged the West at the WIPO Intergovernmental Committee on Intellectual Property and Genetic Resources, Traditional Knowledge and Folklore for recognition of what they see as their intellectual property.[220] To date, there is no end in sight that an agreement will be reached.

A colonial recognition of indigenous creations and inventions could have laid the foundation for subsequent international law reception. This would have been particularly useful for local innovators and creators such as traditional artists and custodians of traditional medicine, among others, who at present, have difficulty in taking advantage of the property rights system to protect their work. Besides, it could have led to high value horizontal foreign direct investment and technology transfer in areas such as indigenous scientific knowledge, research into plant medicine, and other creations and innovations resulting from the exploitation of traditional knowledge.[221] Yet, this vision of local development was not the focus of the colonial project.

Furthermore, the colonial legal system of the British failed to build local intellectual property expertise (or intellectual property "culture") and institutional capacity among their subjects. While the British had a greater emphasis on socializing the legal profession in its colonies and generating an English legal culture, this practice rarely extended to the realm of intellectual property, which remained largely administered from London.[222] Neal Goldman in an extensive study of the British judicial system in the Gold Coast insinuates that the focus of the British government on trade and commerce explain its

218 WIPO, "The WIPO Intergovernmental Committee on Intellectual Property and Genetic Resources, Traditional Knowledge and Folklore," Background Brief No. 2, https://www.wipo.int/publications/en/details.jsp?id=3861&plang=EN.

219 WIPO, "The WIPO Intergovernmental Committee."

220 WIPO, "The WIPO Intergovernmental Committee." Established in 2000, the WIPO Intergovernmental Committee on Intellectual Property and Genetic Resources, Traditional Knowledge and Folklore (IGC) is a forum where WIPO member states discuss the intellectual property issues that arise in the context of access to genetic resources and benefit-sharing as well as the protection of traditional knowledge and traditional cultural expressions. The IGC holds formal negotiations with the objective of reaching agreement on one or more international legal instruments that would ensure the effective protection of genetic resources, traditional knowledge and traditional cultural expressions.

221 Manteaw, "Patents and Development," 7 (see, n. 64).

222 Deere Birkbeck, "Developing Country Perspectives," (see, n. 214).

unwillingness to develop local capacity in intellectual property and administration. The British government failed to respond to repeated pleas by the colonial governors for additional judicial personnel or to spend money on infrastructure improvements or operations.[223]

Instead of training the indigenes to administer the local patent system at the inception of patent law in Ghana, the colonialists took the easy option of no training with the intent of cutting down costs.[224] There was also a lack of trust in the local elite.[225] This showed in the expression of doubt by the Board of Trade in the capability of the Chief Registrar of the Gold Coast to conduct the type of patent examinations envisaged in the 1899 Patent Ordinance.[226] Thus, the paucity of technical expertise to operate an independent patent system in the Gold Coast was highlighted as a reason for the 1925 Patent Ordinance.[227] A similar reason was given by the Attorney General of Nigeria in his advocacy for the adoption of the Patents Ordinance No. 30 of 1916.[228] Local intellectual property offices thus served as "clerical outpost"[229] for the colonial intellectual property office and merely rubber-stamped or extended intellectual property rights granted in Great Britain to the colony.[230] It can thus be said that the colonial patent and copyright system were not backed by adequate education to ensure a proper understanding of both systems and their institutions for socio-economic development. What it rather did was to create a biased

223 Goldman, "Fallible Justice," (see, n. 24).

224 Yankey, *International Patents*, 102 (see, n. 3). (Noting, for instance, that in the Board of Trades letter dated 25 January 1899 addressed to the secretary of state for the colonies (C.O. 96 Gold Coast 189, 349) the Attorney General for the colony had expressed the desire that 'the ordinance must be worked at the least possible expense to the Government).'

225 Goldman, "Fallible Justice," 3–6 (see, n. 24). Merry, "Law and Colonialism," (see, n. 32).

226 Yankey, *International Patents*, 102 (see, n. 3).

227 Manteaw, "Patents and Development," 4–5 (see, n. 64).

228 Yankey, *International Patents*, 115 (see, n. 3), citing the Report on the draft Patents Ordinance, 1916 by the Attorney-General of Nigeria dated 18.2.1916 in C.O. 583, 44, Despatches (Jan–Feb) Nigeria 1916, p. 546. The Attorney General noted that 'it is frequently impossible to obtain locally that expert advice which is required by the authority responsible for deciding whether or not a patent should be granted, and in the circumstances it is submitted that persons desiring to obtain protection in Nigeria, for an alleged invention may probably be required to satisfy first the Patents Office in the United Kingdom that his invention is one for which a patent should be granted.'

229 Mgbeoji, Ikechi. "African patent offices not fit for purpose," in *Innovation & Intellectual Property Collaborative Dynamics in Africa*, eds., Jeremy de Beer, Chris Armstrong, Chidi Ogumanam and Tobias Scchinwetter (Claremont: University of Cape Town Press, 2014), 234–236.

230 Ncube, "Three Centuries and Counting," 419 (see, n. 3).

perception that the intellectual property system was merely about adopting the laws of developed nations.[231]

The combined effect of all of the above (and many more, especially, the post-colonial dimension, which cannot be covered due to the limit in period for the volume) has been the persistence of legal imperialism and neo-colonialism in most countries of Africa. To put it differently, this has subtly led to the systemic integration of African countries into the international intellectual property system (adherence overdrive) and the curious case of countries inadvertently neglecting the flexibilities inherent in the international intellectual property system when formulating national intellectual property laws and policy (compliance overdrive).

7 Conclusion

This chapter explored the unusual circumstances under which the United Kingdom extended its intellectual property laws to its colonies in Africa in the nineteenth and early twentieth century, permitting to explore the variations in treatment in comparison to other colonies – such as the white settler colonies or dominions – and the consequences thereof on Africa. The extension and application of Imperial intellectual property laws to the colonies indeed varied according to region. The British treated their colonies differently in place, time and situation. The African colonies received the treatment that was in the eyes of the British colonizers deserving of them: intellectual property laws were imposed, not borrowed. The imposition of Imperial intellectual property laws was seen as a gift to the continent in all of its civilizing glory. This gift of the law, however, inherently challenged and transformed traditional conceptions of property, time, space, marriage, work and the state. Imperial intellectual property laws sidelined local innovation, creativity and knowledge governance systems (customary law) in Africa as they did not fit the Western concept of privately held rights over intellectual property.

Besides, the Imperial legal system failed to tailor laws to build the innovation and technological capacity of their colonies or to develop local expertise in intellectual property among the colonized. In this regard, intellectual property laws instituted at the peak of colonialism were not well adapted to the needs, priorities and situations of African countries. The same can be said of the corresponding international intellectual property treaties contracted at the time. Thus, commentators think that this colonial bottleneck has contributed to the

231 Manteaw, "Patents and Development," 7 (see, n. 64). (Emphasis added).

asymmetrical vulnerability dependence of African countries on raw materials and natural resources. The outcome is a crisis of underdevelopment and confidence among many African countries, especially, in the aftermath of independence as they set about adhering to and achieving compliance with differing and overlapping intellectual property regimes. This has led to adherence and compliance overdrive. In this sense, Africa is a unique intellectual property laboratory both during the period of colonization and its engagement with the international intellectual property system in the aftermath of independence.

Bibliography

Acquah, Daniel. "Intellectual Property, Developing Countries and the Law and Policy of the European Union: Towards Postcolonial Control of Development." PhD diss., IPR University Center, 2017.

Acquah, Daniel. "Technical Assistance as a Hedge to IP Exclusivity." In *Global Intellectual Property Protection and New Constitutionalism: Hedging Exclusive Rights*, edited by Jonathan Griffiths, and Tuomas Mylly. Oxford: Oxford University Press, 2021. Available on SSRN at https://papers.ssrn.com/sol3/papers.cfm?abstract_id=3682646.

Anghie, Antony. "Finding the Peripheries: Sovereignty and Colonialism in Nineteenth Century International Law." *Harvard International Law Journal* 40, no. 1 (Winter 1999): 1–80.

Anghie, Antony. *Imperialism, Sovereignty, and the Making of International Law*. Cambridge: Cambridge University Press, 2005.

Anghie, Antony. "Imperialism and International Legal Theory." In *The Oxford Handbook of the Theory of International Law*, edited by Anne Orford, and Florian Hoffmann, 156–172. Oxford: Oxford University Press, 2016.

Asher, Gordon. The Development of the Patent System in Canada Since 1767. Agincourt: Canada Law Book Company, 1965. Photocopied from *the Canadian Patent Reporter* 43 (1965): 56–75.

Austen, Ralph A., and Headrick, Daniel. "The Role of Technology in the African Past." *African Studies Review* 26, no. 3–4 (December 1983): 163–184.

Barrigar, R.H., and Robinson C. "Some Notes on the Historical Development of Patent law in Colonial Canada and Other British Colonies." *Intellectual Property Journal* 5 (1990).

Becker Lorca, Arnulf. "Universal International Law: Nineteenth-Century Histories of Imposition and Appropriation." *Harvard International Law Journal* 51, no. 2 (Summer 2010): 475–552.

Beckett, Jason. "Creating Poverty." In *The Oxford Handbook of the Theory of International Law*, edited by Anne Orford, and Florian Hoffmann, 987–1010. Oxford: Oxford University Press, 2016.

Bently, Lionel. "Copyright, Translations, and Relations Between Britain and India in the Nineteenth and Early Twentieth Centuries." *Chicago-Kent Law Review* 82, no. 3 (June 2007): 1181–1240.

Bently, Lionel. "The 'Extraordinary Multiplicity' of Intellectual Property Laws in the British Colonies in the Nineteenth Century." *Theoretical Inquiries in Law* 12, no. 1 (January 2011): 161–200.

Boateng, Boatema. "The Hand of the Ancestors: Time, Cultural Production, and Intellectual Property Law." *Law & Society Review* 47, no. 4 (December 2013): 943–973.

Bodenhausen, Georg H.C. *Guide to the Application of the Paris Convention for the Protection of Industrial Property*. Geneva: BIRPI, 1968.

Bond, Catherine. "'Cabined, Cribbed, Confined, Bound in': Copyright in the Australian Colonies." In *Research Handbook on the History of Copyright Law*, edited by Isabella Alexander, and H. Tomás Gómez-Arostegui, 372–390. Cheltenham: Edward Elgar, 2016.

Bryce, James. *Studies in History and Jurisprudence*. New York: Oxford University Press, 1901.

Chege, John Waruingi. *Copyright Law and Publishing in Kenya*. Nairobi: Kenya Literature Bureau, Nairobi, 1978.

Darby, Philip. *The Three Faces of Imperialism*. New Haven: Yale University Press, 1987.

de Beer, Jeremy, Baarbé, Jeremiah, and Ncube, Caroline B. "The Intellectual Property Treaty Landscape in Africa, 1885 to 2015." Open AIR Working Paper 4, 2017.

Deere Birkbeck, Carolyn. *The Implementation Game: The TRIPS Agreement and the Global Politics of Intellectual Property Reform in Developing Countries*. Oxford: Oxford University Press, 2008.

Deere Birbeck, Carolyn. "Developing Country Perspectives on Intellectual Property in the WTO: Setting the Pre-TRIPS Context." In *Research Handbook on Intellectual Property Law and the WTO*, edited by Carlos Correa. Oxford: Edward Elgar, 2009. Available at SSRN: https://ssrn.com/abstract=1405430.

Dinwoodie, Graeme B., Hennessey, William O., Esc., Perlmutter, Shira, and Austin, Graeme W. *International Intellectual Property Law and Policy*. San Francisco: Matthew Bender & Company, 2001.

Dutfield, Graham. "Traditional Knowledge, Intellectual Property and Pharmaceutical Innovation: What's Left to Discuss?" In *The Sage Handbook on Intellectual Property*, edited by Matthew David, and Debora Halbert, 649–664. Los Angeles: Sage publications, 2014. Sage.

Elias, Taslim Olawale. *Africa and the Development of International Law*, edited and reviewed by Richard Akinjide. Dordrecht: Nijhoff Publishers, 1988.

Ezejiofor, G. "Sources of Nigerian Law." In *Introduction to Nigerian Law*, edited by Cyprian Okechukwu Okonkwo. London: Sweet & Maxwell, 1980.

Feinberg, H.M. "Benin and the Europeans 1485–1897 by A.F.C. Ryder." Review of *Benin and the Europeans 1485–1897*, by Alan Frederick Charles Ryder. *African Studies* 4, no. 2 (1971).

Forbes, Robert J. "The Black Man's Industries." *Geographical Review* 23, no. 2 (April 1933): 230–247.

Fitzpatrick, Peter. "Custom as Imperialism." In *Law, Society and National Identity in Africa*, edited by Jamil M. Abun-Nasr, Ulrich Spellenberg, and Ulrike Wanitzek, 15–30. Hamburg: Helmut Buske Verlag, 1990.

Gervais, Daniel. "The Emergence and Development of Intellectual Property Law in Canada." In *The Oxford Handbook of Intellectual Property Law*, edited by Rochelle Dreyfuss, and Justine Pila, 265–290. Oxford: Oxford University Press, 2018.

Goldman, Neal M. "Fallible Justice: The Dilemma of the British in the Gold Coast, 1874–1944." PhD diss., Graduate Center, City University of New York, 2016.

Government of India: Office of the Controller General of Patents, Designs and Trademarks, Department for Promotion of Industry and Internal Trade, Ministry of Commerce and Industry. "History of Indian Patent System." Page last updated December 20, 2019. http://www.ipindia.nic.in/history-of-indian-patent-system.htm.

Graham, Aaron. "Patents and Invention in Jamaica and the British Atlantic Before 1857." *The Economic History Review* 73, no. 4. (July 2020): 940–963.

Greenberg, Suzanne F. "The WIPO Model Laws for the Protection of Unpatented Know-How: A Comparative Analysis." *International Tax & Business Lawyer* 3, no. 52 (1985): 52–80.

Harbers, Michael J. "International Patent Cooperation." *Stanford Law Review* 20, no. 5 (May 1968): 1000–1029.

Houghton, Peter J., and Mensah, Abraham Y. "Herbal Practitioners and Pharmacists in Ghana." *The Pharmaceutical Journal* 271, no. 7258 (2003): 93–94.

Himonga, Chuma, and Nhlapo, Thandabantu, eds. *African Customary Law in South Africa: Post-Apartheid and Living Law Perspectives*. Cape Town: Oxford University Press Southern Africa, 2014.

Kuruk, Paul. "The Role of Customary Law Under Sui Generis Frameworks of Intellectual Property Rights in Traditional and Indigenous Knowledge." *Indiana International & Comparative Law Review* 17, no. 1 (2007): 67–118.

Kongolo, Tshimanga. "Historical developments of industrial property laws in Africa." *WIPO Journal* 5, no. 1 (2013): 105–117.

Kongolo, Tshimanga. "Historical evolution of copyright legislation in Africa." *WIPO Journal* 5, no. 2 (2014), 163–175.

Long, Pamela O. "Invention, Authorship, 'Intellectual Property,' and the Origin of Patents: Notes Toward a Conceptual History." *Technology and Culture* 32, no. 4 (October 1991): 846–884.

Lund, Henry. *A Treatise on the Substantive Law Relating to Letters Patent for Inventions*. Pennsylvania: T. & J.W. Johnson, 1851.

Lynch, B.M., and Robbins, L.H. "Namoratunga: The First Archeoastronomical Evidence in Sub-Saharan Africa." *Science* 200, no. 4343 (May 1978): 766–768.

Manteaw, Samuel O. "Patents and Development in Ghana: Proposals for Change." *University of Ghana Law Journal* 24 (2008–2010): 111–144.

Melo Araujo, Billy A. *The EU Deep Trade Agenda: Law and Policy*. Oxford: Oxford University Press, 2016.

Merry, Sally Engle. "Law and Colonialism." *Law & Society Review* 24, no. 4 (1991): 889–922.

Mgbeoji, Ikechi. "African Patent Offices Not Fit for Purpose." In *Innovation & Intellectual Property Collaborative Dynamics in Africa*, edited by Jeremy de Beer, Chris Armstrong, Chidi Oguamanam, and Tobias Schonwetter, 234–247. Claremont: University of Cape Town Press, 2014.

Moyse, Pierre-Emanuel. "Canadian Colonial Copyright: The Colony Strikes Back." In *An Emerging Intellectual Property Paradigm: Perspectives from Canada*, edited by Ysolde Gendreau, 107–138. Cheltenham: Edward Elgar, 2008.

Ncube, Caroline B. *Intellectual Property Policy, Law and Administration in Africa: Exploring Continental and Sub-regional Co-operation*. Oxon: Routledge, 2016.

Ncube, Caroline B. "Three Centuries and Counting: The Emergence and Development of Intellectual Property Law in Africa." In *The Oxford Handbook of Intellectual Property Law*, edited by Rochelle Dreyfuss, and Justine Pila, 409–430. Oxford: Oxford University Press, 2018.

Oguamanaam, Chidi. "Wandering Footloose: Traditional Knowledge and the 'Public Domain' revisited." *The Journal of Intellectual Property* 21, no. 3 (March 2018): 306–325.

Okediji, Ruth L. "The International Relations of Intellectual Property: Narratives of Developing Country Participation in the Global Intellectual Property System." *Singapore Journal of International & Comparative Law* 7 (2003): 315–385.

Okediji, Ruth L. "Negotiating the Public Domain in an International Framework for Generic Resources, Traditional Knowledge and Traditional Cultural Expression." In *Protecting Traditional Knowledge: The WIPO Intergovernmental Committee on Intellectual Property and Generic Resources, Traditional Knowledge and Folklore*, edited by Daniel F. Robinson, Ahmed Abdel-Latif, and Pedro Roffe. 141–172. London, Routledge, 2017.

Ola, Kunle. "Evolution and Future Trends of Copyright in Nigeria." *Journal of Open Access to Law* 2, no. 1 (2014): 7–32.

Ouma, Marisella. "The Policy Context for a Commons-Based Approach to Traditional Knowledge in Kenya." In *Innovation and Intellectual Property Collaborative Dynamics in Africa*, edited by Jeremy de Beer, Chris Armstrong, Chidi Ogumanam, and Tobias Schonwetter, 132–150. Claremont: University of Cape Town Press. 2014.

Penrose, Edith T. "International Patenting and the Less-developed Countries." *The Economic Journal* 83, no. 331 (September 1973): 768–786.

Peukert, Alexander. "The Colonial Legacy of the International Copyright System." In *Copyright Africa: How Intellectual Property, Media and Markets Transform Immaterial Goods*, edited by Ute Röchenthaler, and Mamadou Diawara. Canon Pyon: Sean Kingston Publishing, 2016.

Ricketson, Sam. *The Berne Convention for the Protection of Literary and Artistic Works: 1886–1986*. London: Kluwer Centre for Commercial Law Studies, 1987.

Ryder, Alan Frederick Charles. *Benin and the Europeans 1485–1897*. New York: Humanities Press, 1969.

Seville, Catherine. *The Internationalisation of Copyright Law: Books, Buccaneers and the Black Flag in the Nineteenth Century*. Cambridge: Cambridge University Press, 2006.

Schmidhauser, John R. "Legal Imperialism: Its Enduring Impact on Colonial and Post-colonial Judicial Systems." *International Political Review* 13, no. 3 (July 1992): 321–334.

Sikyo, George M., Nyukuri, Elvin, and Wakhungu, Judi W. *Intellectual Property Protection in Africa: Status of Laws, Research and Policy Analysis in Ghana, Kenya, Nigeria, South Africa and Uganda*. Nairobi: Acts Press, 2006.

Singh, Prabhakar, and Mayer, Benoît. *Critical International Law: Postrealism, Postcolonialism, and Transnationalism*. Delhi: Oxford University Press, 2014.

Suthersanen, Uma. "The First Global Copyright Act." Queen Mary School of Law Legal Studies Research Paper No. 106/2012. 2012. Available at SSRN, https://ssrn.com/abstract=2022878.

Suthersanen, Uma, and Gendreau, Ysolde, eds. *A Shifting Empire: 100 Years of the Copyright Act 1911*. Cheltenham: Edward Elgar, 2013.

Umahi, Okechukwu Timothy. "Access to Medicines: the Colonial Impacts on Patent Law of Nigeria." 2011. Available on SSRN, http://papers.ssrn.com/sol3/papers.cfm?abstract_id=1975928.

United International Bureaux for the Protection of Intellectual Property. "Model Law for Developing Countries on Inventions." BIRPI Pub. No. 801(E) (1965).

United Nations. "Universal Copyright Convention." Signed at Geneva on 6 September 1952. http://www.wipo.int/wipolex/en/other_treaties/text.jsp?file_id=172836.

Wadlow, Christopher. "The British Empire Patent 1901–1923: The 'global' patent that never was." *Intellectual Property Quarterly*, no. 4 (2006): 311–346.

Worboys, Micahel. "British Colonial Science Policy, 1918–1939." In *Les Sciences Coloniales: Figures and Institutions*, edited by Patrick Petitjean, 99–112. ORSTOM, 1996.

World Intellectual Property Organization. "Berne Convention for the Protection of Literary and Artistic Works." September 9, 1886, as last revised July 24, 1971, 25 U.S.T. 1341, 828 U.N.T.S. 221, as amended on September 28, 1979.

World Intellectual Property Organization. "International Convention for the Protection of Performers, Producers of Phonograms and Broadcasting Organisations." Done at Rome on October 26, 1961. http://www.wipo.int/wipolex/en/treaties/text.jsp?file_id=289795.

World Intellectual Property Organization. "Paris Convention for the Protection of Industrial Property." March 20, 1883, 13 U.S.T. 2, 828 U.N.T.S. 107, as last revised at the Stockholm Revision Conference, July 14, 1967, 21 U.S.T. 1538, 828 U.N.T.S. 303, and as amended on September 28, 1979.

World Intellectual Property Organization. "The WIPO Intergovernmental Committee on Intellectual Property and Genetic Resources, Traditional Knowledge and Folklore." Background Brief No. 2. https://www.wipo.int/publications/en/details.jsp?id=3861&plang=EN.

Yankey, George Sipa-Adjah. *International Patents and Technology Transfer to Less Developed Countries: The Case of Ghana and Nigeria*. Aldershot: Avebury, 1987.

Yawson, Robert M. "Technology commercialisation and intellectual property rights in Ghana." Paper presented at the International Conference on TRIPS – Next Agenda for Developing Countries, Hyderabad, India 11–12 October, 2002, https://mpra.ub.uni-muenchen.de/id/eprint/33185.

Yelpaala, Kojo. "In Search of a Model Investment Law for Africa." *African Development Bank Law for Development Review*. Forthcoming. Available on SSRN: https://ssrn.com/abstract=1011166.

CHAPTER 10

Early American Federal Trademark Law and the Law of Nations

Zvi S. Rosen

Early U.S. federal trademark law is dominated by the U.S. Supreme Court's unanimous opinion in the *Trade-Mark Cases*,[1] which invalidated the federal trademark laws enacted 1870 through 1876 on constitutional grounds. This case however exists in a broader milieu which is dominated by concerns of reciprocity with treaty counterparties to bilateral treaties – and the power of Congress to pass legislation to enforce those treaties in the absence of a clear grant in the Constitution. The story of U.S. trademark law at the time is the story of a largely isolated economy encountering the broader commercial world, and its legal system adapting to this reality by reckoning with powers Congress would need to prevent the United States from being excluded from the nascent global economy.

1 The Origins of Federal Trademark Law

A series of bills were introduced in Congress to provide for trademark registration through the 1860s, but they were mostly focused on domestic concerns,

1 100 U.S. 82 (1879). The case is also referred to as *Steffens, et al. v. U.S.* The short, practical name "Trade-Mark Cases" was part of the trend towards shorter and more useful case names begun during John William Wallace's tenure as Reporter of Decisions, stemming from his desire to prevent case names from becoming unwieldy since the case name "is only designed for facility of reference." Wallace, John William. *United States Reports*, Preface, 68 U.S. (1 Wallace) xiii–xiv (1863). Wallace's practice in this area and others stood in stark contrast to the reporters who had preceded him, and his methodology was largely criticized. Cohen, Morris L. and O'Connor, Sharon Hamby. *A Guide to the Early Reports of the Supreme Court of the United States* (Littleton, CO: Fred B. Rothman & Company, 1995), 110–112. Many of Wallace's practices were followed by his successor William Tod Otto, who served as reporter for this case. Regarding addressing the case as "The *Trade-Mark Cases*," this is the general custom. Cross, John. "The Lingering Legacy of the Trade-Mark Cases." *Michigan State Law Review* 1 (2008): 367. While the definite article "The" is not part of the title, it is an indispensable way of regarding the decision, otherwise leading to confusion as to whether one is discussing trademark cases more generally. As for the hyphenated form "Trade-Mark," the term seems to have always hyphenated been in that day (as is amply shown by the titles of the citations *infra*), or written as two words, unhyphenated.

 | DOI:10.1163/9789004511439_012

not foreign trade in trademark goods.[2] However, in the latter part of the decade the United States would enter into several treaties respecting foreign trademarks, and there would be a need for legislation to execute them.

1.1 *State and International Trademark Law*

In the first half of the nineteenth century, the common law tort of fraud and deceit developed into common law protection for trademarks, and '[b]y the 1850s, common law rules against passing off and trademark infringement were well-accepted.'[3] As the common law of trademarks began to coalesce, states also began to enact statutes clarifying civil remedies, as well as providing criminal remedies in some cases. In 1845, New York was the first state to pass a trademark law, providing for both criminal and civil remedies[4] but would hardly be the last; prior to 1870, eleven other states would also enact statutes respecting trademarks.[5]

As the common law of trademarks was developing in the United States, it was also developing in the United Kingdom, and this took on a transatlantic tint in the late 1850s when the American Collins Company was successful in a series of suits there to enforce its mark for cutlery.[6] The international dimensions of trademarks were made clearer in 1860, when New York state courts considered cases brought by both British and French trademark holders against alleged American infringers.[7] France passed a trademark law in 1857 'so robust that it survived with only minor changes for another century,' while the United Kingdom passed a trademark law in 1862.[8] However, the French statute made clear that in order to receive protection for their mark in France, a foreigner would need to be from a nation with a diplomatic agreement with

---

2 H.R. 330, 36th Cong., 1860; H.R. 235, 37th Cong., 1862; H.R. 1008, 39th Cong., 1867.

3 McCarthy, J. Thomas. *McCarthy on Trademarks and Unfair Competition*, 4th ed. (n.p.: Thomson West, 2009): § 5:2.

4 N.Y. Laws 304–05 (1845); Barber, Arthur W. "The Constitution and Trade-Marks." *Lawyer and Banker and Southern Bench and Bar Review* 5 (1912): 210–211.

5 Forbes, Francis et al. *Report of The Commissioners Appointed To Revise the Statutes Relating to Patents, Trade and Other Marks, and Trade and Commercial Names*, S. Doc. No. 20 at 91–92 (2d Sess. 1902). The other states were Connecticut (1847); Pennsylvania (1847); Massachusetts (1850); Ohio (1859); Iowa (1860); Michigan (1863); Oregon (1864); Nevada (1865); Kansas (1866); Maine (1866); Missouri (1866). Ibid. Of these laws, eight provided for criminal remedies, two provided for civil and criminal remedies, and two provided civil remedies only. Ibid. Those states only providing criminal remedies presumably meant to complement the civil common-law trademark law.

6 Duguid, Paul. "French Connections: The International Propagation of Trademarks in the Nineteenth Century." *Enterprise & Society* 10 (Mar. 2009): 13.

7 Diguid, "Fresh Connections," 14.

8 Ibid., 6.

France providing bilateral trademark protection.[9] Spurred on by concerns of British trademarks being infringed overseas, especially in Germany, the United Kingdom began negotiating bilateral trademark treaties itself.[10]

The enactment of the 1862 British trademark law was spurred on by its 1859 commercial treaty with Russia, part of the aftermath of the Crimean War, under which Britain was to 'adopt such measures as may be required to' secure protection for Russian trademarks in the United Kingdom.[11] France had already signed a bilateral trademark treaty with Russia in 1857, its first such treaty under the 1857 law.[12] It is unclear why exactly Russia was so enthusiastic about bilateral trademark protection in the mid-19th century, but whatever the reason, Russia would soon be the first trademark counterparty of the United States as well.[13]

1.2 *American Trademark Treaties*

As this was going on the press in the U.S. took occasional notice of what were becoming increasingly frequent international trademark disputes.[14] By 1865 foreign nations were enquiring about the status of trademark law in the United States[15] – it would not be long before this curiosity morphed into negotiation. The first foreign trademark treaty was signed with Russia in 1868,[16] followed shortly thereafter with treaties with Belgium,[17] and

9 Ibid., 16.

10 Dinwoodie, Graeme B., and Janis, Mark D., eds. *Trademark Law and Theory: A Handbook of Contemporary Research* (Cheltenham, UK: Edward Elgar Publishing, 2008), 19.

11 Duguid, "French Connections," 17–18.

12 Ibid., 16–17.

13 Paul DuGuid argues that in fact France was the main interested party and Russia was amenable but not motivated in terms of its own trademark owners, noting from an examination of registrations that "Russian firms showed little interest in trademark reciprocity." Ibid., 20. One can imagine that Russia put it into their commercial treaty with Britain as a sort of best practices, having just agreed to such a treaty with France.

14 Ibid., 13–14 (discussing American opinion in an article on the development of French trademark law).

15 Ashton, J. Hubley, ed. *Trade Marks: State Legislation on Subject of Trade-Marks Noticed*, vol. 11 of *Official Opinions of the Attorneys General of the United States: Advising the President and Heads of Departments in Relation to their Official Duties*, (Washington, DC: Authority of Congress, 1869), 352. (Responding to a letter from the Austrian Minister enquiring about trademark protections in the United States).

16 Malloy, William M. "Additional Article to Treaty of Commerce [US-Russia]," in *Treaties, Conventions, International Acts, Protocols and Agreements Between the United States of America and Other Powers 1776–190* (Washington Government Printing Office, 1910), 2:1524.

17 Malloy, William M. "Additional Article [to Treaty of July 17, 1858]" in *Treaties, Conventions, International Acts, Protocols and Agreements Between the United States of America and Other Powers 1776–190* (Washington Government Printing Office, 1910), 1:86.

France.[18] With each of these treaties, a question would linger as to whether they were self-executing, or whether their enactment required affirmative legislation by congress.

In September 1867 the United States expressed interest in a trademark treaty with Russia, and Russia indicated their willingness to do so in late 1867, proposing that it be drawn along the lines of article 22 of their treaty of commerce with France.[19] The treaty was negotiated during January 1868 in Washington, DC,[20] and signed on January 27.[21] It was transmitted to the Senate on the following day,[22] and ratification was advised that summer.[23] The treaty read, in pertinent part:

> The High Contracting Parties, desiring to secure complete and efficient protection to the manufacturing industry of their respective citizens and subjects, agree that any counterfeiting in one of the two countries of the trade marks affixed in the other on merchandize to show its origin and quality, shall be strictly prohibited and repressed, and shall give ground for an action of damages in favor of the injured party, to be prosecuted in the courts of the country in which the counterfeit shall be proven.
>
> The trade marks in which the citizens or subjects of one of the two countries may wish to secure the right of property in the other, must be lodged exclusively, to wit, the marks of citizens of the United States, in the Department of Manufactures and Inland Commerce, at St. Petersburg, and the marks of Russian subjects, at the Patent Office in Washington.[24]

This treaty's provisions created, for the first time, a registry at the Patent Office (then in the Department of the Interior) for trademarks. They also created a civil cause of action for damages, although whether injunctive relief would

18 Malloy, William M. "1869 Trade-Mark Convention" in *Treaties, Conventions, International Acts, Protocols and Agreements Between the United States of America and Other Powers 1776–190* (Washington Government Printing Office, 1910), 1:534. It has been argued that the French treaty was the most important in spurring the drafting of the 1870 Act. Duguid, "French Connections," 28.

19 Letter from the Chancellor of the Empire of Russia to the United States to Secretary of State William Seward, 1 December 1867. Letter and translation on microfilm in Dept. of State Papers, Nat'l Archives, College Park, MD.

20 U.S. *House Journal.* "Message of the President for the Third Session of the 40th Congress," 40th Cong., 3rd sess., 10 December 1868, 34.

21 U.S. Congress. *Senate Executive Journal.* 40th Cong., 2nd sess., 28 January 1868, 157.

22 Ibid.

23 Ibid., 371–372 (Jul. 25, 1868).

24 Malloy, "1868. Additional Article to Treaty of Commerce [US-Russia]," 1910.

likewise be permitted is less clear. In practice, the Russian trademark treaty would prove a disappointment to US trademark owners, as its limitation to Russian-made articles was ineffectual against German and other counterfeits which were imported into Russia.[25]

The next trademark treaty to come would be with Belgium, later in 1868. Following up on an "intimation" from the minister to Belgium, the Secretary of State authorized him to conclude a trademark convention along the lines of the one concluded with Russia.[26] The Belgian government objected to the phrase 'or repressed' in the Russian Treaty, feeling that it suggested criminal jurisdiction, and also insisted on additional language about marks in the public domain.[27] Aside from these changes the treaty was substantially identical to the Russian treaty in verbiage, and was advised on by the Senate in much shorter order than the Russian treaty.[28]

With these two treaties signed and ratified, the ball began rolling for treaties with more major commercial powers; France was the first. The Emperor Napoleon III noted the trademark treaties in his 1869 Address, and specifically asserted that France was prepared for such an arrangement.[29] Such an arrangement was concluded April 16, 1869, and ratified in short order.[30] In substance it was similar to the Belgian Treaty, save that it fixed that this arrangement was limited by the duration normally given to trademarks in the relevant country. Other treaties would be made throughout the 1870s and beyond, but a question quickly reared its head – need domestic legislation be passed in America as a result of these treaties?

25 "Our Trade with Russia," *New York Tribune*, April 25, 1874, 1.

26 Letter from William Seward, Secretary of State, to Henry Sanford, Ambassador to Belgium, 17 November 1868, in the National Archives.

27 Letter from Henry Sanford, Ambassador to Belgium to William Seward, Secretary of State, 20 December 1868, in the National Archives. This letter also transmitted the proposed treaty and noted that the problem was mostly of American trademarks being infringed in Belgium. Belgium also wanted protections for designs and models, where the situation was the reverse, but the ambassador did not feel that his instructions from the Secretary of State included such authorization. Ibid; Letter from the Belgian Dept. of Interior to Henry Sanford, Ambassador to Belgium, 11 December 1868, in the National Archives.

28 U.S. Congress. *Senate Executive Journal*. 40th Cong., 3rd sess., 28 January 1869, 463–464.

29 "Report on the Conditions of the Empire," Made to the Senate and Legislative Assembly of France (1869). The handwritten translation in the State Department papers says this alludes specifically to the treaty with Russia.

30 U.S. Congress. *Senate Executive Journal*. 41st Cong., 1st sess., 19 April 1869, 219.

1.3 *The Treaty Power*

That treaties are the supreme law of the land, on par with statutes, is set forth in the constitution.[31] Arising out of the Louisiana Purchase and annexation of Florida, the Supreme Court's opinion in *Foster & Elam v. Neilson* was the definitive word at the time regarding whether a treaty is self-executing.[32] In pertinent part, it said:

> A treaty is in its nature a contract between two nations, not a legislative act. It does not generally effect, of itself, the object to be accomplished, especially so far as its operation is infra-territorial; but is carried into execution by the sovereign power of the respective parties to the instrument.
>
> In the United States a different principle is established. Our constitution declares a treaty to be the law of the land. It is, consequently, to be regarded in courts of justice as equivalent to an act of the legislature, whenever it operates of itself without the aid of any legislative provision. But when the terms of the stipulation import a contract, when either of the parties engages to perform a particular act, the treaty addresses itself to the political, not the judicial department; and the legislature must execute the contract before it can become a rule for the Court.[33]

Even one hundred years after *Foster*, it was still one of the few pronouncements on this issue.[34] The Supreme Court did deal with whether a treaty could provide jurisdiction for a cause of action indirectly when it noted that a treaty specifically did not create a cause of action, leading to the possible inference that such a treaty could enact a cause of action, it just did not in the case in question.[35] All of the trademark treaties specifically gave a cause of action in the courts of each nation, and thus were most likely self-executing. Nonetheless, it would only be prudent to put legislation in Congress, both to

---

31 U.S. Const. Art. VI. *See also* U.S. v. Schooner Peggy, 5 U.S. 109–110 (1801). To wit: "The constitution of the United States declares a treaty to be the supreme law of the land. Of consequence its obligation on the courts of the United States must be admitted. It is certainly true that the execution of a contract between nations is to be demanded from, and, in the general, superintended by the executive of each nation, and therefore, whatever the decision of this court may be relative to the rights of parties litigating before it, the claim upon the nation is unsatisfied, may still be asserted. But yet where a treaty is the law of the land, and as such affects the rights of parties litigating in court, that treaty as much binds those rights and is as much to be regarded by the court as an act of congress."

32 Foster & Elam v. Neilson, 27 U.S. 253 (1829).

33 Ibid., 314.

34 Henry, Leslie. "When is a Treaty Self-Executing." *Michigan Law Review* 27 (1928–1929): 776.

35 U.S. v. Ferreira, 54 U.S. 40 (1851).

ensure the execution of the treaties and put greater detail into the procedure of their enforcement.

This leads to the second question … under what authority could Congress pass executory legislation generally? In the 1920 case of *Missouri v. Holland*, the Supreme Court held that the making of a treaty gave Congress the power to enforce its provisions even if Congress would otherwise lack the power to enact the legislation.[36] However, that case was still a half-century away in 1870, and it is unclear to what degree such a power was recognized at the time. The primary tension with such a power is the Tenth Amendment, with its reservation of powers not enumerated to the states. Some have argued that up through *Missouri v. Holland*, the treaty power only permitted Congress to legislate up to the limits of its enumerated powers.[37] Others have argued that the treaty power extended further at the time, and permitted Congress to act even in areas where such action would otherwise be prohibited.[38] While arguments for both sides are compelling, it does not seem that Congress or the Courts took the latter, nationalist, view of the treaty power in either 1870 or 1879.

1.4 *The 1870 Act*

While no record survives, it seems that trademarks were deposited in the Patent Office under these treaties even prior to any formal enactment executing these treaties.[39] This gave the matter a certain urgency, and apropos of these treaties two separate bills were introduced as S. 264 and S. 265 on April 7th, 1869.[40] The former bill assumed that the civil remedies of the Russian Treaty were self-executing, and provided criminal remedies for the infringement of Russian trademarks.[41] The latter bill, by contrast, was proposed simply to execute the treaties that had just been concluded, being proposed "carry into effect the

36 Missouri v. Holland, 252 U.S. 416 (1920). The Supreme Court dealt with the treaty power in 2013–14 in what many thought might be an occasion to revisit *Missouri v. Holland*, but the Supreme Court largely avoided the fundamental treaty power issue. Bond v. United States, 572 U.S. 844 (2014).

37 Bradley, Curtis A. "The Treaty Power and American Federalism." *Michigan Law Review* 97 (1998): 390.

38 Golove, David M. "Treaty-Making and The Nation: The Historical Foundations of The Nationalist Conception of The Treaty Power." *Michigan Law Review* 98 (2000): 1075.

39 Letter from Mr. Bowen, Examiner of Trademarks, to Rep. Hammond, 23 February 1880, 2. Files of the House Committee on the Judiciary in the National Archives. Apparently they were not registered and no record was kept – this was simply his recollection. Ibid.

40 U.S. *Senate Journal*. 41st Cong., 1st sess., 7 April 1869, 133.

41 S.264, 41st Cong., (As introduced Apr. 7, 1869).

stipulations" of trademark treaties more generally.[42] The bills were referred to different committees, and both were referred back and debated on the same day two weeks later.[43] On that day Senator Trumbull noted that the introduction of both bills had been a mistake, and asked that his bill (S. 264) be withdrawn in favor of S. 265.[44] There was some debate over whether the bill added anything to the law, and Senator Sumner said that the purpose of the bill was simply to effectuate the three treaties already signed.[45] Without much more debate, the bill was passed by the Senate.[46] Concurrence was requested from the House,[47] but the House did not take a straightforward approach in concurring with this bill.

Less than a year later, in the second session of the 41st Congress, a slew of bills would be introduced on the subject of foreign trademarks. The first was introduced by Sen. Trumbull (who had also introduced S. 264) as S. 501 on February 7, 1870, and referred to the Committee on the Judiciary.[48] Entitled 'A Bill [to m]ore effectually to provide for the execution of treaties for the protection of the owners of trade marks,' it did not actually create a federal trademark code, but rather gave the Circuit Courts jurisdiction to hear cases under trademark treaties.[49] The second was introduced in the House as H.R. 1824 on April 19, 1870, and doubled the tariff on imported goods bearing a false trademark of American goods.[50] The final one was a fairly limited one, introduced two days later, and dealing solely with imported watches.[51]

---

42 Indeed, the treaty would be sent to the senate by the president a week later, and consented to three days after that. U.S. Congress. *Senate Executive Journal.* 41st Cong., 1st sess., 16 April, 1869, 196.

43 *Congressional Globe*, 41st Cong., 1st sess., 22 April 1869, 2894. S. 264 was referred to the Committee on the Judiciary, while S. 265 was referred to the Committee on Foreign Affairs. Letter from Mr. Bowen to Rep. Hammond.

44 Ibid.

45 Ibid. The argument in the contrary was simply that foreigners could already sue in the federal courts in enforce their common-law trademark rights.

46 Ibid., 2895.

47 Ibid., 2932 (Apr. 23, 1869).

48 U.S. *Senate Journal.* 41st Cong., 2nd sess., 7 February 1870, 209.

49 S.501, 41st Cong. (As introduced Feb. 7, 1869).

50 U.S. *House Journal.* 41st Cong., 2nd sess., 19 April 1870, 640. Compared to the standard tariff on imported goods.

51 U.S. *Senate Journal.* 41st Cong., 2nd sess., 21 April 1870, 529; S.829, 41st Cong. (As introduced Apr. 21, 1870). This bill was sent to the committee on Finance, and reported with minor amendments a week later. U.S. *Senate Journal*, 41st Cong., 28 April 1870, 566. Apparently this bill was meant to address the specific problem of foreign counterfeiting of American watches, which were then imported to the US and sold at lower prices.

These myriad bills from the second session were ultimately distractions. Rather than taking a simple position on concurring with the Senate Bill, the House took a much more ambitious approach, combining the trademark bill with a full revision of the nation's intellectual property laws that was currently occupying the Committees on Patents.[52] Bill H.R. 1714 started out as a patent revision, and then had copyrights added to it. As it came towards completion, trademarks would be added as well.[53]

Rep. Thomas B. Jenckes first brought up this development to the whole Congress on April 14, 1870, in a lengthy explanation of the omnibus bill. The trademark bill received limited mention, first that it simply provided an alternative to state protection, and did not go beyond the contours of common-law trademark protection.[54] He then explained the reasons for introducing a federal trademark law at the present time:

> Concerning trade-marks, we are at present in an anomalous condition, which perhaps is not understood by the House generally. By certain treaties or conventions with Belgium, France, and Russia, we have agreed to recognize the validity of the trade-marks of those countries upon their being registered in the Patent Office of the United States, and to give them the same effect throughout the United States that they have in the country where they originated; and trade-marks recognized by the law of this country have the same effect throughout those European countries as the trademarks secured by the citizens or subjects of those countries. Thus by treaties, which are a part of the supreme law of the land, we have secured to subjects of those three nations rights which are not by national law secured to citizens of the United States. The right, which it is proposed to protect by registration of trademarks are not greater in any sense than those which are secured to citizens of foreign countries. In fact, these provisions are substantially those of the continental nations, and also those of the trade-marks statute of Great Britain, with which country I believe we are also engaged in negotiations for a similar

"A Needed 'Protection,'" *Chicago Tribune*, June 14, 1870, 2; *See also* (untitled article), *New York Tribune*, October 29, 1870, 4 (noting that watch importers had threatened to spend a large sum of money to defeat the bill).

52 The history of the bill more generally can be found at William Patry, *Patry on Copyright* (n.p.: Thomson West, 2007): § 1:33.

53 Patry, "Patry on Copyright." Unfortunately, there is no documentation of when trademarks were added to the bill or the motivation for including them in the omnibus bill – what evidence there is of the committee's deliberations does not include such detail.

54 U.S. Congress. *Congressional Record.* 41st Cong., 2nd sess., 14 April 1870 at 2683.

> treaty. The desirableness of these provisions I have not heard questioned by any one.[55]

Although discussion of technical aspects of the trademark bill would continue for some time, discussions of whether such a trademark law was truly necessary were more or less over. Perhaps even more surprisingly, given the reaction to the trademark bill offered a decade earlier, whether the trademark law was constitutional never came up. Not only is there no discussion of it in the Record, but it seems that there was no discussion of the power of Congress in this area at all.[56] Rep. Orestes Cleveland, one of the members of the Committee of Patents in the House at the time, recalled that "no question was raised on the power of Congress, under the Constitution, to legislate on that subject. My own Impression is that the power of Congress was considered beyond question – taken for granted in fact. Nobody, so far as we knew, having ever raised the point."[57]

While one reason for the lack of questions regarding the act's constitutionality was that bill was created and focused on other areas of intellectual property law, there was more to it than that – the act became law with the main purpose of the trademark sections being to call into effect the treaties that had and would be made with foreign powers. Not only are the aforementioned circumstances strong evidence of that, but the truth of this matter was obvious to contemporary observers.[58] While domestic trademarks were perhaps not absent from the consideration of the 1870 Act, they were neither the impetus for the law nor the prime reason for its passage, and seem to have been of no more than evanescent concern. Given this, the reason for the lack of concern for the constitutionality of the bill becomes apparent – Congress saw themselves as simply executing international treaties. In the next six years Congress would pass a law moving copyright registration of labels to the patent office,[59] and a law providing for criminal remedies for trademark infringement.[60] Neither bill was particularly focused on concerns of international trade, though.

55 Ibid.
56 "The Federal Trade-Mark Statutes." *Albany Law Journal* 19 (Jan. 1879): 5.
57 Ibid.
58 Ibid. ("In order to give full effect to the treaties with Russia, Belgium and France, which were negotiated in aid and encouragement of the commercial relations between the countries mentioned and the United States, Congress enacted the registration act of July, 1870."); Browne, William Henry. preface to *A Treatise on the Law of Trade-Marks* (Boston: Little, Brown, and Company, 1873): v. ("[T]he principal object that [the 1870 act] had in view, it must be confessed, was the matter of reciprocity.")
59 18 Stat.78 § 3 (1874); Reimagining Bleistein.
60 19 Stat. 141 (1876).

2 The Turbulent Decade

For a short period time, federal trademark law bloomed. The constitutionality of the federal trademark was not immediately questioned by the courts or lawyers, new treaties were made, and these laws were applied repeatedly, most famously by the Supreme Court in *McLean v. Fleming*.[61] However, after the criminal trademark act raised the stakes for trademark infringement, both judges and lawyers began to question the constitutionality of the federal trademark laws.

2.1 *New Treaties*

Following the passage of the 1870 act additional trademark treaties had been entered into, including treaties with Austria-Hungary,[62] Germany,[63] Great Britain,[64] and Brazil.[65] Each of these reflected the increasingly international flavor of trademark law. These treaties were not perfect – irreversible damage to the mark might have occurred before a treaty was signed for instance.[66] Even given this, these treaties reflected America's participation in a transatlantic branding marketplace.

The convention with Austria was entered into in 1871, and to American observers was to the benefit of the United States, since counterfeiting of American goods like sewing machines was more common there.[67] That same

61 McLean v. Fleming, 96 U.S. 245 (1877).

62 Malloy, William M. "Trade-Mark Convention between the United States and Austria-Hungary" in *Treaties, Conventions, International Acts, Protocols and Agreements Between the United States of America and Other Powers 1776–190* (Washington Government Printing Office, 1910), 1:47.

63 Malloy, William M. "Article XVII [of Consular Convention between the United States and the German Empire]," in *Treaties, Conventions, International Acts, Protocols and Agreements Between the United States of America and Other Powers 1776–190* (Washington Government Printing Office, 1910), 1:556.

64 Malloy, William M. "Declaration Affording Reciprocal Protection to Trade-Marks between the United States and Great Britain" in *Treaties, Conventions, International Acts, Protocols and Agreements Between the United States of America and Other Powers 1776–190* (Washington Government Printing Office, 1910), 1:737.

65 Malloy, William M. "Agreement Concerning Trade-Mark between the United States and Brazil" in *Treaties, Conventions, International Acts, Protocols and Agreements Between the United States of America and Other Powers 1776–190* (Washington Government Printing Office, 1910), 1:146.

66 Higgins, David M. "'Forgotten Heroes and Forgotten Issues': Business and Trademark History during the Nineteenth Century," *Business History Review* 86, no. 2 (2012): 273, http://www.jstor.org/stable/23239499.

67 "The New Treaty for The Protection of Trade-Marks," *Chicago Tribune*, December 27, 1871, 3. The treaty with Austria was followed shortly thereafter with a special law to protect

year the United States entered into a "Convention Respecting Consuls and Trademarks" with the new German Empire, which despite the name only had one article out of the eighteen on trademarks, and was more generally focused otherwise on setting basic diplomatic relations with united Germany.[68] The treaty with Germany would mirror the treaty with Great Britain in 1877 – instead of setting rules it simply requires reciprocity of treatment and putting subjects of the contracting parties on equal footing as native citizens.[69] This was perhaps unsurprising as Germany and the United States (plus Japan) were the largest counterfeiters of British goods, making simple bilateral trademark relations a priority.[70] All of these nations required registration for protection of a trademark, so it was reasonable to expect that the United States would need to offer registration to fulfill its treaty obligations.[71]

2.2 *Roots of the Trade-Mark Cases*

In 1878, clouds began to darken for the 1870 trademark act. In August of 1878 the Central Law Journal published a two-part article arguing that a trademark is neither a copyright nor a patent, and that trademarks are not covered within the text and spirit of any reasonable construction of the Intellectual Property Clause of the constitution.[72] The Circuit Court in Cincinnati, Ohio, heard a challenge to the act on the basis of the Constitution but held the act constitutional.[73] Later that year the Circuit Court in Milwaukee found the opposite, that the 1870 Act could not be supported by the Constitution.[74]

American patented goods exhibited in Vienna. "Executive documents printed by order of the House of Representatives" (1872–1873), 48–49, https://search.library.wisc.edu/digital/A5M4HQBWHZPLGL8Z/pages/AHCG5FQRKXUTHG8W. It is unclear if they were related but it wouldn't be surprising.

68 U.S. Congress, Senate, *Report of the commissioners appointed to revise the statutes relating to patents, trade and other marks, and trade and commercial names, under act of Congress approved June 4, 1898*, December 4, 1900, 56th Cong. 2nd sess., 1900, S. Doc. 20, 51.

69 Ibid., 51–52. Courts would later qualify that national registration was still required, and simply registering in the country of origin was insufficient. Richter v. Reynolds, 59 F. 577 (3d Cir. 1893).

70 Da Silva Lopes, Teresa, and Casson, Mark. "Brand Protection and the Globalization of British Business," *Business History Review* 86, no. 2 (2012): 308, http://www.jstor.org/stable/23239500.

71 Da Silva Lopes and Casson, "Brand Protection," 57–58.

72 Ritchie, W.M. "Jurisdiction of Federal Courts in Trade-Mark Cases I," *Central Law Journal* 7 (1878): 142 and "Jurisdiction of Federal Courts in Trade-Mark Cases II," *Central Law Journal* 7 (1878): 163.

73 Duwell v. Bohmer, 8 F.Cas.181 (C.C.S.D. Ohio 1878).

74 Leidersdorf v. Flint, 15 F. Case 260 (C.C.E.D. Wisconsin 1878).

All of these cases involved domestic disputes over trademarks, and it was becoming clear that the 1870 Act's lack of a jurisdictional limit posed a Constitutional problem. By this point the Patent Office 'disclaimed [the Intellectual Property Clause] as the basis for [the trademark act],'[75] and thus would have to rely on the commerce clause or treaty power.

A group of prosecutions against knockoff champagne and whiskey sellers would comprise the unlikely genesis of one of the most important cases to deal with the constitution and intellectual property in American History. In retrospect these cases were profoundly different and the commingling of domestic and international trademark concerns would lead to the international aspect of the case being lost.

2.2.1 The International Cases

It had long been the 'prevalent opinion' that a majority of the champagne with foreign labels sold in New York was actually manufactured domestically and given a counterfeit label.[76] As part of the effort to fight this, numerous prosecutions were brought against sellers of champagne in New York who were engaging in such practices.

Emil Steffens was charged with possessing and selling counterfeit trademarks of G.H. Mumm & Co., of Rheims, France, a maker of champagne on May 7, 1878.[77] On the same day, Adolph Wittemann was charged with possessing and selling counterfeit trademarks of Kunkelmann & Co, of Rheims, France, also a maker of champagne.[78] Neither Steffens or Wittemann were actually selling counterfeit champagne, but they were rather label makers whose counterfeit labels would then be attached to American champagne.[79] The two prosecutions were intertwined and would be so regarded throughout

75 Smith, R. McP. "Correspondence," *Central Law Journal* 7 (1878): 198.

76 "A Case of Champagne," *New York Times*, February 20, 1878, 3 (describing a different prosecution).

77 Supreme Court of the United States, *Transcript of Record: U.S. v. Steffens*, January 8, 1879, 1.

78 Supreme Court of the United States, *Transcript of Record: U.S. v. Witteman*, January 11, 1879, 1.

79 "The Trademark Law," *New York Evening Post*, November 19, 1879, 4 (Calling the accused "label makers;" the Post is one of the few sources from that time to use the modern spelling). A small irony of this case is that both Steffens and Witteman would later become highly successful. Emil Steffens would become a rich man in New York as owner of one of the largest lithographing establishments in the country. "Drugged for Evidence," *New York Times*, September 8, 1895, 14 (regarding the divorce of his son). Adolph Witteman would go on to even greater success and fame as the co-owner of the Albertype Company, which produced many postcards and viewbooks. The Historical Society of Pennsylvania. The Albertype Company: Collection V-18 [finding aid], 2004.

their pendency.[80] The defendants retained the same counsel, who plead a general demurrer in both cases on May 13, 1878, asserting simply that the indictments were "not sufficient in law."[81] The demurrer was argued before Judge Charles L. Benedict in the Circuit Court on May 29, 1878.[82] Thereafter the US Attorney for the District took over (the case had been a private complaint at first, although with coordination with the US Attorney), and the demurrer was reargued in mid-October of that year before Judge Benedict and Judge Samuel Blatchford.[83] The Judges were unable to agree, and filed a Certificate of Division of Opinion with the U.S. Supreme Court regarding the question of "Can the [1876 Trademark Act], under which this indictment is found, be upheld, wholly or in part, as a law necessary and proper for carrying into execution any of the powers vested in the Congress by the Constitution of the United States?" This certificate was filed January 8, 1879.[84]

Thus the majority of the *Trade-Mark Cases* came to the Supreme Court. They were ideal cases for the proponents of the Act, involving foreign trademark holders protected by the 1869 treaty with France and by their registrations with the Patent Office under that treaty. The connection with international commerce and treaty obligations of the original act would have been difficult to dispute, and made more prominent. Had it not been for the Ohio case being joined, the outcome may well have been completely different.

2.2.2 The Domestic Case

On December 10, 1878, criminal charges were brought against W.W. Johnson, T.E. McNamara and N.S. Reeder for violations of the 1876 Trademark Act in the Southern District of Ohio.[85] They stood accused of seven slightly varying accounts of violating the trademark of one Charles F. O'Donnell and his assigns for whisky with a label reading "OK."[86] The defendants then filed a demurrer, arguing that the Court was without jurisdiction to hear the case, and that 'are insufficient in law to constitute an offense' – that the act was unconstitutional.[87] Judges John Baxter and Phillip B. Swing (the same Judge as in *Duwell*) could not

80 The case numbers for the cases are even consecutive.
81 Steffens Transcript, 6.
82 Ibid.
83 Letter from Coudert Brothers to Stewart L. Woodford, U.S. District Attorney, June 1878. National Archives New York Division, US Attorney Correspondence; Ibid.
84 Steffens Transcript, 6.
85 Supreme Court of the United States, *Transcript of Record: U.S. v. Johnson*, 1879, 1.
86 Ibid.
87 Ibid., 5. The first argument was a strange one to make, since it was precisely the argument that this same court had ruled against in *Duwell*.

reach an agreement as to whether the act was constitutional, and thus sent the question to the U.S. Supreme Court on February 20, 1879 on Certificate of Division of Opinion. In April 1879 the Attorney General requested that all the pending trademark cases be consolidated and heard together, thus joining this case with the New York cases.[88]

In terms of the statutes in question, this case was not any different than the others. In practice though, the cases were entirely different if the copyright clause would prove insufficient, as would prove the case at the Supreme Court. The fact that the defendants and plaintiffs were from the same state, and that the commerce was primarily local, would make this a hard case for advocates of the law, and quite akin to the facts in *Leidersdorf*. The plaintiffs in this case would also make a wise choice in retaining as their counsel one of the top lawyers in Cincinnati, George Hoadly, who had been already twice offered a position on the Ohio Supreme Court, and would in 1883 become that state's governor. Knowing that the Ohio prosecutions offered them a stronger case, the New York defendants declined to argue separately before the Supreme Court, forcing the act's defenders to focus on the Ohio prosecutions in this consolidated matter. This consolidation more than anything would influence the court's decision on the Commerce Clause.

2.3 *Arguing the Trade-Mark Cases*

As has been seen, the Intellectual Property Clause of the Constitution had already been roundly rejected by the legal community. The Attorney General recognized this, and while in his brief against Wittemann and Steffens the argument was not rejected, nor was it argued. Rather, the Justices were simply provided with the *Duwell* opinion, and no further argument was made on this point.[89] Rowland Cox, in his brief for G.H. Mumm against Emil Steffens, went much further and

> conceded that the power to legislate upon the subject of trade-marks is not deducible from that clause of the Constitution, which provides for

88 Supreme Court of the United States. "Motion to Advance," 100 U.S. 82 (1879), copy on file with Author.

89 Supreme Court of the United States, *The United States v. Steffens: Argument on Behalf of the United States*, 1879, 5. Indeed, the Attorney General asserted immediately thereafter that "We maintain the constitutionality of the statute upon … the Commerce Clause of the Constitution." Ibid. The direct implication is that this is the only argument the government put its faith in.

> the granting of patents and copyrights. It must be sustained, if at all, under the commercial clause and those of a cognate nature.[90]

The brief of Coudert Brothers on behalf of the Kunkelman & Co. against Wittemann did not even mention the Intellectual Property Clause, effectively dismissing it out of hand.[91] Rather, like the Mumm Brief, it argued for the Commerce Clause – and the treaty power. It has been asserted that the treaty power was not argued before the Supreme Court,[92] but this is manifestly untrue – both the Mumm and Kunkelman briefs made this argument.

These briefs show clearly both that the argument later approved in *Missouri v. Holland* was not inconceivable in 1879, but equally how little precedent there was for the notion. In the Mumm Brief counsel was forced to make the naked argument that

> Is it possible to reason that the Government of the United States is without power to make a treaty with Great Britain whereby it may protect the trade-marks of its people within British jurisdiction?
>
> If the Government of the United States has that power, *it has the power to afford reciprocal protection by legislation*. It has the power to provide for the registration of foreign trademarks.
>
> I do not attempt to locate this power. *If the United States are a nation, it exists.*[93]

This argument was essentially rhetoric, and no support was given in favor of it. The Kunkelman Brief treated the issue more extensively, and more in line with the modern scholarly arguments in favor of a robust treaty power, looking back to the writings of the founding fathers. Nonetheless, it too could not find any caselaw in favor of its proposition, rather relying on a fairly similar appeal to logic:

---

90 Mumm and Co., *Argument on Behalf of the U.S.*, 100 U.S. 82 (1879), no. 705, 3 [hereinafter Mumm brief]. Cox was the attorney for G.H. Mumm and Co., representing them from the original criminal action. He was already an authority on trademark law, and would be one of the key advocates in the coming debate leading to the 1881 act. *See* Cox, Rowland, ed. *American Trade-Mark Cases* (1871); Rowland Cox, *American Lawyer* 5 (1897): 353. Interestingly, Rowland Cox was the grandfather of Archibald Cox, Jr., of Watergate fame. Ken Gormley and Elliot Richardson, *Archibald Cox: Conscience of a Nation* (n.p.: Hachette Books, 1997), 4.

91 *Brief on the Part of Kunkelman and Co.*, 100 U.S. 82 (1879), no. 711, 11–13 [hereinafter Kunkelman brief].

92 Cross, John. "The Lingering Legacy of the Trade-Mark Cases," 367–375.

93 Mumm Brief, 12–13 (italics in original).

> [I]f the Statute of 1876 carries out and puts into operation and effect the treaty with France, the power to enact such a law, as the one more immediately under consideration, is clear, unless the treaty be a dead letter, and the obligations incurred by the United States be without any binding force or effect.[94]

Interestingly, a paragraph asserting that the commerce power was sufficient to enact these statutes in relation to the discussion of the treaty power was crossed out of the Kunkelman Brief, indicating that they meant to argue for an independent treaty power, not one powered by the Commerce Clause.[95]

The Briefs for the Attorney General, Mumm, and Kunkelman against the New York defendants all made a similar argument as their core – that the Commerce Clause permits regulation of not only interstate commerce, but also of the instrumentalities therof.[96] The Attorney General and Mumm briefs further asserted that if intrastate activity was incidental to interstate commerce, the regulation could still be upheld.[97]

Although one source asserts that Witteman and Steffens filed briefs with the Court, these do not survive.[98] As such, the only direct evidence of the arguments made against the law is the brief of future governor of Ohio George Hoadly on behalf of the Ohio defendants. That brief is tactically limited to the issues of the defendants in the Johnson case, who were accused of counterfeiting a label owned by another in the same state. The brief specifically focused on the fact that there had been no use of the trademark in interstate commerce, and accordingly the only availing argument would be argument based on the intellectual property clause. The Hoadly brief nowhere mentions the treaty power, even though the argument was raised in the other briefs. The strategy here seems to have been to give the Supreme Court a narrow question on which to resolve the case, without stepping deep into the question of Congressional power regarding international relations. This tactic worked, and the Supreme Court's opinion limited itself to the same issues as the Hoadly brief.

94 Kunkelman Brief, 12.

95 Ibid., 25–26.

96 Supreme Court of the United States, *The United States v. Steffens (No. 705), The United States v. Witteman (No. 711)*, 1878, 6–7 [hereinafter Witteman/Steffens Brief]; Mumm Brief, 21–22; Kunkelman Brief, 26. *Quoting Welton v. Missouri.*

97 Mumm Brief, 6; Witteman/Steffens Brief, 15. *Quoting Wheeling Bridge* Case.

98 Browne, William Henry. "Correspondence: Has Congress Authority to Legislate on the Subject of Trade-Marks," *American Law Review* 1 (1880): 156–157 (Asserting that counsel for Steffens and Witteman filed briefs but did not make oral argument).

The cases were argued on October 22, 1879,[99] early in the October Term of 1879, pursuant to a Motion to Advance the hearing filed by the Attorney General the Previous March.[100] The motion was granted March 31, 1879, with the hearing to be on the second day of the October Term of 1879. Counsel for Witteman and Steffens chose not to make oral argument.[101] Although no transcript exists of George Hoadly's argument on behalf of the Ohio Defendants, William Henry Browne did record a few tidbits from the argument, including that in response to a question from the Court, Hoadly expressly admitted that Congress had the power to regulate trademarks under the Commerce Clause – it was simply a question of how much it could encompass.[102]

The Attorney General's argument then turned to an argument under the embryonic treaty power, couching it at times in terms of the mention that it was also a regulation of international commerce.[103] The Attorney General did not specifically argue that the treaty power went beyond the constraints of the Commerce Clause, however. His argument then shifted back to the Commerce Clause, once again following his brief's argument that incidental regulation of purely intrastate commerce was permissible.[104] His argument closed with a brief mention that even if the act was unconstitutional regarding purely intrastate commerce, it could still be saved and regarded as constitutional regarding acts within Congressional purview under the Commerce Clause.[105]

2.4 *The Decision*

The Supreme Court's unanimous decision in the *Trade-Mark Cases* was announced November 17, 1879, less than a month after the argument.[106] The Court opened with a short discussion of the procedural history of the cases

99 "Forged Trade-Marks," *Washington Post*, October 23, 1879, 4.

100 "Motion to Advance" filed March 28, 1879 in the Witteman Casefile. The motion itself requests a hearing on April 21, 1879, but this was not to be. The motion mentions the interest of the Secretary of State, but a letter implies that the interest of the Secretary of State came at the request of the French Minister. The French Ministry took quite an interest in the case, as its domestic industries were affected both by the specific suits and more general question raised, and as such asked the Supreme Court for a copy of the decision as soon as it was issued. Letter in Steffens Casefile from French Minister. The US Patent Office made a similar request. Letter in Steffens Casefile from Commissioner of Patents.

101 Kunkelman Brief.

102 Ibid.

103 *Trade-Mark Cases*, 100 U.S. at 88. ("The purpose and the natural and reasonable effect of the acts are to ... carry out in good faith and enforce our treaty stipulations on the subject. The act is a regulation of foreign commerce.")

104 *Trade-Mark Cases*, 89–91.

105 Ibid., 91.

106 *Trade-Mark Cases*.

and of trademark law in general,[107] and then addressed the Intellectual Property Clause head-on. The Court found that 'the effort [to defend the law on the grounds of the intellectual property clause] is surrounded with insurmountable difficulties,' and found the law could thus not be constitutionally justified.[108]

The Court then turned to the Commerce Clause as an issue, and was faced with a more problematic question. Not only was there strong authority on both sides, the merits of this argument were starkly different among the different defendants in the consolidated matter. The Court attempted to deal with this in exactly the matter the defendants had hoped they would – they found a resolution which would apply to all defendants equally, relying on a technicality rather than facing the issue head-on. The Court held, without citing authority for the proposition, that a statute premised on the Commerce Clause *must* limit itself, by its own terms, to interstate commerce.[109] The ruling neatly addressed the central problem of the Commerce Clause – the differences between the parties. By looking solely at the statute on its face, the Court was able to avoid discussing whether its ruling would only apply to certain parties or all of them, or avoid a precedent that would say that Congress could regulate intrastate commerce, or could not regulate international commerce.

Finally, the Court turned to the question of whether the statute could only be found partially unconstitutional, and held it could not, for two reasons. The first reason given was that there was no evidence that the trademarks in question were used in interstate or foreign commerce.[110] This assertion is somewhat perverse in light of the fact that the Kunkelman and Mumm trademarks at issue in the New York prosecutions were specifically described as being French in origin, and as such the simplest explanation is that the court was focusing on the Ohio defendants and not really thinking about the fact that 2/3 of the cases in this suit involved French-owned trademarks. The second argument was that the Court cannot read words into a law to limit it and make it constitutional,

107 Ibid., 92.

108 Ibid., 93–94.

109 Ibid., 96. ("When, therefore, Congress undertakes to enact a law, which can only be valid as a regulation of commerce, it is reasonable to expect to find on the face of the law, or from its essential nature, that it is a regulation of commerce with foreign nations, or among the several States, or with the Indian tribes. If not so limited, it is in excess of the power of Congress.")

110 *Trade-Mark Cases*, 100 U.S. at 98. ("First, the indictments in these cases do not show that the trade-marks which are wrongfully used were trade-marks used in that kind of commerce.")

it can only excise them.[111] Since to limit the statute to commerce would add words to the statute, it was beyond the Court's power.

The Court briefly noted that it 'wish[ed] to be understood as leaving untouched the whole question of the treaty-making power over trade-marks, and of the duty of Congress to pass any laws necessary to carry treaties into effect.'[112] As will be discussed below, this statement was peculiar. It was already well-settled that a Court should take any reasonable interpretation to find a law Constitutional.[113] If the argument that the law could be saved under the treaty power was made to the Court – and as demonstrated it was – then one can read a implication that the law could not be saved under the treaty power, as the law which was passed was beyond the scope of what was necessary to carry the treaties into effect.

2.5 *The Reaction*

While the result in the *Trade-Mark Cases* seems inevitable, at least in hindsight, the decision still took the public as a surprise. It even accomplished the rare feat of giving trademark law more than token coverage in the newspapers.

Initial reports of the decision hit the newspapers the day after the case was decided, on November 18, 1879.[114] These articles consisted chiefly of summaries of the decision, and speculation as to its effects, noting that there had already been some 8000 trademark registrations, and 200 more were pending before the Patent Office.[115] The law also brought some $10,000 in revenue

111 Ibid., 98–99.

112 Ibid., 99.

113 "No court ought, unless the terms of an act rendered it unavoidable, to give a construction to it which should involve a violation, however unintentional, of the constitution." Parsons v. Bedford, 3 Pet. 433, 448–449 (1830).

114 "The Validity of Trade Marks," *Atlanta Constitution*, November 18, 1879, 1; "Supreme Court," *Chicago Tribune*, November 18, 1879, 6; "The Trade-Mark Laws Invalid," *New York Times*, November 18, 1879, 1; "An Unconstitutional Law," *Washington Post*, November 18, 1879, 1.

115 "The Trade-Mark Law Swept Away," *New York Times*, November 19, 1879, 4. This number was later clarified – there had been 7,777 registrations from the law's enactment to November 11, 1879. (Untitled Editorial), *New York Times*, November 21, 1879, 4. There had been 2,150 trademarks registered from 1870 to the beginning of 1875, 1,138 in 1875, 959 in 1876, 1,216 in 1877, 1,577 in 1878, and 859 thus far in 1879. Ibid. This amounted to nearly $200,000 in fees paid for the government in return for a 30-year registration. Ibid. By the end of 1879 there had been another 15 registrations, making the total amount 7,792, for a total of $211,960.00 in fees. Letter from H.E. Paine, Commissioner of Patents, to Rep. Armfield, 9 January 1880. Files of the House Committee on the Judiciary in the National Archives. Another 40 were registered in the first two months of 1880. Golove, "Treaty-Making and The Nation."

to the Patent Office annually.[116] In response to the decision the Patent Office released a circular on November 22, announcing that all registrations would be suspended pending further action from the applicants.[117] Further registrations would only be permitted if the person had full knowledge and understanding of the Supreme Court's decision.[118] However, fees could not be refunded absent a specific act from Congress to that effect.[119] Apparently many trademark holders had immediately written to the Patent Office asking for their fees to be refunded, and one went even further and sued the federal government for breach of contract, and requested that the registration fee be returned.[120] The Court of Claims denied the request, holding that "was for him to determine, before paying the fee, whether it was under the statute worth $ 25 to him to have his trade-mark registered,"[121] but of course that did not satisfy those who had paid the registration fee.

One group the decision pleased greatly were those in favor of a more limited federal government in favor of the states. For example, the New York Post published an editorial when word of the decision came down praising the Court for its limitation on Congressional power, and hoping that "we shall hear less henceforth about Congressional regulation of railroad and insurance companies and the like."[122]

The newspapers also reported that this decision would be a 'surprise to many lawyers, as well as a disappointment to the mercantile community.'[123] While it certainly was a surprise, disappointment soon abated as many began to openly assert that for domestic trademarks, common-law rights were sufficient. For instance, the New York Tribune published 'A Talk with a Patent Lawyer,' in which it was noted that the property right in trademarks remained, the only difference was the right to sue in federal court.[124] More importantly, at a meeting of the United States Trade-Mark Association on the afternoon

116 "The Trademark Decision," *Atlanta Daily Constitution*, November 22, 1879, 1.

117 "Registration of Trade-Marks," *New York Times*, November 22, 1879, 12.

118 Ibid.

119 Ibid. This was in part because the contingent fund of the patent office was not large enough to meet the demand for refunded fees. "The Trademark Decision," *Atlanta Daily Constitution*, 1.

120 Woodman v. U.S. (Woodman's Case), 15 Ct.Cl. 541 (Ct. Cl. 1879).

121 Ibid., 545.

122 "Conservative Views of the Constitution," *New York Evening Post*, November 19, 1879, 2.

123 "Trade-Mark Law Swept Away," *New York Times*.

124 "A Talk with a Patent Lawyer," *New York Tribune*, November 22, 1879, 8. The Post published a similar article but the interviewee asserted that the effects of the decision would be more negative, as the 1870 Act had a positive effect on the level of trademark piracy. "The Trademark Law," *New York Evening Post*, 4.

of November 24, Orestes Cleveland, the group's president, asserted that the effects of the decision were not dramatic, and that the main value of the law had been the existence of a registry for trademarks that was useful for proving priority in Court.[125] After further discussion among the members of the USTA it was agreed that new legislation was needed, if solely to provide for the registration of foreign trademarks.[126] While there is little mention in the news of excessive worry on the part of domestic merchants, proprietors of foreign marks were concerned – French merchants in New York had already written their ambassador in Washington asking that he push to enact a new law to enforce the 1869 treaty.[127] The gears of government were already grinding in this direction.

3 A New Trademark Law for International Trade

At a Cabinet meeting on November 18, 1879, it was decided to recommend to Congress that an act to protect foreign trademarks be passed.[128] Domestic trademarks were conspicuously absent from this recommendation, but nonetheless legislative proposals would include an act purely for foreign trademarks as well as an act based on the Commerce Clause to protect interstate trademarks as well.[129]

3.1 *The Immediate Legislative Response*

On December 9, 1879, Rep Robert F. Armfield, a lawyer from North Carolina, introduced his own proposal to remedy the damage done by the Supreme Court.[130] This bill created a registry in Washington for marks used in commerce with foreign nations, Indian tribes, or between states,[131] and allowed

125 "The Trade-Mark Decision," *New York Times*, November 25, 1879, 8.

126 Ibid. This was necessary since other countries such as France would only recognize American marks in their courts if American Courts offered French trademark owners recourse.

127 "Trade-Marks: A Discussion in This City," *New York Tribune*, November 25, 1879, 2.

128 "Meeting of the Cabinet," *Boston Globe*, November 19, 1879, 1; "Trade-Mark Matter in Cabinet," *Washington Post*, November 19, 1879, 2. The matter was apparently discussed again by the cabinet a week later as well. "Trade-Marks: The Recent Decision," *New York Tribune*, November 25, 1879, 2.

129 There was also the proposal for or a constitutional amendment that would allow the revival of the old act which protected even intrastate trademarks, but this was found to be unnecessary and was not enacted. Joint Res. 125, 46th Cong., 1879.

130 H.R. 2593, 46th Cong., 2nd sess., 1879.

131 Ibid., § 2.

for both damages and equitable remedies against infringers of trademarks.[132] The Register of Trademarks would be empowered to decide among claimants regarding who held the valid mark, with the decision reviewable to the *en banc* Supreme Court for the District of Columbia.[133] The bill was then committed to the Committee on Commerce.[134] There is some indication that the bill grew substantially after its first introduction, incorporating a modified version of the 1876 criminal trademark legislation.[135]

A day prior, the *New York Tribune* ran an editorial enquiring into the extent Congress could legislate based solely on the empowerment of a treaty.[136] It noted that a national law was required to effectuate the treaties America had entered into, but felt that 'it will be a new discovery in constitutional law that the President and the Senate can, by making a treaty, enlarge the power of Congress to legislate regarding internal affairs.'[137] This prospect was considered risible, and "any legislation which rests on treaties must run on very narrow limits."[138] The *Tribune* proposed that the solution was to permit Congress to legislate only regarding foreign marks.

While the committee deliberated, individuals in foreign countries, especially England and France, fretted about the state of their trademarks in America.[139] Although only 317 of the nearly 8,000 trademark registrations had been to residents of foreign countries,[140] it stands to reason that a foreign entity would have to be of substantial size and import to have their trademarks used across the oceans. Some felt that trademarks from England were less at risk, since the treaty of 1877 merely restated the existing common law giving reciprocal protection, but it was admitted that for other European nations no such balm existed.[141] Likewise worried were American owners of trademarks abroad, whose marks would only receive reciprocal protection, and since foreign owners currently had no protection, they held the same measure of safety

132 Ibid., § 8.

133 Ibid., § 4. This is the modern-day Court of Appeals for the DC Circuit.

134 U.S. Congress. *Congressional Record*. 46th Cong., 2nd sess., 9 December 1879 at 38.

135 *Id.*, 23 April 1880 at 2704.

136 "Trade-Mark Treaties," *New York Tribune*, December 8, 1879, 4.

137 Ibid.

138 Ibid.

139 "Foreign Trade-Marks," *New York Times*, February 14, 1880, 4.

140 Letter from Mr. Bowen, Examiner of Trademarks, to Rep. Hammond, 6 March 1880. Files of the House Committee on the Judiciary in the National Archives.

141 Weightman, Hugh. "Trade-Marks," *University of Pennsylvania Law Review* (n.d.): 312–313, https://scholarship.law.upenn.edu/cgi/viewcontent.cgi?article=2964&context=penn_law_review.

in their marks.[142] This would give an added urgency to the push for legislation for foreign trademarks, while protection for domestic trademarks would seem far less pressing. This was reflected in the testimony of Mr. Rowland Cox before the House Committee on the Judiciary encouraging a law protecting foreign marks but declining to comment on protection for domestic trademarks.[143] Nearly 100 firms, representing some $200 million in trade (in 1880 dollars) and including many companies with active principals in the USTA, had sent in form petitions requesting that Congress take action regarding foreign trademarks in the US in order to protect American interests abroad.[144] Domestic trademarks were not commented on once, following the policy the USTA had decided on shortly after the Supreme Court's decision.

Within the subcommittee, it seems that Rep. Hammond took the lead.[145] He asked the Trademark Examiner several questions, including whether any marks had been registered prior to the passage of the act of 1870,[146] what states and industries were most highly represented in terms of trademark registrations,[147] and whether the trademark office was profitable.[148] He was also the likely hand behind an unsigned memorandum found in the files of the Committee on the Judiciary laying out how the treaty power provided sufficient authority for a new trademark act.[149]

---

142 Weightman, "Trade-Marks."

143 Prepared Testimony of Mr. Rowland Cox to the House Committee on the Judiciary [January 1880], in the National Archives. The testimony is not dated, but it was likely a number of days after the petitions, which were dated around January 12, 1880. *See* Petition signed of the Singer Company to the House Committee on the Judiciary dated January 12, 1880, in the National Archives. There is no mention of Mr. Cox speaking at any hearing in the newspapers. As noted, *supra*, Mr. Cox was the counsel for G.H. Mumm in the action against Emil Steffens.

144 Cox Prepared Testimony, 1, Form Petition.

145 Nathaniel J. Hammond was the former Attorney General of Georgia and was regarded as one of that state's "chief authorities" on constitutional law. Reed, Thomas Walter. *The History of the University of Georgia* (1949): 556, *available at* http://dlg.galileo.usg.edu/cgi-bin/ebind2html.pl/reed_c05?seq=83.

146 Golove, "Treaty-Making and The Nation," 1–3. As noted, while there had been no actual registrations, there were several marks deposited by foreign nationals pursuant to the treaties. Ibid., 2.

147 Ibid., 3. Medicines, tobacco, and whiskey were the most frequent registrations, about one third of the total amount, so it was suggested that states in which these industries were prominent would be states with the most registrations. Ibid.

148 Ibid., 4. Apparently it was, only costing in administrative costs one third of what it received in fees.

149 Undated and unsigned memorandum in the files of the House Committee on the Judiciary.

The fact that the treaty power was regarded as nebulous and ill-defined at best, and nonexistent at its worst, formed a major obstacle to legislation based primarily on it. In this memorandum, the committee laid out what would become its argument, both in the report it would issue, and in subsequent debate, over the applicability of the treaty power to this matter. Like many who would follow, it was noted that the framers of the constitution had countenanced the treaty power at the very time of the founding, such as the 1790 Treaty with the Cree and the Jay Treaty.[150] Various other historical cases were considered, as well as the caselaw in the Supreme Court regarding treaties, before the court noted the naked core of the argument – that the treaties had imposed an obligation for Congress to act, and Congress must thus have that power.[151]

By early March of 1880, the subcommittee had finished their work and the House Judiciary Committee agreed to proceed with a bill rather than the constitutional amendment.[152] Three days later, the Committee approved a new bill based on the treaty power, and ordered it presented to the full House.[153] At that same meeting, the Committee decided that Congress did not have the authority to legislate regarding interstate trademarks – the Commerce Clause was out.[154]

On the same day, the new bill and accompanying report were presented to Congress.[155] The new bill, H.R. 5088, did not differ much from the Armfield bill (or the 1870 Act), save for one critical fact – it only applied to trademarks used in commerce with foreign nations or Indian tribes.[156] The report which accompanied the bill went into some detail about why this was so, explaining the bill's basis in the treaty power.[157] The Report explained that the committee had engaged in careful consideration as to whether the Commerce Clause empowered Congress to legislate regarding trademarks – and had determined that it

---

150 Ibid., 1.

151 Ibid., 5.

152 "Capital Notes," *Washington Post*, March 10, 1880, 1 (Noting that the Armfield Bill had been adopted on the 9th – it is likely that there was more a general discussion choosing to proceed with a bill rather than the amendment, and that a draft of the new bill was distributed that day). The Committee felt that "the subject was not invested with sufficient importance to warrant a constitutional amendment." "Congressional Committee Work," *New York Times*, March 13, 1880, 5.

153 "Capital Notes," *Washington Post*, 1.

154 Ibid.

155 U.S. *House Journal*. 46th Cong., 2nd sess., 12 March 1880, 769.

156 H.R. 5088, 46th Cong., 1880. As was noted *supra*, the criminal trademark act had already been added, and there were additional technical changes to the bill from the version which was introduced.

157 Committee on the Judiciary, H. Rep. 561, 46th Cong., 1880.

did not.[158] It was felt that a trademark was simply a manufacturer's guarantee, which is not necessary to commerce.[159] However, the necessary and proper clause of the Constitution did give the Congress the power to enact legislation executing treaties validly made by the executive branch with the Senate's consent.[160] The Committee's only stated authority for this proposition was *United States v. Coombs*, a case which seems inapposite.[161] In that case Justice Story held for the Supreme Court that the Commerce Clause extended to acts committed entirely above the high water mark in a single state (specifically salvage of goods from a sinking vessel) because they implicated questions of navigation, and thus commerce, and that Congress may make 'all laws necessary and proper to execute their delegated constitutional powers.'[162] This uncontroversial statement does not lead to the statement that Congress may make all laws necessary and proper to execute powers *not* specifically delegated, but it comprised the sole justification for the treaty power given by the Committee.

When the bill was read, Rep. Hammond provided some background, and revealed that the committee had unanimously felt that trademarks could not be regulated under the Commerce Clause.[163] He went through the relevant cases, many of which had been mentioned by the Supreme Court, regarding whether a trademark was a used in commerce, and concluded that either way, Congress should refrain from exercising power where it was in doubt:

> But valuable as are the opinions of the Supreme Court they should not be the measure of the power we shall exercise in Congress. They pass upon State laws said to conflict with the supreme law, and may give the benefit of doubts in favor of the Federal power or the States as they like. But Congress is co-ordinate with the court and the legislative body of the Government, whose ermine they wear. They must therefore hold Congressional legislation valid unless manifestly and plainly unconstitutional. The only safety, then, is for Congress to solve its doubts against the exercise of power. If it will not, the result is Congress can do all things not plainly forbidden. This is at war with the plan of our fathers. That plan restricted Congress to the exercise of certain delegated powers. One of

158 Ibid., 5 (the first four pages of the report are the Supreme Court's decision).

159 Ibid. It was also noted that only 8000 trademarks were in use the in the United States at the time, but this is fairly clearly erroneous – there were only 8000 registrations of trademarks – it is unknown how many marks were unregistered and protected by common law.

160 Ibid., 6.

161 United States v. Coombs, 37 U.S. 72 (1825).

162 Ibid., 78.

163 Ibid., 2702.

> them was regulating commerce. That power was delegated to the United States that the States might not cripple commerce.[164]

With such an approach in mind, it was clear that not only did the Committee on the Judiciary not feel that they had the power to legislate regarding interstate commerce, they felt they *should not* have such a power out of a concern for federalism. Under such a view the Committee's looking askance at the McCoid amendment makes perfect sense – if the right to legislate regarding domestic trademarks is inappropriate, then likewise an amendment to grant such a right to the federal government is inappropriate.

Rep. Hammond then turned to the question of foreign trademarks, and went through the arguments made in the report as well as the various relevant trademark treaties.[165] He noted that '[m]any foreign trade-marks were lodged [in the Patent Office] before the act of 1870 was passed,' and that "[i]t is plain from the debates that [the 1870 Act] never could have passed had it not been thought important in aid of those treaties."[166] Of the petitions the committee had received, all but one only dealt with the request for an act to uphold America's treaty obligations.[167]

In closing his oration, Rep. Hammond noted that all amendments up to this time had limited the power of the federal government, not enhanced it, and that it was highly undesirable to have the power of the federal government enhanced.[168] It is impossible here to forget that Rep. Hammond was from Georgia, and it was only a decade and a half since the civil war. It is likewise impossible to ignore that three amendments had just been passed over the opposition of the southern states. The time was simply wrong for any expansion of the federal government – implicit was that the federal government was already too powerful.

The debates continued on April 27, 1880, where Rep. McCoid questioned the scope of the treaty power, noting that no treaties had yet been concluded with the Indian Tribes, and thus asking if the treaty power nonetheless permitted regulation of marks used in commerce with them.[169] Pursuant to his belief that a Constitutional amendment was required for a federal trademark law, he set out this in his view the "correct principle" regarding the treaty power was that

164 Ibid., 2703.
165 Ibid., 2703–2704.
166 Ibid., 2704.
167 Ibid. Apparently there was one from Boston in favor of the McCoid amendment.
168 Ibid.
169 Ibid., 2796.

> A treaty does not confer upon Congress a power to legislate as between persons in the state, whether citizens of foreigners, in their internal commerce where that power does not exist without such treaty, incidental to some general power. But a treaty agreeing to legislate in such cases by controlling the transactions between foreign citizens and the people of the United States is void.[170]

To this point Rep. McCoid noted that while the Committee on the Judiciary looked to the treaty power, they had not found any authority for the proposition that a treaty could expand the powers of Congress.[171] Following this, Rep. McCoid went on at great length on the issue, mostly focused on other concerns, but the supporters of the bill largely did not face his comments about the scope of the treaty power head-on, and instead focused on the need for a law. To such end they had a letter from the Secretary of State dated five days earlier entered into the record, explaining that

> from the point of view of the obligations of this Government to the various foreign governments with which trade-mark conventions have been concluded prompt action providing for the registration of the trade-marks is of the greatest importance. The subject is continually being brought to the attention of this Department by the representatives of foreign governments at this capital, who are naturally solicitous for the interests of their countrymen and for the observance of the treaty stipulations. The interests of our own people in foreign countries would also suffer even more seriously by the removal of the protection which the reciprocal provisions of the various trade-mark conventions now furnish them.[172]

In conclusion, the Secretary of state urged "speedy passage" of the trademark bill.[173] Following this, Rep. Lapham took note of the Supreme Court's brief comment that the Court left "untouched" the question of the treaty power, and took this as an endorsement of the treaty power's utility in passing a new trademark law.[174] As a representative of New York, Rep. Lapham also introduced

170 Ibid., 2797.

171 Ibid.

172 Ibid., 2805 (reprinting letter from William M. Evarts, Secretary of State, to Rep. Nathaniel J. Hammond, House Committee on the Judiciary, Apr. 22, 1880).

173 Ibid.

174 Ibid., 2806.

a resolution of the United States Trade-Mark Association, founded only two years earlier, endorsing the trademark bill and urging its passage.[175]

In a twist, Rep. Armfield, who had introduced the bill on which the revised bill was based, expressed his doubts about the revised bill, noting that he was comfortable with the use of the commerce clause for trademarks, including those used interstate, but did not agree on the use of the treaty power.[176] However, because he believed Congress had the power to pass the law under the commerce clause, he continued to support the bill.[177] Somewhat surprisingly, there were never any real defenses of the treaty power raised – beyond a few stray comments from Rep. Hammond the bill's sponsors instead chose to move forward, knowing they had the votes for this needed measure.[178] And indeed they did, although the vote was closer than one might expect, with a substantial minority of members of Congress voting "no."[179]

The Senate received the bill on the 29th, and it was sent to the Committee on the Judiciary.[180] It must have seemed that the bill had considerable momentum, but instead it did not get out of that committee in the second session of the Congress.

3.2 *Passing a New Law*

Shortly before the 46th Congress had adjourned its second session, another bill was sent to the Senate Committee on the Judiciary, which was already considering H.R. 5088.[181] This bill, S. 1751, provided merely for registration and that such registration would be proof of ownership, as the Patent Office was already doing in the wake of the *Trade-Mark Cases*.[182] As such, there was no requirement that the mark be used in interstate or international commerce, although there were criminal sanctions for engaging in any falsehood in procuring registration.[183] While the question of a trademark law waited for Congress to start its third session, there remained occasional reminders of the difficulty of the situation where the trademark law was now in limbo. It was noted that foreign manufacturers were leery of sending their goods to the 1883 World's Fair in

175 The USTA is now the International Trademark Association (INTA), and then as now was comprised of the leading trademark holders.

176 Ibid., 2807.

177 Ibid.

178 Ibid., 2798–2799.

179 Ibid., 2808.

180 Ibid., 2860.

181 S. 1751, 46th Cong., 1880.

182 Ibid., 1–2.

183 Ibid., 4.

New York, and the USTA created a committee to determine the best solution to this problem.[184] At the same time, the USTA was fairly indifferent to the effect of the *Trade-Mark Cases* on domestic marks, feeling that common law protections were generally sufficient.[185]

The Third Session of the 46th Congress began in early December of 1880, and later in the month the Senate Judiciary Committee took up consideration of both bills, assigning them to a subcommittee of Senators Conkling and Davis.[186] Slightly over two months later, the subcommittee reported favorably on H.R. 5088, while recommending that S. 1751 be indefinitely postponed.[187] The 46th Congress was about to end without a trademark law, and the full committee reported back H.R. 5088 favorably and without amendment on the same day.[188] The following day the bill passed the Senate without debate.[189] Two days after that, the President signed H.R. 5088 into law – the very last day of the 46th Congress.[190] After a year of inaction, the Senate passed the bills with remarkable alacrity, but press coverage of the bill's passage was slight – it was mostly ignored in the face of the avalanche of other bills passed at the end of the session.

Not a single nation entered into a trademark treaty with the U.S. in 1879 or 1880. However, passage of the 1881 act served to reassure foreign powers, and within two years of its enactment trademark treaties were signed with Serbia,[191]

---

184 "Property in Trade Marks," *New York Herald*, January 29, 1881, 10 (noting that Belgian manufacturers would not exhibit unless their trademarks were protected); "City And Suburban News," *New York Times*, January 29, 1881, 8; "Foreign Trade Marks and the World's Fair," *New York Herald*, January 31, 1881, 6; *See also* "The New Trade-Marks Law," *New York Times*, March 18, 1881, 4 (discussing the applicability of the new 1881 Act to the fair). The fair was never actually held. *See* "A World's Fair In 1892," *New York Times*, June 25, 1889, 4 (recounting why the 1883 fair never occurred).

185 "Trade-Mark Legislation," *New York Times*, January 18, 1881, 2; "Trade Mark Registry," *New York Herald*, January 18, 1881, 11. The USTA also considered the possibility of applying to the New York legislature to make registrations on its own "with some legal effect and value." *Times*, Ibid.

186 Senate Judiciary Committee Minutes, 46th Cong., 50 (20 December 1880).

187 Ibid., 55 (Feb. 28, 1881).

188 Ibid., 2195 (Feb. 28, 1881).

189 Ibid., 2284 (Mar. 1, 1881).

190 Ibid., 2467 (Mar. 3, 1881).

191 Malloy, William M. "Article XII [of Convention of Commerce and Navigation between the United States and Serbia]," in *Treaties, Conventions, International Acts, Protocols and Agreements Between the United States of America and Other Powers 1776–190* (Washington Government Printing Office, 1910), 2:1616 (all aspects of the treaty were completed well after the 1881 act was passed).

Spain,[192] Italy,[193] and the Netherlands.[194] Two years later in 1883 many nations came together to form the Paris Convention for the Protection of Industrial Property.[195] True to form at the time, the United States was not among the original contracting parties, but somewhat surprisingly waited only four years before joining in 1887.[196] Congress passed no legislation to put the United States into compliance, and the Attorney General of the United States opined that the United States had not executed the Paris Convention in reference to its provisions for patents.[197] However, because the trademark provisions of federal law were entirely reciprocal, they did not pose the same problem and were sufficient to put the Paris Convention into execution in the United States.[198] A reliable federal law of trademarks was clearly needed for the United States to engage in international commerce in trademarked goods, and the 1881 Act at least comprised the minimum acceptable law for those purposes. Given the increasing importance of trademarks, the minimum would be increasingly unsatisfactory.

3.3 *The Problems of the 1881 Act*

With the passage of the 1881 Act, the shadow of the *Trade-Mark Cases* at once grew shorter and stronger. There was once again a federal trademark law, but its coverage was exceedingly scant, pursuant to Congressional understanding

---

192 Malloy, William M. Trade-Mark Convention between the United States and Spain" in *Treaties, Conventions, International Acts, Protocols and Agreements Between the United States of America and Other Powers 1776–190* (Washington Government Printing Office, 1910), 2:1675.

193 Malloy, William M. "1882 Declaration for the Reciprocal Protection of Marks of Manufacture and Trade between the United States and Italy" in *Treaties, Conventions, International Acts, Protocols and Agreements Between the United States of America and Other Powers 1776–190* (Washington Government Printing Office, 1910), 1:984.

194 Malloy, William M. "1883 Exchange of Notes between the Netherlands Legation and the Department of State," in *Treaties, Conventions, International Acts, Protocols and Agreements Between the United States of America and Other Powers 1776–190* (Washington Government Printing Office, 1910), 2:1265.

195 *Paris Convention for the Protection of Industrial Property*, 1883, https://www.wipo.int/treaties/en/ip/paris/.

196 *WIPO-Administered Treaties*, 1887, https://wipolex.wipo.int/en/treaties/parties/remarks/US/2.

197 *Caveats for Patents for Inventions*, vol. 19 of *Official Opinions of the Attorneys General of the United States: Advising the President and Heads of Departments in Relation to their Official Duties*, ed. A.J. Bentley (Washington, DC: Authority of Congress, 1891), 273.

198 Paul, Amasa Copp. *The Law of Trade-marks Including Trade-names and Unfair Competition* (RareBooksClub.com, 1903): §351, *citing* Kerry v. Toupin, 60 F. 272 (1894).

of the Supreme Court's opinion.[199] With the 1881 Act now law, the Federal Government would paradoxically be able to register a far smaller number of marks than it had even a month prior. This drop is simple enough to explain – the practice of registering trademarks never actually ceased, despite the fact that 16 months passed with no trademark law. As noted, the Commissioner of Patents continued to accept registrations, provided the registrant was made aware of the problematic nature of the trademark laws.

Once registrations were started again, it was clear that the Commissioner's authorities were considerably changed. In the appeal of a registrant from the denial of the examiner, the Commissioner of Patents held that the examiner was correct – examiners should once again consider the legality of the patent rather than just registering it mechanically.[200] Beyond the requirement that the trademark is in use in commerce with a foreign nation or Indian tribe, the criteria for registration were the same as they had been prior to the *Trade-Mark Cases*.[201]

In the following years, there would be repeated attempts to bring interstate trademarks within the coverage of the federal trademark laws, the first being in 1885.[202] In this case and in others thereafter the House Committee on Patents would be in favor of such an act, but the House Committee on the Judiciary Would be opposed.[203] In 1895 Rowland Cox, who had advocated that the Congress that it content itself with legislating regarding foreign marks in early 1880, presented a paper advocating expanding coverage of the federal law to include domestic marks, noting that both times and the understanding of the Commerce Clause had changed.[204] In 1898 Commissioners would be appointed to study a revision of the trademark law, and the dissent in particular made clear that the view the commerce clause was not a barrier to a new trademark law including both domestic and foreign marks.[205] Even then,

199 For a discussion of the 1881 Trademark Act, its problems and eventual collapse following the Supreme Court's 1903 decision in *Warner v. Searle* and replacement with the 1905 Act which finally included marks used domestically in interstate commerce, *see* Rosen, Zvi S. "In the Shadow of the Trade-Mark Cases." Chap. 11 in Ghosh, Shubha, ed. *Forgotten Intellectual Property Lore*, ed. Shubha Ghosh (Northampton, MA: Edward Elgar Publishing 2020): 256.

200 "Ex Parte Strasburger," *Official Gazette Patent Office* 20 (28 May 1881): 155.

201 Ibid.

202 H. Rep. 2376, 48th Cong., 2nd sess., 1885 (Committee on Patents).

203 Abdel-Khalik, Jasmine. "To Live in In-'fame'-y: Reconceiving Scandalous Marks as Analogous to Famous Marks," *Cardozo Arts and Entertainment Law Journal* 25, no. 44 (2007): 173.

204 Cox, Rowland. "The Constitution of the United States and its Relation To The Subject Of Trade-Marks," *Albany Law Journal* 51 (1895): 118.

205 Forbes, Francis et al. *Report of The Commissioners*, 91–92. (Dissent of Commissioner Arthur Greeley).

Congress deferred action until the Supreme Court limited the scope of the 1881 Act to cases where the actual infringement was in international commerce, at which point what would become the 1905 Act was passed in a little over a year.[206]

4 The Treaty Power and Trademarks

Regarding the treaty power, the Court explicitly resisted the urge to comment on the power. In turn, the Congress was forced to wrestle with the issue that while it could not find the power to enact legislation to execute treaties in the Constitution's text, such a power needed to exist in order to carry out the power to make treaties. The House Committee on the Judiciary wrestled with this problem and came to a determination that produced no objection from any quarter, even though the existence of a Treaty Power as an independent basis for Congressional action was essentially unknown prior to 1879. For purposes of the treaty power, the true adjudication would be in Congress, and in that inquiry the treaty power began to take on powers it had never assumed before, leading to *Missouri v. Holland* and its progeny a generation later, and the modern era of the treaty power. By contrast, the Treaty Power of this era was limited narrowly to foreign activities.

4.1 *The Nascent Treaty Power*

It is a maxim of legal practice that when an argument is made and presented as 'so obvious to require no support,' it is often entirely lacking in support. This does not make it incorrect, it simply means that the argument is premised on little more than rhetoric. So it was with the *Trade-Mark Cases* – advocates of the constitutionality of the existing trademark laws asserted that the power to make legislation calling treaties into effect must exist – even if no previous example of the power being used could be found. The same arguments were raised the next year in Congress – that a Treaty Power must exist, even if they could not locate particular examples of its prior uses.

There had been a number of times where Congress was called upon to execute a treaty, a treaty which called for appropriations or regulation of commerce, and where the question of whether execution of a treaty was required or discretionary. These examples were not unknown to those drafting the 1881 Trademark Act – in fact a draft of a speech found in the papers of the Judiciary

206 Rosen, Zvi S. "In the Shadow of the Trade-Mark Cases." Chap 11. in *Forgotten Intellectual Property Lore* (Elgar, 2020).

Committee from the 46th Congress enumerates many of the same examples, including the Jay Treaty and 1815 Treaty with Great Britain, along with the then-recent treaty with Hawaii and purchase of Alaska.[207] However, these are not examples of situations where an independent Treaty Power was considered, since it was unnecessary … the constitutionality of the laws to be passed was clear, the question was whether the constitution required their passage.

In her article *Congress's Treaty-Implementing Power in Historical Practice*, Jean Galbraith cites a number of times where an independent Treaty Power was asserted in debated over legislation, in secondary sources, and in an opinion of the Attorney General, none of these instances were raised during the litigation which lead to the *Trade-Mark Cases* or in the debates over the 1881 Trademark Act.[208] Rather, the fact that none of the examples raised by Prof. Galbraith's article were raised at any point in the debates over trademark law from 1879–1881 demonstrates that the Treaty Power was profoundly obscure and poorly understood. Further, while it can be pointed to in certain debates, and perhaps as an unexpressed basis for extradition laws, the Treaty Power had never been the explicit Constitutional basis for a law of Congress as of 1879.

4.2 *The Limits of the Treaty Power*

While the Treaty Power may have been obscure and poorly understood, and while it also was limited in scope, as will be discussed *infra*, Congress did unquestionably decide in 1880–1881 that some limited form of the Treaty Power premised on the necessary and proper clause and the power to make treaties did exist and confer powers beyond Congress's enumerated powers. What Congress did not assert – and indeed their actions strongly suggests a contrary view – is that the Treaty Power allowed Congress to regulate in areas subject to state control under the 10th Amendment.

The obscurity of the Treaty Power – and the relative lack of controversy surrounding its application – owes first and foremost to the sharply limited scope in which it existed in the nineteenth century. In many ways, then as now, asking whether a Treaty Power existed is asking the wrong question. The right question is what the scope of the Treaty Power was – and is. In the nineteenth century, the Treaty Power ended where state power began, and was limited to the arena where the federal government had primacy – that of foreign affairs.

207 Unsigned memorandum, Congressional Committee (1880). Copy on file with author, along with partial transcription.

208 Galbraith, Jean. "Congress's Treaty-Implementing Power in Historical Practice," *William & Mary Law Review* 56 (2014): 59, https://scholarship.law.wm.edu/wmlr/vol56/iss1/3.

As Prof. Galbraith notes, a 1887 House Report on a treaty with the Hawaiian Islands made clear that the Treaty-Making Power ends with the 10th Amendment.[209] This was the generally accepted view through the nineteenth century.[210] Indeed, the standard view through the 19th and much of the 20th century was that the Treaty-Making Power carried with it substantial limitations in scope limiting it to foreign affairs.[211] The arguments made and actions taken in the Courts and Congress regarding trademarks are entirely consonant with the view that the Treaty Power carries with it the same limitation.

Congress felt that in order to legislate under the Treaty Power, only trademarks used internationally could be subject to that legislation. The House Judiciary Committee had before it a bill based on the commerce clause, which included trademarks used in interstate commerce. In order to change the bill's Constitutional rationale to the Treaty Power, it was necessary to excise trademarks which were only used domestically. That the Judiciary Committee felt that such a change was necessary – and that the bill became law with this limitation – demonstrates that a limitation of the Treaty Power to international affairs was understood by all at the time.

Further, although the Supreme Court expressly refused to rule on the Treaty Power question, it is not accurate to say they took no position on the Treaty Power in the *Trade-Mark Cases*. It was already well-settled that a Court should take any reasonable interpretation to find a law Constitutional.[212] Had the trademark laws as of 1879 – without the limitation of international or interstate activity – been constitutional under the Treaty Power, the Supreme Court would have been duty bound to hold the trademark law constitutional.[213] The fact that the Supreme Court did not save the trademark laws with national scope under the Treaty Power leads to the direct inference that they could not be saved by the Treaty Power. In the *Trade-Mark Cases*, the Supreme Court effectively held that to be valid under the Treaty Power, any future trademark law would need a limitation of scope.

---

209 H.R. Rep. No. 49-4177, 1887.

210 Bradley, "The Treaty Power and Federalism," 418–422.

211 Ibid.

212 "No court ought, unless the terms of an act rendered it unavoidable, to give a construction to it which should involve a violation, however unintentional, of the constitution." Parsons v. Bedford, 448–449 (1830).

213 Indeed, this rule was repeated in opinions which Justice Miller (who wrote the opinion in the *Trade-Mark Cases*) joined. *See* Presser v. People of State of Illinois, 116 U.S. 252, 269 (1886) ("[I]t is a rule of construction that a statute must be interpreted so as, if possible, to make it consistent with the constitution and the paramount law.").

In this context, the 1879 editorial in the New York Tribune mocking the assertion of the Treaty Power makes complete sense. The Tribune's editorial commented that 'if will be a new discovery in Constitutional law if the President and the senate can, by making a treaty, enlarge the power of Congress to legislate *affecting internal afairs*.'[214] What is important is not just the questioning of the Treaty Power, but the questioning of the *scope* of the Treaty Power. After noting the absurdity of a truly unbound Treaty Power, the anonymous author concluded "[e]vidently, any legislation which rests on treaties must run within very narrow limits."

The law crafted by Congress to fit the Treaty Power tells us a great deal about what these "narrow limit" are. Had the relevance of a particular area of law to a treaty been all that was needed, then a limitation to international commerce hardly seems necessary. Rather, Congress clearly felt international activity was necessary to be within the scope of the Treaty Power, and thus so crafted the 1881 Trademark Act.

5 Conclusion

America underwent a period of massive industrial and commercial development from the 1850s to the 1880s, and trademarks were part of that development. But even as this happened, America remained somewhat hidebound and proprietary, and the Constitution provided a major limitation the scope of what measures Congress could offer to protect trademarks at the federal level. Constitutional law would continue to develop alongside trademark law, though, and as the cramped view of federal power implied by the trademark cases grew increasingly dated, possibilities for a more robust federal trademark law would finally be realized – in the next century. As this happened the United States was increasingly ready to join a world increasingly networked by international trademark protection.

Acknowledgements

This chapter adapts two previous articles, "In Search of the Trade-Mark Cases: The Nascent Treaty Power and the Turbulent Origins of Federal Trademark Law." *Saint John's Law Review* 83 (2009): 827 and "Treaty Power Justifications for

214 *New York Tribune*, December 8, 1879, 1–8, https://www.loc.gov/resource/sn83030214/1879-12-18/ed-1/?sp=1 (emphasis added).

Early Federal Trademark Laws." *University of Pennsylvania Journal of Constitutional Law Heightened Scrutiny* 16 (2013): 1. Special thanks to Justine Newman, Southern Illinois University MD, JD Candidate, for her research assistance with this chapter.

Bibliography

18 Stat.78 § 3 (1874).

19 Stat. 141 (1876).

Abdel-Khalik, Jasmine. "To Live in In-'fame'-y: Reconceiving Scandalous Marks as Analogous to Famous Marks," *Cardozo Arts and Entertainment Law Journal* 25, no. 44 (2007): 173.

Barber, Arthur W. "The Constitution and Trade-Marks," *Lawyer and Banker and Southern Bench and Bar Review* 5 (1912): 210–211.

Bond v. United States, 572 U.S. 844 (2014).

Bradley, Curtis A. "The Treaty Power and American Federalism." *Michigan Law Review* 97 (1998): 390, 418–422.

Browne, William Henry. "Correspondence: Has Congress Authority to Legislate on the Subject of Trade-Marks," *American Law Review* 1 (1880): 156–157.

Browne, William Henry. preface to *A Treatise on the Law of Trade-Marks* (Boston: Little, Brown, and Company, 1873): v.

"Capital Notes," *Washington Post*, March 10, 1880, 1.

"A Case of Champagne," *New York Times*, February 20, 1878, 3.

Caveats for Patents for Inventions, vol. 19 of *Offical Opinions of the Attorneys General of the United States: Advising the President and Heads of Departments in Relation to their Official Duties*, ed. A.J. Bentley (Washington, DC: Authority of Congress, 1891), 273.

"City And Suburban News," *New York Times*, January 29, 1881, 8.

Cohen, Morris L., and O'Connor, Sharon Hamby. *A Guide to the Early Reports of the Supreme Court of the United States* (Littleton, CO: Fred B. Rothman & Company, 1995), 110–112.

Committee on the Judiciary, H. Rep. 561, 46th Cong., 1880.

"Congressional Committee Work," *New York Times*, March 13, 1880, 5.

Congressional Globe, 41st Cong., 1st sess., 22 April 1869, 2894.

"Conservative Views of the Constitution," *New York Evening Post*, November 19, 1879, 2.

Cox, Rowland. *American Lawyer* 5 (1897): 353.

Cox, Rowland, ed. *American Trade-Mark Cases* (1871).

Cox, Rowland. "The Constitution of the United States and its Relation To The Subject Of Trade-Marks," *Albany Law Journal* 51 (1895): 118.

Cross, John. "The Lingering Legacy of the Trade-Mark Cases," *Michigan State Law Review* 1 (2008): 367–375.

Da Silva Lopes, Teresa, and Casson, Mark. "Brand Protection and the Globalization of British Business," *Business History Review* 86, no. 2 (2012): 308, http://www.jstor.org/stable/23239500.

Dinwoodie, Graeme B., and Janis, Mark D., eds. *Trademark Law and Theory: A Handbook of Contemporary Research* (Cheltenhem, UK: Edward Elgar Publishing, 2008), 19.

"Drugged for Evidence," *New York Times*, September 8, 1895, 14.

Duguid, Paul. "French Connections: The International Propagation of Trademarks in the Nineteenth Century," *Enterprise & Society* 10 (Mar. 2009): 13.

Duwell v. Bohmer, 8 F.Cas.181 (C.C.S.D. Ohio 1878).

"Ex Parte Strasburger," *Official Gazette Patent Office* 20 (28 May 1881): 155.

"Executive documents printed by order of the House of Representatives" (1872–1873), 48–49, https://search.library.wisc.edu/digital/A5M4HQBWHZPLGL8Z/pages/AHCG5FQRKXUTHG8W.

"The Federal Trade-Mark Statutes," *Albany Law Journal* 19 (Jan. 1879): 5.

Forbes, Francis, et al., *Report of The Commissioners Appointed To Revise the Statutes Relating to Patents, Trade and Other Marks, and Trade and Commercial Names*, S. Doc. No. 20, 2nd sess., 1902, 91–92.

"Foreign Trade Marks and the World's Fair," *New York Herald*, January 31, 1881, 6.

"Foreign Trade-Marks," *New York Times*, February 14, 1880, 4.

"Forged Trade-Marks," *Washington Post*, October 23, 1879, 4.

Foster & Elam v. Neilson, 27 U.S. 253 (1829).

Galbraith, Jean. "Congress's Treaty-Implementing Power in Historical Practice, *William & Mary Law Review* 56 (2014): 59, https://scholarship.law.wm.edu/wmlr/vol56/iss1/3.

Golove, David M. "Treaty-Making and The Nation: The Historical Foundations of The Nationalist Conception of The Treaty Power." *Michigan Law Review* 98 (2000): 1075.

Gormley, Ken, and Richardson, Elliot. *Archibald Cox: Conscience of a Nation* (n.p.: Hachette Books, 1997), 4.

Henry, Leslie. "When is a Treaty Self-Executing," *Michigan Law Review* 27 (1928–1929): 776.

Higgins, David M. "'Forgotten Heroes and Forgotten Issues': Business and Trademark History during the Nineteenth Century," *Business History Review* 86, no. 2 (2012): 273, http://www.jstor.org/stable/23239499.

The Historical Society of Pennsylvania. The Albertype Company: Collection V-18 [finding aid], 2004.

H.R. 235, 37th Cong., 1862.

H.R. 330, 36th Cong., 1860.

H.R. 1008, 39th Cong., 1867.

H.R. 2593, 46th Cong., 2nd sess., 1879.

H.R. 5088, 46th Cong., 1880.

H.R. Rep. No. 49-4177, 1887.

H. Rep. 2376, 48th Cong., 2nd sess., 1885.

Joint Res. 125, 46th Cong., 1879.

Kerry v. Toupin, 60 F. 272 (1894).

Leidersdorf v. Flint, 15 F. Case 260 (C.C.E.D. Wisconsin 1878).

Letter from the Belgian Dept. of Interior to Henry Sanford, Ambassador to Belgium, 11 December 1868, in the National Archives.

Letter from Chancellor of the Empire of Russia to the United States to Secretary of State William Seward, 1 December 1867. Letter and translation on microfilm in Dept. of State Papers, Nat'l Archives, College Park, MD.

Letter from Coudert Brothers to Stewart L. Woodford, U.S. District Attorney, June 1878. National Archives New York Division, US Attorney Correspondence.

Letter from Henry Sanford, Ambassador to Belgium to William Seward, Secretary of State, 20 December 1868, in the National Archives.

Letter from H.E. Paine, Commissioner of Patents, to Rep. Armfield, 9 January 1880. Files of the House Committee on the Judiciary in the National Archives.

Letter from Mr. Bowen, Examiner of Trademarks, to Rep. Hammond, 23 February 1880, 2. Files of the House Committee on the Judiciary in the National Archives.

Letter from Mr. Bowen, Examiner of Trademarks, to Rep. Hammond, 6 March 1880. Files of the House Committee on the Judiciary in the National Archives.

Letter from William Seward, Secretary of State, to Henry Sanford, Ambassador to Belgium, 17 November 1868, in the National Archives.

Malloy, William M. "Additional Article [to Treaty of July 17, 1858]" in *Treaties, Conventions, International Acts, Protocols and Agreements Between the United States of America and Other Powers 1776–190* (Washington Government Printing Office, 1910), 1:86.

Malloy, William M. "Additional Article to Treaty of Commerce [US-Russia]," in *Treaties, Conventions, International Acts, Protocols and Agreements Between the United States of America and Other Powers 1776–190* (Washington Government Printing Office, 1910), 2:1524.

Malloy, William M. "Agreement Concerning Trade-Mark between the United States and Brazil" in *Treaties, Conventions, International Acts, Protocols and Agreements Between the United States of America and Other Powers 1776–190* (Washington Government Printing Office, 1910), 1:146.

Malloy, William M. "Article XII [of Convention of Commerce and Navigation between the United States and Serbia]," in *Treaties, Conventions, International Acts, Protocols and Agreements Between the United States of America and Other Powers 1776–190* (Washington Government Printing Office, 1910), 2:1616.

Malloy, William M. "Article XVII [of Consular Convention between the United States and the German Empire]," in *Treaties, Conventions, International Acts, Protocols and Agreements Between the United States of America and Other Powers 1776–190* (Washington Government Printing Office, 1910), 1: 556.

Malloy, William M. "Declaration Affording Reciprocal Protection to Trade-Marks between the United States and Great Britain" in *Treaties, Conventions, International Acts, Protocols and Agreements Between the United States of America and Other Powers 1776–190* (Washington Government Printing Office, 1910), 1: 737.

Malloy, William M. "Trade-Mark Convention between the United States and Austria-Hungary" in *Treaties, Conventions, International Acts, Protocols and Agreements Between the United States of America and Other Powers 1776–190* (Washington Government Printing Office, 1910), 1: 47.

Malloy, William M. "Trade-Mark Convention between the United States and Spain" in *Treaties, Conventions, International Acts, Protocols and Agreements Between the United States of America and Other Powers 1776–190* (Washington Government Printing Office, 1910), 2:1675.

Malloy, William M. "1869 Trade-Mark Convention" in *Treaties, Conventions, International Acts, Protocols and Agreements Between the United States of America and Other Powers 1776–190* (Washington Government Printing Office, 1910), 1: 534.

Malloy, William M. "1882 Declaration for the Reciprocal Protection of Marks of Manufacture and Trade between the United States and Italy" in *Treaties, Conventions, International Acts.*

Malloy, William M. "1883 Exchange of Notes between the Netherlands Legation and the Department of State" in *Treaties, Conventions, International Acts, Protocols and Agreements Between the United States of America and Other Powers 1776–190* (Washington Government Printing Office, 1910), 2: 1265.

McCarthy, J. Thomas. *McCarthy on Trademarks and Unfair Competition*, 4th ed. (n.p.: Thomson West, 2009): § 5: 2.

McLean v. Fleming, 96 U.S. 245 (1877).

"Meeting of the Cabinet," *Boston Globe*, November 19, 1879, 1.

Missouri v. Holland, 252 U.S. 416 (1920).

"Motion to Advance" filed March 28, 1879 in the Witteman Casefile.

"A Needed 'Protection,'" *Chicago Tribune*, June 14, 1870, 2.

"The New Trade-Marks Law," *New York Times*, March 18, 1881, 4.

"The New Treaty for The Protection of Trade-Marks," *Chicago Tribune*, December 27, 1871, 3.

N.Y. Laws. 304–05 (1845).

(Untitled Editorial), *New York Times*, November 21, 1879, 4.

(Untitled Article), *New York Tribune*, October 29, 1870, 4.

New York Tribune, December 8, 1879, 1–8, https://www.loc.gov/resource/sn83030214/1879-12-18/ed-1/?sp=1.

"Our Trade with Russia," *New York Tribune*, April 25, 1874, 1.

Paris Convention for the Protection of Industrial Property, 1883, https://www.wipo.int/treaties/en/ip/paris/.

Patry, William. *Patry on Copyright* (n.p.: Thomson West, 2007): § 1: 33.

Parsons v. Bedford, 3 Pet. 433, 448–449 (1830).

Paul, Amasa Copp. *The Law of Trade-marks Including Trade-names and Unfair Competition* (RareBooksClub.com, 1903): §351, *citing* Kerry v. Toupin, 60 F. 272 (1894).

Petition signed of the Singer Company to the House Committee on the Judiciary dated January 12, 1880, in the National Archives.

Prepared Testimony of Mr. Rowland Cox to the House Committee on the Judiciary [January 1880], in the National Archives.

Presser v. People of State of Illinois, 116 U.S. 252, 269 (1886).

"Property in Trade Marks," *New York Herald*, January 29, 1881, 10.

Protocols and Agreements Between the United States of America and Other Powers 1776–190 (Washington Government Printing Office, 1910), 1: 984.

Reed, Thomas Walter. *The History of the University of Georgia* (1949): 556, *available at* http://dlg.galileo.usg.edu/cgi-bin/ebind2html.pl/reed_c05?seq=83.

"Registration of Trade-Marks," *New York Times*, November 22, 1879, 12.

"Report on the Conditions of the Empire," Made to the Senate and Legislative Assembly of France (1869).

Richter v. Reynolds, 59 F. 577 (3d Cir. 1893).

Ritchie, W.M. "Jurisdiction of Federal Courts in Trade-Mark Cases I," *Central Law Journal* 7 (1878): 142.

Ritchie, W.M. "Jurisdiction of Federal Courts in Trade-Mark Cases II," *Central Law Journal* 7 (1878): 163.

Rosen, Zvi S. "In Search of the Trade-Mark Cases: The Nascent Treaty Power and the Turbulent Origins of Federal Trademark Law," *Saint John's Law Review* 83 (2009): 827.

Rosen, Zvi S. "In the Shadow of the Trade-Mark Cases." Chap. 11 in *Forgotten Intellectual Property Lore*, ed. Shubha Ghosh (Northampton, MA: Edward Elgar Publishing 2020): 256.

Rosen, Zvi S., "Treaty Power Justifications for Early Federal Trademark Laws," *University of Pennsylvania Journal of Constitutional Law Heightened Scrutiny* 16 (2013): 1.

Senate Judiciary Committee Minutes, 46th Cong., 50 (20 December 1880).

Smith, R. McP. "Correspondence," *Central Law Journal* 7 (1878): 198.

Supreme Court." *Chicago Tribune*, November 18, 1879, 6.

S.264, 41st Cong., (As introduced Apr. 7, 1869).

S.501, 41st Cong. (As introduced Feb. 7, 1869).

S.829, 41st Cong. (As introduced Apr. 21, 1870).

S. 1751, 46th Cong., 1880.

"A Talk with a Patent Lawyer," *New York Tribune*, November 22, 1879, 8.

"Trade-Mark Cases," (Steffens, et al. v. U.S.) 100 U.S. 82 (1879).

"The Trademark Decision," *Atlanta Daily Constitution*, November 22, 1879, 1.

"The Trade-Mark Decision," *New York Times*, November 25, 1879, 8.

"The Trademark Law," *New York Evening Post*, November 19, 1879, 4.

"The Trade-Mark Law Swept Away," *New York Times*, November 19, 1879, 4.

"The Trade-Mark Laws Invalid," *New York Times*, November 18, 1879, 1.

"Trade-Mark Legislation," *New York Times*, January 18, 1881, 2.

"Trade-Mark Matter in Cabinet," *Washington Post*, November 19, 1879, 2.

"Trade-Mark Registry," *New York Herald*, January 18, 1881, 11.

"Trade-Mark Treaties," *New York Tribune*, December 8, 1879, 4.

"Trade-Marks: A Discussion in This City," *New York Tribune*, November 25, 1879, 2.

"Trade-Marks: The Recent Decision," *New York Tribune*, November 25, 1879, 2.

Trade Marks: State Legislation on Subject of Trade-Marks Noticed, vol. 11 of *Offical Opinions of the Attorneys General of the United States: Advising the President and Heads of Departments in Relation to their Official Duties*, ed. J. Hubley Ashton (Washington, DC: Authority of Congress, 1869), 352.

"An Unconstitutional Law," *Washington Post*, November 18, 1879, 1.

United States v. Coombs, 37 U.S. 72 (1825).

Unsigned memorandum, Congressional Committee (1880). Copy on file with author, along with partial transcription.

Supreme Court of the United States. "Motion to Advance," 100 U.S. 82 (1879), No. 1070 and 1084.

Supreme Court of the United States, *Transcript of Record: U.S. v. Johnson*, 1879.

Supreme Court of the United States, *Transcript of Record: U.S. v. Steffens*, January 8, 1879.

Supreme Court of the United States, *Transcript of Record: U.S. v. Witteman*, January 11, 1879.

Supreme Court of the United States, *The United States v. Steffens: Argument on Behalf of the United States*, 1879.

Supreme Court of the United States, *The United States v. Steffens (No. 705), The United States v. Witteman (No. 711)*, 1878.

U.S. Congress. *Congressional Record*. 46th Cong., 2nd sess., 9 December 1879 at 38.

U.S. Congress. *Congressional Record*. 41st Cong., 2nd sess., 14 April 1870 at 2683.

U.S. Congress. *Senate Executive Journal*. 40th Cong., 2nd sess., 28 January 1868, 157.

U.S. Congress. *Senate Executive Journal*. 40th Cong., 3rd sess., 28 January 1869, 463–464.

U.S. Congress. *Senate Executive Journal*. 41st Cong., 1st sess., 16 April, 1869, 196.

U.S. Congress, Senate, *Report of the commissioners appointed to revise the statutes relating to patents, trade and other marks, and trade and commercial names, under act of Congress approved June 4, 1898*, December 4, 1900, 56th Cong. 2nd sess., 1900, S. Doc. 20, 51.

U.S. Const. Art. VI.

U.S. *House Journal.* "Message of the President for the Third Session of the 40th Congress," 40th Cong., 3rd sess., 10 December 1868, 34.

U.S. *House Journal.* 41st Cong., 2nd sess., 19 April 1870, 640.

U.S. *House Journal.* 46th Cong., 2nd sess., 12 March 1880, 769.

U.S. *Senate Journal.* 41st Cong., 1st sess., 7 April 1869, 133.

U.S. *Senate Journal.* 41st Cong., 2nd sess., 7 February 1870, 209.

U.S. *Senate Journal.* 41st Cong., 2nd sess., 21 April 1870, 529.

U.S. *Senate Journal*, 41st Cong., 28 April 1870, 566.

U.S. v. Ferreira, 54 U.S. 40 (1851).

U.S. v. Schooner Peggy, 5 U.S. 109–110 (1801).

"The Validity of Trade Marks," *Atlanta Constitution*, November 18, 1879, 1.

Wallace, John William. *United States Reports*, Preface, 68 U.S. (1 Wallace) xiii–xiv (1863).

Weightman, Hugh. "Trade-Marks," *University of Pennsylvania Law Review* (n.d.): 312–313, https://scholarship.law.upenn.edu/cgi/viewcontent.cgi?article=2964&context=penn_law_review.

WIPO-Administered Treaties, 1887, https://wipolex.wipo.int/en/treaties/parties/remarks/US/2.

Woodman v. U.S. (Woodman's Case), 15 Ct.Cl. 541 (Ct. Cl. 1879).

"A World's Fair In 1892," *New York Times*, June 25, 1889, 4.

CHAPTER 11

The Transforming Face of *Terroir*

Unde Venis Geographical Indications?

Devanshi Saxena and Esther van Zimmeren

1 Introduction

> History may teach us that the connection between intellectual property, science and economic development is contingent and local rather than necessary and universal.
>
> ... It would make our examination of intellectual property less Eurocentric.
>
> ... Histories of intellectual property rights would also guard against an overreliance on economic storytellers for an understanding of intellectual property.
>
> PETER DRAHOS[1]

This quote aptly summarizes our inspiration to delve into the history of GI law. GIs were first defined and regulated under the TRIPS Agreement in 1994.[2] This term did not originate out of the blue but has its predecessors in the terms 'indications of source' and 'appellations of origin' in the Paris Convention of 1883,[3] and false indications of source in the Madrid Agreement in 1891.[4] Neither of these treaties defined these terms. In 1958, appellations of origin (AOs) were defined under Art. 2(1) of the Lisbon Agreement as "the geographical denomination of a country, region, or locality, which serves to designate a product originating therein, the quality or characteristics of which are due exclusively or essentially to the geographical environment, including natural

1 Drahos, Peter. *A Philosophy of Intellectual Property*, 2016th ed. (Australia: ANU E Press, 1955), 18.

2 TRIPS: Agreement on Trade-Related Aspects of Intellectual Property Rights, Apr. 15, 1994, Marrakesh Agreement Establishing the World Trade Organization, Annex 1C, 1869 U.N.T.S. 299, 1994 [TRIPS Agreement].

3 Paris Convention for the Protection of Industrial Property 1883, WIPO Lex No. TRT/PARIS/008 [Paris Convention].

4 Madrid Agreement for the Repression of False or Deceptive Indications of Source on Goods 1891, WIPO Lex No. TRT/MADRID-IP/007 [Madrid Agreement (indications of source)].

 | DOI:10.1163/9789004511439_013

and human factors".[5] AOs are one of the terms used to identify products that have a link to the geographical location where they originate, a link which is theoretically more than a mere indication of the source. The TRIPS agreement which remains the most widely ratified international agreement on intellectual property, includes a similar protection for GIs that are defined under Art. 22(1) as "… indications which identify a good as originating in the territory of a Member, or a region or locality in that territory, where a given quality, reputation or other characteristic of the good is essentially attributable to its geographical origin". The TRIPS agreement uses the term GIs for the first time in an international instrument and it has been used once again in the Geneva Act of the Lisbon Agreement under Art. 2 (1).[6]

It has been argued that the definition of GIs under TRIPS can be functionally similar to AOs under the Lisbon Agreement.[7] Both definitions take a broad stand on the link between the product and its origins and it can be further argued that the definition of GIs under the Geneva Act is also not different from AOs. While this "functional" consistency may be good to reiterate the only constant position in this area, i.e., flexibility, we have not come any further in terms of bringing countries together towards a common understanding of these terms and therefore of the link between the product and the origin. This can be explained by the fact that countries who played a major role in the drafting process for these definitions historically did not have a common national practice for protecting origin linked goods and therefore this flexibility was a compromise between the negotiators. Therefore, it is essential to get a better understanding of the roots of the contemporary international GI laws to show why this flexibility was necessary.

The result of this drafting process is a fragmented and incoherent international law on GIs in a globalized world. While uniformity in this area may not be desirable and feasible amongst all the WTO member countries that are obliged to implement the TRIPS Agreement, the wide variety of GI protection regimes make way for legal uncertainty. Moreover, producers who may see some benefits from registering a GI after navigating the domestic GI

---

5 Lisbon Agreement for the Protection of Appellations of Origin and their International Registration 1958 (as amended on September 28, 1979), WIPO Lex No. TRT/LISBON/001 [Lisbon Agreement].

6 Geneva Act of the Lisbon Agreement on Appellations of Origin and Geographical Indications (as adopted on May 20, 2015), WIPO Lex No. TRT/LISBON/009 [Geneva Act].

7 Gervais, Daniel. "The Lisbon Agreement's Misunderstood Potential," *The WIPO Journal*, no. 1 (2009): 87; Gervais, Daniel. "Geographical Indications under TRIPS," in *Research Handbook on Intellectual Property and Geographical Indications* (Cheltenham: Edward Elgar, 2016), 129.

protection regime may end up lost in a sea of protection regimes when it comes to international registration. In cases where a particular product has enough national importance, it may even be taken up by lead negotiators of a certain Free-Trade Agreement to be included in the list of GIs exchanged between the two countries concerned, which may be helpful for that product but undesirable for those who pursue legal certainty, consistency and equal opportunities.

Above all, GIs in contemporary times are supposed to communicate the link between the product and the geographical origin to the consumer. If there is no certainty in the law on the required link between the product and the place, it prevents consumers from having an accurate idea of what to expect from GI protected products. In our historical analysis, we also highlight that consumer protection was actually not the primary motivation for installing a GI regime but today it is an important and explicit rationale for GI protection.[8] Before we begin the historical analysis, we give a couple of disclaimers about the scope and focus of the chapter.

The link between the product and the *terroir* has undergone a transformation since its origins in 19th century French law to the current articulation of this link in the Lisbon Agreement (See Box. 1 for an explanation on *terroir*). As pointed out before, the TRIPS Agreement is the first agreement that used the term GIs. Other concepts such as AOs and indications of source are primarily used in European countries. In non-European countries trademarks enjoy a much longer heritage.[9] It is not clear whether and to what extent the law of trademarks in different jurisdictions historically required a link to the origin. This chapter focuses on the history of GIs, as such and does not examine the potential requirement of link to the origin in jurisdictions that traditionally have used trademark law even though today trademark law is one way through which WTO member states implement Art. 22.1, TRIPS. This is because the space that the typical rationale of trademark law (link between the product and the producer; not necessarily the geographical origin) leaves to the protection of the link between the product and the origin is typically less than what GI law demands.

8 See Section 2 on National Developments in France.

9 Okediji, Ruth L. "The International Intellectual Property Roots of Geographical Indications," *Chicago-Kent Law Review* 82 (2007): 1335.

What is *terroir*?[10]

Terroir is a French concept used to describe the relationship between the product and the geographical origin. It eludes easy definitions that can apply in all contexts and cannot be easily translated in other languages; however, some scholars have tried to define it as follows:

> ... area or terrain, usually rather small, whose soil and micro-climate impart distinctive qualities to food products
>
> BARHAM 2016

> ... having physical and agricultural origins, based on the *terre* or territorial bases of the word and of the concept [...] Additionally, *terroir* has a human dimension, originating from the fact that to express the quality of the land, human intervention is required. As such *savoir-faire*, knowledge, traditions, and the social characteristics of *terroir* are also features that *terroir* can evoke.
>
> SPIELMANN et al. 2012

> ... The true concept is not easily grasped but includes physical elements of the vineyard habitat- the vine, subsoil, siting, drainage, and micro-climate. Beyond the measurable ecosystem, there is an additional dimension – the spiritual aspect that recognizes the joys, the heartbreaks, the pride, the sweat, and the frustrations of its history.
>
> WILSON 1998 cited in BARHAM 2016

Ethnographer Laurence Bérard has evaluated the concept right from its historical roots in the French experience of nation building to its modern use in the "taste of *terroir*" movement. She writes that the concept is uniquely French and has been used as a conceptual framework in various fields viz. law, geography, anthropology, sociology, urban planning, agrarian studies, marketing and development studies. Even though rooted in tradition, *terroir* is not considered to be fixed and can be influenced by

10 For more information on the concept of *terroir*, see: Bérard, Laurence. "Terroir and the Sense of Place," in *Research Handbook on Intellectual Property and Geographical Indications* (Cheltenham: Edward Elgar, 2016), 72–91; Spielmann, Nathalie, and Gélinas-Chebat, Claire. "Terroir? That's Not How I Would Describe It," *International Journal of Wine Business Research* 24, no. 4 (2012): 254–70.

"locality" (Bérard and Marchenay 1998). In view of its multi-dimensional nature, its implementation in practice has not been smooth e.g., to define appellations of origins in France outside the wine industry or in the use of *produits de terroir* label without there being sufficient linkage with the *terroir*. It's interpretation outside France in countries with colonial histories for instance has also been problematic because of how *terroir* studies have been used to define land boundaries (Bassett et al. 2007 cited in Bérard 2016).

Secondly, the history of GIs cannot be dissociated from the extent of political participation of different countries in the international decision-making process regarding GI harmonization. What finally ended up on the table during the formative years of modern GI law, starting from the Paris Convention down to the TRIPS Agreement reflects the legal traditions of a select group of countries. The Art. 22.1 definition of GIs with all its flexibilities has evolved from a law against fraudulent labelling practices in France. It is possible that different legal traditions for distinguishing origin linked products existed in other countries within and outside Europe. There could also have been a transfer of European legal traditions owing to the colonial past of countries. We can see one such example in the case of Pisco, a brandy that originated in Peru when it was colonized by Spain. After formal decolonization and Chile's victory against the Bolivian-Peruvian alliance in the War of the Pacific (1879–1884), Pisco's territory was divided between Peru and Chile.[11] Pisco is well-studied due to competing claims made by both Peru and Chile at the world stage.

Mitchell and Terry explain how Pisco became important for the national identity of Peru and Chile as both countries became independent and maintained their colonial borders.[12] While it has been suggested that Pisco is a bi-national product for both Peru and Chile considering the "close political, social commercial and cultural bonds" between the two in the past, there is no such agreement between the countries.[13] Chile recognized Pisco as an AO through

11 Jerry T. Mitchell, and William C. Terry, "Contesting Pisco: Chile, Peru and the Politics of Trade," *Geographical Review* 101, no. 4 (2011): 518–35.

12 Mitchell and Terry, 518. "Pisco's origins coincide with Spanish colonization. The colony, then part of the Viceroyalty of Peru, included both modern Chile and Peru. Grapes brought from Europe and originally meant for general consumption and wine production found a second use in pisco production when the Spanish crown prohibited wine exports that would compete with Spain's domestic industry (Gotkine 2002; Vallejos 2004; Olivares C. 2005)", p. 524.

13 Lacoste, Pablo. "A Bi-National Appellation of Origin: Pisco in Chile and Peru," *Chilean Journal of Agricultural Research* 73, no. 4 (2013): 424.

an executive order in 1931 and Peru did the same in 1991.[14] To this date the countries present competing claims to Pisco and have sought to get it recognized in other countries in all possible ways.[15] The Chilean use of tax-reforms to encourage viticulture in the 20th century has been compared to the Spanish approach for Vino de Alicante which was an AO.[16] However, the extent to which colonization affected the relationship between the settlers and the indigenous population in Peru and Chile in relation to Pisco[17]; or the extent to which subsequent events shaped the governance of Pisco or impacted the national regime for GI protection that these countries have today; or the role (if any) that Peru and Chile played/could have played in the formation of the regional/international approach to GIs should be a subject of sophisticated historical analysis elsewhere. Pisco is only one example in a long list of traditional and cultural products whose histories have been tarnished by the violence of colonialism and sometimes that heritage cannot be recreated, repatriated or reclaimed.[18] Acquah's chapter in this book can be referred here, for the argument that western notions of intellectual property were introduced by the European powers in the colonies in Africa. This does not mean that pre-existing practices and systems of knowledge governance were unworkable, any less organized or needed 'civilizing'. A systematic, in-depth study of historical legal traditions on GIs outside the context of the modern IP treaties is outside the scope of this chapter. We do not conduct that exercise here but see value in conducting such an exercise especially when reviewing domestic GI regimes. The central argument in this paper that there has been a dilution of the legally required link between a product and its *terroir*, can certainly benefit from such an analysis. Countries that see merit in protecting GIs – not only in order to comply with the TRIPS agreement or other bilateral agreements which impose a form of protection but because of a grounded historical domestic rationale can offer

14 Both countries enacted this protection before the harmonizing influence of the TRIPS agreement. Lacoste, 424.

15 Özreisoğlu, Ayşe Kübra. "Who Owns the Geographical Indication Pisco, Peru or Chile?," *Law Blogs Maastricht*, 2019, https://www.maastrichtuniversity.nl/blog/2019/03/who-owns-geographical-indication-pisco-peru-or-chile.

16 Lacoste, "A Bi-National Appellation of Origin: Pisco in Chile and Peru."

17 Lacoste. The authors mention records of a dispute between Don Pedro, the main producer of Pisco in Chile and the "Indians of the Pisco land grant" in Peruvian part of the territory.

18 Some other examples can be found in this chapter by Sengupta where she discovers the histories of some agricultural and handcrafted products from Bengal. Mayuree Sengupta, "Folklore vs Intellectual Property in Bengal since the Seventeenth Century: A Study," in *Forgotten Intellectual Property Lore* (Cheltenham: Edward Elgar, 2020), 160–75.

insights for international GI law. It would, however, require a direct examination of national archives which goes beyond the scope of the current contribution. In this sense, we acknowledge that our analysis may also sometimes be influenced by the lens adopted by the authors of secondary literature that we studied and the primary sources used by them. The value of our contribution lies in linking these different analyses and exploring them from the specific perspective of link to the origin.

With these key disclaimers in mind, in Section 2 we start our journey from 19th century France. Though there are other examples of regulation of origin linked products, e.g., a proclamation in the UK in 1419 prohibiting mixing of wine between regions and requiring an origin label or establishment of quality zones for Rioja and Tuscan wine-grape growing regions in 1560s,[19] the evolution of the French *appellation d'origine contrôlée* has been trendsetting. The developments post-French revolution in the wine industry in France are significant because of their reverberations in the formation of EU's agricultural policy in 1992, the strength of French representations during the TRIPS negotiations and finally their impact today on other countries. Morris's chapter in this book argues that "private merchant's lobbying, knowledge, networks and technological achievements were central to the formation of the international legal system on industrial innovation in the 1880s", and this is also true for the development of international law on GIs.[20] Alongside the descriptive lens of history focusing on the origins, we focus on the link to the *terroir* and its connection to the rationale of GI protection. We also include international developments in the late 1800s alongside the French developments and connect this discussion to broader trends in the development of international law. This is followed by reflections on GIs at the European and International level in Section 3. Finally, we present reflections on the evolving rationale of protection of GIs and the governance framework in Section 4 on the basis of the historical analysis conducted in parts 2 and 3.

19 Gangjee, Dev. *Relocating the Law of Geographical Indications* (Cambridge: Cambridge University Press, 2011), 81.

20 Mengistie and Blakeney write that the international agreements that introduced indications of source were largely driven by the lobbyists from the wine industry from France, Spain and Portugal. Mengistie, Getachew, and Blakeney, Michael. "Geographical Indications and the Scramble for Africa," *African Journal of International and Comparative Law* 25 (2017): 200.

2 Origin Linked Indications and Appellations in the 19th and Early 20th Century

Though GI law historians trace its historical origins to ancient Rome and ancient Greece, a charter regulating trade in wine in Yugoslavia in 1222 is perhaps the earliest recorded reference.[21] Vadim Mantrov cites other records of European GIs Parmiggiano and Comté that date back to the 13th century, wine regulations in 1718 in Switzerland for Neuchtâtel and Neuenstadt and an example of Washington potatoes in the 18th century in the US.[22] However, no country is as well studied as France. This is due to the influence of French laws on GI law adopted in modern treaties such as the Paris Convention, the Lisbon Agreement and TRIPS.[23] This is also the reason why France is the reference point in this contribution. France has a long history of protecting origin-linked products widely discussed in the literature.[24] The production of Roquefort cheese for example was restricted to the Roquefort-sur-Soulzon region since the early 15th century.[25] A systematic analysis has been conducted by historian Alessandro Stanziani, tracing French law on origin-linked products right after the French Revolution up to the early beginnings of what we know as *appellation d'origine contrôlée* today (1789–1914).[26] The regulation on wine-production during this period, much like today, was influenced by a variety of interests,

21 Mantrov, Vadim. *EU Law on Indications of Geographical Origin: Theory and Practice* (Cham: Springer, 2014), 33; O'Connor, Bernard. *The Law of Geographical Indications* (London: Cameron May, 2004), 21.

22 Ibid.

23 The role of France as one of the colonial powers that led the internationalization of French/EU style system of GI protection in former colonies/French territories, e.g., in Francophone African countries Burkina Faso, Cameroon, Côte d'Ivoire and Guinèe, is also noteworthy here. See Mengistie and Blakeney, "Geographical Indications and the Scramble for Africa," 212.

24 Stanziani, Alessandro. "French Collective Wine Branding in the Nineteenth-Twentieth Centuries," in *Research Handbook on Intellectual Property and Geographical Indications* (Cheltenham: Edward Elgar, 2016), 13–45; Marie-Vivien, Delphine et al. "Are French Geographical Indications Losing Their Soul? Analysing Recent Developments in Governance of the Link to the Origin in France," *World Development* 19 (2017): 25–34; Marie-Vivien, Delphine. *The Protection of Geographical Indications in India: A New Perspective on the French and European Experience* (New Delhi: Sage Publications, 2015); Gangjee, *Relocating the Law of Geographical Indications*; Bérard, "Terroir and the Sense of Place."

25 Mitchell and Terry, "Contesting Pisco: Chile, Peru and the Politics of Trade," 521. However, a law specific to Roquefort was promulgated only in 1925. Law on the appellation of origin Roquefort, 26 July 1925, JO 30 July 1925, p. 7190, cited in Marie-Vivien, *The Protection of Geographical Indications in India: A New Perspective on the French and European Experience*, 27.

26 Stanziani, "French Collective Wine Branding in the Nineteenth-Twentieth Centuries."

namely, those of the winegrowers (later associations of winegrowers), wine traders and wine merchants and the State. The actors involved in early regulation of the wine industry were winegrowers, big and small, traders, trade associations, commissions composed of experts such as geographers, hygienists, agronomics, agronomy professors, the judiciary and the legislature.[27] The underlying concern during this period of winemaking regulation was prevention of fraud and adulteration.

Stanziani explains that since wine was not subject to any standardization for methods of production, it was not easy for wine producers and traders to prevent its counterfeiting. The interests of winegrowers and traders were not always aligned on whether there should be any standardization in the industry and whether the *terroir* should play any role in such standardization. The interests also diverged based on preferences for the quality of the product and for high quantities. In the beginning, there was a desire to prevent the names of wine regions from becoming generic. While this was not possible to regulate internationally (the lack of extra-territorial jurisdiction and mutual agreements between countries unlike today's FTAs), the law of July 1824,[28] was the first step to regulate wine production within France. This law penalized the use of a place name on an industrial product other than that of the origin and using the appearance of a wine producing region following adulteration. The 'origin' as per judicial decisions was interpreted broadly – place of manufacture for industrial products and of harvest for natural products.[29]

Between 1835–1845, because trade became more international and there were more complaints on fraud and adulteration, there was a need felt for stricter controls. The purpose of further regulation at this stage was to regulate trade and competition and the interests of the consumer were not a priority.[30] Further regulation still did not lead to standardization as at this stage wine producers did not agree on the efficiency of such measures.[31] No provisions existed on the protection of trademarks (note: neither Paris Convention nor the Madrid Agreement were signed at this point) which was a problem for the producers. However, a Court of Cassation ruling in 1847 held that wines are manufactured products and winegrowers have the right to "brand the vessels

27 Stanziani.

28 Law of July 28, 1824 Relating to Alterations or Assumptions of Names in Manufactured Products (1825) 7 Law Bulletin no.19 (Loi du 28 juillet 1824 Relative aux Altérations ou Suppositions de Noms dans les Produits Fabriques (1825) 7 Bulletin des Lois no 19).

29 Court of Cassation, 16 June 1847 and 12 July 1845, Sirey 47.1.521, 45.1.842, cited in Stanziani, "French Collective Wine Branding in the Nineteenth-Twentieth Centuries," 17.

30 Stanziani, 18–19.

31 Stanziani, 18.

containing their wine with a stamp signaling this vineyard".[32] Until 1847, producers were selling their wines by subscription and could control the prices, however after 1847, these prices collapsed. In 1855, there was a national exhibition where producers and traders agreed on the classification for the main areas of wine.[33] Following this agreement a law on trademarks and brands was adopted in 1857.[34] This law also partially influenced the draft of Art. 10 of the Paris Convention in 1883.[35] Gangjee writes that even though this law dealt with trademarks, Art. 19 of the Law of 1857 prohibited the false use of a French place of manufacture.[36] This law however, did not protect collective marks and did not include any requirements for standardized methods of production.[37]

Between 1845 and 1887, Stanziani refers to several judicial decisions on the use of the name Champagne.[38] In an 1887 case, the Court of Cassation decided that the name would be reserved for producers whose wines were "grown and made" in the Champagne region.[39] During this period, the link between the product and the place remained broadly defined, though there was already a sense of *terroir* taking shape, i.e., the value of the environmental factors in giving the product its quality.[40] At this stage no requirement of standardization

32 Pouillet, E. (1883) Traité des marques de fabrique et de la concurrence déloyale en tous genres, (Paris: Marchal et Billard) cited in Genevieve Teil, "Protecting Appellations of Origin: One Hundred Years of Efforts and Debates," in *The Importance of Place: Geographical Indications as a Tool for Local and Regional Development*, Ius Gentium: Comparative Perspectives on Law and Justice 58 (Cham: Springer, 2017), 155.

33 Stanziani, "French Collective Wine Branding in the Nineteenth-Twentieth Centuries," 19.

34 Loi sur les Marques de Fabrique et de Commerce, du 23 Juin 1857. Reproduced with an English translation in Reports Relative to Legislation in Foreign Countries on the Subject of Trade Marks 54 PP 585 (C. 596) (1872) 32–47, cited in Gangjee, *Relocating the Law of Geographical Indications*, 33.

35 Gangjee, 33. The original text of art. 10 of the Paris Convention, 1883 read as follows, "The provisions of the preceding Article [art 9 providing for seizure on importation for unlawful use of trademarks or trade names] shall apply to any goods which falsely bear as an indication of source the name of a *specified locality*, when such indication is joined to a trade name of a fictitious character or used with fraudulent intention. [...] Any manufacturer or trader engaged in the manufacture of or trade in such goods and established in the locality falsely indicated as the source shall be deemed an interested party." Arpad Bogsch, *The Paris Convention for the Protection of Industrial Property from 1883 to 1983* (Geneva: International Bureau of Intellectual Property, 1983), 216.

36 Gangjee, *Relocating the Law of Geographical Indications*, 34.

37 Rapport fait au nom de la commission chargée d'examiner le projet de loi relatif aux marques de fabrique et de commerce par Busson, député au corps législatif, cited in Stanziani, "French Collective Wine Branding in the Nineteenth-Twentieth Centuries," 20.

38 Stanziani, "French Collective Wine Branding in the Nineteenth-Twentieth Centuries."

39 Stanziani, citing Court of Cassation, 19 July 1887, AN F 12 6969, Sirey 88-2-209.

40 Stanziani, 20–21.

in methods of production was imposed. Different stakeholders involved in the production and sale of the wines, vineyard proprietors, farmers, traders and brokers, all had their interests in the regulation of winemaking and they did not agree on these issues. Producer's associations became stronger during this period thanks to the importance of freedom of association.[41] Interestingly, many of the concerns of the producers and the governance concerns during this period, mirror the concerns of GI producers in current times.

Before we continue describing the legal developments in France, we must mention the phylloxera-crisis that had a huge impact on the flourishing wine industry in France and other European countries in this period and also shaped the legal developments. In 1863, the pest phylloxera common in Eastern and Central America was introduced unintentionally to France where it started causing damage to grape vines in the southern Rhône region.[42] The outbreak further spread to the Bordeaux region and between 1874 and 1900 continued to spread in other European countries including Spain, Italy, Switzerland and Portugal.[43] It is estimated that the agricultural sector in France suffered a loss in the range of 16–22% from this crisis, massively reducing the incomes of vineyard proprietors and laborers.[44] The farmers did not have financial support from the government to overcome this crisis.[45] With reduced yields for grapes, they imported raisins for wine production or wines from other European countries (before the pest had penetrated those vineyards) and French-Algeria; from Chile as well as from the US and faced high rates of domestic taxation.[46] They used several techniques to counter the effect of the pest including grafting of American pest resistant vines and blending wines from outside the main wine producing regions.[47] While useful to sustain the wine industry temporarily, such imports began to compete with the French grape wines after the crisis. Consumers also seemed to have developed an affinity for raisin wines which

41 Stanziani, 21.

42 Tello, Javier et al. "Major Outbreaks in the Nineteenth Century Shaped Grape Phylloxera Contemporary Genetic Structure in Europe," *Scientific Reports* 9, no. 17540 (2019): 1–11.

43 Tello et al.

44 Banerjee, Abhijit et al. "Long-Run Health Impacts of Income Shocks: Wine and Phylloxera in Nineteenth-Century France," *The Review of Economics and Statistics* 92, no. 4 (2010): 714; Paul Leroy Beaulieu, "Wine Production in France," *Journal of the Statistical Society of London* 48, no. 3 (1885): 469–82.

45 Beaulieu, "Wine Production in France."

46 Beaulieu; Teil, "Protecting Appellations of Origin: One Hundred Years of Efforts and Debates," 152–53.

47 Beaulieu, "Wine Production in France"; Stanziani, "French Collective Wine Branding in the Nineteenth-Twentieth Centuries."

were cheaper to produce than grape wines.[48] To add to this, a high rate of fraud and adulteration in wine sales continued.[49] The adulteration harmed the reputation of French wine and also harmed its exports.[50]

Meanwhile, the concept of industrial property was taking shape at the international level, primarily for the protection of inventions to be exhibited during the Vienna international exposition of 1873,[51] amongst other international exhibitions (see also, the chapter by Morris in this book). In the Vienna exposition several industrial goods were exhibited including agricultural and manufactured products such as wine, beer and several food preparations. A resolution was also passed to protect the products of intellectual work, primarily inventions, in all 'civilized nations'.[52] Other important conferences for this area of law were the Paris Conferences of 1880 and 1883. The 1880 Congress was attended by the delegates of 21 states namely, Argentina, Austria, Belgium, Brazil, France, Guatemala, Hungary, Italy, Luxemburg, the Netherlands, Norway, Portugal, Russia, Salvador, Sweden, Switzerland, Turkey, UK, Uruguay, US, Venezuela.[53] During this conference a draft containing the definition of industrial property (Art. 1) prepared by an official of the French Ministry of Foreign Affairs, Charles Jagerschmidt was accepted. Industrial property was defined then as relating "not only to the products of industry in the strict sense, but also to agricultural products (wines, grain, fruit, cattle, etc.), and mineral products which are put into trade (mineral waters, etc.)".[54] Three years later, after going through multiple drafts 11 states namely, Belgium, Brazil, France, Guatemala, Italy, the Netherlands, Portugal, Salvador, Serbia, Spain and Switzerland gave their assent to the Paris Convention text on 20 March 1883.[55]

48 Teil, "Protecting Appellations of Origin: One Hundred Years of Efforts and Debates," 153.

49 Marie-Vivien, *The Protection of Geographical Indications in India: A New Perspective on the French and European Experience*, 25; Beaulieu, "Wine Production in France," 480–81.

50 Beaulieu, "Wine Production in France," 480.

51 Blakeney, Michael. "The International Protection of Industrial Property: From the Paris Convention to the TRIPS Agreement," WIPO National Seminar on Intellectual Property (Cairo, 2003), https://www.wipo.int/meetings/en/doc_details.jsp?doc_id=16104.

52 Blakeney, 3.

53 Blakeney, 4. We will systematically mention the countries involved in negotiations and signing treatments as this indicates the variety of countries involved and some key countries that were more or less involved in the early years of GI law development.

54 Final Protocol of 20th March 1883, Paris Convention for the Protection of Industrial Property, WIPO Lex No. TRT/PARIS/008.

55 Art. 1, Paris Convention.

While scholars question the place of GI law as part of intellectual property law even in contemporary times,[56] the Paris Convention was the first international agreement that used the terms 'indications of source' and 'appellations of origin' as industrial property alongside patents, trademarks, etc.[57] Being mentioned alongside those industrial property rights led some to doubt as to whether natural products were also covered. In order to overcome those doubts natural products were specifically included under Art. 1(3) of the Paris Convention.[58] Neither of these terms are defined in the Convention but they can be understood as requiring all member countries to enact laws to prevent the use of false indications of source. This is because at the time using a false indication of source pertaining to the product's geography or otherwise was illegal in many countries but this law was not strongly enforced.[59] The reference to these terms as a separate intellectual property in the Paris Convention was opposed by some states. For instance, delegates from Italy, Poland and Hungary questioned whether a separate reference was needed when indications of source were already protected under unfair competition laws and penal laws.[60] In hindsight, it seems that it was unwise to not define 'indications of source' at this stage. Scholars argue that the term 'indications of source' translated by WIPO from the French *indications de provenance* does not accurately capture the state of national law.[61] *Provenance* means to 'issue from a place' i.e., there is a historical association of the product with the place in the minds of the people living there.[62] The result of this gap in translation

56 Gervais, Daniel. "Traditional Innovation and the Ongoing Debate on the Protection of Geographical Indications," in *Indigenous People's Innovation: Intellectual Property Pathways to Development* (Ebook: ANU E Press, 2012), 121–46, https://library.oapen.org/bitstream/handle/20.500.12657/33574/459872.pdf?sequence=1#page=145; Stern, Stephen. "Are GIs IP?," *European Intellectual Property Review* 29, no. 2 (2007): 39–42.

57 Art 1(2), Paris Convention. These terms can, in a limited sense, be considered predecessors to the definition of GIs in the TRIPS Agreement but that discussion follows later on.

58 Gangjee, *Relocating the Law of Geographical Indications*, 25 and 37.

59 Bogsch, *The Paris Convention for the Protection of Industrial Property from 1883 to 1983*, 22.

60 Gangjee, *Relocating the Law of Geographical Indications*, 25.

61 Gangjee, 37.

62 Bérard, Laurence, and Marchenay, Philippe. *From Localised Products to Geographical Indications* (Bourg-en-Bresse: CNRS Ressources des terroirs, 2008), 10, https://www.ethno-terroirs.cnrs.fr/IMG/pdf/Localized_Products_to_GI.pdf. The authors differentiate between provenance and origin. Provenance, they argue gives a "historical depth". It means "to issue from a place" as opposed to "to be from a place". "Historical precedents give a place meaning and lead to a shift in status. The timespan in question may range from several centuries to just a few decades, but there is a definite sense of historical precedence. […] in order to understand the diversity of localized products we need to look at the cultural criteria that link a place with a particular history and social group. This

is that the relevance of regional reputation for the Paris Convention at this stage is unclear. However, by examining the rationale of protection from the negotiating history, namely, preventing counterfeiting and unfair competition, Gangjee argues that the law at this time period was "incidentally" about consumer protection, while the core rationale was protecting producer's and trader's interests.[63]

Art. 14 of the Convention provided for the possibility of revisions to the Convention with a view to introduce improvements.[64] To this end member states agreed to meet successively in one of the states that were party to the Convention. Several revisions took place between 1886 and 1967. Art. 15 of the Convention specified that the members had the right to make 'special arrangements' for the protection of industrial property separately between them, in so far as these arrangements do not contravene the provisions of the present Convention.[65] At the second conference for the revision of the Convention at Madrid hosted by the International Bureau (the secretariat for the administration of the Paris Convention) and the Spanish Government in 1890–91, two texts were proposed as special agreements. One was for the international registration of trademarks and another for the repression of false indications of origin.[66] It is at the same conference that the Madrid Agreement Concerning the International Registration of Marks 1891,[67] was adopted by Belgium, Guatemala, Italy, the Netherlands, Norway, Portugal, Spain, Sweden and Switzerland. The second text i.e., the Madrid Agreement for the Repression of False or Deceptive Indications of Source on Goods,[68] was adopted by Brazil, France, Great Britain, Guatemala, Norway, Portugal, Spain, Switzerland and Tunis.

The Madrid Agreement (indications of source) much like the Paris Convention did not provide a definition for indications of source. However, this can be inferred from the articles. Member states agreed to provide laws for seizure upon importation of goods carrying a false indication of source where the indication refers to one of the member countries (Art. 1). Art. 3 allowed the seller to indicate a different country than the one in which the

approach allows us to distinguish between different kinds of products, concentrating first on those that make sense at a local level…."

63 Gangjee, *Relocating the Law of Geographical Indications*, 37–38.

64 Art. 14, Paris Convention.

65 Art. 15, Paris Convention.

66 Blakeney, "The International Protection of Industrial Property: From the Paris Convention to the TRIPS Agreement," 6.

67 WIPO Lex No. TRT/MADRID-GP/008 [Madrid Agreement (marks)].

68 Madrid Agreement (indications of source).

sale takes place, but in that case any such address or name should be clearly indicated and it can be the name of the country, or the place of manufacture or production. An indication of source could thus be defined as any indication that communicates the geographical origin of the product, which could be a country or a smaller unit within it; an inquiry based on the principles derived for trademark law.[69] Art 4 gave the power to the courts of the member states to decide which "appellations" on account of their generic character escape the provisions of the Agreement however, regional appellations for wine were excluded from such an exemption. This special treatment to wines is noteworthy as it has been cited as the origin for the special treatment for wines and spirits under Art. 23 of the TRIPS Agreement.[70] Both prior to and after the Madrid Agreement, countries used a diverse set of laws to protect indications of source.[71] The Agreement itself provided for different options, law on seizure upon importation, import prohibition, "any other actions and remedies available in such cases to nationals under the laws of such country" or sanctions provided by trademark law (art. 1).[72] Evidently, trademark law has always remained a key tool to guard against false indications of source.

In France meanwhile, a general law was passed on 1 August 1905 in response to the growing concerns of the producers vis. high competition from foreign wines and high rates of fraud and adulteration in the sale of wines domestically.[73] This law reiterated the obligation in the Law of 1857 to respect

69 Gangjee, *Relocating the Law of Geographical Indications*, 27–28.

70 Escudero, Sergio. 'International protection of geographical indications and developing countries', TRADE working papers no. 10, South Centre, Geneva, cited in Rangnekar, Dwijen. "Geographical Indications, A Review of Proposals at the TRIPS Council: Extending Article 23 to Products Other than Wines and Spirits," UNCTAD-ICTSD Project on IPRS and Sustainable Development (Geneva, 2003), http://citeseerx.ist.psu.edu/viewdoc/download?doi=10.1.1.297.8212&rep=rep1&type=pdf.

71 "… for Germany it is the law against unfair competition of 1896, supplemented by the trade mark legislation of 1894; Austria lacks any specific laws but is considering their enactment; Belgium relies on its Penal Code, as do Italy and the Netherlands; Brazil's response is found in the trade mark law of 1897, including detailed provisions for seizure by customs authorities; Spain has bespoke ordinances prohibiting fraudulent marking for specific products; Britain relies on the penal provisions of the Merchandise Marks regime supplemented by customs regulations; Russia draws upon customs rules and procedures to regulate origin marks; Japan, Norway, the Dominican Republic, Serbia and Tunisia apparently do not have any relevant laws and so on." Pelletier, M., and Vidal-Naquet, E. La Convention d'Union pour la Protection de la Proprie´te´ Industrielle du 20 Mars 1883 (Larose & Forcel, Paris 1902), 258–62, cited in Gangjee, *Relocating the Law of Geographical Indications*, 29.

72 Art. 1, Madrid Agreement (indications of source).

73 Law of 1 August 1905 on the fight against frauds in the sale of goods and adulteration of foodstuff and agricultural products, JO 5 August 1905, no. 210, cited in Marie-Vivien,

the appellation of origin of products. It was aimed to tackle fraud in the sale of origin-linked goods and adulteration of origin-linked foodstuff and agricultural product. Art. 1 of the law penalized anyone who had deceived or attempted to deceive the 'contracting party' about the "nature, substantial qualities, the composition and the useful principles of any good or about their variety, their origin when, according to convention or customs, the false designation of the goods' variety or origin will have to be considered as the main cause for the sale".[74] It allowed administrative regulations for identifying and delimiting the origin of the goods, "… or regional appellation and appellations of particular vineyards which buyers might request on invoices, on packaging or on the products themselves as a guarantee from sellers, as well as necessary exterior or apparent indications to ensure the honesty of the sale and offer."[75] For the sake of clarity, a second law was passed in 1908 stating that such delimitation will be based on "local and constant customs".[76] The Law of 1905 already seems to be differentiated from trademarks by mentioning an area of production, a regional appellation, though not a collective right. Six products were identified and production areas were defined by an expert commission by 1908, which was however not accepted by the producers nor the traders and trade associations and riots followed.[77] The frustrations were related to the vagueness of the delimitation and the lack of recognition for the quality of the wine.[78]

In June 1911 a new bill was introduced in the French parliament seeking to guide the judiciary in defining the wine regions and granting exclusive protections to producers in a region.[79] As per this bill, judges were to consider the quality of the wine in addition to its origin, nature and composition.[80] But how do you define the quality of the product? There was no agreement whether the quality of the product should be linked to a (delimited) region. In July 1911, the bill was revised and quality of the product was not considered relevant for

The Protection of Geographical Indications in India: A New Perspective on the French and European Experience, 26.

74 Teil, "Protecting Appellations of Origin: One Hundred Years of Efforts and Debates," 157.

75 Teil, 157.

76 Teil, 158; Marie-Vivien, *The Protection of Geographical Indications in India: A New Perspective on the French and European Experience*, 26.

77 Marie-Vivien, *The Protection of Geographical Indications in India: A New Perspective on the French and European Experience*, 26; Stanziani, "French Collective Wine Branding in the Nineteenth-Twentieth Centuries," 24–25.

78 Teil, "Protecting Appellations of Origin: One Hundred Years of Efforts and Debates," 158–59.

79 Stanziani, "French Collective Wine Branding in the Nineteenth-Twentieth Centuries," 28.

80 Stanziani, 28.

delimitation in this version.[81] This version was also protested and was followed by more parliamentary debates and further revisions to the bill.[82] On the one hand, wine producers were against any standards, while on the other hand traders were pushing for standards to be able to guarantee "unvarying tastes".[83] There was no agreement amongst producers on the 'traditional' methods of production of wines, though supporters of regional appellations had started campaigning for such definitions citing the interest of consumers.[84]

Further developments in this area were halted due to the First World War. Several members of the Paris Union entered into bilateral treaties which included a higher level of protection for indications of source than mentioned in the Paris Convention.[85] After the war, the law of 1919 was passed allowing any producer who wanted an appellation to register for it, without the requirement of meeting any production criteria.[86] The power to determine the boundaries lay with the court and producers could challenge the unregistered use of the appellations in the court.[87] Through this legislation a collective right of producers was introduced.[88] The law at this stage favored *'usages locaux, loyaux et constants'* (local, loyal and constant use). However, these terms were not defined clearly in the law or by the courts.[89] In the absence of such definitions, there was a surplus of wine in the market and the industry continued to

---

81 Stanziani, 30.

82 See also, Zappalaglio, Andrea. *The Transformation of EU Geographical Indications Law* (Oxon: Routledge, 2021), 49, who writes that, "… until 1913, the idea of protecting the substantive qualities of the products, determined also by terroir was a minority concept".

83 Stanziani, "French Collective Wine Branding in the Nineteenth-Twentieth Centuries," 37.

84 Stanziani, 25.

85 France entered into treaties with Austria, Belgium, Czechoslovakia, Finland, Latvia, Luxembourg, Norway, and Poland. Ladas, Stephen. *Patents, Trademarks, and Related Rights* (1975) cited in Simon, Lori E. "Appellations of Origin: The Continuing Controversey," *Northwestern Journal of International Law and Business* 5, no. 1 (1983): 132–56.

86 OECD, "Appellations of Origin and Geographical Indications in IECD Member Countries: Economic and Legal Implications," Working Party on Agricultural Policies and Markets of the Committee for Agriculture Joint Working Party of the Committee for Agriculture and the Trade Committee (OECD, 2000), http://www.oecd.org/official documents/publicdisplaydocumentpdf/?cote=COM/AGR/APM/TD/WP%282000%2915/FINAL&doclanguage=En.

87 Law of 6 May 1919 on the protection of appellations of origin, JO 8 May 1919, p. 4726; cited in Marie-Vivien, *The Protection of Geographical Indications in India: A New Perspective on the French and European Experience*, 26.

88 Gangjee, *Relocating the Law of Geographical Indications*, 103.

89 Marie-Vivien, *The Protection of Geographical Indications in India: A New Perspective on the French and European Experience*, 26–27; Stanziani, "French Collective Wine Branding in the Nineteenth-Twentieth Centuries," 37.

be in crisis due to decreasing demands and competition from foreign wines.[90] In 1927, the 1919 law was modified to allow an appellation for wines based on geographical area and type of grape.[91] Zappalaglio finds that when this law was introduced by Joseph Capus, a member of the parliament, his intention was to reinterpret 'local, loyal and constant use' to refer to both the physical and the human links.[92] In fact, he finds that this was the first time terroir was defined in the French parliament as a combination of the three natural factors – the variety of the grapes, the soil and the climate.[93] Nonetheless, the issue of standardization was still not settled. In 1934, after several attempts to tackle the wine surplus, a new law was passed incentivizing winegrowers to uproot vine plants and to stop growing hybrids. This led to an adverse reaction by the producers who started selling their surplus under false names.[94]

These frustrations culminated in the winegrowers of Bordeaux proposing a decree at the national conference of winegrowers' association that was eventually accepted by the government and resulted in the Decree of July 1935.[95] This is the decree that gave shape to the modern *Appellations d' Origine Contrôlée* (AOC). This decree espoused growing demands from agricultural producers and traders to limit the area of production for a specific type of product. Moreover, finally a solution was found to answer the demands for standardization.[96] A committee was formed to demarcate vineyards – the *Comité National des Appellations d'Origine* (CNAO) which in 1947 became the *Institut National des Appellations d'Origine* (INAO). Certain hybrids were banned and there was a requirement to identify an area of production that has geological conditions suited for the respective vines.[97]

The Laws of 1919, 1927 and the Decree of 1935 are the basis for the modern understanding of AOs. The strong French legal tradition on GIs also played a

90 Stanziani, "French Collective Wine Branding in the Nineteenth-Twentieth Centuries," 37.

91 Erica A. Farmer, "Codifying Consensus and Constructing Boundaries: Setting the Limits of Appellation d'origine Contrôlée Protection in Bordeaux, France," *Political and Legal Anthropology Review* 37, no. 1 (2014): 140.

92 Zappalaglio, *The Transformation of EU Geographical Indications Law*, 54.

93 Zappalaglio, 54.

94 Stanziani, "French Collective Wine Branding in the Nineteenth-Twentieth Centuries," 37–38.

95 Decree-law of July 30, 1935 relating to the Defense of the Wine Market and the Economic Regulation of Alcohol, JO 31 July 1935, p. 8314.

96 Some judicial rulings were already moving in this direction. Marie-Vivien gives an example of a court on the AO Lentilles du Puy where court refers to product characteristics. Marie-Vivien, *The Protection of Geographical Indications in India: A New Perspective on the French and European Experience*, 27.

97 Gangjee, *Relocating the Law of Geographical Indications*, 106.

crucial role in the formation of the EU strategy on legal protection for GIs in the 90s (see Section 3). In 1966, after France signed the Lisbon Agreement, a clear definition of appellations was given in the law amending the law of 1919: "geographical name of a country, region, or locality, which serves to designate a product originating therein, the quality and characteristics of which are due exclusively or essentially to the geographical environment, including natural and human factors."[98] The French AOC system remained limited to wines for the next couple of decades and it was only in 1990 that it was extended to other agricultural products.[99]

The French system for appellations of origins, at least for wines, is heavily influenced by the idea of *terroir*.[100] But it is not correct to say that all registered AOCs in France are necessarily an ode to their *terroir*. The process of demarcating the territory includes compromises and can exclude certain regions and producers. The interpretations of the terms 'local, loyal and constant use' by the French court shows that if a producer could show the same conditions of production in terms of physical characteristics of the land, they could use the appellation even when the production was happening beyond the demarcated area.[101] Though these laws made a link to the natural and human factors in the definition of the geographical region of protection and for defining local, loyal, constant, use; the purpose of the appellation was not to valorize *terroir* or to inform the consumer about the origins.[102] The purpose was, "to provide the producer with a guaranteed income while offering a stable normative framework for negotiating innovation".[103] The organization and lobbying of producers and traders and the identification of a commercial interest shared by the producers was important for this result. This was a system that worked for a group of wine producers in one part of the world.

98 Law of 6 July 1966 amending and completing the Law of 6 May 1919, JO 7 July 1966, cited in Marie-Vivien, *The Protection of Geographical Indications in India: A New Perspective on the French and European Experience*, 29.

99 Law No. 90-558 of 2 July 1990 relating to appellations of origin controls of agricultural or food products, raw or processed, JO 6 July 1990, p. 155, cited in Gangjee, *Relocating the Law of Geographical Indications*, 111. See also, Marie-Vivien et al., "Are French Geographical Indications Losing Their Soul? Analyzing Recent Developments in Governance of the Link to the Origin in France," 26.

100 Bérard, "Terroir and the Sense of Place," 79.

101 *Syndicat Viticole de Sauternes et de Barsac v. Chaumel et Autres* [1935] *Propriété Industrielle* 76 (Bordeaux Court of Appeal, 19 February 1934); cited in Gangjee, *Relocating the Law of Geographical Indications*, 110.

102 Stanziani, "French Collective Wine Branding in the Nineteenth-Twentieth Centuries," 40.

103 Stanziani, 40.

The French experience of problem-solving in the wine industry had a significant impact in inspiring similar regulations at the regional and international level. This can be seen as an example of "globalized localism", in international law, a form of globalization defined by de Sousa Santos as "a local phenomenon that is successfully globalized".[104] Dutfield and Suthersanen have called the TRIPS Agreement as an example of globalized localism where "generalized principles recognized initially in a few countries force the remaining nations to adopt broadly similar intellectual property laws".[105] The story of GIs, as the following text in this chapter will show, is similar.

In Europe there were other countries dealing with fraud and adulteration in the wine sector as well, but none had an impact as significant as France on the regional and international level. In Spain and Italy 'denominations' of origin had a similar background as in France – the wine industry (that actually was inspired by the French developments).[106] The first Spanish law on denominations in the wine industry was passed in 1933 following France's example.[107] In Italy, a need was felt to regulate against fraud and adulteration and the first attempts began in 1899 with a bill to define "wine", which was passed in 1904.[108] As per Zappalaglio's research, subsequent developments in Italy introduced a system of regulation of wines which was much more bottom-up than the French system.[109] Instead of top-down delimitation of regions, Italy tried to protect "typical wines" by letting the consortia for the protection of wines decide upon the zone of the production and the production methods. However, this system was not considered efficient by the wine producers who found it "vague and arbitrary" leading to its reform in 1930.[110] The Royal Law Decree 62/1930 stated that the areas of production were to be identified by the

---

104 Sousa Santos, Boaventura de. *Toward a New Legal Common Sense: Law, Globalization, and Emancipation*, 3rd ed. (Cambridge: Cambridge University Press, 2020), 215.

105 Dutfield, Graham, and Suthersanen, Uma. *Dutfield and Suthersanen on Global Intellectual Property Law*, 2nd ed. (Cheltenham: Edward Elgar, 2020), 3.

106 Pulido Polo, Marta. "Historia Jurídica de Las Indicaciones Geográficas: Una Perspectiva Desde La Gestión de La Comunicación En Las Instituciones," *Estudios Institucionales* 3, no. 4 (2016): 7–24; Planas, Jordi. "State Intervention in Wine Markets in the Early 20th Century: Why Was It so Different in France and Spain?," *Journal of Iberian and Latin American Economic History* 35, no. 2 (2016): 177.

107 Wine statute of 1933, first approved by Decree on 8 September 1932 and then an act was passed 26 May 1933. Planas, "State Intervention in Wine Markets in the Early 20th Century: Why Was It so Different in France and Spain?," 178.

108 Legge 11 Luglio 1904 n 388, portante disposizioni per combattere le frodi nella preparazione e nel commercio dei vini, GURI 26 July 1904 n 388, Zappalaglio, *The Transformation of EU Geographical Indications Law*, 60.

109 Zappalaglio, 62–64.

110 Zappalaglio, 62.

Ministry of Agriculture as per the guidelines established by the government.[111] The Decree, inspired by the French developments in this period, also redefined "typical wines" as, "wines (…) that, having an origin ascertained on the basis of the place of production, the soil, the grapevines and the techniques of preparation, are characterized by constant organoleptic features".[112] Finally, in 1963 the first law on denominations of origin entered into force in Italy to comply with European Community law.[113] Alternative approaches to connecting the product to the place were found using unfair competition law in the UK and Germany, which did not have the same experiences from the wine industry or the influence of the idea of *terroir*.[114]

Scholars have observed difficulties in expanding the French AOC system beyond the boundaries of France.[115] *Terroir* is assumed to be the basis of the system. It is assumed that an appellation and other GI laws modelled on appellations such as the Protected Designation of Origin (PDO) and the AO defined in the Lisbon Agreement should have a link to the origin in the same way as French AOC products (presumably) have.[116] What happens then to other products such as traditional food preparations or manufactured and handmade products that do not have the same strong kind of attachment to the *terroir* and that are not as dependent on the physical environment of the place as much as the local customs or *savoir faire*? Could this new method of protection

111 Regio Decreto Legge 11 Gennaio 1930 n 62, contenente disposizioni per la difesa dei vini tipici italiani, Zappalaglio, 63.

112 Zappalaglio, 63.

113 Italy implemented the International Convention on the Use of Designations of Origin and Names for Cheeses (Stresa Convention) in 1953 through the Presidential Decree No. 1099 of 18 November 1953. OECD, "Appellations of Origin and Geographical Indications in IECD Member Countries: Economic and Legal Implications," 62.

114 Gangjee, *Relocating the Law of Geographical Indications*, 116. Gangjee delves elsewhere into the history of German law to show the history of a non-*terroir* approach pre-Europeanisation of *terroir* namely, the law of unfair competition. A 1902 law prevented "deceptive advertising with respect to inter alia the origin and quality of the goods in question, with the additional possibility of extended protection under the general prohibition against conduct which is contrary to honest commercial practices …" Dev Gangjee, "Melton Mowbray and the GI Pie in the Sky: Exploring Cartographies of Protection," *Intellectual Property Quarterly* 3 (2006): 291–306.

115 Barham, Elizabeth. "'Translating Terroir' Revisited: The Global Challenge of French AOC Labelling," in *Research Handbook on Intellectual Property and Geographical Indications* (Cheltenham: Edward Elgar, 2016), 46–71; Farmer, "Codifying Consensus and Constructing Boundaries: Setting the Limits of Appellation d'origine Contrôlée Protection in Bordeaux, France", 138.

116 Farmer, "Codifying Consensus and Constructing Boundaries: Setting the Limits of Appellation d'origine Contrôlée Protection in Bordeaux, France", 138–9.

of origin-linked products exist beyond the wine industry?[117] These questions were being raised when French proposals for appellations reached the stage of reform of the European Common Agricultural Policy (CAP) in the late 20th century.[118] But before that regional expansion was realized, the Lisbon Agreement was adopted which followed the philosophy of AOCs in France in its definition of AOs.

3 Reflections on Contemporary GIs Based on the Past

This section describes the extension of the AOC system in Europe first, in the wine industry leading up to the early beginnings of the PDOs and Protected Geographical Indications (PGIs) under the EU Quality Schemes Regulation (1992). International legislations namely, the Lisbon Agreement and TRIPS, are discussed alongside. We acknowledge that this book is primarily aimed at providing a historical analysis of IP law up to the 1920s, but we would like to argue that our historical analysis becomes more valuable when we can show the evolution of GI law from the 19th and early 20th century into the 21st century. The historical analysis can be employed to get a better understanding of contemporary issues in GI law. Therefore, throughout this section we will reflect on lessons that have been (but should not) or could have been used to clarify the law. This is followed by a final reflection on the evolving rationale for protection of GIs from the past to the present and the concomitant evolutions in the governance of GIs in Section 4.

By the time the European Economic Community (EEC) was established by the Treaty of Rome in 1957, some sort of protection of origin-linked products already existed in the founding member countries. The regimes of protection were influenced by the definition of AOs in the Lisbon Agreement which was in turn heavily influenced by French regulation on AOCs in the wine industry.[119]

117 Even in France, AOCs were limited to wines and it is only in 1990 that they were extended to other agricultural products; Marie-Vivien et al., "Are French Geographical Indications Losing Their Soul? Analysing Recent Developments in Governance of the Link to the Origin in France," 26.

118 Gangjee, "Melton Mowbray and the GI Pie in the Sky: Exploring Cartographies of Protection." These questions continue to be raised in the context of recent discussions on geographical indications for non-agricultural products in Europe and for the protection of manufactured/handmade products around the world.

119 Gangjee, *Relocating the Law of Geographical Indications*, chap. 3. Gangjee explains this influence in his 2011 book wherein he also draws a link between the French AOC on protection of appellations outside the wine industry by referring to the International Convention on the Use of Appellations of Origin and Denominations of Cheeses 1951.

EEC member countries Belgium, France, Germany, Italy, Luxembourg and the Netherlands met during the Stresa Conference in 1958 to discuss the path towards a Common Agricultural Policy (CAP) identifying the importance of a European agricultural community as a priority for all member countries but especially for France as a major agricultural exporter.[120] Since boosting the agricultural sector was important, the French AOC system was considered to be useful to promote the "rent-seeking" that it allowed.[121] The Lisbon Agreement was signed in the same year (1958) that the principles of the CAP were set out.

The Lisbon Agreement entered into force in 1966 with only two European countries (France and Portugal) ratifying it at the beginning in addition to Cuba, Haiti, Israel and Mexico. Italy and Hungary joined in soon followed by other countries who were mainly composed of former French colonies.[122] The Lisbon Agreement was the first agreement to consider a separate protection for appellations of origin at the international level. The purpose of the Agreement was to go beyond the Paris Convention and the Madrid Agreement (Indications of source), recognizing appellations as a separate category

---

This Convention was ratified by Austria, Denmark, France, Italy, The Netherlands, Norway and Switzerland before the EEC was formed and refers to the 'local, loyal and uninterrupted usage' criteria used for the French AOCs.

120 "Economically, the formation of a common market and customs union required the inclusion of agriculture and food, simply because of the importance of food in both production and consumption patterns of the time. Politically, the essential compromise between German and French national interests required that France, as the predominant agricultural producer within the EEC, gain remunerative Community agricultural markets to offset the competitiveness of German industry in a common market." Harvey, David. "What Does the History of the Common Agricultural Policy Tell Us?," in *Research Handbook on EU Agriculture Law* (Cheltenham: Edward Elgar, 2015), 7. This difference in priorities between France and Germany would have an impact on the formation of the EU PDO and PGI regime later.

121 Spoerer explains that rent-seeking can be justified politically by for example considering their welfare impacts or the contribution of farmers to the society. Spoerer, Mark. "Agricultural Protection and Support in the European Economic Community, 1962–92: Rent-Seeking or Welfare Policy?," *European Review of Economic History* 19 (2015): 195–214. GIs are considered "rent-seeking" instruments by economists. As GIs counter informational asymmetry by providing information about the origin and the quality of a product, they allow producers to extract much higher revenues than is "justified" when compared to the investment. Gangjee, *Relocating the Law of Geographical Indications*, 82; Landi, Chiara, and Stefani, Gianluca. "Rent Seeking and Political Economy of Geographical Indication Foods," *Agribusiness* 31, no. 4 (2015): 543–63.

122 Micara, Anna G. "The Geneva Act of the Lisbon Agreement for the Protection of Appellations of Origin and Their International Registration: An Assessment of a Controversial Agreement," *International Review of Intellectual Property and Competition Law* 47 (2016): 677.

and providing for its international registration similar to what the Madrid Agreement (Marks) allowed for trademarks.[123] The agreement defined AOs (Art. 2.1 cited above) and instituted an international registration system for AOs (Art. 5). During the negotiations, Germany was opposed to the definition of AOs as a special kind of indication that also required specific product characteristics as well as the use of the term AO itself.[124] This is curious because during the negotiations on the Art. 1(2) of the Paris Convention Germany had presented a proposal to include appellations of origin as a sub-type of indications of source.[125] Art. 1(2) of the Lisbon agreement states that countries party to this agreement "undertake to protect on their territories, in accordance with the terms of this Agreement, the appellations of origin of products of the other countries of the Special Union, recognized and protected as such in the country of origin". Some countries raised the concern that there was no equivalent protection in their domestic laws that could satisfy the narrow scope of the Agreement (Germany, Sweden, Denmark).[126] France countered that the term was already in use domestically, as well as in Spain, Italy and Hungary. Scholars note that despite the use of 'as such' in this clause and the AOC style definition, the intention of the negotiating parties to the treaty was not to impose the AO style of protection on all member countries.[127] However, it was perceived in this restrictive fashion and has remained a particularly unpopular agreement (with only 30 parties) to date. The Geneva Act of the Lisbon Agreement,[128] tries to address this by supplying a definition of geographical indications alongside the AO definition and also expressly stating under Art. 10 (1) that "Each Contracting Party shall be free to choose the type

123 Daciana Boloş, Mihaela. "Appellation of Origin vs. Geographical Indications. Terminological Debates during the Lisbon Treaty 1958," *Studia Universitatis Petru Maior – History* 1 (2011): 275.

124 The negotiating history of the Lisbon Agreement can be found in Actes De la Conférence De Lisbonne, 6–31 Octobre 1958, <https://www.wipo.int/export/sites/www/treaties/en/documents/prep-docs/1958_oct_Lisbon-fr.pdf> accessed on 15 January 2021. For an English translation of the arguments, See Daciana Boloş, "Appellation of Origin vs. Geographical Indications. Terminological Debates during the Lisbon Treaty 1958."

125 "Actes De La Conférence De Lisbonne" (Neuchatel (Suisse), 1963), 771–75, https://www.wipo.int/export/sites/www/treaties/en/documents/prep-docs/1958_oct_Lisbon-fr.pdf.

126 Daciana Boloş, "Appellation of Origin vs. Geographical Indications. Terminological Debates during the Lisbon Treaty 1958."

127 Micara, "The Geneva Act of the Lisbon Agreement for the Protection of Appellations of Origin and Their International Registration: An Assessment of a Controversial Agreement," 678; Gervais, "The Lisbon Agreement's Misunderstood Potential," 90. This is similar to the intention of the countries in the Paris Convention. "Actes De La Conférence De Lisbonne," 771–75.

128 Geneva Act.

of legislation under which it establishes the protection stipulated in this Act, provided that such legislation meets the substantive requirements of this Act."

The Lisbon 'system' is composed of the Lisbon Agreement for the International Registration of Appellations of Origins,[129] which came into force in 1966 and subsequent Acts, out of which the Geneva Act is the latest. Despite the low number of signatories, the agreement is path-breaking in signaling a new era for GI protection. Whether its enforcement is going to have a positive or a negative consequence depends on the lens one uses to analyze it. With a broader and flexible approach to the definition of GIs, the Geneva Act is a textbook example of international legislations that are bound to entail many compromises to remain acceptable by a large number of member states. In addition, this compromise is a step towards solidifying the laws that do not require a strong link to the *terroir*, i.e., the people and the place.[130] We argue that though it is not necessary that this link is made using the French understanding of *terroir*, a dilution of this link is incoherent with the increasing relevance of sustainable development as a rationale for GI protection.

In 1962 the EEC launched the CAP based on the principle of the free internal market for agricultural and food products and adopting common prices.[131] In July 1992, a reform of the CAP was announced which introduced the Quality Schemes Regulation for agricultural products and foodstuffs.[132] Between 1962 and 1992, several new member states joined and the EEC was reformed into the EU. The respective competence of EU member states and the EU in GI matters was refined and tested at the CJEU.[133] It was established that while member states can regulate on IP matters, domestic IP laws cannot prejudice the free movement of goods within the EU and the competition provisions of the treaties.[134]

The influence of the German approach to unfair competition and the importance of the consumer in the context of the EU internal market law and the CAP meant that the focus of appellations law shifted from the producer to

129 Lisbon Agreement.

130 See information box 'What is *Terroir?*', p. 9.

131 Harvey, "What Does the History of the Common Agricultural Policy Tell Us?," 8.

132 Council Regulation No 2081/92 of 14 July 1992 on the protection of geographical indications and designations of origin for agricultural products and foodstuffs [1992] L208/1.

133 For an understanding of the reasons behind the EU's competence to legislate on geographical indications, See Brouwer, Onno. "Community Protection of Geographical Indications and Specific Character as a Means of Enhancing Foodstuff Quality," *Common Market Law Review* 28, no. 3 (1991): 624.

134 Pila, Justine, and Torremans, Paul. *European Intellectual Property Law* (Oxford: Oxford University Press, 2016), 52–55.

also include the consumer.[135] Gangjee refers to this as the reputational link to the origin and explains that 1992 Regulation on PDOs and PGIs tried to reconcile the French and the German approach to GIs.[136] The French idea was that it is the *terroir* that provides the reputation to the product while the German approach was to also consider 'reputation' of the product in the minds of the consumer as having a link to the origin on its own. This is an important distinction and it did come up again when TRIPS was being negotiated.[137] The 1992 Regulation ended up defining two different types of GIs in the Quality Schemes Regulation. Art. 2 of the regulation defines a designation of origin and a geographical indication. First it explains that designation of origin means "the name of a region, a specific place or, in exceptional cases, a country, used to describe an agricultural product or a foodstuff: [...] originating in that region, specific place or country, and *the quality or characteristics of which are essentially or exclusively due to a particular geographical environment with its inherent natural and human factors*, and the production, processing and preparation of which take place in the defined geographical area. Second, geographical indication means the name of a region, a specific place or, in exceptional cases, a country, used to describe an agricultural product or a foodstuff: [...] originating in that region, specific place or country, and [...] which possesses a *specific quality, reputation or other characteristics attributable to that geographical origin* and the production and/or processing and/or preparation of which take place in the defined geographical area." The two types of GIs are considered to reflect the compromise between the two positions on GIs amongst the member states.[138] The PDO due to its symbolic allegiance to the idea of *terroir* was considered favorable for some member states who had domestic GI legislations modelled after the AOs under the Lisbon Agreement e.g., France, Italy and Spain. Whereas the PGI was considered favorable for countries that did not have a *sui generis* GI protection and instead relied on judge made unfair competition laws such as Germany and the UK.

The PDO was also considered by some to be a stronger or superior form of protection because of its supposed attention to the *quality* of the product that

135 Brouwer, "Community Protection of Geographical Indications and Specific Character as a Means of Enhancing Foodstuff Quality," 622.

136 Gangjee, "Melton Mowbray and the GI Pie in the Sky: Exploring Cartographies of Protection."

137 Gervais, "The Lisbon Agreement's Misunderstood Potential," 93–94.

138 Zappalaglio, Andrea. "The Protection of Geographical Indications: Ambitions and Concrete Limitations," *Edinburgh Student Law Review* 89 (2015): 599.

was due to the distinctiveness provided by the origin.[139] Yet another reason could be that a system based on PDOs, in theory, protects the *terroir* by rewarding long standing traditions and know-how of the producers and by encouraging traditional practices. If this is true and could be shown, then it would also be one reason to justify the excessive rent-seeking.[140] Others dismiss the need for PDOs as a separate category if the focus is on the quality of the product. Writing in 1991, Brouwer argued that PDOs were unnecessary and trademarks or existing labelling schemes for origin-linked products would have sufficed because, "Good quality could reside in the concept of traditional skills and culinary arts or in new products arising from better techniques or culinary innovation. Trademarks and labels do not concede or enhance the intrinsic quality of a product."[141] Therefore, according to Brouwer we should be honest about the purpose of PDOs as a marketing tool rather than a quality enhancing appellation. While marketing is one of the functions PDOs fulfil, more recently several authors have been recognizing that PDOs can also protect innovation and creativity in GI specifications.[142] This reflects the growing understanding that standardizations mentioned in the PDO can be fluid and aren't necessarily fixed. Others have expressed concern about the assumed 'authenticity' of PDO products due to the fact that the creation of a PDO essentially requires a compromise between the different actors and the registration system may leave

139 Bérard (n 16) 83 discusses the proposal in 2012 to combine PDOs and PGIs which she asserts would have resulted in a definition closer to PGI and not the PDO because of France's role in positioning PDOs as a superior form of GIs.

140 This is to say that a PDO style protection of a product is not necessarily effective. GIs rely on other domestic laws, government support and on local governance methods for their efficiency. "The success of GIs in Europe clearly relies upon a whole range of other supports and subsidies as well as a legal context in which human rights are 'constitutionalized' within IP rights protections. Without such supports and normative framings, however, GIs cannot simply be transplanted and expected to function in the same way." Coombe, Rosemary J., and Malik, S. Ali. "Transforming the Work of Geographical Indications to Decolonize Racialized Labor and Support Agroecology," *UC Irvine Law Review* 8 (2018): 367.

141 Brouwer, "Community Protection of Geographical Indications and Specific Character as a Means of Enhancing Foodstuff Quality," 631.

142 See Van Moerland, Anke. "Geographical Indications and Innovation, What Is the Connection?," in *The Innovation Society and Intellectual Property*, European Intellectual Property Institutes Network Series (Cheltenham: Edward Elgar, 2019), 59–86; Quiñones Ruiz, Xiomara et al. "How Are Food Geographical Indications Evolving? – An Analysis of EU GI Amendments," *British Food Journal* 120, no. 8 (2018): 1876–87; Gocci, Alessandro and Luetge, Christoph. "The Synergy of Tradition and Innovation Leading to Sustainable Geographical Indication Products: A Literature Review," *Journal of Management and Sustainability* 10, no. 1 (2020): 152–61.

out a host of local actors.[143] This refers to the fact that the process of creation of a GI necessarily requires drawing boundaries and this comes with the risk of exclusion of certain producers if the process is poorly governed. Despite these resistances the PDO and PGI system came into existence and continues to this day.[144]

The French AO definition had a far-reaching impact at the European (Regulation 1992), the international level (Lisbon Agreement) and framed the discussions during the TRIPS negotiations.[145] The TRIPS Agreement is an Annex to the Marrakesh Agreement establishing the World Trade Organization,[146] and brought intellectual property rights out from the pure ambit of the World Intellectual Property Organization (WIPO) into the ambit of the trade and the WTO. TRIPS is widely considered as a major step in harmonizing international intellectual property law including GI law. Before TRIPS the number of countries negotiating each of the WIPO administered treaties (Paris, Madrid, Lisbon) were limited.[147] However, when TRIPS was on the table under the ambit of the WTO, the number of countries that were participating in the negotiations as well as those being affected by the consequences of the Agreement were far more.[148] Another noteworthy consequence of intellectual property law being negotiated under TRIPS as part of a trade agreement was the objective with which countries came to the table. While some countries sought to ensure that their manner of protecting GIs would not be threatened, others who did not protect GIs so efficiently or had little interest in international harmonization of these rights were forced to accept intellectual property protection provisions as part of the package-deal to be able to benefit under the WTO rules. According to Dutfield and Suthersanen the motivation for the inclusion of GIs during TRIPS negotiations was the proposals made by the EU and Switzerland.[149]

143 Faure, Muriel. "An Agricultural Product 'Refined' into a Cultural Object: Beaufort Cheese in the Northern Alps," *Terrain* 33 (1999): 81–92; Coombe, Rosemary J., and Aylwin, Nicole. "Bordering Diversity and Desire: Using Intellectual Property to Mark Place-Based Products," *Environment and Planning* 43 (2011): 2034.

144 In addition, in 2012 three new quality schemes have been introduced namely: "traditional specialties guaranteed", "mountain products" and "products of island farming". Art. 18, 31 and 32 Regulation (EU) No 1151/2012 of the European Parliament and of the Council of 21 November 2012 on quality schemes for agricultural products and foodstuffs, L 343/1.

145 Okediji, "The International Intellectual Property Roots of Geographical Indications," 1341.

146 TRIPS Agreement (n 2).

147 Currently the number of Contracting Parties to the Paris, Madrid and Lisbon treaties are 177, 36 and 30 respectively.

148 164 countries are currently members of the WTO.

149 Dutfield and Suthersanen, *Dutfield and Suthersanen on Global Intellectual Property Law*, 268.

In line with our argumentation on the impact of the French AOCs regime on the Lisbon Agreement, the compromise solution in the EU Quality Schemes Regulation of 1992, the role of the EU and Switzerland in the TRIPs negotiations on GIs again led to a proposal for a compromise solution for the two main approaches towards GIs at the EU level. Namely, one that considered reputation in the minds of the consumers as enough to recognize a link to the origin (unfair competition approach) and the other that requires a connection to the natural and human factors of the origin (*sui generis/terroir* approach).[150]

The TRIPS negotiators had the difficult task of harmonizing multiple approaches used for regulating GIs globally. These ranged from *sui generis* AO regimes to trademark law protection to unfair competition laws and the common law remedy against passing off.[151] The TRIPS agreement addressed these differences by opting for a flexible definition for GIs and to this date, safeguarding 'flexibility' as to the definitions and regime for protection is the only harmonization that has taken place on this topic internationally. In addition to this flexibility, there is a hierarchical position for GI products with wines at the top.[152] There is no intellectual property policy-based reason for this hierarchical position other than the fact that the level of protection envisaged in art. 22 was considered insufficient by the European Communities.[153] Considering the influence of the wine industry on the conceptualization of the concept of GIs, this does not seem surprising. Okediji points out that "the outcome of the TRIPS Agreement on GIs reflected the triumph of methods and processes of production divorced from social contexts that might cause a return to considerations of the value of the product over the symbol."[154] This flexibility com-

150 The Swiss proposal actually reads as follows: "A geographical indication is any direct or indirect reference to the geographical origin of a product, including characteristics or qualities which are related to that origin ... [while] an appellation of origin is a qualified geographical indication denominating a country, region or locality indicating that a product is originating therefrom and has *qualities, reputation or other characteristic which are essentially or exclusively attributable to the geographical origin, including human or natural factors*. A denomination which has acquired a geographical character in relation to a product which has such qualities, reputation or characteristics is also deemed to be appellation of origin." Swiss proposal tabled on May 14, 1990, MTN.GNG/NG11/W/73 cited in Gervais, 'The Lisbon Agreement's Misunderstood Potential' (n 6) 91.

151 Dutfield and Suthersanen, *Dutfield and Suthersanen on Global Intellectual Property Law*, 238.

152 Spirits were added to art. 23 towards the end of the negotiations. Daniel Gervais, *The TRIPS Agreement: Drafting History and Analysis*, 3rd ed. (London: Sweet & Maxwell, 2008); Rangnekar, "Geographical Indications, A Review of Proposals at the TRIPS Council: Extending Article 23 to Products Other than Wines and Spirits," 23.

153 For a discussion See Gangjee, *Relocating the Law of Geographical Indications*, 237–44.

154 Okediji, "The International Intellectual Property Roots of Geographical Indications," 1350.

promise also persists with the Geneva Act of the Lisbon Agreement which can be seen as a fresh attempt to bring GIs back into the multilateral arena.[155]

As a consequence, countries continue to use different methods and they can even use combinations of methods to produce the effects visualized under Art. 22.1 TRIPS. For example, countries with a *sui generis* GI law can have a trademark flavor in terms of actual protection e.g. in India, allowing for GI registration as a collective right and requiring a description to be attached but not going beyond to enforce the conditions laid down in the GI specifications, a key feature of *sui generis* regimes.[156] On the other hand, collective trademark regimes can have quite detailed specifications protecting more of the human or environmental elements of the origin, an approach that resembles *sui generis* regimes, e.g. in case of Rooibos tea in South Africa.[157] Thus, today countries use *sui generis* laws, trademark laws, unfair competition and common law remedies against passing off. A connection has even been made between urban planning and GI protection by Dutfield and Suthersanen using an example of the Savile Row street for tailored suits in London which has been granted a protected status by the local city council.[158] Gervais beautifully summarizes the TRIPS compromise as follows: "TRIPS [...] seems to blend the normative heft of Lisbon in protecting geographically-dependent quality, characteristics or reputation, with the symbolic flexibility of the Madrid Agreement by encompassing broadly any indication that would point to a particular geographic origin provided, however, that a certain quality or characteristic (and/or reputation) is attributable to that origin."[159]

155 Geneva Act. The Geneva Act of the Lisbon Agreement adds a definition of the geographical indication as defined under TRIPS to the existing AO definition, thereby allowing all countries to register their products in the Lisbon register which was so far restricted to the registration of AOs. In 2020 the Geneva Act came into force after the ratification by the EU in 2019.

156 In this respect see the definition of 'permissive' and 'prescriptive' ways of implementing GIs in Dominique Barjolle and others, 'The Role of the State for Geographical Indications of Coffee: Case Studies from Colombia and Kenya' (2017) 98 World Development 105, 114 where the authors state that permissive states govern GIs much like trademarks. This study is also a good example of States enforcing sui generis laws having a trademark flavor (Colombia) and states having trademark laws being prescriptive in enforcing a specification for better quality management (Kenya for Coffee in this case).

157 Blakeney, Michael. "Geographical Indications and Environmental Protections," *Frontiers of Law in China* 12, no. 2 (2017): 166.

158 Dutfield and Suthersanen, *Dutfield and Suthersanen on Global Intellectual Property Law*, 268.

159 Gervais, "The Lisbon Agreement's Misunderstood Potential," 92.

4 Reflections Based on the Descriptive Historical Analysis

We begin this final Section with our observations on the comparison of the evolution of GI law in the 19th and early 20th century with general trends in international law. Thereafter we discuss some of the key findings of our descriptive historical analysis of the legal framework focusing on the different approaches towards GI protection that have evolved over time at the national, European and international level. We then link our findings to recent suggestions to reconsider sustainable development as a new rationale for GI protection. We argue that for GIs to fulfill this role a link between the product and the human or natural characteristics of the origin is essential. Our argument first focuses on the evolving rationale for GI protection and is followed by a subsection on the governance framework, which – in our opinion – is important as a reflection of the underlying rationale for GI protection and for ensuring an effective implementation of this changing rationale.

4.1 *Colonization, European Modernity and Globalization*

What we today refer to as international GI law emerged from local developments in France. As a result of the complex influences of imperialism, European modernity and globalization, these developments were included in major international treaties that the rest of the world was obliged to implement in their domestic systems. European rationality/modernity in this period is understood as the hidden coloniality of knowledge and the coloniality of power wherein rationality/modernity emerged not only as a separation of the state with church and religion but also in the restructuring of power and imagination of humanism and society as excluding non-Western peoples.[160] With Europe imagining itself to be at the center of world history, the enlightenment ideals were accompanied with the 'white man's burden' of emancipating and civilizing the rest of the world.[161] The 'civilizing' narrative of the Law of Nations,[162] in the 19th and early 20th century is identifiable in the origin story

160 Quijano, Aníbal. "Coloniality and Modernity/Rationality," *Cultural Studies* 21, no. 2–3 (2007): 168–78.

161 Mignolo, Walter D. "Delinking: The Rhetoric of Modernity, the Logic of Coloniality and the Grammar of Decolonization," *Cultural Studies* 21, no. 2–3 (2007): 449–514. "The rhetoric of modernity works through the imposition of 'salvation', whether as Christianity, civilization, modernization and development after WWII or market democracy after the fall of the Soviet Union."

162 Spitra, Sebastian M. "Civilisation, Protection, Restitution: A Critical History of International Cultural Heritage Law in the 19th and 20th Century," *Journal of the History of International Law* 22, no. 2–3 (2020): 329–54.

of GI law as we know it today. As Morris notes in his chapter the countries that could participate in the discussions on the Paris Convention were limited by European conceptions of civilization and the colonized peoples were themselves exhibits in the late 19th century technological exhibitions. International GI law was not and is not a universal law. Dutfield and Suthersanen note that until recently implementation of intellectual property was a matter of compliance rather than policy making in developing countries.[163] In the same vein, Acquah writes in his chapter here that intellectual property law was not borrowed by the colonized states but was imposed on them to enable and justify the extraction of wealth through colonialism. After the Berlin Conference of 1884–1885, African countries were partitioned between the European countries of Britain, France, Portugal, Germany and Belgium. Intellectual property law was imposed on African countries through their colonial 'masters'.[164] Mengistie and Blakeney have specifically traced the role of GIs in the European 'Scramble for Africa' and show how European countries enlisted the support of former African colonies for implementing EU style *sui generis* protection laws (e.g. Algeria, Morocco, Tunisia, Benin, Burkina Faso, Cameroon, Chad, Congo and so on).[165] As we have mentioned before, the evolution of GI law can also be seen as an example of globalized localism, wherein the laws driven by a small group of powerful countries, or even a single country are imposed on the rest of the world. The story of European economic development that justified the expansion of GI law continued with the expansion of globalization and of world trade of GI products. Raustiala and Munzer convincingly argue that the current debates in GI protection are not driven by philosophical justifications but by political interests and accurately predicted in 2007 that the continuing progress of globalization and economic liberalization will keep supporting propertization and commodification through international law.[166]

4.2 *Evolving Rationales*

In the previous sections (2–3), we have shown that today multiple approaches to protect GIs are being adopted at the national, European and international

163 Dutfield and Suthersanen, *Dutfield and Suthersanen on Global Intellectual Property Law*, 10.

164 See also Okediji, Ruth. "The International Relations of Intellectual Property: Narratives of Developing Country Participation in the Global Intellectual Property System," *Singapore Journal of International & Comparative Law* 7 (2003): 315–85.

165 Mengistie and Blakeney, "Geographical Indications and the Scramble for Africa", 211–16.

166 Raustiala, Kal, and Munzer, Stephen R. "The Global Struggle over Geographical Indications," *The European Journal of International Law* 18, no. 2 (2007): 337–65; Peukert, Alexander. "Intellectual Property and Development – Narratives and Their Empirical Validity," *The Journal of World Intellectual Property* 20, no. 2 (2017): 4–5.

level, though some approaches are more prominent (more effectively promoted by countries concerned) than others. Three of those approaches towards protection emphasize the link between the product and the human and natural aspects of the origin to different extents: a *terroir*-based appellation, a TRIPS based GI and a collective trademark. Out of these it is the *terroir*-based appellation that demands the strongest link to the origin, whether human or natural, followed by the GI as defined under TRIPS and then the trademark-style protection that requires the least strong link to the origin. The extension of *terroir*-based appellations outside France through international treaties such as Lisbon and TRIPS and bilateral agreements has, however, resulted in the dilution of the link to the origin.

Despite the dilution of the link to the origin in the way terroir-based appellations were implemented in different countries, the underlying rationales for GI protection have been extended in a direction that seems to presuppose a strong link to the origin. The rationales given today for the protection of GIs range from preventing unfair competition and fraud (link to the origin generally less important) to protection of the environment and sustainable development (link to the origin essential). Calboli and Marie-Vivien suggest for instance more concretely that GIs can support various UN Sustainable Development Goals (SDGs) (SDG2 – Zero Hunger, SDG9 – Industry, Innovation and Infrastructure, SDG12 – Responsible Consumption and Production, SDG 15 – Life on Land, etc.) because of their potential to valorize the natural and human elements of a place but they also note the skepticism against GIs in this respect.[167] The sustainable development rationale stretches the capacity of what GIs (even appellations) as defined under the current legislations have traditionally been designed to do. Achieving such objectives would require more effort from all actors involved, especially the producers who are lucky enough to participate in the GI process, third-party private actors, civil society organizations as well as the State.

Our analysis in Section 2 illustrates that the original rationale of protection in early and late 19th century France was to regulate trade and prevent unfair competition, fraud and adulteration. The law therefore reflected this purpose and prevented false origin-labelling. The positive externality of this protection

---

167 See, Calboli, Irene, and Marie-Vivien, Delphine. "One Size Does Not Fit All: The Roles of the State and the Private Sector in the Governance Framework of Geographical Indications," in *The Cambridge Handbook of Public-Private Partnerships, Intellectual Property Governance, and Sustainable Development* (Cambridge: Cambridge University Press, 2018), 312. where the authors suggest that GIs can support various SDGs (SDG2 – Zero Hunger, SDG9 – Industry, Innovation and Infrastructure, SDG12 – Responsible Consumption and Production, etc.), but also note the skepticism against GIs in this respect.

was correct information to the producer, helping with origin-based marketing and building a reputation for the product. The protection of products was fragmented, and legislation was introduced for individual products wherever the producer's lobbies were able to gain influence and respond to major risks and market crisis. There was a difference of opinion amongst the actors involved – the wine producers (who did not have a uniform view in the first place) and the traders on whether the focus of legislation should be the quality of the product or the quantity. There were differing views amongst trade associations and the producers on the desirability of standardization in methods of production but eventually by 1935 there was overpowering support for definition of methods of production in the wine regions. These debates lasted decades and were backed up by labor associations and benefiting from the freedom of association.[168] During this time the importance of protection of consumer interests also gradually became a more important rationale for the national regimes.

The objective of the Lisbon Agreement was effective international protection for AOs but firstly, to create a separate space for AOs out of the shadows of trademarks.[169] The rationale for GI protection at that time following our historical description was to promote the standardization in the production of wines and other agricultural products to increase their distinctiveness in international markets. If more countries adopted the AO approach, European producers who were already protecting their products as AOs could protect their products in the international market along the same lines as their domestic protection. At the EU level, the case law of the CJEU firmly positioned GIs at the interface between the free movement of goods (internal market), the protection of consumers and last but not least supporting the European agricultural sector. Analyzing in detail whether the Quality Schemes legislative framework of 1992 has been able to achieve these very different combined rationales goes beyond the scope of this chapter. However, we can point out that there are some noteworthy criticisms in the literature.[170]

168 See Stanziani, "French Collective Wine Branding in the Nineteenth-Twentieth Centuries."

169 Gangjee, *Relocating the Law of Geographical Indications*, 127–28.

170 See Brouwer (n 99) for early criticisms on the necessity of the Quality Schemes; Stanziani (n 16) refers to several other criticisms: the high cost of setting up collective designations, the multiplicity of AOCs in France which actually prevent consumers from knowing a brand, etc. See also, Hughes, Justin. "The Limited Promise of Geographical Indications for Farmers in Developing Countries," in *Geographical Indications at the Crossroads of Trade, Development and Culture* (Cambridge University Press, 2017), 61–86. From the point of view of producers as well, the awareness of Quality Schemes is not evenly distributed in Europe and the assumption that PDOs would exclude human elements of *terroir* is also an obstacle. Martijn Huysmans and Johan Swinnen, "No Terroir in the Cold? A Note on

When we examine the adopted rationale(s) for GI protection in the TRIPS agreement, the view becomes even more blurry: the 19th century AO has been stretched beyond its limits and breaks up into multiple approaches. The TRIPS agreement tried to provide a flexible definition, but the domestic rationales remain relevant and one can see their influence in the resistance to reduce the flexibilities at the TRIPS level and in bilateral negotiations between countries. As is to be expected with an agreement adopted in the context of the WTO, the emphasis in terms of the rationale for protecting GIs focuses much more on stimulating international trade and offering a level playing field by facilitating recognition of domestic products with trading partners,[171] and by ensuring compliance with the requirements in the TRIPS Agreement and with bilateral trade agreements.[172] Obviously, this shift in emphasis does not help rescue the existing lack of coherence between the domestic rationales of protection and the legal regime used.

The international harmonization of GIs is a compelling project which is nowhere near complete. Proponents of GIs have pointed to several positive externalities of GIs to convince naysayers of the added value of GI protection. Some of these positive externalities concern socio-economic development of rural areas, preservation of the environment, biodiversity conservation, rights of indigenous populations over their land, etc.[173]

4.3 *Importance of the Governance Framework*

One consequence of the fact that the historical roots of GI protection are closely associated with the idea of *terroir* is that the governance of GI evokes the image of human intervention with the product in an organized fashion and

---

the Geography of Geographical Indications," *Journal of Agricultural Economics* 70, no. 2 (2019): 550–59.

171 See Marie-Vivien, Delphine. 'Protection of Geographical Indications in ASEAN Countries: Convergences and Challenges to Awakening Sleeping Geographical Indications' (2020) 23 *Journal of World Intellectual Property* 328, 331–332 for influence of US and EU GI protection regimes on ASEAN countries.

172 Van Moerland, Anke. "Do Developing Countries Have a Say? Bilateral and Regional Intellectual Property Negotiations with the EU," *International Review of Intellectual Property and Competition Law* 48, no. 7 (November 2017): 760–83.

173 Marie-Vivien, Delphine, and Chabrol, Didier. "Geographical Indications, Biodiversity and Poor Communities: The Opportunity of Geographical Indications to Provide Protection of Traditional Indigenous Biodiversity Products and Benefits to Poor Agricultural Communities. A Desk Study on Six Target Countries: Cambodia, Laos, Indonesia, Vietnam, Ethiopia, Mauritania," 2014; Rangnekar, Dwijen. "The Socio-Economics of Geographical Indications: A Review of Empirical Evidence from Europe," Project Report (Warwick, 2003); Vandecandelaere, Emilie et al. "Strengthening Sustainable Food Systems through Geographical Indications" (Rome, 2018).

of fair and inclusive collective organization. While this is possible to achieve, this image is unlikely to be accurate in all cases. This is where the governance framework for GI protection becomes important. The governance framework is also closely interrelated with the rationale. In fact, the specific underlying rationale of GI protection adopted in a particular country determines whether a country opts for a *sui generis* (IP) regime or a trademark regime and it has an impact on the design of the governance framework and the level of interference of different stakeholders in the GI management process.[174] Furthermore, the selected legal regime also needs to be well aligned with the governance framework; and the set-up of the governance framework will determine the respective roles and responsibilities of the various stakeholders. Marie-Vivien and Biénabe have explained the relation between the justifications for institutionalizing GI as an IP right and for selecting a particular type of IP regime. They posit that *sui generis* GI systems are based on seeing GIs as a 'natural right' and thus demand a high level of state interference whereas trademark systems are based on a utilitarian doctrine where state intervention is restricted to the setting up of the GI and the governance is primarily by the right holders.[175] They mention the impact of other rationales such as the stimulation of international trade and environmental sustainability on governance as well. In view of its broad definitions and flexibility the international legal framework does not impose substantial restrictions in terms of the selection of the legal regime and the governance framework.

The governance framework used in different jurisdictions has also changed with time. With the evolution of rationales, the range and role of actors has also evolved. In the French wine industry these were producers, traders and the state. Today, in addition, there are internal market concerns in case of the EU, interests of other states as per the obligations under bilateral trade agreements, consumers as well as third-party private actors in various capacities. This can be in the form of public-private partnerships or complete outsourcing of certification or monitoring to private actors.[176] Considering the

174 See, Marie-Vivien, Delphine, and Biénabe, Estelle. "The Multifaceted Role of the State in the Protection of Geographical Indications: A Worldwide Review," *World Development* 98 (2017): 3.

175 See also, Le Goffic, Caroline, and Zappalaglio, Andrea. 'The Role Played by the US Government in Protecting Geographical Indications', *World Development* 98 (2017: 35) where the authors draw commonalities between the US Collective trademark system, the American Viticulture Areas and the EU *sui generis* system to show that there is public intervention even beyond the registration phase.

176 See, Marie-Vivien and others (n 16) for a historical overview of the role of state in the AOC process in France.

importance of a good governance framework for GI and the evolving rationales of GI protection in the direction of sustainable development, GI governance has become multi-dimensional as it operates at many levels and involves many different stakeholders.[177] As mentioned above, while the variety of rationales for protection has increased, the legally required link to the origin has loosened. This creates uncertainty for governance as well. It is pertinent that the so-called new world countries that are currently in the process of re-evaluating their GI protection regimes, thoughtfully identify the rationales of protection in their domestic context and construct a tailored GI governance framework accordingly (e.g., steps of the process, top-down/bottom-up, level of state intervention, roles of stakeholders in the different steps of the process, accountability). Without such a careful re-evaluation, the GI regime may entail significant risks, such as the exclusion of producers from their cultural heritage, abandonment of traditional methods, creation of product specifications in case of agricultural products that can result in reduced diversity,[178] lack of trust in the GI process amongst stakeholders including producers and consumers, and weak enforcement of GI regimes.[179] To counter these risks, state intervention is considered necessary but the exact level of state intervention should be decided on an individual basis. Calboli and Marie-Vivien conducted a comparative analysis of governance models in France, India and Singapore and argue that even though countries choose their own governance models as per the circumstances, the State should remain in charge in some stages of the GI management process, such as, examining and approving GI specifications and monitoring infringement post-registration.[180] They conclude that even though no ideal distribution of responsibilities between the state and the

177 See also, Marie-Vivien and Biénabe, "The Multifaceted Role of the State in the Protection of Geographical Indications: A Worldwide Review," 4. They identify four levels of governance: meta-rules at the international level, macro-rules at the national level, meso-rules at the sub-national level and micro-rules at the local level.

178 See the example of Tequila and Feni in the following studies: Bowen, Sarah and Valenzuela Zapata, Ana. "Geographical Indications, Terroir, and Socioeconomic and Ecological Sustainability: The Case of Tequila," *Journal of Rural Studies* 25 (2009): 108–19; Rangnekar, Dwijen. "Remaking Place: The Social Construction of a Geographical Indication for Feni," *Environment and Planning* 43 (2011): 2043–59.

179 See Van Moerland, 'Governance Systems of Geographical Indications' (n 167) 82–84 for an understanding of loopholes in EU law that can reduce consumer trust in the GI process. Van Moerland further makes recommendations for governance processes that can help stimulate trust in GIs.

180 Calboli and Marie-Vivien, "One Size Does Not Fit All: The Roles of the State and the Private Sector in the Governance Framework of Geographical Indications."

private actors can be recommended, there should always be a balance if states want to achieve the modern rationales of GI protection.

Finally, another important consideration for GI governance considering the new rationale of sustainable development is the necessity of integration of GIs with other areas of law, such as human rights law as well as the importance of multi-disciplinarity. Chon (borrowing from Sunder's conception of IP and Sen's capabilities approach to development) argues that IP rights in general are no longer being looked at only as public goods but are being expected to fulfill human development goals.[181] GI governance if allowed to be coherent with this new rationale will need to be more dynamic, innovative and adaptive. The entry of non-traditional actors (e.g., FAO, UNCTAD, development-agencies, third-party private actors combining CSR objectives with GI marketing, etc.) is one sign of change. Now the ball is in the court of countries to develop governance processes that appropriately respond to the rationales for protection.

5 Conclusion

In this chapter we have traced the development of GI law from its origins in early 19th century France to the latest Geneva Act of the Lisbon Agreement which came into force in 2020. We show how the law has evolved, how the rationales for protection have expanded and how the GI governance has become more dynamic. We asked whether it is time to reharmonize GI law with a stronger link to the *terroir*, that gives equal importance to the human and the environmental aspects. In short, yes, we must think about such a re-harmonization. However, a more nuanced answer is that the concept of *terroir* that would fit within this reconceptualization of GI law is much broader than espoused by 19th century French law regulating AOCs. Moreover, what is really needed is for countries to develop an appropriate governance framework and institutional capacities that allow for greater participation by producers in determining their GI regime. This would allow for a GI system that enshrines better protections for the human and natural environment of the product if the rationale is sustainable development.

Our descriptive historical analysis shows that origin-linked products have been regulated before the 19th century and in the early 19th century; however,

181 Chon, Margaret. "Recasting Intellectual Property in Light of The U.N. Sustainable Development Goals: Toward Global Knowledge Governance," *American University International Law Review* 34, no. 4 (2019): 763–85.

this regulation was fragmented. One can find national regulations for individual products or a group of products through an isolated executive decision such as an ordinance or an executive decree. The rationales of those regulations were in general to prevent fraud and adulteration, to discourage free riding on the reputation of another product and to allow fair trade for the producers. It is only in the early 20th century that we see legislations with the rationale of regulating the quality of the product or consumer protection.

The developments in France on AOCs added the concept of *terroir* from the wine industry into the discussion. While the concept of *terroir* is uniquely French and has been useful in a French context, there may be other concepts unique to other regions in other countries that define the relationship between the product and the place.[182] *Terroir* need not be the cornerstone of GI laws and therefore transplanted worldwide. The legitimacy and assumed success of the approach lay in the collective organization and lobbying power of (a select) group of producers. Europeanisation of an aspect of *terroir* began with the wine legislations. Around the same time, the Lisbon Agreement embodying AOs entered into force. This brought attention to the concept of *terroir* protection at a regional and international level. This was further subsumed into the CAP reform and the Quality Schemes Regulation of 1992. With the expansion of *terroir* beyond its borders and beyond the wine industry began the process of loosening of the link between the product and the place, more specifically between the natural and/or human factors of the origin and the product. At the same time, French lobbying for *terroir* continued. Merits of *terroir* were shown not only in the form of economic benefit for the producers but also on the collective organization of the producers, the biodiversity of the region, the marketing value of the product and the dissemination of correct information to the consumer about the quality of the product. The French example has been studied extensively by GI scholars and it has been shown that even in the homeland of *terroir* the law did not actually *require* a strong link to be proven.

Naturally, this trend of loosening of the link was transferred also outside the French legal system. The European system of PDOs has been touted to be inspired by the AOC in France. Recent studies show that products protected as PDOs do not necessarily have such a strong link with the origin and the original difference between PGI and PDOs related to the link of origin is at the risk of becoming blurred. Outside the EU, while there may be systems of protection of origin linked products and there are examples of products that are strongly linked to local identity, the formal protection of these products as

182 Bérard, "Terroir and the Sense of Place."

an IP right is a result of the European project of internationalization of GI law that continues to this day.[183] Countries that are in the process of constructing their own GI protection strategy should carefully evaluate domestic rationales of protection that go beyond compliance with TRIPS (which anyway contains minimal requirements), compliance with FTAs or international trade. A systematic comparison of GI protection regimes was outside the scope of this chapter and we did not engage with arguments on whether *sui generis* regimes are better suited to meet the new rationale of sustainable development. But so far as maintaining a link with the human and environmental aspects of a product is concerned, well-tailored *sui generis* regimes and within those *terroir*-based-appellations appear to be more appropriate for guaranteeing that link. This further depends of course on the governance of the appellation. As shown by Marie-Vivien and others in the case of France, a shift towards third-party based certifications and standardization as a *sine qua non* for quality management can limit the participation of producer organizations leading to frustrations with the GI management process.[184] These frustrations can lead to lack of trust in the GI regime as a whole. Whether there should be a re-harmonization of GI law at the international level, albeit minimal, in order to create more coherence in terms of the different rationales for protection and with effective participation from all countries is also a question that can benefit from more comparative analysis of different GI legal regimes and associated governance frameworks.

Acknowledgements

The authors are grateful to P. Sean Morris, Zvi Rosen and the two anonymous reviewers of this book for their helpful comments about previous versions of this chapter. Any errors are our own.

183 Mengistie and Blakeney, "Geographical Indications and the Scramble for Africa," 211. "Generally, those African countries with a French colonial heritage have adopted *sui generis* geographical indications legislation along the lines of EU laws, which reflect the French approach to *sui generis* protection of geographical indications." See also, Van Moerland, "Do Developing Countries Have a Say? Bilateral and Regional Intellectual Property Negotiations with the EU."

184 Marie-Vivien et al., "Are French Geographical Indications Losing Their Soul? Analysing Recent Developments in Governance of the Link to the Origin in France."

Bibliography

"Actes De La Conférence De Lisbonne." Neuchatel (Suisse), 1963. https://www.wipo.int/export/sites/www/treaties/en/documents/prep-docs/1958_oct_Lisbon-fr.pdf.

Banerjee, Abhijit, Duflo, Esther, Postel-Vinay, Gilles, and Watts, Tim. "Long-Run Health Impacts Of Income Shocks: Wine And Phylloxera In Nineteenth-Century France." *The Review of Economics and Statistics* 92, no. 4 (2010): 714–28.

Barham, Elizabeth. "'Translating Terroir' Revisited: The Global Challenge of French AOC Labelling." In *Research Handbook on Intellectual Property and Geographical Indications*, 46–71. Cheltenham: Edward Elgar, 2016.

Barjolle, Dominique, Quinones-Ruiz, Xiomara, Bagal, Monique, and Comoe, Hermann. "The Role of the State for Geographical Indications of Coffee: Case Studies from Colombia and Kenya." *World Development* 98 (2017): 105–19.

Beaulieu, Paul Leroy. "Wine Production in France." *Journal of the Statistical Society of London* 48, no. 3 (1885): 469–82.

Bérard, Laurence. "Terroir and the Sense of Place." In *Research Handbook on Intellectual Property and Geographical Indications*, 72–91. Cheltenham: Edward Elgar, 2016.

Bérard, Laurence, and Marchenay, Philippe. *From Localised Products to Geographical Indications*. Bourg-en-Bresse: CNRS Ressources des terroirs, 2008. https://www.ethno-terroirs.cnrs.fr/IMG/pdf/Localized_Products_to_GI.pdf.

Blakeney, Michael. "Geographical Indications and Environmental Protections." *Frontiers of Law in China* 12, no. 2 (2017): 162–74.

Blakeney, Michael. "The International Protection of Industrial Property: From the Paris Convention to the TRIPS Agreement." WIPO National Seminar on Intellectual Property. Cairo, 2003. https://www.wipo.int/meetings/en/doc_details.jsp?doc_id=16104.

Bogsch, Arpad. *The Paris Convention for the Protection of Industrial Property from 1883 to 1983*. Geneva: International Bureau of Intellectual Property, 1983.

Bowen, Sarah, and Valenzuela Zapata, Ana. "Geographical Indications, Terroir, and Socioeconomic and Ecological Sustainability: The Case of Tequila." *Journal of Rural Studies* 25 (2009): 108–19.

Brouwer, Onno. "Community Protection of Geographical Indications and Specific Character as a Means of Enhancing Foodstuff Quality." *Common Market Law Review* 28, no. 3 (1991): 615–46.

Calboli, Irene, and Marie-Vivien, Delphine. "One Size Does Not Fit All: The Roles of the State and the Private Sector in the Governance Framework of Geographical Indications." In *The Cambridge Handbook of Public-Private Partnerships, Intellectual Property Governance, and Sustainable Development*, 308–29. Cambridge: Cambridge University Press, 2018.

Chon, Margaret. "Recasting Intellectual Property in Light of The U.N. Sustainable Development Goals: Toward Global Knowledge Governance." *American University International Law Review* 34, no. 4 (2019): 763–85.

Coombe, Rosemary J., and Aylwin, Nicole. "Bordering Diversity and Desire: Using Intellectual Property to Mark Place-Based Products." *Environment and Planning* 43 (2011): 2027–42.

Coombe, Rosemary J., and Ali Malik, S. "Transforming the Work of Geographical Indications to Decolonize Racialized Labor and Support Agroecology." *UC Irvine Law Review* 8 (2018): 363–412.

Daciana Boloş, Mihaela. "Appellation of Origin vs. Geographical Indications. Terminological Debates during the Lisbon Treaty 1958." *Studia Universitatis Petru Maior – History* 1 (2011): 275–82.

Drahos, Peter. *A Philosophy of Intellectual Property*. 2016th ed. Australia: ANU E Press, 1955.

Dutfield, Graham, and Suthersanen, Uma. *Dutfield and Suthersanen on Global Intellectual Property Law*. 2nd ed. Cheltenham: Edward Elgar, 2020.

Farmer, Erica A. "Codifying Consensus and Constructing Boundaries: Setting the Limits of Appellation d'origine Contrôlée Protection in Bordeaux, France." *Political and Legal Anthropology Review* 37, no. 1 (2014): 126–44.

Faure, Muriel. "An Agricultural Product 'Refined' into a Cultural Object: Beaufort Cheese in the Northern Alps." *Terrain* 33 (1999): 81–92.

Gangjee, Dev. "Melton Mowbray and the GI Pie in the Sky: Exploring Cartographies of Protection." *Intellectual Property Quarterly* 3 (2006): 291–306.

Gangjee, Dev. *Relocating the Law of Geographical Indications*. Cambridge: Cambridge University Press, 2011.

Gervais, Daniel. "Geographical Indications under TRIPS." In *Research Handbook on Intellectual Property and Geographical Indications*, 123–45. Cheltenham: Edward Elgar, 2016.

Gervais, Daniel. "The Lisbon Agreement's Misunderstood Potential." *The WIPO Journal*, no. 1 (2009): 87–102.

Gervais, Daniel. *The TRIPS Agreement: Drafting History and Analysis*. 3rd ed. London: Sweet & Maxwell, 2008.

Gervais, Daniel. "Traditional Innovation and the Ongoing Debate on the Protection of Geographical Indications." In *Indigenous People's Innovation: Intellectual Property Pathways to Development*, 121–46. Ebook: ANU E Press, 2012. https://library.oapen.org/bitstream/handle/20.500.12657/33574/459872.pdf?sequence=1#page=145.

Gocci, Alessandro, and Luetge, Christoph. "The Synergy of Tradition and Innovation Leading to Sustainable Geographical Indication Products: A Literature Review." *Journal of Management and Sustainability* 10, no. 1 (2020): 152–61.

Harvey, David. "What Does the History of the Common Agricultural Policy Tell Us?" In *Research Handbook on EU Agriculture Law*, 3–40. Cheltenham: Edward Elgar, 2015.

Hughes, Justin. "The Limited Promise of Geographical Indications for Farmers in Developing Countries." In *Geographical Indications at the Crossroads of Trade, Development and Culture*, 61–86. Cambridge University Press, 2017.

Huysmans, Martijn, and Swinnen, Johan. "No Terroir in the Cold? A Note on the Geography of Geographical Indications." *Journal of Agricultural Economics* 70, no. 2 (2019): 550–59.

Lacoste, Pablo. "A Bi-National Appellation of Origin: Pisco in Chile and Peru." *Chilean Journal of Agricultural Research* 73, no. 4 (2013): 424–29.

Landi, Chiara, and Stefani, Gianluca. "Rent Seeking and Political Economy of Geographical Indication Foods." *Agribusiness* 31, no. 4 (2015): 543–63.

Le Goffic, Caroline, and Zappalaglio, Andrea. "The Role Played by the US Government in Protecting Geographical Indications." *World Development* 98 (2017): 35–44.

Mantrov, Vadim. *EU Law on Indications of Geographical Origin: Theory and Practice*. Cham: Springer, 2014.

Marie-Vivien, Delphine. "Protection of Geographical Indications in ASEAN Countries: Convergences and Challenges to Awakening Sleeping Geographical Indications." *Journal of World Intellectual Property* 23 (2020): 328–49.

Marie-Vivien, Delphine. *The Protection of Geographical Indications in India: A New Perspective on the French and European Experience*. New Delhi: Sage Publications, 2015.

Marie-Vivien, Delphine, Be'rard, L., Boutonnet, J., and Casabianca, F. "Are French Geographical Indications Losing Their Soul? Analysing Recent Developments in Governance of the Link to the Origin in France." *World Development* 19 (2017): 25–34.

Marie-Vivien, Delphine, and Biénabe, Estelle. "The Multifaceted Role of the State in the Protection of Geographical Indications: A Worldwide Review." *World Development* 98 (2017): 1–11.

Marie-Vivien, Delphine, and Chabrol, Didier. "Geographical Indications, Biodiversity and Poor Communities: The Opportunity of Geographical Indications to Provide Protection of Traditional Indigenous Biodiversity Products and Benefits to Poor Agricultural Communities. A Desk Study on Six Target Countries: Cambodia, Laos, Indonesia, Vietnam, Ethiopia, Mauritania," 2014.

Mengistie, Getachew, and Blakeney, Michael. "Geographical Indications and the Scramble for Africa." *African Journal of International and Comparative Law* 25 (2017): 199–220.

Micara, Anna G. "The Geneva Act of the Lisbon Agreement for the Protection of Appellations of Origin and Their International Registration: An Assessment of a Controversial Agreement." *International Review of Intellectual Property and Competition Law* 47 (2016): 673–96.

Mignolo, Walter D. "Delinking: The Rhetoric of Modernity, the Logic of Coloniality and the Grammar of Decolonization." *Cultural Studies* 21, no. 2–3 (2007): 449–514.

Mitchell, Jerry T., and Terry, William C. "Contesting Pisco: Chile, Peru and the Politics of Trade." *Geographical Review* 101, no. 4 (2011): 518–35.

O'Connor, Bernard. *The Law of Geographical Indications*. London: Cameron May, 2004.

OECD. "Appellations of Origin and Geographical Indications in IECD Member Countries: Economic and Legal Implications." Working Party on Agricultural Policies and Markets of the Committee for Agriculture Joint Working Party of the Committee for Agriculture and the Trade Committee. OECD, 2000. http://www.oecd.org/officialdocuments/publicdisplaydocumentpdf/?cote=COM/AGR/APM/TD/WP%282000%2915/FINAL&doclanguage=En.

Okediji, Ruth. "The International Relations of Intellectual Property: Narratives of Developing Country Participation in the Global Intellectual Property System." *Singapore Journal of International & Comparative Law* 7 (2003): 315–85.

Okediji, Ruth L. "The International Intellectual Property Roots of Geographical Indications." *Chicago-Kent Law Review* 82 (2007): 1329–65.

Özreisoğlu, Ayşe Kübra. "Who Owns the Geographical Indication Pisco, Peru or Chile?" *Law Blogs Maastricht*. 2019. https://www.maastrichtuniversity.nl/blog/2019/03/who-owns-geographical-indication-pisco-peru-or-chile.

Peukert, Alexander. "Intellectual Property and Development – Narratives and Their Empirical Validity." *The Journal of World Intellectual Property* 20, no. 2 (2017): 2–23.

Pila, Justine, and Torremans, Paul. *European Intellectual Property Law*. Oxford: Oxford University Press, 2016.

Planas, Jordi. "State Intervention in Wine Markets in the Early 20th Century: Why Was It so Different in France and Spain?" *Journal of Iberian and Latin American Economic History* 35, no. 2 (2016): 175–206.

Polo, Marta Pulido. "Historia Jurídica de Las Indicaciones Geográficas: Una Perspectiva Desde La Gestión de La Comunicación En Las Instituciones." *Estudios Institucionales* 3, no. 4 (2016): 7–24.

Quijano, Aníbal. "Coloniality and Modernity/Rationality." *Cultural Studies* 21, no. 2–3 (2007): 168–78.

Quiñones Ruiz, Xiomara, Forster, Hanna, Penker, Marianne, Belletti, Giovanni, Marescotti, Andrea, Scaramuzzi, Silvia, Broscha, Kristina, Braito, Michael, and Altenbuchner, Christine. "How Are Food Geographical Indications Evolving? – An Analysis of EU GI Amendments." *British Food Journal* 120, no. 8 (2018): 1876–87.

Rangnekar, Dwijen. "Geographical Indications, A Review of Proposals at the TRIPS Council: Extending Article 23 to Products Other than Wines and Spirits." UNCTAD-ICTSD Project on IPRS and Sustainable Development. Geneva, 2003. http://citeseerx.ist.psu.edu/viewdoc/download?doi=10.1.1.297.8212&rep=rep1&type=pdf.

Rangnekar, Dwijen. "Remaking Place: The Social Construction of a Geographical Indication for Feni." *Environment and Planning* 43 (2011): 2043–59.

Rangnekar, Dwijen. "The Socio-Economics of Geographical Indications: A Review of Empirical Evidence from Europe." Project Report. Warwick, 2003.

Raustiala, Kal, and Munzer, Stephen R. "The Global Struggle over Geographical Indications." *The European Journal of International Law* 18, no. 2 (2007): 337–65.

Sengupta, Mayuree. "Folklore vs Intellectual Property in Bengal since the Seventeenth Century: A Study." In *Forgotten Intellectual Property Lore*, 160–75. Cheltenham: Edward Elgar, 2020.

Simon, Lori E. "Appellations of Origin: The Continuing Controversey." *Northwestern Journal of International Law and Business* 5, no. 1 (1983): 132–56.

Sousa Santos, Boaventura de. *Toward a New Legal Common Sense: Law, Globalization, and Emancipation*. 3rd ed. Cambridge: Cambridge University Press, 2020.

Spielmann, Nathalie, and Gélinas-Chebat, Claire. "Terroir? That's Not How I Would Describe It." *International Journal of Wine Business Research* 24, no. 4 (2012): 254–70.

Spitra, Sebastian M. "Civilisation, Protection, Restitution: A Critical History of International Cultural Heritage Law in the 19th and 20th Century." *Journal of the History of International Law* 22, no. 2–3 (2020): 329–54.

Spoerer, Mark. "Agricultural Protection and Support in the European Economic Community, 1962–92: Rent-Seeking or Welfare Policy?" *European Review of Economic History* 19 (2015): 195–214.

Stanziani, Alessandro. "French Collective Wine Branding in the Nineteenth-Twentieth Centuries." In *Research Handbook on Intellectual Property and Geographical Indications*, 13–45. Cheltenham: Edward Elgar, 2016.

Stern, Stephen. "Are GIs IP?" *European Intellectual Property Review* 29, no. 2 (2007): 39–42.

Teil, Genevieve. "Protecting Appellations of Origin: One Hundred Years of Efforts and Debates." In *The Importance of Place: Geographical Indications as a Tool for Local and Regional Development*, 147–72. Ius Gentium: Comparative Perspectives on Law and Justice 58. Cham: Springer, 2017.

Tello, Javier, Mammerler, Roswitha, Čajić, Marko, and Forneck, Astrid. "Major Outbreaks in the Nineteenth Century Shaped Grape Phylloxera Contemporary Genetic Structure in Europe." *Scientific Reports* 9, no. 17540 (2019): 1–11.

Van Moerland, Anke. "Do Developing Countries Have a Say? Bilateral and Regional Intellectual Property Negotiations with the EU." *International Review of Intellectual Property and Competition Law* 48, no. 7 (November 2017): 760–83.

Van Moerland, Anke. "Geographical Indications and Innovation, What Is the Connection?" In *The Innovation Society and Intellectual Property*, 59–86. European Intellectual Property Institutes Network Series. Cheltenham: Edward Elgar, 2019.

Van Moerland, Anke. “Governance Systems of Geographical Indications.” In *Restoring Trust in Trade*, 67–84. Oxford: Hart, 2019.

Vandecandelaere, Emilie, Teyssier, Catherine, Barjolle, Dominique, Jeanneaux, Philippe, Fournier, Stephane, and Beucherie, Olivier. “Strengthening Sustainable Food Systems through Geographical Indications.” Rome, 2018.

Zappalaglio, Andrea. “The Protection of Geographical Indications: Ambitions and Concrete Limitations.” *Edinburgh Student Law Review* 89 (2015): 89–102.

Zappalaglio, Andrea. *The Transformation of EU Geographical Indications Law*. Oxon: Routledge, 2021.

Index

www.ingramcontent.com/pod-product-compliance
Lightning Source LLC
Chambersburg PA
CBHW071328230926
51849CB00002B/336
* 9 7 8 9 0 0 4 4 3 9 8 1 8 *